How to Use the Maps in *The Essential World History, Third Edition*

Here are some basic map concepts that will help you to get the most out of the maps in this textbook.

- ◻ Always look at the scale, which allows you to determine the distance in miles or kilometers between locations on the map.

- ◻ Examine the legend carefully. It explains the colors and symbols used on the map.

- ◻ Note the locations of mountains, rivers, oceans, and other geographic features, and consider how these would affect such human activities as agriculture, commerce, travel, and warfare.

- ◻ Read the map caption thoroughly. It provides important information, sometimes not covered in the text itself, and poses a thought question to encourage you to think beyond the mere appearance of the map and make connections across chapters, regions, and concepts.

- ◻ Several "spot maps" appear in each chapter, to allow you to view in detail smaller areas that may not be apparent in larger maps. For example, a spot map in Chapter 12 lets you zoom in on Charlemagne's Empire.

- ◻ Many of the text's maps also carry a globe icon, which indicates that they or similar maps appear in interactive form at http://worldrc.wadsworth.com/

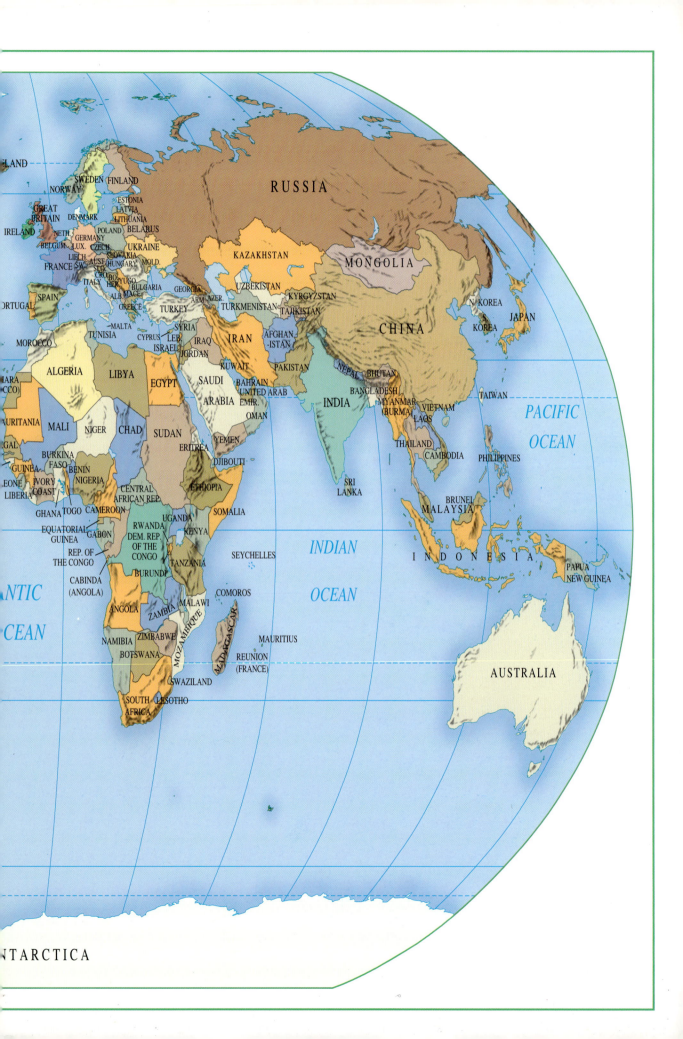

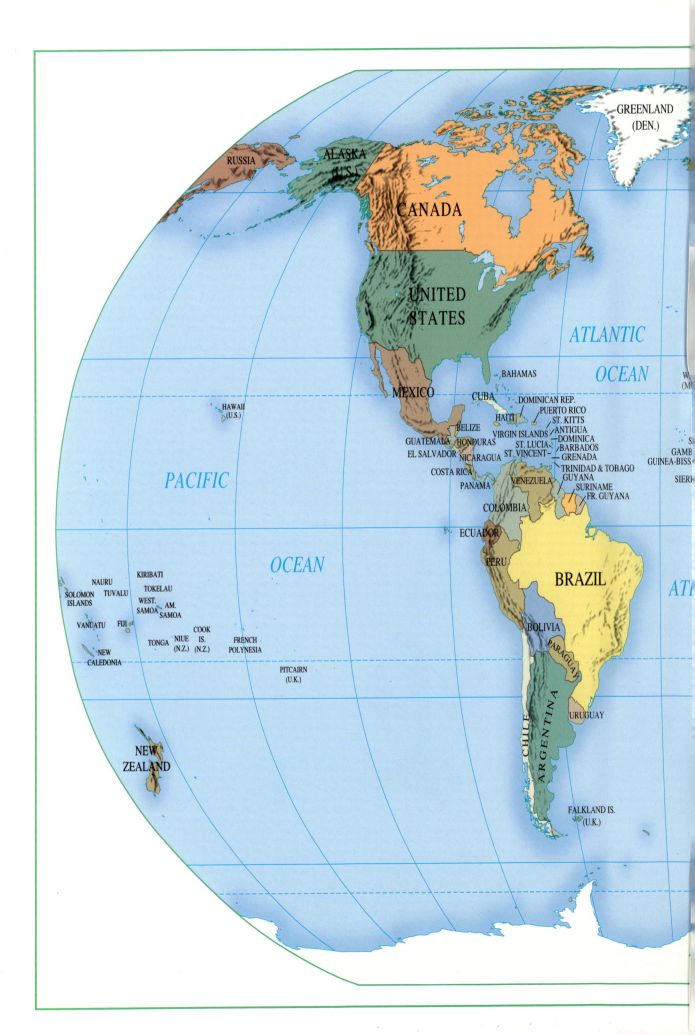

GREENLAND
(DEN.)

RUSSIA

ALASKA
(U.S.)

CANADA

UNITED
STATES

ATLANTIC

OCEAN

BAHAMAS

HAWAII
(U.S.)

MEXICO

CUBA

DOMINICAN REP.
PUERTO RICO
HAITI   ST. KITTS
BELIZE   ANTIGUA
              VIRGIN ISLANDS DOMINICA
GUATEMALA HONDURAS ST. LUCIA BARBADOS
EL SALVADOR NICARAGUA ST. VINCENT GRENADA
          COSTA RICA   TRINIDAD & TOBAGO
                     PANAMA VENEZUELA GUYANA
                                  SURINAME
                            FR. GUYANA
                 COLOMBIA

GUINEA-BISS

ECUADOR

PACIFIC

PERU

OCEAN

KIRIBATI
NAURU   TOKELAU
SOLOMON TUVALU
ISLANDS   WEST.
          SAMOA AM.
                SAMOA
VANUATU FIJI
              COOK
          NIUE IS.
TONGA (N.Z.) (N.Z.) FRENCH
                    POLYNESIA

NEW
CALEDONIA

PITCAIRN
(U.K.)

BRAZIL

BOLIVIA

PARAGUAY

URUGUAY

CHILE

ARGENTINA

NEW
ZEALAND

FALKLAND IS.
(U.K.)

W.
(MC

SI

GAMB

SIER

AT

THE ESSENTIAL WORLD HISTORY TO 1500

THIRD EDITION

THE ESSENTIAL
WORLD HISTORY
TO 1500

WILLIAM J. DUIKER

The Pennsylvania State University

JACKSON J. SPIELVOGEL

The Pennsylvania State University

WADSWORTH
CENGAGE Learning™

Australia • Brazil • Japan • Korea • Mexico • Singapore • Spain • United Kingdom • United States

**The Essential World History to 1500,
Third Edition**
William J. Duiker, Jackson J. Spielvogel

Publisher: Clark Baxter

Senior Development Editor: Sue Gleason

Assistant Editor: Jessica Kim

Editorial Assistant: Kristen Judy

Technology Project Manager: David Lionetti

Marketing Manager: Janise Fry

Marketing Assistant: Teresa Jessen

Advertising Project Manager: Tami Strang

Project Manager, Editorial Production:
Katy German

Creative Director: Rob Hugel

Art Director: Maria Epes

Print Buyer: Doreen Suruki

Permissions Editor: Sarah D'Stair

Production Service: Orr Book Services

Text and Cover Designer: Kathleen Cunningham

Photo Researcher: ImageQuest

Copy Editor: Pat Lewis

Cover Image: Akbar's journey to Agra by water in
1562. Painting from the Akbarnama. Gouache on
paper. Mughal. (CT36528) Victoria and Albert
Museum, London, Great Britain. Victoria & Albert
Museum, London/Art Resource, NY

Compositor: International Typesetting
and Composition

For product information and technology assistance, contact us at
Cengage Learning Customer & Sales Support, 1-800-354-9706

For permission to use material from this text or product,
submit all requests online at **cengage.com/permissions**
Further permissions questions can be e-mailed to
permissionrequest@cengage.com

Library of Congress Control Number: 2006939303

ISBN-13: 978-0-495-09767-9

ISBN-10: 0-495-09767-5

Wadsworth
25 Thomson Place
Boston, MA 02210
USA

Cengage Learning products are represented in Canada by Nelson Education, Ltd.

For your course and learning solutions, visit **academic.cengage.com**

Purchase any of our products at your local college store or at our preferred online
store **www.ichapters.com**

Printed in the United States of America
3 4 5 6 7 10 09 08

$\mathcal{W}$ILLIAM J. DUIKER is liberal arts professor emeritus of East Asian studies at The Pennsylvania State University. A former U.S. diplomat with service in Taiwan, South Vietnam, and Washington, D.C., he received his doctorate in Far Eastern history from Georgetown University in 1968, where his dissertation dealt with the Chinese educator and reformer Cai Yuanpei. At Penn State, he has written widely on the history of Vietnam and modern China, including the widely acclaimed *The Communist Road to Power in Vietnam* (revised edition, Westview Press, 1996), which was selected for a Choice Outstanding Academic Book Award in 1982–1983 and 1996–1997. Other recent books are *China and Vietnam: The Roots of Conflict* (Berkeley, 1987), *Sacred War: Nationalism and Revolution in a Divided Vietnam* (McGraw-Hill, 1995), and *Ho Chi Minh: A Life* (Hyperion, 2000). While his research specialization is in the field of nationalism and Asian revolutions, his intellectual interests are considerably more diverse. He has traveled widely and has taught courses on the History of Communism and non-Western civilizations at Penn State, where he was awarded a Faculty Scholar Medal for Outstanding Achievement in the spring of 1996.

To Yvonne,
for adding sparkle to this book, and to my life
W.J.D.

$\mathcal{J}$ACKSON J. SPIELVOGEL is associate professor emeritus of history at The Pennsylvania State University. He received his Ph.D. from The Ohio State University, where he specialized in Reformation history under Harold J. Grimm. His articles and reviews have appeared in such journals as *Moreana, Journal of General Education, Catholic Historical Review, Archiv für Reformationsgeschichte,* and *American Historical Review.* He has also contributed chapters or articles to *The Social History of the Reformation, The Holy Roman Empire: A Dictionary Handbook, Simon Wiesenthal Center Annual of Holocaust Studies,* and *Utopian Studies.* His work has been supported by fellowships from the Fulbright Foundation and the Foundation for Reformation Research. At Penn State, he helped inaugurate the Western civilization course as well as a popular course on Nazi Germany. His book *Hitler and Nazi Germany* was published in 1987 (fifth edition, 2005). He is the author of *Western Civilization* published in 1991 (sixth edition, 2006). Professor Spielvogel has won five major university-wide teaching awards. During the year 1988–1989, he held the Penn State Teaching Fellowship, the university's most prestigious teaching award. In 1996, he won the Dean Arthur Ray Warnock Award for Outstanding Faculty Member and in 2000 received the Schreyer Honors College Excellence in Teaching Award.

To Diane,
whose love and support made it all possible
J.J.S.

BRIEF CONTENTS

DETAILED CONTENTS

11 THE EAST ASIAN RIMLANDS: EARLY JAPAN, KOREA, AND VIETNAM   238

12 THE MAKING OF EUROPE   259

CHRONOLOGIES

MAPS

PREFACE

$\mathcal{F}$OR SEVERAL MILLION YEARS after primates first appeared on the surface of the earth, human beings lived in small communities, seeking to survive by hunting, fishing, and foraging in a frequently hostile environment. Then suddenly, in the space of a few thousand years, there was an abrupt change of direction as human beings in a few widely scattered areas of the globe began to master the art of cultivating food crops. As food production increased, the population in those areas rose correspondingly, and people began to congregate in larger communities. Governments were formed to provide protection and other needed services to the local population. Cities appeared and became the focal point of cultural and religious development. Historians refer to this process as the beginnings of civilization.

For generations, historians in Europe and the United States pointed to the rise of such civilizations as marking the origins of the modern world. Courses on Western civilization conventionally began with a chapter or two on the emergence of advanced societies in Egypt and Mesopotamia and then proceeded to ancient Greece and the Roman Empire. From Greece and Rome, the road led directly to the rise of modern civilization in the West.

There is nothing inherently wrong with this approach. Important aspects of our world today can indeed be traced back to these early civilizations, and all human beings the world over owe a considerable debt to their achievements. But all too often this interpretation has been used to imply that the course of civilization has been linear in nature, leading directly from the emergence of agricultural societies in ancient Mesopotamia to the rise of advanced industrial societies in Europe and North America. Until recently, most courses on world history taught in the United States routinely focused almost exclusively on the rise of the West, with only a passing glance at other parts of the world, such as Africa, India, and East Asia. The contributions made by those societies to the culture and technology of our own time were often passed over in silence.

Two major reasons have been advanced to justify this approach. Some have argued that it is more important that young minds understand the roots of their own heritage than that of peoples elsewhere in the world. In many cases, however, the motivation for this Eurocentric approach has been the belief that since the time of Socrates and Aristotle Western civilization has been the sole driving force in the evolution of human society.

Such an interpretation, however, represents a serious distortion of the process. During most of the course of human history, the most advanced civilizations have been not in the West, but in East Asia or the Middle East. A relatively brief period of European dominance culminated with the era of imperialism in the late nineteenth century, when the political, military, and economic power of the advanced nations of the West spanned the globe. During recent generations, however, that dominance has gradually eroded, partly as the result of changes taking place within Western societies and partly because new centers of development are emerging elsewhere on the globe—notably in East Asia, where the growing economic strength of China and Japan and many of their neighbors has led to the now familiar prediction that the twenty-first century will be known as the Pacific Century.

World history, then, has been a complex process in which many branches of the human community have taken an active part, and the dominance of any one area of the world has been a temporary rather than a permanent phenomenon. It will be our purpose in this book to present a balanced picture of this story, with all respect for the richness and diversity of the tapestry of the human experience. Due attention must be paid to the rise of the West, of course, since that has been the most dominant aspect of world history in recent centuries. But the contributions made by other peoples must be given adequate consideration as well, not only in the period prior to 1500 when the major centers of civilization were located in Asia, but also in our own day, where a multipolar picture of development is clearly beginning to emerge.

Anyone who wishes to teach or write about world history must decide whether to present the topic as an integrated whole or as a collection of different cultures. The world that we live in today, of course, is in many respects an interdependent one in terms of economics as well as culture and communications, a reality that is often expressed by the phrase "global village." The convergence of peoples across the surface of the earth into an integrated world system began in early times and intensified after the rise of capitalism in the early modern era. In growing recognition of this trend, historians trained in global history, as well as instructors in the growing number of world history courses, have now begun to speak and write of a "global approach" that turns attention away from the study of individual civilizations and focuses instead on the "big picture" or, as the world historian Fernand Braudel termed it, interpreting world history as a river with no banks.

On the whole, this development is to be welcomed as a means of bringing the common elements of the evolution of human society to our attention. But there is a problem involved in this approach. For the vast majority of their time on earth, human beings have lived in partial or virtually total isolation from each other. Differences in climate, location, and geographical features have created human societies very different from each other in culture and historical experience. Only in relatively recent times—(the commonly accepted date has long been the beginning of the age of European exploration at the end of the fifteenth century, but some would now push it back to the era of the Mongol empire or even further)— have cultural interchanges begun to create a common "world system," in which events taking place in one part of the world are rapidly transmitted throughout the globe, often with momentous consequences. In recent generations, of course, the process of global interdependence has been proceeding even more rapidly. Nevertheless, even now the process is by no means complete, as ethnic and regional differences continue to exist and to shape the course of world history. The tenacity of these differences and sensitivities is reflected not only in the rise of internecine conflicts in such divergent areas as Africa, India, and Eastern Europe, but also in the emergence in recent years of such regional organizations as the Organization of African Unity, the Association for the Southeast Asian Nations, and the European Union.

The second problem is a practical one. College students today are all too often not well informed about the distinctive character of civilizations such as China and India and, without sufficient exposure to the historical evolution of such societies, will assume all too readily that the peoples in these countries have had historical experiences similar to ours and will respond to various stimuli in a similar fashion to those living in Western Europe or the United States. If it is a mistake to ignore those forces that link us together, it is equally a mistake to underestimate those factors that continue to divide us and to differentiate us into a world of diverse peoples.

Our response to this challenge has been to adopt a global approach to world history while at the same time attempting to do justice to the distinctive character and development of individual civilizations and regions of the world. The presentation of individual cultures will be especially important in Parts I and II, which cover a time when it is generally agreed that the process of global integration was not yet far advanced. Later chapters will begin to adopt a more comparative and thematic approach, in deference to the greater number of connections that have been established among the world's peoples since the fifteenth and sixteenth centuries. Part V will consist of a series of chapters that will center on individual regions of the world while at the same time focusing on common problems related to the Cold War and the rise of global problems such as overproduction and environmental pollution.

We have sought balance in another way as well. Many textbooks tend to simplify the content of history courses by emphasizing an intellectual or political perspective or, most recently, a social perspective, often at the expense of sufficient details in a chronological framework. This approach is confusing to students whose high school social studies programs have often neglected a systematic study of world history. We have attempted to write a well-balanced work in which political, economic, social, religious, intellectual, cultural, and military history have been integrated into a chronologically ordered synthesis.

To enliven the past and let readers see for themselves the materials that historians use to create their pictures of the past, we have included primary sources (boxed documents) in each chapter that are keyed to the discussion in the text. The documents include examples of the religious, artistic, intellectual, social, economic, and political aspects of life in different societies and reveal in a vivid fashion what civilization meant to the individual men and women who shaped it by their actions. We have added questions to help guide students in analyzing the documents, as well as references to related documents that are available online.

Each chapter has a lengthy introduction and conclusion to help maintain the continuity of the narrative and to provide a synthesis of important themes. Anecdotes in the chapter introductions convey more dramatically the major theme or themes of each chapter. Timelines, at the end of each chapter enable students to see the major developments of an era at a glance and within cross-cultural categories, while the more detailed chronologies reinforce the events discussed in the text. An annotated bibliography at the end of each chapter reviews the most recent literature on each period and also gives references to some of the older, "classic" works in each field.

Updated maps and extensive illustrations serve to deepen the reader's understanding of the text. Map captions are designed to enrich students' awareness of the importance of geography to history, and numerous spot maps enable students to see at a glance the region or subject being discussed in the text. In addition, special globe icons indicate maps for which an interactive version appears on the Web site. The maps have also been revised where needed. To facilitate understanding of cultural movements, illustrations of artistic works discussed in the text are placed near the discussions. Chapter outlines and focus and critical thinking questions have been combined in a new format at the beginning of each chapter to help students with an overview and guide them to the main subjects of each chapter. A glossary of important terms (now boldfaced in the text when they are introduced and defined) and a pronunciation guide are provided at the back of the book to maximize reader comprehension.

After reexamining the entire book and analyzing the comments and reviews of many colleagues who have found the book to be a useful instrument for introducing their students to world history, we have also made a number of other changes for the third edition. In the first place, we have reorganized the material by ending Part II at 1500, reversing the order of Chapters 13 and 14, and redoing Chapter 12, "The Making of Europe." The Renaissance is now covered in Chapter 12, and Chapter 14, "Europe Transformed: Reform and State Building," begins with the Reformation. Chapter 5, now titled "The First World Civilization: Rome, China, and the Emergence of the Silk Road," includes a discussion of both the Roman and Han Chinese empires.

Second, we have sought to strengthen the global framework of the book, but not at the expense of reducing the attention assigned to individual regions of the world. New comparative essays have been added to each chapter. Keyed to the seven major themes of world history (see p. xxiii), these essays enable us to more concretely draw comparisons and contrasts across geographical, cultural, and chronological lines. Moreover, additional comparative material has been added to each chapter to help students be aware of similar developments globally. Among other things, this material includes new comparative sections as well as comparative illustrations in each chapter that are keyed to the seven major themes of world history. We hope that these techniques will assist instructors who wish to encourage their students to adopt a comparative approach to their understanding of the human experience.

Third, this new edition contains additional information on the role of women in world history. In conformity with our own convictions, as well as what we believe to be recent practice in the field, we have tried where possible to introduce such material at the appropriate point in the text, rather than to set aside separate sections devoted exclusively to women's issues.

Finally, a number of new illustrations, boxed documents, and maps have been added, and the bibliographies have been revised to take account of newly published material. The chronologies and maps have been fine-tuned as well, to help the reader locate in time and space the multitude of individuals and place names that appear in the book. To keep up with the ever-growing body of historical scholarship, new or revised material has been added throughout the book on many topics.

Chapter 1   The Code of Hammurabi; urbanization in the first civilizations; gender issues in Mesopotamia; and new section, "The Spread of Egyptian Influence: Nubia." New comparative illustration on early writing. New comparative essay, "From Hunter-Gatherers and Herders to Farmers."

Chapter 2   New material on Hinduism and Buddhism, and ancient Indian achievements in mathematics. New comparative essay, "Writing and Civilization."

Chapter 3   New material on early Chinese religion compared with that in Mesopotamia and Greece; the evolution of autocratic rule in ancient China; and bronze-casting factories. New comparative illustration on early agricultural technology. New comparative essay, "The Use of Metals."

Chapter 4   New material on Hellenistic urbanization; trade and cultural diffusion; Alexander's connections to the East; Greek science in the classical and Hellenistic periods; Minoan Crete; the effects of colonization; and the development of Athenian democracy, especially under Pericles. New comparative essay, "Demos and Despots."

Chapter 5   New material on trade between Rome and China; slaves; the crises of the third century and the end of the Western Empire; and new section, "The Glorious Han Empire (202 B.C.E. – 221 C.E.)." New comparative essay, "Rulers and Gods."

Chapter 6   New material on the Maya; Caral and Chavín de Huantar; environmental problems in ancient South America; and the Anasazi. New comparative essay, "History and the Environment."

Chapter 7   New material on early Islam; early Muslim brotherhoods; and iconoclasm in Islam. New comparative essay, "Trade and Civilization."

Chapter 8   New material on the Husuni Kubwa; comparison of building techniques of the Inka and Great Zimbabwe; the Khoi and the San; and African wood carving. New comparative essay, "The Migration of Peoples." New spot map of the Swahili coast.

Chapter 9   New comparative illustration of rock architecture. New comparative essay, "Caste, Class, and Family."

Chapter 10   New material on the Silk Road and the School of Mind compared with Greek philosophy. New comparative essay, "The Spread of Technology."

Chapter 11   New comparative essay, "Feudal Orders Around the World."

Chapter 12   New material on decentralization versus centralization of state power in the Middle Ages and Renaissance and long-distance trade with the East. New comparative essay, "The Role of Disease."

Chapter 13   New material on the Middle Passage and an overall assessment of the Age of Exploration. New comparative illustration of Christianity in Asia. New comparative essay, "Marriage in the Early Modern World."

Chapter 14   New material on Jesuit missionary activities in Asia. New comparative essay, "Marriage in the Early Modern World."

Chapter 15   New material on Safavid Iran. New comparative illustration of war commemorations. New comparative essay, "The Changing Face of War."

Chapter 16   New comparative essay, "Population Explosion."

Chapter 17   New comparative essay, "The Scientific Revolution."

Chapter 18   New material on nationalism and a changed interpretation of the Battle of Königgrätz. New comparative essay, "The Industrial Revolution."

Chapter 19   New material on trade unions and Canada. New comparative essay, "The Rise of Nationalism."

Chapter 20   New comparative illustration on cultural influences. New comparative essay, "Imperialism: The Balance Sheet."

Chapter 21   New comparative illustration of female rulers. New comparative essay, "Imperialism and the Global Environment."

Chapter 22   New material on the Russian Revolution; casualties of World War I; genocide of Armenians by Turks at end of World War I; and Dadaism. New comparative essay, "A Revolution in the Arts."

Chapter 23   New material on women's rights in India and early twentieth-century nation building in Iraq. New comparative essay, "Out of the Doll's House."

Chapter 24   New material on Japanese motives for expansion; the Japanese path to war; and Japan in the war. New comparative essay, "Paths to Modernization."

Chapter 25   New comparative illustration, "The Iron Curtain Falls." New comparative essay, "One World, One Environment." New map of the Chinese civil war; new spot map of South Vietnam at war.

Chapter 26   New comparative essay, "Family and Society in an Era of Change."

Chapter 27   New section on the European Union. New material on Yugoslavia; immigration laws in Europe; and postmodernism. All nations updated to the present. New comparative essay, "From the Industrial to the Technological Revolution." New spot map of Central America.

Chapter 28   New material on Muslim fundamentalism and the growth of Islam in the West, and society and culture in the Middle East. All nations updated to the present. New comparative illustration on traditional patterns in the countryside. New comparative essay, "Religion and Society." New spot map of present-day Iraq.

Chapter 29   All nations updated to the present. New comparative illustration on the new technology. New comparative essay, "Global Village or Clash of Civilizations?"

Because courses in world history at American and Canadian colleges and universities follow different chronological divisions, a one-volume comprehensive edition, a two-volume edition of this text, and a volume covering events to 1500 are being made available to fit the needs of instructors. Teaching and learning ancillaries include:

Multimedia Manager for World History with Instructor's Resources: A Microsoft® Powerpoint® Tool   Includes the Instructor's Manual, Resource Integration Guide (grids that link each chapter of the text to instructional ideas and corresponding supplemental resources), ExamView® computerized testing, and Microsoft® PowerPoint® slides with lecture outlines and images that can be used as offered, or customized by importing personal lecture slides or other material. ExamView allows you to create, deliver, and customize tests and study guides (both print and online) in minutes with its easy-to-use assessment and tutorial system. It offers both a Quick Test Wizard and an Online Test Wizard that guide you step by step through the process of creating tests, while its "what you see is what you get" capability allows you to see the test you are creating on the screen exactly as it will print or display online. You can build tests of up to 250 questions using up to 12 question types. Using ExamView's complete word-processing capabilities, you can enter an unlimited number of new questions or edit existing questions.

Instructor's Manual with Test Bank   Prepared by Eugene Larson, Los Angeles Pierce College. Includes chapter outlines reflecting the main headings; class lecture/discussion topics; thought/discussion questions for the boxed documents; possible student projects; and examination questions (essay, identification, and 50 multiple-choice questions, the latter with correct answers and text page references indicated). Available on the Book Companion Site and the Multimedia Manager.

Transparency Acetates for World History   Each package contains more than 100 four-color map images from the text and other sources. Packages are three-hole punched and shrinkwrapped. Map commentary is provided by James Harrison, Siena College.

Sights and Sounds of History   Prepared by David Redles, Cuyahoga Community College. Short, focused VHS video clips, photos, artwork, animations, music, and dramatic readings are used to bring life to historical topics and events which are most difficult for students to appreciate from a textbook alone. For example, students will experience the grandeur of Versailles and the defeat felt by a German soldier at Stalingrad. The video segments average 4 minutes in length and make excellent lecture launchers.

JoinIn™ on TurningPoint®—World History JoinIn™ on TurningPoint® is the easiest way to turn your lecture hall into a personal, fully interactive experience for your students. JoinIn turns your ordinary PowerPoint® application into powerful audience response software, allowing you to take attendance, poll students on key issues to spark discussion, check student comprehension of difficult concepts, collect student demographics to better assess student needs, and even administer quizzes without collecting papers or grading. In addition, we provide interactive slide sets for many of our leading products that you can modify and merge with any existing PowerPoint lecture slides for a seamless classroom presentation.

Music CDs   Available to instructors upon request, these CDs include musical selctions from Henry Purcell through Ravi Shankar to enrich lectures. A correlation guide is available in the Resource Integration Guide in the Multimedia Manager and the Multimedia Manager.

HistoryNow   Available via access card, this web-based intelligent study system saves time for students and instructors by providing a complete package of diagnostic quizzes, a personalized study plan, integrated multimedia, over 450 primary source readings, and an instructor gradebook.

HistoryUnbound: Online Explorations in World History   *HistoryUnbound's* online modules bring the past to life through seamless integration of interactive maps and timelines, images, and primary-source readings. Available as a bundle item or as a standalone product, the *HistoryUnbound* access code is packaged with a text-specific Correlation Guide.

Wadsworth History Resource Center   Wadworth History Resource Centers (http://worldrc.wadsworth.com/) for American History, World History, and Western Civilization have significantly expanded! Now chronologically organized with a user-friendly timeline navigation bar, these centers act as a primary source e-reader with over 300 primary source documents and feature numerous resources, such as timelines, photos, interactive maps, exercises, and more. Your students obtain access to the appropriate resource center when you package an access code with any Wadsworth Cengage Learning history textbook. Access codes are available free when packaged with most new books and at a nominal price when packaged with our Cengage Learning Advantage Books. If need be, you can also order it by itself. All access codes last for one complete year. Demo the resource centers at http://history.wadsworth.com, by clicking on your area (American, Western Civilization,

World Civilization) on the left-hand navigation bar, and then contact your local representative for ordering details.

Book Companion Web Site

academic.cengage.com/history/duiker

Both instructors and students will enjoy the chapter-by-chapter resources for Duiker and Spielvogel's *World History*, with access to the Wadsworth World History Resource Center. Text-specific content for students includes interactive maps, interactive timelines, tutorial quizzes, glossary, hyperlinks, InfoTrac College Edition exercises, Internet activities, and an annotated bibliography. Instructors also have access to the Instructor's Manual and PowerPoint slides (access code required). From the History homepage, instructors and students can access many selections, such as primary source documents, interactive simulations, an Internet Guide for History, a career center, lessons on surfing the web, the World History Image Bank, and links to great history-related web sites.

The Journey of Civilization Prepared by David Redles, Cuyahoga Community College. This CD-ROM takes the student on 18 interactive journeys through history. Enhanced with QuickTime movies, animations, sound clips, maps, and more, the journeys allow students to engage in history as active participants rather than as readers of past events. Contact your local sales representative for bundle pricing.

Migrations in Modern World History 1500–2000 CD-ROM with User Guide (Student Version) An interactive multimedia curriculum on CD-ROM developed by Patrick Manning and the World History Center at Northeastern University. *Migration* goes beyond the mere chronicling of migratory paths. Over 400 primary source documents in *Migration* provide a springboard to explore a wide range of global issues in social, cultural, economic, and political history during the period 1500–2000.

InfoTrac® College Edition with InfoMarks® Now available, free four-month access to InfoTrac® College Edition's online database of more than 18 million reliable, full-length articles from 5,000 academic journals and periodicals (including *the New York Times, Science, Forbes,* and *USA Today*) includes access to InfoMarks—stable URLs that can be linked to articles, journals, and searches. InfoMarks allow you to use a simple "copy and paste" technique to create instant and continually updated online readers, content services, bibliographies, elecronic "reserve" readings, and current topic sites. And incorporating InfoTrac College Edition into your course is easy—references to this virtual library are built into many of our texts in margins, exercises, and so forth. In addition, ask about other InfoTrac College Edition resources available, including InfoMarks print and online readers with readings, activities, and exercises hand selected to work with the text. And to help students use the research they gather, their free four-month subscription to InfoTrac College Edition includes access to InfoWrite, a complete set of online critical thinking and paper writing tools. To take a quick tour of InfoTrac

College Edition, visit http://www.infotrac-college.com/ and select the "User Demo." (Journals subject to change. Certain restrictions may apply. For additional information, please consult your local Cengage Learning representative.)

A Civilization Primer, 5th Edition This proven supplement for the introductory Western civilization course, by Edward M. Anson, University of Arkansas, Little Rock, is designed to help history students develop their knowledge of core social science concepts and terminology. This brief text defines and clarifies the basics of history, culture, religion, government, economics, and geography.

Document Exercise Workbook for World History, 3rd Edition Prepared by Donna Van Raaphorst, Cuyahoga Community College, this two-volume workbook provides a collection of exercises based around primary source documents in history. Contact your local sales representative for bundle pricing.

Magellan World History Atlas Available to bundle with any history text. Contains 44 four-color historical maps, including The Conflict in Afghanistan, 2001, and States of the World, 2001. Contact your local sales representative for bundle pricing.

Map Exercise Workbook, 3rd Edition Prepared by Cynthia Kosso, Northern Arizona University, this two-volume workbook features approximately 30 map exercises. Designed to help students feel comfortable with maps by having them work with different kinds of maps to identify places and improve their geographic understanding of world history. Contact your local sales representative for bundle pricing.

Scientific American—Ancient Civilizations Bring your students into current activity in the field with *Scientific American* magazine. As an exclusive offer from Cengage Learning, this magazine is available as a bundle item for your course. This issue includes coverage by region, including such topics as the Iceman, Death Cults of Prehistoric Malta, Keys to the Lost Indus Cities, Women and Men at Catalhuyuk, Rock Art in Southern Africa, Life and Death in Nabada, Tapestry of Power in a Mesopotamian City, Daily Life in Ancient Egypt, Great Zimbabwe, Precious Metal Objects of the Middle Sican, Life in the Provinces of the Aztec Empire, Reading the Bones of La Florida, and more.

Sources of World History This two-volume reader, edited by Mark Kishlansky, Harvard University, is a collection of primary source documents designed to supplement any world history text. Provides a balance of constitutional documents, political theory, philosophy, imaginative literature, and social description. Contact your local sales representative for bundle pricing.

Primary Source Reader for World History Edited by Elsa A. Nystrom, Kennesaw State University. A thoughtful collection of important primary source documents essential to world history, this two-volume reader is an affordable supplement for students and a valuable complement to any world history or world civilization class. More than 50 percent of the primary source documents are non-Western, giving students a broad perspective on the history of the world. The readings are divided by eras and organized according to principal themes, such as religion, law and government, and everyday life. Each group of readings has a section describing the signficance of subsequent readings and how those readings interrelate. Individual readings include a headnote and various study questions intended to guide student reading and understanding.

A Custom Reader for Western Civilization Written by leading educators and historians, this fully customizable reader of primary and secondary sources, appropriate for the text's European coverage, is enhanced with an online collection of visual sources, including maps, animations and interactive exercises. Each reading also comes with an introduction and a series of review questions. To learn more visit CengageCustom.com or call Cengage Custom Publishing at 1-800-355-9983.

ACKNOWLEDGMENTS

BOTH AUTHORS GRATEFULLY acknowledge that without the generosity of many others, this project could not have been completed.

William Duiker would like to thank Kumkum Chatterjee and On-cho Ng for their helpful comments about issues related to the history of India and premodern China. His longtime colleague Cyril Griffith, now deceased, was a cherished friend and a constant source of information about modern Africa. Art Goldschmidt has been of invaluable assistance in reading several chapters of the manuscript, as well as in unraveling many of the mysteries of Middle Eastern civilization. Finally, he remains profoundly grateful to his wife, Yvonne V. Duiker, Ph.D. She has not only given her usual measure of love and support when this appeared to be an insuperable task, but she has also contributed her own time and expertise to enrich the sections on art and literature, thereby adding life and sparkle to this, as well as the earlier editions of the book. To her, and to his daughters Laura and Claire, he will be forever thankful for bringing joy to his life.

Jackson Spielvogel would like to thank Art Goldschmidt, David Redles, and Christine Colin for their time and ideas. Daniel Haxall and Kathryn Spielvogel of The Pennsylvania State University provided valuable assistance with materials on postwar art, popular culture, and Postmodern art and thought. Above all, he thanks his family for their support. The gifts of love, laughter, and patience from his daughters, Jennifer and Kathryn, his sons, Eric and Christian, and daughters-in-law, Liz and Laurie, and his son-in-law, Daniel, were invaluable. Diane, his wife and best friend, provided him with editorial assistance, wise counsel, and the loving support that made a project of this magnitude possible.

Thanks to Wadsworth's comprehensive review process, many historians were asked to evaluate our manuscript. We are grateful to the following for the innumerable suggestions that have greatly improved our work. This edition's map reviewers (asterisked) deserve our particular thanks.

Henry Abramson
Florida Atlantic University

Eric H. Ash
Wayne State University

William Bakken
Rochester Community College

Suzanne Balch-Lindsay
Eastern New Mexco University

Michael E. Birdwell
Tennessee Technological University

*Connie Brand
Meridien Community College

Eileen Brown
Norwalk Community College

Thomas Cardoza
University of California, San Diego

Alistair Chapman
Westmont College

Nupur Chaudhuri
Texas Southern University

Richard Crane
Greensboro College

Wade Dudley
East Carolina University

E.J. Fabyan
Vincennes University

Kenneth Faunce
Washington State University

Jamie Garcia
Hawaii Pacific University

Steven Gosch
University of Wisconsin— Eau Claire

Donald Harreld
Brigham Young University

Janine C. Hartman
University of Connecticut

Greg Havrilcsak
University of Michigan—Flint

Thomas Hegerty
University of Tampa

Sanders Huguenin
University of Science and Arts of Oklahoma

Ahmed Ibrahim
Southwest Missouri State University

C. Barden Keeler
Gulf Coast High School

Marilynn Fox Kokoszka
Orchard Ridge Campus, Oakland Community College

James Krippner-Martinez
Haverford College

Oscar Lansen
University of North Carolina— Charlotte

David Leinweber
Oxford College, Emory University

Susie Ling
Pasadena City College

*Moira Maguire
University of Arkansas—Little Rock

Andrew McGreevy
Ohio University

Daniel Miller
Calvin College

Michael Murdock
Brigham Young University

Elsa A. Nystrom
Kennesaw State University

S. Mike Pavelec
Hawaii Pacific University

Randall L. Pouwels
University of Central Arkansas

Margaret Power
Illinois Institute of Technology

Pamela Sayre
Henry Ford Community College

Philip Curtis Skaggs
Grand Valley State University

Laura Smoller
University of Arkansas at Little Rock

Beatrice Spade
University of Southern Colorado

Jeremy Stahl
Middle Tennessee State University

Kate Transchel
California State University, Chico

Justin Vance
Hawaii Pacific University

Lorna VanMeter
Ball State University

Michelle White
University of Tennessee at Chattanooga

Edna Yahil
Washington State University— Swiss Center

The authors are truly grateful to the people who have helped us to produce this book. We especially want to thank Clark Baxter, whose faith in our ability to do this project was inspiring. Sue Gleason thoughtfully and cheerfully guided the overall development of the third edition, and Kristen Tatoe orchestrated the preparation of outstanding teaching and learning ancillaries. Pat Lewis was, as usual, an outstanding copyeditor. Sarah Evertson provided valuable assistance in obtaining permissions for the illustrations. John Orr, of Orr Book Services, was as cooperative and cheerful as he was competent in matters of production management.

A NOTE TO STUDENTS ABOUT LANGUAGES AND THE DATING OF TIME

ONE OF THE MOST difficult challenges in studying world history is coming to grips with the multitude of names, words, and phrases in unfamiliar languages. Unfortunately, this problem has no easy solution. We have tried to alleviate the difficulty, where possible, by providing an English-language translation of foreign words or phrases, a glossary, and a pronunciation guide. The issue is especially complicated in the case of Chinese, since two separate systems are commonly used to transliterate the spoken Chinese language into the Roman alphabet. The Wade-Giles system, invented in the nineteenth century, was the most frequently used until recent years, when the pinyin system was adopted by the People's Republic of China as its own official form of transliteration. We have opted to use the latter, since it appears to be gaining acceptance in the United States, but the initial use of a Chinese word is accompanied by its Wade-Giles equivalent in parentheses for the benefit of those who may encounter the term in their outside reading.

In our examination of world history, we need also to be aware of the dating of time. In recording the past, historians try to determine the exact time when events occurred. World War II in Europe, for example, began on September 1, 1939, when Adolf Hitler sent German troops into Poland, and ended on May 7, 1945, when Germany surrendered. By using dates, historians can place events in order and try to determine the development of patterns over periods of time.

If someone asked you when you were born, you would reply with a number, such as 1988. In the United States, we would all accept that number without question, because it is part of the dating system followed in the Western world (Europe and the Western Hemisphere). In this system, events are dated by counting backward or forward from the birth of Christ (assumed to be the year 1). An event that took place 400 years before the birth of Christ would most commonly be dated 400 B.C. (before Christ). Dates after the birth of Christ are labeled as A.D. These letters stand for the Latin words *anno domini*, which mean "in the year of the Lord" (or the year of the birth of Christ). Thus an event that took place 250 years after the birth of Christ is written A.D. 250, or in the year of the Lord 250. It can also be written as 250, just as you would not give your birth year as A.D. 1988, but simply 1988.

Some historians now prefer to use the abbreviations B.C.E. ("before the common era") and C.E. ("common era") instead of B.C. and A.D. This is especially true of world historians who prefer to use symbols that are not so Western or Christian oriented. The dates, of course, remain the same. Thus, 1950 B.C.E. and 1950 B.C. would be the same year, as would A.D. 40 and 40 C.E. In keeping with the current usage by many world historians, this book will use the terms B.C.E. and C.E.

Historians also make use of other terms to refer to time. A decade is 10 years; a century is 100 years; and a millennium is 1,000 years. The phrase fourth century B.C.E. refers to the fourth period of 100 years counting backward from 1, the assumed date of the birth of Christ. Since the first century B.C.E would be the years 100 B.C.E. to 1 B.C.E., the fourth century B.C.E would be the years 400 B.C.E. to 301 B.C.E. We could say, then, that an event in 350 B.C.E. took place in the fourth century B.C.E.

The phrase fourth century C.E. refers to the fourth period of 100 years after the birth of Christ. Since the first period of 100 years would be the years 1 to 100, the fourth period or fourth century would be the years 301 to 400. We could say, then, for example, that an event in 350 took place in the fourth century. Likewise, the first millennium B.C.E refers to the years 1000 B.C.E to 1 B.C.E; the second millennium C.E refers to the years 1001 to 2000.

The dating of events can also vary from people to people. Most people in the Western world use the Western calendar, also known as the Gregorian calendar after Pope Gregory XIII who refined it in 1582. The Hebrew calendar, on the other hand, uses a different system in which the year 1 is the equivalent of the Western year 3760 B.C.E, considered by Jews to be the date of the creation of the world. Thus, the Western year 2007 will be the year 5767 on the Jewish calendar. The Islamic calendar begins year 1 on the day Muhammad fled Mecca, which is the year 622 on the Western calendar.

THEMES FOR UNDERSTANDING
WORLD HISTORY

As they pursue their craft, historians often organize their material on the basis of themes that enable them to ask and try to answer basic questions about the past. Such is our intention here. In preparing the third edition of this book, we have selected several major themes that we believe are especially important in understanding the course of world history. These themes transcend the boundaries of time and space and have relevance to all cultures since the beginning of the human experience.

In the chapters that follow, we will refer to these themes frequently as we advance from the prehistoric era to the present. Where appropriate, we shall make comparisons across cultural boundaries, or across different time periods. To facilitate this process, we have included a comparative essay in each chapter that focuses on a particular theme within the specific time period dealt with in that section of the book. For example, the comparative essays in Chapters 1 and 6 deal with the human impact on the natural environment during the premodern era, while those in Chapters 21 and 25 discuss the issue during the age of imperialism and in the contemporary world. Each comparative essay is identified with a particular theme, although it will be noted that many essays deal with several themes at the same time.

We have sought to illustrate these themes through the use of comparative illustrations in each chapter. These illustrations are comparative in nature and seek to encourage the reader to think about thematic issues in cross-cultural terms, while not losing sight of the unique characteristics of individual societies. Our seven themes, each divided into two subtopics, are listed below.

1. *Politics and Government*   The study of politics seeks to answer certain basic questions that historians have about the structure of a society: How were people governed? What was the relationship between the ruler and the ruled? What people or groups of people (the political elites) held political power? What actions did people take to guarantee their security or change their form of government?

2. *Arts and Ideas*   We cannot understand a society without looking at its culture, or the common ideas, beliefs, and patterns of behavior that are passed on from one generation to the next. Culture includes both high culture and popular culture. High culture consists of the writings of a society's thinkers and the works of its artists. A society's popular culture is the world of ideas and experiences of ordinary people. Today the media have embraced the term popular culture to describe the current trends and fashionable styles.

3. *Religion and Philosophy*   Throughout history, people have sought to find a deeper meaning to human life. How have the world's great religions, such as Hinduism, Buddhism, Judaism, Christianity, and Islam, influenced people's lives? How have they spread to create new patterns of culture in other parts of the world?

4. *Family and Society*   The most basic social unit in human society has always been the family. From a study of family and social patterns, we learn about the different social classes that make up a society and their relationships with one another. We also learn about the role of gender in individual societies. What different roles did men and women play in their societies? How and why were those roles different?

5. *Science and Technology*   For thousands of years, people around the world have made scientific discoveries and technological innovations that have changed our world. From the creation of stone tools that made farming easier to advanced computers that guide our airplanes, science and technology have altered how humans have related to their world.

6. *Earth and the Environment*   Throughout history, peoples and societies have been affected by the physical world in which they live. Climatic changes alone have been an important factor in human history. Through their economic activities, peoples and societies, in turn, have also made an impact on their world. Human activities have affected the physical environment and even endangered the very existence of entire societies and species.

7. *Interaction and Exchange*   Many world historians believe that the exchange of ideas and innovations is the driving force behind the evolution of human societies. The introduction of agriculture, writing and printing, metal working, and navigational techniques, for example, spread gradually from one part of the world to other regions and eventually changed the face of the entire globe. The process of cultural and technological exchange took place in various ways, including trade, conquest, and the migration of peoples.

THIRD EDITION

THE ESSENTIAL WORLD HISTORY TO 1500

I

THE FIRST CIVILIZATIONS AND THE RISE OF EMPIRES (PREHISTORY TO 500 C.E.)

FOR HUNDREDS OF THOUSANDS of years, human beings lived in small communities, seeking to survive by hunting, fishing, and foraging in an often hostile environment. Then, in the space of a few thousand years, there was an abrupt change of direction as human beings in a few widely scattered areas of the globe began to master the art of cultivating food crops. As food production increased, the population in such areas grew, and people began to congregate in larger communities. Cities appeared and became centers of cultural and religious development. Historians refer to these changes as the beginnings of civilization.

How and why did the first civilizations arise? What role did cross-cultural contacts play in their development? What was the nature of the relationship between these permanent settlements and nonagricultural peoples living elsewhere in the world? Finally, what brought about the demise of these early civilizations, and what legacy did they leave for their successors in the region? The first civilizations that emerged in Mesopotamia, Egypt, India, and China in the fourth and third millennia B.C.E. all shared a number of basic characteristics. Each developed in a river valley that was able to provide the agricultural resources needed to maintain a large population.

The appearance of these sedentary societies had a major impact on the social organizations, religious beliefs, and ways of life of the peoples living within their boundaries. With the increase in population and the development of centralized authority came the emergence of cities. Within the cities, new forms of livelihood appeared to satisfy the growing need for social services and consumer goods. Some people became artisans or merchants, while others became warriors, scholars, or priests. In some cases, the physical divisions within the first cities reflected the strict hierarchical character of the society as a whole, with a royal palace surrounded by an imposing wall and separate from the remainder of the urban population.

Although the emergence of the first civilizations led to the appearance of major cities, the vast majority of the population undoubtedly consisted of peasants or slaves working on the lands of the wealthy. In general, rural peoples were less affected by the change than their urban counterparts. Farmers continued to live in simple mud-and-thatch huts, and many still faced severe legal restrictions on their freedom of action and movement. Slavery was still commonly practiced in virtually all ancient societies.

Within these civilizations, the nature of social organization and relationships also began to change. As the concept of private property spread, people were less likely to live in large kinship groups, and the concept of the nuclear family became increasingly prevalent. Gender roles came to be differentiated, with men working in the fields or at various specialized occupations and women remaining in the home. Wives were less likely to be viewed as partners than as possessions under the control of their husbands.

These new civilizations were also the scene of significant religious and cultural developments. All of them gave birth to new religions as a means of explaining the functioning of the forces of nature. The approval of gods was deemed crucial

to a community's chances of success, and a professional class of priests emerged to govern relations with the divine world.

Writing was an important development in the evolution of these new civilizations. Eventually, all of them used writing as a primary means of communication and of creative expression.

From the beginnings of the first civilizations around 3000 B.C.E., there was an ongoing movement toward the creation of larger territorial states with more sophisticated systems of control. This process reached a high point in the first millennium B.C.E. Between 1000 and 500 B.C.E., the Assyrians and Persians amassed empires that encompassed large areas of the ancient Middle East. The conquests of Alexander the Great in the fourth century B.C.E. created an even larger, if short-lived, empire that soon divided into four kingdoms. Later, the western portion of these kingdoms as well as the Mediterranean world and much of western Europe fell subject to the mighty empire of the Romans. At the same time, much of India became part of the Mauryan Empire. Finally, in the last few centuries B.C.E., the Qin and Han dynasties of China created a unified Chinese empire.

At first, these new civilizations had relatively little contact with peoples in the surrounding regions. But there is growing evidence that a pattern of regional trade had begun to develop in the Middle East, and probably in southern and eastern Asia as well, at a very early date. As the population increased, the volume of trade undoubtedly rose with it, and the new civilizations began to move outward to acquire new lands and access needed resources. As they expanded, they began to encounter peoples along the periphery of their growing empires.

Not much evidence has survived to chronicle the nature of these first encounters, but it is likely that the results varied widely according to time and place. In some cases, the growing civilizations found it relatively easy to absorb isolated communities of agricultural or food-gathering peoples whom they encountered. Such was the case in southern China and in the southern part of the South Asian peninsula. But in other instances, notably among the nomadic or semi-nomadic peoples in central and northeastern Asia, the problem was more complicated and often resulted in bitter and extended conflict.

Contacts between these nomadic or seminomadic peoples and settled civilizations probably developed gradually over an extended period of time. Often the relationship, at least at the outset, was mutually beneficial, as each needed goods produced by the other. Nomadic peoples in Central Asia also served as an important conduit for goods and ideas between sedentary civilizations and were transporting goods over long distances as early as 3000 B.C.E. Overland trade throughout southwestern Asia was already well established by the third millennium B.C.E.

Eventually, the relationship between the settled peoples and the nomadic peoples became increasingly characterized by conflict. Where conflict occurred, the governments of the sedentary civilizations used a variety of techniques to resolve the problem, including negotiations, conquest, or alliance with other pastoral peoples to isolate their primary tormentors.

In the end, these early civilizations collapsed not only as a result of nomadic invasions but also because of their own weaknesses, which made them increasingly vulnerable to attacks along the frontier. Some of their problems were political, and others were related to climatic change or environmental problems.

The fall of the ancient empires did not mark the end of civilization, of course, but rather a transition to a new stage of increasing complexity in the evolution of human society. ◈

THE FIRST CIVILIZATIONS: THE PEOPLES OF WESTERN ASIA AND NORTH AFRICA

Ruins of the ancient Sumerian city of Uruk

© Nik Wheeler/CORBIS

*I*N 1849, A DARING YOUNG ENGLISHMAN made a hazardous journey into the deserts and swamps of southern Iraq. Braving high winds and temperatures that reached 120 degrees Fahrenheit, William Loftus led a small expedition southward along the banks of the Euphrates River in search of the roots of civilization. As he said, "From our childhood we have been led to regard this place as the cradle of the human race."

Guided by native Arabs into the southernmost reaches of Iraq, Loftus and his small band of explorers were soon overwhelmed by what they saw. He wrote, "I know of nothing more exciting or impressive than the first sight of one of these great piles, looming in solitary grandeur from the surrounding plains and marshes." One of these piles, known to the natives as the mound of Warka, contained the ruins of Uruk, one of the first cities in the world and part of one of the world's first civilizations.

Southern Iraq, known to ancient peoples as Mesopotamia, was one area in the world where civilization began. In the fertile valleys of large rivers—the Tigris and Euphrates in Mesopotamia, the Nile in Egypt, the Indus in India, and the Yellow River in China—intensive agriculture became capable of supporting large groups of people. In these regions, civilization was born. The first civilizations emerged in western Asia (now known as the Middle East) and North Africa, where people developed the organized societies that we associate with civilization.

Before considering the early civilizations of western Asia and North Africa, however, we must briefly examine humankind's prehistory and observe how human beings made the shift from hunting and gathering to agricultural communities and ultimately to cities. ◆

The First Humans

The earliest humanlike creatures—known as **hominids**—lived in Africa three to four million years ago. Called australopithecines, or "southern ape-men," by their discoverers, they flourished in eastern and southern Africa and were the first hominids to make simple stone tools. Australopithecines were also bipedal—that is, they walked upright on two legs, a trait that enabled them to move over long distances and use their arms and legs for different purposes.

In 1959, Louis and Mary Leakey discovered a new form of hominid in Africa that they labeled *Homo habilis* ("handy human"). The Leakeys believed that *Homo habilis,* which had a brain almost 50 percent larger than that of the australopithecines, was the earliest toolmaking hominid. Their larger brains and ability to walk upright allowed these hominids to become more sophisticated in the search for meat, seeds, and nuts for nourishment.

A new phase in early human development occurred around 1.8 million years ago with the emergence of *Homo erectus* ("upright human"). A more advanced human form, *Homo erectus* made use of larger and more varied tools and was the first hominid to leave Africa and move into Europe and Asia.

The Emergence of *Homo sapiens*

Around 250,000 years ago, a crucial phase in human development began with the emergence of *Homo sapiens* ("wise human"). By 100,000 B.C.E., two groups of *Homo sapiens* had developed. One type was the Neanderthal, whose remains were first found in the Neander River valley in Germany. Neanderthal remains have since been found in both Europe and the Middle East and have been dated to between 100,000 and 30,000 B.C.E. Neanderthals relied on a variety of stone tools and were the first early people to bury their dead.

The first anatomically modern humans, known as *Homo sapiens sapiens* ("wise, wise human"), appeared in Africa between 200,000 and 150,000 years ago. Recent evidence indicates that they began to spread outside Africa around 100,000 years ago. Map 1.1 shows probable dates for different movements, although many of these dates are still controversial. By 30,000 B.C.E., *Homo sapiens sapiens* had replaced the Neanderthals, who had largely become extinct, and by 10,000 B.C.E., members of the *Homo sapiens sapiens* species could be found throughout the world. By that time, it was the only human species left. All humans today, whether Europeans, Australian Aborigines, or Africans, belong to the same subspecies of human being.

The Hunter-Gatherers of the Paleolithic Age

One of the basic distinguishing features of the human species is the ability to make tools. The earliest tools were made of stone, and so the early period of human history (c. 2,500,000–10,000 B.C.E.) has been designated the **Paleolithic Age** (*paleolithic* is Greek for "old stone").

For hundreds of thousands of years, humans relied on hunting and gathering for their daily food. Paleolithic people had a close relationship with the world around them, and over a period of time, they came to know what animals to hunt and what plants to eat. They gathered wild nuts, berries, fruits, and a variety of wild grains and green plants. Around the world, they captured and consumed different animals, including buffalo, horses, bison, reindeer, and fish.

The hunting of animals and the gathering of wild plants no doubt led to certain patterns of living. Paleolithic people probably lived in small bands of twenty or thirty. They were nomadic, moving from place to place to follow animal migrations and vegetation cycles. Over the years, tools became more refined and more useful. The invention of the spear and later the bow and arrow made hunting considerably easier. Harpoons and fishhooks made of bone increased the catch of fish.

Both men and women were responsible for finding food—the chief work of Paleolithic people. Because women bore and raised the children, they generally stayed close to the camps, but they played an important role in acquiring food, gathering berries, nuts, and grains. Men hunted the wild animals, an activity that took them far from camp. Because both men and women played important roles in providing for the band's survival, scientists have argued that a rough equality existed between men and women.

These groups of Paleolithic people, especially those who lived in cold climates, found shelter in caves. Over time, they created new types of shelter as well. Perhaps the most common was a simple structure of wood poles or sticks covered with animal hides. The systematic use of fire, which archaeologists believe began around 500,000 years ago, made it possible for the caves and shelters to have light and heat. Fire also enabled early humans to cook their food, which made it taste better, last longer, and, in the case of some plants such as wild grain, easier to digest.

The making of tools and the use of fire—two important technological innovations of Paleolithic peoples—remind us how crucial the ability to adapt was to human survival. But Paleolithic peoples did more than just survive. The cave paintings of large animals found in southwestern France and northern Spain bear witness to the cultural activity of Paleolithic peoples. A cave discovered in southern France in 1994 contains more than three hundred

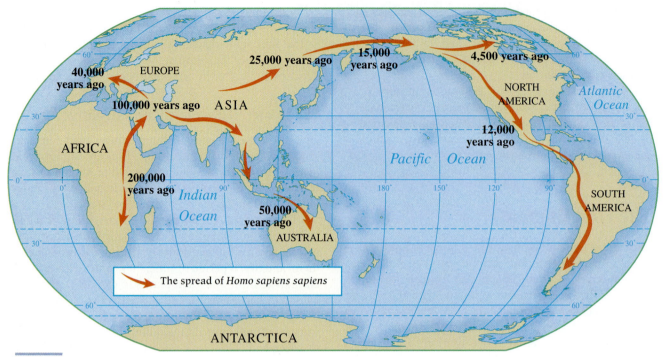

MAP 1.1 **The Spread of *Homo sapiens sapiens*.** *Homo sapiens sapiens* spread from Africa beginning about 100,000 years ago. Living and traveling in small groups, these anatomically modern humans were hunter-gatherers. ❓ Given that some diffusion of humans occurred during ice ages, how might such climate change affect humans and their movements, especially from Asia to Australia and Asia to North America?

🌐 View an animated version of this map or related maps at http://worldrc.wadsworth.com/

paintings of lions, oxen, owls, panthers, and other animals. Most of these are animals that Paleolithic people did not hunt, which suggests that they were painted for religious or decorative purposes.

The Neolithic Revolution, c. 10,000–4000 B.C.E.

The end of the last ice age around 10,000 B.C.E. was followed by what is called the **Neolithic Revolution** because it ushered in the New Stone Age (*neolithic* is Greek for "new stone"). The name New Stone Age is misleading, however. Although Neolithic peoples made a new type of polished stone axes, this was not the most significant change they introduced.

A Revolution in Agriculture The biggest change was the shift from hunting animals and gathering plants for sustenance to producing food by systematic agriculture. The planting of grains and vegetables provided a regular supply of food, while the taming of animals, such as sheep, goats, cattle, and pigs, added a steady source of meat, milk, and fibers such as wool for clothing. The growing of crops and the taming of food-producing animals created a new relationship between humans and nature, which historians speak of as an agricultural revolution. Revolutionary change is dramatic and requires great effort, but the ability to acquire food on a regular basis gave humans greater control over their environment and enabled them

to give up their nomadic ways of life and live in settled communities.

Systematic agriculture developed independently in different areas of the world between 8000 and 5000 B.C.E. Inhabitants of the Middle East began cultivating wheat and barley and domesticating pigs, cattle, goats, and sheep by 8000 B.C.E. From the Middle East, farming spread into southeastern Europe and by 4000 B.C.E. was well established in central Europe and the coastal regions of the Mediterranean. The cultivation of wheat and barley also spread from western Asia into the Nile valley of Egypt by 6000 B.C.E. and soon spread up the Nile to other areas of Africa. In the woodlands and tropical forests of Central Africa, a separate farming system emerged with the growing of tubers or root crops such as yams and tree crops such as bananas. The cultivation of wheat and barley also moved eastward into the highlands of northwestern and central India between 7000 and 5000 B.C.E. By 5000 B.C.E., rice was being cultivated in Southeast Asia, and it soon spread into southern China. In northern China, the cultivation of millet and the domestication of pigs and dogs seem well established by 6000 B.C.E. In the Western Hemisphere, Mesoamericans (inhabitants of present-day Mexico and Central America) domesticated beans, squash, and maize (corn) as well as dogs and fowl between 7000 and 5000 B.C.E. (see the comparative essay "From Hunter-Gatherers and Herders to Farmers" on p. 7).

FROM HUNTER-GATHERERS AND HERDERS TO FARMERS

EARTH & ENVIRONMENT

About ten thousand years ago, human beings began to practice the cultivation of crops and the domestication of animals. The first farmers undoubtedly used simple techniques and still relied primarily on other forms of food production, such as hunting, foraging, and pastoralism, or herding. The real breakthrough came when farmers began to cultivate crops along the floodplains of river systems. The advantage was that crops grown in such areas were not as dependent on rainfall and therefore produced a more reliable harvest. An additional benefit was that the sediment carried by the river waters deposited nutrients in the soil, thus enabling the farmer to cultivate a single plot of ground for many years without moving to a new location. Thus, the first truly sedentary (nonmigratory) societies were born.

The spread of river valley agriculture in various parts of Asia and Africa was the decisive factor in the rise of the first civilizations. The increase in food production in these regions led to a significant growth in population, while efforts to control the flow of water to maximize the irrigation of cultivated areas and to protect the local inhabitants from hostile forces outside the community provoked the first steps toward cooperative activities on a large scale. The need to oversee the entire process brought about the emergence of an elite that was eventually transformed into a government.

We shall investigate this process in the next several chapters as we explore the rise of civilizations in the Mediterranean, the Middle East, South Asia, China, and the Americas. We shall also raise a number of important questions: Why did human communities in some areas that had the capacity to support agriculture not take the leap to farming? Why did other groups that had managed to master the cultivation of crops not take the next step to create large and advanced societies? Finally, what happened to the existing communities of hunter-gatherers who were overrun or driven out as the agricultural revolution spread its way rapidly throughout the world?

Over the years, a number of possible reasons, some of them biological, others cultural or environmental in nature, have been advanced to explain such phenomena. According to Jared Diamond, in his highly acclaimed work *Guns, Germs, and Steel: The Fates of Human Societies,* the ultimate causes of such differences lie not within the character or cultural values of the resident population, but in the nature of the local climate and topography. These influence the degree to which local crops and animals can be put to human use and then be transmitted to adjoining regions. In Mesopotamia, for example, the widespread availability of edible crops, such as wheat and barley, helped promote the transition to agriculture in the region. At the same time, the lack of land barriers between Mesopotamia and its neighbors to the east and west facilitated the rapid spread of agricultural techniques and crops to climatically similar regions in the Indus River valley and Egypt.

Consequences of the Neolithic Revolution The growing of crops on a regular basis gave rise to relatively permanent settlements, which historians refer to as Neolithic farming villages or towns. Although Neolithic villages appeared in Europe, India, Egypt, China, and Mesoamerica, the oldest and most extensive ones were located in the Middle East. Çatal Hüyük, located in modern Turkey, had walls that enclosed 32 acres, and its population probably reached six thousand inhabitants during its high point from 6700 to 5700 B.C.E. People lived in simple mudbrick houses that were built so close to one another that there were few streets. To get to their homes, people had to walk along the rooftops and enter the house through a hole in the roof.

The Neolithic agricultural revolution had far-reaching consequences. Once people settled in villages or towns, they built houses for protection and other structures for the storage of goods. As organized communities stored food and accumulated material goods, they began to engage in trade. People also began to specialize in certain crafts, and a division of labor developed. Pottery was made from clay and baked in a fire to make it hard. The pots were used for cooking and to store grains. Woven baskets were also used for storage. Stone tools became refined as flint blades were used to make sickles and hoes for use in the fields. Vegetable fibers from such plants as flax and cotton were used to make thread that was woven into cloth. In the course of the Neolithic Age, many of the food plants consumed today came to be cultivated.

The change to systematic agriculture in the Neolithic Age also had consequences for the relationship between men and women. Men assumed the primary responsibility for working in the fields and herding animals, jobs that kept them away from the home. Women remained behind, caring for the children, weaving clothes, and performing other household tasks that required considerable labor. In time, as work outside the home was increasingly perceived as more important than work done at home, men came to play the more dominant role in society, a pattern that persisted until our own times.

Other patterns set in the Neolithic Age also proved to be enduring elements of human history. Fixed dwellings, domesticated animals, regular farming, a division of labor, men holding power—all of these are part of the human story.

Statues from Ain Ghazal. These life-size statues made of plaster and bitumen were discovered in 1984 in Ain Ghazal, an archaeological site near Amman, Jordan. Dating from 6500 B.C.E., they are among the oldest known statues of the human figure. Although they appear lifelike, their features are considered generic rather than portraits of individual faces. The purpose and meaning of these sculptures may never be known.

Courtesy of the Hashemite Kingdom of Jordan, Dept. of Antiquities

For all of our scientific and technological progress, human survival still depends on the growing and storing of food, an accomplishment of people in the Neolithic Age. The Neolithic Revolution was truly a turning point in human history.

Between 4000 and 3000 B.C.E., significant technical developments began to transform the Neolithic towns. The invention of writing enabled records to be kept, and the use of metals marked a new level of human control over the environment and its resources. Already before 4000 B.C.E., artisans had discovered that metal-bearing rocks could be heated to liquefy metals, which could then be cast in molds to produce tools and weapons that were more useful than stone instruments. Copper was the first metal to be used for producing tools, but after 4000 B.C.E., metalworkers in western Asia discovered that combining copper and tin formed bronze, a much harder and more durable metal than copper alone. Its widespread use has led historians to speak of the Bronze Age from around 3000 to 1200 B.C.E.; thereafter, bronze was increasingly replaced by iron.

At first, Neolithic settlements were hardly more than villages, but as their inhabitants mastered the art of farming, more complex human societies gradually emerged. As wealth increased, these societies began to develop armies and to wall off their cities for protection. By the beginning of the Bronze Age, the concentration of larger numbers of people in river valleys was leading to a whole new pattern for human life.

The Emergence of Civilization

As we have seen, early human beings formed small groups and developed a simple culture that enabled them to survive. As human societies grew and developed greater complexity, civilization came into being. A **civilization** is a complex culture in which large numbers of people share a variety of common elements. Historians have identified a number of basic characteristics of civilization, including the following:

1. *An urban focus.* Cities became the centers for political, economic, social, cultural, and religious development.
2. *New political and military structures.* An organized government bureaucracy arose to meet the administrative demands of the growing population, and armies were organized to gain land and power.
3. *A new social structure based on economic power.* While kings and an upper class of priests, political leaders, and warriors dominated, there also existed a large group of free common people (farmers, artisans, craftspeople) and, at the very bottom socially, a class of slaves.
4. *The development of more complexity in a material sense.* Abundant agricultural yields created opportunities for economic specialization as a surplus of goods enabled some people to work in occupations other than farming. The demand of ruling elites for luxury items encouraged artisans and craftspeople to create new products. As urban populations exported finished goods in exchange for raw materials from neighboring populations, organized trade grew substantially.
5. *A distinct religious structure.* The gods were deemed crucial to the community's success, and professional priestly classes, as stewards of the gods' property, regulated relations with the gods.
6. *The development of writing.* Kings, priests, merchants, and artisans began to use writing to keep records.

7. *New and significant artistic and intellectual activity.* For example, monumental architectural structures, usually religious, occupied a prominent place in urban environments.

The first civilizations that developed in Mesopotamia and Egypt will be examined in detail in this chapter. But civilizations also developed independently in other parts of the world. Between 3000 and 1500 B.C.E., the valleys of the Indus River in India supported a flourishing civilization that extended hundreds of miles from the Himalayas to the coast of the Arabian Sea (see Chapter 2). Another river valley civilization emerged along the Yellow River in northern China about four thousand years ago (see Chapter 3). Under the Shang dynasty of kings, which ruled from 1750 to 1122 B.C.E., this civilization contained impressive cities with huge city walls and royal palaces.

Scholars have believed for a long time that civilization emerged only in these four areas—in the fertile river valleys of the Tigris and Euphrates, the Nile, the Indus, and the Yellow River. Recently, however, archaeologists have discovered two other early civilizations. One of these flourished in Central Asia (in what are now the republics of Turkmenistan and Uzbekistan) around four thousand years ago. People in this civilization built mudbrick buildings, raised sheep and goats, had bronze tools, used a system of irrigation to grow wheat and barley, and had a writing system.

Central Asian Civilization

Another early civilization was discovered in the Supe River valley of Peru, in South America. At the center of this civilization was the city of Caral, which flourished around 2600 B.C.E. It contained buildings for officials, apartment buildings, and grand residences, all built of stone. The inhabitants of Caral also developed a system of irrigation by diverting a river more than a mile upstream into their fields.

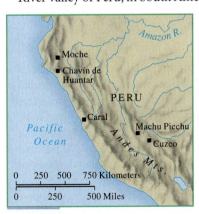
Caral, Peru

Civilization in Mesopotamia

The Greeks spoke of the valley between the Tigris and Euphrates rivers as Mesopotamia, the "land between the rivers." The region receives little rain, but the soil of the plain of southern Mesopotamia was enlarged and enriched over the years by layers of silt deposited by the two rivers. In late spring, the Tigris and Euphrates overflow their banks and deposit their fertile silt, but since this flooding depends on the melting of snows in the upland mountains where the rivers begin, it is irregular and sometimes catastrophic. In such circumstances, farming could be accomplished only with human intervention in the form of irrigation and drainage ditches. A complex system was required to control the flow of the rivers and produce the crops. Large-scale irrigation made possible the expansion of agriculture in this region, and the abundant food provided the material base for the emergence of civilization in Mesopotamia.

The City-States of Ancient Mesopotamia

The creators of the first Mesopotamian civilization were the Sumerians, a people whose origins remain unclear. By 3000 B.C.E., they had established a number of independent cities, including Eridu, Ur, Uruk, Umma, and Lagash (see Map 1.2). As the cities expanded, they came to exercise political and economic control over the surrounding countryside, forming city-states, which were the basic units of Sumerian civilization.

Sumerian Cities Sumerian cities were surrounded by walls. Uruk, for example, was encircled by a wall 6 miles long with defense towers located along it every 30 to 35 feet. City dwellings, built of sun-dried bricks, included both the small flats of peasants and the larger dwellings of the civic and priestly officials. Although Mesopotamia had little stone or wood for building purposes, it did have plenty of mud. Mudbricks, easily shaped by hand, were left to bake in the hot sun until they were hard enough to use for building. People in Mesopotamia were remarkably creative with mudbricks, inventing the arch and the dome and constructing some of the largest brick buildings in the world.

The most prominent building in a Sumerian city was the temple, which was dedicated to the chief god or goddess of the city and often built atop a massive stepped tower called a **ziggurat**. The Sumerians believed that gods and goddesses owned the cities, and much wealth was used to build temples to these deities and elaborate houses for the priests and priestesses who served them. Priests and priestesses, who supervised the temples and their property, had much power. Eventually, however, ruling power in Sumerian city-states passed into the hands of kings.

Sumerians viewed kingship as divine in origin—kings, they believed, derived their power from the gods and were the agents of the gods. As one person said in a petition to his king: "You in your judgment, you are the son of Anu [god of the sky]; Your commands, like the work of a god, cannot be reversed. Your words, like rain pouring down from heaven, are without number."[1] Regardless of their origins, kings had power—they led armies, supervised the

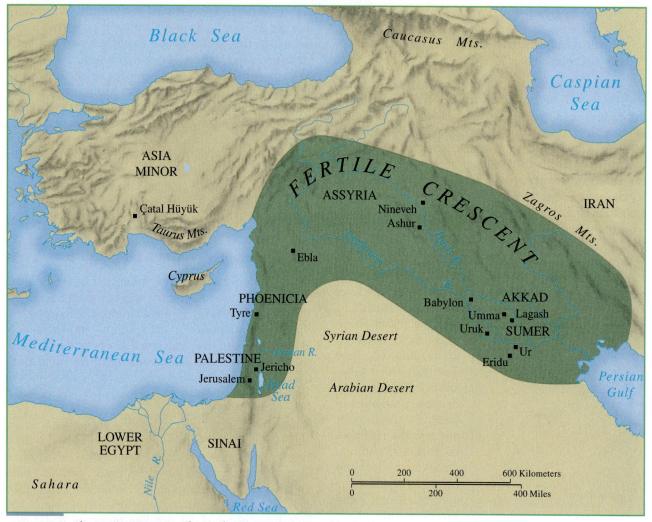

MAP 1.2 **The Ancient Near East.** The Fertile Crescent encompassed land with access to water at the Persian Gulf, the Mediterranean Sea, and the Tigris and Euphrates rivers. Employing flood management and irrigation systems, the peoples of the region established civilizations based on agriculture. These civilizations developed writing, law codes, and economic specialization. ❓ What geographic aspects of the Mesopotamian city-states made conflict between them likely? 🌐 **View an animated version of this map or related maps at** http://worldrc.wadsworth.com/

building of public works, and organized workers for the irrigation projects on which Mesopotamian farming depended. The army, the government bureaucracy, and the priests and priestesses all aided the kings in their rule.

Economy and Society The economy of the Sumerian city-states was primarily agricultural, but commerce and industry became important as well. The people of Mesopotamia produced woolen textiles, pottery, and metalwork. The Sumerians imported copper, tin, and timber in exchange for dried fish, wool, barley, wheat, and metal goods. Traders traveled by land to the edge of the Mediterranean in the west and by sea to India in the east. The introduction of the wheel, which had been invented around 3000 B.C.E. by nomadic people living in the region north of the Black Sea, led to carts with wheels that made the transport of goods easier.

Sumerian city-states contained three major social groups—nobles, commoners, and slaves. Nobles included royal and priestly officials and their families. Commoners were the nobles' clients who worked for the palace and temple estates and other free citizens who worked as farmers, merchants, fishers, and craftspeople. At least 90 percent of the population was engaged in farming. Slaves belonged to palace officials, who used them in building projects; to temple officials, who used mostly female slaves to weave cloth and grind grain; and to rich landowners, who used them for farming and domestic work.

Empires in Ancient Mesopotamia

As the number of Sumerian city-states grew and expanded, new conflicts arose as city-state fought city-state for control of land and water. Located in the flat

TABLE 1.1 **Some Semitic Languages**

Akkadian	*Assyrian*	Hebrew
Arabic	*Babylonian*	*Phoenician*
Aramaic	*Canaanitic*	*Syriac*

NOTE: Languages in italic type are no longer spoken.

land of Mesopotamia, the Sumerian city-states were also open to invasion. To the north of the Sumerian city-states were the Akkadians. We call them a Semitic people because of the language they spoke (see Table 1.1). Around 2340 B.C.E., Sargon, leader of the Akkadians, overran the Sumerian city-states and established an empire that included most of Mesopotamia as well as lands westward to the Mediterranean. Attacks from neighboring hill peoples eventually caused the Akkadian empire to fall, and its end by 2100 B.C.E. brought a return to the system of warring city-states. It was not until 1792 B.C.E. that a new empire came to control much of Mesopotamia. Leadership came from Babylon, a city-state north of Akkad, where Hammurabi ruled over the Amorites or Old Babylonians, a large group of Semitic-speaking seminomads.

Hammurabi's Empire Hammurabi (1792–1750 B.C.E.) employed a well-disciplined army of foot soldiers who carried axes, spears, and copper or bronze daggers. He learned to divide his opponents and subdue them one by one. Using such methods, he gained control of Sumer and Akkad, creating a new Mesopotamian kingdom with its capital at Babylon.

Hammurabi, the man of war, was also a man of peace who took a strong interest in state affairs. He built temples, defensive walls, and irrigation canals; encouraged trade; and brought about an economic revival. Indeed, Hammurabi saw himself as a shepherd to his people: "I am indeed the shepherd who brings peace, whose scepter is just. My benevolent shade was spread over my city. I held the people of the lands of Sumer and Akkad safely on my lap."[2] After his death, however, a series of weak kings were unable to keep Hammurabi's empire united, and it finally fell to new invaders.

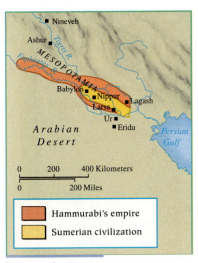

Hammurabi's Empire

The Code of Hammurabi Hammurabi is best remembered for his law code, a collection of 282 laws. This collection provides considerable insight into almost every aspect of everyday life in Mesopotamia and gives us a priceless glimpse of the values of this early society (see the box on p. 12).

The Code of Hammurabi reveals a society with a system of strict justice. Penalties for criminal offenses were severe and varied according to the social class of the victim. A crime against a member of the upper class (a noble) by a member of the lower class (a commoner) was punished more severely than the same offense against a member of the lower class. Moreover, the principle of "an eye for an eye, a tooth for a tooth" was fundamental to this system of justice. This meant that punishments should fit the crime: "If a free man has destroyed the eye of a member of the aristocracy, they shall destroy his eye." Hammurabi's code also had an impact on legal ideas in Southwest Asia for hundreds of years, as the following verse from the Hebrew Bible (Leviticus 24:19–20) demonstrates: "If anyone injures his neighbor, whatever he has done must be done to him: fracture for fracture, eye for eye, tooth for tooth. As he has injured the other, so he is to be injured."

The largest category of laws in the Code of Hammurabi focused on marriage and the family. Parents arranged marriages for their children. After marriage, the two parties signed a marriage contract; without it, no one was considered legally married. While the husband provided a bridal payment, the woman's parents were responsible for a dowry to the new husband.

As in many patriarchal societies, women possessed fewer privileges and rights in marriage than men. A woman's place was in the home, and failure to fulfill her expected duties was grounds for divorce. If she was not able to bear children or tried to leave home to engage in business, her husband could divorce her. Furthermore, a wife who was a "gadabout, . . . neglecting her house [and] humiliating her husband," could be drowned.

Sexual relations were strictly regulated as well. Husbands, but not wives, were permitted sexual activity outside marriage. A wife and her lover caught committing adultery were pitched into the river, although if the husband pardoned his wife, the king could pardon the guilty man. Incest was strictly forbidden. If a father had incestuous relations with his daughter, he would be banished. Incest between a son and his mother resulted in both being burned.

Fathers ruled their children as well as their wives. Obedience was duly expected: "If a son has struck his father, he shall cut off his hand." If a son committed a serious enough offense, his father could disinherit him. Hammurabi's law code covered almost every aspect of people's lives.

The Culture of Mesopotamia

A spiritual worldview was of fundamental importance to Mesopotamian culture. To the peoples of Mesopotamia, the gods were living realities who affected all aspects of life. It was crucial, therefore, that the correct hierarchies be observed. Leaders could prepare armies for war, but success really depended on a favorable relationship with the gods. This helps explain the importance of the priestly class and the reason why even the kings took great care to dedicate offerings and monuments to the gods.

THE CODE OF HAMMURABI

FAMILY & SOCIETY

Although there were earlier Mesopotamian law codes, Hammurabi's is the most complete. The law code emphasizes the principle of retribution ("an eye for an eye") and punishments that vary according to social status. Punishments could be severe. Marriage and family affairs also play a large role in the code. The following examples illustrate these concerns.

What do these points of law from the Code of Hammurabi reveal to you about Mesopotamian society?

The Code of Hammurabi

25. If fire broke out in a free man's house and a free man, who went to extinguish it, cast his eye on the goods of the owner of the house and has appropriated the goods of the owner of the house, that free man shall be thrown into that fire.

129. If the wife of a free man has been caught while lying with another man, they shall bind them and throw them into the water. If the husband of the woman wishes to spare his wife, then the king in turn may spare his subject.

131. If a free man's wife was accused by her husband, but she was not caught while lying with another man, she shall make affirmation by god and return to her house.

196. If a free man has destroyed the eye of a member of the aristocracy, they shall destroy his eye.

198. If he has destroyed the eye of a commoner or broken the bone of a commoner, he shall pay one mina of silver.

199. If he has destroyed the eye of a free man's slave or broken the bone of a free man's slave, he shall pay one-half his value.

209. If a free man struck another free man's daughter and has caused her to have a miscarriage, he shall pay ten shekels of silver for her fetus.

210. If that woman has died, they shall put his daughter to death.

211. If by a blow he has caused a commoner's daughter to have a miscarriage, he shall pay five shekels of silver.

212. If that woman has died, he shall pay one-half mina of silver.

213. If he struck a free man's female slave and has caused her to have a miscarriage, he shall pay two shekels of silver.

214. If that female slave has died, he shall pay one-third mina of silver.

CENGAGENOW To read the entire code, enter the *CengageNOW* documents area using the access card that is available for *The Essential World History.*

The Importance of Religion   The physical environment had an obvious impact on the Mesopotamian view of the universe. Ferocious floods, heavy downpours, scorching winds, and oppressive humidity were all part of the Mesopotamian climate. These conditions and the resulting famines easily convinced Mesopotamians that this world was controlled by supernatural forces, which often were not kind or reliable. In the presence of nature, people in Mesopotamia could easily feel helpless, as this poem relates:

> *The rampant flood which no man can oppose,*
> *Which shakes the heavens and causes earth to tremble,*
> *In an appalling blanket folds mother and child,*
> *Beats down the canebrake's full luxuriant greenery,*
> *And drowns the harvest in its time of ripeness.*[3]

The Mesopotamians discerned cosmic rhythms in the universe and accepted its order but perceived that it was not completely safe because of the presence of willful, powerful cosmic powers that they identified with gods and goddesses.

With its nearly three thousand gods and goddesses animating all aspects of the universe, Mesopotamian religion was a form of **polytheism.** The four most important deities were An, god of the sky and hence the most important force in the universe; Enlil, god of wind; Enki, god of the earth, rivers, wells, and canals, as well as inventions and crafts; and Ninhursaga, a goddess associated with soil, mountains, and vegetation, who came to be worshiped as a mother goddess, the "mother of all children," who manifested her power by giving birth to kings and conferring the royal insignia on them.

The Cultivation of New Arts and Sciences   The realization of writing's great potential was another aspect of Mesopotamian culture. Around 3000 B.C.E., the Sumerians invented a **cuneiform** ("wedge-shaped") system of writing. Using a reed stylus, they made wedge-shaped impressions on clay tablets, which were then baked or dried in the sun. Once dried, these tablets were virtually indestructible, and the several hundred thousand that have been found so far have provided a valuable source of information for modern scholars. Sumerian writing began as pictures of concrete objects that evolved into simplified signs, leading eventually to a phonetic system that made possible the written expression of abstract ideas.

Writing was important because it enabled a society to keep records and maintain knowledge of previous practices and events. Writing also made it possible for people to communicate ideas in new ways, which is especially evident in the most famous piece of Mesopotamian literature,

From *Atlas of Ancient America*, by Michael Coe, Dean Snow, and Elizabeth Benson/Andromeda Oxford Limited, Oxford, England

Pictographic sign, c. 3100 B.C.E.	✳	⌣	≈	🌾	⋁	▽		⊔	
Interpretation	star	?sun over horizon	?stream	ear of barley	bull's head	bowl	head + bowl	lower leg	?shrouded body
Cuneiform sign, c. 2400 B.C.E.	✳								
Cuneiform sign c. 700 B.C.E. (turned through 90°)									
Phonetic value*	dingir, an	u$_4$, ud	a	še	gu$_4$	nig$_2$, ninda	ku$_2$	du, gin, gub	lu$_2$
Meaning	god, sky	day, sun	water, seed, son	barley	ox	food, bread	to eat	to walk, to stand	man

*Some signs have more than one phonetic value and some sounds are represented by more than one sign; for example, u$_4$ means the fourth sign with the phonetic value *u*.

The Development of Cuneiform Writing. This chart shows the evolution of writing from pictographic signs around 3100 B.C.E. to cuneiform signs by about 700 B.C.E. Note that the sign for star came to mean "god" or "sky." Pictographic signs for *head* and *bowl* came eventually to mean "to eat" in their simplified cuneiform version.

 COMPARATIVE ILLUSTRATION

ARTS & IDEAS

Early Writing. Pictured at left is the upper part of the cone of Uruinimgina, an example of cuneiform script from an early Sumerian dynasty. The first Egyptian writing was also pictographic, as shown in the hieroglyphs in this detail from the mural in the tomb of Ramesses I. In Central America, the Mayan civilization had a well-developed writing system, also based on hieroglyphs, as seen below in this text carved on a stone platform in front of the Palace of the Large Masks in Kabah, Mexico.

the *Epic of Gilgamesh*, a poem that records the exploits of a legendary king, Gilgamesh, who embarks on a search for the secret of immortality. But his efforts fail; Gilgamesh remains mortal. The desire for immortality, one of humankind's great searches, ends in complete frustration. "Everlasting life," as this Mesopotamian epic makes clear, is only for the gods.

People in Mesopotamia also made outstanding achievements in mathematics and astronomy. In math, the Sumerians devised a number system based on 60, using combinations of 6 and 10 for practical solutions. They used geometry to measure fields and erect buildings. In astronomy, the Sumerians made use of units of 60 and charted the heavenly constellations. They based their calendar on twelve lunar months and brought it into harmony with the solar year by adding an extra month from time to time.

Egyptian Civilization: "The Gift of the Nile"

"The Egyptian Nile," wrote one Arab traveler, "surpasses all the rivers of the world in sweetness of taste, in length of course and usefulness. No other river in the world can show such a continuous series of towns and villages along its banks." The Nile River was crucial to the development of Egyptian civilization (see the box on p. 15). Egypt, like Mesopotamia, was a river valley civilization.

The Importance of Geography

The Nile is a unique river, beginning in the heart of Africa and coursing northward for thousands of miles. It is the longest river in the world. The Nile was responsible for creating an area several miles wide on both banks of the river that was fertile and capable of producing abundant harvests. The "miracle" of the Nile was its annual flooding. The river rose in the summer from rains in Central Africa, crested in Egypt in September and October, and left a deposit of silt that enriched the soil. The Egyptians called this fertile land the "Black Land" because it was dark in color from the silt and the lush crops that grew on it. Beyond these narrow strips of fertile fields lay the deserts (the "Red Land"). About 100 miles before it empties into the Mediterranean, the river splits into two major branches, forming the delta, a triangular-shaped territory called Lower Egypt to distinguish it from Upper Egypt, the land upstream to the south (see Map 1.3). Egypt's important cities developed at the apex of the delta.

The Nile, unlike Mesopotamia's rivers, flooded gradually and, most often, predictably, and the river itself was seen as life-enhancing, not life-threatening. Although a system of organized irrigation was still necessary, the small villages along the Nile could make the effort without the massive state intervention that was required in Mesopotamia. Egyptian civilization consequently tended to remain more rural, with many small villages congregated along a narrow band on both sides of the Nile.

The surpluses of food that Egyptian farmers grew in the fertile Nile valley made Egypt prosperous. But the Nile also served as a unifying factor in Egyptian history. In ancient times, the Nile was the fastest way to travel through the land, making both transportation and communication easier. Winds from the north pushed sailboats south, and the current of the Nile carried them north.

Unlike Mesopotamia, which was subject to constant invasion, Egypt had natural barriers that gave it some protection from invasion. These barriers included deserts to the west and east; cataracts (rapids) on the southern part of the Nile, which made defense relatively easy; and the Mediterranean Sea to the north.

The regularity of the Nile floods and the relative isolation of the Egyptians created a sense of security and a feeling of changelessness. To the ancient Egyptians, when the Nile flooded each year, "the fields laugh and people's faces light up." Unlike people in Mesopotamia, Egyptians faced life with a spirit of confidence in the stability of things. Ancient Egyptian civilization was characterized by a remarkable degree of continuity for thousands of years.

The Importance of Religion

Religion, too, provided a sense of security and timelessness for the Egyptians. Actually, they had no word for religion because it was an inseparable element of the world order to which Egyptian society belonged. The Egyptians were polytheistic and had a remarkable number of gods associated with heavenly bodies and natural forces. Two groups, sun gods and land gods, came to have special importance, hardly surprising in view of the importance to Egypt's well-being of the sun, the river, and the fertile land along its banks. The sun was the source of life and hence worthy of worship. The sun god took on different forms and names, depending on his specific role. He was worshiped as Atum in human form and as Re, who had a human body but the head of a falcon. The Egyptian ruler took the title of "Son of Re," since he was seen as an earthly form of Re. River and land deities included Osiris and Isis with their child Horus, who was related to the Nile and to the sun as well. Osiris became especially important as a symbol of resurrection or rebirth.

The Course of Egyptian History: The Old, Middle, and New Kingdoms

Modern historians have divided Egyptian history into three major periods known as the Old Kingdom, the Middle Kingdom, and the New Kingdom. All were periods of long-term stability characterized by strong leadership from

THE SIGNIFICANCE OF THE NILE RIVER AND THE PHARAOH

RELIGION & PHILOSOPHY

Two of the most important sources of life for the ancient Egyptians were the Nile River and the pharaoh. Egyptians perceived that the Nile made possible the abundant food that was a major source of their well-being. This *Hymn to the Nile*, probably from the nineteenth and twentieth dynasties in the New Kingdom, expresses the gratitude Egyptians felt for the Nile.

How do these two hymns underscore the importance of the Nile River and the institution of the pharaoh to Egyptian civilization?

Hymn to the Nile

> Hail to you, O Nile, that issues from the earth and comes to keep Egypt alive! . . .
>
> He that waters the meadows which Re created, in order to keep every kid alive.
>
> He that makes to drink the desert and the place distant from water: that is his dew coming down from heaven. . . .
>
> The lord of fishes, he who makes the marsh-birds to go upstream. . . .
>
> He who makes barley and brings emmer into being, that he may make the temples festive.
>
> If he is sluggish, then nostrils are stopped up, and everybody is poor. . . .
>
> When he rises, then the land is in jubilation, then every belly is in joy, every backbone takes on laughter, and every tooth is exposed.
>
> The bringer of good, rich in provisions, creator of all good, lord of majesty, sweet of fragrance. . . .

> He who makes every beloved tree to grow, without lack of them.

The Egyptian king, or pharaoh, was viewed as a god and the absolute ruler of Egypt. His significance and the gratitude of the Egyptian people for his existence are evident in this hymn from the reign of Sesotris III (c. 1880–1840 b.c.e.).

Hymn to the Pharaoh

> He has come unto us that he may carry away Upper Egypt; the double diadem [crown of Upper and Lower Egypt] has rested on his head.
>
> He has come unto us and has united the Two Lands; he has mingled the reed with the bee [symbols of Lower and Upper Egypt].
>
> He has come unto us and has brought the Black Land under his sway; he has apportioned to himself the RedLand.
>
> He has come unto us and has taken the Two Lands under his protection; he has given peace to the Two River-banks.
>
> He has come unto us and has made Egypt to live; he has banished its suffering.
>
> He has come unto us and has made the people to live; he has caused the throat of the subjects to breathe. . . .
>
> He has come unto us and has done battle for his boundaries; he has delivered them that were robbed.

CENGAGENOW To read a full version of *Hymn to the Nile*, enter the *CengageNOW* documents area using the access card that is available for *The Essential World History*.

---

dynasties of kings, freedom from invasion, construction of temples and pyramids, and considerable intellectual and cultural activity. Between the periods of stability were ages of political chaos and invasion known as the Intermediate Periods.

The Old Kingdom The history of Egypt begins around 3100 B.C.E. when King Menes united the villages of both Upper and Lower Egypt into a single kingdom and created the first Egyptian royal dynasty. Henceforth the ruler would be called "king of Upper and Lower Egypt," and the royal crown would be a double diadem, signifying the unification of all Egypt. Just as the Nile united Upper and Lower Egypt physically, kingship served to unite the two areas politically (see the box above).

The Old Kingdom encompassed the third through sixth dynasties of Egyptian kings, lasting from around 2686 to 2125 B.C.E. It was an age of prosperity and splendor, made visible in the construction of the greatest and largest pyramids in Egypt's history. Kingship was a divine institution in ancient Egypt and formed part of a universal scheme: "What is the king of Upper and Lower Egypt? He is a god by whose dealings one lives, the father and mother of all men, alone by himself, without an equal."[4] In obeying their king, subjects helped maintain the cosmic order. A breakdown in royal power meant that citizens were offending divinity and weakening the universal structure. Among the various titles of Egyptian kings, **pharaoh** (originally meaning "great house" or "palace," referring to the royal palace) eventually became the most common.

Although theoretically absolute in their power, in practice Egyptian kings did not rule alone. By the fourth dynasty, a bureaucracy with regular procedures had developed. In time, Egypt was divided into provinces or nomes, as they were later called by the Greeks—twenty-two in Upper Egypt and twenty in Lower Egypt. A governor, called a *nomarch* by the Greeks, was head of each nome and was responsible to the king.

The Pyramids One of the great achievements of Egyptian civilization, the building of pyramids, occurred in the time of the Old Kingdom. Pyramids were built as part of a

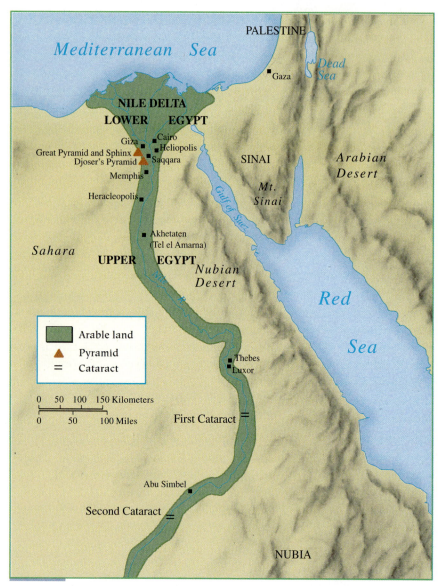

MAP 1.3 Ancient Egypt. Egyptian civilization centered on the life-giving water and flood silts of the Nile River, with most of the population living in Lower Egypt, where the river splits to form the Nile delta. Most of the pyramids, built during the Old Kingdom, are clustered south and west of Cairo. ❓ How did the lands to the east and west of the river make invasions of Egypt difficult?

larger complex of buildings dedicated to the dead—in effect, a city of the dead. The area included a large pyramid for the king's burial, smaller pyramids for his family, and several mastabas, rectangular structures with flat roofs used as tombs for the pharaoh's noble officials.

The tombs were well prepared for their residents, their rooms furnished and stocked with numerous supplies, including chairs, boats, chests, weapons, games, dishes, and a variety of food. The Egyptians believed that human beings had two bodies—a physical one and a spiritual one, which they called the *ka*. If the physical body was properly preserved (by mummification) and the tomb was furnished with all the objects of regular life, the *ka* could return and continue to live, surrounded by earthly comforts, despite the death of the physical body.

The largest and most magnificent of all the pyramids was built under King Khufu. Constructed at Giza around 2540 B.C.E., this famous Great Pyramid covers 13 acres, measures 756 feet at each side of its base, and stands 481 feet high. Its four sides are precisely oriented to the four points of the compass. The interior included a grand gallery to the burial chamber, which was built of granite and housed a lidless sarcophagus for the pharaoh's body. The Great Pyramid still stands as a visible symbol of the power of Egyptian kings of the Old Kingdom. No pyramid built later ever matched its size or splendor. The pyramid was not only the king's tomb but also an important symbol of royal power. It could be seen from miles away, reminding people of the glory, might, and wealth of the ruler who was regarded as a living god on earth.

The Middle Kingdom Despite the theory of divine order, the Old Kingdom eventually collapsed, ushering in a period of chaos that lasted about 150 years. Finally, a new royal dynasty managed to gain control of all Egypt and inaugurated the Middle Kingdom, a new period of stability lasting from about 2055 to 1650 B.C.E. Egyptians later portrayed the Middle Kingdom as a golden age, a clear indication of its stability.

As evidence of its newfound strength, Egypt began a period of expansion. Lower Nubia was conquered, and fortresses were built to protect the new southern frontier. The government also sent armies into Palestine and Syria, although they did not remain there. Pharaohs also sent traders to Kush, Syria, Mesopotamia, and Crete.

A new concern of the pharaohs for the people was a feature of the Middle Kingdom. In the Old Kingdom, the pharaoh had been viewed as an inaccessible god-king. Now he was portrayed as the shepherd of his people who must build public works and provide for the public welfare. Pharaohs of the Middle Kingdom undertook a number of helpful projects. The draining of swampland in the Nile delta provided thousands of acres of new farmland.

Chaos and a New Order: The New Kingdom The Middle Kingdom came to an end around 1650 B.C.E. with

Nubians in Egypt. During the New Kingdom, Egypt expanded to the north, into Palestine and Syria, and to the south, into the African kingdom of Nubia. Nubia had first emerged as an African kingdom around 2300 B.C.E. Nubians arriving in Egypt with bags and rings of gold are shown here in a fourteenth-century B.C.E. painting from an Egyptian official's tomb in Nubia. Nubia was a rich source of gold for the Egyptians.

the invasion of Egypt by a people from western Asia known to the Egyptians as the Hyksos. The Hyksos used horse-drawn war chariots and overwhelmed the Egyptian soldiers, who fought from donkey carts. For almost a hundred years, the Hyksos ruled much of Egypt, but the conquered took much from their conquerors. From the Hyksos, the Egyptians learned to use bronze in making new farming tools and weapons. They also mastered the military skills of the Hyksos, especially the use of horse-drawn war chariots.

Eventually, a new line of pharaohs—the eighteenth dynasty—made use of the new weapons to throw off Hyksos domination, reunite Egypt, establish the New Kingdom (c. 1550–1070 B.C.E.), and launch the Egyptians along a new militaristic path. During the period of the New Kingdom, Egypt created an empire and became the most powerful state in the Middle East.

Massive wealth aided the power of the New Kingdom pharaohs. The Egyptian rulers showed their wealth by building new temples. Queen Hatshepsut (c. 1503–1480 B.C.E.), one of the first women to become pharaoh in her own right, built a great temple at Deir el Bahri near Thebes. Hatshepsut was succeeded by her nephew, Thutmosis III (c. 1480–1450 B.C.E.), who led seventeen military campaigns into Syria and Palestine and even reached the Euphrates River. Egyptian forces occupied Palestine and Syria and also moved westward into Libya.

The eighteenth dynasty was not without its troubles, however. Amenhotep IV (c. 1364–1347 B.C.E.) introduced the worship of Aten, god of the sun disk, as the sole god. Amenhotep changed his own name to Akhenaten ("It is well with Aten") and closed the temples of other gods. Akhenaten's attempt at religious change failed. It was too much to ask Egyptians to abandon their traditional ways and beliefs, especially since they saw the destruction of the old gods as subversive of the very cosmic order on which Egypt's survival and continuing prosperity depended. At the same time, Akhenaten's preoccupation with his religious revolution caused him to ignore foreign affairs and led to the loss of both Syria and Palestine. Akhenaten's changes were soon undone after his death by the boy-pharaoh Tutankhamen, who restored the old gods. The eighteenth dynasty itself came to an end in 1333.

The nineteenth dynasty managed to restore Egyptian power one more time. Under Rameses II (c. 1279–1213 B.C.E.), the Egyptians regained control of Palestine, but new invasions in the thirteenth century by the Sea Peoples, as the Egyptians called them, destroyed Egyptian power in Palestine and drove the Egyptians back within their old frontiers. The days of Egyptian empire were ended, and the New Kingdom itself expired with the end of the twentieth dynasty in 1070. For the next thousand years, despite periodic revivals of strength, Egypt was dominated by Libyans, Nubians, Persians, and finally Macedonians after the conquest of Alexander the Great (see Chapter 4). In the first century B.C.E., Egypt became a province in Rome's mighty empire.

Society and Daily Life in Ancient Egypt

For thousands of years, Egyptian society managed to maintain a simple structure, organized along hierarchical lines with the god-king at the top. The king was surrounded by an upper class of nobles and priests who participated in the elaborate rituals of life that surrounded the pharaoh. This ruling class ran the government and managed its own landed estates, which provided much of its wealth.

Below the upper classes were merchants and artisans. Merchants engaged in an active trade up and down the Nile

Early Dynastic Period (Dynasties 1–2)	c. 3100–2686 B.C.E.
Old Kingdom (Dynasties 3–6)	c. 2686–2125 B.C.E.
First Intermediate Period (Dynasties 7–10)	c. 2125–2055 B.C.E.
Middle Kingdom (Dynasties 11–12)	c. 2055–1650 B.C.E.
Second Intermediate Period (Dynasties 13–17)	c. 1650–1550 B.C.E.
New Kingdom (Dynasties 18–20)	c. 1550–1070 B.C.E.
Postempire (Dynasties 21–31)	c. 1070–30 B.C.E.

as well as in town and village markets. Some merchants also engaged in international trade; they were sent by the king to Crete and Syria, where they obtained wood and other products. Expeditions traveled into Nubia for ivory and down the Red Sea to Punt for incense and spices. Eventually, trade links were established between ports in the Red Sea and countries as far away as the Indonesian archipelago. Egyptian artisans made an incredible variety of well-built and beautiful goods: stone dishes; painted boxes made of clay; wooden furniture; gold, silver, and copper tools and containers; paper and rope made of papyrus; and linen clothing.

The largest number of people in Egypt simply worked the land. In theory, the king owned all the land but granted out portions of it to his subjects. Large sections were in the possession of nobles and the temple complexes. Most of the lower classes were serfs or common people, bound to the land, who cultivated the estates. They paid taxes in the form of crops to the king, nobles, and priests, lived in small villages or towns, and provided military service and forced labor for building projects.

Ancient Egyptians had a very positive attitude toward daily life on earth. They married young (girls at twelve, boys at fourteen) and established a home and family. The husband was master in the house, but wives were respected and in charge of the household and education of the children. From a book of wise sayings (called "instructions") came this advice: "If you are a man of standing, you should found your household and love your wife at home as is fitting. Fill her belly; clothe her back. . . . Make her heart glad as long as you live."[5] Women's property and inheritance remained in their hands, even in marriage. Although most careers and public offices were closed to women, some did operate businesses. Peasant women worked long hours in the fields and at numerous domestic tasks. Upper-class women could function as priestesses, and four queens even became pharaohs in their own right.

The Culture of Egypt: Art and Writing

Commissioned by kings or nobles for either temples or tombs, Egyptian art was largely functional. Wall paintings and statues of gods and kings in temples served a spiritual purpose. They were an integral part of the performance of ritual, which was thought necessary to preserve the cosmic order and hence the well-being of Egypt. Likewise, the mural scenes and sculptured figures found in the tombs had a specific function. They were supposed to assist the journey of the deceased into the afterworld.

Egyptian art was also formulaic. Artists and sculptors were expected to observe a strict canon of proportions that determined both form and presentation. This canon gave Egyptian art a distinctive appearance for thousands of years. Especially characteristic was the convention of combining the profile, semiprofile, and frontal views of the human body in relief work and painting in order to represent each part of the body accurately. This fashion created an art that was highly stylized yet still allowed distinctive features to be displayed.

Writing in Egypt emerged during the first two dynasties. The Greeks later labeled Egyptian writing **hieroglyphics,** meaning "priest carvings" or "sacred writings." Hieroglyphs were sacred characters used as picture signs that depicted objects and had a sacred value at the same time. Although hieroglyphs were later simplified for writing purposes into two scripts, they never developed into an alphabet. Egyptian hieroglyphs were initially carved in stone, but later the two simplified scripts were written on papyrus, paper made from the reeds that grew along the Nile.

The Spread of Egyptian Influence: Nubia

The civilization of Egypt had an impact on other peoples in the lands of the eastern Mediterranean. Egyptian products have been found in Crete and Cretan products in Egypt (see Chapter 4). Egyptian influence is also evident in early Greek statues. The Egyptians also had an impact on peoples to the south in sub-Saharan Africa in an area known historically as Nubia (the northern part of modern Sudan). In fact, some archaeologists have recently suggested that the first true African kingdom may have been located in Nubia rather than Egypt.

Whatever the truth of this conjecture, it is clear that contacts between the upper and lower Nile had been established by the late third millennium B.C.E., when Egyptian merchants traveled to Nubia to obtain ivory, ebony, frankincense, and leopard skins. A few centuries later, Nubia had become an Egyptian tributary. At the end of the second millennium B.C.E., Nubia profited from the disintegration of the Egyptian New Kingdom to become the independent state of Kush. Egyptian influence continued, however, as Kushite culture borrowed extensively from Egypt, including religious beliefs, the practice of interring kings in pyramids, and hieroglyphs.

Although its economy was probably founded primarily on agriculture and animal husbandry, Kush developed into

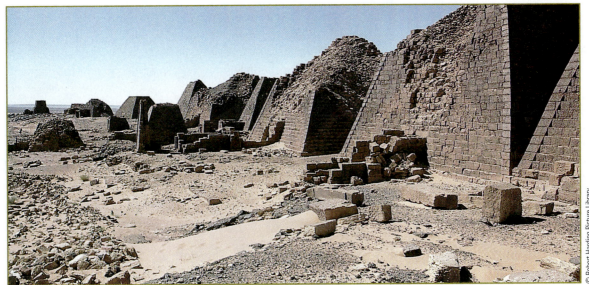

The Pyramids at Meroë. The kingdom of Kush borrowed much of its culture from the Egyptian empire to the north while placing its own imprint on all imports. Kushite rulers, for example, modeled their political institutions after those of the pharaohs, but governmental authority was somewhat more decentralized, and monarchical power was apparently limited by the influence of priests and the local aristocracy. The pyramids at Meroë, on the banks of the Nile River, are another example. Younger, smaller, unpointed at the top, and more standardized in size and shape than their famous counterparts at Giza, they remain a dramatic reminder of the glory of ancient Kush. Some scholars speculate that the idea of erecting pyramids came from the natural hillocks and sand dunes found in the region of the Nile River valley, although pyramids were built in many early societies.

a major trading state in Africa that endured for hundreds of years. Its commercial activities were stimulated by the discovery of iron ore in a floodplain near the river at Meroë. Strategically located at the point where a land route across the desert to the south intersected the Nile River, Meroë eventually became the capital of the state. In addition to iron products, Kush supplied goods from Central and East Africa, notably ivory, gold, ebony, and slaves, to the Roman Empire, Arabia, and India. At first, goods were transported by donkey caravans to the point where the river north was navigable. By the last centuries of the first millennium B.C.E., however, the donkeys were being replaced by camels, newly introduced from the Arabian peninsula.

New Centers of Civilization

Our story of civilization so far has been dominated by Mesopotamia and North Africa. But significant developments were also taking place on the fringes of these civilizations. Agriculture had spread into the Balkan peninsula of Europe by 6500 B.C.E., and by 4000 B.C.E., Neolithic peoples in southern France, central Europe, and the coastal regions of the Mediterranean had domesticated animals and begun to farm largely on their own.

One outstanding feature of late Neolithic Europe was the building of megalithic structures. **Megalith** is Greek for "large stone." The first megalithic structures were built around 4000 B.C.E., more than a thousand years before the great pyramids were built in Egypt. Between 3200 and 1500 B.C.E., standing stones placed in circles or lined up in rows were erected throughout the British Isles and northwestern France. Other megalithic constructions have been found as far north as Scandinavia and as far south as the islands of Corsica, Sardinia, and Malta. Archaeologists have demonstrated that the stone circles were used as observatories not only to detect such simple astronomical phenomena as the midwinter and midsummer sunrises but also to make such sophisticated observations as the major and minor standstills of the moon.

The Role of Nomadic Peoples

On the fringes of civilization lived nomadic peoples who depended on hunting and gathering, herding, and sometimes a bit of farming for their survival. Most important were the pastoral nomads who on occasion overran civilized communities and created their own empires. Pastoral nomads domesticated animals for both food and clothing and moved along regular migratory routes to provide steady sources of nourishment for their animals.

Stonehenge. By far the most famous megalithic construction, Stonehenge in England consists of a series of concentric rings of standing stones. Its construction sometime between 2100 and 1900 B.C.E. was no small accomplishment. The eighty bluestones used at Stonehenge weighed 4 tons each and were transported to the site from 135 miles away. Like other megalithic structures, Stonehenge indicates a remarkable awareness of astronomy on the part of its builders, as well as an elaborate coordination of workers.

© Adam Woolfit/Robert Harding Picture Library

The Indo-Europeans were among the most important nomadic peoples. These groups spoke languages derived from a single parent tongue. Indo-European languages include Greek, Latin, Persian, Sanskrit, and the Germanic languages (see Table 1.2). The original Indo-European-speaking peoples were probably based somewhere in the steppe region north of the Black Sea or in southwestern Asia, in modern Iran or Afghanistan, but around 2000 B.C.E., they began to move into Europe, India, and western Asia. One group of Indo-Europeans who moved into Asia Minor and Anatolia (modern Turkey) around 1750 B.C.E. coalesced with the native peoples to form the Hittite kingdom, with its capital at Hattusha (Bogazköy in modern Turkey).

Between 1600 and 1200 B.C.E., the Hittites created their own empire in western Asia and even threatened the power of the Egyptians. The Hittites were the first of the Indo-European peoples to use iron, which enabled them to construct weapons that were stronger and cheaper to make because of the widespread availability of iron ore. But around 1200 B.C.E., new waves of invading Indo-European peoples destroyed the Hittite empire. The destruction of the Hittite kingdom and the weakening of Egypt around 1200 B.C.E. temporarily left no dominant powers in western Asia, allowing a patchwork of petty kingdoms and city-states to emerge, especially in Syria and Palestine. The Phoenicians were one of these peoples.

The Phoenicians

A Semitic-speaking people, the Phoenicians lived in Palestine along the Mediterranean coast on a narrow band of land 120 miles long. Their newfound political independence after the demise of Hittite and Egyptian power helped the Phoenicians expand the trade that was already the foundation of their prosperity. The Phoenicians improved their ships and became great international sea traders. They charted new routes, not only in the Mediterranean but also in the Atlantic Ocean, where they sailed north to Britain and south along the west coast of Africa. The Phoenicians established a number of colonies in the western Mediterranean; Carthage, the most famous, was located on the North African coast.

Culturally, the Phoenicians are best known for their alphabet. They simplified their writing by using twenty-two different signs to represent the sounds of their speech. These twenty-two characters or letters could be used to spell out all the words in the Phoenician language. Although the Phoenicians were not the only people to invent an alphabet, theirs would have special significance because it was eventually passed on to the Greeks. From the ancient Greek alphabet came the modern Greek, Roman, and Cyrillic alphabets in use today.

TABLE 1.2   Some Indo-European Languages

Subfamily	Languages
Indo-Iranian	*Sanskrit*, Persian
Balto-Slavic	Russian, Serbo-Croatian, Czech, Polish, Lithuanian
Hellenic	Greek
Italic	*Latin*, Romance languages (French, Italian, Spanish, Portuguese, Romanian)
Celtic	Irish, Gaelic
Germanic	Swedish, Danish, Norwegian, German, Dutch, English

NOTE: Languages in italic type are no longer spoken.

The "Children of Israel"

To the south of the Phoenicians lived another group of Semitic-speaking people known as the Israelites. Although they were a minor factor in the politics of the region, their **monotheism**—belief in one God—known as Judaism, later influenced both Christianity and Islam and flourished as a world religion in its own right. The Israelites had a tradition concerning their origins and history that was eventually written down as part of the Hebrew Bible, known to Christians as the Old Testament. Many scholars today doubt that the early books of the Hebrew Bible reflect the true history of the early Israelites. They argue that the early books of the Bible, written centuries after the events described, preserve only what the Israelites came to believe about themselves and that recent archaeological evidence often contradicts the details of the biblical account. What is generally agreed, however, is that between 1200 and 1000 B.C.E., the Israelites emerged as a distinct group of people, possibly organized in tribes or a league of tribes, who established a united kingdom known as Israel.

The United and Divided Kingdoms By the time of King Solomon (c. 970–930 B.C.E.), the Israelites had established control over all of Palestine (see Map 1.4) and made Jerusalem the capital of a united kingdom. Solomon did even more to strengthen royal power. He expanded the government and army and was especially active in extending the trading activities of the Israelites. Solomon is best known for his building projects, of which the most famous was the Temple in Jerusalem. The Israelites viewed the Temple as the symbolic center of their religion and hence of the kingdom of Israel itself. Under Solomon, ancient Israel was at the height of its power.

After Solomon's death, tensions between the northern and southern tribes led to the establishment of two separate kingdoms—the kingdom of Israel, composed of ten northern tribes, with its capital eventually at Samaria, and the kingdom of Judah, consisting of two southern tribes, with its capital at Jerusalem. In 722 B.C.E., the Assyrians overran the kingdom of Israel and deported many Hebrews to other parts of the Assyrian Empire. These dispersed Hebrews (the "ten lost tribes") merged with neighboring peoples and gradually lost their identity.

The southern kingdom of Judah managed for a while to retain its independence as Assyrian power declined, but a new enemy soon appeared on the horizon. The Chaldeans defeated Assyria, conquered the kingdom of Judah, and completely destroyed Jerusalem in 586 B.C.E. Many upper-class people from Judah were deported to Babylon, the memory of which is still evoked in the words of Psalm 137:

By the rivers of Babylon, we sat and wept when we remembered Zion. . . .

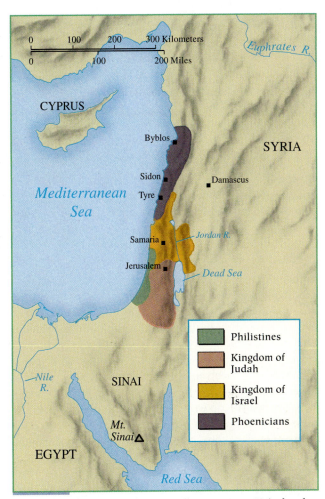

MAP 1.4 **Palestine in the First Millennium B.C.E.** United under Saul, David, and Solomon, greater Israel split into two states—Israel and Judah—after the death of Solomon. With power divided, the Israelites could not resist invasions that dispersed many Hebrews from Palestine. Some, such as the "ten lost tribes," never returned. Others were sent to Babylon but were later allowed to return under the rule of the Persians. **?** Why was Israel more vulnerable to the Assyrian Empire than Judah was?

How can we sing the songs of the Lord while in a foreign land?
If I forget you, O Jerusalem, may my right hand forget its skill.
May my tongue cling to the roof of my mouth if I do not remember you,
if I do not consider Jerusalem my highest joy.[6]

But the Babylonian captivity of the people of Judah did not last. A new set of conquerors, the Persians, destroyed the Chaldean kingdom and allowed the people of Judah to return to Jerusalem and rebuild their city and Temple. The revived kingdom of Judah remained under Persian control until the conquests of Alexander the Great in the fourth century B.C.E. The people of Judah survived, eventually becoming known as the Jews and giving their name to Judaism, the religion of Yahweh, the Jewish God.

THE COVENANT AND THE LAW: THE BOOK OF EXODUS

RELIGION & PHILOSOPHY

According to the biblical account, it was during the exodus from Egypt that the Israelites made their covenant with Yahweh. They agreed to obey their God and follow his law. In return, Yahweh promised to take special care of his chosen people. This selection from the Book of Exodus describes the making of the covenant and God's commandments to the Israelites.

What was the nature of the covenant between Yahweh and the Hebrews? What was its moral significance for the Hebrew people? How might you explain its differences from Hammurabi's Code?

Exodus 19:1–8

In the third month after the Israelites left Egypt—on the very day—they came to the Desert of Sinai. After they set out from Rephidim, they entered the Desert of Sinai, and Israel camped there in the desert in front of the mountain. Then Moses went up to God, and the Lord called to him from the mountain, and said, "This is what you are to say to the house of Jacob and what you are to tell the people of Israel: 'You yourselves have seen what I did to Egypt, and how I carried you on eagles' wings and brought you to myself. Now if you obey me fully and keep my covenant, then out of all nations you will be my treasured possession. Although the whole earth is mine, you will be for me a kingdom of priests and a holy nation.' These are the words you are to speak to the Israelites." So Moses went back and summoned the elders of the people and set before them all the words the Lord had commanded him to speak. The

people all responded together, "We will do everything the Lord has said." So Moses brought their answer back to the Lord.

Exodus 20:1–3, 7–17

And God spoke all these words, "I am the Lord your God, who brought you out of Egypt, out of the land of slavery. You shall have no other gods before me. . . . You shall not misuse the name of the Lord your God, for the Lord will not hold anyone guiltless who misuses his name. Remember the Sabbath day by keeping it holy. Six days you shall labor and do all your work, but the seventh day is a Sabbath to the Lord your God. On it you shall not do any work, neither you, nor your son or daughter, nor your man-servant or maidservant, nor your animals, nor the alien within your gates. For in six days the Lord made the heavens and the earth, the sea, and all that is in them, but he rested on the seventh day. Therefore the Lord blessed the Sabbath day and made it holy. Honor your father and your mother, so that you may live long in the land the Lord your God is giving you. You shall not murder. You shall not commit adultery. You shall not steal. You shall not give false testimony against your neighbor. You shall not covet your neighbor's house. You shall not covet your neighbor's wife, or his manservant or maidservant, his ox or donkey, or anything that belongs to your neighbor."

CENGAGENOW To read a full version of this document, enter the CengageNOW documents area using the access card that is available for *The Essential World History*.

The Spiritual Dimensions of Israel   According to the Jewish conception, there is but one God called Yahweh, who is the creator of the world and everything in it. This omnipotent creator was not removed from the life he had created. A just and good God, he expected goodness from his people and would punish them if they did not obey his will. Still, he was primarily a God of mercy and love: "The Lord is gracious and compassionate, slow to anger and rich in love. The Lord is good to all; he has compassion on all he has made."[7] Each individual could have a personal relationship with this being.

Three aspects of the Jewish religious tradition had special significance: the covenant, law, and the prophets. The Israelites believed that during the exodus from Egypt, when Moses had supposedly led his people out of bondage toward the promised land, God made a covenant or contract with the tribes of Israel, who believed that Yahweh had spoken to them through Moses (see the box above). The Israelites promised to obey Yahweh and follow his law. In return, Yahweh promised to take special care of his chosen people, "a peculiar treasure unto me above all people."

This covenant between Yahweh and his chosen people could be fulfilled, however, only by Hebrew obedience to the law of God. Most important were the ethical concerns that stood at the center of the law. These commandments spelled out God's ideals of behavior: "You shall not murder. You shall not commit adultery. You shall not steal."[8] True freedom consisted of following God's moral standards voluntarily. If people chose to ignore the good, then suffering and evil would follow.

The Israelites believed that certain religious teachers, called prophets, were sent by God to serve as his voice to his people. The golden age of prophecy began in the mid-eighth century B.C.E. and continued during the time when the people of Israel and Judah were threatened by Assyrian and Chaldean conquerors. These "men of God" went through the land warning the Israelites that they had failed to keep God's commandments and would be punished for breaking the covenant: "I will punish you for all your iniquities."

Out of the words of the prophets came new concepts that enriched the Jewish tradition. The prophets embraced a concern for all humanity. All nations would someday

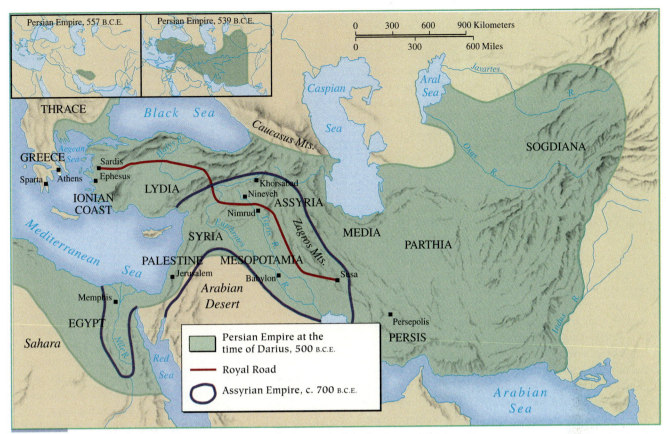

MAP 1.5 **The Assyrian and Persian Empires.** Cyrus the Great united the Persians and led them in a successful conquest of much of the Near East, including most of the lands of the Assyrian Empire. By the time of Darius, the Persian Empire was the largest the world had yet seen. ❓ How did Persian policies attempt to overcome the difficulties of governing far-flung provinces? 🌐 **View an animated version of this map or related maps at** http://worldrc.wadsworth.com/

come to the God of Israel: "All the earth shall worship you." This vision encompassed the establishment of peace for all the nations of the world. In the words of the prophet Isaiah: "He will judge between the nations and will settle disputes for many people. They will beat their swords into plowshares and their spears into pruning hooks. Nation will not take up sword against nation, nor will they train for war anymore."[9]

Although the prophets developed a sense of universalism, the demands of the Jewish religion (the need to obey God) eventually encouraged a separation between the Jews and their non-Jewish neighbors. Unlike most other peoples of the Middle East, the Jews could not simply be amalgamated into a community by accepting the gods of their conquerors and their neighbors.

The Rise of New Empires

A small and independent Israelite state could exist only as long as no larger state dominated western Asia. New empires soon arose, however, and conquered vast stretches of the ancient world.

The Assyrian Empire

The first of these empires was formed in Assyria, located on the upper Tigris River. The Assyrians were a Semitic-speaking people who exploited the use of iron weapons to establish an empire that by 700 B.C.E. included Mesopotamia, parts of the Iranian plateau, sections of Asia Minor, Syria, Palestine, and Egypt down to Thebes (see Map 1.5). But in less than a hundred years, internal strife and resentment of Assyrian rule led subject peoples to rebel against it. The capital city of Nineveh fell to a coalition of Chaldeans and Medes in 612 B.C.E., and seven years later, the rest of the empire was finally divided between the two powers.

At its height, the Assyrian Empire was ruled by kings whose power was considered absolute. The Assyrians developed an efficient system of communication to administer their empire more effectively. They established a network of staging posts throughout the empire and used relays of horses (mules or donkeys in the mountains) to carry messages.

The Assyrians were outstanding conquerors. Over many years of practice, they developed good military leaders and fighters. The Assyrian army was large, well organized,

THE ASSYRIAN MILITARY MACHINE

POLITICS & GOVERNMENT

The Assyrians achieved a reputation for possessing a mighty military machine. They were able to use a variety of military tactics and were successful whether they were waging guerrilla warfare, fighting set battles, or laying siege to cities. In these three selections, Assyrian kings boast of their military conquests.

Based on their own descriptions, what did Assyrian kings believe was important for military success? Do you think their accounts may be exaggerated? Why?

King Sennacherib (704–681 B.C.E.) Describes a Battle with the Elamites in 691

At the command of the god Ashur, the great Lord, I rushed upon the enemy like the approach of a hurricane. . . . I put them to rout and turned them back. I transfixed the troops of the enemy with javelins and arrows. . . . I cut their throats like sheep. . . . My prancing steeds, trained to harness, plunged into their welling blood as into a river; the wheels of my battle chariot were bespattered with blood and filth. I filled the plain with the corpses of their warriors like herbage. . . . As to the sheikhs of the Chaldeans, panic from my onslaught overwhelmed them like a demon. They abandoned their tents and fled for their lives, crushing the corpses of their troops as they went. . . . In their terror they passed scalding urine and voided their excrement into their chariots.

King Sennacherib Describes His Siege of Jerusalem in 701

As to Hezekiah, the Jew, he did not submit to my yoke, I laid siege to 46 of his strong cities, walled forts, and the countless small villages in their vicinity, and conquered

them by means of well-stamped earth-ramps, and battering-rams brought thus near to the walls combined with the attack by foot soldiers, using mines, breeches, as well as sapper work. I drove out of them 200,150 people, young and old, male and female, horses, mules, donkeys, camels, big and small cattle beyond counting, and considered them booty. Himself I made a prisoner in Jerusalem, his royal residence, like a bird in a cage. I surrounded him with earthwork in order to molest those who were leaving his city's gate.

King Ashurbanipal (669–626 B.C.E.) Describes His Treatment of Conquered Babylon

I tore out the tongues of those whose slanderous mouths had uttered blasphemies against my god Ashur and had plotted against me, his god-fearing prince; I defeated them completely. The others, I smashed alive with the very same statues of protective deities with which they had smashed my own grandfather Sennacherib—now finally as a belated burial sacrifice for his soul. I fed their corpses, cut into small pieces, to dogs, pigs, . . . vultures, the birds of the sky, and also to the fish of the ocean. After I had performed this and thus made quiet again the hearts of the great gods, my lords, I removed the corpses of those whom the pestilence had felled, whose leftovers after the dogs and pigs had fed on them were obstructing the streets, filling the places of Babylon, and of those who had lost their lives through the terrible famine.

CENGAGENOW To read full versions of these documents, enter the *CengageNOW* documents area using the access card that is available for *The Essential World History*.

and disciplined. A force of infantrymen was its core, accompanied by cavalrymen and horse-drawn war chariots that were used as platforms for shooting arrows. Moreover, the Assyrians had the first large armies equipped with iron weapons.

The Assyrian military machine used terror as an instrument of warfare (see the box above). As a matter of regular policy, the Assyrians laid waste the land in which they were fighting, smashing dams, looting and destroying towns, setting crops on fire, and cutting down trees, particularly fruit trees. The Assyrians were especially known for committing atrocities on their captives. King Ashurnasirpal recorded this account of his treatment of prisoners:

> 3,000 of their combat troops I felled with weapons. . . . Many of the captives taken from them I burned in a fire. Many I took alive; from some of these I cut off their hands to the wrist, from others I cut off their noses, ears and fingers; I put out the eyes of many of the soldiers. . . . I burned their young men and women to death.[10]

The Persian Empire

After the collapse of the Assyrian Empire, the Chaldeans, under their king Nebuchadnezzar II (605–562 B.C.E.), made Babylonia the leading state in western Asia. Nebuchadnezzar rebuilt Babylon as the center of his empire, giving it a reputation as one of the great cities of the ancient world. But the splendor of Chaldean Babylonia proved to be short-lived when Babylon fell to the Persians in 539 B.C.E.

The Persians were an Indo-European-speaking people who lived in southwestern Iran. Primarily nomadic, the Persians were organized in tribes until the Achaemenid family managed to unify them. One of its members, Cyrus (559–530 B.C.E.), created a powerful Persian state that stretched from Asia Minor in the west to western India in the east. In 539, Cyrus entered Meospotamia and captured Babylon. His treatment of Babylonia showed remarkable restraint and wisdom. Babylonia was made into a Persian province, but many

Darius, the Great King. Darius ruled the Persian Empire from 521 to 486 B.C.E. He is shown here on his throne in Persepolis, a new capital city that he built. In his right hand, Darius holds the royal staff. In his left hand, he grasps a lotus blossom with two buds, a symbol of royalty.

government officials were kept in their positions. Cyrus also issued an edict permitting the Jews, who had been brought to Babylon in the sixth century B.C.E., to return to Jerusalem with their sacred temple objects and to rebuild their Temple as well.

To his contemporaries, Cyrus the Great deserved to be called the Great. He must have been an unusual ruler for his time, a man who demonstrated considerable wisdom and compassion in the conquest and organization of his empire. Unlike the Assyrian rulers of an earlier empire, he had a reputation for mercy. Medes, Jews, Babylonians—all accepted him as their legitimate ruler.

Cyrus' successors extended the territory of the Persian Empire. His son Cambyses (530–522 B.C.E.) undertook a successful invasion of Egypt. Darius (521–486 B.C.E.) added a new Persian province in western India that extended to the Indus River and then moved into Europe, conquering Thrace and creating the largest empire the world had yet seen. His contact with the Greeks led him to undertake an invasion of the Greek mainland (see Chapter 4).

Civil Administration and the Military

Darius strengthened the basic structure of the Persian government by creating a more rational division of the empire into twenty provinces called **satrapies.** Each province was ruled by a governor or satrap, literally a "protector of the kingdom." Satraps collected tributes, were responsible for justice and security, raised military levies for the royal army, and normally commanded the military forces within their satrapies. In terms of real power, the satraps were miniature kings who created courts imitative of the Great King's.

An efficient system of communication was crucial to sustaining the Persian Empire. Well-maintained roads facilitated the rapid transit of military and government personnel. One in particular, the so-called Royal Road (see Map 1.5), stretched from Sardis, the center of Lydia in Asia Minor, to Susa, the chief capital of the Persian Empire. Like the Assyrians, the Persians established way stations equipped with fresh horses for the king's messengers.

In this vast administrative system, the Persian king occupied an exalted position. All subjects were the king's servants, and he, the Great King, was the source of all justice, possessing the power of life and death over everyone. At its height, much of the power of the Persian Empire depended on the military. By the time of Darius, the Persian monarchs had created a standing army of professional soldiers. This army was truly international in character, composed of contingents from the various peoples who made up the empire. At its core was a cavalry force of ten thousand and an elite infantry force of the same size known as the Immortals because they were never allowed to fall below ten thousand in number. When one was killed, he was immediately replaced.

After Darius, Persian kings became more and more isolated at their courts, surrounded by luxuries provided by immense quantities of gold and silver that flowed into their treasuries, located in the capital cities. Both their hoarding of wealth and their later overtaxation of their subjects are seen as crucial factors in the ultimate weakening of the Persian Empire.

Persian Religion: Zoroastrianism Of all the Persians' cultural contributions, the most original was their religion, **Zoroastrianism.** According to Persian tradition, Zoroaster was born in 660 B.C.E. After a period of wandering and solitude, he experienced revelations that caused him to be revered as a prophet of the "true religion." His teachings were eventually written down in the third century B.C.E. in the *Zend Avesta*, the sacred book of Zoroastrianism.

Like the Hebrews', Zoroaster's spiritual message was monotheistic. To Zoroaster, Ahuramazda was the only god, and the religion he preached was the only perfect one.

Ahuramazda (the "Wise Lord") was the supreme deity who brought all things into being. According to Zoroaster, Ahuramazda also possessed qualities that all humans should aspire to, such as good thought, right, and piety. Although Ahuramazda was supreme, he was not unopposed. At the beginning of the world, the good spirit of Ahuramazda was opposed by the evil spirit (later identified with Ahriman).

Humans also played a role in this cosmic struggle between good and evil. Ahuramazda, the creator, gave all humans free will and the power to choose between right and wrong. The good person chooses the right way of Ahuramazda. Zoroaster taught that there would be an end to the struggle between good and evil. Ahuramazda would eventually triumph, and at the last judgment at the end of the world, the final separation of good and evil would occur. Individuals, too, would be judged. Each soul faced a final evaluation of its actions. If a person had performed good deeds, he or she would achieve paradise; if evil deeds, the soul would be thrown into an abyss of torment.

CONCLUSION

THE PEOPLES OF MESOPOTAMIA and North Africa, like the peoples of India and China, built the first civilizations. They developed cities and struggled with the problems of organized states. They developed writing to keep records and to preserve and create literature. They constructed monumental architecture to please their gods, symbolize their power, and glorify their culture. They developed new political, military, social, and religious structures to deal with the basic problems of human existence and organization. These first literate civilizations left detailed records that allow us to view how they grappled with three of the fundamental problems that humans have pondered: human relationships, the nature of the universe, and the role of divine forces in the cosmos. Although other peoples would provide different answers from those of the Mesopotamians and the Egyptians, the people of these cultures posed the questions, gave answers, and wrote them down. Human memory begins with the creation of civilizations.

By the middle of the second millennium B.C.E., the creative impulse of the Mesopotamian and Egyptian civilizations was beginning to wane. Around 1200 B.C.E.,

the decline of the Hittites and the Egyptians had created a power vacuum that allowed a number of small states to emerge and flourish temporarily. All of them were eventually overshadowed by the rise of the great empires of the Assyrians and the Persians. The Assyrian Empire had been the first to unite almost all of the ancient Middle East. Even larger was the empire of the Great Kings of Persia. The many years of peace that the Persian Empire brought to the Middle East facilitated trade and the general well-being of its peoples. It is no wonder that many peoples expressed their gratitude for being subjects of the Great Kings of Persia. Among these peoples were the Israelites, who created no empire but nevertheless left an important spiritual legacy. The evolution of monotheism created in Judaism one of the world's great religions; moreover, Judaism influenced the development of both Christianity and Islam.

The Persians had also extended their empire to the Indus River, which brought them into contact with another river valley civilization that had developed independently of the civilizations in the Middle East and Egypt. It is to South Asia that we now turn.

CHAPTER NOTES

1. Quoted in Amélie Kuhrt, *The Ancient Near East, c. 3000–330 B.C.* (London, 1995), vol. 1, p. 68.
2. Quoted in Marc Van de Mieroop, *A History of the Ancient Near East, ca. 3000–323 B.C.* (Oxford, 2004), p. 106.
3. Quoted in Thorkild Jacobsen, "Mesopotamia," in Henri Frankfort et al., *Before Philosophy* (Baltimore, 1949), p. 139.
4. Quoted in Milton Covensky, *The Ancient Near Eastern Tradition* (New York, 1966), p. 51.
5. Ibid., p. 413.
6. Psalms 137:1, 4–6.

TIMELINE

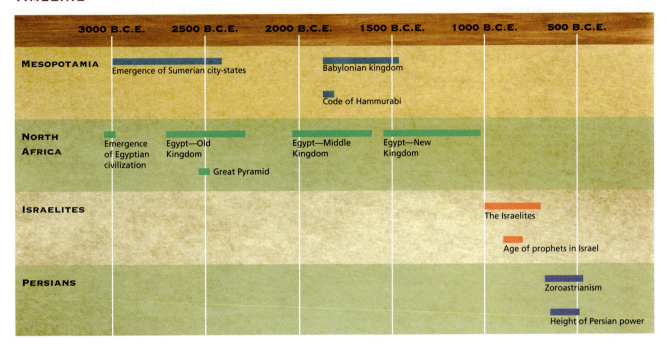

	3000 B.C.E.	2500 B.C.E.	2000 B.C.E.	1500 B.C.E.	1000 B.C.E.	500 B.C.E.
MESOPOTAMIA	Emergence of Sumerian city-states		Babylonian kingdom			
			Code of Hammurabi			
NORTH AFRICA	Emergence of Egyptian civilization	Egypt—Old Kingdom	Egypt—Middle Kingdom	Egypt—New Kingdom		
		Great Pyramid				
ISRAELITES					The Israelites	
					Age of prophets in Israel	
PERSIANS					Zoroastrianism	
					Height of Persian power	

7. Psalms 145:8–9.
8. Exodus 20:13–15.
9. Isaiah 2:4.
10. Quoted in H. W. F. Saggs, *The Might That Was Assyria* (London, 1984), pp. 261–262.

SUGGESTED READING

To examine some of the issues raised in the comparative essay for Chapter 1, see **J. Diamond, *Guns, Germs, and Steel: The Fates of Human Societies*** (New York, 1997). The following works are of considerable value in examining the prehistory of humankind: **R. Leakey, *The Making of Mankind*** (London, 1981); **R. J. Wenke, *Patterns in Prehistory: Humankind's First Three Million Years,*** 4th ed. (New York, 1999); and **P. Mellars and C. Stringer, *The Human Revolution*** (Edinburgh, 1989). For a study of the role of women in early human society, see **E. Barber, *Women's Work: The First 20,000 Years*** (New York, 1994).

An excellent reference tool on the ancient Near East can be found in **P. Bienkowski and A. Milward, eds., *Dictionary of the Ancient Near East*** (Philadelphia, 2000). A very competent general survey of the ancient Near East is **M. Van de Mieroop, *A History of the Ancient Near East, ca. 3000–323 B.C.*** (Oxford, 2004). For a detailed survey, see **A. Kuhrt, *The Ancient Near East, c. 3000–330 B.C.,*** 2 vols. (London, 1996). On the economic and social history of the ancient Near East, see **D. C. Snell, *Life in the Ancient Near East*** (New Haven, Conn., 1997).

General works on ancient Mesopotamia include **J. N. Postgate, *Early Mesopotamia: Society and Economy at the Dawn of History*** (London, 1992), and **S. Lloyd, *The Archaeology of Mesopotamia,*** rev. ed. (London, 1984). A beautifully illustrated survey can be found in **M. Roaf, *Cultural Atlas of Mesopotamia and the Ancient Near East*** (New York, 1996). For a reference work on daily life, see **S. Bertman, *Handbook to Life in Ancient Mesopotamia*** (New York, 2003).

For a good introduction to ancient Egypt, see the beautifully illustrated works by **M. Hayes, *The Egyptians*** (New York, 1997);

J. Baines and J. Málek, *The Cultural Atlas of the World: Ancient Egypt* (Alexandria, Va., 1991); and **D. P. Silverman,** ed., ***Ancient Egypt*** (New York, 1997). Other general surveys include **N. Grant, *The Egyptians*** (New York, 1996); **I. Shaw,** ed., ***The Oxford History of Ancient Egypt*** (New York, 2000); and **N. Grimal, *A History of Ancient Egypt,*** trans. I. Shaw (Oxford, 1992). Daily life in ancient Egypt can be examined in **E. Strouhal, *Life of the Ancient Egyptians*** (Norman, Okla., 1992). An important study on women is **G. Robins, *Women in Ancient Egypt*** (Cambridge, Mass., 1993).

For a good account of Phoenician domestic history and overseas expansion, see **D. Harden, *The Phoenicians,*** rev. ed. (Harmondsworth, England, 1980). See also **M. E. Aubet, *The Phoenicians and the West: Politics, Colonies and Trade*** (Cambridge, 1993), and **G. Markoe, *Phoenicians*** (London, 2000). There is an enormous literature on ancient Israel. Two good studies on the archaeological aspects are **A. Mazar, *Archaeology of the Land of the Bible*** (New York, 1992), and **A. Ben-Tor,** ed., ***The Archaeology of Ancient Israel*** (New Haven, Conn., 1992). For historical narratives, see especially **J. Bright, *A History of Israel,*** 3d ed. (Philadelphia, 1981), a fundamental study; the survey by **M. Grant, *The History of Ancient Israel*** (New York, 1984); and **H. Shanks, *Ancient Israel: A Short History from Abraham to the Roman Destruction of the Temple*** (Englewood Cliffs, N.J., 1988). For a general study on the religion of the Hebrews, see **W. J. Doorly, *The Religion of Israel*** (New York, 1997). On the origins of the Israelites, see **W. G. Dever, *Who Were the Early Israelites and Where Did They Come From?*** (Grand Rapids, Mich., 2003).

A detailed account of Assyrian political, economic, social, military, and cultural history is **H. W. F. Saggs, *The Might That Was Assyria*** (London, 1984). The classic work on the Persian Empire is **A. T. Olmstead, *History of the Persian Empire*** (Chicago, 1948), but a more recent work by **J. M. Cook, *The Persian Empire*** (New York, 1983), provides new material and fresh interpretations. Also of value is **J. Curtis, *Ancient Persia*** (Cambridge, Mass., 1990). On the history of Zoroastrianism, see **S. A. Nigosian, *The Zoroastrian Faith: Tradition and Modern Research*** (New York, 1993).

InfoTrac College Edition

Visit this chapter's InfoTrac College Edition/Research activities at the *Essential World History* Companion Website for activities related to the first civilizations.

CENGAGENOW **for Duiker and Spielvogel's *The Essential World History, Third Edition***

Enter *CengageNOW* using the access card that is available with this text. *CengageNOW* will assist you in understanding the content in this chapter with lesson plans generated for your needs, as well as provide you with a connection to the *Wadsworth World History Resource Center* (see description at the right for details).

Enter the Resource Center using either your *CengageNow* access card or your standalone access card for the *Wadsworth World History Resource Center*. Organized by topic, this website includes quizzes; images; over 350 primary source documents; interactive simulations, maps, and timelines; movie explorations; and a wealth of other resources. You can read the following documents, and many more, at http://worldrc.wadsworth.com/

> *Enuma Elish*
>
> Herodotus, *History,* book 2, chapters 124–127

Visit the *Essential World History* Companion Website for chapter quizzes and more.

> academic.cengage.com/history/duiker

ANCIENT INDIA

CHAPTER OUTLINE AND FOCUS QUESTIONS

The Emergence of Civilization in India: Harappan Society

☐ What were the chief features of Harappan civilization, and in what ways was it similar to the civilizations that arose in North Africa and Mesopotamia?

The Arrival of the Aryans

☐ What were some of the distinctive features of the class system introduced by the Aryan peoples, and what effect did the class system have on Indian civilization?

Escaping the Wheel of Life: The Religious World of Ancient India

☐ What are the main tenets of Hinduism and Buddhism, and how did each religion influence Indian civilization?

The Rule of the Fishes: India After the Mauryas

☐ Why was India unable to maintain a unified empire in the first millennium B.C.E., and how was the Mauryan Empire temporarily able to overcome the tendencies toward disunity?

The Exuberant World of Indian Culture

☐ In what ways did the culture of ancient India resemble and differ from the cultural experience of ancient Mesopotamia and Egypt?

CRITICAL THINKING

☐ What are some of the key factors that explain why India became one of the first regions to create an advanced technological society in the ancient world? To what degree does it merit comparison with Mesopotamia and North Africa as the site of the first civilizations?

Krishna and Arjuna preparing for battle

𝒜RJUNA WAS DESPONDENT as he prepared for battle. In the opposing army were many of his friends and colleagues, some of whom he had known since childhood. In despair, he turned for advice to Krishna, his chariot driver, who, unknown to Arjuna, was in actuality an incarnation of the Indian deity Vishnu. "Do not despair of your duty," Krishna advised his friend.

> To be born is certain death,
>   to the dead, birth is certain.
>
> It is not right that you should sorrow
>   for what cannot be avoided. . . .
> If you do not fight this just battle
>   you will fail in your own law
> and in your honor,
>   and you will incur sin.

Krishna's advice to Arjuna is contained in the Bhagavad Gita, one of India's most sacred classical writings, and reflects one of the key tenets in Indian philosophy—the belief in reincarnation, or rebirth of the soul. It also points up the importance of doing one's duty without regard for the consequences. Arjuna was a warrior, and according to Aryan tribal tradition, he was obliged to follow the code of his class. "There is more joy in doing one's own duty badly," advised Krishna, "than in doing another man's duty well."

In advising Arjuna to fulfill his obligation as a warrior, the author of the Bhagavad Gita, writing around the second century B.C.E. about a battle that took place almost a thousand years earlier, was by implication urging all readers to adhere to their own responsibility as members of one of India's major classes. Henceforth, this hierarchical vision of a society divided into groups, each with clearly distinct roles, would become a defining characteristic of Indian history.

The Bhagavad Gita is part of a larger work that deals with the early history of the Aryan peoples who entered India from beyond the mountains north of the Khyber Pass between 1500 and 1000 B.C.E. When the Aryans, a pastoral people speaking a branch of the Indo-European family of languages, arrived in India, the subcontinent had already had a thriving civilization for almost two thousand years. The Indus valley civilization, although not as well known today as the civilizations of Mesopotamia and North Africa, was just as old; and its political, social, and cultural achievements were also impressive. That civilization, known to historians by the names of its two major cities, Harappa and Mohenjo-Daro, emerged in the late fourth millennium B.C.E., flourished for over one thousand years, and then came to an abrupt end about 1500 B.C.E. It was soon replaced by a new society dominated by the Aryan peoples. The new civilization that emerged represented a rich mixture of the two cultures—Harappan and Aryan—and evolved over the next three thousand years into what we know today as India. ◇

The Emergence of Civilization in India: Harappan Society

Although today this beautiful mosaic of peoples and cultures has been broken up into a number of separate independent states, the region still possesses a coherent history that despite its internal diversity is recognizably Indian.

A Land of Diversity

India was and still is a land of diversity, which is evident in its languages and cultures as well as in its physical characteristics. India possesses an incredible array of languages. It has a deserved reputation, along with the Middle East, as a cradle of religion. Two of the world's major religions, Hinduism and Buddhism, originated in India.

In its size and diversity, India seems more like a continent than a single country. That diversity begins with the geographic environment. The Indian subcontinent, shaped like a spade hanging from the southern ridge of Asia, is composed of a number of core regions. In the far north are the Himalayan and Karakoram mountain ranges, home to the highest mountains in the world. Directly south of the

Himalayas and the Karakoram range is the rich valley of the Ganges, India's "holy river" and one of the core regions of Indian culture. To the west is the Indus River valley. Today, the latter is a relatively arid plateau that forms the backbone of the modern state of Pakistan, but in ancient times, it enjoyed a more balanced climate and served as the cradle of Indian civilization.

South of India's two major river valleys lies the Deccan, a region of hills and an upland plateau that extends from the Ganges valley to the southern tip of the Indian subcontinent. The interior of the plateau is relatively hilly and dry, but the eastern and western coasts are occupied by lush plains, which are historically among the most densely populated regions of India. Off the southeastern coast is the island known today as Sri Lanka. Although Sri Lanka is now a separate country quite distinct politically and culturally from India, the island's history is intimately linked with that of its larger neighbor.

In this vast region lives a rich mixture of peoples: people speaking one of the languages in the Dravidian family, who probably descended from the Indus River culture that flourished at the dawn of Indian civilization, over four thousand years ago; Aryans, descended from the pastoral peoples who flooded southward from Central Asia in the second millennium B.C.E.; and hill peoples, who may have lived in the region prior to the rise of organized societies and thus may have been the earliest inhabitants of all.

Harappan Civilization: A Fascinating Enigma

In the 1920s, archaeologists discovered agricultural settlements dating back well over six thousand years in the lower reaches of the Indus River valley in modern Pakistan. Those small mudbrick villages eventually gave rise to the sophisticated human communities that historians call Harappan civilization. Although today the area is relatively arid, during the third and fourth millennia B.C.E., it evidently received much more abundant rainfall, and the valleys of the Indus River and its tributaries supported a thriving civilization that may have covered a total area of over 600,000 square miles, from the Himalayas to the coast of the Indian Ocean. More than seventy sites have been unearthed since the area was first discovered in the 1850s, but the main sites are at the two major cities, Harappa, in the Punjab, and Mohenjo-Daro, nearly 400 miles to the south near the mouth of the Indus River (see Map 2.1).

The origin of the Harappans is still debated, but some scholars have suggested on the basis of ethnographic and linguistic analysis that the language and physical characteristics of the Harappans were similar to those of the Dravidian-speaking peoples who live in the Deccan Plateau today. If that is so, Harappa is not simply a dead civilization but a part of the living culture of the Indian subcontinent.

Political and Social Structures In several respects, Harappan civilization closely resembled the cultures of Mesopotamia and the Nile valley. Like them, it probably began in tiny farming villages scattered throughout the

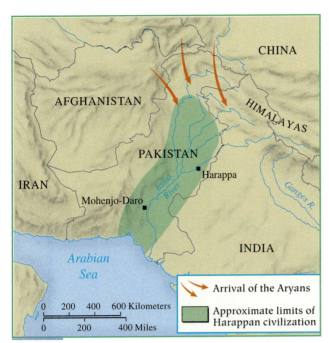

MAP 2.1 **Ancient Harappan Civilization.** This map shows the location of the first civilization that arose in the Indus River valley, which today is located in Pakistan. ❓ Based on this map, why do you think Harappan civilization resembled those of Mesopotamia and Egypt?

river valley, some dating back to as early as 6500 or 7000 B.C.E. These villages thrived and grew until, by the middle of the third millennium B.C.E., they could support a privileged ruling elite living in walled cities of considerable magnitude and affluence. The center of power was the city of Harappa, which was surrounded by a brick wall over 40 feet thick at its base and more than $3\frac{1}{2}$ miles in circumference. The city was laid out on an essentially rectangular grid, with some streets as wide as 30 feet. Most buildings were constructed of kiln-dried mudbricks and were square in shape, reflecting the grid pattern. At its height, the city may have had as many as eighty thousand inhabitants, as large as some of the most populous urban centers in Sumerian civilization.

Both Harappa and Mohenjo-Daro were divided into large walled neighborhoods, with narrow lanes separating the rows of houses. Houses varied in size, with some as high as three stories, but all followed the same general plan based on a square courtyard surrounded by rooms. Bathrooms featured an advanced drainage system, which carried wastewater out to drains located under the streets and thence to sewage pits beyond the city walls.

Unfortunately, Harappan writing has not yet been deciphered, so historians know relatively little about the organization of the Harappan state (see the comparative essay "Writing and Civilization" on p. 33). However, recent archaeological evidence suggests that unlike its contemporaries in Egypt and Sumer, Harappa was not a centralized monarchy claiming divine origins but a collection of over fifteen hundred towns and cities loosely connected by ties of trade and alliance and ruled by a coalition of landlords and rich merchants. There

were no royal precincts or imposing burial monuments, and there are few surviving stone or terra-cotta images that might represent kings, priests, or military commanders. It is possible however, that religion had advanced beyond the stage of spirit worship to belief in a single god or goddess of fertility. Presumably, priests at court prayed to this deity to maintain the fertility of the soil and guarantee the annual harvest.

As in Mesopotamia and Egypt, the Harappan economy was based primarily on agriculture.

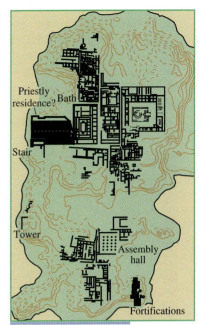

The City of Mohenjo-Daro

Wheat, barley, rice, and peas were apparently the primary crops. The presence of cotton seeds at various sites suggests that the Harappan peoples may have been the first to master the cultivation of this useful crop and possibly introduced it, along with rice, to other societies in the region. But Harappa also developed an extensive trading network that extended to Sumer and other civilizations to the west. Textiles and foodstuffs were apparently imported from Sumer in exchange for metals such as copper, lumber, precious stones, and various types of luxury goods. Much of this trade was conducted by ship via the Persian Gulf, although some undoubtedly went by land.

Harappan Culture Archaeological remains indicate that the Indus valley peoples possessed a culture as sophisticated in some ways as that of the Sumerians to the west. The aesthetic quality of some Harappan pottery and sculpture is superb, rivaling equivalent work produced elsewhere. Sculpture was the Harappans' highest artistic achievement. Some artifacts possess a wonderful vitality of expression. Fired clay seals show a deft touch in carving animals such as elephants, tigers, rhinoceros, and antelope, and figures made of copper or terra-cotta show a lively sensitivity and a sense of grace and movement.

Writing was another achievement of Harappan society and dates back at least to the beginning of the third millennium B.C.E. Unfortunately, the only surviving examples of Harappan writing are the pictographic symbols inscribed on the clay seals. The script contained more than four hundred characters, but most are too stylized to be identified by their shape, and scholars have thus far been unable to decipher them. There are no apparent links with Mesopotamian scripts, although, like the latter, Harappan writing may have been used primarily to record commercial transactions. Until the script is deciphered, much about the Harappan civilization must remain, as one historian termed it, a fascinating enigma.

The City of the Dead.   Mohenjo-Daro (below) was one of the two major cities of the ancient Indus River civilization. In addition to rows on rows of residential housing, it had a ceremonial center, with palatial residence and a sacred bath that was probably used by the priests as a means of achieving ritual purity. The bath is reminiscent of water tanks in modern Hindu temples, such as the Minakshi Temple in Madurai (on the right), where the faithful wash their feet prior to religious devotion. Water was an integral part of Hindu temple complexes, as symbolically it represented Vishnu's cosmic ocean and Shiva's reception of the holy Ganges on his head. Psychologically, water was a vital necessity in India's arid climate.

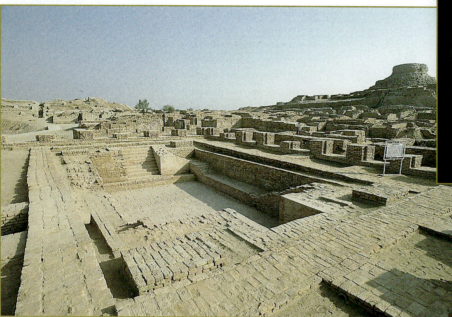

The Arrival of the Aryans

One of the great mysteries of Harappan civilization is how it came to an end. Archaeologists working at Mohenjo-Daro have discovered signs of first a gradual decay and then a sudden destruction of the city and its inhabitants

Harappan Seals. The Harappan peoples, like their contemporaries in Mesopotamia, developed a writing system to record their spoken language. Unfortunately, it has not yet been deciphered. Most extant examples of Harappan writing are found on fired clay seals depicting human figures and animals. These seals have been found in houses and were probably used to identify the owners of goods for sale. Other seals may have been used as amulets or have had other religious significance. Several depict religious figures or ritualistic scenes of sacrifice.

around 1500 B.C.E. Many of the surviving skeletons have been found in postures of running or hiding, reminiscent of the ruins of the Roman city of Pompeii, destroyed by the eruption of Mount Vesuvius in 79 C.E.

These tantalizing signs of flight before a sudden catastrophe led some scholars to surmise that the city of Mohenjo-Daro (the name was applied by archaeologists and means "city of the dead") and perhaps the remnants of Harappan civilization were destroyed by the Aryans, nomads from the north, who arrived in the subcontinent around the middle of the second millennium B.C.E. Aryan oral tradition recounts the occurrence of battles between "Aryans" and "Desas" in the second millennium B.C.E. As in Mesopotamia and the Nile valley, most contacts between pastoral and agricultural peoples proved unstable and often ended in armed conflict. Nevertheless, it is doubtful that the Aryan peoples were directly responsible for the final destruction of Mohenjo-Daro. More likely, Harappan civilization had already fallen on hard times, perhaps as a result of climatic change in the Indus valley. Archaeologists have found clear signs of social decay, including evidence of trash in the streets, neglect of public services, and overcrowding in urban neighborhoods. Mohenjo-Daro itself may have been destroyed by an epidemic or by natural phenomena such as floods, an earthquake, or a shift in the course of the Indus River. If that was the case, the Aryans arrived at a time when the Harappan culture's moment of greatness had already passed.

WRITING AND CIVILIZATION

In the year 3250 B.C.E., King Scorpion of Egypt issued an edict announcing a major victory for his army over rival forces in the region.

Inscribed in limestone on a cliff face in the Nile River valley, that edict is perhaps the oldest surviving historical document in the world today.

According to prehistorians, human beings began to create the first spoken language about 50,000 years ago. As human beings spread from Africa to other continents, that first system gradually fragmented into innumerable separate languages. By the time the agricultural revolution began about 10,000 years ago, there were perhaps nearly twenty distinct language families in existence around the world (see Map 2.2).

During the later stages of the agricultural revolution, the first writing systems also began to be created in various regions around the world. The first successful efforts were apparently achieved in Mesopotamia and Egypt, but knowledge of writing soon spread to peoples along the shores of the Mediterranean and in the Indus River valley in South Asia. Wholly independent systems were also invented in China and Mesoamerica. Writing was used for a variety of purposes. King Scorpion's edict suggests that one reason was to enable a ruler to communicate with his subjects on matters of official concern. In other cases, the purpose was to enable human beings to communicate with supernatural forces. In China and Egypt, for example, priests used writing to communicate with the gods. In Mesopotamia and in the Indus River valley, merchants used writing to record commercial and other legal transactions. Finally, writing was also used to present ideas in new ways, giving rise to such early Mesopotamian literature as *The Epic of Gilgamesh*.

How did such early written languages evolve into the complex systems in use today? In almost all cases, the first systems consisted of pictographs, pictorial images of various concrete objects such as trees, water, cattle, body parts, and the heavenly bodies. Eventually, such signs became more stylized to facilitate transcription—much as we often use a cursive script instead of block printing today. Finally, and most important for their future development, these pictorial images began to take on specific phonetic meaning so that they could represent sounds in the written language. Most sophisticated written systems eventually evolved to a phonetic script, based on an alphabet of symbols to represent all sounds in the spoken language, but others went only part way by adding phonetic signs to the individual character to suggest pronunciation while keeping part of the original pictograph to indicate meaning. Most of the latter systems, such as hieroglyphics in Egypt and cuneiform in Mesopotamia, eventually became extinct, but the ancient Chinese writing system survives today, although in changed form.

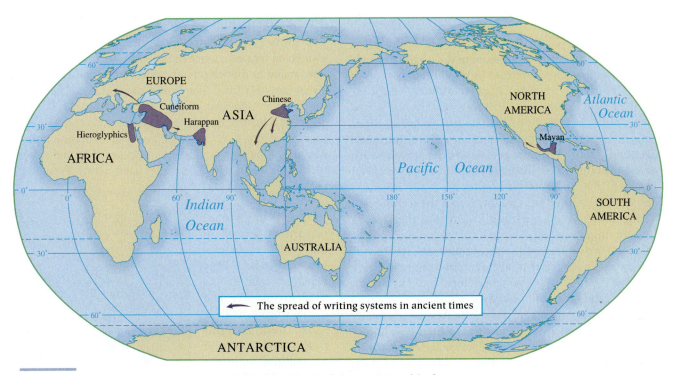

MAP 2.2 **Writing Systems in the Ancient World.** One of the chief characteristics of the first civilizations was the development of a system of written communication. ❓ Based on the comparative essay, in what ways were these first writing systems similar, and how were they different?

ANCIENT INDIA   33

The Dancing Girl. Relatively little has survived reflecting the creative talents of the Harappan peoples. This 5-inch bronze figure of a young dancer in repose is one of the few surviving metal sculptures from Mohenjo-Daro. The detail and grace of her stance reflect the skill of the artist who molded her four thousand years ago.

The Early Aryans

Historians know relatively little about the origins and culture of the Aryans before they entered India, although they were part of the extensive group of Indo-European-speaking peoples who inhabited vast areas in what is now Siberia and the steppes of Central Asia. Whereas other Indo-European-speaking peoples moved westward and eventually settled in Europe, the Aryans moved south across the Hindu Kush into the plains of northern India. Between 1500 and 1000 B.C.E., they gradually advanced eastward from the Indus valley, across the fertile plain of the Ganges, and later southward into the Deccan Plateau until they had eventually extended their political mastery over the entire subcontinent and its Dravidian-speaking inhabitants, although indigenous culture survived to remain a prominent element in the evolution of traditional Indian civilization.

After they settled in India, the Aryans gradually adapted to the geographic realities of their new homeland and abandoned the pastoral life for agricultural pursuits. They were assisted by the introduction of iron, which probably came from the Middle East, where it had first been introduced by the Hittites (see Chapter 1) about 1500 B.C.E. The invention of the iron plow, along

with the development of irrigation, allowed the Aryans and the local inhabitants to clear the dense jungle growth along the Ganges River and transform the Ganges valley into one of the richest agricultural regions in all of South Asia. The Aryans also developed their first writing system—based on the **Aramaic** script used in the Middle East—and were thus able to transcribe the legends that previously had been passed down from generation to generation by memory. Most of what is known about the early Aryans is based on oral traditions passed on in the Rig Veda, an ancient work that was written down after the Aryans arrived in India (the Rig Veda is one of several Vedas, or collections of sacred instructions and rituals).

As in other Indo-European societies, each of the various Aryan tribes was led by a chieftain, called a *raja* ("prince"), who was assisted by a council of elders composed of other leading members of the tribe; like them, he was normally a member of the warrior class, called the *kshatriya.* The chief derived his power from his ability to protect his tribe from rival groups, an ability that was crucial in the warring kingdoms and shifting alliances that were typical of early Aryan society. Though the *rajas* claimed to be representatives of the gods, they were not viewed as gods themselves (see the box on p. 35).

As Indian society grew in size and complexity, the chieftains began to be transformed into kings, usually called *maharajas* ("great princes"). Nevertheless, the tradition that the ruler did not possess absolute authority remained strong. Like all human beings, the ruler was required to follow the *dharma,* a set of laws that set behavioral standards for all individuals and classes in Indian society (see the boxes on pp. 36 and 37).

The Impact of the Greeks While competing groups squabbled for precedence in India, powerful new empires were rising to the west. First came the Persian Empire of Cyrus and Darius. Then came the Greeks. After two centuries of sporadic rivalry and warfare, the Greeks achieved a brief period of regional dominance in the late fourth century B.C.E. with the rise of Macedonia under Alexander the Great. Alexander had heard of the riches of India, and in 330 B.C.E., after conquering Persia, he launched an invasion of the east (see Chapter 4). In 326 B.C.E., his armies arrived in the plains of northwestern India. They departed almost as suddenly as they had come, leaving in their wake Greek administrators and a veneer of cultural influence that would affect the area for generations to come.

Alexander the Great's Movements in Asia

THE ORIGINS OF KINGSHIP

POLITICS & GOVERNMENT

Both India and China had a concept of a golden age in the remote past that provided a model for later governments and peoples to emulate. This passage from the famous Indian epic the Mahabharata describes a three-stage process in the evolution of government in human society. Yudhishthira and Bhishma are two of the main characters in the story.

What is the author's purpose here? How does this vision compare with the views then current on the reasons for the emergence of political leadership? How does it compare with Chinese theories regarding the mandate of Heaven (see Chapter 3)?

The Mahabharata

Yudhisthira said: "This word 'king' [raja] is so very current in this world, O Bharata; how has it originated? Tell me that O grandfather."

Bhishma said: "Currently, O best among men, do you listen to everything in its entirety—how kingship originated first during the golden age [krtayuga]. Neither kingship nor king was there in the beginning, neither scepter [danda] nor the bearer of a scepter. All people protected one another by means of righteous conduct, O Bharata, men eventually fell into a state of spiritual lassitude. Then delusion overcame them. Men were thus overpowered by infatuation, O leader of men, on account of the delusion of understanding; their sense of righteous conduct was lost. When understanding was lost, all men, O best of the Bharatas, overpowered by infatuation, became victims of greed. Then they sought to acquire what should not be acquired. Thereby, indeed, O lord, another vice, namely, desire overcame them. Attachment then attacked them, who had become victims of desire. Attached to objects of sense, they did not discriminate between what should be said and what should not be said, between the edible and inedible and between right and wrong. When this world of men had been submerged in dissipation, all spiritual knowledge [brahman] perished; and when spiritual knowledge perished, O king, righteous conduct also perished."

When spiritual knowledge and righteous conduct perished, the gods were overcome with fear, and fearfully sought refuge with Brahma, the creator. Going to the great lord, the ancestor of the worlds, all the gods, afflicted with sorrow, misery, and fear, with folded hands said: "O Lord, the eternal spiritual knowledge, which had existed in the world of men, has perished because of greed, infatuation, and the like, therefore we have become fearful. Through the loss of spiritual knowledge, righteous conduct also has perished, O God. Therefore, O Lord of the three worlds, mortals have reached a state of indifference. Verily, we showered rain on earth, but mortals showered rain [i.e., oblations] up to heaven. As a result of the cessation of ritual activity on their part, we faced a serious peril. O grandfather, decide what is most beneficial to use under these circumstances."

Then, the self-born lord said to all those gods: "I will consider what is most beneficial; let your fear depart, O leaders of the gods."

Thereupon he composed a work consisting of a hundred thousand chapters out of his own mind, wherein righteous conduct [dharma], as well as material gain [artha] and enjoyment of sensual pleasures [kama] were described. This group, known as the threefold classification of human objectives, was expounded by the self-born lord; so, too, a fourth objective, spiritual emancipation [moksha], which aims at a different goal, and which constitutes a separate group by itself.

Then the gods approached Vishnu, the lord of creatures, and said: "Indicate to us that one person among mortals who alone is worthy of the highest eminence." Then the blessed lord god Narayana reflected, and brought forth an illustrious mind-born son, called Virajas [who, in this version of the origins of the Indian state, became the first king].

CENGAGENOW To read more of the Mahabharata, enter the *CengageNOW* documents area using the access card that is available for *The Essential World History.*

The Mauryan Empire

The Alexandrian conquest was only a brief interlude in the history of the Indian subcontinent, but it played a formative role, for on the heels of Alexander's departure came the rise of the first dynasty to control much of the region. The founder of the new state, who took the royal title Chandragupta Maurya (324–301 B.C.E.), drove out the Greek administrators who had remained after the departure of Alexander and solidified his control over the northern Indian plain. He established the capital of his new Mauryan Empire at Pataliputra (modern Patna) in the Ganges valley (see Map 2.3 on p. 45).

Little is known of Chandragupta Maurya's empire. Most accounts of his reign rely on a lost work written by Megasthenes, a Greek ambassador to the Mauryan court, in about 302 B.C.E. Chandragupta Maurya was apparently advised by a brilliant court official named Kautilya, whose name has been attached to a treatise on politics called the *Arthasastra* (see the box on p. 36). The work actually dates from a later time, but it may well reflect Kautilya's ideas.

Although the author of the *Arthasastra* follows Aryan tradition in stating that the happiness of the king lies in the happiness of his subjects, the treatise also asserts that when the sacred law of the *dharma* and practical politics

The Duties of a King

Kautilya, India's earliest known political philosopher, was an adviser to the Mauryan rulers. The *Arthasastra*, though written down at a later date, very likely reflects his ideas. This passage sets forth some of the necessary characteristics of a king, including efficiency, diligence, energy, compassion, and concern for the security and welfare of the state. In emphasizing the importance of results rather than motives, Kautilya resembles the Italian Renaissance thinker Machiavelli. But in focusing on winning popular support as the means of becoming an effective ruler, the author echoes the view of the Chinese philosopher Mencius, who declared that the best way to win the empire is to win the people (see Chapter 3).

To whom was the author of this document directing his advice? How do the ideas expressed here compare with those of political thinkers during the time of Confucius in China and of Socrates and Plato in classical Greece?

The *Arthasastra*

Only if a king is himself energetically active do his officers follow him energetically. If he is sluggish, they too remain sluggish. And, besides, they eat up his works. He is thereby easily overpowered by his enemies. Therefore, he should ever dedicate himself energetically to activity. . . .

A king should attend to all urgent business; he should not put it off. For what has been thus put off becomes either difficult or altogether impossible to accomplish.

The vow of the king is energetic activity; his sacrifice is constituted of the discharge of his own administrative duties; his sacrificial fee [to the officiating priests] is his impartiality of attitude toward all; his sacrificial consecration is his anointment as king.

In the happiness of the subjects lies the happiness of the king; in their welfare, his own welfare. The welfare of the king does not lie in the fulfillment of what is dear to him; whatever is dear to the subjects constitutes his welfare.

Therefore, ever energetic, a king should act up to the precepts of the science of material gain. Energetic activity is the source of material gain; its opposite, of downfall.

In the absence of energetic activity, the loss of what has already been obtained and of what still remains to be obtained is certain. The fruit of one's works is achieved through energetic activity—one obtains abundance of material prosperity.

CENGAGENOW To read more from the *Arthasastra*, enter the *CengageNOW* documents area using the access card that is available for *The Essential World History*.

---

collide, the latter must take precedence: "Whenever there is disagreement between history and sacred law or between evidence and sacred law, then the matter should be settled in accordance with sacred law. But whenever sacred law is in conflict with rational law, then reason shall be held authoritative."[1] The *Arthasastra* also emphasizes ends rather than means, achieved results rather than the methods employed. For this reason, it has often been compared to Machiavelli's famous political treatise of the Italian Renaissance, *The Prince*, written more than a thousand years later (see Chapter 12).

As described in the *Arthasastra*, Chandragupta Maurya's government was highly centralized and even despotic: "It is power and power alone which, only when exercised by the king with impartiality, and in proportion to guilt, over his son or his enemy, maintains both this world and the next."[2] The king possessed a large army and a secret police responsible to his orders (according to the Greek ambassador Megasthenes, Chandragupta Maurya was chronically fearful of assassination, a not unrealistic concern for someone who had allegedly come to power by violence). Reportedly, all food was tasted in his presence, and

he made a practice of never sleeping twice in the same bed in his sumptuous palace. To guard against corruption, a board of censors was empowered to investigate cases of possible malfeasance and incompetence within the bureaucracy.

The ruler's authority beyond the confines of the capital may often have been limited, however. The empire was divided into provinces that were ruled by governors. At first, most of these governors were appointed by and reported to the ruler, but later the position became hereditary. The provinces themselves were divided into districts, each under a chief magistrate appointed by the governor. At the base of the government pyramid was the village, where the vast majority of the Indian people lived. The village was governed by a council of elders; membership in the council was normally hereditary and was shared by the wealthiest families in the village.

Caste and Class: Social Structures in Ancient India

When the Aryans arrived in India, they already possessed a strong class system based on a ruling warrior class and

SOCIAL CLASSES IN ANCIENT INDIA

FAMILY & SOCIETY

The Law of Manu is a set of behavioral norms allegedly prescribed by India's mythical founding ruler, Manu. The treatise was probably written in the first or second century B.C.E. The following excerpt describes the various social classes in India and their prescribed duties. Many scholars doubt that the social system in India was ever as rigid as it was portrayed here, and some suggest that upper-class Indians may have used the idea of *varna* to enhance their own status in society.

How might the class system in ancient India, as described here, be compared with social class divisions in other societies in Asia? Why do you think the class system as described here developed in India? What is the difference between the class system (varna) *and the* jati?

The Law of Manu

For the sake of the preservation of this entire creation, the Exceedingly Resplendent One [the Creator of the Universe] assigned separate duties to the classes which had sprung from his mouth, arms, thighs, and feet.

Teaching, studying, performing sacrificial rites, so too making others perform sacrificial rites, and giving away and receiving gifts—these he assigned to the [*brahmins*].

Protection of the people, giving away of wealth, performance of sacrificial rites, study, and nonattachment to sensual pleasures—these are, in short, the duties of a *kshatriya*.

Tending of cattle, giving away of wealth, performance of sacrificial rites, study, trade and commerce, usury, and agriculture—these are the occupations of a *vaisya*.

The Lord has prescribed only one occupation [*karma*] for a *sudra*, namely, service without malice of even these other three classes.

Of created beings, those which are animate are the best; of the animate, those which subsist by means of their intellect; of the intelligent, men are the best; and of men, the [*brahmins*] are traditionally declared to be the best.

The code of conduct—prescribed by scriptures and ordained by sacred tradition—constitutes the highest *dharma;* hence a twice-born person, conscious of his own Self [seeking spiritual salvation], should be always scrupulous in respect of it.

CENGAGENOW To read a full version of *The Law of Manu,* enter the *CengageNOW* documents area using the access card that is available for *The Essential World History.*

---

other social groupings characteristic of a pastoral society. On their arrival in India, they encountered peoples living in an agricultural society and assigned them to a lower position in the community. The result was a set of social institutions and class divisions that have persisted with only minor changes down to the present day.

The Class System At the base of the social system that emerged from the clash of cultures was the concept of the hierarchical division of society into separate classes on the basis of the functions assigned to each class. In a sense, it became an issue of color, because the Aryans, a primarily light-skinned people, were contemptuous of the indigenous population, who were dark. Light skin came to imply high status, whereas dark skin suggested the opposite.

The concept of color, however, was only the physical manifestation of a division that took place in Indian society on the basis of economic functions. Indian classes (called **varna,** literally, "color," and commonly but mistakenly known as "castes" in English) did not simply reflect an informal division of labor. Instead, at least in theory, they were a set of rigid social classifications that determined not only one's occupation but also one's status in society and one's hope for ultimate salvation (see the section "Escaping the Wheel of Life" later in this chapter). There

were five major *varna* in Indian society in ancient times. At the top were two classes, collectively viewed as the aristocracy, which clearly represented the ruling elites in Aryan society prior to their arrival in India: the priests and the warriors (see the box above).

The priestly class, known as the **brahmins,** was usually considered to be at the top of the social scale. Descended from seers who had advised the ruler on religious matters in Aryan tribal society (*brahmin* meant "one possessed of **Brahman,**" a term for the supreme god in the Hindu religion), they were eventually transformed into an official class after their religious role declined in importance. Megasthenes described this class as follows:

From the time of their conception in the womb they are under the care and guardianship of learned men who go to the mother and . . . give her prudent hints and counsels, and the women who listen to them most willingly are thought to be the most fortunate in their offspring. After their birth the children are in the care of one person after another, and as they advance in years their masters are men of superior accomplishments. The philosophers reside in a grove in front of the city within a moderate-sized enclosure. They live in a simple style and lie on pallets of straw and [deer] skins. They abstain from animal food and sexual pleasures, and occupy their time in listening to serious discourse and in imparting knowledge to willing ears.[3]

The second class was the *kshatriya,* the warriors. Although often listed below the *brahmins* in social status, many *kshatriyas* were probably descended from the ruling warrior class in Aryan society prior to the conquest of India and thus may have originally ranked socially above the *brahmins,* although they were ranked lower in religious terms. Like the *brahmins,* the *kshatriyas* were originally identified with a single occupation—fighting—but as the character of Aryan society changed, they often switched to other forms of employment.

The third-ranked class in Indian society was the **vaisya** (literally, "commoner"). The *vaisyas* were usually viewed in economic terms as the merchant class. Some historians have speculated that the *vaisyas* were originally guardians of the tribal herds but that after settling in India, many moved into commercial pursuits. Megasthenes noted that members of this class "alone are permitted to hunt and keep cattle and to sell beasts of burden or to let them out on hire. In return for clearing the land of wild beasts and birds which infest sown fields, they receive an allowance of corn from the king. They lead a wandering life and dwell in tents."[4] Although this class was ranked below the first two in social status, it shared with them the privilege of being considered **"twice-born,"** a term used to refer to males who had undergone a ceremony at puberty whereby they were initiated into adulthood and introduced into Indian society.

Below the three "twice-born" classes were the **sudras,** who represented the great bulk of the Indian population. The *sudras* were not considered fully Aryan, and the term probably originally referred to the indigenous population. Most *sudras* were peasants or artisans or worked at other forms of manual labor. They had only limited rights in society.

At the lowest level of Indian society, and in fact not even considered a legitimate part of the class system itself, were the untouchables (also known as outcastes, or **pariahs**). The untouchables probably originated as a slave class consisting of prisoners of war, criminals, ethnic minorities, and other groups considered outside Indian society. Even after slavery was outlawed, the untouchables were given menial and degrading tasks that other Indians would not accept, such as collecting trash, handling dead bodies, or serving as butchers or tanners (handling dead meat). According to the estimate of one historian, they may have accounted for a little more than 5 percent of the total population of India in antiquity.

The life of the untouchables was extremely demeaning. They were not considered human, and their very presence was considered polluting to members of the other *varna.* No Indian would touch or eat food handled or prepared by an untouchable. Untouchables lived in special ghettos and were required to tap two sticks together to announce their presence when they traveled outside their quarters so that others could avoid them.

Technically, the class divisions were absolute. Individuals supposedly were born, lived, and died in the same class. In practice, some upward or downward mobility probably took place, and there was undoubtedly some flexibility in economic functions. But throughout most of Indian history, class taboos remained strict. Members were generally not permitted to marry outside their class (although in practice, men were occasionally allowed to marry below their class but not above it).

The *Jati* The people of ancient India did not belong to a particular class as individuals but as part of a larger kinship group commonly referred to as the **jati** (in Portuguese, *casta,* which evolved into the English term *caste*), a system of extended families that originated in ancient India and still exists in somewhat changed form today. Although the origins of the *jati* system are unknown (there are no indications of strict class distinctions in Harappan society), the *jati* eventually became identified with a specific kinship group living in a specific area and carrying out a specific function in society. Each *jati* was identified with a particular *varna,* and each had, at least in theory, its own separate economic function.

Thus, *jatis* were the basic social organization into which traditional Indian society was divided. Each *jati* was itself composed of hundreds or thousands of individual nuclear families and was governed by its own council of elders. Membership in this ruling council was usually hereditary and was based on the wealth or social status of particular families within the community.

In theory, each *jati* was assigned a particular form of economic activity. Obviously, though, not all families in a given *jati* could take part in the same vocation, and as time went on, members of a single *jati* commonly engaged in several different lines of work. Sometimes an entire *jati* would have to move its location in order to continue a particular form of activity. In other cases, a *jati* would adopt an entirely new occupation in order to remain in a certain area. Such changes in habitat or occupation introduced the possibility of movement up or down the social scale. In this way, an entire *jati* could sometimes engage in upward mobility, even though it was not possible for individuals, who were tied to their class identity for life.

The class system in ancient India may sound highly constricting, but there were persuasive social and economic reasons why it survived for so many centuries. In the first place, it provided an identity for individuals in a highly hierarchical society. Although an individual might rank lower on the social scale than members of other classes, it was always possible to find others ranked even lower. Perhaps equally important, the *jati* was a primitive form of welfare system. Each was obliged to provide for any of its members who were poor or destitute. The *jati* also provided an element of stability in a society that all too often was in a state of political instability.

Daily Life in Ancient India

Beyond these rigid social stratifications was the Indian family. Not only was life centered around the family, but the family, not the individual, was the most basic unit in society.

The Family   The ideal social unit was an extended family, with three generations living under the same roof. It was essentially patriarchal, except along the Malabar coast, near the southwestern tip of the subcontinent, where a matriarchal form of social organization prevailed down to modern times. In the rest of India, the oldest male traditionally possessed legal authority over the entire family unit.

The family was linked together in a religious sense by a series of commemorative rites to ancestral members. This ritual originated in the Vedic era and consisted of family ceremonies to honor the departed and to link the living and the dead. The male family head was responsible for leading the ritual. At his death, his eldest son had the duty of conducting the funeral rites.

The importance of the father and the son in family ritual underlined the importance of males in Indian society. Male superiority was expressed in a variety of ways. Women could not serve as priests (although in practice, some were accepted as seers), nor were they normally permitted to study the Vedas. In general, males had a monopoly on education, since the primary goal of learning to read was to carry on family rituals. In high-class families, young men began Vedic studies with a *guru* (teacher). Some then went on to higher studies in one of the major cities. The goal of such an education might be either professional or religious.

Marriage   In general, only males could inherit property, except in a few cases where there were no sons. According to law, a woman was always considered a minor. Divorce was prohibited, although it sometimes took place. According to the *Arthasastra,* a wife who had been deserted by her husband could seek a divorce. Polygamy was fairly rare and apparently occurred mainly among the higher classes, but husbands were permitted to take a second wife if the first was barren. Producing children was an important aspect of marriage, both because children provided security for their parents in old age and because they were a physical proof of male potency. Child marriage was common for young girls, whether because of the desire for children or because daughters represented an economic liability to their parents. But perhaps the most graphic symbol of women's subjection to men was the ritual of **sati** (often written *suttee*), which required the wife to throw herself on her dead husband's funeral pyre. The Greek visitor Megasthenes reported "that he had heard from some persons of wives burning themselves along with their deceased husbands and doing so gladly; and that those women who refused to burn themselves were held in disgrace."[5] All in all, it was undoubtedly a difficult existence. According to the *Law of Manu,* an early treatise on social organization and behavior in ancient India, probably written in the first or second century B.C.E., women were subordinated to men—first to their father, then to their husband, and finally to their sons:

She should do nothing independently
    even in her own house.
In childhood subject to her father,
    in youth to her husband,
and when her husband is dead to her sons,
    she should never enjoy independence. . . .

She should always be cheerful,
    and skillful in her domestic duties,
with her household vessels well cleansed,
    and her hand tight on the purse strings. . . .

Though he be uncouth and prone to pleasure,
    though he have no good points at all,
the virtuous wife should ever
    worship her lord as a god.[6]

The Role of Women   At the root of female subordination to the male was the practical fact that as in most agricultural societies, men did most of the work in the fields. Females were viewed as having little utility outside the home and indeed were considered an economic burden, since parents were obliged to provide a dowry to acquire a husband for a daughter. Female children also appeared to offer little advantage in maintaining the family unit, since they joined the families of their husbands after the wedding ceremony.

Despite all of these indications of female subjection to the male, there are numerous signs that in some ways women often played an influential role in Indian society, and the Hindu code of behavior stressed that they should be treated with respect. Indians appeared to be fascinated by female sexuality, and tradition held that women often used their sexual powers to achieve domination over men. The author of the Mahabharata, a vast epic of early Indian society, complained that "the fire has never too many logs, the ocean never too many rivers, death never too many living souls, and fair-eyed woman never too many men." Despite the legal and social constraints, women often played an important role within the family unit, and many were admired and honored for their talents. It is probably significant that paintings and sculpture from ancient and medieval India frequently show women in a role equal to that of men.

Homosexuality was not unknown in India. It was condemned in the law books, however, and generally ignored by literature, which devoted its attention entirely to erotic heterosexuality. The *Kamasutra,* a textbook on sexual practices and techniques dating from the second century C.E. or slightly thereafter, mentions homosexuality briefly and with no apparent enthusiasm.

The Economy

The arrival of the Aryans did not drastically change the economic character of Indian society. Not only did most Aryans take up farming, but it is likely that agriculture expanded rapidly under Aryan rule with the invention of the iron plow and the spread of northern Indian culture into the Deccan Plateau. One consequence of this process was to shift the focus of Indian culture from the Indus valley farther eastward to the Ganges River valley, which even today is one of the most densely populated regions on earth. The flatter areas in the Deccan Plateau and in the coastal plains were also turned into cropland.

Indian Farmers For most Indian farmers, life was harsh. Among the most fortunate were those who owned their own land, although they were required to pay taxes to the state. Many others were sharecroppers or landless laborers. They were subject to the vicissitudes of the market and often paid exorbitant rents to their landlord. Concentration of land in large holdings was limited by the tradition of dividing property among all the sons, but large estates worked by hired laborers or rented out to sharecroppers were not uncommon, particularly in areas where local *rajas* derived much of their wealth from their property.

Another problem for Indian farmers was the unpredictability of the climate. India is in the monsoon zone. The monsoon is a seasonal wind pattern in southern Asia that blows from the southwest during the summer months and from the northeast during the winter. The southwest monsoon is commonly marked by heavy rains. When the rains were late, thousands starved, particularly in the drier areas, which were especially dependent on rainfall. Strong governments attempted to deal with such problems by building state-operated granaries and maintaining the irrigation works; but strong governments were rare, and famine was probably all too common. The staple crops in the north were wheat, barley, and millet, with wet rice common in the fertile river valleys. In the south, grain and vegetables were supplemented by various tropical products, cotton, and spices such as pepper, ginger, cinnamon, and saffron.

Trade and Manufacturing By no means were all Indians farmers. As time passed, India became one of the most advanced trading and manufacturing civilizations in the ancient world. After the rise of the Mauryas, India's role in regional trade began to expand, and the subcontinent became a major transit point in a vast commercial network that extended from the rim of the Pacific to the Middle East and the Mediterranean Sea. This regional trade went both by sea and by camel caravan. Maritime trade across the Indian Ocean may have begun as early as the fifth century B.C.E. It extended eastward as far as Southeast Asia and China and southward as far as the straits between Africa and the island of Madagascar. Westward went spices, teakwood, perfumes, jewels, textiles, precious stones and ivory, and wild animals. In return, India received gold, tin, lead, and wine. The subcontinent had, indeed, become a major crossroads of trade in the ancient world.

India's expanding role as a manufacturing and commercial hub of the ancient world was undoubtedly a spur to the growth of the state. Under Chandragupta Maurya, the central government became actively involved in commercial and manufacturing activities. It owned mines and vast crown lands and undoubtedly earned massive profits from its role in regional commerce. Separate government departments were established for trade, agriculture, mining, and the manufacture of weapons, and the movement of private goods was vigorously taxed. Nevertheless, a significant private sector also flourished; it was dominated by great caste guilds, which monopolized key sectors of the economy. A money economy probably came into operation during the second century B.C.E., when copper and gold coins were introduced from the Middle East. This in turn led to the development of banking.

Escaping the Wheel of Life: The Religious World of Ancient India

Like Indian politics and society, Indian religion is a blend of Aryan and Dravidian culture. The intermingling of those two civilizations gave rise to an extraordinarily complex set of religious beliefs and practices, filled with diversity and contrast. Out of this cultural mix came two of the world's great religions, Buddhism and Hinduism, and several smaller ones, including Jainism and Sikhism.

Hinduism

Evidence about the earliest religious beliefs of the Aryan peoples comes primarily from sacred texts such as the Vedas, a set of four collections of hymns and religious ceremonies transmitted by memory through the centuries by Aryan priests. Many of these religious ideas were probably common to all of the Indo-European peoples before their separation into different groups at least four thousand years ago. Early Aryan beliefs were based on the common concept of a pantheon of gods and goddesses representing great forces of nature similar to the immortals of Greek mythology. The Aryan ancestor of the Greek father-god Zeus, for example, may have been the deity known in early Aryan tradition as Dyaus (see Chapter 4).

The parent god Dyaus was a somewhat distant figure, however, who was eventually overshadowed by other, more functional gods possessing more familiar human traits. For a while, the primary Aryan god was the great warrior god Indra. Indra summoned the Aryan tribal peoples to war and was represented in nature by thunder. Later, Indra declined in importance and was replaced by Varuna, lord of justice. Other gods and goddesses represented various forces of nature or the needs of human beings, such as fire, fertility, and wealth.

The concept of sacrifice was a key element in Aryan religious belief in Vedic times. As in many other ancient cultures, the practice may have begun as human sacrifice, but later animals were used as substitutes. The priestly class, the *brahmins,* played a key role in these ceremonies.

Another element of Indian religious belief in ancient times was the ideal of asceticism. Although there is no reference to such practices in the Vedas, by the sixth century B.C.E., self-discipline, which involved subjecting oneself to painful stimuli or even self-mutilation, had begun to replace sacrifice as a means of placating or communicating with the gods. Apparently, the original motive for asceticism was to achieve magical powers, but later, in the Upanishads (a set of commentaries on the Vedas compiled in the sixth century B.C.E.), it was seen as a means of spiritual meditation that would enable the practitioner to reach beyond material reality to a world of truth and bliss beyond earthly joy and sorrow: "Those who practice penance and faith in the forest, the tranquil ones, the knowers of truth, living the life of wandering mendicancy—they depart, freed from passion, through the door of the sun, to where dwells, verily . . . the imperishable Soul."[7] It is possible that another motive was to permit those with strong religious convictions to communicate directly with metaphysical reality without having to rely on the priestly class at court.

Asceticism, of course, has been practiced in other religions, including Christianity and Islam, but it seems particularly identified with **Hinduism,** the religion that emerged from early Indian religious tradition. Eventually, asceticism evolved into the modern practice of body training that we know as *yoga* ("union"), which is accepted today as a meaningful element of Hindu religious practice.

Reincarnation Another new concept also probably began to appear around the time the Upanishads were written—the idea of **reincarnation.** This is the idea that the individual soul is reborn in a different form after death and progresses through several existences on the wheel of life until it reaches its final destination in a union with the Great World Soul, *Brahman.* Because life is harsh, this final release is the objective of all living souls. From this concept comes the term **Brahmanism,** referring to the early form of Aryan religious tradition.

A key element in this process is the idea of *karma*—that one's rebirth in a next life is determined by one's *karma* (actions) in this life. Hinduism, as it emerged from Brahmanism in the first century C.E., placed all living species on a vast scale of existence, including the four classes and the untouchables in human society. The current status of an individual soul, then, is not simply a cosmic accident but the inevitable result of actions that that soul has committed in a past existence.

At the top of the scale are the *brahmins,* who by definition are closest to ultimate release from the law of reincarnation. The *brahmins* are followed in descending order by the other classes in human society and the world of the beasts. Within the animal kingdom, an especially high position is reserved for the cow, which even today is revered by Hindus as a sacred beast. Some have speculated that the cow's sacred position may have descended from the concept of the sacred bull in Harappan culture.

The concept of *karma* is governed by the *dharma,* a law regulating human behavior. The *dharma* imposes different requirements on different individuals depending on their status in society. Those high on the social scale, such as *brahmins* and *kshatriyas,* are held to a more strict form of behavior than are *sudras.* The *brahmin,* for example, is expected to abstain from eating meat, because that would entail the killing of another living being, thus interrupting its *karma.*

How the concept of reincarnation originated is not known, although it was apparently not unusual for early peoples to believe that the individual soul would be reborn in a different form in a later life. In any case, in India the concept may have had practical causes as well as consequences. In the first place, it tended to provide religious sanction for the rigid class divisions that had begun to emerge in Indian society after the arrival of the Aryans, and it provided moral and political justification for the privileges of those on the higher end of the scale.

At the same time, the concept of reincarnation provided certain compensations for those lower on the ladder of life. For example, it gave hope to the poor that if they behaved properly in this life, they might improve their condition in the next. It also provided a means for unassimilated groups such as ethnic minorities to find a place in Indian society while at the same time permitting them to maintain their distinctive way of life.

The ultimate goal of achieving "good" *karma,* as we have seen, was to escape the cycle of existence. To the sophisticated, the nature of that release was a spiritual union of the individual soul with the Great World Soul, *Brahman,* described in the Upanishads as a form of dreamless sleep, free from earthly desires. Such a concept, however, was undoubtedly too ethereal for the average Indian, who needed a more concrete form of heavenly salvation, a place of beauty and bliss after a life of disease and privation.

Hindu Gods and Goddesses It was probably for this reason that the Hindu religion—in some ways so otherworldly and ascetic—came to be peopled with a multitude of very human gods and goddesses. It has been estimated that the Hindu pantheon contains more than 33,000 deities. Only a small number are primary ones, however, notably the so-called trinity of gods: Brahman the Creator, Vishnu the Preserver, and Shiva (originally the Vedic god Rudra) the Destroyer. Although Brahman (sometimes in his concrete form called Brahma) is considered to be the highest god, Vishnu and Shiva take precedence in the devotional exercises of many Hindus, who can be roughly divided into Vishnuites and Shaivites. In addition to the trinity of gods, all of whom have wives with readily identifiable roles and personalities, there are countless minor deities, each again with his or her own specific function, such as bringing good fortune, arranging a good marriage, or guaranteeing a son in childbirth.

The rich variety and earthy character of many Hindu deities are misleading, however, for many Hindus regard the multitude of gods as simply different manifestations of one ultimate reality. The various deities also provide a useful means for ordinary Indians to personify their religious feelings. Even though some individuals among the early

Courtesy of William J. Duiker

Dancing Shiva. The Hindu deity Shiva is often presented in the form of a bronze statue, performing a cosmic dance in which he simultaneously creates and destroys the universe. While his upper right hand creates the cosmos, his upper left hand reduces it in flames, and the lower two hands offer eternal blessing. Shiva's dancing statues present to his followers the visual message of his power and compassion.

Aryans attempted to communicate with the gods through animal sacrifice or asceticism, most Indians undoubtedly sought to satisfy their own individual religious needs through devotion, which they expressed through ritual ceremonies and offerings at a Hindu temple. Such offerings were not only a way to seek salvation but also a means of satisfying all the aspirations of daily life.

Over the centuries, then, Hinduism changed radically from its origins in Aryan tribal society and became a religion of the vast majority of the Indian people. Concern with a transcendental union between the individual soul and the Great World Soul contrasted with practical desires for material wealth and happiness; ascetic self-denial contrasted with an earthy emphasis on the pleasures and values of sexual union between marriage partners. All of these became aspects of Hinduism, the religion of 70 percent of the Indian people.

Buddhism: The Middle Path

In the sixth century B.C.E., a new doctrine appeared in northern India that soon began to rival Hinduism's popularity throughout the subcontinent. This new doctrine was called Buddhism.

The Life of Siddhartha Gautama   The historical founder of Buddhism, Siddhartha Gautama, was a native of a small principality in the foothills of the Himalaya Mountains in what is today southern Nepal. He was born in the mid-sixth century B.C.E., the son of a ruling *kshatriya* family. According to tradition, the young Siddhartha was raised in affluent surroundings and trained, like many other members of his class, in the martial arts. On reaching maturity, he married and began to raise a family. At the age of twenty-nine, however, he suddenly discovered the pain of illness, the sorrow of death, and the degradation caused by old age in the lives of ordinary people and exclaimed: "Would that sickness, age, and death might be forever bound!" From that time on, he decided to dedicate his life to determining the cause and seeking the cure for human suffering.

To find the answers to these questions, Siddhartha abandoned his home and family and traveled widely. At first, he tried to follow the model of the ascetics, but he eventually decided that self-mortification did not lead to a greater understanding of life and abandoned the practice. Then one day, after a lengthy period of meditation under a tree, he finally achieved enlightenment as to the meaning of life and spent the remainder of his life preaching it. His conclusions, as embodied in his teachings, became the philosophy (or as some would have it, the religion) of Buddhism. According to legend, the Devil (the Indian term is *Mara*) attempted desperately to tempt him with political power and the company of beautiful girls. But Siddhartha Gautama resisted:

> *Pleasure is brief as a flash of lightning*
> *Or like an autumn shower, only for a moment. . . .*
> *Why should I then covet the pleasures you speak of?*
> *I see your bodies are full of all impurity:*
> *Birth and death, sickness and age are yours.*
> *I seek the highest prize, hard to attain by men—*
> *The true and constant wisdom of the wise.*[8]

How much the modern doctrine of Buddhism resembles the original teachings of Siddhartha Gautama is open to debate, since much time has elapsed since his death and original texts relating his ideas are lacking. Nor is it certain that Siddhartha even intended to found a new religion or doctrine. In some respects, his ideas could be viewed as a reformist form of Hinduism, designed to transfer responsibility from the priests to the individual, much as Martin Luther saw Protestantism as a reformation of Christianity. Siddhartha accepted much of the belief system of Hinduism, if not all of its practices. For example, he accepted the concept of reincarnation and the role of *karma* as a means of influencing the movement of individual souls up and down in the scale of life. He followed Hinduism in praising nonviolence and borrowed the idea of living a life of simplicity and chastity from the ascetics. Moreover, his vision of metaphysical reality—commonly known as **Nirvana**—is closer to the Hindu concept of *Brahman* than it is to the Christian concept of heavenly salvation. Nirvana, which involves an extinction of selfhood and a final reunion with the Great World Soul, is sometimes likened to a dreamless sleep or to a kind of "blowing out" (as of a

RELIGION & PHILOSOPHY

COMPARATIVE ILLUSTRATION

The Buddha and Jesus. As Buddhism evolved, transforming Gautama Buddha from mortal to god, Buddhist art changed as well. The representation of the Buddha in statuary and in relief panels began to illustrate the story of his life. Here the infant Siddhartha Gautama is seen emerging from the hip of his mother, Queen Maya, dressed in Greek-style draperies. Also shown is a fifth-century mosaic showing Jesus as the Good Shepherd. Notice that the heads of both the Buddha and Jesus are surrounded by a halo. The halo—or circle of light—is an ancient symbol of divinity. In ancient Hindu, Greek, and Roman art, the heads of gods were shown to emit a sunlike divine radiance. Early kings adopted crowns of gold and precious gems to symbolize their own divine authority.

candle). Buddhists occasionally remark that someone who asks for a description does not understand the concept.

At the same time, the new doctrine differed from existing Hindu practices in a number of key ways. In the first place, Siddhartha denied the existence of an individual soul. To him, the Hindu concept of **Atman**—the individual soul—meant that the soul was subject to rebirth and thus did not achieve a complete liberation from the cares of this world. In fact, Siddhartha denied the ultimate reality of the material world in its entirety and taught that it was an illusion to be transcended. Siddhartha's idea of achieving Nirvana was based on his conviction that the pain, poverty, and sorrow that afflict human beings are caused essentially by their attachment to the things of this world. Once worldly cares are abandoned, pain and sorrow can be overcome. With this knowledge comes **bodhi,** or wisdom (source of the term *Buddhism* and the familiar name for Gautama the Wise: Gautama Buddha).

Achieving this understanding is a key step on the road to Nirvana, which, as in Hinduism, is a form of release from the wheel of life. According to tradition, Siddhartha transmitted this message in a sermon to his disciples in a deer park at Sarnath (see the box on p. 44), not far from the modern city of Benares (also known as Varanasi). Like so many messages, it is deceptively simple and is enclosed in four noble truths: life is suffering; suffering is caused by desire; the way to end suffering is to end desire; and the way to end desire is to avoid the extremes of a life of vulgar materialism and a life of self-torture and to follow the **Middle Path.** This Middle Path, which is also known as the Eightfold Way, calls for right knowledge, right purpose, right speech, right conduct, right occupation, right effort, right awareness, and right meditation.

Buddhism also differed from Hinduism in its relative egalitarianism. Although Siddhartha accepted the idea of reincarnation (and hence the idea that human beings differ

HOW TO ACHIEVE ENLIGHTENMENT

RELIGION & PHILOSOPHY

One of the most famous passages in Buddhist literature is the sermon at Sarnath, which Siddhartha Gautama delivered to his followers in a deer park outside the holy city of Varanasi (Benares), in the Ganges River valley. Here he set forth the key ideas that would define Buddhist beliefs for centuries to come.

How did Siddhartha Gautama reach the conclusion that the "Four Noble Truths" are the proper course in living a moral life? How do his ideas compare with the biblical Ten Commandments or with the moral teachings of Confucius?

The Sermon at Benares

Thus have I heard: at one time the Lord dwelt at Benares at Isipatana in the Deer Park. There the Lord addressed the five monks:—

"These two extremes, monks, are not to be practiced by one who has gone forth from the world. What are the two? That conjoined with the passions and luxury, low, vulgar, common, ignoble, and useless; and that conjoined with self-torture, painful, ignoble, and useless. Avoiding these two extremes the Tathagata has gained the enlightenment of the Middle Path, which produces insight and knowledge and tends to calm, to higher knowledge, enlightenment, Nirvana.

"And what, monks, is the Middle Path, of which the Tathagata has gained enlightenment, which produces insight and knowledge, and tends to calm, to higher knowledge, enlightenment, Nirvana? This is the noble Eightfold Way: namely, right view, right intention, right speech, right action, right livelihood, right effort, right mindfulness, right concentration. This, monks, is the Middle Path, of which the Tathagata has gained enlightenment, which produces insight and knowledge, and tends to calm, to higher knowledge, enlightenment, Nirvana.

1. Now this, monks, is the noble truth of pain: birth is painful, old age is painful, sickness is painful, death is painful, sorrow, lamentation, dejection, and despair are painful. Contact with unpleasant things is painful, not getting what one wishes is painful. In short the five groups of graspings are painful.
2. Now this, monks, is the noble truth of the cause of pain: the craving, which tends to rebirth, combined with pleasure and lust, finding pleasure here and there; namely, the craving for passion, the craving for existence, the craving for nonexistence.
3. Now this, monks, is the noble truth of the cessation of pain, the cessation without a remainder of craving, the abandonment, forsaking, release, nonattachment.
4. Now this, monks, is the noble truth of the way that leads to the cessation of pain: this is the noble Eightfold Way; namely, right view, right intention, right speech, right action, right livelihood, right effort, right mindfulness, right concentration.

"And when, monks, in these four noble truths my due knowledge and insight with its three sections and twelve divisions was well purified, then, monks, . . . I had attained the highest complete enlightenment. This I recognized. Knowledge arose in me, insight arose that the release of my mind is unshakable; this is my last existence; now there is no rebirth."

CENGAGENOW To read more writings of Siddhartha Gautama, enter the *CengageNOW* documents area using the access card that is available for *The Essential World History.*

---

as a result of *karma* accumulated in a previous existence), he rejected the Hindu division of humanity into rigidly defined classes based on previous reincarnations and taught that all human beings could aspire to Nirvana as a result of their behavior in this life—a message that likely helped Buddhism win support among people at the lower end of the social scale.

In addition, Buddhism was much simpler than Hinduism. Siddhartha rejected the panoply of gods that had become identified with Hinduism and forbade his followers to worship his person or his image after his death. In fact, many Buddhists view Buddhism as a philosophy rather than a religion.

After Siddhartha Gautama's death in 480 B.C.E., dedicated disciples carried his message the length and breadth of India. Buddhist monasteries were established throughout the subcontinent, and temples and **stupas** (stone towers housing relics of the Buddha) sprang up throughout the countryside.

Women were permitted to join the monastic order but only in an inferior position. As Siddhartha had explained, women are "soon angered," "full of passion," and "stupid": "That is the reason . . . why women have no place in public assemblies . . . and do not earn their living by any profession." Still, the position of women tended to be better in Buddhist societies than it was elsewhere in ancient India.

Jainism   During the next centuries, Buddhism began to compete actively with Hindu beliefs, as well as with another new faith known as **Jainism.** Jainism was founded by Mahavira, a contemporary of Siddhartha Gautama. Resembling Buddhism in its rejection of the reality of the material world, Jainism was more extreme in practice. Whereas Siddhartha Gautama called for the "middle way" between passion and luxury and pain and self-torture, Mahavira preached a doctrine of extreme simplicity to his followers, who kept no possessions and

Female Earth Spirit. This 2,200-year-old earth spirit, sculpted on a sandstone gatepost from the Buddhist stupa at Bharhut, illustrates how earlier Indian representations of the fertility goddess were incorporated into Buddhist art. Women were revered as powerful fertility symbols, represented first on Harappan seals, later on Buddhist shrines, and later still on Hindu temples. Voluptuous and idealized, these earth spirits could allegedly cause a tree to blossom if they merely touched a branch with their arm or wrapped a leg around its trunk.

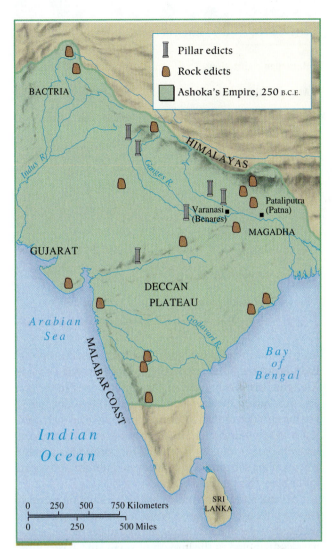

MAP 2.3   The Empire of Ashoka. Ashoka, the greatest of Indian monarchs, reigned over the Mauryan dynasty in the third century B.C.E. This map shows the extent of his empire, with the location of the pillar edicts that were erected along major trade routes. ❔ Why do you think the pillars and rocks were placed where they were?

relied on begging for a living. Some even rejected clothing and wandered through the world naked. Perhaps because of its insistence on a life of poverty, Jainism failed to attract enough adherents to become a major doctrine and never received official support. According to tradition, however, Chandragupta Maurya accepted Mahavira's doctrine after abdicating the throne and fasted to death in a Jain monastery.

Ashoka, a Buddhist Monarch   Buddhism received an important boost when Ashoka, the grandson of Chandragupta Maurya, converted to Buddhism in the third century B.C.E. Ashoka (269–232 B.C.E.) is widely considered the greatest ruler in the history of India. By his own admission, as noted in rock edicts placed around his kingdom, Ashoka began his reign conquering, pillaging, and killing, but after his conversion to Buddhism, he began to regret his bloodthirsty past and attempted to rule benevolently.

Ashoka directed that banyan trees and shelters be placed along the road to provide shade and rest for weary travelers. He sent Buddhist missionaries throughout India and ordered the erection of stone pillars with official edicts and Buddhist inscriptions to instruct people in the proper way (see Map 2.3). According to tradition, his son converted the island of Sri Lanka to Buddhism, and the peoples there accepted a tributary relationship with the Mauryan Empire.

The Rule of the Fishes: India After the Mauryas

After Ashoka's death in 232 B.C.E., the Mauryan Empire began to decline. In 183 B.C.E., the last Mauryan ruler was overthrown by one of his military commanders, and India slipped back into disunity. A number of new kingdoms, some of them perhaps influenced by the memory of the Alexandrian conquests, arose along the fringes of the subcontinent in

CHRONOLOGY Ancient India

Harappan civilization	c. 2600–1900 B.C.E.
Arrival of the Aryans	c. 1500 B.C.E.
Life of Gautama Buddha	c. 560–480 B.C.E.
Invasion of India by Alexander the Great	326 B.C.E.
Mauryan dynasty founded	324 B.C.E.
Reign of Chandragupta Maurya	324–301 B.C.E.
Reign of Ashoka	269–232 B.C.E.
Collapse of Mauryan dynasty	183 B.C.E.
Rise of Kushan kingdom	c. first century C.E.

Bactria, known today as Afghanistan. In the first century C.E., Indo-European-speaking peoples fleeing from the nomadic Xiongnu warriors in Central Asia seized power in the area and proclaimed the new Kushan kingdom (see Chapter 9). For the next two centuries, the Kushanas extended their political sway over northern India as far as the central Ganges valley, while other kingdoms scuffled for predominance elsewhere on the subcontinent. India would not see unity again for another five hundred years.

Several reasons for India's failure to maintain a unified empire have been proposed. Some historians suggest that a decline in regional trade during the first millennium C.E. may have contributed to the growth of small land-based kingdoms, which drew their primary income from agriculture. The tenacity of the Aryan tradition with its emphasis on tribal rivalries may also have contributed. Although the Mauryan rulers tried to impose a more centralized organization, clan loyalties once again came to the fore after the collapse of the Mauryan dynasty. Furthermore, the behavior of the ruling class was characterized by what Indians call the "rule of the fishes," which glorified warfare as the natural activity of the king and the aristocracy. The *Arthasastra,* which set forth a model of a centralized Indian state, assumed that war was the "sport of kings." Still, this was not an uneventful period in the history of India, as Indo-Aryan ideas continued to spread toward the south while both major religions, Hinduism and Buddhism, evolved in new directions.

The Exuberant World of Indian Culture

Few cultures in the world are as rich and varied as that of India. Most societies excel in some forms of artistic and literary achievement and not in others, but India has produced great works in almost all fields of cultural endeavor—art and sculpture, science, architecture, and literature.

Literature

The earliest known Indian literature consists of the four Vedas, which were passed down orally from generation to generation until they were finally written down after the Aryans arrived in India. The Rig Veda dates from the second millennium B.C.E. and consists of over a thousand hymns that were used at religious ceremonies. The other three Vedas were written considerably later and contain instructions for performing ritual sacrifices and other ceremonies.

The language of the Vedas was **Sanskrit,** part of the Indo-European family of languages. After the Aryans entered India, Sanskrit gradually declined as a spoken language and was replaced in northern India by a simpler tongue known as **Prakrit.** Nevertheless, Sanskrit continued to be used as the language of the bureaucracy and literary expression for many centuries after that and, like Latin in medieval Europe, served as a common language of communication between various regions of India. In the south, a variety of Dravidian languages continued to be spoken.

After the development of a new writing system sometime in the first millennium B.C.E., India's holy literature was probably inscribed on palm leaves stitched together into a book somewhat similar to the bamboo strips used during the same period in China. Also written for the first time were India's great historical epics, the Mahabharata and the Ramayana. Both of these epics may have originally been recited at religious ceremonies, but they are essentially historical writings that recount the martial exploits of great Aryan rulers and warriors.

The Mahabharata, consisting of more than ninety thousand stanzas, was probably written about 100 B.C.E. and describes in great detail a war between cousins for control of the kingdom about 1000 B.C.E. Interwoven in the narrative are many fantastic legends of the Hindu gods. Above all, the Mahabharata is a tale of moral confrontations. The most famous section of the book is the Bhagavad Gita, a sermon by the legendary Indian figure Krishna on the eve of a major battle. In this sermon, Krishna sets forth one of the key ethical maxims of Indian society: in taking action, one must be indifferent to success or failure and consider only the moral rightness of the act itself.

The Ramayana, written at about the same time, is much shorter than the Mahabharata. It is an account of a semilegendary ruler named Rama who, as the result of a palace intrigue, is banished from the kingdom and forced to live as a hermit in the forest. Later, he fights the demon-king of Sri Lanka (Ceylon), who has kidnapped his beloved wife, Sita. Like the Mahabharata, the Ramayana is strongly imbued with religious and moral significance. Rama himself is portrayed as the ideal Aryan hero, a perfect ruler and an ideal son, while Sita projects the supreme duty of female chastity and wifely loyalty to her husband. The Ramayana is a story of the triumph of good over evil, duty over self-indulgence, and generosity over selfishness. It combines filial and erotic love, conflicts of human passion, character analysis, and poetic descriptions of nature.

Carved Chapels. Carved out of solid rock cliffs during the Mauryan dynasty, (left photo) rock chambers served as meditation halls for traveling Buddhist monks. Initially, they resembled freestanding shrines of wood and thatch from the Vedic period but evolved into magnificent chapels carved deep into the mountainside such as this one at Karli (left). Working downward from the top, the stone cutters removed tons of rock while sculptors embellished and polished the interior decor. Notice the rounded vault and multicolumned sides reminiscent of Roman basilicas in the West. This style would reemerge in medieval chapels such as the one shown here in southern France (right).

The Ramayana also has all the ingredients of an enthralling adventure: giants, wondrous flying chariots, invincible arrows and swords, and magic potions and mantras. One of the real heroes of the story is the monkey-king Hanuman, who flies from India to Sri Lanka to set the great battle in motion. It is no wonder that for millennia the Ramayana, including a hugely popular TV version produced in recent years, has remained a favorite among Indians of all age groups.

Architecture and Sculpture

After literature, the greatest achievements of early Indian civilization were in architecture and sculpture. Some of the earliest examples of Indian architecture stem from the time of Emperor Ashoka, when Buddhism became the religion of the state. Until the time of the Mauryas, Aryan buildings had been constructed of wood. With the rise of the empire, stone began to be used as artisans arrived in India seeking employment after the destruction of the Persian Empire by Alexander. Many of these stone carvers accepted the patronage of Emperor Ashoka, who used them to spread Buddhist ideas throughout the subcontinent.

There were three main types of religious structure: the pillar, the stupa, and the rock chamber. During Ashoka's reign, many stone columns were erected alongside roads to commemorate the events in the Buddha's life and mark pilgrim routes to holy places. Weighing up to 50 tons each and rising as high as 32 feet, these polished sandstone pillars were topped with a carved capital, usually depicting lions uttering the Buddha's message. Ten remain standing today.

A stupa was originally meant to house a relic of the Buddha, such as a lock of his hair or a branch of the famous Bodhi tree, and was constructed in the form of a burial mound (the pyramids in Egypt also derived from burial mounds). Eventually, the stupa became a place for devotion and the most familiar form of Buddhist architecture. It rose to considerable heights and was surmounted with a spire, possibly representing the stages of existence en route to Nirvana. According to legend, Ashoka ordered the construction of 84,000 stupas throughout India to promote the Buddha's message. A few survive today.

The final form of early Indian architecture is the rock chamber carved out of a cliff on the side of a mountain. Ashoka began the construction of these chambers to provide rooms to house monks or wandering ascetics and to serve as halls for religious ceremonies. The chambers were rectangular in form, with pillars, an altar, and a vault, reminiscent of Roman basilicas in the West. The three most famous chambers of this period are at Bhaja, Karli, and Ajanta; this last one contains twenty-nine rooms.

All three forms of architecture were embellished with decorations. Consisting of detailed reliefs and free-standing statues of deities, other human figures, and animals, these decorations are permeated with a sense of nature and the vitality of life. Many reflect an amalgamation of popular and sacred themes, of Buddhist, Vedic, and pre-Aryan religious motifs, such as male and female earth spirits. Until the second century C.E., Siddhartha Gautama was represented only through symbols, such as the wheel of life, the Bodhi tree, and the footprint, perhaps because artists deemed it improper to portray him in human form, since he had escaped his corporal confines into enlightenment. After the spread of Mahayana Buddhism in the second century, when the Buddha began to be portrayed as a god, his image began to appear in stone as an object for divine worship.

By this time, India had established its own unique religious art. The art is permeated by sensuousness and exuberance and is often overtly sexual. These scenes are meant to express otherworldly delights, not the pleasures of this world. The sensuous paradise that adorned the religious art of ancient India represented salvation and fulfillment for the ordinary Indian.

Science

Our knowledge of Indian science is limited by the paucity of written sources, but it is evident that ancient Indians had amassed an impressive amount of scientific knowledge in a number of areas. Especially notable was their work in mathematics, where they devised the numerical system that we know as "Arabic numerals" and use today, and in astronomy, where they charted the movements of the heavenly bodies and recognized the spherical nature of the earth at an early date. Their ideas of physics were similar to those of the Greeks; matter was divided into the five elements of earth, air, fire, water, and ether. Many of their technological achievements are impressive, notably the quality of their textiles and the massive stone pillars erected during the reign of Ashoka. The pillars weighed up to 50 tons each and were transported many miles to their final destination.

CONCLUSION

WHILE THE PEOPLES OF NORTH AFRICA and the Middle East were actively building the first civilizations, a similar process was getting under way in the Indus River valley. Much has been learned about the nature of the Indus valley civilization in recent years, but without written records, there are inherent limits to our understanding. How did the Harappan people deal with the fundamental human problems mentioned at the close of Chapter 1? The answers remain tantalizingly elusive.

As often happened elsewhere, however, the collapse of Harappan civilization did not lead to the total disappearance of its culture. The new society that eventually emerged throughout the subcontinent after the coming of the Aryans was clearly an amalgam of two highly distinctive cultures, Aryan and Dravidian, each of which made a significant contribution to the politics, the social institutions, and the creative impulse of ancient Indian civilization.

With the rise of the Mauryan dynasty in the fourth century B.C.E., the distinctive features of a great civilization begin to be clearly visible. It was extensive in its scope, embracing the entire Indian subcontinent and eventually, in the form of Buddhism and Hinduism, spreading to China and Southeast Asia. But the underlying ethnic, linguistic, and cultural diversity of the Indian people posed a constant challenge to the unity of the state. After the collapse of the Mauryas, the subcontinent would not come under a single authority again for several hundred years.

In the meantime, another great experiment was taking place far to the northeast, across the Himalaya Mountains. Like many other civilizations of antiquity, the first Chinese state was concentrated on a major river system. And like them, too, its political and cultural achievements eventually spread far beyond their original habitat. In the next chapter, we turn to the civilization of ancient China.

CHAPTER NOTES

1. Quoted in R. Lannoy, *The Speaking Tree: A Study of Indian Culture and Society* (London, 1971), p. 318.
2. The quotation is from ibid., p. 319. Note also that the *Law of Manu* says that "punishment alone governs all created beings. . . . The whole world is kept in order by punishment, for a guiltless man is hard to find."
3. Strabo's *Geography*, bk. 15, quoted in M. Edwardes, *A History of India: From the Earliest Times to the Present Day* (London, 1961), p. 55.
4. Ibid., p. 54.

TIMELINE

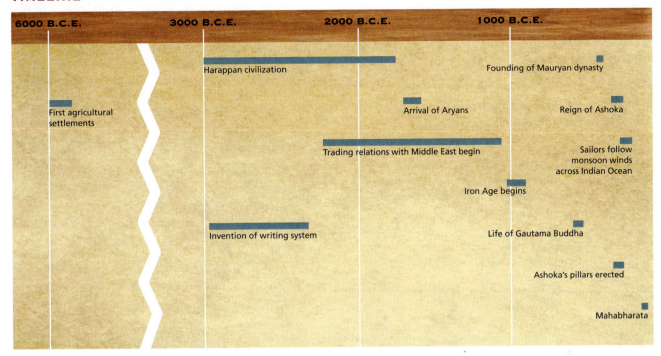

| 6000 B.C.E. | 3000 B.C.E. | 2000 B.C.E. | 1000 B.C.E. |

First agricultural settlements

Harappan civilization

Arrival of Aryans

Founding of Mauryan dynasty

Reign of Ashoka

Trading relations with Middle East begin

Sailors follow monsoon winds across Indian Ocean

Iron Age begins

Invention of writing system

Life of Gautama Buddha

Ashoka's pillars erected

Mahabharata

5. Ibid., p. 57.
6. From the *Law of Manu,* quoted in A. L. Basham, *The Wonder That Was India* (London, 1961), pp. 180–181.
7. Mundaka Upanishad 1:2, quoted in W. T. de Bary et al., eds., *Sources of Indian Tradition* (New York, 1966), pp. 28–29.
8. Quoted in A. K. Coomaraswamy, *Buddha and the Gospel of Buddhism* (New York, 1964), p. 34.

SUGGESTED READING

Several standard histories of India provide a good overview of the ancient period. One of the most readable and reliable is **S. Wolpert, *New History of India,*** 3d ed. (New York, 1989).

By far the most informative and readable narrative on the cultural history of India in premodern times is still **A. L. Basham, *The Wonder That Was India*** (London, 1961), which, although somewhat out of date, contains informative sections on prehistory, economy, language, art and literature, society, and everyday life. **R. Thapar, *Early India: From the Origins to AD 1300*** (London, 2002), provides a recent view by an Indian historian.

Because of the relative paucity of archaeological exploration in South Asia, evidence for the Harappan period is not as voluminous as for areas such as Mesopotamia and the Nile valley. Some of the best work has been written by scholars who actually worked at the sites. For a recent account, see **J. M. Kenoyer, *Ancient Cities of the Indus Valley Civilization*** (Karachi, 1998). A somewhat more extensive study is **B. Allchin** and **R. Allchin, *The Birth of Indian Civilization, India and Pakistan Before 500 B.C.*** (New York, 1968). For a detailed and well-illustrated analysis, see **G. L. Possehl,** ed., ***The Harappan Civilization: A Contemporary Perspective*** (Amherst, N.Y., 1983). Commercial relations between Harappa and its neighbors are treated in **S. Ratnagar, *Encounters: The Westerly Trade of the Harappan Civilization*** (Oxford, 1981).

There are a number of good books on the introduction of Buddhism into Indian society. Buddha's ideals are presented in **P. Williams** (with **A. Tribe**), ***Buddhist Thought: A Complete Introduction to the Indian Tradition*** (London, 2000). Also see **H. Nakamura** and **M. B. Dasgupta, *Indian Buddhism: A Survey with Bibliographical Notes*** (New Delhi, 1987). **H. Akira, *A History of Indian Buddhism: From Sakyamuni to Early Mahayana*** (Honolulu, 1990), provides a detailed analysis of early activities by Siddhartha Gautama and his followers. The intimate relationship between Buddhism and commerce is discussed in **Liu Hsin-ju, *Ancient India and Ancient China: Trades and Religious Exchanges*** (Oxford, 1988).

There are a number of excellent surveys of Indian art, including the comprehensive **S. L. Huntington, *The Art of Ancient India: Buddhist, Hindu, Jain*** (New York, 1985), and the concise ***Indian Art,*** rev. ed. (London, 1997) by **R. Craven.** See also **V. Dehejia's *Devi: The Great Goddess*** (Washington, D.C., 1999) and ***Indian Art*** (London, 1997).

Many editions of Sanskrit literature are available in English translation. Many are available in the multivolume ***Harvard Oriental Series.*** For a shorter annotated anthology of selections from the Indian classics, consult **S. N. Hay,** ed., ***Sources of Indian Tradition,*** 2 vols. (New York, 1988), or **J. B. Alphonso-Karkala, *An Anthology of Indian Literature,*** 2d rev. ed. (New Delhi, 1987), put out by the Indian Council for Cultural Relations.

The Mahabharata and Ramayana have been rewritten for 2,500 years. Fortunately, the vibrant versions, retold by **William Buck** and condensed to 400 pages each, reproduce the spirit of the originals and enthrall today's imagination. See **W. Buck, *Mahabharata*** (Berkeley, Calif., 1973) and ***Ramayana*** (Berkeley, Calif., 1976). On the role played by women writers in ancient India, see **S. Tharu** and **K. Lalita,** eds., ***Women Writing in India: 600 B.C. to the Present,*** vol. 1 (New York, 1991).

For additional information on the invention of the first writing system, see **J. T. Hooker,** ed., ***Reading the Past: Ancient Writing from Cuneiform to the Alphabet*** (London, 1990), and A. Hurley, ***The Alphabet: The History, Evolution, and Design of the Letters We Use Today*** (New York, 1995).

InfoTrac College Edition

Visit this chapter's InfoTrac College Edition/Research activities at the *Essential World History* Companion Website for activities related to ancient India.

CENGAGENOW **for Duiker and Spielvogel's** *The Essential World History, Third Edition*

Enter *CengageNOW* using the access card that is available with this text. *CengageNOW* will assist you in understanding the content in this chapter with lesson plans generated for your needs, as well as provide you with a connection to the *Wadsworth World History Resource Center* (see description at the right for details).

WORLD HISTORY
RESOURCE CENTER

Enter the Resource Center using either your *CengageNOW* access card or your standalone access card for the *Wadsworth World History Resource Center.* Organized by topic, this website includes quizzes; images; over 350 primary source documents; interactive simulations, maps, and timelines; movie explorations; and a wealth of other resources. You can read the following documents, and many more, at http://worldrc.wadsworth.com/

The Law of Manu

The Rig Veda

Visit the *Essential World History* Companion Website for chapter quizzes and more.

academic.cengage.com/history/duiker

3

CHINA IN ANTIQUITY

CHAPTER OUTLINE AND FOCUS QUESTIONS

The Dawn of Chinese Civilization

▢ How did geography influence the civilization that arose in China?

The Zhou Dynasty

▢ What were the major tenets of Confucianism, Legalism, and Daoism, and what role did each play in early Chinese history?

The Rise of the Chinese Empire: The Qin Dynasty (221–206 B.C.E.)

▢ What role did nomadic peoples play in early Chinese history? How did that role compare with conditions in other parts of Asia?

Daily Life in Ancient China

▢ What were the key aspects of social and economic life in early China?

Chinese Culture

▢ What were the chief characteristics of the Chinese writing system? How did it differ from scripts used in Egypt and Mesopotamia?

CRITICAL THINKING

▢ The civilization of ancient China resembles those of its contemporaries in Mesopotamia and North Africa in several respects, but the contrasts were equally significant. What were some of these differences, and how might geography and the environment have been factors in determining them?

Confucius and his disciples

© Topham/The Image Works

𝒯HE MASTER SAID: "If the government seeks to rule by decree, and to maintain order by the use of punishment, the people will seek to evade punishment and have no sense of shame. But if government leads by virtue and governs through the rules of propriety, the people will feel shame and seek to correct their mistakes."

That statement is from the *Analects,* a collection of remarks by the Chinese philosopher Confucius that were gathered together by his disciples and published after his death in the fifth century B.C.E. Confucius lived at a time when Chinese society was in a state of increasing disarray. The political principles that had governed society since the founding of the Zhou dynasty six centuries earlier were widely ignored, and squabbling principalities scuffled for primacy as the power of the Zhou court steadily declined. The common people groaned under the weight of an oppressive manorial system that left them at the mercy of their aristocratic lords.

In the midst of this turmoil, Confucius traveled the length of the kingdom observing events and seeking employment as a political counselor. In the process, he attracted a number of disciples, to whom he expounded a set of ideas that in later years served as the guiding principles for the Chinese empire. Some of his ideas are strikingly modern in their thrust. Among them is the revolutionary proposition that government depends on the will of the people.

But Confucius was not simply a radical thinker opposed to all traditional values. To the contrary, the principles that Confucius sought to instill into his society had, in his view, all been previously established many centuries in the past—during an alleged "Golden Age" at the dawn of Chinese history. In that sense, Confucius was a profoundly conservative thinker, seeking to preserve elements in Chinese history that had been neglected by his contemporaries. The dichotomy between tradition and change was thus a key component in Confucian philosophy that would be reflected in many ways over the course of the next 2,500 years of Chinese history.

The civilization that produced Confucius had originated more than fifteen hundred years earlier along the two great river systems of East Asia, the Yellow and the Yangtze. This vibrant new civilization, which we know today as ancient China, expanded gradually over its neighboring areas. By the third century B.C.E., it had emerged as a great empire, as well as the dominant cultural and political force in the entire region.

Like Sumer, Harappa, and Egypt, the civilization of ancient China began as a collection of autonomous villages cultivating food crops along a major river system. Improvements in agricultural techniques led to a food surplus and the growth of an urban civilization characterized by more complex political and social institutions, as well as new forms of artistic and intellectual creativity.

Like its counterparts elsewhere, ancient China faced the challenge posed by the appearance of pastoral peoples on its borders. Unlike Harappa, Sumer, and Egypt, however, ancient China was able to surmount that challenge, and many of its institutions and cultural values survived intact down to the beginning of the twentieth century. For that reason, Chinese civilization is sometimes described as the oldest continuous civilization on earth. ◇

The Dawn of Chinese Civilization

According to Chinese legend, Chinese society was founded by a series of rulers who brought the first rudiments of civilization to the region nearly five thousand years ago. The first was Fu Xi (Fu Hsi), the ox-tamer, who "knotted cords for hunting and fishing," domesticated animals, and introduced the beginnings of family life. The second was Shen Nong (Shen Nung), the divine farmer, who "bent wood for plows and hewed wood for plowshares." He taught the people the techniques of agriculture. Last came Huang Di (Huang Ti), the Yellow Emperor, who "strung a piece of wood for the bow, and whittled little sticks of wood for the arrows." Legend credits Huang Di with

creating the Chinese system of writing, as well as with inventing the bow and arrow.[1] Modern historians, of course, do not accept the literal accuracy of such legends but view them instead as part of the process whereby early peoples attempt to make sense of the world and their role in it. Nevertheless, such re-creations of a mythical past often contain an element of truth. Although there is no clear evidence that the "three sovereigns" actually existed, their achievements do symbolize some of the defining characteristics of Chinese civilization: the interaction between nomadic and agricultural peoples, the importance of the family as the basic unit of Chinese life, and the development of a unique system of writing.

The Land and People of China

Human communities have existed in China for several hundred thousand years. Sometime around the eighth millennium B.C.E., the early peoples living along the riverbanks of northern China began to master the cultivation of crops. A number of these early agricultural settlements were in the neighborhood of the Yellow River, where they gave birth to two Neolithic societies known to archaeologists as the **Yangshao** and the **Longshan** cultures (sometimes identified in terms of their pottery as the painted and black pottery cultures, respectively). Similar communities have been found in the Yangtze valley in central China and along the coast to the south. The southern settlements were based on the cultivation of rice rather than dry crops such as millet, barley, and wheat, but they were as old as those in the north. Thus, agriculture, and perhaps other elements of early civilization, may have developed spontaneously in several areas of China rather than radiating outward from one central region.

At first, these simple Neolithic communities were hardly more than villages, but as the inhabitants mastered the rudiments of agriculture, they gradually gave rise to more sophisticated and complex societies. In a pattern that we have already seen elsewhere, civilization gradually spread from these nuclear settlements in the valleys of the Yellow and Yangtze rivers to other lowland areas of eastern and central China. The two great river valleys, then, can be considered the core regions in the development of Chinese civilization.

Although these densely cultivated valleys eventually became two of the great food-producing areas of the ancient world, China is more than a land of fertile fields. In fact, only 12 percent of the total land area is arable, compared with 23 percent in the United States. Much of the remainder consists of mountains and deserts that ring the country on its northern and western frontiers.

This often arid and forbidding landscape is a dominant feature of Chinese life and has played a significant role in Chinese history. The geographic barriers served to isolate the Chinese people from advanced agrarian societies in other parts of Asia. The frontier regions in the Gobi Desert, Central Asia, and the Tibetan plateau

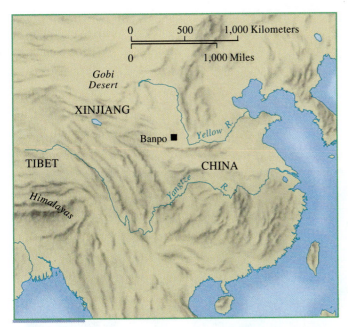

Neolithic China

maintains that the founder was a ruler named Yu, who is also credited with introducing irrigation and draining the floodwaters that periodically threatened to inundate the northern China plain. The Xia dynasty was replaced by a second dynasty, the Shang, around the sixteenth century B.C.E. The late Shang capital at Anyang, just north of the Yellow River in north-central China, has been excavated by archaeologists. Among the finds were thousands of so-called oracle bones, ox and chicken bones or turtle shells that were used by Shang rulers for divination (seeking to foretell future events by interpreting divine signs) and to communicate with the gods. The inscriptions on these oracle bones are the earliest known form of Chinese writing and provide much of our information about the beginnings of civilization in China. They describe a culture gradually emerging from the Neolithic to the early Bronze Age.

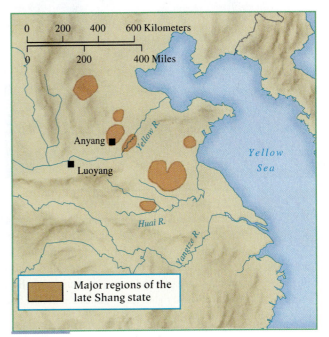

Shang China

were sparsely inhabited by peoples of Mongolian, Indo-European, or Turkish extraction. Most were pastoral societies, and like the other river valley civilizations, their contacts with the Chinese were often characterized by mutual distrust and conflict. Although less numerous than the Chinese, many of these peoples possessed impressive skills in war and were sometimes aggressive in seeking wealth or territory in the settled regions south of the Gobi Desert. Over the next two thousand years, the northern frontier became one of the great fault lines of conflict in Asia as Chinese armies attempted to protect precious farmlands from marauding peoples from beyond the frontier. When China was unified and blessed with capable rulers, it could usually keep the nomadic intruders at bay and even bring them under a loose form of Chinese administration. But in times of internal weakness, China was vulnerable to attack from the north, and on several occasions, nomadic peoples succeeded in overthrowing native Chinese rulers and setting up their own dynastic regimes.

From other directions, China normally had little to fear. To the east lay the China Sea, a lair for pirates and the source of powerful typhoons that occasionally ravaged the Chinese coast but otherwise rarely a source of concern. South of the Yangtze River was a hilly region inhabited by a mixture of peoples of varied language and ethnic stock who lived by farming, fishing, or food gathering. They were gradually absorbed in the inexorable expansion of Chinese civilization.

The Shang Dynasty

Historians of China have traditionally dated the beginning of Chinese civilization to the founding of the Xia (Hsia) dynasty more than four thousand years ago. Although the precise date for the rise of the Xia is in dispute, recent archaeological evidence confirms its existence. Legend

Political Organization China under the Shang dynasty was a predominantly agricultural society ruled by an aristocratic class whose major occupation was war. One ancient chronicler complained that "the big affairs of state consist of sacrifice and soldiery."[2] Combat was carried on by means of two-horse chariots. The appearance of chariots in China in the mid-second millennium B.C.E. coincides roughly with similar developments elsewhere, leading some historians to suggest that the Shang ruling class may originally have invaded China from elsewhere in Asia. But items found in Shang burial mounds are similar to Longshan pottery, implying that the Shang ruling elites were linear descendants of the indigenous Neolithic peoples in the area. If that was the case, the Shang may have acquired their knowledge of horse-drawn chariots through contact with the peoples of neighboring regions.

Some recent support for that assumption has come from evidence unearthed in the sandy wastes of Xinjiang,

COMPARATIVE ILLUSTRATION

RELIGION & PHILOSOPHY

The Afterlife and Prized Possessions. Like the pharaohs in Egypt, Chinese rulers filled their tombs with prized possessions from daily life. It was believed that if the tombs were furnished and stocked with supplies, including chairs, boats, chests, weapons, games, and dishes, the spiritual body could continue its life despite the death of the physical body. At left, we see the remains of a chariot and horses in a burial pit in Hebei province in China that dates from the early Zhou dynasty. At right, we see a small model boat from the tomb of Tutankhamun in the Valley of the Kings in Egypt.

China's far-northwestern province. There archaeologists have discovered corpses dating back as early as the second millennium B.C.E. with physical characteristics that are clearly European. They are also clothed in textiles similar to those worn at the time in Europe, suggesting that they may have been members of an Indo-European migration from areas much farther to the west. If that is the case, they were probably familiar with advances in chariot making that occurred a few hundred years earlier in southern Russia and Kazakhstan. By about 2000 B.C.E., spoked wheels were being deposited at grave sites in Ukraine and also in the Gobi Desert, just north of the great bend of the Yellow River. It is thus likely that the new technology became available to the founders of the Shang dynasty and may have aided their rise to power in northern China.

The Shang king ruled with the assistance of a central bureaucracy in the capital city. His realm was divided into a number of territories governed by aristocratic chieftains, but the king appointed these chieftains and could apparently depose them at will. He was also responsible for the defense of the realm and controlled large armies that often fought on the fringes of the kingdom. The transcendent importance of the ruler was graphically displayed in the ritual sacrifices undertaken at his death, when hundreds of his retainers were buried with him in the royal tomb.

As the inscriptions on the oracle bones make clear, the Chinese ruling elite believed in the existence of supernatural forces and thought that they could communicate with those forces to obtain divine intervention on matters of this world. In fact, the purpose of the oracle bones was to communicate with the gods. This evidence also suggests that the king was already being viewed as an intermediary between heaven and earth. In fact, an early Chinese character for king (王) consists of three horizontal lines connected by a single vertical line; the middle horizontal line represents the king's place between human society and the divine forces in nature.

Shell and Bone Writing. The earliest known form of true writing in China dates back to the Shang dynasty and was inscribed on shells or animal bones. Questions for the gods were scratched on bones, which cracked after being exposed to fire. The cracks were then interpreted by sorcerers. The questions often expressed practical concerns: Will it rain? Will the king be victorious in battle? Will he recover from his illness? Originally composed of pictographs and ideographs four thousand years ago, Chinese writing has evolved into an elaborate set of symbols that combine meaning and pronunciation in a single character.

The early Chinese also had a clear sense of life in the hereafter. Though some of the human sacrifices discovered in the royal tombs were presumably intended to propitiate the gods, others were meant to accompany the king or members of his family on the journey to the next world. From this conviction would come the concept of the **veneration of ancestors** (mistakenly known in the West as "ancestor worship") and the practice, which continues to the present day in many Chinese communities, of burning replicas of physical objects to accompany the departed on their journey to the next world.

Social Structures   In the Neolithic period, the farm village was apparently the basic social unit of China, at least in the core region of the Yellow River valley. Villages were organized by clans rather than by nuclear family units, and all residents probably took the common clan name of the entire village. In some cases, a village may have included more than one clan. At Banpo (Pan P'o), an archaeological site near modern Xian that dates back at least eight thousand years, the houses in the village are separated by a ditch, which some scholars think may have served as a divider between two clans. The individual dwellings at Banpo housed nuclear families, but a larger building in the village was apparently used as a clan meeting hall. The tribal origins of Chinese society may help explain the continued importance of the joint family in traditional China, as well as the relatively small number of family names in Chinese society. Even today there are only about four hundred commonly used family names in a society of more than one billion people, and the colloquial name for the common people in China today is "the old hundred names."

By Shang times, the classes were becoming increasingly differentiated. It is likely that some poorer peasants did not own their farms but were obliged to work the land of the chieftain and other elite families in the village. The aristocrats not only made war and served as officials (indeed, the first Chinese character for *official* originally meant "warrior"), but they were also the primary landowners. In addition to the aristocratic elite and the peasants, there were a small number of merchants and artisans, as well as slaves, probably consisting primarily of criminals or prisoners taken in battle.

The Shang are perhaps best known for their mastery of the art of bronze casting. Utensils, weapons, and ritual objects made of bronze (see the comparative essay "The Use of Metals" on p. 56) have been found in royal tombs in urban centers throughout the area known to be under Shang influence. It is also clear that the Shang had achieved a fairly sophisticated writing system that would eventually spread throughout East Asia and evolve into the written language that is still used in China today.

The Zhou Dynasty

In the eleventh century B.C.E., the Shang dynasty was overthrown by an aggressive young state located somewhat to the west of Anyang, the Shang capital, and near the great bend of the Yellow River as it begins to flow

THE USE OF METALS

SCIENCE & TECHNOLOGY

Around 6000 B.C.E., people in western Asia discovered how to use metals. They soon realized the advantage in using metal rather than stone to make both tools and weapons. Metal could be shaped more exactly, allowing artisans to make more refined tools and weapons with sharp edges and more precise shapes. Copper, silver, and gold, which were commonly found in their elemental form, were the first metals to be used. These were relatively soft and could be easily pounded into different shapes. But an important step was taken when people discovered that a rock that contained metal could be heated to liquefy the metal (a process called smelting). The liquid metal could then be poured into molds of clay or stone to make precisely shaped tools and weapons.

Copper was the first metal to be used in making tools. The first known copper smelting furnace, dated to 3800 B.C.E., was found in the Sinai. At about the same time, however, artisans in Southeast Asia discovered that tin could be added to copper to make bronze. By 3000 B.C.E., artisans in West Asia were also making bronze. Bronze has a lower melting point that makes it easier to cast, but it is also a harder metal than copper and corrodes less. By 1400 B.C.E., the Chinese were making bronze decorative objects as well as battle-axes and helmets. The widespread use of bronze has led historians to speak of the period from around 3000 to 1200 B.C.E. as the Bronze Age, although this is somewhat misleading in that many peoples continued to use stone tools and weapons even after bronze became available.

But there were limitations to the use of bronze. Tin was not as available as copper, which made bronze tools and weapons expensive. After 1200 B.C.E., bronze was increasingly replaced by iron, which was probably first used around 1500 B.C.E. in western Asia, where the Hittites made new weapons from it. Between 1500 and 600 B.C.E., iron making spread across Europe, North Africa, and Asia. Bronze continued to be used, but mostly for jewelry and other domestic purposes. Iron was used to make tools and weapons with sharper edges. Because iron weapons were cheaper than bronze ones, larger numbers of warriors could be armed, and wars could be fought on a larger scale.

Iron was handled differently from bronze: it was heated until it could be beaten into a desired shape. Each hammering produced increased strength for the metal. This wrought iron, as it was called, was typical of iron manufacturing in the West until the late Middle Ages. In China, however, the use of heat-resistant clay in the walls of their blast furnaces raised temperatures to 1,537 degrees Celsius, enabling artisans in the fourth century B.C.E. to liquefy iron so that it too could be cast in a mold. Europeans would not develop such blast furnaces until the fifteenth century C.E.

© The Trustees of The British Museum

Bronze Axhead. This axhead was made around 2000 B.C.E. by pouring liquid metal into an ax-shaped mold of clay or stone. Artisans would then polish the surface of the ax to produce a sharp cutting edge.

directly eastward to the sea. The new dynasty, which called itself the Zhou (Chou), survived for about eight hundred years and was thus the longest-lived dynasty in the history of China. According to tradition, the last of the Shang rulers was a tyrant who oppressed the people (Chinese sources assert that he was a degenerate who built "ponds of wine" and ordered the composing of lustful music that "ruined the morale of the nation"),[3] leading the ruler of the principality of Zhou to revolt and establish a new dynasty.

The Zhou located their capital in their home territory, near the present-day city of Xian. Later they established a second capital city at modern Luoyang, farther to the east, to administer new territories captured from the Shang. This established a pattern of eastern and western capitals that would endure off and on in China for nearly two thousand years.

Political Structures

The Zhou dynasty (1045–221 B.C.E.) adopted the political system of its predecessors, with some changes. The Shang practice of dividing the kingdom into a number of territories governed by officials appointed by the king was continued under the Zhou. At the apex of the government hierarchy was the Zhou king, who was served by a bureaucracy of growing size and complexity. It now included several ministries responsible for rites, education, law, and public works. Beyond the capital, the Zhou kingdom was divided into a number of principalities, governed by members of the hereditary aristocracy, who were appointed by the king and were at least theoretically subordinated to his authority.

The Mandate of Heaven But the Zhou kings also introduced some innovations. According to the *Rites of Zhou,* one of the oldest surviving documents on statecraft, the Zhou dynasty ruled China because it possessed the **"mandate of Heaven."** According to this concept, Heaven (viewed as an impersonal law of nature rather than as an anthropomorphic deity) maintained order in the universe through the Zhou king, who thus ruled as a representative of Heaven but not as a divine being. The king, who was selected to rule because of his talent and virtue, was then responsible for governing the people with compassion and efficiency. It was his duty to appease the gods in order to protect the people from natural calamities or bad harvests. But if the king failed to rule effectively, he could, theoretically at least, be overthrown and replaced by a new ruler. As noted earlier, this idea was used to justify the Zhou conquest of the Shang. Eventually, the concept of the heavenly mandate would become a cardinal principle of Chinese statecraft.[4] Each founder of a new dynasty would routinely assert that he had earned the mandate of Heaven, and who could disprove it except by overthrowing the king? As a pragmatic Chinese proverb put it, "He who wins is the king; he who loses is the rebel."

In asserting that the ruler had a direct connection with the divine forces presiding over the universe, Chinese tradition reflected a belief that was prevalent in all ancient civilizations. But whereas in some societies, notably in Mesopotamia and Greece (see Chapter 4), the gods were seen as capricious and not subject to human understanding, in China, Heaven was viewed as an essentially benevolent force devoted to universal harmony and order that could be influenced by positive human action. Was this attitude a consequence of the fact that the Chinese environment, though subject to some of the same climatic vicissitudes that plagued other parts of the world, was somewhat more predictable and beneficial than in climatically harsh regions like the Middle East?

By the sixth century B.C.E., the Zhou dynasty began to decline. As the power of the central government disintegrated, bitter internal rivalries arose among the various principalities, where the governing officials had succeeded in making their positions hereditary at the expense of the king. As the power of these officials grew, they began to regulate the local economy and seek reliable sources of revenue for their expanding armies, such as a uniform tax system and government monopolies on key commodities such as salt and iron.

Economy and Society

During the Zhou dynasty, the essential characteristics of Chinese economic and social institutions began to take shape. The Zhou continued the pattern of land ownership that had existed under the Shang: the peasants worked on lands owned by their lord but also had land of their own that they cultivated for their own use. The practice was called the **well field system,** since the Chinese character for well (井) resembles a simplified picture of the division of the farmland into nine separate segments. Each peasant family tilled an outer plot for its own use and then joined with other families to work the inner one for the hereditary lord. How widely this system was used is unclear, but it represented an ideal described by Confucian scholars of a later day. As the following poem indicates, life for the average farmer was a difficult one. The "big rat" is probably a reference to the high taxes imposed on the peasants by the government or lord.

> Big rat, big rat
> Do not eat my millet!
> Three years I have served you,
> But you will not care for me.
> I am going to leave you
> And go to that happy land;
> Happy land, happy land,
> Where I will find my place.[5]

Trade and manufacturing were carried out by merchants and artisans, who lived in walled towns under the direct control of the local lord. Merchants did not operate independently but were considered the property of the local lord and on occasion could even be bought and sold like chattels. A class of slaves performed a variety of menial tasks and perhaps worked on local irrigation projects. Most of them were probably prisoners of war captured during conflicts with the neighboring principalities. Scholars do not know how extensive slavery was in ancient times, but slaves probably did not constitute a large portion of the total population.

The period of the later Zhou, from the sixth to the third century B.C.E., was an era of significant economic growth and technological innovation, especially in agriculture. During that time, large-scale water control projects were undertaken to regulate the flow of rivers and distribute water evenly to the fields, as well as to construct canals to facilitate the transport of goods from one region to another. Perhaps the most impressive technological achievement of the period was the construction of the massive water control project on the Min River, a tributary of the Yangtze. This system of canals and spillways, which was put into operation by the state of Qin a few years prior to the end of the Zhou dynasty, diverted excess water from the river into the local irrigation network and watered an area populated by as many as five million people. The system is still in use today, over two thousand years later.

Food production was also stimulated by a number of advances in farm technology. By the mid-sixth century B.C.E., the introduction of iron had led to the development of iron plowshares, which permitted deep plowing for the first time. Other innovations dating from the later Zhou were the use of natural fertilizer, the collar harness,

Courtesy of William J. Duiker

Courtesy of William J. Duiker

COMPARATIVE ILLUSTRATION

Early Agricultural Technology. For centuries, farmers across the globe have adopted various techniques to guarantee the flow of adequate amounts of water to their crops. One of the most effective ways to irrigate fields in hilly regions is to construct terraces to channel the flow of water from higher elevations in the most effective manner. Shown on the left is a hillside terrace in northern China, an area where dry crops like oats and millet have been cultivated since the sixth millennium B.C.E. The illustration on the right shows a terraced hillside in the southwestern corner of the Arabian peninsula. Excavations show that terraced agriculture has been practiced in mountainous parts of the peninsula for as long as five thousand years.

and the technique of leaving land fallow to preserve or replenish nutrients in the soil. By the late Zhou dynasty, the cultivation of wet rice had become one of the prime sources of food in China. Although rice was difficult and time-consuming to produce, it replaced other grain crops in areas with a warm climate because of its good taste, relative ease of preparation, and high nutritional value.

The advances in agriculture, which enabled the population of China to rise as high as twenty million people during the late Zhou era, were also undoubtedly a major factor in the growth of commerce and manufacturing. During the late Zhou, economic wealth began to replace noble birth as the prime source of power and influence. Utensils made of iron became more common, and trade developed in a variety of useful commodities, including cloth, salt, and various manufactured goods.

One of the most important items of trade in ancient China was silk. There is evidence of silkworm raising as early as the Neolithic period. Remains of silk material have been found on Shang bronzes, and a large number of fragments have been recovered in tombs dating from the mid-Zhou era. Silk cloth was used not only for clothing and quilts but also to wrap the bodies of the dead prior to burial. Fragments have been found throughout Central Asia and as far away as Athens, suggesting that the famous Silk Road stretching from central China westward to the Middle East and the Mediterranean Sea was in operation as early as the fifth century B.C.E. (see Chapter 10).

With the development of trade and manufacturing, China began to move toward a money economy. The first form of money, as in much of the rest of the world, may have been seashells (the Chinese character for goods or property contains the ideographic symbol for "shell": 貝),

but by the Zhou dynasty, pieces of iron shaped like a knife or round coins with a hole in the middle so they could be carried in strings of a thousand were being used. Most ordinary Chinese, however, simply used a system of barter. Taxes, rents, and even the salaries of government officials were normally paid in grain.

The Hundred Schools of Ancient Philosophy

In China, as in other great river valley societies, the birth of civilization was accompanied by the emergence of an organized effort to comprehend the nature of the cosmos and the role of human beings within it. Speculation over such questions began in the very early stages of civilization and culminated at the end of the Zhou era in the "hundred schools" of ancient philosophy, a wide-ranging debate over the nature of human beings, society, and the universe.

Early Beliefs   The first hint of religious belief in ancient China comes from relics found in royal tombs of Neolithic times. By then, the Chinese had already developed a religious sense beyond the primitive belief in the existence of spirits in nature. The Shang had begun to believe in the existence of one transcendent god, known as Shang Di, who presided over all the forces of nature. As time went on, the Chinese concept of religion evolved from a vaguely anthropomorphic god to a somewhat more impersonal symbol of universal order known as Heaven (*Tian,* or *T'ien*). There was also much speculation among Chinese intellectuals about the nature of the cosmic order. One of the earliest ideas was that the universe was divided into two primary forces of good and evil, light and dark, male and female, called the *yang* and the *yin,* represented symbolically by the sun (*yang*) and the moon (*yin*). According to this theory, life was a dynamic process of interaction between the forces of *yang* and *yin*. Early Chinese could attempt only to understand the process and perhaps to have some minimal effect on its operation. They could not hope to reverse it. It is sometimes asserted that this belief has contributed to the heavy element of fatalism in Chinese popular wisdom. The Chinese have traditionally believed that bad times will be followed by good times, and vice versa.

The belief that there was some mysterious "law of nature" that could be interpreted by human beings led to various attempts to predict the future, such as the Shang oracle bones and other methods of divination. Philosophers invented ways to interpret the will of nature, while shamans, playing a role similar to the *brahmins* in India, were employed at court to assist the emperor in his policy deliberations until at least the fifth century C.E. One of the most famous manuals used for this purpose was the *Yi Jing* (*I Ching*), known in English as the *Book of Changes*.

Confucianism Such efforts to divine the mysterious purposes of Heaven notwithstanding, Chinese thinking about metaphysical reality also contained a strain of pragmatism, which is readily apparent in the ideas of the great philosopher Confucius. Confucius (the name is the Latin form of his honorific title, Kung Fuci, or K'ung Fu-tzu, meaning Master Kung) was born in the state of Lu (in the modern province of Shandong) in 551 B.C.E. After reaching maturity, he apparently hoped to find employment as a political adviser in one of the principalities into which China was divided at that time, but he had little success in finding a patron. Nevertheless, he made an indelible mark on history as an independent (and somewhat disgruntled) political and social philosopher.

In conversations with his disciples contained in the *Analects*, Confucius often adopted a detached and almost skeptical view of Heaven. "You are unable to serve man," he commented on one occasion, "how then can you hope to serve the spirits? While you do not know life, how can you know about death?" In many instances, he appeared to advise his followers to revere the deities and the ancestral spirits but to keep them at a distance. Confucius believed it was useless to speculate too much about metaphysical questions. Better by far to assume that there was a rational order to the universe and then concentrate one's attention on ordering the affairs of this world.[6]

Confucius' interest in philosophy, then, was essentially political and ethical. The universe was constructed in such a way that if human beings could act harmoniously in accordance with its purposes, their own affairs would prosper. Much of his concern was with human behavior. The key to proper behavior was to behave in accordance with the **Dao** (Way). Confucius assumed that all human beings had their own *Dao,* depending on their individual role in life, and it was their duty to follow it. Even the ruler had his own *Dao,* and he ignored it at his peril, for to do so could mean the loss of the mandate of Heaven. The idea of the *Dao* is reminiscent of the concept of *dharma* in ancient India and played a similar role in governing the affairs of society.

Two elements in the Confucian interpretation of the *Dao* are particularly worthy of mention. The first is the concept of duty. It was the responsibility of all individuals to subordinate their own interests and aspirations to the broader needs of the family and the community. Confucius assumed that if each individual worked hard to fulfill his or her assigned destiny, the affairs of society as a whole would prosper as well. In this respect, it was important for the ruler to set a good example. If he followed his "kingly way," the beneficial effects would radiate throughout society (see the box on p. 60).

The second key element is the idea of humanity, sometimes translated as "human-heartedness." This concept involves a sense of compassion and empathy for others. It is similar in some ways to Christian concepts, but with a subtle twist. Where Christian teachings call on human beings to "behave toward others as you would have them behave toward you," the Confucian maxim is put in a different way: "Do not do unto others what you would not wish done to yourself." To many Chinese, this attitude symbolizes an element of tolerance in the Chinese character that has not always been practiced in other societies.[7]

Confucius may have considered himself a failure because he never attained the position he wanted, but many of his contemporaries found his ideas appealing, and in the generations after his death, his message spread widely throughout China. Confucius was an outspoken critic of his times and lamented the disappearance of what he regarded as the Golden Age of the early Zhou.

In fact, however, Confucius was not just another disgruntled Chinese conservative mourning the passing of the good old days; rather, he was a revolutionary thinker, many of whose key ideas looked forward rather than backward. Perhaps his most striking political idea was that the government should be open to all men of superior quality, not limited to those of noble birth. As one of his disciples reports in the *Analects:* "The Master said, by nature, men are nearly alike; by practice, they get to be wide apart."[8] Confucius undoubtedly had himself in mind as one of those "superior" men, but the rapacity of the hereditary lords must have added strength to his convictions.

The concept of rule by merit was, of course, not an unfamiliar idea in the China of his day; the *Rites of Zhou* had clearly stated that the king himself deserved to rule because of his talent and virtue, rather than as the result of noble birth. In practice, however, aristocratic privilege must often have opened the doors to political influence, and many of Confucius' contemporaries must have regarded his appeal for government by talent as both exciting and dangerous. Confucius did not explicitly question the right of the hereditary aristocracy to play a leading role in the political process, nor did his ideas have much effect in his lifetime. Still, they introduced a new

THE WAY OF THE GREAT LEARNING

RELIGION & PHILOSOPHY

Few texts exist today that were written by Confucius himself. Most were written or edited by his disciples. The following text, titled *The Great Learning*, was probably written two centuries after Confucius' death, but it illustrates his view that good government begins with the cultivation of individual morality and proper human relationships at the basic level. This conviction that to bring peace to the world, you must cultivate your own person continued to win general approval down to modern times. There are interesting similarities between such ideas and the views expressed in the Indian treatise *Arthasastra*, discussed in Chapter 2.

Compare these views, which reflect one of the most basic elements in Confucian thought—that proper moral behavior must begin at the level of the individual if it is to succeed within the framework of the larger community—with moral teachings expressed in other ancient civilizations. Would the Indian political adviser Kautilya, for example, agree with such views?

The Great Learning

The Way of the Great Learning consists in clearly exemplifying illustrious virtue, in loving the people, and in resting in the highest good.

Only when one knows where one is to rest can one have a fixed purpose. Only with a fixed purpose can one achieve calmness of mind. Only with calmness of mind can one attain serene repose. Only in serene repose can one carry on careful deliberation. Only through careful deliberation can one have achievement. Things have their roots and branches; affairs have their beginning and end. He who knows what comes first and what comes last comes himself near the Way.

The ancients who wished clearly to exemplify illustrious virtue throughout the world would first set up good government in their states. Wishing to govern well their states, they would first regulate their families. Wishing to regulate their families, they would first cultivate their persons. Wishing to cultivate their persons, they would first rectify their minds. Wishing to rectify their minds, they would first seek sincerity in their thoughts. Wishing for sincerity in their thoughts, they would first extend their knowledge. The extension of knowledge lay in the investigation of things. For only when things are investigated is knowledge extended; only when knowledge is extended are thoughts sincere; only when thoughts are sincere are minds rectified; only when minds are rectified are our persons cultivated; only when our persons are cultivated are our families regulated; only when families are regulated are states well governed; and only when states are well governed is there peace in the world.

From the emperor down to the common people, all, without exception, must consider cultivation of the individual character as the root. If the root is in disorder, it is impossible for the branches to be in order. To treat the important as unimportant and to treat the unimportant as important—this should never be. This is called knowing the root; this is called the perfection of knowledge.

CENGAGENOW To read more of *The Great Learning*, enter the CengageNOW documents area using the access card that is available for *The Essential World History*.

---

concept that was later implemented in the form of a bureaucracy selected through a civil service examination.

Confucius' ideas, passed on to later generations through the *Analects* as well as through writings attributed to him, had a strong impact on Chinese political thinkers of the late Zhou period, a time when the existing system was in disarray and open to serious question. But as with most great thinkers, Confucius' ideas were sufficiently ambiguous to be interpreted in contradictory ways. Some, like the philosopher Mencius (370–290 B.C.E.), stressed the humanistic side of Confucian ideas, arguing that human beings were by nature good and hence could be taught their civic responsibilities by example. He also stressed that the ruler had a duty to govern with compassion:

> It was because Chieh and Chou lost the people that they lost the empire, and it was because they lost the hearts of the people that they lost the people. Here is the way to win the empire: win the people and you win the empire. Here is the way to win the people: win their hearts and you win the people. Here is the way to win their hearts: give them and share with them what they like, and do not do to them what they do not like. The people turn to a human ruler as water flows downward or beasts take to wilderness.[9]

Here is a prescription for political behavior that could win wide support in our own day. Other thinkers, however, rejected Mencius' rosy view of human nature and argued for a different approach.

Legalism One school of thought that became quite popular during the "hundred schools" era in ancient China was the philosophy of Legalism. Taking issue with the view of Mencius and other disciples of Confucius that human nature was essentially good, the Legalists argued that human beings were by nature evil and would follow the correct path only if coerced by harsh laws and stiff punishments. These thinkers were referred to as the School of Law because they rejected the Confucian view that government by "superior men" could solve society's problems and argued instead for a system of impersonal laws.

The Legalists also disagreed with the Confucian belief that the universe has a moral core. They therefore believed that only firm action by the state could bring about social order. Fear of harsh punishment, more than

Confucius and Lao Tzu. It is not likely that the two ancient Chinese philosophers ever met, for little is known about the life of Lao Tzu, but according to tradition the two allegedly held a face-to-face meeting. The discussion must have been interesting, for their points of view about the nature of reality were diametrically opposed. The Chinese have managed to preserve both traditions throughout history, however, perhaps a reflection of the dualities represented in the Chinese approach to life. A similar duality existed among Platonists and Aristotelians in ancient Greece (see Chapter 4).

the promise of material reward, could best motivate the common people to serve the interests of the ruler. Because human nature was essentially corrupt, officials could not be trusted to carry out their duties in a fair and even-handed manner, and only a strong ruler could create an orderly society. All human actions should be subordinated to the effort to create a strong and prosperous state subject to his will.

Daoism One of the most popular alternatives to **Confucianism** was the philosophy of **Daoism** (frequently spelled Taoism). According to Chinese tradition, the Daoist school was founded by a contemporary of Confucius popularly known as Lao Tzu (Lao Zi), or the Old Master. Many modern scholars, however, are skeptical that Lao Tzu actually existed.

Obtaining a clear understanding of the original concepts of Daoism is difficult because its primary document, a short treatise known as the *Dao De Jing* (sometimes translated as *The Way of the Tao*), is an enigmatic book whose interpretation has baffled scholars for centuries. The opening line, for example, explains less what the *Dao* is than what it is not: "The Tao [Way] that can be told of is not the eternal Tao. The name that can be named is not the eternal name."[10]

Nevertheless, the basic concepts of Daoism are not especially difficult to understand. Like Confucianism, Daoism does not anguish over the underlying meaning of the cosmos. Rather, it attempts to set forth proper forms of behavior for human beings here on earth. In most other respects, however, Daoism presents a view of life and its ultimate meaning that is almost diametrically opposed to that of Confucianism. Where Confucian doctrine asserts that it is the duty of human beings to work hard to improve life here on earth, Daoists contend that the true way to interpret the will of Heaven is not action but inaction *(wu wei).* The best way to act in harmony with the universal order is to act spontaneously and let nature take its course (see the box on p. 62).

Such a message could be very appealing to people who were uncomfortable with the somewhat rigid flavor of the Confucian work ethic and preferred a more individualistic approach. This image would eventually find graphic expression in Chinese landscape painting, which in its classical form would depict naturalistic scenes of mountains, water, and clouds and underscore the fragility and smallness of individual human beings.

Daoism achieved considerable popularity in the waning years of the Zhou dynasty. It was especially popular among intellectuals, who may have found it appealing as an escapist antidote in a world characterized by growing disorder.

Popular Beliefs Daoism also played a second role as a loose framework for popular spiritualistic and animistic beliefs among the common people. Popular Daoism was less a philosophy than a religion; it comprised a variety of rituals and forms of behavior that were regarded as a means of achieving heavenly salvation or even a state of immortality on earth. Daoist sorcerers practiced various types of mind- or body-training exercises in the hope of achieving power, sexual prowess, and long life. It was primarily this form of Daoism that survived into a later age.

The philosophical forms of Confucianism and Daoism did not provide much meaning to the mass of the population, for whom philosophical debate over the ultimate meaning of life was not as important as the daily struggle for survival. Even among the elites, interest in the occult and in astrology was high, and magicoreligious ideas coexisted with interest in natural science and humanistic philosophy throughout the ancient period.

For most Chinese, Heaven was not a vague, impersonal law of nature, as it was for many Confucian and Daoist intellectuals, but a terrain peopled with innumerable gods and spirits of nature, both good and evil, who existed in trees, mountains, and streams as well as in heavenly bodies. As human beings mastered the techniques of farming, they called on divine intervention to

THE DAOIST ANSWER TO CONFUCIANISM

RELIGION & PHILOSOPHY

The *Dao De Jing* (*The Way of the Tao*) is the great classic of philosophical Daoism (Taoism). Traditionally attributed to the legendary Chinese philosopher Lao Tzu (Old Master), it was probably written sometime during the era of Confucius. This opening passage illustrates two of the key ideas that characterize Daoist belief: it is impossible to define the nature of the universe, and "inaction" (not Confucian "action") is the key to ordering the affairs of human beings.

What is Lao Tzu, the presumed author of this document, trying to express about the basic nature of the universe? Is there a moral order that can be comprehended by human thought? What would Lao Tzu have to say about Confucian moral teachings?

The Way of the Tao

The Tao that can be told of is not the eternal Tao;
The name that can be named is not the eternal name.
The Nameless is the origin of Heaven and Earth;
The Named is the mother of all things.

Therefore let there always be nonbeing, so we may see
    their subtlety.
And let there always be being, so we may see their
    outcome.
The two are the same,
But after they are produced, they have different names.
They both may be called deep and profound.
Deeper and more profound,

The door of all subtleties!
When the people of the world all know beauty
    as beauty,
There arises the recognition of ugliness.
When they all know the good as good,
There arises the recognition of evil.
Therefore:
Being and nonbeing produce each other;
Difficult and easy complete each other;
Long and short contrast each other;
High and low distinguish each other;
Sound and voice harmonize each other;
Front and behind accompany each other.

Therefore the sage manages affairs without action
And spreads doctrines without words.
All things arise, and he does not turn away from
    them.
He produces them but does not take possession of
    them.
He acts but does not rely on his own ability.
He accomplishes his task but does not claim
    credit for it.
It is precisely because he does not claim credit that his
    accomplishment remains with him.

CENGAGENOW To read more selections from the *Dao De Jing*, enter the *CengageNOW* documents area using the access card that is available for *The Essential World History*.

---

guarantee a good harvest. Other gods were responsible for the safety of fishers, transportation workers, or prospective mothers.

Another aspect of popular religion was the belief that the spirits of deceased human beings lived in the atmosphere for a time before ascending to heaven or descending to hell. During that period, surviving family members had to care for the spirits through proper ritual, or they would become evil spirits and haunt the survivors.

Thus, in ancient China, human beings were offered a variety of interpretations of the nature of the universe. Confucianism satisfied the need for a rational doctrine of nation building and social organization at a time when the existing political and social structure was beginning to disintegrate. Philosophical Daoism provided a more sensitive approach to the vicissitudes of fate and nature, and a framework for a set of diverse animistic beliefs at the popular level. But neither could satisfy the deeper emotional needs that sometimes inspire the human spirit. Neither could effectively provide solace in a time of sorrow or the hope of a better life in the hereafter. Something else would be needed to fill the gap.

The Rise of the Chinese Empire: The Qin Dynasty (221–206 B.C.E.)

During the last two centuries of the Zhou dynasty (the fourth and third centuries B.C.E.), the authority of the king became increasingly nominal, and several of the small principalities into which the Zhou kingdom had been divided began to evolve into powerful states that presented a potential challenge to the Zhou ruler himself. Chief among these were Qu (Ch'u) in the central Yangtze valley, Wu in the Yangtze delta, and Yue (Yueh) along the southeastern coast. At first, their mutual rivalries were in check, but by the late fifth century B.C.E., competition intensified into civil war, giving birth to the so-called Period of the Warring States (see the box on p. 64). Powerful principalities vied with each other for preeminence and largely ignored the now purely titular authority of the Zhou court (see Map 3.1). New forms of warfare also emerged with the invention of iron weapons and the introduction of the foot soldier. Cavalry, too, made its first appearance, armed with the powerful crossbow.

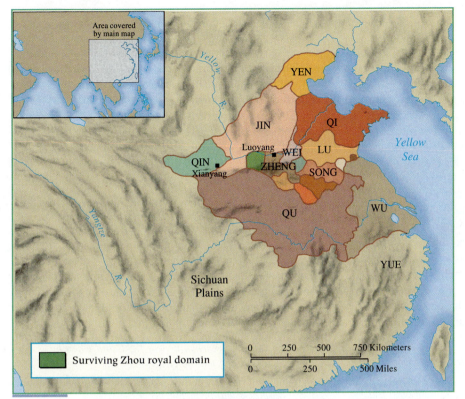

MAP 3.1 **China During the Period of the Warring States.** From the fifth to the third centuries B.C.E., China was locked in a time of civil strife known as the Period of the Warring States. This map shows the Zhou dynasty capital at Luoyang, along with the major states that were squabbling for precedence in the region. The state of Qin would eventually suppress its rivals and form the first unified Chinese empire, with its capital at Xianyang (near modern Xian). ❓ Why did most of the early states emerge in areas adjacent to China's two major river systems, the Yellow and Yangtze?

history as Qin Shi Huangdi (Ch'in Shih Huang Ti), or the First Emperor of Qin. A man of forceful personality and immense ambition, Qin Shi Huangdi had ascended to the throne of Qin in 246 B.C.E. at the age of thirteen. Described by the famous Han dynasty historian Sima Qian as having "the chest of a bird of prey, the voice of a jackal, and the heart of a tiger," the new king of Qin found the Legalist views of his adviser Li Su (Li Ssu) only too appealing. In 221 B.C.E. Qin Shi Huangdi defeated the last of his rivals and founded a new dynasty with himself as emperor.

Political Structures

The Qin dynasty transformed Chinese politics. Philosophical doctrines that had proliferated during the late Zhou period were prohibited, and Legalism was adopted as the official ideology. Those who opposed the policies of the new regime were punished and sometimes executed, while books presenting ideas contrary to the official orthodoxy were publicly put to the torch, perhaps the first example of book burning in history (see the box on p. 65).

Legalistic theory gave birth to a number of fundamental administrative and political developments, some of which would survive the Qin and serve as a model for future dynasties. In the first place, unlike the Zhou, the Qin was a highly centralized state. The central bureaucracy was divided into three primary ministries: a civil authority, a military authority, and a censorate, whose inspectors surveyed the efficiency of officials throughout the system. This would later become standard administrative procedure for future Chinese dynasties.

Below the central government were two levels of administration: provinces and counties. Unlike the Zhou system, officials at these levels did not inherit their positions but were appointed by the court and were subject to dismissal at the emperor's whim. Apparently, some form of merit system was used, although there is no evidence that selection was based on performance in an examination. The civil servants may have been chosen on the recommendation of other government officials. A penal code provided for harsh punishments for all wrongdoers. Officials were watched

Eventually, the relatively young state of Qin, located in the original homeland of the Zhou, became a key player in these conflicts. Benefiting from a strong defensive position in the mountains to the west of the great bend of the Yellow River, as well as from their control of the rich Sichuan plains, the Qin gradually subdued their main rivals through conquest or diplomatic maneuvering. In 221 B.C.E., the Qin ruler declared the establishment of a new dynasty, the first truly unified government in Chinese history.

One of the primary reasons for the triumph of the Qin was probably the character of the Qin ruler, known to

The Qin Empire, 221–206 B.C.E.

CHINA IN ANTIQUITY **63**

THE ART OF WAR

POLITICS & GOVERNMENT

With the possible exception of the nineteenth-century German military strategist Karl von Clausewitz, there is probably no more famous or respected writer on the art of war than the ancient Chinese thinker Sun Tzu. Yet surprisingly little is known about him. Recently discovered evidence suggests that he lived sometime in the fifth century B.C.E., during the chronic conflict of the Period of Warring States, and that he was an early member of an illustrious family of military strategists who advised Zhou rulers for more than two hundred years. But despite the mystery surrounding his life, there is no doubt of his influence on later generations of military planners. Among his most avid followers in modern times have been the revolutionary leaders Mao Zedong and Ho Chi Minh, as well as the Japanese military strategists who planned the attacks on Port Arthur and Pearl Harbor.

The following brief excerpt from his classic *The Art of War* provides a glimmer into the nature of his advice, still so timely today.

Why are the ideas of Sun Tzu about the art of war still so popular among military strategists after 2,500 years? How might he advise U.S. and other leaders to deal with the problem of international terrorism today?

Selections from Sun Tzu

Sun Tzu said:

"In general, the method for employing the military is this: . . . Attaining one hundred victories in one hundred battles is not the pinnacle of excellence. Subjugating the enemy's army without fighting is the true pinnacle of excellence. . . .

"Thus the highest realization of warfare is to attack the enemy's plans; next is to attack their alliances; next to attack their army; and the lowest is to attack their fortified cities.

"This tactic of attacking fortified cities is adopted only when unavoidable. Preparing large movable protective shields, armored assault wagons, and other equipment and devices will require three months. Building earthworks will require another three months to complete. If the general cannot overcome his impatience but instead launches an assault wherein his men swarm over the walls like ants, he will kill one-third of his officers and troops, and the city will still not be taken. This is the disaster that results from attacking [fortified cities].

"Thus one who excels at employing the military subjugates other people's armies without engaging in battle, captures other people's fortified cities without attacking them, and destroys others people's states without prolonged fighting. He must fight under Heaven with the paramount aim of 'preservation.' . . .

"In general, the strategy of employing the military is this: If your strength is ten times theirs, surround them; if five, then attack them; if double, then divide your forces. If you are equal in strength to the enemy, you can engage him. If fewer, you can circumvent him. If outmatched, you can avoid him. . . .

"Thus there are five factors from which victory can be known:

"One who knows when he can fight, and when he cannot fight, will be victorious.
"One who recognizes how to employ large and small numbers will be victorious.
"One whose upper and lower ranks have the same desires will be victorious.
"One who, fully prepared, awaits the unprepared will be victorious.
"One whose general is capable and not interfered with by the ruler will be victorious.

"These five are the Way (Tao) to know victory. . . .

"Thus it is said that one who knows the enemy and knows himself will not be endangered in a hundred engagements. One who does not know the enemy but knows himself will sometimes be victorious, sometimes meet with defeat. One who knows neither the enemy nor himself will invariably be defeated in every engagement."

CENGAGE**NOW** To read more of *The Art of War,* enter the CengageNOW documents area using the access card that is available for *The Essential World History.*

---

by the censors, who reported directly to the throne. Those guilty of malfeasance in office were executed.

Society and the Economy

Qin Shi Huangdi, who had a passion for centralization, unified the system of weights and measures, standardized the monetary system and the written forms of Chinese characters, and ordered the construction of a system of roads extending throughout the empire. He also attempted to eliminate the remaining powers of the landed aristocrats and divided their estates among the peasants, who were now taxed directly by the state. He thus eliminated potential rivals and secured tax revenues for the central government. Members of the aristocratic clans were required to live in the capital city at Xianyang (Hsienyang), just north of modern Xian, so that the court could monitor their activities. Such a system may not have been advantageous to the peasants in all respects, however, since the central government could now collect taxes more

MEMORANDUM ON THE BURNING OF BOOKS

Li Su, the author of the following passage, was a chief minister of the First Emperor of Qin. An exponent of Legalism, Li Su hoped to eliminate all rival theories on government. His recommendation to the emperor on the subject was recorded by the Han dynasty historian Sima Qian. The emperor approved the proposal and ordered all books contrary to the spirit of Legalist ideology to be destroyed on pain of death. Fortunately, some texts were preserved by being hidden or even memorized by their owners and were thus available to later generations. For centuries afterward, the First Emperor of Qin and his minister were singled out for criticism because of their intolerance and their effort to control the very minds of their subjects. Totalitarianism, it seems, is not exclusively a modern concept.

Why does the Legalist thinker Li Su feel that his proposal to destroy dangerous ideas is justified? Are there examples of similar thinking in our own time? Are there occasions when it might be permissible to outlaw unpopular ideas?

Sima Qian, *Historical Records*

In earlier times the empire disintegrated and fell into disorder, and no one was capable of unifying it. Thereupon the various feudal lords rose to power. In their discourses they all praised the past in order to disparage the present and embellished empty words to confuse the truth. Everyone cherished his own favorite school of learning and criticized what had been instituted by the authorities. But at present Your Majesty possesses a unified empire, has regulated the distinctions of black and white, and has firmly established for yourself a position of sole supremacy. And yet these independent schools, joining with each other, criticize the codes of laws and instructions. Hearing of the promulgation of a decree, they criticize it, each from the standpoint of his own school. At home they disapprove of it in their hearts; going out they criticize it in the thoroughfare. They seek a reputation by discrediting their sovereign; they appear superior by expressing contrary views, and they lead the lowly multitude in the spreading of slander. If such license is not prohibited, the sovereign power will decline above and partisan factions will form below. It would be well to prohibit this.

Your servant suggests that all books in the imperial archives, save the memoirs of Ch'in, be burned. All persons in the empire, except members of the Academy of Learned Scholars, in possession of the *Book of Odes,* the *Book of History,* and discourses of the hundred philosophers should take them to the local governors and have them indiscriminately burned. Those who dare to talk to each other about the *Book of Odes* and the *Book of History* should be executed and their bodies exposed in the marketplace. Anyone referring to the past to criticize the present should, together with all members of his family, be put to death. Officials who fail to report cases that have come under their attention are equally guilty. After thirty days from the time of issuing the decree, those who have not destroyed their books are to be branded and sent to build the Great Wall. Books not to be destroyed will be those on medicine and pharmacy, divination by the tortoise and milfoil, and agriculture and arboriculture. People wishing to pursue learning should take the officials as their teachers.

CENGAGENOW To read more of Sima Qian's writings, enter the *CengageNOW* documents area using the access card that is available for *The Essential World History.*

---

effectively and mobilize the peasants for military service and for various public works projects.

The Qin dynasty was equally unsympathetic to the merchants, whom it viewed as parasites. Private commercial activities were severely restricted and heavily taxed, and many vital forms of commerce and manufacturing, including mining, wine making, and the distribution of salt, were placed under a government monopoly.

Qin Shi Huangdi was equally aggressive in foreign affairs. His armies continued the gradual advance to the south that had taken place during the final years of the Zhou dynasty, extending the border of China to the edge of the Red River in modern Vietnam. To supply the Qin armies operating in the area, the Grand Canal was dug to provide direct inland navigation from the Yangtze River in central China to what is now the modern city of Guangzhou (Canton) in the south.

Beyond the Frontier: The Nomadic Peoples and the Great Wall

The main area of concern for the Qin emperor, however, was in the north, where a nomadic people, known to the Chinese as the Xiongnu (Hsiung-nu) and possibly related to the Huns (see Chapter 5), had become increasingly active in the area of the Gobi Desert. The area north of the Yellow River had been sparsely inhabited since prehistoric times. During the Qin period, the climate of northern China was somewhat milder and moister than it is today, and parts of the region were heavily forested. The local population probably lived by hunting and fishing, practicing limited forms of agriculture, or herding animals such as cattle or sheep.

As the climate gradually became drier, people were forced to rely increasingly on animal husbandry as a means of livelihood. Their response was to master the art of riding on horseback and to adopt the nomadic life. Organized loosely into communities consisting of a number of kinship groups, they ranged far and wide in search of pasture for their herds of cattle, goats, or sheep. As they moved seasonally from one pasture to another, they often traveled several hundred miles carrying their goods and their circular felt tents, called *yurts*.

But the new way of life presented its own challenges. Increased food production led to a growing population, which in times of drought outstripped the available resources. Rival groups then competed for the best pastures. After they mastered the art of fighting on horseback sometime during the middle of the first millennium B.C.E., territorial warfare became commonplace throughout the entire frontier region from the Pacific Ocean to Central Asia.

By the end of the Zhou dynasty in the third century B.C.E., the nomadic Xiongnu posed a serious threat to the security of China's northern frontier, and a number of Chinese principalities in the area began to build walls and fortifications to keep them out. But warriors on horseback possessed significant advantages over the infantry of the Chinese.

Qin Shi Huangdi's answer to the problem was to strengthen the walls to keep the marauders out. In Sima Qian's words:

> [The] First Emperor of the Ch'in dispatched Meng T'ien to lead a force of a hundred thousand men north to attack the barbarians. He seized control of all the lands south of the Yellow River and established border defenses along the river, constructing forty-four walled district cities overlooking the river and manning them with convict laborers transported to the border for garrison duty. Thus he utilized the natural mountain barriers to establish the border defenses, scooping out the valleys and constructing ramparts and building installations at other points where they were needed. The whole line of defenses stretched over ten thousand *li* [a *li* is one-third of a mile] from Lin-t'ao to Liao-tung and even extended across the Yellow River and through Yang-shan and Pei-chia.[11]

Today, of course, we know Qin Shi Huangdi's project as the Great Wall, which extends nearly 4,000 miles from the sandy wastes of Central Asia to the sea. It is constructed of massive granite blocks, and its top is wide enough to serve as a roadway for horse-drawn chariots. Although the wall that appears in most photographs today was built 1,500 years after the Qin, during the Ming dynasty, some of the walls built by the Qin remain standing. Their construction was a massive project that required the efforts of thousands of laborers, many of whom met their deaths there and, according to legend, are now buried within the wall.

The Fall of the Qin

The Legalist system put in place by the First Emperor of Qin was designed to achieve maximum efficiency as well as total security for the state. It did neither. Qin Shi Huangdi was apparently aware of the dangers of factions within the imperial family and established a class of **eunuchs** (males whose testicles have been removed) who served as personal attendants for himself and female members of the royal family. The original idea may have been to restrict the influence of male courtiers, and the eunuch system later became a standard feature of the Chinese imperial system. But as confidential advisers to the royal family, eunuchs were in a position of influence. The rivalry between the "inner" imperial court and the "outer" court of bureaucratic officials led to tensions that persisted until the end of the imperial system.

By ruthlessly gathering control over the empire into his own hands, Qin Shi Huangdi had hoped to establish a rule that, in the words of Sima Qian, "would be enjoyed by his sons for ten thousand generations." In fact, his centralizing zeal alienated many key groups. Landed aristocrats and Confucian intellectuals, as well as the common people, groaned under the censorship of thought and speech, harsh taxes, and forced labor projects. "He killed men," recounted the historian, "as though he thought he could never finish, he punished men as though he were afraid he would never get around to them all, and the whole world revolted against him."[12] Shortly after the emperor died in 210 B.C.E., the dynasty quickly descended into factional rivalry, and four years later it was overthrown.

The disappearance of the Qin brought an end to an experiment in absolute rule that later Chinese historians would view as a betrayal of humanistic Confucian principles. But in another sense, the Qin system was a response—though somewhat extreme—to the problems of administering a large and increasingly complex society. Although later rulers would denounce Legalism and enthrone Confucianism as the new state orthodoxy, in practice they would make use of a number of the key tenets of Legalism to administer the empire and control the behavior of their subjects.

Daily Life in Ancient China

Few social institutions have been as closely identified with China as the family. As in most agricultural civilizations, the family served as the basic economic and social unit in society. In traditional China, however, it took on an almost sacred quality as a microcosm of the entire social order.

The Role of the Family

In Neolithic times, the farm village, organized around the clan, was the basic social unit in China, at least in the core region of the Yellow River valley. Even then, however, the smaller family unit was becoming more important, at least among the nobility, who attached considerable significance to the ritual veneration of their immediate ancestors.

During the Zhou dynasty, the family took on increasing importance, in part because of the need for cooperation in agriculture. The cultivation of rice, which had become the primary crop along the Yangtze River and in the provinces to the south, is highly labor-intensive. The seedlings must be planted in several inches of water in a nursery bed and then transferred individually to the paddy beds, which must be irrigated constantly. During the harvest, the stalks must be cut and the kernels carefully separated from the stalks and husks. As a result, children—and the labor they supplied—were considered essential to the survival of the family, not only during their youthful years but also later, when sons were expected to provide for their parents. Loyalty to family members came to be considered even more important than loyalty to the broader community or the state. Confucius commented that it is the mark of a civilized society that a son should protect his father even if the latter has committed a crime against the community.

At the crux of the concept of family was the idea of **filial piety,** which called on all members of the family to subordinate their personal needs and desires to the patriarchal head of the family. More broadly, it created a hierarchical system in which every family member had his or her place. All Chinese learned the **five relationships** that were the key to a proper social order. The son was subordinate to the father, the wife to her husband, the younger brother to the older brother, and all were subject to their king. The final relationship was the proper one between friend and friend. Only if all members of the family and the community as a whole behaved in a properly filial manner would society function effectively.

A stable family system based on obedient and hardworking members can serve as a bulwark for an efficient government, but putting loyalty to the family and the clan over loyalty to the state can also present a threat to a centralizing monarch. For that reason, the Qin dynasty attempted to destroy the clan system in China and assert the primacy of the state. Legalists even imposed heavy taxes on any family with more than two adult sons in order to break down the family concept. The Qin reportedly also originated the practice of organizing several family units into larger groups of five and ten families that would exercise mutual control and surveillance. Later dynasties continued the practice under the name of the **Bao-jia** (*Pao-chia*) **system.**

But the efforts of the Qin to eradicate or at least reduce the importance of the family system ran against tradition and the dynamics of the Chinese economy, and under the Han dynasty, which succeeded the Qin in 202 B.C.E., the family revived and increased in importance. With official encouragement, the family system began to take on the character that it would possess until our own day. The family was not only the basic economic unit; it was also the basic social unit for education, religious observances, and training in ethical principles.

Lifestyles

We know much more about the lifestyle of the elites than that of the common people in ancient China. The first houses were probably constructed of wooden planks, but later Chinese mastered the art of building in tile and brick. By the first millennium B.C.E., most public buildings and the houses of the wealthy were probably constructed in this manner. By Han times, most Chinese probably lived in simple houses of mud, wooden planks, or brick with thatch or occasionally tile roofs. But in some areas, especially the loess (pronounced "less," a type of soil common in North China) regions of northern China, cave dwelling remained common down to modern times. The most famous cave dweller of modern times was Mao Zedong, who lived in a cave in Yan'an during his long struggle against Chiang Kai-shek.

Chinese houses usually had little furniture; most people squatted or sat with their legs spread out on the packed mud floor. Chairs were apparently not introduced until the sixth or seventh century C.E. Clothing was simple, consisting of cotton trousers and shirts in the summer and wool or burlap in the winter.

The staple foods were millet in the north and rice in the south. Other common foods were wheat, barley, soybeans, mustard greens, and bamboo shoots. In early times, such foods were often consumed in the form of porridge, but by the Zhou dynasty, stir-frying in a wok was becoming common. When possible, the Chinese family would vary its diet of grain foods with vegetables, fruit (including pears, peaches, apricots, and plums), and fish or meat; but for most, such additions to the daily plate of rice, millet, or soybeans were a rare luxury.

Alcohol in the form of ale was drunk at least by the higher classes and by the early Zhou era had already begun to inspire official concern. According to the *Book of History*, "King Wen admonished . . . the young nobles . . . that they should not ordinarily use spirits; and throughout all the states he required that they should be drunk only on occasion of sacrifices, and that then virtue should preside so that there might be no drunkenness."[13]

Cities

Most Chinese, then as now, lived in the countryside. But as time went on, cities began to play a larger role in Chinese society. The first towns were little more than forts for the local aristocracy; they were small in size and limited in population. By the Zhou era, however, larger towns, usually located on the major trade routes, began to combine administrative and economic functions, serving as regional markets or manufacturing centers. Such cities were usually surrounded by a wall and a moat, and a raised platform might be built within the walls to provide a place for ritual ceremonies and housing for the ruler's family.

The Humble Estate: Women in Ancient China

Male dominance was a key element in the social system of ancient China. As in many traditional societies, the male was considered of transcendent importance because of his role as food procurer or, in the case of farming communities, food producer. In ancient China, men worked in the fields and women raised children and served in the home. This differential in sexual roles goes back to prehistoric times and is embedded in Chinese creation myths. According to legend, Fu Xi's wife Nu Wa assisted her husband in organizing society by establishing the institution of marriage and the family. Yet Nu Wa was not just a household drudge. After Fu Xi's death, she became China's first female sovereign.

During ancient times, women apparently did not normally occupy formal positions of authority, but they often became a force in politics, especially at court where wives of the ruler or other female members of the royal family were often influential in palace intrigues. Such activities were frowned on, however, as the following passage from the *Book of Songs* attests:

> *A clever man builds a city,*
> *A clever woman lays one low;*
> *With all her qualifications, that clever woman*
> *Is but an ill-omened bird.*
> *A woman with a long tongue*
> *Is a flight of steps leading to calamity;*
> *For disorder does not come from heaven,*
> *But is brought about by women.*
> *Among those who cannot be trained or taught*
> *Are women and eunuchs.*[14]

The nature of gender relationships was also graphically demonstrated in the Chinese written language. The character for man (男) combines the symbols for strength and rice field, while the character for woman (女) represents a person in a posture of deference and respect. The character for peace (安) is a woman under a roof. A wife is symbolized by a woman with a broom. Male chauvinism has deep linguistic roots in China.

Chinese Culture

Modern knowledge about artistic achievements in ancient civilizations is limited because often little has survived the ravages of time. Fortunately, many ancient civilizations, such as Egypt and Mesopotamia, were located in relatively arid areas where many artifacts were preserved, even over thousands of years. In more humid regions, such as China and South Asia, the cultural residue left by the civilizations of antiquity has been adversely affected by climate.

As a result, relatively little remains of the cultural achievements of the prehistoric Chinese aside from Neolithic pottery and the relics found at the site of the Shang dynasty capital at Anyang. In recent years, a rich trove from the time of the Qin Empire has been unearthed near the tomb of Qin Shi Huangdi near Xian in central China and at Han tombs nearby. But little remains of the literature of ancient China and almost none of the painting, architecture, and music.

Metalwork and Sculpture

Discoveries at archaeological sites indicate that ancient China was a society rich in cultural achievement. The pottery found at Neolithic sites such as Longshan and Yangshao exhibits a freshness and vitality of form and design, and the ornaments, such as rings and beads, show a strong aesthetic sense.

Bronze Casting The pace of Chinese cultural development began to quicken during the Shang dynasty, which ruled in northern China from the sixteenth to the eleventh century B.C.E. At that time, objects cast in bronze began to appear. Various bronze vessels were produced for use in preparing and serving food and drink in the ancestral rites. Later vessels were used for decoration or for dining at court.

The method of casting used was one reason for the extraordinary quality of Shang bronze work. Bronze workers in most ancient civilizations used the lost-wax method, for which a model was first made in wax. After a clay mold had been formed around it, the model was heated so that the wax would melt away, and the empty space was filled with molten metal. In China, clay molds composed of several sections were tightly fitted together prior to the introduction of the liquid bronze. This technique, which had evolved from ceramic techniques used during the Neolithic period, enabled the artisans to apply

Courtesy of William J. Duiker

A Shang Wine Vessel. Used initially as food containers in royal ceremonial rites during the Shang dynasty, Chinese bronzes were the product of an advanced technology unmatched by any contemporary civilization. This wine vessel displays a deep green patina as well as a monster motif, complete with large globular eyes, nostrils, and fangs, typical of many Shang bronzes. Known as the *taotie,* this fanciful beast is normally presented in silhouette as two dragons face to face so that each side forms half of the mask. Although the *taotie* presumably served as a guardian force against evil spirits, scholars are still not aware of its exact significance for early Chinese peoples.

the design directly to the mold and thus contributed to the clarity of line and rich surface decoration of the Shang bronzes.

Bronze casting became a large-scale business, and more than ten thousand vessels of an incredible variety of form and design survive today. Factories were located not only in the Yellow River valley but also in Sichuan Province, in southern China. The art of bronze working continued into the Zhou and the Han dynasties, but the quality and originality declined. The Shang bronzes remain the pinnacle of creative art in ancient China.

One reason for the decline of bronze casting in China was the rise in popularity of iron. Iron making developed in China around the ninth or eighth century B.C.E., much later than in the Middle East, where it had

been mastered almost a millennium earlier. Once familiar with the process, however, the Chinese quickly moved to the forefront. Ironworkers in Europe and the Middle East, lacking the technology to achieve the high temperatures necessary to melt iron ore for casting, were forced to work with wrought iron, a cumbersome and expensive process. By the fourth century B.C.E., the Chinese had invented the technique of the blast furnace, powered by a person operating a bellows. They were therefore able to manufacture cast-iron ritual vessels and agricultural tools centuries before an equivalent technology appeared in the West.

The First Emperor's Tomb In 1974, in a remarkable discovery, farmers digging a well about 35 miles east of Xian unearthed a number of terra-cotta figures in an underground pit about one mile east of the burial mound of the First Emperor of Qin. Chinese archaeologists sent to work at the site discovered a vast terra-cotta army that they believed was a re-creation of Qin Shi Huangdi's imperial guard, which was to accompany the emperor on his journey to the next world.

One of the astounding features of the terra-cotta army is its size. The army is enclosed in four pits that were originally encased in a wooden framework, which has since disintegrated. More than a thousand figures have been unearthed in the first pit, along with horses, wooden chariots, and seven thousand bronze weapons. Archaeologists estimate that there are more than six thousand figures in that pit alone.

Equally impressive is the quality of the work. Slightly larger than life-size, the figures were molded of finely textured clay and then fired and painted. The detail on the uniforms is realistic and sophisticated, but the most striking feature is the individuality of the facial features of the soldiers. Apparently, ten different head shapes were used and were then modeled further by hand to reflect the variety of ethnic groups and personality types in the army.

The discovery of the terra-cotta army also shows that the Chinese had come a long way from the human sacrifices that had taken place at the death of Shang sovereigns more than a thousand years earlier. But the project must have been ruinously expensive and is additional evidence of the burden the Qin ruler imposed on his subjects. One historian has estimated that one-third of the national income in Qin and Han times may have been spent on preparations for the ruler's afterlife. The emperor's mausoleum has not yet been unearthed, but it is enclosed in a mound nearly 250 feet high and is surrounded by a rectangular wall nearly 4 miles around. According to the Han historian Sima Qian, the ceiling is a replica of the heavens, while the floor contains a relief model of the entire Qin kingdom, with rivers flowing in mercury. According to tradition, traps were set within the mausoleum to prevent intruders, and the workers applying the final touches were buried alive in the tomb with its secrets.

Qin Shi Huangdi's Tomb. The First Emperor of Qin ordered the construction of an elaborate mausoleum, an underground palace complex protected by an army of terra-cotta soldiers and horses to accompany him on his journey to the afterlife. This massive formation of six thousand life-size armed soldiers, discovered accidentally by farmers in 1974, reflects Qin Shi Huangdi's grandeur and power.

Language and Literature

Precisely when writing developed in China cannot be determined, but certainly by Shang times, as the oracle bones demonstrate, the Chinese had developed a simple but functional script. Like many other languages of antiquity, it was primarily ideographic and pictographic in form. Symbols, usually called "characters," were created to represent an idea or to form a picture of the object to be represented. For example, the Chinese characters for mountain (山), the sun (日), and the moon (月) were meant to represent the objects themselves. Other characters, such as "big" (大) (a man with his arms outstretched), represent an idea. The word "east" (東) symbolizes the sun coming up behind the trees.

Each character, of course, would be given a sound by the speaker when pronounced. In other cultures, this process led to the abandonment of the system of ideographs and the adoption of a written language based on phonetic symbols. The Chinese language, however, has never entirely abandoned its original ideographical format, although the phonetic element has developed into a significant part of the individual character. In that sense, the Chinese written language is virtually unique in the world today.

One reason the language retained its ideographic quality may have been the aesthetics of the written characters. By the time of the Han dynasty, if not earlier, the written language came to be seen as an art form as well as a means of communication, and calligraphy became one of the most prized forms of painting in China.

Even more important, if the written language had developed in the direction of a phonetic alphabet, it could no longer have served as the written system for all the peoples of an expanding civilization. Although the vast majority spoke a tongue derived from a parent Sinitic language (a system distinguished by its variations in pitch, a characteristic that gives Chinese its lilting quality even today), the languages spoken in various regions of the country differed from each other in pronunciation and to a lesser degree in vocabulary and syntax; for the most part, they were (and are today) mutually unintelligible.

The Chinese answer to this problem was to give all the spoken languages the same writing system. Although any character might be pronounced differently in different regions of China, that character would be written the same way (after the standardization undertaken under the Qin) no matter where it was written. This system of written characters could be read by educated Chinese from one end of the country to the other. It became the language of the bureaucracy and the vehicle for the transmission of Chinese culture to all Chinese from the Great Wall to the southern border and even beyond. The written language, however, was not identical with the spoken. Written Chinese evolved a totally separate vocabulary and grammatical structure from the spoken tongues. As a result, those who used it required special training.

The earliest extant form of Chinese literature dates from the Zhou dynasty. It was written on silk or strips of bamboo and consisted primarily of historical records such as the *Rites of Zhou,* philosophical treatises such as the *Analects* and *The Way of the Tao,* and poetry, as recorded in *The Book of Songs* and the *Song of the South.* In later years, when Confucian principles had been elevated to a state ideology, the key works identified with the Confucian school were integrated into a set of so-called Confucian Classics. These works became required reading for generations of Chinese schoolchildren and introduced them to the forms of behavior that would be required of them as adults.

Music

From early times in China, music was viewed not just as an aesthetic pleasure but also as a means of achieving political order and refining the human character. In fact, music may have originated as an accompaniment to sacred rituals at the royal court. According to the *Historical Records,* a history written during the Han dynasty: "When our sage-kings of the past instituted rites and music, their objective was far from making people indulge in the . . . amusements of singing and dancing. . . . Music is produced to purify the heart, and rites introduced to rectify the behavior."[15] Eventually, however, music began to be appreciated for its own sake as well as to accompany singing and dancing.

A wide variety of musical instruments were used, including flutes, various stringed instruments, bells and chimes, drums, and gourds. Bells cast in bronze were first used as musical instruments in the Shang period; they were hung in rows and struck with a wooden mallet. The finest were produced during the mid-Zhou era and are considered among the best examples of early bronze work in China.

By the late Zhou era, bells had begun to give way as the instrument of choice to strings and wind instruments, and the purpose of music shifted from ceremony to entertainment. This led conservative critics to rail against the onset of an age of debauchery.

Ancient historians stressed the relationship between music and court life, but it is highly probable that music, singing, and dancing were equally popular among the common people. The *Book of History,* purporting to describe conditions in the late third millennium B.C.E., suggests that ballads emanating from the popular culture were welcomed at court. Nevertheless, court music and popular music differed in several respects. Among other things, popular music was more likely to be motivated by the desire for pleasure than for the purpose of law and order and moral uplift. Those differences continued to be reflected in the evolution of music in China down to modern times.

CONCLUSION

*O*F THE GREAT CLASSICAL CIVILIZATIONS discussed in Part I of this book, China was the last to come into full flower. By the time the Shang began to emerge as an organized state, the societies in Mesopotamia and the Nile valley had already reached an advanced level of civilization. Unfortunately, not enough is known about the early stages of these civilizations to allow us to determine why some developed earlier than others, but one likely reason for China's late arrival was that it was virtually isolated from other emerging centers of culture elsewhere in the world and thus was compelled to develop essentially on its own. Only at the end of the first millennium B.C.E. did China come into regular contact with other civilizations in South Asia, the Middle East, and the Mediterranean.

Once embarked on its own path toward the creation of a complex society, however, China achieved results that were in all respects the equal of its counterparts elsewhere. During the glory years of the Han dynasty, China extended the boundaries of its empire far into the sands of Central Asia and southward along the coast of the South China Sea into what is now Vietnam (see Chapter 5).

One reason for China's striking success was undoubtedly that unlike its contemporary civilizations, it long was able to fend off the danger from nomadic peoples (along the northern frontier). By the second century B.C.E., however, the Xiongnu were looming ominously, and tribal warriors began to nip at the borders of the empire. While China was strong, the problem was manageable, but when internal difficulties began to corrode the unity of the state, it became increasingly vulnerable to the threat from the north and entered its own time of troubles.

In the meantime, another great civilization was beginning to take form on the northern shores of the Mediterranean Sea. Unlike China and the other ancient societies discussed thus far, this new civilization in Europe was based as much on trade as on agriculture. Yet the political and cultural achievements of ancient Greece were the equal of any of the great human experiments that had preceded it and soon began to exert a significant impact on the rest of the ancient world.

CHAPTER NOTES

1. *Book of Changes,* quoted in Chang Chi-yun, *Chinese History of Fifty Centuries,* vol. 1, *Ancient Times* (Taipei, 1962), pp. 15, 31, and 65.

2. Ibid., p. 381.

3. Quoted in E. N. Anderson, *The Food of China* (New Haven, Conn., 1988), p. 21.

4. According to Chinese tradition, the *Rites of Zhou* was written by the Duke of Zhou himself near the time of the founding of the

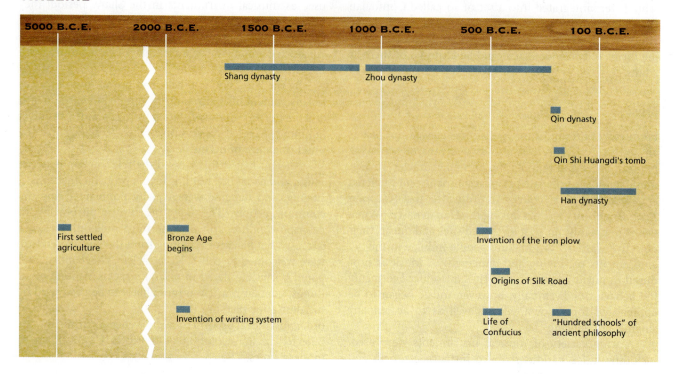

| 5000 B.C.E. | 2000 B.C.E. | 1500 B.C.E. | 1000 B.C.E. | 500 B.C.E. | 100 B.C.E. |

Shang dynasty

Zhou dynasty

Qin dynasty

Qin Shi Huangdi's tomb

Han dynasty

First settled agriculture

Bronze Age begins

Invention of the iron plow

Origins of Silk Road

Invention of writing system

Life of Confucius

"Hundred schools" of ancient philosophy

Zhou dynasty. However, modern historians believe that it was written much later, perhaps as late as the fourth century B.C.E.

5. From *The Book of Songs*, quoted in S. de Grazia, ed., *Masters of Chinese Political Thought: From the Beginnings to the Han Dynasty* (New York, 1973), pp. 40–41.

6. *Confucian Analects* (Lun Yu), ed. J. Legge (Taipei, 1963), 11:11 and 6:20.

7. Ibid., 15:23.

8. Ibid., 17:2.

9. *Book of Mencius* (Meng Zi), 4A:9, quoted in W. T. de Bary et al., eds., *Sources of Chinese Tradition* (New York, 1960), p. 107.

10. Quoted in de Bary, *Sources of Chinese Tradition*, p. 53.

11. B. Watson, *Records of the Grand Historian of China* (New York, 1961), vol. 2, pp. 155, 160.

12. Ibid., pp. 32, 53.

13. C. Waltham, *Shu Ching: Book of History* (Chicago, 1971), p. 154.

14. Quoted in H. A. Giles, *A History of Chinese Literature* (New York, 1923), p. 19.

15. Chang Chi-yun, *Chinese History of Fifty Centuries*, vol. 1, p. 183.

SUGGESTED READING

Several general histories of China provide a useful overview of the period of antiquity. Perhaps the best known is the classic *East Asia: Tradition and Transformation* (Boston, 1973), by **J. K. Fairbank, E. O. Reischauer,** and **A. M. Craig.** For an authoritative overview of the ancient period, see **M. Loewe** and **E. L. Shaughnessy,** *The Cambridge History of Ancient China from the Origins of Civilization to 221 B.C.* (Cambridge, 1999). Political and social maps of China can be found in **A. Herrmann,** *A Historical Atlas of China* (Chicago, 1966).

The period of the Neolithic era and the Shang dynasty has received increasing attention in recent years. For an impressively documented and annotated overview, see **Kwang-chih Chang,** *Shang Civilization* (New Haven, Conn., 1980) and *Studies in Shang*

Archaeology (New Haven, Conn., 1982). **D. Keightley,** *The Origins of Chinese Civilization* (Berkeley, Calif., 1983), presents a number of interesting articles on selected aspects of the period.

The Zhou and Qin dynasties have also received considerable attention. The former is exhaustively analyzed in **Cho-yun Hsu** and **J. M. Linduff,** *Western Zhou Civilization* (New Haven, Conn., 1988), and **Li Xueqin,** *Eastern Zhou and Qin Civilizations* (New Haven, Conn., 1985). The latter is a translation of an original work by a mainland Chinese scholar and is especially interesting for its treatment of the development of the silk industry and the money economy in ancient China. On bronze casting, see **E. L. Shaughnessy,** *Sources of Eastern Zhou History* (Berkeley, Calif., 1991).

The philosophy of ancient China has attracted considerable attention from Western scholars. For excerpts from all the major works of the "hundred schools," consult **W. T. de Bary** and **I. Bloom,** eds., *Sources of Chinese Tradition,* vol. 1 (New York, 1999). On Confucius, see **B. W. Van Norden,** ed., *Confucius and the Analects: New Essays* (Oxford, 2002). Also see **F. Mote,** *Intellectual Foundations of China,* 2d ed. (New York, 1989).

For works on general culture and science, consult the illustrated work by **R. Temple,** *The Genius of China: 3000 Years of Science, Discovery, and Invention* (New York, 1986), and **J. Needham,** *Science in Traditional China: A Comparative Perspective* (Boston, 1981). See also **E. N. Anderson,** *The Food of China* (New Haven, Conn., 1988). Environmental issues are explored in **M. Elvin,** *The Retreat of the Elephants: An Environmental History of China* (New Haven, Conn., 2004).

For an introduction to classical Chinese literature, consult the three standard anthologies: **Liu Wu-Chi,** *An Introduction to Chinese Literature* (New York, 1961); **V. H. Mair,** ed., *The Columbia Anthology of Traditional Chinese Literature* (New York, 1994); and **S. Owen,** ed., *An Anthology of Chinese Literature: Beginnings to 1911* (New York, 1996). For a comprehensive introduction to Chinese art, consult **M. Sullivan,** *The Arts of China,* 4th ed. (Berkeley, Calif., 1999), with good illustrations in color. Also see **M. Tregear,** *Chinese Art,* rev. ed. (London, 1997), and *Art Treasures in China* (New York, 1994). Also of interest is

P. B. Ebrey, *The Cambridge Illustrated History of China* (Cambridge, 1999). For recent finds, consult **J. Rowson,** *Mysteries of Ancient China: New Discoveries from the Early Dynasties* (New York, 1996). On music, see **J. F. So,** ed., *Music in the Age of Confucius* (Washington, D.C., 2000).

InfoTrac College Edition

Visit this chapter's InfoTrac College Edition/Research activities at the *Essential World History* Companion Website for activities related to ancient China.

CENGAGENOW **for Duiker and Spielvogel's** *The Essential World History, Third Edition*

Enter *CengageNOW* using the access card that is available with this text. *CengageNOW* will assist you in understanding the content in this chapter with lesson plans generated for your needs, as well as provide you with a connection to the *Wadsworth World History Resource Center* (see description at the right for details).

4

THE CIVILIZATION OF THE GREEKS

CHAPTER OUTLINE AND FOCUS QUESTIONS

Early Greece

☐ How did the geography of Greece affect Greek history, and why was Homer used as the basis for Greek education?

The Greek City-States (c. 750–c. 500 B.C.E.)

☐ What was the *polis*, or city-state, and how did the city-states of Athens and Sparta differ?

The High Point of Greek Civilization: Classical Greece

☐ What did the Greeks mean by democracy, and in what ways was the Athenian political system a democracy?

The Rise of Macedonia and the Conquests of Alexander

☐ How was Alexander the Great able to amass his empire, and what was his legacy?

The World of the Hellenistic Kingdoms

☐ How did the political and social institutions of the Hellenistic world differ from those of classical Greece?

CRITICAL THINKING

☐ In what ways did the culture of the Hellenistic period differ from that of the classical period, and what do those differences suggest about society in the two periods?

A statue of Pericles in Athens

akg-images/John Hios

DURING THE ERA OF CIVIL WAR in China known as the Period of the Warring States, a civil war also erupted on the northern shores of the Mediterranean Sea. In 431 B.C.E., two very different Greek city-states—Athens and Sparta—fought for domination of the Greek world. The people of Athens felt secure behind their walls and in the first winter of the war held a public funeral to honor those who had died in battle. On the day of the ceremony, the citizens of Athens joined in a procession, with the relatives of the dead wailing for their loved ones. As was the custom in Athens, one leading citizen was asked to address the crowd, and on this day it was Pericles who spoke to the people. He talked about the greatness of Athens and reminded the Athenians of the strength of their political system: "Our constitution," he said, "is called a democracy because power is in the hands not of a minority but of the whole people. When it is a question of settling private disputes, everyone is equal before the law. Just as our political life is free and open, so is our day-to-day life in our relations with each other. . . . Here each individual is interested not only in his own affairs but in the affairs of the state as well."

In this famous funeral oration, Pericles gave voice to the ideal of democracy and the importance of the individual, ideals that were quite different from those of some other ancient societies, in which the individual was subordinated to a larger order based on obedience to an exalted ruler. The Greeks asked some basic questions about human life: What is the nature of the universe? What is the purpose of human existence? What is our relationship to divine forces? What constitutes a community? What constitutes a state? What is truth, and how do we realize it? Not only did the Greeks answer these questions, but they also derived a system of logical, analytical thought to examine them. Their answers and their system of rational thought laid the intellectual foundation of Western civilization's understanding of the human condition.

The remarkable story of ancient Greek civilization begins with the arrival of the Greeks around 1900 B.C.E. By the eighth century B.C.E., the characteristic institution of ancient Greek life, the *polis*, or city-state, had emerged. Greek civilization flourished and reached its height in the classical era of the fifth century B.C.E., but the inability of the Greek states to end their fratricidal warfare eventually left them vulnerable to the Macedonian king Philip II and helped bring an end to the era of independent Greek city-states.

Although the city-states were never the same after their defeat by the Macedonian monarch, this defeat did not bring an end to the influence of the Greeks. Philip's son Alexander led the Macedonians and Greeks on a spectacular conquest of the Persian Empire and opened the door to the spread of Greek culture throughout the Middle East. ◇

Early Greece

Geography played an important role in Greek history. Compared to Mesopotamia and Egypt, Greece occupied a small area, a mountainous peninsula that encompassed only 45,000 square miles of territory, about the size of the state of Louisiana. The mountains and the sea were especially significant. Much of Greece consists of small plains and river valleys surrounded by mountain ranges 8,000 to 10,000 feet high. The mountains isolated Greeks from one another, causing Greek communities to follow their own separate paths and develop their own ways of life. Over a period of time, these communities became so fiercely attached to their independence that they were only too willing to fight one another to gain advantage. No doubt the small size of these independent Greek communities fostered participation in political affairs and unique cultural expressions, but the rivalry among them also led to the internecine warfare that ultimately devastated Greek society.

The sea also influenced Greek society. Greece had a long seacoast, dotted by bays and inlets that provided numerous harbors. The Greeks also inhabited a number of islands to the west, south, and particularly the east of the Greek mainland. It is no accident that the Greeks became seafarers who sailed out into the Aegean and Mediterranean seas to make contact with the outside world and later to establish colonies that would spread Greek civilization throughout the Mediterranean.

Greek topography helped determine the major territories into which Greece was ultimately divided (see Map 4.1). South of the Gulf of Corinth was the Peloponnesus, virtually an island connected to the mainland by a narrow isthmus. Consisting mostly of hills, mountains, and small valleys, the Peloponnesus was home to the city-state of Sparta. Northeast of the Peloponnesus was the Attic peninsula (or Attica), the site of Athens, hemmed in by mountains to the north and west and surrounded by the sea to the south and east. Northwest of Attica was Boeotia in central Greece, with its chief city of Thebes. To the north of Boeotia was Thessaly, which contained the largest plains and became a great producer of grain and horses. To the north of Thessaly lay Macedonia, which was of minor importance in Greek history until 338 B.C.E., when the Macedonian king conquered the Greeks.

Minoan Crete

The earliest civilization in the Aegean region emerged on the large island of Crete, southeast of the Greek mainland. A Bronze Age civilization that used metals, especially bronze, in making weapons had been established there by 2800 B.C.E. This civilization was discovered at the turn of the twentieth century by the English archaeologist Arthur Evans, who named it "Minoan" after Minos, a legendary king of Crete. In language and religion, the Minoans were not Greek, although they did have some influence on the peoples of the Greek mainland.

Evans's excavations on Crete at the beginning of the twentieth century unearthed an enormous palace complex at Knossus, near modern Heracleion. The remains revealed a prosperous culture with Knossus as the apparent center of a far-ranging "sea empire" based on trade.

The Minoan civilization reached its height between 2000 and 1450 B.C.E. The palace at Knossus, the royal seat of the kings, was an elaborate structure that included numerous private living rooms for the royal family and workshops for making decorated vases, ivory figurines, and jewelry. Even bathrooms, with elaborate drains, like those found at Mohenjo-Daro in India, formed part of the complex. The rooms were decorated with brightly colored frescoes showing sporting events and nature scenes.

The centers of Minoan civilization on Crete suffered a sudden and catastrophic collapse around 1450 B.C.E. Some historians believe that a tidal wave triggered by a powerful volcanic eruption on the island of Thera was responsible for the devastation, but most historians maintain that the

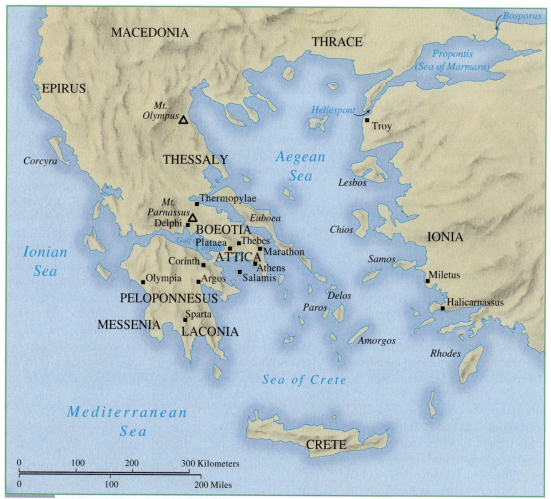

MAP 4.1 Ancient Greece (c. 750–338 B.C.E.). Between 750 and 500 B.C.E., Greek civilization witnessed the emergence of the city-state as the central institution in Greek life and the Greeks' colonization of the Mediterranean and Black seas. Classical Greece lasted from about 500 to 338 B.C.E. and encompassed the high points of Greek civilization in the arts, science, philosophy, and politics, as well as the Persian Wars and the Peloponnesian War. ▨ How does the geography of Greece help explain the rise and development of the Greek city-state? 🌐 **View an animated version of this map or related maps at** http://worldrc.wadsworth.com/

destruction was the result of invasion and pillage by mainland Greeks known as the Mycenaeans.

The First Greek State: Mycenae

The term *Mycenaean* is derived from Mycenae, a fortified site excavated by an amateur German archaeologist, Heinrich Schliemann, starting in 1870. Mycenae was one center in a civilization that flourished between 1600 and 1100 B.C.E. The Mycenaean Greeks were part of the Indo-European family of peoples (see Chapter 1) who spread from their original location into southern and western Europe, India, and Persia. One group entered the territory of Greece from the north around 1900 B.C.E. and eventually managed to gain control of the Greek mainland and develop a civilization.

Mycenaean civilization, which reached its high point between 1400 and 1200 B.C.E., consisted of a number of powerful monarchies that resided in fortified palace complexes. Like Mycenae, they were built on hills and surrounded by gigantic stone walls. These various centers of power probably formed a loose confederacy of independent states, with Mycenae being the strongest. The Mycenaeans were warriors who prided themselves on their heroic deeds in battle. Some scholars believe that the Mycenaeans spread outward and conquered Crete. The most famous of their supposed military adventures has come down to us in the epic poetry of Homer (see "Homer" later in this chapter). Did the Mycenaean

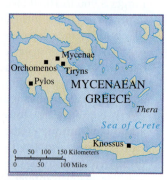

Minoan Crete and Mycenaean Greece

Greeks, led by Agamemnon, king of Mycenae, sack the city of Troy on the northwestern coast of Asia Minor around 1250 B.C.E.? Ever since Schliemann began his excavations in 1870, scholars have debated this question. Many believe that Homer's account does have a basis in fact, even if the details have become shrouded in mystery.

By the late thirteenth century B.C.E., Mycenaean Greece was showing signs of serious trouble. Mycenae itself was torched around 1190 B.C.E., and other Mycenaean centers show similar patterns of destruction as new waves of Greek-speaking invaders moved into Greece from the north. By 1100, Mycenaean culture was coming to an end, and the Greek world was entering a new period of considerable insecurity.

The Greeks in a Dark Age (c. 1100–c. 750 B.C.E.)

After the collapse of Mycenaean civilization, Greece entered a difficult era of declining population and falling food production; not until 850 B.C.E. did farming—and Greece itself—revive. Because of both the difficult conditions and the fact that we have few records to help us reconstruct what happened in this period, historians refer to it as the Dark Age.

During the Dark Age, large numbers of Greeks left the mainland and migrated across the Aegean Sea to various islands and especially to the southwestern shore of Asia Minor, a strip of territory that came to be called Ionia. Two other major groups of Greeks settled in established parts of Greece. The Aeolians from northern and central Greece colonized the large island of Lesbos and the adjacent mainland. The Dorians established themselves in southwestern Greece, especially in the Peloponnesus, as well as on some south Aegean islands, including Crete.

As trade and economic activity began to recover, iron replaced bronze in the construction of weapons, making them affordable for more people. At some point in the eighth century B.C.E., the Greeks adopted the Phoenician alphabet to give themselves a new system of writing. Near the very end of the Dark Age appeared the work of Homer, who has come to be viewed as one of the great poets of all time.

Homer   The first great epics of early Greece, the *Iliad* and the *Odyssey*, were based on stories that had been passed down from generation to generation. It is generally assumed that early in the eighth century B.C.E., Homer made use of these oral traditions to compose the *Iliad*, his epic poem of the Trojan War. The war began after Paris, a prince of Troy, kidnapped Helen, wife of the king of the Greek state of Sparta, outraging all the Greeks. Under the leadership of the Spartan king's brother, Agamemnon of Mycenae, the Greeks attacked Troy. After ten years of combat, the Greeks finally sacked the city. The *Iliad* is not so much the story of the war itself, however, as it is the tale of the Greek hero Achilles and how the "wrath of Achilles"

led to disaster. The *Odyssey*, Homer's other masterpiece, is an epic romance that recounts the journeys of another Greek hero, Odysseus, after the fall of Troy and his eventual return to his wife, Penelope, after twenty years.

The Greeks regarded the *Iliad* and the *Odyssey* as authentic history as recorded by one poet, Homer. The epics gave the Greeks an idealized past, a legendary age of heroes, and the poems became standard texts for the education of generations of Greek males. As one Athenian stated, "My father was anxious to see me develop into a good man . . . and as a means to this end he compelled me to memorize all of Homer."[1] The values Homer inculcated were essentially the aristocratic values of courage and honor (see the box on p. 78). It was important to strive for the excellence befitting a hero, which the Greeks called *arete*. In the warrior-aristocratic world of Homer, *arete* is won in struggle or contest. Through his willingness to fight, the hero protects his family and friends, preserves his own honor and his family's, and earns his reputation. In the Homeric world, aristocratic women, too, were expected to pursue excellence. For example, Odysseus' wife, Penelope, remains faithful to her husband and displays great courage and intelligence in preserving their household during her husband's long absence.

To a later generation of Greeks, these heroic values formed the core of aristocratic virtue, a fact that explains the tremendous popularity of Homer as an educational tool. Homer gave the Greeks a universally accepted model of heroism, honor, and nobility. But in time, as city-states proliferated in Greece, new values of cooperation and community also transformed what the Greeks learned from Homer.

The Greek City-States (c. 750–c. 500 B.C.E.)

During the Dark Age, Greek villages gradually expanded and evolved into independent city-states. By the eighth century B.C.E., the city-state, or what the Greeks called a **polis** (plural, *poleis*), had emerged as a unique and fundamental institution in Greek society.

The *Polis*

In the most basic sense, a *polis* could be defined as a small but autonomous political unit in which all major political, social, and religious activities were carried out at one central location. The *polis* consisted of a city, town, or village and its surrounding countryside. The city, town, or village was the focus, a central point where the citizens of the *polis* could assemble for political, social, and religious activities. In some *poleis*, this central meeting point was a hill, like the Acropolis at Athens, which could serve as a place of refuge during an attack and later in some sites came to be the religious center on which temples and public monuments were erected. Below the acropolis would be an *agora*, an open

HOMER'S IDEAL OF EXCELLENCE

ARTS & IDEAS

The *Iliad* and the *Odyssey*, which the Greeks believed were both written by Homer, were used as basic texts for the education of Greeks for hundreds of years during antiquity. This passage from the *Iliad*, describing the encounter between Hector, prince of Troy, and his wife, Andromache, illustrates the Greek ideal of gaining honor through combat. At the end of the passage, Homer also reveals what became the Greek attitude toward women: they are supposed to spin and weave and take care of their households and children.

What important ideals for Greek men and women are revealed in this passage from the Iliad? *How do the women's ideals compare with those for ancient Indian and Chinese women?*

Homer, *Iliad*

Hector looked at his son and smiled, but said nothing. Andromache, bursting into tears, went up to him and put her hand in his. "Hector," she said, "you are possessed. This bravery of yours will be your end. You do not think of your little boy or your unhappy wife, whom you will make a widow soon. Some day the Achaeans [Greeks] are bound to kill you in a massed attack. And when I lose you I might as well be dead. . . . I have no father, no mother, now. . . . I had seven brothers too at home. In one day all of them went down to Hades' House. The great Achilles of the swift feet killed them all. . . .

"So you, Hector, are father and mother and brother to me, as well as my beloved husband. Have pity on me now; stay here on the tower; and do not make your boy an orphan and your wife a widow. . . ."

"All that, my dear," said the great Hector of the glittering helmet, "is surely my concern. But if I hid myself like a coward and refused to fight, I could never face the Trojans

and the Trojan ladies in their trailing gowns. Besides, it would go against the grain, for I have trained myself always, like a good soldier, to take my place in the front line and win glory for my father and myself. . . ."

As he finished, glorious Hector held out his arms to take his boy. But the child shrank back with a cry to the bosom of his girdled nurse, alarmed by his father's appearance. He was frightened by the bronze of the helmet and the horsehair plume that he saw nodding grimly down at him. His father and his lady mother had to laugh. But noble Hector quickly took his helmet off and put the dazzling thing on the ground. Then he kissed his son, dandled him in his arms, and prayed to Zeus and the other gods: "Zeus, and you other gods, grant that this boy of mine may be, like me, preeminent in Troy; as strong and brave as I; a mighty king of Ilium. May people say, when he comes back from battle, 'Here is a better man than his father.' Let him bring home the bloodstained armor of the enemy he has killed, and make his mother happy."

Hector handed the boy to his wife, who took him to her fragrant breast. She was smiling through her tears, and when her husband saw this he was moved. He stroked her with his hand and said, "My dear, I beg you not to be too much distressed. No one is going to send me down to Hades before my proper time. But Fate is a thing that no man born of woman, coward or hero, can escape. Go home now, and attend to your own work, the loom and the spindle, and see that the maidservants get on with theirs. War is men's business; and this war is the business of every man in Ilium, myself above all."

CENGAGENOW To read Book 1 of the *Iliad,* enter the *CengageNOW* documents area using the access card that is available for *The Essential World History.*

---

space or plaza that served both as a market and as a place where citizens could assemble.

Poleis could vary greatly in size, from a few square miles to a few hundred square miles. They also varied in population. Athens had a population of about 250,000 by the fifth century B.C.E. But most *poleis* were much smaller, consisting of only a few hundred to several thousand people.

Although our word *politics* is derived from the Greek term *polis*, the *polis* itself was much more than just a political institution. It was, above all, a community of citizens who shared a common identity and common goals. As a community, the *polis* consisted of citizens with political rights (adult males), citizens with no political rights (women and children), and noncitizens (slaves and resident aliens). All citizens of a *polis* possessed fundamental rights, but these rights were coupled with responsibilities.

The loyalty that citizens had to their city-states also had a negative side, however. City-states distrusted one another, and the division of Greece into fiercely patriotic sovereign units helped bring about its ruin.

A New Military System: The Hoplites As the *polis* developed, so did a new military system. Greek fighting had previously been dominated by aristocratic cavalrymen, who reveled in individual duels with enemy soldiers. By 700 B.C.E., however, a new military order came into being that was based on **hoplites,** heavily armed infantrymen who wore bronze or leather helmets, breastplates, and greaves (shin guards). Each carried a round shield, a short sword, and a thrusting spear about 9 feet long. Hoplites advanced into battle as a unit, the tightly ordered **phalanx,** usually eight ranks deep. As long as the hoplites kept their order, were not outflanked, and did not break, they

The Hoplite Forces. The Greek hoplites were infantrymen equipped with large round shields and long thrusting spears. In battle, they advanced in tight phalanx formation and were dangerous opponents as long as this formation remained unbroken. This vase painting of the seventh century B.C.E. shows two groups of hoplite warriors engaged in battle. The piper on the left is leading another line of soldiers preparing to enter the fray.

either secured victory or at the very least suffered no harm. If the phalanx broke its order, however, it was easily routed. Thus, the safety of the phalanx depended on the solidarity and discipline of its members. As one poet of the seventh century B.C.E. noted, a good hoplite was a "short man . . . with a courageous heart, not to be uprooted from the spot where he plants his legs."[2]

The hoplite force had political as well as military repercussions. The aristocratic cavalry was now outdated. Since each hoplite provided his own armor, men of property, both aristocrats and small farmers, made up the new phalanx. Those who could become hoplites and fight for the state could also challenge aristocratic control.

Colonization and the Growth of Trade

Between 750 and 550 B.C.E., large numbers of Greeks left their homeland to settle in distant lands. The growing gulf between rich and poor, overpopulation, and the development of trade were all factors that led to the establishment of colonies. Invariably, each colony saw itself as an independent *polis* whose links to the mother *polis* (*metropolis*) were not political but based on sharing common social, economic, and religious practices.

In the western Mediterranean, new Greek settlements were established along the coastline of southern Italy, southern France, eastern Spain, and northern Africa west of Egypt. To the north, the Greeks set up colonies in Thrace, where they sought good farmland to grow grains. Greeks also settled along the shores of the Black Sea and secured the approaches to it with cities on the Hellespont and Bosporus, most notably Byzantium, site of the later Constantinople (Istanbul). In establishing these settlements, the Greeks spread their culture throughout the Mediterranean basin. Moreover, colonization helped the Greeks foster a greater sense of Greek identity. Before the eighth century, Greek communities were mostly isolated from one another, leaving many neighboring states on unfriendly terms. Once Greeks from different communities went abroad and found peoples with different languages and customs, they became more aware of their own linguistic and cultural similarities.

Colonization also led to increased trade and industry. The Greeks on the mainland sent their pottery, wine, and olive oil to these areas; in return, they received grains and metals from the west and fish, timber, wheat, metals, and slaves from the Black Sea region. In many *poleis,* the expansion of trade and industry created a new group of rich men who desired political privileges commensurate with their wealth but found them impossible to gain because of the power of the ruling aristocrats.

Tyranny in the Greek *Polis*

The aspirations of the new industrial and commercial groups laid the groundwork for the rise of **tyrants** in the seventh and sixth centuries B.C.E. These men were not necessarily oppressive or wicked, as our word *tyrant* connotes. Greek tyrants were rulers who came to power in an unconstitutional way; a tyrant was not subject to the law. Many tyrants were actually aristocrats who opposed the control of the ruling aristocratic faction in their cities. Support for the tyrants, however, came from the new rich, who made their money in trade and industry, as well as from poor peasants, who were becoming increasingly indebted to landholding aristocrats. Both groups were opposed to the domination of political power by aristocratic **oligarchies** (an oligarchy is rule by a few).

Once in power, the tyrants built new marketplaces, temples, and walls that not only glorified the city but also enhanced their own popularity. Tyrants also favored the interests of merchants and traders. Despite these achievements, however, **tyranny** was largely extinguished by the end of the sixth century B.C.E. Greeks believed in the rule of law, and tyranny made a mockery of that ideal.

Although tyranny did not last, it played a significant role in the evolution of Greek history by ending the rule of narrow aristocratic oligarchies. Once the tyrants were eliminated, the door was open to the participation of more people in governing the affairs of the community. Although this trend culminated in the development of democracy in some communities, in other states expanded oligarchies of one kind or another managed to remain in power. Greek states exhibited considerable variety in their governmental structures; this can perhaps best be seen by examining the two most famous and most powerful Greek city-states, Sparta and Athens.

Sparta

Located in the southeastern Peloponnesus, Sparta, like other Greek states, faced the need for more land. Instead of sending its people out to found new colonies, the Spartans conquered the neighboring Laconians and later, beginning around 730 B.C.E., undertook the conquest of neighboring Messenia despite its larger size and population. Messenia possessed a large, fertile plain ideal for growing grain. After its conquest in the seventh century B.C.E., many Messenians, like some of the Laconians earlier, were made **helots** (the name is derived from a Greek word for "capture") and forced to work for the Spartans. To ensure control over their conquered Laconian and Messenian *helots,* the Spartans made a conscious decision to establish a military state.

The New Sparta Between 800 and 600 B.C.E., the Spartans instituted a series of reforms that are associated with the name of the lawgiver Lycurgus (see the box on p. 81). Although historians are not sure that Lycurgus ever existed, there is no doubt about the result of the reforms: the lives of Spartans were now rigidly organized and tightly controlled (to this day, the word *spartan* means "highly self-disciplined"). Boys were taken from their mothers at the age of seven and put under control of the state. They lived in military-style barracks, where they were subjected to harsh discipline to make them tough and given an education that stressed military training and obedience to authority. At twenty, Spartan males were enrolled in the army for regular military service. Although allowed to marry, they continued to live in the barracks and ate all their meals in public dining halls with fellow soldiers. Meals were simple; the famous Spartan black broth consisted of a piece of pork boiled in blood, salt, and vinegar, prompting a visitor who ate in a public mess to remark that he now understood why Spartans were not afraid to die. At thirty, Spartan males were allowed to vote in the assembly and live at home, but they remained in military service until the age of sixty.

While their husbands remained in military barracks, Spartan women lived at home. Because of this separation, Spartan women had greater freedom of movement and greater power in the household than was common elsewhere in Greece. Spartan women were expected to exercise and remain fit to bear and raise healthy children. Like the men, Spartan women engaged in athletic exercises in the nude. Many Spartan women upheld the strict Spartan values, expecting their husbands and sons to be brave in war. The story is told that as a Spartan mother was burying her son, an old woman came up to her and said, "You poor woman, what a misfortune." "No," replied the other, "because I bore him so that he might die for Sparta and that is what has happened, as I wished."[3]

The Spartan State The so-called Lycurgan reforms also reorganized the Spartan government, creating an oligarchy. Two kings were primarily responsible for military affairs and served as the leaders of the Spartan army on its campaigns. A group of five men, known as the ephors, were elected each year and were responsible for the education of youth and the conduct of all citizens. A council of elders, composed of the two kings and twenty-eight citizens over the age of sixty, decided on the issues that would be presented to an assembly. This assembly of all male citizens did not debate but only voted on the issues put before it by the council of elders.

To make their new military state secure, the Spartans deliberately turned their backs on the outside world. Foreigners, who might bring in new ideas, were discouraged from visiting Sparta. Nor were Spartans, except for military reasons, allowed to travel abroad where they might

The Lycurgan Reforms

POLITICS & GOVERNMENT

To maintain their control over the conquered Messenians, the Spartans instituted the reforms that created their military state. In this account of the lawgiver Lycurgus, who may or may not have been a real person, the Greek historian Plutarch discusses the effect of these reforms on the treatment and education of boys.

What does this passage from Plutarch's account of Lycurgus reveal about the nature of the Spartan state? Why would this whole program have been distasteful to the Athenians?

Plutarch, *Lycurgus*

Lycurgus was of another mind; he would not have masters bought out of the market for his young Spartans, . . . nor was it lawful, indeed, for the father himself to breed up the children after his own fancy; but as soon as they were seven years old they were to be enrolled in certain companies and classes, where they all lived under the same order and discipline, doing their exercises and taking their play together. Of these, he who showed the most conduct and courage was made captain; they had their eyes always upon him, obeyed his orders, and underwent patiently whatsoever punishment he inflicted; so that the whole course of their education was one continued exercise of a ready and perfect obedience. The old men, too, were spectators of their performances, and often raised quarrels and disputes among them, to have a good opportunity of finding out their different characters, and of seeing which would be valiant, which a coward, when they should come to more dangerous encounters. Reading and writing they gave them, just enough to serve their turn; their chief care was to make them good subjects, and to teach them to endure pain and conquer in battle. To this end, as they grew in years, their discipline was proportionately increased; their heads were close-clipped, they were accustomed to go barefoot, and for the most part to play naked.

After they were twelve years old, they were no longer allowed to wear any undergarments; they had one coat to serve them a year; their bodies were hard and dry, with but little acquaintance of baths and unguents; these human indulgences they were allowed only on some few particular days in the year. They lodged together in little bands upon beds made of the rushes which grew by the banks of the river Eurotas, which they were to break off with their hands with a knife; if it were winter, they mingled some thistle down with their rushes, which it was thought had the property of giving warmth. By the time they were come to this age there was not any of the more hopeful boys who had not a lover to bear him company. The old men, too, had an eye upon them, coming often to the grounds to hear and see them contend either in wit or strength with one another, and this as seriously . . . as if they were their fathers, their tutors, or their magistrates; so that there scarcely was any time or place without someone present to put them in mind of their duty, and punish them if they had neglected it.

[Spartan boys were also encouraged to steal their food.] They stole, too, all other meat they could lay their hands on, looking out and watching all opportunities, when people were asleep or more careless than usual. If they were caught, they were not only punished with whipping, but hunger, too, being reduced to their ordinary allowance, which was but very slender, and so contrived on purpose, that they might set about to help themselves, and be forced to exercise their energy and address. This was the principal design of their hard fare.

CENGAGENOW To read more of Plutarch's *Life of Lycurgus,* enter the *CengageNOW* documents area using the access card that is available for *The Essential World History*.

---

pick up new ideas that might be dangerous to the stability of the state. Likewise, Spartan citizens were discouraged from studying philosophy, literature, or the arts, any subject that might encourage new thoughts. The art of war was the Spartan ideal, and all other arts were frowned upon.

Athens

By 700 B.C.E., Athens had established a unified *polis* on the peninsula of Attica. Although early Athens had been ruled by a monarchy, by the seventh century B.C.E. it had fallen under the control of its aristocrats. They possessed the best land and controlled political life by means of a council of nobles, assisted by a board of nine archons. Although there was an assembly of full citizens, it possessed few powers.

Near the end of the seventh century B.C.E., Athens faced political turmoil because of serious economic problems.

Increasing numbers of Athenian farmers found themselves sold into slavery when they were unable to repay loans they had obtained from their aristocratic neighbors. Repeatedly, there were cries to cancel the debts and give land to the poor.

The ruling Athenian aristocrats responded to this crisis in 594 B.C.E. by giving full power to Solon, a reform-minded aristocrat, to make changes. Solon canceled all land debts, outlawed new loans based on humans as collateral, and freed people who had fallen into slavery for debts. He refused, however, to carry out land redistribution. Thus, Solon's reforms, though popular, did not truly solve Athens's problems. Aristocratic factions continued to vie for power, and poor peasants could not get land. Internal strife finally led to the very institution Solon had hoped to avoid—tyranny. Pisistratus, an aristocrat, seized power in 560 B.C.E. Pursuing a foreign policy that aided

DEMOS AND *DESPOTS*

POLITICS & GOVERNMENT

The origins of modern government lie in the agricultural revolution, when sedentary peoples began to seek organized protection from threats and dangers arising from within and outside the community. Influential figures, known to sociologists as "big men," emerged as community leaders in farm villages or pastoral communities to provide protection and to perform other services of importance to the local population. As these societies grew in size and complexity, such informal authority figures began to assume greater power and influence and to surround themselves with relatives and retainers serving as a ruling elite. By the time of the emergence of ancient civilizations, the former "big men" had begun to assume divine or semidivine powers to ensure their hereditary status and bolster their authority over their subjects. Examples appeared in Egypt with the reign of kings around 3100 B.C.E., in Mesopotamia a few hundred years later, and in China by the end of the second millennium B.C.E.

The power of these rulers over their subject peoples was not necessarily absolute. In many cases (see Chapter 2) government was decentralized rather than focused on one single authority. In China under the Zhou dynasty, the concept that the ruler governed by divine mandate (the mandate of Heaven) became widely accepted. With this concept came the belief that if the ruler did not govern effectively, he could be overthrown and replaced by a new ruler. This view culminated with the ideas of the Zhou dynasty philosopher Confucius, and his disciple Mencius, who declared that "the people are first in importance, the nation is next, while the ruler is of the least importance, since it is the people who make him the Son of Heaven."

But it was in the region of the Mediterranean Sea that the most effective statement against the power of the ruler was proclaimed. In the sixth century B.C.E., political thinkers in Greece—notably in the city-state of Athens—began to reject the idea of the *despot* (from the Greek word for "master"), which they identified with the rulers of the Persian Empire, in favor of government based on the will of the people (in Greek, *demos*). Such views represent the first glimmerings of the modern concept of *democracy*. The Greek experiment was brief, however, as despotic forces soon brought an end to Athenian democracy. On the nearby Italian peninsula to the west, an early Roman Republic was eventually replaced by a monarchy based on the divine power of the emperor. But the vision of democracy did not entirely vanish and was revived with even greater force in Europe and North America at the end of the eighteenth century.

Athenian trade, Pisistratus remained popular with the mercantile and industrial classes. But the Athenians rebelled against his son and ended the tyranny in 510 B.C.E. When the aristocrats attempted to reestablish an aristocratic oligarchy, Cleisthenes, another aristocratic reformer, opposed their plan and, with the backing of the Athenian people, gained the upper hand in 508 B.C.E.

Cleisthenes set up a "council of five hundred" that supervised foreign affairs and the treasury and proposed laws that would be voted on by the assembly. The Athenian assembly, composed of all male citizens, was given final authority in the passing of laws after free and open debate. Since the assembly of citizens now had the central role in the Athenian political system, the reforms of Cleisthenes had created the foundations for Athenian democracy (see the comparative essay "*Demos* and Depots" above).

The High Point of Greek Civilization: Classical Greece

Classical Greece is the name given to the period of Greek history from around 500 B.C.E. to the conquest of Greece by the Macedonian king Philip II in 338 B.C.E. Many of the cultural contributions of the Greeks occurred during this period. The age began with a mighty confrontation between the Greek states and the mammoth Persian Empire.

The Challenge of Persia

As the Greeks spread throughout the Mediterranean, they came into contact with the Persian Empire to the east. The Ionian Greek cities in western Asia Minor had already fallen subject to the Persian Empire by the mid-sixth century B.C.E. An unsuccessful revolt by the Ionian cities in 499 B.C.E., assisted by the Athenians, led the Persian ruler Darius to seek revenge by attacking the mainland Greeks. In 490 B.C.E., the Persians landed an army on the plain of Marathon, only 26 miles from Athens. The Athenians and their allies were clearly outnumbered, but the Greek hoplites charged across the plain of Marathon and crushed the Persian forces.

Xerxes, the new Persian monarch after the death of Darius in 486 B.C.E., vowed revenge and planned to invade Greece. In preparation for the attack, some of the Greek states formed a defensive league under Spartan leadership, while the Athenians pursued a new military policy by undertaking the development of a navy. By the time of the Persian invasion in 480 B.C.E., the Athenians had produced a fleet of about two hundred vessels.

Xerxes led a massive invasion force into Greece: close to 150,000 troops, almost seven hundred naval ships, and hundreds of supply ships to keep the large army fed. The Greeks tried to delay the Persians at the pass of Thermopylae, along the main road into central Greece. A Greek force numbering close to nine thousand men, under the leadership of a Spartan king and his contingent of three hundred Spartans, held off the Persian army for several days. The Spartan troops were especially brave. When told that Persian arrows would darken the sky in battle, one Spartan warrior supposedly responded: "That is good news. We will fight in the shade!" Unfortunately for the Greeks, a traitor told the Persians about a mountain path that would allow them to outflank the Greek force. The Spartans fought to the last man.

The Athenians, now threatened by the onslaught of the Persian forces, abandoned their city. While the Persians sacked and burned Athens, the Greek fleet remained offshore near the island of Salamis and challenged the Persian navy. Although the Greeks were outnumbered, they managed to outmaneuver the Persian fleet and utterly defeated it. A few months later, early in 479 B.C.E., the Greeks formed the largest Greek army seen up to that time and decisively defeated the Persian army at Plataea, northwest of Attica. The Greeks had won the war and were free to pursue their own destiny.

The Growth of an Athenian Empire in the Age of Pericles

After the defeat of the Persians, Athens took over the leadership of the Greek world against the Persians by forming a defensive alliance called the Delian League in the winter of 478–477 B.C.E. Its main headquarters was on the island of Delos, but its chief officials, including the treasurers and commanders of the fleet, were Athenian. Under the leadership of the Athenians, the Delian League pursued the attack against the Persian Empire. Virtually all of the Greek states in the Aegean were liberated from Persian control. In 454 B.C.E., the Athenians moved the treasury from Delos to Athens. By controlling the Delian League, Athens had created an empire.

At home, Athenians favored the new imperial policy, especially after 461 B.C.E., when an aristocrat named Pericles began to play an important political role. Under Pericles, Athens embarked on a policy of expanding democracy at home and its new empire abroad. This period of Athenian and Greek history, which historians have subsequently labeled the Age of Pericles, witnessed the height of Athenian power and the culmination of its brilliance as a civilization.

In the Age of Pericles, the Athenians became deeply attached to their democratic system. The sovereignty of the people was embodied in the assembly, which consisted of all male citizens over eighteen years of age. In the mid-fifth century, that was probably a group of about 43,000. Not all attended, however, and the number present at the meetings, which were held every ten days on a hillside east of the Acropolis, seldom reached 6,000. The assembly passed all laws and made final decisions on war and foreign policy.

Routine administration of public affairs was handled by a large body of city magistrates, usually chosen by lot without regard to class and usually serving only one-year terms. This meant that many male citizens held public office at some time in their lives. A board of ten officials known as generals (*strategoi*) was elected by public vote to guide affairs of state, although their power depended on the respect they had attained. Generals were usually wealthy aristocrats, although the people were free to select otherwise. The generals could be reelected, enabling individual leaders to play an important political role. Pericles' frequent reelection (fifteen times) as one of the ten generals made him one of the leading politicians between 461 and 429 B.C.E.

Pericles expanded the Athenians' involvement in democracy, which is what by now the Athenians had come to call their form of government. Power was in the hands of the people; male citizens voted in the assemblies and served as jurors in the courts. Lower-class citizens were now eligible for public offices formerly closed to them. Pericles also introduced state pay for officeholders, including the widely held jury duty. This meant that even poor citizens could hold public office and afford to participate in public affairs. Nevertheless, although the Athenians developed a system of government, unique in its time, in which citizens had equal rights and the people were the government, aristocrats continued to hold the most important offices, and many people, including women, slaves, and foreigners residing in Athens, were not given the same political rights.

Under Pericles, Athens also became the leading center of Greek culture. The Persians had destroyed much of the city during the Persian Wars, but Pericles used the treasury money of the Delian League to launch a massive rebuilding program. New temples and statues soon proclaimed the greatness of Athens. Art, architecture, and philosophy flourished, and Pericles broadly boasted that Athens had become the "school of Greece." But the achievements of Athens alarmed the other Greek states, especially Sparta, and soon all Greece was confronted with a new war.

The Great Peloponnesian War and the Decline of the Greek States

During the forty years after the defeat of the Persians, the Greek world came to be divided into two major camps: Sparta and its supporters and the Athenian maritime empire. Sparta and its allies feared the growing Athenian empire. Then, too, Athens and Sparta had built two very different kinds of societies, and neither was able to tolerate the other's system. A series of disputes finally led to the outbreak of war in 431 B.C.E.

At the beginning of the war, both sides believed they had winning strategies. The Athenians planned to remain behind the protective walls of Athens; the overseas empire

The Great Peloponnesian War (431–404 B.C.E)

and the navy would keep them supplied. Pericles knew that the Spartans and their allies could beat the Athenians in open battles, which was the chief aim of the Spartan strategy. The Spartans and their allies attacked Athens, hoping that the Athenians would send out their army to fight beyond the walls. But Pericles was convinced that Athens was secure behind its walls and stayed put.

In the second year of the war, however, plague devastated the crowded city of Athens and wiped out possibly one-third of the population. Pericles himself died the following year (429 B.C.E.), a severe loss to Athens. Despite the decimation of the plague, the Athenians fought on in a struggle that dragged on for another twenty-five years. A crushing blow came in 405 B.C.E., when the Athenian fleet was destroyed at Aegospotami on the Hellespont. Athens was besieged and surrendered in 404 B.C.E., its walls torn down, its navy disbanded, and its empire destroyed. The war was finally over.

The Great Peloponnesian War weakened the major Greek states and led to new alliances among them. The next seventy years of Greek history are a sorry tale of efforts by Sparta, Athens, and Thebes, a new Greek power, to dominate Greek affairs. In continuing their petty wars, the Greeks remained oblivious to the growing power of Macedonia to their north.

The Culture of Classical Greece

Classical Greece saw a period of remarkable intellectual and cultural growth throughout the Greek world, and Periclean Athens was the most important center of classical Greek culture.

The Writing of History   History as we know it, as a systematic analysis of past events, was introduced to the Western world by the Greeks. Herodotus (c. 484–c. 425 B.C.E.) wrote *History of the Persian Wars,* a work commonly regarded as the first real history in Western civilization. The central theme of Herodotus' work is the conflict between the Greeks and the Persians, which he viewed as a struggle between Greek freedom and Persian despotism. Herodotus traveled extensively and questioned many people for his information. He was a master storyteller and sometimes included fanciful material, but he was also capable of exhibiting a critical attitude toward the materials he used.

Thucydides (c. 460–c. 400 B.C.E.) was by far the better historian, widely acknowledged as the greatest historian of the ancient world. Thucydides was an Athenian and a participant in the Peloponnesian War. A defeat in battle led the Athenian assembly to send him into exile, which gave him the opportunity to continue to write his *History of the Peloponnesian War.*

Unlike Herodotus, Thucydides was not concerned with underlying divine forces or gods as explanatory causal factors in history. He saw war and politics in purely rational terms, as the activities of human beings. He examined the causes of the Peloponnesian War in a clear and objective fashion, placing much emphasis on accuracy and the precision of his facts. Thucydides also provided remarkable insight into the human condition. He believed that political situations recur in similar fashion and that the study of history is of great value in understanding the present.

Greek Drama   Drama as we know it in Western culture originated with the Greeks. Plays were presented in outdoor theaters as part of religious festivals. The form of Greek plays remained rather stable. Three male actors who wore masks acted all the parts, and a chorus, also male, spoke lines that explained what was going on.

The first Greek dramas were tragedies, plays based on the suffering of a hero and usually ending in disaster. Aeschylus (525–456 B.C.E.) is the first tragedian whose plays are known to us. As was customary in Greek tragedy, his plots are simple, and the entire drama focuses on a single tragic event and its meaning. Greek tragedies were sometimes presented in a trilogy (a set of three plays) built around a common theme. The only complete trilogy we possess, called the *Oresteia,* was composed by Aeschylus. The theme of this trilogy is derived from Homer. Agamemnon, the king of Mycenae, returns a hero from the defeat of Troy. His wife, Clytemnestra, avenges the sacrificial death of her daughter Iphigenia by murdering Agamemnon, who had been responsible for Iphigenia's

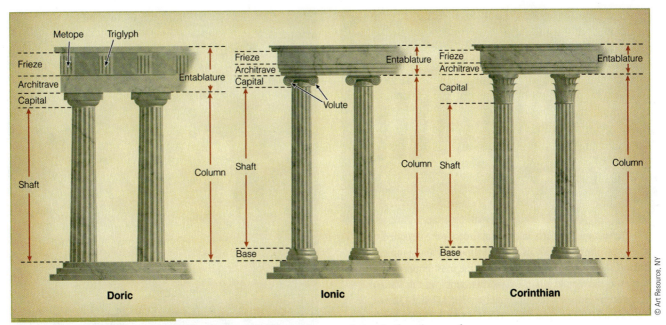

Doric, Ionic, and Corinthian Orders. The Greeks used different shapes and sizes in the columns of their temples. The Doric order, evolved first in the Dorian Peloponnesus, consisted of thick, fluted columns with simple capitals (the decorated tops of the columns). The Greeks considered the Doric order grave, dignified, and masculine. The Ionic style was first developed in western Asia Minor and consisted of slender columns with spiral-shaped capitals. The Greeks characterized the Ionic order as slender, elegant, and feminine in principle. Corinthian columns, with their more detailed capitals modeled after acanthus leaves, came later, near the end of the fifth century B.C.E.

death. In the second play of the trilogy, Agamemnon's son Orestes avenges his father by killing his mother. Orestes is then pursued by the avenging Furies, who torment him for killing his mother. Evil acts breed evil acts, and suffering is the human lot, suggests Aeschylus. In the end, however, reason triumphs over the forces of evil.

Another great Athenian playwright was Sophocles (c. 496–406 B.C.E.), whose most famous play was *Oedipus the King*. In this play, the oracle of Apollo foretells how a man (Oedipus) will kill his own father and marry his mother. Despite all attempts at prevention, the tragic events occur. Although it appears that Oedipus suffered the fate determined by the gods, Oedipus also accepts that he himself as a free man must bear responsibility for his actions: "It was Apollo, friends, Apollo, that brought this bitter bitterness, my sorrows, to completion. But the hand that struck me was none but my own."[4]

The third outstanding Athenian tragedian, Euripides (c. 485–406 B.C.E.), moved beyond his predecessors by creating more realistic characters. His plots became more complex, with a greater interest in real-life situations. Euripides was controversial; he questioned traditional moral and religious values. For example, he was critical of the traditional view that war was glorious and portrayed war as brutal and barbaric.

Greek tragedies dealt with universal themes still relevant to our day. They probed such problems as the nature of good and evil, the rights of the individual, the nature of divine forces, and the essence of human beings. Over and over, the tragic lesson was repeated: humans were free and

yet could operate only within limitations imposed by the gods. To strive to do the best may not always gain a person success in human terms but is nevertheless worthy of the endeavor. Greek pride in human accomplishment and independence is real. As the chorus chanted in Sophocles' *Antigone:* "Is there anything more wonderful on earth, our marvelous planet, than the miracle of man?"[5]

The Arts: The Classical Ideal The artistic standards established by the Greeks of the classical period have largely dominated the arts of the Western world. Greek art was concerned with expressing eternally true ideals. Its subject matter was basically the human being, expressed harmoniously as an object of great beauty. The classical style, based on the ideals of reason, moderation, symmetry, balance, and harmony in all things, was meant to civilize the emotions.

In architecture, the most important form was the temple, dedicated to a god or goddess. At the center of Greek temples were walled rooms that housed the statues of deities and treasuries where gifts to the gods and goddesses were safeguarded. These central rooms were surrounded by a screen of columns that make Greek temples open structures rather than closed ones. The columns were originally made of wood but were changed to marble in the fifth century B.C.E.

Some of the finest examples of Greek classical architecture were built in fifth-century Athens. The most famous building, regarded as the greatest example of the classical Greek temple, was the Parthenon, built between

The Parthenon. The arts in classical Greece were designed to express the eternal ideals of reason, moderation, symmetry, balance, and harmony. In architecture, the most important form was the temple, and the classical example of this kind of architecture is the Parthenon, built between 447 and 432 B.C.E. Located on the Acropolis, the Parthenon was dedicated to Athena, the patron goddess of Athens, but it also served as a shining example of the power and wealth of the Athenian empire.

447 and 432 B.C.E. Consecrated to Athena, the patron goddess of Athens, the Parthenon was also dedicated to the glory of the city-state and its inhabitants. The structure typifies the principles of classical architecture: calmness, clarity, and the avoidance of superfluous detail.

Greek sculpture also developed a classical style. Statues of the male nude, the favorite subject of Greek sculptors, exhibited relaxed attitudes; their faces were self-assured, their bodies flexible and smoothly muscled. Although the figures possessed natural features that made them lifelike, Greek sculptors sought to achieve not realism but a standard of ideal beauty. Polyclitus, a fifth-century sculptor, wrote a treatise (now lost) on proportion that he illustrated in a work known as the *Doryphoros*. His theory maintained that the use of ideal proportions, based on mathematical ratios found in nature, could produce an ideal human form, beautiful in its perfected and refined features. This search for ideal beauty was the dominant feature of classical sculpture.

The Greek Love of Wisdom   In classical Greece, Athens became the foremost intellectual and artistic center. Its reputation is perhaps strongest of all in philosophy, a Greek term that means "love of wisdom." Socrates, Plato, and Aristotle raised basic questions that have been debated for more than two thousand years; these are still largely the same philosophical questions we wrestle with today.

Socrates (469–399 B.C.E.) left no writings, but we know about him from his pupils. Socrates was a stonemason whose true love was philosophy. He taught a number of pupils, although not for pay, because he believed that the goal of education was solely to improve the individual. His approach, still known as the **Socratic method,** uses a question-and-answer technique to lead pupils to see things for themselves using their own reason. Socrates believed that all knowledge was within each person; only

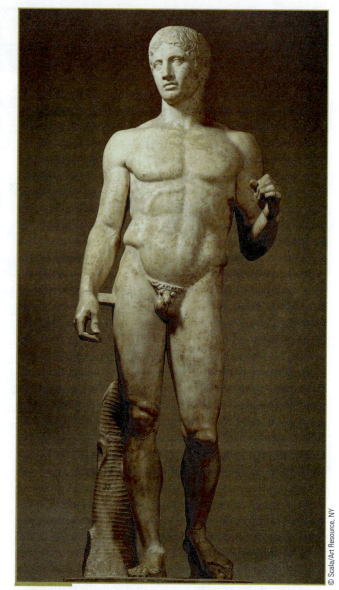

Doryphoros. This statue, known as the *Doryphoros,* or spear-carrier, is by the fifth-century B.C.E. sculptor Polyclitus, who believed it illustrated the ideal proportions of the human figure. Classical Greek sculpture moved away from the stiffness of earlier figures but retained the young male nude as the favorite subject matter. The statues became more lifelike, with relaxed poses and flexible, smooth-muscled bodies. The aim of sculpture, however, was not simply realism but rather the expression of ideal beauty.

critical examination was needed to call it forth. This was the real task of philosophy, since "the unexamined life is not worth living."

Socrates questioned authority, and this soon led him into trouble. Athens had had a tradition of free thought and inquiry, but defeat in the Peloponnesian War had created an environment intolerant of open debate and soul-searching. Socrates was accused and convicted of corrupting the youth of Athens by his teaching and sentenced to death.

One of Socrates' disciples was Plato (c. 429–347 B.C.E.), considered by many the greatest philosopher of Western civilization. Unlike his master Socrates, who wrote nothing,

Plato wrote a great deal. He was fascinated with the question of reality: How do we know what is real? According to Plato, a higher world of eternal, unchanging Ideas or Forms has always existed. To know these Forms is to know truth. These ideal Forms constitute reality and can be apprehended only by a trained mind, which, of course, is the goal of philosophy. The objects that we perceive with our senses are simply reflections of the ideal Forms. They are shadows; reality is in the Forms themselves.

Plato's ideas of government were set out in the dialogue titled *The Republic*. Based on his experience in Athens, Plato had come to distrust the workings of democracy. It was obvious to him that individuals could not attain an ethical life unless they lived in a just and rational state. Plato's search for the just state led him to construct an ideal state in which the population was divided into three basic groups. At the top was an upper class of philosopher-kings: "Unless . . . political power and philosophy meet together . . . there can be no rest from troubles . . . for states, nor yet, as I believe, for all mankind."[6] The second group were those who showed courage; they would be the warriors who protected society. All the rest made up the masses, essentially people driven not by wisdom or courage but by desire. They would be the producers of society—the artisans, tradespeople, and farmers. Contrary to common Greek custom, Plato also stressed that men and women should have the same education and equal access to all positions.

Plato established a school at Athens known as the Academy. One of his pupils, who studied there for twenty years, was Aristotle (384–322 B.C.E.). Aristotle did not accept Plato's theory of ideal Forms. Instead he believed that by examining individual objects, we can perceive their form and arrive at universal principles; but these principles are a part of things themselves and do not exist as a separate higher world of reality beyond material things. Aristotle's interests, then, lay in analyzing and classifying things based on thorough research and investigation. His interests were wide-ranging, and he wrote treatises on an enormous number of subjects: ethics, logic, politics, poetry, astronomy, geology, biology, and physics.

Like Plato, Aristotle wished for an effective form of government that would rationally direct human affairs. Unlike Plato, he did not seek an ideal state but tried to find the best form of government by a rational examination of existing governments. For his *Politics*, Aristotle examined the constitutions of 158 states and identified three good forms of government: monarchy, aristocracy, and constitutional government. He favored constitutional government as the best form for most people.

Aristotle's philosophical and political ideas played an enormous role in the development of Western thought during the Middle Ages (see Chapter 12). So did his ideas on women. Aristotle maintained that women were biologically inferior to men: "A woman is, as it were, an infertile male. She is female in fact on account of a kind of inadequacy." Therefore, according to Aristotle, women must be subordinated to men, not only in the community but also in marriage: "The association between husband and wife is clearly an aristocracy. The man rules by virtue of merit, and in the sphere that is his by right; but he hands over to his wife such matters as are suitable for her."[7]

Greek Religion

As was the case throughout the ancient world, Greek religion played an important role in Greek society and was intricately connected to every aspect of daily life; it was both social and practical. Public festivals, which originated from religious practices, served specific functions: boys were prepared to be warriors, girls to be mothers. Since religion was related to every aspect of life, citizens had to have a proper attitude toward the gods. Religion was a civic cult necessary for the well-being of the state. Temples dedicated to a god or goddess were the major buildings of Greek society.

The poetry of Homer gave an account of the gods that provided Greek religion with a definite structure. Over a period of time, most Greeks came to accept a common religion based on twelve chief gods and goddesses who were thought to live on Mount Olympus, the highest mountain in Greece. Among the twelve were Zeus, the chief god and father of many other gods; Athena, goddess of wisdom and crafts; Apollo, god of the sun and poetry; Aphrodite, goddess of love; and Poseidon, brother of Zeus and god of the seas and earthquakes.

Greek religion did not have a body of doctrine, nor did it focus on morality. It gave little or no hope of life after death for most people. Because the Greeks wanted the gods to look favorably on their activities, ritual assumed enormous importance in Greek religion. Prayers were often combined with gifts to the gods based on the principle "I give so that you, the gods, will give in return." Yet the Greeks were well aware of the capricious nature of the gods, who were assigned recognizably human qualities and often engaged in fickle or even vengeful behavior toward other deities or human beings.

Festivals also developed as a way to honor the gods and goddesses. Some of these (the Panhellenic celebrations) came to have international significance and were held at special locations, such as those dedicated to the worship of Zeus at Olympia or to Apollo at Delphi. Numerous events were held in honor of the gods at the great festivals, including athletic competitions to which all Greeks were invited. The first such games were held at the Olympic festival in 776 B.C.E. and then held every four years thereafter to honor Zeus. Initially, the Olympic contests consisted of foot races and wrestling, but later boxing, javelin throwing, and various other contests were added.

As another practical side of Greek religion, Greeks wanted to know the will of the gods. To do so, they made use of the oracle, a sacred shrine dedicated to a god or goddess who revealed the future. The most famous was the oracle of Apollo at Delphi, located on the side of Mount Parnassus, overlooking the Gulf of Corinth. At Delphi, a priestess, thought to be inspired by Apollo, listened to questions. Her responses were then interpreted

HOUSEHOLD MANAGEMENT AND THE ROLE OF THE ATHENIAN WIFE

FAMILY & SOCIETY

In the Athens of the fifth century B.C.E., a woman's place was in the home. She had two major responsibilities: the bearing and raising of children and the management of the household. In this dialogue on estate management, Xenophon relates the advice of an Attican gentleman on how to train a wife.

What does the selection from Xenophon tell you about the role of women in the Athenian household? How do these requirements compare with those applied in ancient India and ancient China?

Xenophon, *Oeconomicus*

[Ischomachus addresses his new wife.] For it seems to me, dear, that the gods with great discernment have coupled together male and female, as they are called, chiefly in order that they may form a perfect partnership in mutual service. For, in the first place, that the various species of living creatures may not fail, they are joined in wedlock for the production of children. Secondly, offspring to support them in old age is provided by this union, to human beings, at any rate. Thirdly, human beings live not in the open air, like beasts, but obviously need shelter. Nevertheless, those who mean to win stores to fill the covered place, have need of someone to work at the open-air occupations; since plowing, sowing, planting, and grazing are all such open-air employments; and these supply the needful food. . . . For he made

the man's body and mind more capable of enduring cold and heat, and journeys and campaigns; and therefore imposed on him the outdoor tasks. To the woman, since he has made her body less capable of such endurance, I take it that God has assigned the indoor tasks. And knowing that he had created in the woman and had imposed on her the nourishment of the infants, he meted out to her a larger portion of affection for newborn babes than to the man. . . . Now since we know, dear, what duties have been assigned to each of us by God, we must endeavor, each of us, to do the duties allotted to us as well as possible. . . .

Your duty will be to remain indoors and send out those servants whose work is outside, and superintend those who are to work indoors, and to receive the incomings, and distribute so much of them as must be spent, and watch over so much as is to be kept in store, and take care that the sum laid by for a year be not spent in a month. And when wool is brought to you, you must see that cloaks are made for those that want them. You must see too that the dry corn is in good condition for making food. One of the duties that fall to you, however, will perhaps seem rather thankless: you will have to see that any servant who is ill is cared for.

CENGAGENOW To read other works by Xenophon, enter the *CengageNOW* documents area using the access card that is available for *The Essential World History*.

---

by the priests and given in verse form to the person asking questions. Representatives of states and individuals traveled to Delphi to consult the oracle of Apollo. Responses were often enigmatic and at times even politically motivated. Croesus, the king of Lydia in Asia Minor who was known for his incredible wealth, sent messengers to the oracle at Delphi, asking "whether he shall go to war with the Persians." The oracle replied that if Croesus attacked the Persians, he would destroy a mighty empire. Overjoyed to hear these words, Croesus made war on the Persians but was crushed by his enemy. A mighty empire *was* destroyed—Croesus' own.

Daily Life in Classical Athens

The *polis* was, above all, a male community: only adult male citizens took part in public life. In Athens, this meant the exclusion of women, slaves, and foreign residents, or roughly 85 percent of the population of Attica. There were perhaps 150,000 citizens of Athens proper, of whom about 43,000 were adult males who exercised political power. Resident foreigners, who numbered about 35,000, received the protection of the laws but were also subject to some of the responsibilities of citizens, including military service and the funding of festivals. The remaining social group, the slaves, numbered around 100,000. Most slaves in Athens worked in the home as cooks and maids or worked

in the fields. Some were owned by the state and worked on public construction projects.

The Athenian economy was largely based on agriculture and trade. Athenians grew grains, vegetables, and fruit for local consumption. Grapes and olives were cultivated for wine and olive oil, which were used locally and also exported. The Athenians raised sheep and goats for wool and dairy products. Because of the size of the population and the lack of abundant fertile land, Athens had to import 50 to 80 percent of its grain, a staple in the Athenian diet. Trade was thus very important to the Athenian economy.

Family and Relationships   The family was a central institution in ancient Athens. It was composed of husband, wife, and children, along with other dependent relatives and slaves who were part of the economic unit. The family's primary social function was to produce new citizens.

Women were citizens who could participate in most religious cults and festivals, but they were otherwise excluded from public life. They could not own property beyond personal items and always had a male guardian. An Athenian woman was expected to be a good wife. Her foremost obligation was to bear children, especially male children who would preserve the family line. Moreover, a wife was to take care of her family and her house, either doing the household work herself or supervising the slaves who did the actual work (see the box above).

Male homosexuality was also a prominent feature of Athenian life. The Greek homosexual ideal was a relationship between a mature man and a young male. While the relationship was frequently physical, the Greeks also viewed it as educational. The older male (the "lover") won the love of his "beloved" through his value as a teacher and the devotion he demonstrated in training his charge. In a sense, this love relationship was seen as a way of initiating young males into the male world of political and military dominance. The Greeks did not feel that the coexistence of homosexual and heterosexual predilections created any special problems for individuals or their society.

The Rise of Macedonia and the Conquests of Alexander

While the Greek city-states were caught up in fighting each other, a new and ultimately powerful kingdom to their north was emerging in its own right. To the Greeks, the Macedonians were little more than barbarians, a mostly rural folk organized into tribes rather than city-states. Not until the late fifth century B.C.E. did Macedonia emerge as a kingdom of any importance. But when Philip II (359–336 B.C.E.) came to the throne, he built an efficient army and turned Macedonia into the strongest power in the Greek world—one that was soon drawn into the conflicts among the Greeks.

The Athenians at last took notice of the new contender. Fear of Philip led them to ally with a number of other Greek states and confront the Macedonians at the Battle of Chaeronea, near Thebes, in 338 B.C.E. The Macedonian army crushed the Greeks, and Philip quickly gained control of all Greece, bringing an end to the freedom of the Greek city-states. He insisted that the Greek states form a league and then cooperate with him in a war against Persia. Before Philip could undertake his invasion of Asia, however, he was assassinated, leaving the task to his son Alexander.

Alexander the Great

Alexander was only twenty when he became king of Macedonia. He was in many ways prepared to rule by his father, who had taken Alexander along on military campaigns and had given him control of the cavalry at Chaeronea. After his father's assassination, Alexander moved quickly to assert his authority, securing the Macedonian frontiers and quashing a rebellion in Greece. He then turned to his father's dream, the invasion of the Persian Empire.

Alexander's Conquests There is no doubt that Alexander was taking a chance in attacking Persia, which was still a strong state. In the spring of 334 B.C.E., Alexander entered Asia Minor with an army of some 37,000 men.

Bust of Alexander the Great. This bust of Alexander the Great is a Roman copy of the head of a statue, possibly by Lysippus. Alexander was partial to Lysippus' portraits, believing that the sculptor was the only one who had the ability to portray Alexander's true essence. Alexander claimed to be descended from Heracles, a Greek hero worshiped as a god, and as pharaoh of Egypt, he gained recognition as a living deity. It is reported that one of his statues, now lost, showed Alexander gazing at Zeus; on the base of the statue were the words "I place the earth under my sway; you, O Zeus, keep Olympus."

About half were Macedonians, the rest Greeks and other allies. The cavalry, which would play an important role as a striking force, numbered about 5,000. By the following spring, the entire western half of Asia Minor was in Alexander's hands (see Map 4.2). Meanwhile, the Persian king, Darius III, mobilized his forces to stop Alexander's army, but the subsequent Battle of Issus resulted in yet another Macedonian success. Alexander then turned south, and by the winter of 332, Syria, Palestine, and Egypt were under his control.

In 331 B.C.E., Alexander turned east and fought a decisive battle with the Persians at Gaugamela, northwest of Babylon. After his victory, Alexander entered Babylon and then proceeded to the Persian capitals at Susa and Persepolis, where he took possession of vast quantities of gold and silver. By 330, Alexander was again on the march, pursuing Darius. After Darius was killed by one of his own men, Alexander took the title and office of the Great King of the Persians. Over the next three years, he moved east and northeast, as far as modern Pakistan. By

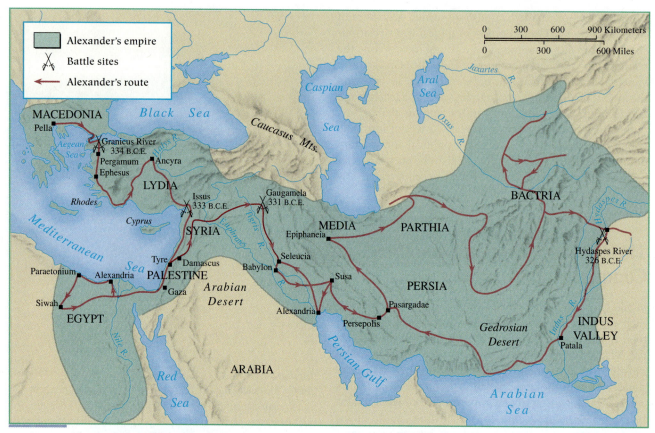

MAP 4.2 **The Conquests of Alexander the Great.** In just twelve years, Alexander the Great conquered vast territories. Dominating lands from west of the Nile to east of the Indus, he brought the Persian Empire, Egypt, and much of the Middle East under his control and laid the foundations for the Hellenistic world. **?** Approximately how far did he and his troops travel during those twelve years, and what kinds of terrain did they encounter on their journey?

summer 327 B.C.E., he had entered India, which at that time was divided into a number of warring states. In 326 B.C.E., Alexander and his armies arrived in the plains of northwestern India. At the Battle of the Hydaspes River, Alexander won a brutally fought battle (see the box on p. 91). When Alexander made clear his determination to march east to conquer more of India, his soldiers, weary of campaigning year after year, mutinied and refused to go further. Alexander returned to Babylon, where he planned more campaigns. But in June 323 B.C.E., weakened by wounds, fever, and probably excessive alcohol, he died at the age of thirty-two.

The Legacy of Alexander Alexander is one of the most puzzling great figures in history. Historians relying on the same sources give vastly different pictures of him. Some portray him as an idealistic visionary and others as a ruthless Machiavellian. How did Alexander the Great view himself? We know that he sought to imitate Achilles, the warrior-hero of Homer's *Iliad*. Alexander kept a copy of the *Iliad*—and a dagger—under his pillow. He also claimed to be descended from

Heracles, the Greek hero who came to be worshiped as a god.

Regardless of his ideals, motives, or views about himself, one fact stands out: Alexander ushered in a new age, the Hellenistic era. The word *Hellenistic* is derived from a Greek word meaning "to imitate Greeks." It is an appropriate term to describe an age that saw the extension of the Greek language and ideas to the non-Greek world of the Middle East. Alexander's destruction of the Persian monarchy opened up opportunities for Greek engineers, intellectuals, merchants, administrators, and soldiers. Those who followed Alexander and his successors participated in a new political unity based on the principle of monarchy. His vision of empire no doubt inspired the Romans, who were the ultimate heirs of Alexander's political legacy.

But Alexander also left a cultural legacy. As a result of his conquests, Greek language, art, architecture, and literature spread throughout the Middle East. The urban centers of the Hellenistic age, many founded by Alexander and his successors, became springboards for the diffusion of Greek culture. While the Greeks spread

ALEXANDER MEETS AN INDIAN KING

INTERACTION & EXCHANGE

In his campaigns in India, Alexander fought a number of difficult battles. At the Battle of the Hydaspes River, he faced a strong opponent in the Indian king Porus. After defeating Porus, Alexander treated him with respect, according to Arrian, Alexander's ancient biographer.

What do we learn from Arrian's account about Alexander's military skills and Indian methods of fighting?

Arrian, *The Campaigns of Alexander*

Throughout the action Porus had proved himself a man indeed, not only as a commander but as a soldier of the truest courage. When he saw his cavalry cut to pieces, most of his infantry dead, and his elephants killed or roaming riderless and bewildered about the field, his behaviour was very different from that of the Persian King Darius: unlike Darius, he did not lead the scramble to save his own skin, but so long as a single unit of his men held together, fought bravely on. It was only when he was himself wounded that he turned the elephant on which he rode and began to withdraw. . . . Alexander, anxious to save the life of this great soldier, sent . . . [to him] an Indian named Meroes, a man he had been told had long been Porus's friend. Porus listened to Meroes's message, stopped his elephant, and dismounted; he was much distressed by thirst, so when he had

revived himself by drinking, he told Meroes to conduct him with all speed to Alexander.

Alexander, informed of his approach, rode out to meet him. . . . When they met, he reined in his horse, and looked at his adversary with admiration: he was a magnificent figure of a man, over seven feet high and of great personal beauty; his bearing had lost none of its pride; his air was of one brave man meeting another, of a king in the presence of a king, with whom he had fought honourably for his kingdom.

Alexander was the first to speak. "What," he said, "do you wish that I should do with you?" "Treat me as a king ought," Porus is said to have replied. "For my part," said Alexander, pleased by his answer, "your request shall be granted. But is there not something you would wish for yourself? Ask it." "Everything," said Porus, "is contained in this one request."

The dignity of these words gave Alexander even more pleasure, and he restored to Porus his sovereignty over his subjects, adding to his realm other territory of even greater extent. Thus he did indeed use a brave man as a king ought, and from that time forward found him in every way a loyal friend.

CENGAGENOW To read more from Arrian's *Campaigns of Alexander*, enter the *CengageNOW* documents area using the access card that is available for *The Essential World History*.

---

their culture in the East, they were also inevitably influenced by Eastern ways. Thus, Alexander's legacy was one of the earmarks of the Hellenistic era: the clash and fusion of different cultures.

The World of the Hellenistic Kingdoms

The united empire that Alexander assembled through his conquests crumbled soon after his death. All too soon, the most important Macedonian generals were engaged in a struggle for power, and by 300 B.C.E., four Hellenistic kingdoms had emerged as the successors to Alexander (see Map 4.3): Macedonia under the Antigonid dynasty, Syria and the East under the Seleucids, the Attalid kingdom of Pergamum in western Asia Minor, and Egypt under the Ptolemies. All were eventually conquered by the Romans.

Political Institutions and the Role of Cities

Alexander had planned to fuse Macedonians, Greeks, and easterners in his new empire by using Persians as officials and encouraging his soldiers to marry native women. The Hellenistic monarchs who succeeded him, however, relied only on Greeks and Macedonians to form the new ruling

class. Even those easterners who did advance to important government posts had learned Greek, the language in which all government business was transacted. The Greek ruling class was determined to maintain its privileged position.

Alexander had founded numerous new cities and military settlements, and Hellenistic kings did likewise. The new population centers varied considerably in size and importance. Military settlements, intended to maintain order, might consist of only a few hundred men. The new independent cities attracted thousands of people. One of these new cities, Alexandria in Egypt, had become the largest city in the Mediterranean region by the first century B.C.E.

Hellenistic rulers encouraged a massive spread of Greek colonists to the Middle East. Greeks and Macedonians provided not only recruits for the army but also a pool of civilian administrators and workers who contributed to economic development. Even architects, engineers, dramatists, and actors were in demand in the new Greek cities. Many Greeks and Macedonians were quick to see the advantages of moving to the new urban centers and gladly sought their fortunes in the Middle East. The Greek cities of the Hellenistic era became the chief agents in the spread of Greek culture in the Middle East—as far east, in fact, as modern Afghanistan and India.

Reign of Philip II	359–336 B.C.E.
Battle of Chaeronea; conquest of Greece	338 B.C.E.
Reign of Alexander the Great	336–323 B.C.E.
Alexander's invasion of Asia	334 B.C.E..
Battle of Gaugamela	331 B.C.E.
Fall of Persepolis	330 B.C.E.
Alexander's entry into India	327 B.C.E.
Death of Alexander	323 B.C.E.

Culture in the Hellenistic World

Although the Hellenistic kingdoms encompassed vast territories and many diverse peoples, the Greeks provided a sense of unity as a result of the diffusion of Greek culture throughout the Hellenistic world. The Hellenistic era was a period of considerable cultural accomplishment in many areas, especially science and philosophy. Although these achievements occurred throughout the Hellenistic world, certain centers, especially the great city of Alexandria,

stood out. Alexandria became home to poets, writers, philosophers, and scientists—scholars of all kinds. The library there became the largest in ancient times, with more than 500,000 scrolls.

The founding of new cities and the rebuilding of old ones provided numerous opportunities for Greek architects and sculptors. The Hellenistic monarchs were particularly eager to spend their money to beautify and adorn the cities within their states. The buildings of the Greek homeland—gymnasiums, baths, theaters, and temples—lined the streets of these cities.

Both Hellenistic monarchs and rich citizens patronized sculptors. Hellenistic sculptors traveled throughout this world, attracted by the material rewards offered by wealthy patrons. These sculptors maintained the technical skill of the classical period, but they moved away from the idealism of fifth-century classicism to a more emotional and realistic art, which is evident in numerous statues of old women, drunks, and little children at play. Hellenistic artistic styles even affected artists in India (see the comparative illustration on p. 93).

A Golden Age of Science   The Hellenistic era witnessed a more conscious separation of science from

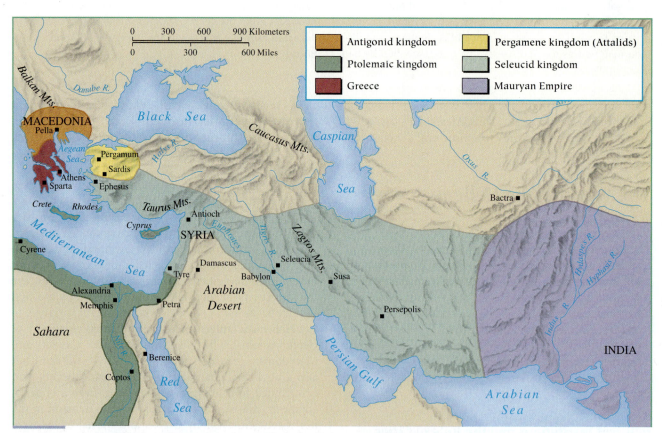

MAP 4.3   **The World of the Hellenistic Kingdoms.** Alexander died unexpectedly at the age of thirty-two and did not designate a successor. Upon his death, his generals struggled for power, eventually establishing four monarchies that spread Hellenistic culture and fostered trade and economic development. ❓ Based solely on the map, which kingdom do you think was the most prosperous and powerful? Why? 🌎 **View an animated version of this map or related maps at** http://worldrc.wadsworth.com/

The Art Archive/Kanellopoulos Museum Athens/Dagli Orti.

© Borromeo/Art Resource, NY

Hellenistic Sculpture and a Greek-Style Buddha. Greek architects and sculptors were highly valued throughout the Hellenistic world. Shown on the left is a terra-cotta statuette of a draped young woman, made as a tomb offering near Thebes, probably around 300 B.C.E. The incursion of Alexander into the western part of India resulted in some Greek cultural influences there, especially during the Hellenistic era. During the first century B.C.E., Indian sculptors in Gandhara, which today is part of Pakistan, began to create statues of the Buddha. The Buddhist Gandharan style combined Indian and Hellenistic artistic traditions, which is evident in the stone sculpture of Buddha on the right. Note the wavy hair topped by a bun tied with a ribbon, also a feature of earlier statues of Greek deities. This Buddha is also seen wearing a Greek-style toga.

philosophy. In classical Greece, what we would call the physical and life sciences had been divisions of philosophical inquiry. Nevertheless, by the time of Aristotle, the Greeks had already established an important principle of scientific investigation—empirical research or systematic observation as the basis for generalization. In the Hellenistic age, the sciences tended to be studied in their own right.

By far the most famous of the scientists of the Hellenistic period was Archimedes (287–212 B.C.E.). Archimedes was especially important for his work on the geometry of spheres and cylinders and for establishing the value of the mathematical constant pi. Archimedes was also a practical inventor. He may have devised the so-called Archimedean screw used to pump water out of mines and to lift irrigation water. During the Roman siege of his native city of Syracuse, he constructed a number of devices to thwart the attackers. Archimedes' accomplishments inspired a wealth of semilegendary stories. Supposedly, he discovered specific gravity by observing the water he displaced in his bath and became so excited by his realization that he jumped out of the water and ran home naked, shouting, "Eureka!" ("I have found it"). He is said to have emphasized the importance of levers by proclaiming to the king of Syracuse: "Give me a lever and a place to stand on, and I will move the earth." The king was so impressed that he encouraged Archimedes to lower his sights and build defensive weapons instead.

Philosophy While Alexandria became the renowned cultural center of the Hellenistic world, Athens remained the prime center for philosophy. Even after Alexander the Great, the home of Socrates, Plato, and Aristotle continued to attract the most illustrious philosophers from the Greek world, who chose to establish their schools there. New schools of philosophical thought reinforced Athens's reputation as a philosophical center.

Epicurus (341–270 B.C.E.), the founder of **Epicureanism,** established a school in Athens near the end of the fourth century B.C.E. Epicurus believed that human beings were free to follow self-interest as a basic motivating force. Happiness was the goal of life, and the means to achieve it was the pursuit of pleasure, the only true good. But pleasure was not meant in a physical, hedonistic sense (which is what our word *epicurean* has come to mean) but rather referred to freedom from emotional turmoil and worry. To achieve this kind of pleasure, one had to free oneself from public affairs and politics. But this was not a renunciation of all social life, for to Epicurus, a life could be complete only when it was based on friendship. Epicurus' own life in Athens was an embodiment of his teachings. He and his friends created their own private community where they could pursue their ideal of true happiness.

Another school of thought was **Stoicism,** which became the most popular philosophy of the Hellenistic world and later flourished in the Roman Empire as well. It was the product of a teacher named Zeno (335–263 B.C.E.), who came to Athens and began to teach in a public colonnade known as the Painted Portico (the *Stoa Poikile*—hence Stoicism). Like Epicureanism, Stoicism was concerned with how individuals find happiness. But Stoics took a radically different approach to the problem. To them, happiness, the supreme good, could be found only by living in harmony with the divine will, by which people gained inner peace. Life's problems could not disturb these people, and they could bear whatever life offered (hence our word *stoic*). Unlike Epicureans, Stoics did not believe in the need to separate oneself from the world and politics. Public service was regarded as noble, and the real Stoic was a good citizen and could even be a good government official.

Both Epicureanism and Stoicism focused primarily on human happiness, and their popularity would suggest a fundamental change in the Greek lifestyle. In the classical Greek world, the happiness of individuals and the meaning of life were closely associated with the life of the *polis*. One found fulfillment in the community. In the Hellenistic kingdoms, the sense that one could find fulfillment through life in the *polis* had weakened. People sought new philosophies that offered personal happiness, and in the cosmopolitan world of the Hellenistic states, with their mixtures of peoples, a new openness to thoughts of universality could also emerge. For some people, Stoicism embodied this larger sense of community.

CONCLUSION

*U*NLIKE THE GREAT CENTRALIZED EMPIRES of the Persians and the Chinese, ancient Greece consisted of a large number of small, independent city-states, most of which had only a few thousand inhabitants. Yet these ancient Greeks created a civilization that was the fountainhead of Western culture. Socrates, Plato, and Aristotle established the foundations of Western philosophy. Western literary forms are largely derived from Greek poetry and drama. Greek notions of harmony, proportion, and beauty have remained the touchstones for all subsequent Western art. A rational method of inquiry, so important to modern science, was conceived in ancient Greece. Many political terms are Greek in origin, and so are concepts of the rights and duties of citizenship, especially as they were conceived in Athens, the world's first great democracy. Especially during their classical period, the Greeks raised and debated the fundamental questions about the purpose of human existence, the structure of human society, and the nature of the universe that have concerned thinkers ever since.

Yet despite all these achievements, there remains an element of tragedy about Greek civilization. Notwithstanding their brilliant accomplishments, the Greeks were unable to rise above the divisions and rivalries that caused them to fight each other and undermine their own civilization. Of course, their cultural contributions have outlived their political struggles. And the Hellenistic era, which emerged after the Greek city-states had lost their independence, made possible the spread of Greek ideas to larger areas.

During the Hellenistic period, Greek culture extended throughout the Middle East and made an impact wherever it was carried. Although the Hellenistic world achieved a degree of political stability, by the late third century B.C.E. signs of decline were beginning to multiply. Few Greeks realized the danger to the Hellenistic world of the growing power of Rome. But soon the Romans would inherit Alexander's empire and Greek culture, and we now turn to them to try to understand what made them such successful conquerors.

CHAPTER NOTES

1. Xenophon, *Symposium*, trans. O. J. Todd (Harmondsworth, England, 1946), 3:5.
2. Quoted in Thomas R. Martin, *Ancient Greece* (New Haven, Conn., 1996), p. 62.
3. The words from Plutarch are quoted in E. Fantham et al., *Women in the Classsical World* (New York, 1994), p. 64.
4. Sophocles, *Oedipus the King*, trans. David Grene (Chicago, 1959), pp. 68–69.
5. Sophocles, *Antigone*, trans. Don Taylor (London, 1986), p. 146.
6. Plato, *The Republic*, trans. F. M. Cornford (New York, 1945), pp. 178–179.
7. Quotations from Aristotle are in Sue Blundell, *Women in Ancient Greece* (London, 1995), pp. 106, 186.

SUGGESTED READING

Good general introductions to Greek history include **T. R. Martin**, *Ancient Greece* (New Haven, Conn., 1996); **P. Cartledge,** *The Cambridge Illustrated History of Ancient Greece* (Cambridge, 1998); and **S. B. Pomeroy** et al., *Ancient Greece: A Political, Social, and Cultural History* (New York, 1998).

Early Greek history is examined in **O. Murray,** *Early Greece,* 2d ed. (Cambridge, Mass., 1993). On colonization, see **J. Boardman,** *The Greeks Overseas,* rev. ed. (Baltimore, 1980). On tyranny, see **J. F. McGlew,** *Tyranny and Political Culture in Ancient Greece* (Ithaca, N.Y., 1993). On Sparta, see **P. Cartledge,** *Spartan Reflections* (Berkeley, Calif., 2001) and *The Spartans* (New York, 2003). On early Athens, see the still valuable **A. Jones,** *Athenian Democracy* (London, 1957), and **R. Osborne,** *Demos* (Oxford, 1985). The

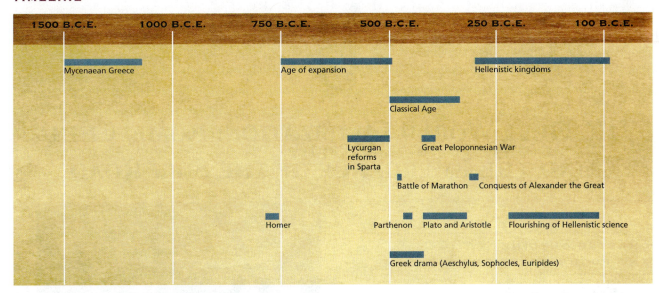

1500 B.C.E.	1000 B.C.E.	750 B.C.E.	500 B.C.E.	250 B.C.E.	100 B.C.E.

Mycenaean Greece

Age of expansion

Hellenistic kingdoms

Classical Age

Lycurgan reforms in Sparta

Great Peloponnesian War

Battle of Marathon   Conquests of Alexander the Great

Homer

Parthenon   Plato and Aristotle

Flourishing of Hellenistic science

Greek drama (Aeschylus, Sophocles, Euripides)

Persian Wars are examined in **P. Green,** *The Greco-Persian Wars* (Berkeley, Calif., 1996).

A general history of classical Greece can be found in **J. R. Davies,** *Democracy and Classical Greece,* 2d ed. (Cambridge, Mass., 1993). Important works on Athens include **C. W. Fornara** and **L. J. Samons II,** *Athens from Cleisthenes to Pericles* (Berkeley, Calif., 1991); **D. Stockton,** *The Classical Athenian Democracy* (Oxford, 1990); and **D. Kagan,** *Pericles of Athens and the Birth of Democracy* (New York, 1991). The best way to examine the Great Peloponnesian War is to read the work of Thucydides, *History of the Peloponnesian War,* trans. **R. Warner** (Harmondsworth, England, 1954). An excellent recent history is **D. Kagan,** *The Peloponnesian War* (New York, 2003).

A good brief study of Greek art is **J. Boardman,** *Greek Art* (London, 1985). On sculpture, see **A. Stewart,** *Greek Sculpture: An Exploration* (New Haven, Conn., 1990). A basic survey of architecture is **H. W. Lawrence,** *Greek Architecture,* rev. ed. (Harmondsworth, England, 1983). On Greek drama, see the general work by **J. De Romilly,** *A Short History of Greek Literature* (Chicago, 1985). On Greek philosophy, a detailed study is available in **W. K. C. Guthrie,** *A History of Greek Philosophy,* 6 vols. (Cambridge, 1962–1981). On Greek religion, see **J. N. Bremmer,** *Greek Religion* (Oxford, 1994).

On the family and women, see **C. B. Patterson,** *The Family in Greek History* (New York, 1998); **E. Fantham,** et al., *Women in the Classical World* (New York, 1994); and **S. Blundell,** *Women in Ancient Greece* (Cambridge, Mass., 1995).

The best general surveys of the Hellenistic era are **F. W. Walbank,** *The Hellenistic World* (Cambridge, Mass., 1993), and **G. Shipley,** *The Greek World After Alexander, 323–30 B.C.* (New York, 2000). There are considerable differences of opinion on Alexander the Great. Good biographies include **R. L. Fox,** *Alexander the Great* (London, 1973); **P. Cartledge,** *Alexander the Great* (New York, 2004); **N. G. L. Hammond,** *The Genius of Alexander the Great* (Chapel Hill, N.C., 1997); **G. M. Rogers,** *Alexander* (New York, 2004); and **P. Green,** *Alexander of Macedon* (Berkeley, Calif., 1991).

The various Hellenistic monarchies can be examined in **N. G. L. Hammond** and **F. W. Walbank,** *A History of Macedonia,* vol. 3, *336–167 B.C.* (Oxford, 1988); **S. Sherwin-White** and **A. Kuhrt,** *From Samarkand to Sardis: A New Approach to the Seleucid Empire* (Berkeley, Calif., 1993); and **N. Lewis,** *Greeks in Ptolemaic Egypt* (Oxford, 1986).

For a general introduction to Hellenistic culture, see **J. Onians,** *Art and Thought in the Hellenistic Age* (London, 1979). The best general survey of Hellenistic philosophy is **A. A. Long,** *Hellenistic Philosophy: Stoics, Epicureans, Skeptics,* 2d ed. (London, 1986). A superb work on Hellenistic science is **G. E. R. Lloyd,** *Greek Science After Aristotle* (London, 1973). On the entry of Rome into the Hellenistic world, see the basic work by **E. S. Gruen,** *The Hellenistic World and the Coming of Rome,* 2 vols. (Berkeley, Calif., 1984).

 InfoTrac College Edition

Visit this chapter's InfoTrac College Edition/Research activities at the *Essential World History* Companion Website for activities related to ancient Greece.

CENGAGENOW **for Duiker and Spielvogel's *The Essential World History, Third Edition***

Enter *CengageNOW* using the access card that is available with this text. *CengageNOW* will assist you in understanding the content in this chapter with lesson plans generated for your needs, as well as provide you with a connection to the *Wadsworth World History Resource Center* (see description below for details).

WORLD HISTORY
RESOURCE CENTER

Enter the Resource Center using either your *CengageNOW* access card or your standalone access card for the *Wadsworth World History Resource Center.* Organized by topic, this website includes quizzes; images; over 350 primary source documents; interactive simulations, maps, and timelines; movie explorations; and a wealth of other resources. You can read the following documents, and many more, at **http://worldrc.wadsworth.com/**

Homer, *Odyssey,* Bk. 1

Plato, *Republic,* Bks. 5 and 6

Visit the *Essential World History* Companion Website for chapter quizzes and more.

academic.cengage.com/history/duiker

THE FIRST WORLD CIVILIZATION: ROME, CHINA, AND THE EMERGENCE OF THE SILK ROAD

CHAPTER OUTLINE AND FOCUS QUESTIONS

Early Rome and the Republic

- What policies and institutions help explain the Romans' success in conquering Italy? How did Rome achieve its empire from 264 to 133 B.C.E., and what problems did Rome face as a result of its growing empire?

The Roman Empire at Its Height

- What were the chief features of the Roman Empire at its height in the second century C.E.?

Crisis and the Late Empire

- What reforms did Diocletian and Constantine institute, and to what extent were the reforms successful?

Transformation of the Roman World: The Development of Christianity

- What characteristics of Christianity enabled it to grow and ultimately to triumph?

The Glorious Han Empire (202 B.C.E.–221 C.E.)

- What were the chief features of the Han Empire?

CRITICAL THINKING

- In what ways were the Roman Empire and the Han Chinese Empire similar, and in what ways were they different?

Horatius defending the bridge as envisioned by Charles Le Brun, a seventeenth-century French painter

ALTHOUGH THE ASSYRIANS, PERSIANS, AND INDIANS under the Mauryan dynasty had created empires, they were neither as large nor as well controlled as the Han and Roman Empires that flourished at the beginning of the first millennium C.E. They were the largest political entities the world had yet seen. The Han Empire extended from Central Asia to the Pacific Ocean; the Roman Empire encompassed the lands around the Mediterranean, parts of the Middle East, and western and central Europe. Although there were no diplomatic contacts between the two civilizations, the Silk Road linked the two great empires together commercially.

Roman history is the remarkable story of how a group of Latin-speaking people, who established a small community on a plain called Latium in central Italy, went on to conquer all of Italy and then the entire Mediterranean world. Why were the Romans able to do this? Scholars do not really know all the answers, but the Romans had their own explanation. Early Roman history is filled with legendary tales of the heroes who made Rome great. One of the best known is the story of Horatius at the bridge. Threatened by attack from the neighboring Etruscans, Roman farmers abandoned their fields and moved into the city, where they would be protected by the walls. One weak point in the Roman defenses, however, was a wooden bridge over the Tiber River. Horatius was on guard at the bridge when a sudden assault by the Etruscans caused many Roman troops to throw down their weapons and flee. Horatius urged them to make a stand at the bridge; when they hesitated, he told them to destroy the bridge behind him while he held the Etruscans back. Astonished at the sight of a single defender, the confused Etruscans threw their spears at Horatius, who caught them on his shield and barred the way. By the time the Etruscans were about to overwhelm the lone defender, the Roman soldiers had brought down the bridge. Horatius then dived fully armed into the water and swam safely to the other side through a hail of arrows. Rome had been saved by the courageous act of a Roman who knew his duty and was determined to carry it out. Courage, duty, determination—these qualities would serve the many Romans who believed that it was their divine mission to rule nations and peoples. As one writer proclaimed: "By heaven's will, my Rome shall be capital of the world." ◇

Early Rome and the Republic

Italy is a peninsula extending about 750 miles from north to south (see Map 5.1). It is not very wide, however, averaging about 120 miles across. The Apennines form a ridge down the middle of Italy that divides west from east. Nevertheless, Italy has some fairly large fertile plains that are ideal for farming. Most important are the Po River valley in the north; the plain of Latium, on which Rome was located; and Campania to the south of Latium. To the east of the Italian peninsula is the Adriatic Sea and to the west the Tyrrhenian Sea, bounded by the large islands of Corsica and Sardinia. Sicily lies just west of the "toe" of the boot-shaped Italian peninsula.

Geography had an impact on Roman history. Although the Apennines bisected Italy, they were less rugged than the mountain ranges of Greece and did not divide the peninsula into many small isolated communities. Italy also possessed considerably more productive agricultural land than Greece, enabling it to support a large population. Rome's location was favorable from a geographic point of view. Located 18 miles inland on the Tiber River, Rome had access to the sea and yet was far enough inland to be safe from pirates. Built on seven hills, it was easily defended.

Moreover, the Italian peninsula juts into the Mediterranean, making Italy an important crossroads between the western and eastern ends of the sea. Once Rome had unified Italy, involvement in Mediterranean affairs was natural. And after the Romans had conquered their Mediterranean empire, governing it was made easier by Italy's central location.

MAP 5.1 **Ancient Italy.** Ancient Italy was home to several groups. Both the Etruscans in the north and the Greeks in the south had a major influence on the development of Rome. ❓ Once Rome conquered the Etruscans, Sabines, Samnites, and other local groups, what aspects of the Italian peninsula helped make it defensible against outside enemies? 🌐 **View an animated version of this map or related maps at** http://worldrc.wadsworth.com/

Early Rome

According to Roman legend, Rome was founded by twin brothers, Romulus and Remus, in 753 B.C.E., and archaeologists have found that by the eighth century B.C.E., a village of huts had been built on the tops of Rome's hills. The early Romans, basically a pastoral people, spoke Latin, which, like Greek, belongs to the Indo-European family of languages (see Table 1.2 in Chapter 1). The Roman historical tradition also maintained that early Rome (753–509 B.C.E.) had been under the control of seven kings and that two of the last three had been Etruscans, people who lived north of Rome in Etruria. Historians believe that the king list may have some historical accuracy. What is certain is that Rome did fall under the influence of the Etruscans for about a hundred years during the period of the kings and that by the beginning of the sixth century, under Etruscan influence, Rome began to emerge as a city. The Etruscans were

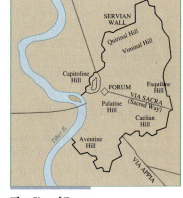

The City of Rome

CINCINNATUS SAVES ROME: A ROMAN MORALITY TALE

POLITICS & GOVERNMENT

There is perhaps no better account of how the virtues of duty and simplicity enabled good Roman citizens to prevail during the travails of the fifth century B.C.E. than Livy's account of Cincinnatus. He was chosen dictator, supposedly in 457 B.C.E., to defend Rome against the attacks of the Aequi. The position of dictator was a temporary expedient used only in emergencies; the consuls would resign, and a leader with unlimited power would be appointed for a limited period (usually six months). In this account, Cincinnatus did his duty, defeated the Aequi, and returned to his simple farm in just fifteen days.

What values did Livy emphasize in his account of Cincinnatus? How important were those values to Rome's success? Why did Livy say he wrote his history? As a writer in the Augustan Age, would he have pleased or displeased Augustus with such a purpose?

Livy, *The Early History of Rome*

The city was thrown into a state of turmoil, and the general alarm was as great as if Rome herself were surrounded. Nautius was sent for, but it was quickly decided that he was not the man to inspire full confidence; the situation evidently called for a dictator, and, with no dissentient voice, Lucius Quinctius Cincinnatus was named for the post.

Now I would solicit the particular attention of those numerous people who imagine that money is everything in this world, and that rank and ability are inseparable from wealth: let them observe that Cincinnatus, the one man in whom Rome reposed all her hope of survival, was at that moment working a little three-acre farm . . . west of the Tiber, just opposite the spot where the shipyards are today. A mission from the city found him at work on his land—digging a ditch, maybe, or plowing. Greetings were exchanged, and he was asked—with a prayer for divine blessing on himself and his country—to put on his toga and hear the Senate's instructions. This naturally surprised him, and, asking if all were well, he told his wife Racilia to run to their cottage and fetch his toga. The toga was brought, and wiping the grimy sweat from his hands and face he put it on; at once the envoys from the city saluted him, with congratulations, as Dictator, invited him to enter Rome, and informed him of the terrible danger of Municius' army. A state vessel was waiting for him on the river, and on the city bank he was welcomed by his three sons who had come to meet him, then by other kinsmen and friends, and finally by nearly the whole body of senators. Closely attended by all these people and preceded by his lictors he was then escorted to his residence through streets lined with great crowds of common folk who, be it said, were by no means so pleased to see the new Dictator, as they thought his power excessive and dreaded the way in which he was likely to use it.

[Cincinnatus proceeds to raise an army, march out, and defeat the Aequi.]

In Rome the Senate was convened by Quintus Fabius the City Prefect, and a decree was passed inviting Cincinnatus to enter in triumph with his troops. The chariot he rode in was preceded by the enemy commanders and the military standards, and followed by his army loaded with its spoils. . . . Cincinnatus finally resigned after holding office for fifteen days, having originally accepted it for a period of six months.

CENGAGENOW To read more of Livy's writings, enter the *CengageNOW* documents area using the access card that is available for *The Essential World History.*

---

responsible for an outstanding building program. They constructed the first roadbed of the chief street through Rome, the Sacred Way, before 575 B.C.E. and oversaw the development of temples, markets, shops, streets, and houses. By 509 B.C.E., supposedly when the monarchy was overthrown and a republican form of government was established, a new Rome had emerged, essentially a result of the fusion of Etruscan and native Roman elements. After Rome had expanded over its seven hills and the valleys in between, the Servian Wall was built in the fourth century B.C.E. to surround the city.

The Roman Republic

The transition from monarchy to a republican government was not easy. Rome felt threatened by enemies from every direction and, in the process of meeting these threats, embarked on a military course that led to the conquest of the entire Italian peninsula.

The Roman Conquest of Italy At the beginning of the Republic, Rome was surrounded by enemies, including the Latin communities on the plain of Latium. If we are to believe Livy, one of the chief ancient sources for the history of the early Roman Republic, Rome was engaged in almost continuous warfare with these enemies for the next hundred years. In his account, Livy provided a detailed narrative of Roman efforts. Many of his stories were legendary in character; writing in the first century B.C.E., he used his stories to teach Romans the moral values and virtues that had made Rome great. These included tenacity, duty, courage, and especially discipline (see the box above).

By 340 B.C.E., Rome had crushed the Latin states in Latium. During the next fifty years, the Romans waged a successful struggle with hill peoples from central Italy and then came into direct contact with the Greek communities. The Greeks had arrived on the Italian peninsula in large numbers during the age of Greek colonization (750–550 B.C.E.; see Chapter 4). Initially, the Greeks settled

© Larry Mulvehill/Photo Researchers, Inc.

© China Tourism Press/Getty Images

COMPARATIVE ILLUSTRATION

Roman and Chinese Roads. The Romans built a remarkable system of roads. After laying a foundation with gravel, which allowed for drainage, the Roman builders placed flagstones, closely fitted together. Unlike other peoples who built similar kinds of roads, the Romans did not follow the contours of the land but made their roads as straight as possible to facilitate communications and transportation, especially for military purposes. Seen here is a view of the Via Appia (Appian Way), built in 312 B.C.E. under the leadership of the censor and consul Appius Claudius (Roman roads were often named after the great Roman families who encouraged their construction). The Via Appia (shown on the map) was meant to make it easy for Roman armies to march from Rome to the newly conquered city of Capua, a distance of 152 miles. Under the Empire, roads were extended to provinces throughout the Mediterranean, parts of western and eastern Europe, and into western Asia. By the beginning of the fourth century C.E., the Roman Empire contained 372 major roads covering 50,000 miles.

Like the Roman Empire, the Han Empire relied on roads constructed with stone slabs for the movement of military forces. The First Emperor of Qin was responsible for the construction of 4,350 miles of roads, and by the end of the second century C.E., China had almost 22,000 miles of roads. Although roads in both the Roman and Chinese Empires were originally constructed for military purposes, they came to be used to facilitate communications and commercial traffic.

in southern Italy and then crept around the coast and up the peninsula. The Greeks had much influence on Rome. They cultivated olives and grapes, passed on their alphabet, and provided artistic and cultural models through their sculpture, architecture, and literature. By 267 B.C.E., the Romans had completed the conquest of southern Italy by defeating the Greek cities. After crushing the remaining Etruscan states to the north in 264 B.C.E., Rome had conquered most of Italy.

To rule Italy, the Romans devised the Roman Confederation. Under this system, Rome allowed some peoples—especially the Latins—to have full Roman citizenship. Most of the remaining communities were made allies. They remained free to run their own local affairs but were required to provide soldiers for Rome. Moreover, the Romans made it clear that loyal allies could improve their status and even have hope of becoming

Roman citizens. The Romans had found a way to give conquered peoples a stake in Rome's success.

In the course of their expansion throughout Italy, the Romans had pursued consistent policies that help explain their success. The Romans were superb diplomats who excelled in making the correct diplomatic decisions. In addition, the Romans were not only good soldiers but also persistent ones. The loss of an army or a fleet did not cause them to quit but spurred them on to build new armies and new fleets. Finally, the Romans had a practical sense of strategy. As they conquered, the Romans established colonies—fortified towns—at strategic locations throughout Italy. By building roads to these settlements and connecting them, the Romans created an impressive communications and military network that enabled them to rule effectively and efficiently (see the comparative illustration "Roman and Chinese Roads" above). By insisting on military service from the allies in the Roman Confederation, Rome essentially mobilized the entire military manpower of all Italy for its wars.

The Roman State   After the overthrow of the monarchy, Roman nobles, eager to maintain their position of power, established a republican form of government. The chief executive officers of the Roman Republic were the **consuls** and **praetors.** Two consuls, chosen annually, administered the government and led the Roman army into battle. In 366 B.C.E., the office of praetor was created. The praetor was in charge of civil law (law as it applied to Roman citizens), but he could also lead armies and govern Rome when the consuls were away from the city. As the Romans' territory expanded, they added another praetor to judge cases in which one or both people were noncitizens. The Roman state also had a number of administrative officials who handled specialized duties, such as the administration of financial affairs and supervision of the public games of Rome.

The Roman **senate** came to hold an especially important position in the Roman Republic. The senate or council of elders was a select group of about three hundred men who served for life. The senate could only advise the magistrates, but this advice was not taken lightly and by the third century B.C.E. had virtually the force of law.

The Roman Republic had a number of popular assemblies. By far the most important was the **centuriate assembly.** Organized by classes based on wealth, it was structured in such a way that the wealthiest citizens always had a majority. This assembly elected the chief magistrates and passed laws. Another assembly, the **council of the plebs,** came into being as a result of the struggle of the orders.

This struggle arose as a result of the division of early Rome into two groups, the **patricians** and the **plebeians.** The patricians were great landowners, who constituted an aristocratic governing class. Only they could be consuls, magistrates, and senators. The plebeians constituted the considerably larger group of nonpatrician large landowners, less wealthy landholders, artisans, merchants, and small farmers. Although they, too, were citizens, they did not have the same rights as the patricians. Both patricians and plebeians could vote, but only the patricians could be elected to governmental offices. Both had the right to make legal contracts and marriages, but intermarriage between patricians and plebeians was forbidden. At the beginning of the fifth century B.C.E., the plebeians began a struggle to seek both political and social equality with the patricians.

The struggle between the patricians and plebeians dragged on for hundreds of years, but it led to success for the plebeians. The council of the plebs, a popular assembly for plebeians only, was created in 471 B.C.E., and new officials, known as **tribunes of the plebs,** were given the power to protect plebeians against arrest by patrician magistrates. A new law allowed marriages between patricians and plebeians, and in the fourth century B.C.E., plebeians were permitted to become consuls.

Finally, in 287 B.C.E., the council of the plebs received the right to pass laws for all Romans.

The struggle between the patricians and plebeians, then, had a significant impact on the development of the Roman state. Theoretically, by 287 B.C.E., all Roman citizens were equal under the law, and all could strive for political office. But in reality, as a result of the right of intermarriage, a select number of patrician and plebeian families formed a new senatorial aristocracy that came to dominate the political offices. The Roman Republic had not become a democracy.

The Roman Conquest of the Mediterranean (264–133 B.C.E.)

After their conquest of the Italian peninsula, the Romans found themselves face to face with a formidable Mediterranean power—Carthage. Founded around 800 B.C.E. on the coast of North Africa by Phoenicians, Carthage had flourished and assembled an enormous empire in the western Mediterranean. By the third century B.C.E., the Carthaginian Empire included the coast of northern Africa, southern Spain, Sardinia, Corsica, and western Sicily. The presence of Carthaginians in Sicily, so close to the Italian coast, made the Romans apprehensive. In 264 B.C.E., the two powers began a lengthy struggle for control of the western Mediterranean (see Map 5.2).

In the First Punic War (the Latin word for Phoenician was *Punicus*), the Romans resolved to conquer Sicily. The Romans—a land power—realized that they could not win the war without a navy and promptly developed a substantial naval fleet. After a long struggle, a Roman fleet defeated the Carthaginian navy off Sicily, and the war quickly came to an end. In 241 B.C.E., Carthage gave up all rights to Sicily and had to pay an indemnity. Sicily became the first Roman province.

Carthage vowed revenge and extended its domains in Spain to compensate for the territory lost to Rome. When the Romans encouraged one of Carthage's Spanish allies to revolt against Carthage, Hannibal, the greatest of the Carthaginian generals, struck back, beginning the Second Punic War (218–201 B.C.E.).

This time, the Carthaginian strategy aimed at bringing the war home to the Romans and defeating them in their own backyard. Hannibal crossed the Alps with an army of thirty to forty thousand men and inflicted a series of defeats on the Romans. At Cannae in 216 B.C.E., the Romans lost an army of almost forty thousand men. Rome seemed on the brink of disaster but refused to give up, raised yet another army, and began to reconquer some of the Italian cities that had gone over to Hannibal's side. They also sent troops to Spain, and by 206 B.C.E., Spain was freed of the Carthaginians.

The Romans then took the war directly to Carthage, forcing the Carthaginians to recall Hannibal from Italy. At the Battle of Zama in 202 B.C.E., the Romans crushed Hannibal's forces, and the war was over. By the peace treaty signed in 201 B.C.E., Carthage lost Spain, which

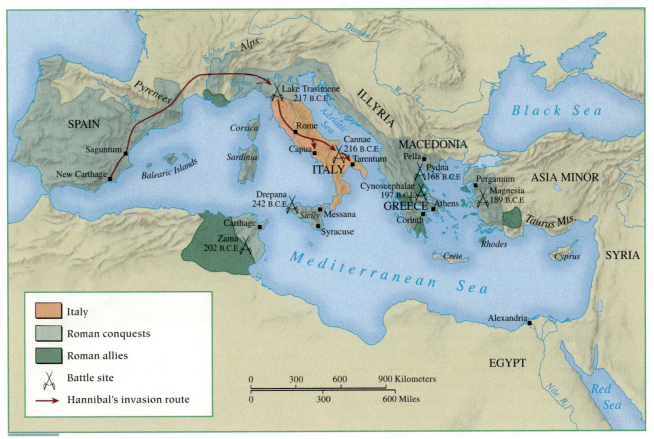

MAP 5.2 **Roman Conquests in the Mediterranean, 264–133 B.C.E.** Beginning with the Punic Wars, Rome expanded its holdings, first in the western Mediterranean at the expense of Carthage and later in Greece and western Asia Minor. ❓ What aspects of Mediterranean geography, combined with the territorial holdings and aspirations of Rome and the Carthaginians, made the Punic Wars more likely?

became another Roman province. Rome had become the dominant power in the western Mediterranean.

Fifty years later, the Romans fought their third and final struggle with Carthage. In 146 B.C.E., Carthage was destroyed. For ten days, Roman soldiers burned and pulled down all of the city's buildings. The inhabitants—fifty thousand men, women, and children—were sold into slavery. The territory of Carthage became a Roman province called Africa.

During its struggle with Carthage, Rome also became involved in problems with the Hellenistic states in the eastern Mediterranean, and after the defeat of Carthage, Rome turned its attention there. In 148 B.C.E., Macedonia was made a Roman province, and two years later, Greece was placed under the control of the Roman governor of Macedonia. In 133 B.C.E., the king of Pergamum deeded his kingdom to Rome, giving Rome its first province in Asia. Rome was now master of the Mediterranean Sea.

The Decline and Fall of the Roman Republic (133–31 B.C.E.)

By the middle of the second century B.C.E., Roman domination of the Mediterranean Sea was complete. Yet the

process of creating an empire had weakened the internal stability of Rome, leading to a series of crises that plagued the empire for the next hundred years.

Growing Unrest and a New Role for the Roman Army By the second century B.C.E., the senate had become the effective governing body of the Roman state. It comprised three hundred men, drawn primarily from the landed aristocracy; they remained senators for life and held the chief magistracies of the Republic. The senate directed the wars of the third and second centuries and took control of both foreign and domestic policy, including financial affairs.

Of course, these aristocrats formed only a tiny minority of the Roman people. The backbone of the Roman state had traditionally been the small farmers. But over time, many small farmers had found themselves unable to compete with large, wealthy landowners and had lost their lands. By taking over state-owned land and by buying out small peasant owners, these landed aristocrats had amassed large estates (called *latifundia*) that used slave labor. Thus, the rise of the *latifundia* contributed to a decline in the number of small citizen farmers who were available for military service. Moreover, many of these small farmers drifted to the cities, especially Rome, forming a large class of landless poor.

End of Latin revolts	340 B.C.E.
Creation of the Roman Confederation	338 B.C.E.
First Punic War	264–241 B.C.E.
Second Punic War	218–201 B.C.E.
Battle of Cannae	216 B.C.E.
Roman seizure of Spain	206 B.C.E.
Battle of Zama	202 B.C.E.
Third Punic War	149–146 B.C.E.
Macedonia made a Roman province	148 B.C.E.
Destruction of Carthage	146 B.C.E.
Kingdom of Pergamum to Rome	133 B.C.E.

© Scala/Art Resource, NY

Caesar. Conqueror of Gaul and member of the First Triumvirate, Julius Caesar is perhaps the best-known figure of the late Republic. Caesar became dictator of Rome in 47 B.C.E. and after his victories in the civil war was made dictator for life. Some members of the senate who resented his power assassinated him in 44 B.C.E. Pictured is a marble copy of the bust of Caesar.

Some aristocrats tried to remedy this growing economic and social crisis. Two brothers, Tiberius and Gaius Gracchus, came to believe that the underlying cause of Rome's problems was the decline of the small farmer. To help the landless poor, they bypassed the senate by having the council of the plebs pass land-reform bills that called for the government to reclaim public land held by large landowners and to distribute it to landless Romans. Many senators, themselves large landowners whose estates included large areas of public land, were furious. A group of senators took the law into their own hands and murdered Tiberius in 133 B.C.E. Gaius later suffered the same fate. The attempts of the Gracchus brothers to bring reforms had opened the door to further violence. Changes in the Roman army soon brought even worse problems.

In the closing years of the second century B.C.E., a Roman general named Marius began to recruit his armies in a new way. The Roman army had traditionally been a conscript army of small farmers who were landholders. Marius recruited volunteers from both the urban and rural poor who possessed no property. These volunteers swore an oath of loyalty to the general, not the senate, and thus inaugurated a professional-type army that might no longer be subject to the state. Moreover, to recruit these men, a general would promise them land, forcing generals to play politics in order to get laws passed that would provide the land for their veterans. Marius had created a new system of military recruitment that placed much power in the hands of the individual generals.

The Collapse of the Republic The first century B.C.E. was characterized by two important features: the jostling for power of a number of powerful individuals and the civil wars generated by their conflicts. Three individuals came to hold enormous military and political power—Crassus, Pompey, and Julius Caesar. Crassus was known as the richest man in Rome and led a successful military command against a major slave rebellion. Pompey had returned from a successful military command in Spain in 71 B.C.E. and had been hailed as a military hero. Julius

Caesar also had a military command in Spain. In 60 B.C.E., Caesar joined with Crassus and Pompey to form a coalition that historians call the First Triumvirate (*triumvirate* means "three-man rule").

The combined wealth and power of these three men was enormous, enabling them to dominate the political scene and achieve their basic aims: Pompey received a command in Spain, Crassus a command in Syria, and Caesar a special military command in Gaul (modern France). When Crassus was killed in battle in 53 B.C.E., it left two powerful men with armies in direct competition. During his time in Gaul, Caesar had conquered all of Gaul and gained fame, wealth, and military experience as well as an army of seasoned veterans who were loyal to him. When leading senators endorsed Pompey as the less harmful to their cause and voted for Caesar to lay down his command and return as a private citizen to Rome, Caesar refused. He chose to keep his army and moved into Italy illegally by crossing the Rubicon, the river that formed the southern boundary of his province. Caesar marched on Rome and defeated the forces of Pompey and his allies, leaving Caesar in complete control of the Roman government.

Caesar was officially made **dictator** in 47 B.C.E. and three years later was named dictator for life. Realizing the need for reforms, he gave land to the poor and increased the senate to nine hundred members. He also reformed the calendar by introducing the Egyptian solar year of 365 days (with later changes in 1582, it became the basis of our own calendar). Caesar planned much more in the way of building projects and military adventures in the East, but in 44 B.C.E., a group of leading senators assassinated him.

Within a few years after Caesar's death, two men had divided the Roman world between them—Octavian, Caesar's heir and grandnephew, taking the western portion and Antony, Caesar's ally and assistant, the eastern half. But the empire of the Romans, large as it was, was still too small for two masters, and Octavian and Antony eventually came into conflict. Antony allied himself closely with the Egyptian queen Cleopatra VII. At the Battle of Actium in Greece in 31 B.C.E., Octavian's forces smashed the army and navy of Antony and Cleopatra, who both fled to Egypt, where they committed suicide a year later. Octavian, at the age of thirty-two, stood supreme over the Roman world. The civil wars were ended. And so was the Republic.

The Roman Empire at Its Height

With the victories of Octavian, peace finally settled on the Roman world. Although civil conflict still erupted occasionally, the new imperial state constructed by Octavian experienced remarkable stability for the next two hundred years. The Romans imposed their peace on the largest empire established in antiquity.

The Age of Augustus (31 B.C.E.–14 C.E.)

In 27 B.C.E., Octavian proclaimed the "restoration of the Republic." He understood that only traditional republican forms would satisfy the senatorial aristocracy. At the same time, Octavian was aware that the Republic could not be fully restored. Although he gave some power to the senate, Octavian in reality became the first Roman emperor. The senate awarded him the title of Augustus, "the revered one"—a fitting title in view of his power that had previously been reserved for gods. Augustus proved highly popular, but the chief source of his power was his continuing control of the army. The senate gave Augustus the title of *imperator* (our word *emperor*), or commander in chief.

Augustus maintained a standing army of twenty-eight legions or about 150,000 men (a legion was a military unit of about 5,000 troops). Only Roman citizens could be legionaries, while subject peoples could serve as auxiliary forces, which numbered around 130,000 under Augustus. Augustus was also responsible for setting up a **praetorian guard** of roughly 9,000 men who had the important task of guarding the emperor.

While claiming to have restored the Republic, Augustus inaugurated a new system for governing the provinces. Under the Republic, the senate had appointed the governors of the provinces. Now certain provinces were given to the emperor, who assigned deputies known as legates to govern them. The senate continued to name the governors of the remaining provinces, but the authority of Augustus enabled him to overrule the senatorial governors and establish a uniform imperial policy.

Augustus also stabilized the frontiers of the Roman Empire. He conquered the central and maritime Alps and then expanded Roman control of the Balkan peninsula up to the Danube River. His attempt to conquer Germany failed when three Roman legions were massacred in 9 C.E. by a coalition of German tribes. His defeats in Germany taught Augustus that Rome's power was not unlimited and also devastated him; for months, he would beat his head on a door, shouting "Varus [the defeated Roman general in Germany], give me back my legions!"

Augustus died in 14 C.E. after dominating the Roman world for forty-five years. He had created a new order while placating the old by restoring traditional values. By the time of his death, his new order was so well established that few agitated for an alternative. Indeed, as the Roman historian Tacitus pointed out, "Practically no one had ever seen truly Republican government.... Political equality was a thing of the past; all eyes watched for imperial commands."[1]

The Early Empire (14–180)

There was no serious opposition to Augustus' choice of his stepson Tiberius as his successor. By his actions, Augustus established the Julio-Claudian dynasty; the next four successors of Augustus were related to the family of Augustus or that of his wife, Livia.

Several major tendencies emerged during the reigns of the Julio-Claudians (14–68 C.E.). In general, more and more of the responsibilities that Augustus had given to the senate tended to be taken over by the emperors, who also instituted an imperial bureaucracy, staffed by talented freedmen, to run the government on a daily basis. As the Julio-Claudian successors of Augustus acted more openly as real rulers rather than "first citizens of the state," the opportunity for arbitrary and corrupt acts also increased. Nero (54–68), for example, freely eliminated people he wanted out of the way, including his own mother, whose murder he arranged. Without troops, the senators proved unable to oppose these excesses, but the Roman legions finally revolted. Abandoned by his guards, Nero chose to commit suicide by stabbing himself in the throat after uttering his final words, "What an artist the world is losing in me!"

The Five Good Emperors (96–180) Many historians see the *Pax Romana* (the Roman peace) and the prosperity it engendered as the chief benefits of Roman rule during the first and second centuries C.E. These benefits were especially noticeable during the reigns of the five so-called **good emperors.** These rulers treated the ruling classes with respect, maintained peace in the empire, and supported generally beneficial domestic policies. Though absolute monarchs, they were known for their tolerance and diplomacy. By adopting capable men as their sons and successors, the first four of these emperors reduced the chances of succession problems.

Under the five good emperors, the powers of the emperor continued to expand at the expense of the senate. Increasingly, imperial officials appointed and directed by

MAP 5.3 **The Roman Empire from Augustus to Trajan (14–117).** Augustus and later emperors continued the expansion of the Roman Empire, adding more resources but also increasing the tasks of administration and keeping the peace. Compare this map with Map 5.2. ❓ Which of Trajan's acquisitions were relinquished during Hadrian's reign? Why? 🌐 **View an animated version of this map or related maps** at http://worldrc.wadsworthcom/

the emperor took over the running of the government. The good emperors also extended the scope of imperial administration to areas previously untouched by the imperial government. Trajan (98–117) implemented an alimentary program that provided state funds to assist poor parents in raising and educating their children. The good emperors were widely praised for their extensive building programs. Trajan and Hadrian (117–138) were especially active in constructing public works—aqueducts, bridges, roads, and harbor facilities—throughout the empire.

Frontiers and the Provinces Although Trajan extended Roman rule into Dacia (modern Romania), Mesopotamia, and the Sinai peninsula (see Map 5.3), his successors recognized that the empire was overextended and returned to Augustus' policy of defensive imperialism. Hadrian withdrew Roman forces from much of Mesopotamia. Although he retained Dacia and Arabia, he went on the defensive in his frontier policy by reinforcing the fortifications along a line connecting the Rhine and Danube rivers and building

a defensive wall 80 miles long across northern Britain to keep the Scots out of Roman Britain. By the end of the second century, the Roman forces were established in permanent bases behind the frontiers.

At its height in the second century C.E., the Roman Empire was one of the greatest states the world had seen. It covered about 3.5 million square miles and had a population, like that of Han China, estimated at more than fifty million. While the emperors and the imperial administration provided a degree of unity, considerable leeway was given to local customs, and the privileges of Roman citizenship were extended to many people throughout the empire. In 212, the emperor Caracalla completed the process by giving Roman citizenship to every free inhabitant of the empire. Latin was the language of the western part of the empire, while Greek was used in the east. Roman culture spread to all parts of the empire and freely mixed with Greek culture, creating what has been called Greco-Roman civilization.

The administration and cultural life of the Roman Empire depended greatly on cities and towns. A provincial governor's staff was not large, so it was left to local city officials to act as Roman agents in carrying out many government functions, especially those related to taxes. Most towns and cities were not large by modern standards. The largest was Rome, but there were also some large cities in the east: Alexandria in Egypt numbered more than 300,000 inhabitants. In the west, cities were usually small, with only a few thousand inhabitants. Cities were important in the spread of Roman culture, law, and the Latin language, and they resembled one another with their temples, markets, amphitheaters, and other public buildings.

Prosperity in the Early Empire

The Early Empire was a period of considerable prosperity. Internal peace resulted in unprecedented levels of trade. Merchants from all over the empire came to the chief Italian ports of Puteoli on the Bay of Naples and Ostia at the mouth of the Tiber. Long-distance trade beyond the Roman frontiers also developed during the Early Empire. Developments in both the Roman and Chinese Empires helped foster the growth of this trade. Although both empires built roads chiefly for military purposes, the roads also came to be used to facilitate trade. Moreover, by creating large empires, the Romans and Chinese not only established internal stability but also pacified bordering territories, thus reducing the threat that bandits posed to traders. As a result, merchants developed a network of trade routes that brought these two great empires into commercial contact. Most important was the overland Silk Road, a regular caravan route between West and East (see "Imperial Expansion and the Origins of the Silk Road" later in this chapter).

Despite the profits from trade and commerce, agriculture remained the chief pursuit of most people and the underlying basis of Roman prosperity. Although the large *latifundia* still dominated agriculture, especially in southern and central Italy, small peasant farms continued to flourish, particularly in Etruria and the Po valley. Although large estates concentrating on sheep and cattle raising used slaves, the lands of some *latifundia* were also worked by free tenant farmers who paid rent in labor, produce, or sometimes cash.

The prosperity of the Roman world left an enormous gulf between rich and poor. The development of towns and cities, so important to the creation of any civilization, is based largely on the agricultural surpluses of the countryside. In ancient times, the margin of surplus produced by each farmer was relatively small. Therefore, the upper classes and urban populations had to be supported by the labor of a large number of agricultural producers, who never found it easy to produce much more than for themselves.

Culture and Society in the Roman World

One of the notable characteristics of Roman culture and society is the impact of the Greeks. Greek ambassadors, merchants, and artists traveled to Rome and spread Greek thought and practices. After their conquest of the Hellenistic kingdoms, Roman generals shipped Greek manuscripts and artworks back to Rome. Multitudes of educated Greek slaves labored in Roman households. Rich Romans hired Greek tutors and sent their sons to Athens to study. As the Roman poet Horace said, "Captive Greece took captive her rude conqueror." Greek thought captivated the less sophisticated Roman minds, and the Romans became willing transmitters of Greek culture.

Roman Literature   The Latin literature that first emerged in the third century B.C.E. was strongly influenced by Greek models. It was not until the last century of the Republic that the Romans began to produce a new poetry in which Latin poets were able to use various Greek forms to express their own feelings about people, social and political life, and love.

The high point of Latin literature was reached in the age of Augustus, often called the golden age of Latin literature. The most distinguished poet of the Augustan Age was Virgil (70–19 B.C.E.). The son of a small landholder in northern Italy, he welcomed the rule of Augustus and wrote his greatest work in the emperor's honor. Virgil's masterpiece was the *Aeneid*, an epic poem clearly intended to rival the work of Homer. The connection between Troy and Rome is made in the poem when Aeneas, a hero of Troy, survives the destruction of that city and eventually settles in Latium—establishing a link between Roman civilization and Greek history. Aeneas is portrayed as the ideal Roman—his virtues are duty, piety, and faithfulness. Virgil's overall purpose was to show that Aeneas had fulfilled his mission to establish the Romans in Italy and thereby start Rome on its divine mission to rule the world.

> Let others fashion from bronze more lifelike, breathing
>   images—
> For so they shall—and evoke living faces from marble;
> Others excel as orators, others track with their instruments
> The planets circling in heaven and predict when stars
>   will appear.
> But, Romans, never forget that government is your medium!
> Be this your art:—to practise men in the habit of peace,
> Generosity to the conquered, and firmness against
>   aggressors.[2]

As Virgil expressed it, ruling was Rome's gift.

Roman Art   The Romans were also dependent on the Greeks for artistic inspiration. The Romans developed a taste for Greek statues, which they placed not only in public buildings but also in their private houses. The Romans' own portrait sculpture was characterized by an intense realism that included even unpleasant physical details. Wall paintings and frescoes in the homes of the rich realistically depicted landscapes, portraits, and scenes from mythological stories.

The Romans excelled in architecture, a highly practical art. Although they continued to adapt Greek styles and made use of colonnades and rectangular structures, the Romans were also innovative. They made considerable use of curvilinear forms: the arch, vault, and dome. The Romans

Roman Aqueduct. The engineering skills of the Romans enabled them to build massive constructions, including aqueducts such as this one in southern France, known as the Pont du Gard. The Pont du Gard is a three-story bridge built of blocks of stone without cement, at the top of which was a channel that carried water. Nîmes received its water from a source 30 miles away. Since gravity kept the water flowing, channels holding the water had to have a gradual decline from the source of the water to its final destination. The Pont du Gard, which crosses the Gardon River outside Nîmes, was built to the exact height needed to maintain the flow of water into the city.

were also the first people in antiquity to use concrete on a massive scale. They constructed huge buildings—public baths, such as those of Caracalla, and amphitheaters capable of seating fifty thousand spectators. These large buildings were made possible by Roman engineering skills. These same skills were put to use in constructing roads, aqueducts, and bridges: a network of 50,000 miles of roads linked all parts of the empire, and in Rome, almost a dozen aqueducts kept the population of one million supplied with water.

Roman Law   One of Rome's chief gifts to the Mediterranean world of its day and to later generations was its system of law. Rome's first code of laws was the Twelve Tables of 450 B.C.E., but that was designed for a simple farming society and proved inadequate for later needs. So, from the Twelve Tables, the Romans developed a system of civil law that applied to all Roman citizens. As Rome expanded, problems arose between citizens and noncitizens and also among noncitizen residents of the empire. Although some of the rules of civil law could be used in these cases, special rules were often needed. These rules gave rise to a body of law known as the law of nations, defined as the part of the law that applied to both Romans and foreigners. Under the influence of Stoicism, the Romans came to identify their law of nations with **natural law,** or universal law based on reason. This enabled them to establish standards of justice that applied to all people.

These standards of justice included principles that we would immediately recognize. A person was regarded as innocent until proved otherwise. People accused of wrongdoing were allowed to defend themselves before a judge. A judge, in turn, was expected to weigh evidence carefully before arriving at a decision. These principles lived on long after the fall of the Roman Empire.

The Roman Family   At the heart of the Roman social structure stood the family, headed by the *paterfamilias*—the dominant male. The household also included the wife, sons with their wives and children, unmarried daughters, and slaves. Like the Greeks, Roman males believed that females needed male guardians. The *paterfamilias* exercised that authority; upon his death, sons or nearest male relatives assumed the role of guardians.

Fathers arranged the marriages of daughters. In the Republic, women married "with legal control" passing from father to husband. By the mid-first century B.C.E., the dominant practice had changed to "without legal control," which meant that married daughters officially remained within the father's legal power. Since the fathers of most married women were dead, not being in the "legal control" of a husband entailed independent property rights that forceful women could translate into considerable power within the household and outside it.

Some parents in upper-class families provided education for their daughters by hiring private tutors or sending them to primary schools. At the age when boys were entering secondary schools, however, girls were pushed into marriage. The legal minimum age for marriage was twelve, although fourteen was a more common age in practice (for males, the legal minimum age was fourteen, and most men married later). Although some Roman doctors warned that early pregnancies could be dangerous for young girls, early marriages persisted because women died at a relatively young age. A good example is Tullia, Cicero's beloved daughter. She was married at sixteen, widowed at twenty-two, remarried one year later, divorced at twenty-eight, remarried at twenty-nine, and divorced at thirty-three. She died at thirty-four, which was not unusually young for women in Roman society.

By the second century C.E., significant changes were occurring in the Roman family. The *paterfamilias* no longer had absolute authority over his children; he could no longer sell his children into slavery or have them put to death. Moreover, the husband's absolute authority over his wife also disappeared, and by the late second century, upper-class Roman women had considerable freedom and independence.

Slaves and Their Masters   Although slavery was a common institution throughout the ancient world, no people possessed more slaves or relied so much on slave labor as the Romans eventually did. Slaves were used in many ways in Roman society. The rich owned the most and the best. In the late Roman Republic, it became a badge of prestige to be attended by many slaves. Greek slaves were in much demand as tutors, musicians, doctors, and

A Roman Lady. Roman women, especially those of the upper class, developed comparatively more freedom than women in classical Athens despite the persistent male belief that women required guardianship. This mural decoration was found in the remains of a villa destroyed by the eruption of Mount Vesuvius.

artists. Roman businessmen would employ them as shop assistants or craftspeople. Slaves were also used as farm laborers; in fact, huge gangs of slaves worked the large landed estates under pitiful conditions. Many slaves of all nationalities were used as menial household workers, such as cooks, waiters, cleaners, and gardeners. Contractors used slave labor to build roads, aqueducts, and other public structures.

The treatment of Roman slaves varied. There are numerous instances of humane treatment by masters and situations where slaves even protected their owners from danger out of gratitude and esteem. Slaves were also subject to severe punishments, torture, abuse, and hard labor that drove some to run away, despite the stringent laws Romans had against aiding a runaway slave. Some slaves revolted against their owners and even murdered them, causing some Romans to live in unspoken fear of their slaves (see the box on p. 108).

Near the end of the second century B.C.E., large-scale slave revolts occurred in Sicily, where enormous gangs of slaves were subjected to horrible working conditions on large landed estates. The most famous uprising on the Italian peninsula occurred in 73 B.C.E. Led by a gladiator named Spartacus, the revolt broke out in southern Italy and involved seventy thousand slaves. Spartacus managed to defeat several Roman armies before being trapped and killed in southern Italy in 71 B.C.E. Six thousand of his followers were crucified, the traditional form of execution for slaves.

Imperial Rome   At the center of the colossal Roman Empire was the ancient city of Rome. Truly a capital city, Rome had the largest population of any city in the empire, close to one million by the time of Augustus. Only Chang'an, the imperial capital of the Han Empire in China, had a comparable population during this time.

Both food and entertainment were provided on a grand scale for the inhabitants of Rome. The poet Juvenal said of the Roman masses: "But nowadays, with no vote to sell, their motto is 'Couldn't care less.' Time was when their plebiscite elected generals, heads of state, commanders of legions: but now they've pulled in their horns, there's only two things that concern them: Bread and Circuses."[3] Public spectacles were provided by the emperor as part of the great religious festivals celebrated by the state. Most famous were the gladiatorial shows, which took place in amphitheaters. Perhaps the most famous was the amphitheater known as the Colosseum, constructed in Rome to seat fifty thousand spectators. In most cities and towns, amphitheaters were the biggest buildings, rivaled only by the circuses (arenas) for races and the public baths.

Gladiatorial games were held from dawn to dusk. Contests to the death between trained fighters formed the central focus of these games, but the games included other forms of entertainment as well. Criminals of all ages and both genders were sent into the arena without weapons to face certain death from wild animals who would tear them to pieces. Numerous types of animal contests were also held: wild beasts against each other, such as bears against buffaloes; staged hunts with men shooting safely from behind iron bars; and gladiators in the arena with bulls, tigers, and lions. It is recorded that five thousand beasts killed in one day of games when Emperor Titus inaugurated the Colosseum in 80 C.E.

Crisis and the Late Empire

During the reign of Marcus Aurelius, the last of the five good emperors, a number of natural catastrophes struck Rome. To many Romans, these natural disasters seemed to portend an ominous future for Rome. New problems arose soon after the death of Marcus Aurelius in 180.

Crises in the Third Century

In the course of the third century, the Roman Empire came near to collapse. Military monarchy under the

THE ROMAN FEAR OF SLAVES

FAMILY & SOCIETY

The lowest stratum of the Roman population consisted of slaves. They were used extensively in households, at the court, as artisans in industrial enterprises, as business managers, and in numerous other ways. Although some historians have argued that slaves were treated more humanely during the Early Empire, these selections by the Roman historian Tacitus and the Roman statesman Pliny indicate that slaves still rebelled against their masters because of mistreatment. Many masters continued to live in fear of their slaves, as witnessed by the saying "As many enemies as you have slaves."

What do these texts reveal about the practice of slavery in the Roman Empire? What were Roman attitudes toward the events discussed in them?

Tacitus, *The Annals of Imperial Rome*

Soon afterwards the City Prefect, Lucius Pedanius Secundus, was murdered by one of his slaves [61 C.E.]. Either Pedanius had refused to free the murderer after agreeing to a price, or the slave, in a homosexual infatuation, found competition from his master intolerable. After the murder, ancient custom required that every slave residing under the same roof must be executed. But a crowd gathered, eager to save so many innocent lives; and rioting began. The senatehouse was besieged. Inside, there was feeling against excessive severity, but the majority opposed any change. Among the latter was Gaius Cassius Longinus, who when his turn came spoke as follows. . . .

"An ex-consul has been deliberately murdered by a slave in his own home. None of his fellow-slaves prevented or betrayed the murderer, though the senatorial decree threatening the whole household with execution still stands. Exempt them from the penalty if you like. But then, if the City Prefect was not important enough to be immune; who will be? Who will have enough slaves to protect him if Pedanius' four hundred were too few? Who can rely on his household's help

if even fear for their own lives does not make them shield us?" [The sentence of death was carried out.]

Pliny the Younger to Acilius

This horrible affair demands more publicity than a letter—Larcius Macedo, a senator and ex-praetor, has fallen a victim to his own slaves. Admittedly he was a cruel and overbearing master, too ready to forget that his father had been a slave, or perhaps too keenly conscious of it. He was taking a bath in his house at Formiae when suddenly he found himself surrounded; one slave seized him by the throat while the others struck his face and hit him in the chest and stomach and—shocking to say—in his private parts. When they thought he was dead they threw him onto the hot pavement, to make sure he was not still alive. Whether unconscious or feigning to be so, he lay there motionless, thus making them believe that he was quite dead. Only then was he carried out, as if he had fainted with the heat, and received by his slaves who had remained faithful, while his concubines ran up, screaming frantically. Roused by their cries and revived by the cooler air he opened his eyes and made some movement to show that he was alive, it being now safe to do so. The guilty slaves fled, but most of them have been arrested and a search is being made for the others. Macedo was brought back to life with difficulty, but only for a few days; at least he died with the satisfaction of having revenged himself, for he lived to see the same punishment meted out as for murder. There you see the dangers, outrages, and insults to which we are exposed. No master can feel safe because he is kind and considerate; for it is their brutality, not their reasoning capacity, which leads slaves to murder masters.

CENGAGENOW To read other works by Tacitus and Pliny, enter the *CengageNOW* documents area using the access card that is available for *The Essential World History*.

Severan rulers (193–235), which restored order after a series of civil wars, was followed by military anarchy. For the next forty-nine years, the Roman imperial throne was occupied by anyone who had the military strength to seize it—a total of twenty-two emperors, only two of whom did not meet a violent death. At the same time, the empire was beset by a series of invasions, no doubt exacerbated by the civil wars. In the east, the Sassanid Persians made inroads into Roman territory. Germanic tribes also poured into the empire. Not until the end of the third century were most of the boundaries restored.

Invasions, civil wars, and plague came close to causing an economic collapse of the Roman Empire in the third century. There was a noticeable decline in trade and small industry, and the labor shortage caused by the

plague affected both military recruiting and the economy. Farm production deteriorated significantly as fields were ravaged by invaders or, even more often, by the defending Roman armies. The monetary system began to collapse as a result of debased coinage and inflation. Armies were needed more than ever, but financial strains made it difficult to pay and enlist more soldiers. By the mid-third century, the state had to hire Germans to fight under Roman commanders.

The Late Roman Empire

At the end of the third and beginning of the fourth centuries, the Roman Empire gained a new lease on life through the efforts of two strong emperors, Diocletian and Constantine. The Roman Empire was virtually transformed into a new state: the so-called Late Empire, which included a new governmental structure, a rigid economic and social system, and a new state religion—Christianity (see "Transformation of the Roman World: The Development of Christianity" later in this chapter).

The Reforms of Diocletian and Constantine Both Diocletian (284–305) and Constantine (306–337) expanded imperial control by strengthening and enlarging the administrative bureaucracies of the Roman Empire. A hierarchy of officials exercised control at the various levels of government. The army was enlarged, and mobile units were set up that could be quickly moved to support frontier troops when the borders were threatened.

Constantine's biggest project was the construction of a new capital city in the east, on the site of the Greek city of Byzantium on the shores of the Bosporus. Eventually renamed Constantinople (modern Istanbul), the city was developed for defensive reasons and had an excellent strategic location. Calling it his "New Rome," Constantine endowed the city with a forum, large palaces, and a vast amphitheater.

Location of the "New Rome"

The political and military reforms of Diocletian and Constantine greatly enlarged two institutions—the army and the civil service—that drained most of the public funds. Though more revenues were needed to pay for the army and bureaucracy, the population was not growing, so the tax base could not be expanded. To ensure the tax base and keep the empire going despite the shortage of labor, the emperors issued edicts that forced people to remain in their designated vocations. Basic jobs, such as bakers and shippers, became hereditary. The fortunes of free tenant farmers also declined. Soon they found themselves bound to the land by large landowners who took advantage of depressed agricultural conditions to enlarge their landed estates.

The End of the Western Empire Constantine had reunited the Roman Empire and restored a semblance of order. After his death, however, the empire continued to divide into western and eastern parts, which had virtually become two independent states by 395. In the course of the fifth century, while the empire in the east remained intact under the Roman emperor in Constantinople, the administrative structure of the empire in the west collapsed and was replaced by an assortment of Germanic kingdoms. The process was a gradual one, beginning with the movement of Germans into the empire.

Although the Romans had established a series of political frontiers along the Rhine and Danube rivers, Romans and Germans often came into contact across these boundaries. Until the fourth century, the empire had proved capable of absorbing these people without harm to its political structure. In the late fourth century, however, the Germanic tribes came under new pressure when the Huns, a fierce tribe of nomads from the steppes of Asia who may have been related to the Xiongnu, the invaders of the Han Empire in China, moved into the Black Sea region, possibly attracted by the riches of the empire to its south. One of the groups displaced by the Huns was the Visigoths, who moved south and west, crossed the Danube into Roman territory, and settled down as Roman allies. But the Visigoths soon revolted, and the Roman attempt to stop them at Adrianople in 378 led to a crushing defeat for Rome.

Increasing numbers of Germans now crossed the frontiers. In 410, the Visigoths sacked Rome. Vandals poured into southern Spain and Africa, Visigoths into Spain and Gaul. The Vandals crossed into Italy from North Africa and ravaged Rome again in 455. By the middle of the fifth century, the western provinces of the Roman Empire had been taken over by Germanic peoples who were in the process of setting up independent kingdoms. At the same time, a semblance of imperial authority remained in Rome, although the real power behind the throne tended to rest in the hands of important military officials known as masters of the soldiers. These military commanders controlled the government and dominated the imperial court. In 476, Odoacer, a new master of the soldiers, himself of German origin, deposed the Roman emperor, the boy Romulus Augustulus. To many historians, the deposition of Romulus signaled the end of the Roman Empire in the west. Of course, this is only a symbolic date, as much of direct imperial rule had already been lost in the course of the fifth century.

Transformation of the Roman World: The Development of Christianity

The rise of Christianity marked a fundamental break with the dominant values of the Greco-Roman world. To understand the rise of Christianity, we must first examine both the religious environment of the Roman world and the Jewish background from which Christianity emerged.

The Roman state religion focused on the worship of a pantheon of Greco-Roman gods and goddesses, including Juno, the patron goddess of women; Minerva, the goddess of craftspeople; Mars, the god of war; and Jupiter Optimus Maximus ("best and greatest"), who became the patron deity of Rome and assumed a central place in the religious life of the city. The Romans believed that the observance of proper ritual by state priests brought them into a right relationship with the gods, thereby guaranteeing security, peace, and prosperity, and that their success in creating an empire confirmed the favor of the gods. As the

RULERS AND GODS

RELIGION & PHILOSOPHY

All of the world's earliest civilizations believed that there was a close relationship between rulers and gods. In Egypt, pharaohs were considered gods whose role was to maintain the order and harmony of the universe in their own kingdom. In the words of an Egyptian hymn, "What is the king of Upper and Lower Egypt? He is a god by whose dealings one lives, the father and mother of all men, alone by himself, without an equal." In Mesopotamia, India, and China, rulers were thought to rule with divine assistance. Kings were often seen as rulers who derived their power from the gods and who were the agents or representatives of the gods. In ancient India, rulers claimed to be representatives of the gods because they were descended from Manu, the first man who had been made a king by Brahman, the chief god. Many Romans certainly believed that their success in creating an empire was a visible sign of divine favor.

Their supposed connection to the gods also caused rulers to seek divine aid in the affairs of the world. This led to the art of divination, or an organized method to discover the intentions of the gods. In Mesopotamian and Roman society, one form of divination involved the examination of the livers of sacrificed animals;

features seen in the livers were interpreted to foretell events to come. The Chinese used oracle bones to receive advice from supernatural forces that were beyond the power of human beings. Questions to the gods were scratched on turtle shells or animal bones, which were then exposed to fire. Shamans then interpreted the meaning of the resulting cracks on the surface of the shells or bones as messages from supernatural forces. The Greeks divined the will of the gods by use of the oracle, a sacred shrine dedicated to a god or goddess who revealed the future in response to a question.

Underlying all of these divinatory practices was a belief in a supernatural universe, that is, a world in which divine forces were in charge and in which humans were dependent for their own well-being on those divine forces. It was not until the Scientific Revolution of the modern world that many people began to believe in a natural world that was not governed by spiritual forces.

Fitzwilliam Museum, University of Cambridge

Vishnu. Brahma the Creator, Shiva the Destroyer, and Vishnu the Preserver are the three chief Hindu gods of India. Vishnu is known as the Preserver because he mediates between Brahma and Shiva and is thus responsible for maintaining the stability of the universe.

---

first-century B.C.E. politician Cicero claimed, "We have overcome all the nations of the world because we have realized that the world is directed and governed by the gods."[4]

The polytheistic Romans were extremely tolerant of other religions. They allowed the worship of native gods and goddesses throughout their provinces and even adopted some of the local deities. In addition, beginning with Augustus, emperors were often officially made gods by the Roman senate, thus bolstering support for the emperors (see the comparative essay "Rulers and Gods" above).

The desire for a more emotional spiritual experience led many people to the mystery religions of the Hellenistic east, which flooded into the western Roman world during the Early Empire. The mystery religions offered their followers entry into a higher world of reality and the promise of a future life superior to the present one.

In addition to the mystery religions, the Romans' expansion into the eastern Mediterranean also brought them into contact with the Jews. Roman involvement with the Jews began in 63 B.C.E., and by 6 C.E., Judaea (which embraced the old Jewish Kingdom of Judah) had been made a province and placed under the direction of a Roman

procurator. But unrest continued, augmented by divisions among the Jews themselves. One group, the Essenes, awaited a Messiah who would save Israel from oppression, usher in the kingdom of God, and establish paradise on earth. Another group, the Zealots, were militant extremists who advocated the violent overthrow of Roman rule. A Jewish revolt in 66 C.E. was crushed by the Romans four years later. The Jewish Temple in Jerusalem was destroyed, and Roman power once more stood supreme in Judaea.

The Rise of Christianity

Jesus of Nazareth (c. 6 B.C.E.–c. 29 C.E.) was a Palestinian Jew who grew up in Galilee, an important center of the militant Zealots. Jesus' message was simple. He reassured his fellow Jews that he did not plan to undermine their traditional religion. What was important was not strict adherence to the letter of the law but the transformation of the inner person: "So in everything, do to others what you would have them do to you, for this sums up the Law and the Prophets."[5] God's command was simple—to love God and one another: "Love the Lord your God with all

CHRISTIAN IDEALS: THE SERMON ON THE MOUNT

RELIGION & PHILOSOPHY

Christianity was one of many religions competing for attention in the Roman Empire during the first and second centuries. The rise of Christianity marked a fundamental break with the value system of the upper-class elites who dominated the world of classical antiquity. As these excerpts from the Sermon on the Mount in the Gospel of Saint Matthew illustrate, Christians emphasized humility, charity, brotherly love, and a belief in the inner being and a spiritual kingdom superior to this material world. These values and principles were not those of classical Greco-Roman civilization as exemplified in the words and deeds of its leaders.

What were the ideals of early Christianity? How do they differ from the values and principles of classical Greco-Roman civilization? Compare this sermon to the Buddha's sermon on the Four Noble Truths from Chapter 2. How are they different? How are they similar?

The Gospel According to Saint Matthew

Now when he saw the crowds, he went up on a mountainside and sat down. His disciples came to him, and he began to teach them, saying:

> *Blessed are the poor in spirit: for theirs is the kingdom of heaven.*
> *Blessed are those who mourn: for they will be comforted.*
> *Blessed are the meek: for they will inherit the Earth.*
> *Blessed are those who hunger and thirst for righteousness: for they will be filled.*
> *Blessed are the merciful: for they will be shown mercy.*
> *Blessed are the pure in heart: for they will see God.*
> *Blessed are the peacemakers: for they will be called sons of God.*
> *Blessed are those who are persecuted because of righteousness: for theirs is the kingdom of heaven. . . .*

You have heard that it was said, "Eye for eye, and tooth for tooth." But I tell you, Do not resist an evil person. If someone strikes you on the right cheek, turn to him the other also. . . .

You have heard that it was said, "Love your neighbor, and hate your enemy." But I tell you, Love your enemies and pray for those who persecute you. . . .

Do not store up for yourselves treasures on Earth, where moth and rust destroy, and where thieves break in and steal. But store up for yourselves treasures in heaven, where moth and rust do not destroy, and where thieves do not break in and steal. For where your treasure is, there your heart will be also. . . .

No one can serve two masters. Either he will hate the one and love the other, or he will be devoted to the one and despise the other. You cannot serve both God and Money.

Therefore I tell you, do not worry about your life, what you will eat or drink; or about your body, what you will wear. Is not life more important than food, and the body more important than clothes? Look at the birds of the air; they do not sow or reap or store away in barns, and yet your heavenly Father feeds them. Are you not much more valuable than they? . . . So do not worry, saying, What shall we eat? or What shall we drink? or What shall we wear? For the pagans run after all these things, and your heavenly Father knows that you need them. But seek first his kingdom and his righteousness, and all these things will be given to you as well.

CENGAGENOW To read the entire sermon, enter the *CengageNOW* documents area using the access card that is available for the *The Essential World History*.

---

your heart and with all your soul and with all your mind and with all your strength. The second is this: Love your neighbor as yourself."[6] In the Sermon on the Mount (see the box above), Jesus presented the ethical concepts—humility, charity, and brotherly love—that would form the basis of the value system of medieval Western civilization.

To the Roman authorities of Palestine, however, Jesus was a potential revolutionary who might transform Jewish expectations of a messianic kingdom into a revolt against Rome. Therefore, Jesus found himself denounced on many sides, and the procurator Pontius Pilate ordered his crucifixion. But that did not solve the problem. A few loyal followers of Jesus spread the story that Jesus had overcome death, had been resurrected, and had then ascended into heaven. The belief in Jesus' resurrection became an important tenet of Christian doctrine. Jesus was now hailed as "the anointed one" (*Christ* in Greek), the Messiah who would return and usher in the kingdom of God on earth.

Christianity began, then, as a religious movement within Judaism and was viewed that way by Roman authorities for many decades. One of the prominent figures in early Christianity, however, Paul of Tarsus (c. 5–c. 67), believed that the message of Jesus should be preached not only to Jews but to Gentiles (non-Jews) as well. Paul taught that Jesus was the savior, the son of God, who had come to earth to save all humans, who were all sinners as a result of Adam's sin of disobedience against God. By his death, Jesus had atoned for the sins of all humans and made possible their reconciliation with God and hence their salvation. By accepting Jesus as their savior, they too could be saved.

The Spread of Christianity

At first, Christianity spread slowly. Although the teachings of early Christianity were mostly disseminated by

Jesus and His Apostles. Pictured is a fourth-century C.E. fresco from a Roman catacomb depicting Jesus and his apostles. Catacombs were underground cemeteries where early Christians buried their dead. Christian tradition holds that in times of imperial repression, Christians withdrew to the catacombs to pray and even hide.

the preaching of convinced Christians, written materials also appeared. Among them were a series of letters or epistles written by Paul outlining Christian beliefs for different Christian communities. Some of Jesus' disciples may also have preserved some of the sayings of the master in writing and would have passed on personal memories that became the basis of the written gospels—the "good news" concerning Jesus—which were written down between 50 and 150 and which attempted to give a record of Jesus' life and teachings and formed the core of the New Testament.

Although Jerusalem was the first center of Christianity, its destruction by the Romans in 70 C.E. dispersed the Christians and left individual Christian churches with considerable independence. By 100, Christian churches had been established in most of the major cities of the east and in some places in the western part of the empire. Many early Christians came from the ranks of Hellenized Jews and the Greek-speaking populations of the east. But in the second and third centuries, an increasing number of followers came from Latin-speaking peoples.

Initially, the Romans did not pay much attention to the Christians, whom they regarded at first as simply another Jewish sect. As time passed, however, the Roman attitude toward Christianity began to change. The Romans tolerated other religions as long as they did not threaten public order or public morals. Many Romans came to view Christians as harmful to the Roman state because they refused to worship the state gods and emperors. Nevertheless, Roman persecution of Christians in the first and second centuries was only sporadic and local, never systematic. In the second century, Christians were largely ignored as harmless. By the end of the reigns of the five good emperors, Christians still represented a small minority, but one of considerable strength.

The Triumph of Christianity

Christianity grew slowly in the first century, took root in the second, and by the third had spread widely. Why was Christianity able to attract so many followers? First, the Christian message had much to offer the Roman world. The promise of salvation, made possible by Jesus' death and resurrection, made a resounding impact on a world full of suffering and injustice. Christianity seemed to imbue life with a meaning and purpose beyond the simple material things of everyday reality. Second, Christianity seemed familiar. It was regarded as simply another mystery religion, offering immortality as the result of the sacrificial death of a savior-god. At the same time, it offered more than the other mystery religions did. Jesus had been a human figure who was easy to relate to.

Moreover, the sporadic persecution of Christians by the Romans in the first and second centuries, which did little to stop the growth of Christianity, in fact served to strengthen Christianity as an institution in the second and third centuries by causing it to become more organized. Crucial to this change was the emerging role of the bishops, who began to assume more control over church communities. The Christian church was creating a well-defined hierarchical structure in which the bishops and clergy were salaried officers separate from the laity or regular church members.

As the Christian church became more organized, some emperors in the third century responded with more systematic persecutions, but their schemes failed. The last great persecution was at the beginning of the fourth century, but by that time, Christianity had become too strong to be eradicated by force. After Constantine became the first Christian emperor, Christianity flourished. Although Constantine was not baptized until the end of his life, in 313 he issued the Edict of Milan officially tolerating Christianity. Under Theodosius the Great (378–395), it was made the official religion of the Roman Empire. In less than four centuries, Christianity had triumphed.

The Glorious Han Empire (202 B.C.E.–221 C.E.)

During the same centuries that saw the height of Roman civilization, China was also the home of a great empire. The fall of the Qin dynasty in 206 B.C.E. had been followed by a brief period of civil strife as aspiring successors competed for hegemony. Out of this strife emerged one of the greatest and most durable dynasties in Chinese history—the Han. The Han dynasty would later become so closely identified with the advance of Chinese civilization that even today the Chinese sometimes refer to themselves as "people of Han" and to their language as the "language of Han."

The founder of the Han dynasty was Liu Bang (Liu Pang), a commoner of peasant origin who would be known historically by his title of Han Gaozu (Han Kao Tsu, or Exalted Emperor of Han). Under his strong rule and that of his successors, the new dynasty quickly moved to consolidate its control over the empire and promote the welfare of its subjects. Efficient and benevolent, at least by the standards of the time, Gaozu maintained the centralized political institutions of the Qin but abandoned its harsh Legalistic approach to law enforcement. Han rulers discovered in Confucian principles a useful foundation for the creation of a new state philosophy. Under the Han, Confucianism began to take on the character of an official ideology.

Confucianism and the State

The integration of Confucian doctrine with Legalist institutions, creating a system generally known as **State Confucianism,** did not take long to accomplish. In doing this, the Han rulers retained many of the Qin institutions. For example, they borrowed the tripartite division of the central government into civilian and military authorities and a censorate. The government was headed by a "grand council" including representatives from all three segments of government. The Han also retained the system of local government, dividing the empire into provinces and districts.

Finally, the Han continued the Qin system of selecting government officials on the basis of merit rather than birth. Shortly after founding the new dynasty, Emperor Gaozu decreed that local officials would be asked to recommend promising candidates for public service. Thirty years later, in 165 B.C.E., the first known **civil service examination** was administered to candidates for positions in the bureaucracy. Shortly after that, an academy was established to train candidates. Nevertheless, the first candidates were almost all from aristocratic or other wealthy families, and the Han bureaucracy itself was still dominated by the traditional hereditary elite. Still, the principle of selecting officials on the basis of talent had been established and would eventually become standard practice.

Under the Han dynasty, the population increased rapidly—by some estimates rising from about twenty million to over sixty million at the height of the dynasty—creating a growing need for a large and efficient bureaucracy to maintain the state in proper working order. Unfortunately, the Han were unable to resolve all of the problems left over from the past. Factionalism at court remained a serious problem and undermined the efficiency of the central government.

The Economy

Han rulers also retained some of the economic and social policies of their predecessors. In rural areas, they saw that a free peasantry paying taxes directly to the state would both limit the wealth and power of the great noble families and increase the state's revenues. The Han had difficulty preventing the recurrence of the economic inequities that had characterized the last years of the Zhou, however (see the box on p. 114). The land taxes were relatively light, but the peasants also faced a number of other exactions, including military service and forced labor of up to one month annually. Although the use of iron tools brought new lands under the plow and food production increased steadily, the trebling of the population under the Han eventually reduced the average size of the individual farm plot to about one acre per capita, barely enough for survival. As time went on, many poor peasants were forced to sell their land and become tenant farmers, paying rents ranging up to half of the annual harvest. Thus, land once again came to be concentrated in the hands of the powerful landed clans, which often owned thousands of acres worked by tenants.

Although such economic problems contributed to the eventual downfall of the dynasty, in general the Han era was one of unparalleled productivity and prosperity. The period was marked by a major expansion of trade, both domestic and foreign. This was not necessarily due to official encouragement. In fact, the Han were as suspicious of private merchants as their predecessors had been and levied stiff taxes on trade in an effort to limit commercial activities. Merchants were also subject to severe social constraints. They were disqualified from seeking office, restricted in their place of residence, and viewed in general as parasites providing little true value to Chinese society.

The state itself directed much trade and manufacturing; it manufactured weapons, for example, and operated shipyards, granaries, and mines. The government also moved cautiously into foreign trade, mostly with neighboring areas in Central and Southeast Asia, although trade relations were established with countries as far away as India and the Mediterranean, where active contacts were maintained with the Roman Empire (see Map 5.4). Some of this long-distance trade was carried by sea through southern ports like Guangzhou, but more was transported by overland caravans on the Silk Road (see Chapter 10) and other routes that led westward into Central Asia.

New technology contributed to the economic prosperity of the Han era. Significant progress was achieved in

AN EDICT FROM THE EMPEROR

According to Confucian doctrine, Chinese monarchs ruled with the mandate of Heaven so long as they properly looked after the welfare of their subjects. One of their most important responsibilities was to maintain food production at a level sufficient to feed their people. Natural calamities such as floods, droughts, and earthquakes were interpreted as demonstrations of displeasure with the "Son of Heaven" on earth. In this edict, Emperor Wendi (r. 180–157 B.C.E.) wonders whether he has failed in his duty to carry out his imperial *Dao* (Way), thus incurring the wrath of Heaven. After the edict was issued in 163 B.C.E., the government took steps to increase the grain harvest, bringing an end to the food shortages.

What reasons does Emperor Wendi advance to explain the decline in grain production in China? What are the possible solutions that he proposes? Does his approach meet the requirements for official behavior raised by Chinese philosophers such as Mencius?

Han Shu (History of the Han Dynasty)

For the past years there have been no good harvests, and our people have suffered the calamities of flood, drought, and pestilence. We are deeply grieved by this, but being ignorant and unenlightened, we have been unable to discover where the blame lies. We have considered whether our administration has been guilty of some error or our actions of some fault. Have we failed to follow the Way of Heaven or to obtain the benefits of Earth? Have we caused disharmony in human affairs or neglected the gods that they do not accept our offerings? What has brought on these things? Have the provisions for our officials been too lavish or have we indulged in too many unprofitable affairs? Why is the food of the people so scarce? When the fields are surveyed, they have not decreased, and when the people are counted they have not grown in number, so that the amount of land for each person is the same as before or even greater. And yet there is a drastic shortage of food. Where does the blame lie? Is it that too many people pursue secondary activities to the detriment of agriculture? Is it that too much grain is used to make wine or too many domestic animals are being raised? I have been unable to attain a proper balance between important and unimportant affairs. Let this matter be debated by the chancellor, the nobles, the high officials, and learned doctors. Let all exhaust their efforts and ponder deeply whether there is some way to aid the people. Let nothing be concealed from us!

---

such areas as textile manufacturing, water mills, and iron casting; skill at ironworking led to the production of steel a few centuries later. Paper was invented under the Han, and the development of the rudder and fore-and-aft rigging permitted ships to sail into the wind for the first time. Thus equipped, Chinese merchant ships carrying heavy cargoes could sail throughout the islands of Southeast Asia and into the Indian Ocean.

Imperial Expansion and the Origins of the Silk Road

The Han emperors continued the process of territorial expansion and consolidation that had begun under the Zhou and the Qin. Han rulers, notably Han Wudi (Han Wu Ti, or Martial Emperor of Han), successfully completed the assimilation into the empire of the regions south of the Yangtze River, including the Red River delta in what is today northern Vietnam. Han armies also marched westward as far as the Caspian Sea, pacifying nomadic tribal peoples and extending China's boundary far into Central Asia (see Map 5.5 on p. 116).

The latter project apparently was originally planned as a means to fend off pressure from the nomadic Xiongnu peoples, who periodically threatened Chinese lands from their base area north of the Great Wall. In 138 B.C.E., Emperor Wudi dispatched the courtier Zhang Qian (Chang Ch'ien) on a mission westward into Central Asia to seek alliances with peoples living in the area against the common Xiongnu menace. Zhang Qian returned home with ample information about political and economic conditions in Central Asia. The new knowledge provoked the Han court to establish the first Chinese military presence in the area of the Taklamakan Desert and the Tian Shan (Heavenly Mountains). Eventually, this area would become known to the Chinese people as Xinjiang, or "New Region."

Chinese commercial exchanges with peoples in Central Asia now began to expand dramatically. Eastward into China came grapes, precious metals, glass objects, and horses from Persia and Central Asia. Horses were of particular significance because Chinese military strategists had learned of the importance of cavalry in their battles against the Xiongnu and sought the sturdy Ferghana horses of Bactria to increase their own military effectiveness. In return, China exported silk, above all, to countries to the west.

Silk, a filament created from the cocoons of silkworms, had been produced in China since the fourth millennium B.C.E. Eventually, knowledge of the wonder product reached the outside world, and Chinese silk exports began to rise dramatically. By the second century B.C.E., the first items made from silk reached the Mediterranean Sea, stimulating the first significant contacts between China and Rome, its great counterpart in

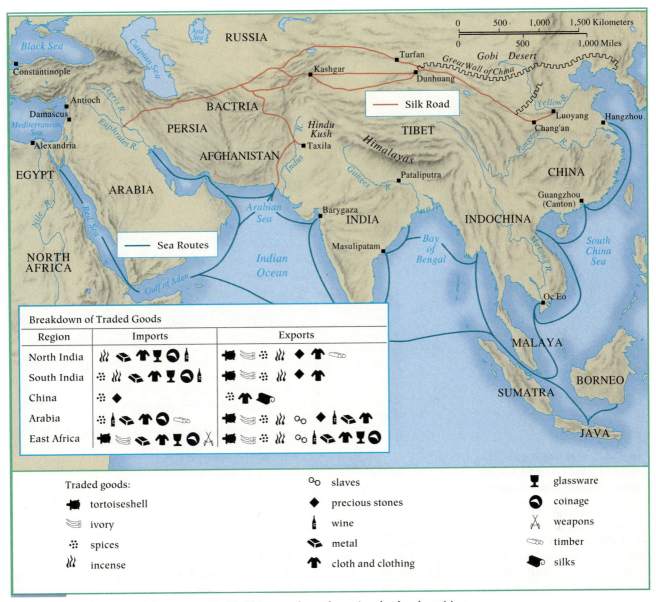

Traded goods:

tortoiseshell	slaves	glassware
ivory	precious stones	coinage
spices	wine	weapons
incense	metal	timber
	cloth and clothing	silks

MAP 5.4 **Trade Routes of the Ancient World.** This map shows the various land and maritime routes that extended from China toward other civilizations that were located to the south and west of the Han Empire. The various goods that were exchanged are identified at the bottom of the map. ❓ Why do you think China had so few imports? What other patterns do you see?

the west. The bulk of the trade went overland through Central Asia (thus earning this route its current name as the Silk Road), although significant exchanges also took place via the maritime route (see Chapter 9). Silk became a popular craze among Roman elites, leading to a vast outflow of silver from Rome to China and provoking the Roman emperor Tiberius to grumble that "the ladies and their baubles are transferring our money to foreigners."

The silk trade also stimulated a degree of mutual curiosity between the two great civilizations, but not much mutual knowledge or understanding. Roman authors like Pliny and the geographer Strabo (who speculated that silk was produced from the leaves of a silk

tree) wrote of a strange land called "Seres" far to the east, while Chinese sources mentioned the empire of "Great Qin" at the far end of the Silk Route to the west. So far as is known, no personal or diplomatic contacts between the two civilizations ever took place. But two great empires at either extreme of the Eurasian supercontinent had for the first time been linked together in a commercial relationship.

Social Changes

Under the Han dynasty, Chinese social institutions evolved into more complex forms than had been the case in past eras. The emergence of a free peasantry resulted in a

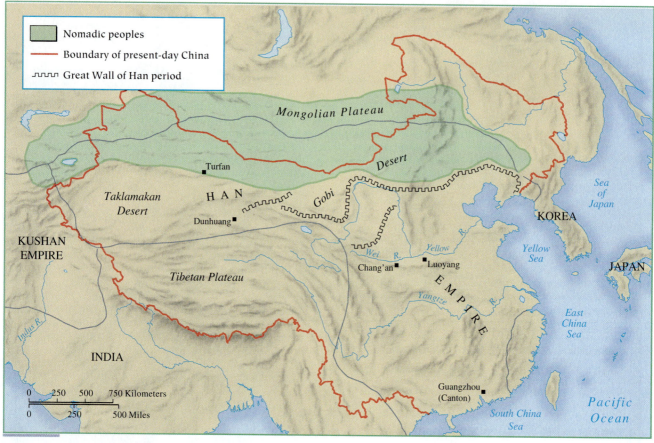

MAP 5.5 **The Han Empire.** This map shows the territory under the control of the Han Empire at its greatest extent during the first century B.C.E. Note the Great Wall's placement relative to nomadic peoples. ❓ How did the expansion of Han rule to the west parallel the Silk Road?

strengthening of the nuclear family, although the joint family—the linear descendant of the clan system in the Zhou dynasty—continued to hold sway in much of the countryside. The vast majority of Chinese continued to live in rural areas, but the number of cities, mainly at the junction of rivers and trade routes, was on the increase. The largest was the imperial capital of Chang'an, which was one of the great cities of the ancient world and rivaled Rome in magnificence. The city covered a total area of nearly 16 square miles and was enclosed by a 12-foot earthen wall surrounded by a moat. Twelve gates provided entry into the city, and eight major avenues run east-west or north-south. Each avenue was nearly 150 feet wide; a center strip in each avenue was reserved for the emperor, whose palace and gardens occupied nearly half of the southern and central parts of the city.

Religion and Culture

The Han dynasty's adoption of Confucianism as the official philosophy of the state did not have much direct impact on the religious beliefs of the Chinese people. Although official sources sought to flesh out the scattered metaphysical references in the Confucian canon with a more coherent cosmology, the pantheon of popular religion was still peopled by local deities and spirits of nature, some connected with popular Daoism. Sometime in the first century C.E., however, a new salvationist faith appeared on the horizon. Merchants from Central Asia carrying their wares over the Silk Road brought the Buddhist faith to China for the first time. At first, its influence was limited, as no Buddhist text was translated into Chinese from the original Sanskrit until the fifth century C.E. But the terrain was ripe for the introduction of a new religion into China, and the first Chinese monks departed for India shortly after the end of the Han dynasty.

Cultural attainments under the Han dynasty tended in general to reflect traditional forms, although there was considerable experimentation with new forms of expression. In literature, poetry and philosphical essays continued to be popular, but historical writing became the primary form of literary creativity. Historians such as Sima Qian and Ban Gu (the dynasty's official historian and the older brother of the female historian Ban Zhao) wrote works that became models for later dynastic histories. These historical works combined political and social history with biographies of key figures. Like so much literary work in China, their primary purpose was moral and political—to explain the underlying reasons for the rise and fall of individual human beings and dynasties.

Painting—often in the form of wall frescoes—became increasingly popular, although little has survived the ravages of time. In the plastic arts, bronze was steadily being replaced by iron as a medium of choice. Less rare, it was better able to satisfy the growing popular demand during a time of increasing economic affluence.

The Decline and Fall of the Han

In 9 C.E., the reformist official Wang Mang, who was troubled by the plight of the peasants, seized power from the Han court and declared the foundation of the Xin (New) dynasty. The empire had been crumbling for decades. As frivolous or depraved rulers amused themselves with the pleasures of court life, the power and influence of the central government began to wane, and the great noble families filled the vacuum, amassing vast landed estates and transforming free farmers into tenants. Wang Mang tried to confiscate the great estates, restore the ancient well field system, and abolish slavery. In so doing, however, he alienated powerful interests, who conspired to overthrow him. In 23 C.E., beset by administrative chaos and a collapse of the frontier defenses, Wang Mang was killed in a coup d'état.

For a time, strong leadership revived some of the glory of the early Han. The court did attempt to reduce land taxes and carry out land resettlement programs. The growing popularity of nutritious crops like rice, wheat, and soybeans, along with the introduction of new crops such as alfalfa and grapes, helped boost food production. But the monopoly of land and power by the great landed families continued. Weak rulers were isolated within their imperial chambers and dominated by eunuchs and other powerful figures at court. Official corruption and the concentration of land in the hands of the wealthy led to

CHRONOLOGY The Han Dynasty	
Overthrow of Qin dynasty	206 B.C.E.
Formation of Han dynasty	202 B.C.E.
Reign of Emperor Wudi	141–87 B.C.E.
Zhang Qian's first mission to Central Asia	138–126 B.C.E.
First silk goods arrive in Europe	Second century B.C.E.
Wang Mang interregnum	9–23 C.E.
First Buddhist merchants arrive in China	First century C.E.
Collapse of Han dynasty	221 C.E.

widespread peasant unrest. The Han also continued to have problems with the Xiongnu beyond the Great Wall to the north. Nomadic raids on Chinese territory continued intermittently to the end of the dynasty, once reaching almost to the gates of the capital city.

Buffeted by insurmountable problems within and without, in the late second century C.E., the dynasty entered a period of inexorable decline. The population of the empire, which had been estimated at about sixty million in China's first census in the year 2 C.E., had shrunk to less than one-third that number two hundred years later. In the early third century C.E., the dynasty was finally brought to an end when power was seized by Cao Cao (Ts'ao Ts'ao), a general known to later generations as one of the main characters in the famous Chinese epic *The Romance of the Three Kingdoms*. But Cao Cao was unable to consolidate his power, and China entered a period of almost constant anarchy and internal division, compounded by invasions by northern tribal peoples. The next great dynasty did not arise until the beginning of the seventh century, four hundred years later.

Courtesy of William J. Duiker

Han Dynasty Horse. This terracotta horse head is a striking example of Han artistry. Although the Chinese had domesticated the smaller Mongolian pony as early as 2000 B.C.E., it was not until toward the end of the first millennium B.C.E. that the Chinese acquired horses as a result of military expeditions into Central Asia. Admired for their power and grace, horses made of terra-cotta or bronze were often placed in Qin and Han tombs. This magnificent head suggests the divine power that the Chinese of this time attributed to horses.

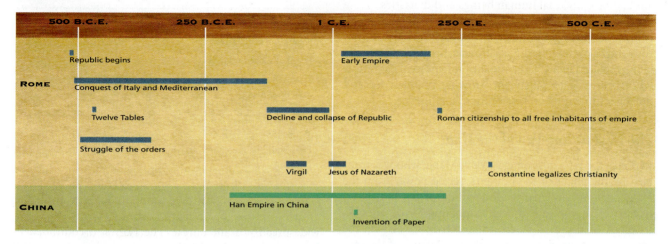

	500 B.C.E.	250 B.C.E.	1 C.E.	250 C.E.	500 C.E.

ROME

Republic begins

Conquest of Italy and Mediterranean

Early Empire

Twelve Tables

Decline and collapse of Republic

Roman citizenship to all free inhabitants of empire

Struggle of the orders

Virgil

Jesus of Nazareth

Constantine legalizes Christianity

CHINA

Han Empire in China

Invention of Paper

CONCLUSION

$\mathcal{A}$T THE BEGINNING OF THE FIRST MILLENNIUM C.E., two great empires—the Roman Empire in the West and the Han Empire in the East—dominated large areas of the world. Although there was little contact between them, the Han Empire and the Roman Empire had some remarkable similarities. Both empires lasted for centuries, and both had remarkable success in establishing centralized control over their empires. They built elaborate systems of roads in order to rule efficiently and relied on provincial officials, and especially on towns and cities, for local administration. In both empires, settled conditions led to a high level of agricultural production that sustained large populations, estimated at between fifty and sixty million in each empire. Although both empires expanded into areas that had different languages, ethnic groups, and ways of life, they managed to carry their legal and political institutions, their technical skills, and their languages throughout their empires.

The Roman and Han Empires had similar social and economic structures. The family stood at the heart of the social structure, with the male head of the family as all-powerful. Duty, courage, obedience, discipline—all were values inculcated by the family that helped make the empires strong. The wealth of both societies also depended on agriculture. Although a free peasantry was a backbone of strength and stability in each, the gradual conversion of free peasants into tenant farmers by wealthy landowners was common to both societies and ultimately served to undermine the power of their imperial governments.

Of course, there were also significant differences. Social mobility was less limited in Rome than in China. And merchants were more highly regarded and allowed more freedom in Rome than they were in China. The dynastic principle in China added a strong element of stability. With the mandate of Heaven, Chinese rulers had the authority to command by a mandate from divine forces that was easily passed on to other family members. Although Roman emperors were accorded divine status by the Roman senate after their death, accession to the Roman imperial throne depended less on solid dynastic principles and more on pure military force. As a result, over a period of centuries, Chinese imperial authority was far more stable.

Despite the differences, one major similarity remains—like the Han Empire, the Roman Empire was eventually faced with overwhelming problems. Both empires suffered from overexpansion, and both fortified their long borders with walls, forts, and military garrisons to guard against invasions of nomadic peoples. Both empires were eventually overcome by these peoples: the Han dynasty was weakened by the incursions of the Xiongnu, and the western Roman Empire eventually collapsed in the face of incursions by the Germanic peoples. Nevertheless, a significant difference between these two contemporary empires remained. Although the Han dynasty collapsed, the Chinese imperial tradition, as well as the class structure and set of values that sustained it, continued, and the Chinese Empire, under new dynasties, continued into the twentieth century as a single political entity. The Roman Empire, on the other hand, collapsed and lived on only as an idea.

Nevertheless, Roman achievements were bequeathed to the future. The Romance languages of today (French, Italian, Spanish, Portuguese, and Romanian) are based on Latin. Western practices of impartial justice and trial by jury owe much to Roman law. As great builders, the Romans left monuments to their skills throughout Europe, some of which, such as aqueducts and roads, are still in use today. Aspects of Roman administrative practices survived in the Western world for centuries. The Romans also preserved the intellectual heritage of the Greco-Roman world of antiquity. Nevertheless, while many aspects of the Roman world would continue, the heirs of Rome created new civilizations—European, Islamic, and Byzantine—that would carry on yet another stage in the development of human society.

CHAPTER NOTES

1. Tacitus, *The Annals of Imperial Rome,* trans. Michael Grant (Harmondsworth, England, 1964), p. 31.
2. Virgil, *The Aeneid,* trans. C. Day Lewis (Garden City, N.Y., 1952), p. 154.
3. Juvenal, *The Sixteen Satires,* trans. P. Green (New York, 1967), sat. 10, p. 207.
4. Quoted in Chester Starr, *Past and Future in Ancient History* (Lanham, Md., 1987), pp. 38–39.
5. Matthew 7:12.
6. Mark 12:30–31.

SUGGESTED READING

For a general account of Roman history, see **M.T. Boatwright, D. J. Gargola,** and **R. J. A. Talbert,** *The Romans: From Village to Empire* (New York, 2004). Good surveys of the Roman Republic include **M. H. Crawford,** *The Roman Republic,* 2d ed. (Cambridge, Mass., 1993); **H. H. Scullard,** *History of the Roman World, 753-146 B.C.,* 4th ed. (London, 1978); **M. Le Glay, J.-L. Voisin,** and **Y. Le Bohec,** *A History of Rome,* trans. **A. Nevill** (Oxford, 1996); and **A. Kamm,** *The Romans* (London, 1995). The history of early Rome is well covered in **T. J. Cornell,** *The Beginnings of Rome: Italy and Rome from the Bronze Age to the Punic Wars (c. 1000–264 B.C.)* (London, 1995).

Accounts of Rome's expansion in the Mediterranean world are provided by **J.-M. David,** *The Roman Conquest of Italy,* trans. **A. Nevill** (Oxford, 1996), and **R. M. Errington,** *The Dawn of Empire: Rome's Rise to World Power* (Ithaca, N.Y., 1971). On Rome's struggle with Carthage, see **A. Goldsworthy,** *The Punic Wars* (New York, 2001).

An excellent account of basic problems in the late Republic can be found in **M. Beard** and **M. H. Crawford,** *Rome in the Late Republic* (London, 1984). The classic work on the fall of the Republic is **R. Syme,** *The Roman Revolution* (Oxford, 1960). Also valuable are **D. Shotter,** *The Fall of the Roman Republic* (London, 1994), and **E. Hildinger,** *Swords Against the Senate: The Rise of the Roman Army and the Fall of the Republic* (Cambridge, Mass., 2002).

Good surveys of the Early Roman Empire include **P. Garnsey** and **R. Saller,** *The Roman Empire: Economy, Society and Culture* (London, 1987); **C. Wells,** *The Roman Empire,* 2d ed. (London, 1992); and **M. Goodman,** *The Roman World, 44 B.C.–A.D. 180* (London, 1997). The Roman army is examined in **A. Goldsworthy,** *The Complete Roman Army* (London, 2003).

A good survey of Roman literature can be found in **R. M. Ogilvie,** *Roman Literature and Society* (Harmondsworth, England, 1980). On Roman art and architecture, see **R. Ling,** *Roman Painting* (New York, 1991); **D. E. Kleiner,** *Roman Sculpture* (New Haven, Conn., 1992); and **M. Wheeler,** *Roman Art and Architecture* (London, 1964). A general study of daily life in Rome is **F. Dupont,** *Daily Life in Ancient Rome* (Oxford, 1994). On the city of Rome, see **O. F. Robinson,** *Ancient Rome: City Planning and Administration* (New York, 1992). On the Roman family, see **S. Dixon,** *The Roman Family* (Baltimore, 1992). Roman women are examined in **R. Baumann,** *Women and Politics in Ancient Rome* (New York, 1995). On slavery, see **K. R. Bradley,** *Slavery and Society at Rome* (New York, 1994). On the gladiators, see **T. Wiedemann,** *Emperors and Gladiators* (New York, 1992).

On the Late Roman Empire, see **A. Cameron,** *The Later Roman Empire* (Cambridge, Mass., 1993). On the fourth century, see **T. D. Barnes,** *The New Empire of Diocletian and Constantine* (Cambridge, Mass., 1982). Studies analyzing the aristocratic circles, the barbarian invasions, and the military problem include **E. A. Thompson,** *Romans and Barbarians* (Madison, Wis., 1982); **A. Ferrill,** *The Fall of the Roman Empire: The Military Explanation* (London, 1986); and **P. Heather,** *The Fall of the Roman Empire: A New History of Rome and the Barbarians* (New York, 2006). On the relationship between the Romans and the Germans, see **T. S. Burns,** *Rome and the Barbarians, 100 B.C.–A.D. 400* (Baltimore, 2003).

For a general introduction to early Christianity, see **J. Court** and **K. Court,** *The New Testament World* (Cambridge, 1990). Useful works on early Christianity include **W. H. C. Frend,** *The Rise of Christianity* (Philadelphia, 1984), and **R. MacMullen,** *Christianizing the Roman Empire* (New Haven, Conn., 1984). For a detailed analysis of Christianity in the 30s and 40s of the first century C.E., see **J. D. Crossan,** *The Birth of Christianity* (New York, 1998). On Christian women, see **D. M. Scholer,** ed., *Women in Early Christianity* (New York, 1993), and **R. Kraemer,** *Her Share of the Blessings: Women's Religion Among the Pagans, Jews and Christians in the Graeco-Roman World* (Oxford, 1995).

There are a number of useful books on the Han dynasty. **Zhongshu Wang,** *Han Civilization* (New Haven, Conn., 1982), presents evidence from the mainland on excavations from Han tombs and the old imperial capital of Chang'an. Also see the lavishly illustrated *Han Civilization of China* (Oxford, 1982) by **M. P. Serstevens.**

 InfoTrac College Edition
Visit this chapter's InfoTrac College Edition/Research activities at the *Essential World History* Companion Website for activities related to Rome and Han China.

CENGAGENOW **for Duiker and Spielvogel's** *The Essential World History, Third Edition*
Enter *CengageNOW* using the access card that is available with this text. *CengageNOW* will assist you in understanding the content in this chapter with lesson plans generated for your needs, as well as provide you with a connection to the *Wadsworth World History Resource Center* (see description below for details).

WORLD HISTORY
RESOURCE CENTER

Enter the Resource Center using either your *CengageNOW* access card or your standalone access card for the *Wadsworth World History Resource Center*. Organized by topic, this website includes quizzes; images; over 350 primary source documents; interactive simulations, maps, and timelines; movie explorations; and a wealth of other resources. You can read the following documents, and many more, at http://worldrc.wadsworth.com/

Plutarch, *Life of Caesar*

Virgil, *The Aeneid,* bk. I

Visit the *Essential World History* Companion Website for chapter quizzes and more: academic.cengage.com/history/duiker

THE IMMEDIATE CONSEQUENCES of the fall of Rome and the Han dynasty were a precipitous drop in world trade and a general decline of prosperity throughout the known world. But new societies eventually rose on the ashes of the ancient empires. Although many were different in key respects from those they replaced, they still carried the legacy of their predecessors. In the meantime, the forces that had been unleashed in the civilizations of antiquity sent out strands of influence that were laying the basis for new societies elsewhere in the world: south of the Sahara in western and eastern Africa, where new societies were beginning to take shape;

TIMELINE

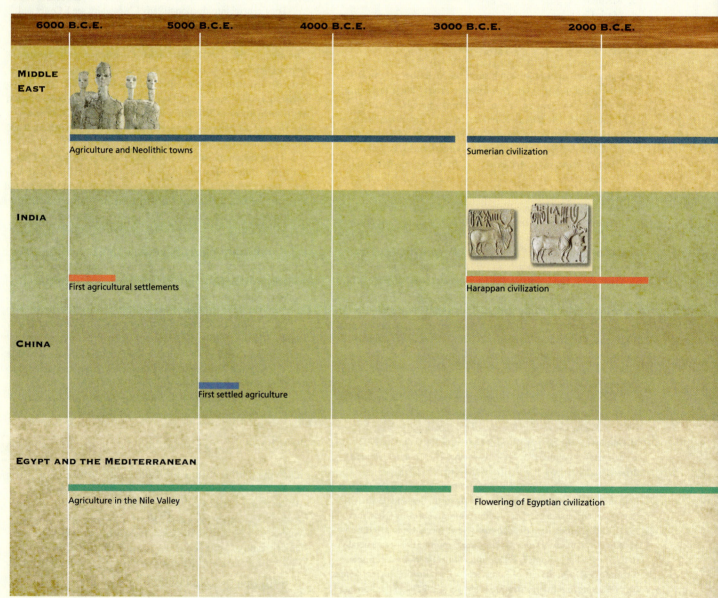

	6000 B.C.E.	5000 B.C.E.	4000 B.C.E.	3000 B.C.E.	2000 B.C.E.
MIDDLE EAST	Agriculture and Neolithic towns			Sumerian civilization	
INDIA	First agricultural settlements			Harappan civilization	
CHINA		First settled agriculture			
EGYPT AND THE MEDITERRANEAN	Agriculture in the Nile Valley			Flowering of Egyptian civilization	

beyond the Alps in central Europe, where the Germanic peoples were in the process of forming a new society; in southeastern Asia, where the influence of India and China was beginning to help shape new societies among the trading and agricultural societies in the region; and across the Sea of Japan in the Japanese islands, where native rulers would import Chinese ideas to form a new civilization uniquely their own. In the meantime, new civilizations were on the verge of creation across the oceans in the continents of North and South America.

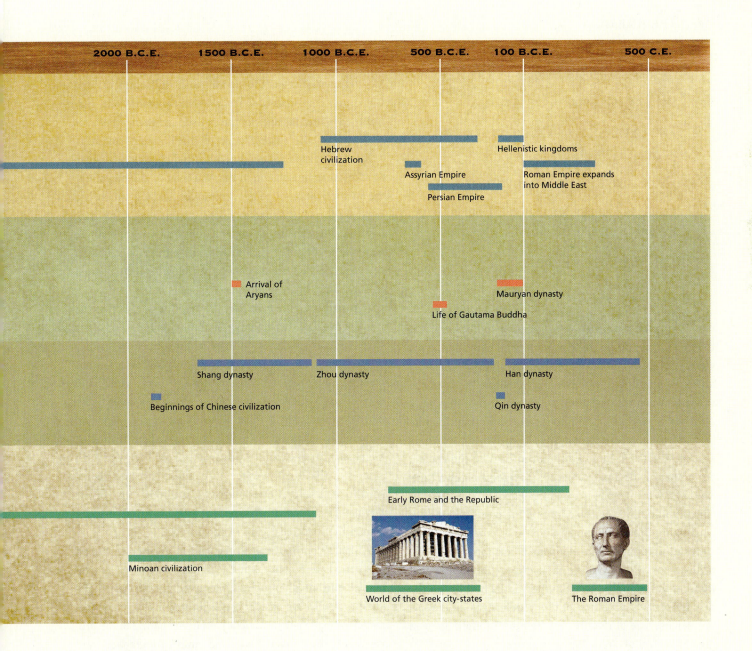

| 2000 B.C.E. | 1500 B.C.E. | 1000 B.C.E. | 500 B.C.E. | 100 B.C.E. | 500 C.E. |

Hebrew civilization

Hellenistic kingdoms

Assyrian Empire

Roman Empire expands into Middle East

Persian Empire

Arrival of Aryans

Mauryan dynasty

Life of Gautama Buddha

Shang dynasty

Zhou dynasty

Han dynasty

Beginnings of Chinese civilization

Qin dynasty

Early Rome and the Republic

Minoan civilization

World of the Greek city-states

The Roman Empire

II

NEW PATTERNS OF CIVILIZATION

*B*Y THE BEGINNING of the first millennium C.E., the great states of the ancient world were in decline; some were even at the point of collapse. On the ruins of these ancient empires, new patterns of civilization began to take shape between 400 and 1500 C.E. In some cases, these new societies were built on the political and cultural foundations of their predecessors. The Tang dynasty in China and the Guptas in India both looked back to the ancient period to provide an ideological model for their own time. The Byzantine Empire carried on parts of the classical Greek tradition while also adopting the powerful creed of Christianity from the Roman Empire. In other cases, new states incorporated some elements of the former classical civilizations while heading in markedly different directions, as in the Arabic states in the Middle East and in the new European civilization of the Middle Ages. In Europe, the Renaissance of the fifteenth century brought an even greater revival of Greco-Roman culture.

During this period, a number of significant forces were at work in human society. The concept of civilization gradually spread from the heartland regions of the Middle East, the Mediterranean basin, the South Asian subcontinent, and China into new areas of the world—sub-Saharan Africa, central and western Europe, Southeast Asia, and even the islands of Japan, off the eastern edge of the Eurasian landmass. Across the oceans, unique but advanced civilizations began to take shape in isolation in the Americas. In the meantime, the vast migration of peoples continued, leading not only to bitter conflicts but also to increased interchanges of technology and ideas. The result was the transformation of separate and distinct cultures and civilizations into an increasingly complex and vast world system embracing not only technology and trade but also ideas and religious beliefs.

As had been the case during antiquity, the Middle East was the heart of this activity. The Arab Empire, which took shape after the death of Muhammad in the early seventh century, provided the key link in the revived trade routes through the region. Muslim traders—both Arab and Berber—opened contacts with West African societies south of the Sahara, while their ships followed the monsoon winds eastward as far as the Spice Islands in Southeast Asia. Merchants from Central Asia carried goods back and forth along the Silk Road between the Middle East and China. For the next several hundred years, the great cities of the Middle East—Mecca, Damascus, and Baghdad—became among the wealthiest in the known world.

Islam's contributions to the human experience during this period were cultural and technological as well as economic. Muslim philosophers preserved the works of the ancient Greeks for posterity, Muslim scientists and mathematicians made new discoveries about the nature of the universe and the human body, and Arab cartographers and historians mapped the known world and speculated about the fundamental forces in human society.

But the Middle East was not the only or necessarily even the primary contributor to the spread of civilization during this period. While the Arab Empire became the linchpin of trade between the Mediterranean and eastern and southern Asia, a new center of primary importance in world trade was emerging in East Asia, focused on China. China had been a major participant in regional trade during the Han dynasty, when its silks were already being transported to Rome via Central Asia, but its role had declined after the fall of the Han. Now, with the rise of the great Tang and Song dynasties, China reemerged as a major commercial power in East Asia, trading by sea with Southeast Asia and Japan and by land with the nomadic peoples of Central Asia. Like the Middle East, China was also a prime source of new technology. From China came paper, printing, the compass, and gunpowder. The double-hulled Chinese junks that entered the Indian Ocean during the Ming dynasty were slow and cumbersome but extremely seaworthy and capable of carrying substantial quantities of goods over long distances. Many inventions arrived in Europe by way of India or the Middle East, and their Chinese origins were therefore unknown in the West.

Increasing trade on a regional or global basis also led to the exchange of ideas. Buddhism was brought to China by merchants, and Islam first arrived in sub-Saharan Africa and the Indonesian archipelago in the same manner. Merchants were not the only means by which religious and cultural ideas spread, however. Sometimes migration, conquest, or relatively peaceful processes played a part. The case of the Bantu-speaking peoples in Central Africa is apparently an example of peaceful expansion; and although Islam sometimes followed the path of Arab warriors, they rarely imposed their religion by force on the local population. In some instances, as with the Mongols, the conquerors made no

effort to convert others to their own religions. By contrast, Christian monks, motivated by missionary fervor, converted many of the peoples of central and eastern Europe. Roman Catholic monks brought Latin Christianity to the Germanic and western Slavic peoples, and monks from the Byzantine Empire largely converted the southern and eastern Slavic populations to Eastern Orthodox Christianity.

Another characteristic of the period between 500 and 1500 C.E. was the almost constant migration of nomadic and seminomadic peoples. Dynamic forces in the Gobi Desert, Central Asia, the Arabian peninsula, and Central Africa provoked vast numbers of peoples to abandon their homelands and seek their livelihood elsewhere. Sometimes the migration was peaceful. More often, however, migration produced violent conflict and sometimes invasion and subjugation. As had been the case during antiquity, the most active source of migrants was Central Asia. The region later gave birth to the fearsome Mongols, whose armies advanced to the gates of central Europe and conquered China in the thirteenth century. Wherever they went, they left a train of enormous destruction and loss of life. Inadvertently, the Mongols were also the source of a new wave of epidemics that swept through much of Europe and the Middle East in the fourteenth century. The spread of the plague—known at the time as the Black Death—took much of the population of Europe to an early grave.

But there was another side to the era of nomadic expansion. Even the invasions of the Mongols—the "scourge of God," as Europeans of the thirteenth and fourteenth centuries called them—had constructive as well as destructive consequences. After their initial conquests, for a brief period of three generations, the Mongols provided an avenue for trade throughout the most extensive empire (known as the Pax Mongolica) the world had yet seen. ◇

The Spanish conquest of the Aztecs

© The Granger Collection, New York

𝕴N AUGUST 1519, five hundred Spanish soldiers of fortune left their anchorage near the modern city of Veracruz on the Gulf of Mexico and began the long trek from the coast across the dusty plateau of Mexico to the capital of the Aztecs. At their head was Hernán Cortés, a Spanish conquistador who had just burned the ship on which he arrived to ensure that his followers would not launch a mutiny and sail back to Europe. In Tenochtitlán, the Aztec capital located at what is now Mexico City, Emperor Moctezuma received the news of the foreigners' presence and awaited their arrival with anticipation. According to Aztec legend, one of their ancestors, the godlike Quetzalcoatl, had left the area hundreds of years earlier, vowing to return one day to reclaim his heritage. Could this stranger with his band of men be Quetzalcoatl or his representative? When Cortés and his forces, now accompanied by a crowd of people they had encountered en route, reached the vicinity of Moctezuma's capital, the two men met face to face. With this encounter, the last barrier between the Old World and the previously unknown civilizations in the Western Hemisphere had been bridged, and a new era dawned. ◈

The Peopling of the Americas

The Aztecs were only the latest in a series of sophisticated societies that had sprung up at various locations in North and South America since human beings first crossed the Bering Strait several millennia earlier. Most of these early peoples, today often referred to as **Amerindians,** lived by hunting and fishing or by food gathering. But by the second millennium B.C.E., the first organized societies, based on the cultivation of agriculture, began to take root in Central and South America. One key area of development was on the plateau of central Mexico. Another was in the lowland regions along the Gulf of Mexico and extending into modern Guatemala. A third was in the central Andes Mountains, adjacent to the Pacific coast of South America. Others were just beginning to emerge in the river valleys and Great Plains of North America.

For the next two thousand years, these societies developed in isolation from their counterparts elsewhere in the world. This lack of contact with other human beings deprived them of access to technological and cultural developments taking place in Africa, Asia, and Europe. They did not know of the wheel, for example, and their written languages were rudimentary compared to equivalents in complex civilizations in other parts of the globe. But in other respects, their cultural achievements were the equal of those realized elsewhere. When the first European explorers arrived in the Americas at the turn of the sixteenth century, they described much that they observed in glowing terms.

The First Americans

When the first human beings arrived in the Western Hemisphere has long been a matter of dispute. In the centuries following the voyages of Christopher Columbus, speculation centered on the possibility that the first settlers to reach the American continents had crossed the Atlantic Ocean. Were they the lost tribes of Israel? Were they Phoenician seafarers from Carthage? Were they refugees from the legendary lost continent of Atlantis? In all cases, the assumption was that they were relatively recent arrivals.

By the mid-nineteenth century, under the influence of the new Darwinian concept of evolution, a new theory developed. It proposed that the peopling of America had taken place much earlier as a result of the migration of small communities across the Bering Strait. Recent evidence, including numerous physical similarities between some early Americans and contemporary peoples living in northeastern Asia, has confirmed this hypothesis. The debate on when the migrations began continues, however. The archaeologist Louis Leakey, one of the pioneers in the search for the origins of humankind in Africa, suggested that the first hominids may have arrived in America as long as 100,000 years ago. Others estimate that the first Americans were members of *Homo sapiens sapiens* who crossed from Asia by foot between 10,000 and 15,000 years ago in pursuit of herds of bison and caribou that moved into the area in search of grazing land at the end of the last ice age. A recently discovered site at Cactus Hill, in central Virginia, shows signs of human habitation as early as 15,000 years ago. Genetic evidence now suggests the possibility of an earlier date, perhaps as early as 29,000 years ago. And other recent discoveries indicate that some early settlers may have originally come from Africa rather than from Asia. The question has not yet been definitively answered.

Nevertheless, it is now generally accepted that human beings were living in the Americas at least 15,000 years ago. They gradually spread throughout the North American continent and had penetrated almost to the southern tip of South America by about 10,000 B.C.E. These first Americans were hunters and food gatherers who lived in small nomadic communities close to the source of their food supply. Although it is not known when agriculture was first practiced, beans and squash seeds have been found at sites that date back at least 8,000 years. The cultivation of maize (corn), and perhaps other crops as well, appears to have been under way in the lowland regions near the modern city of Veracruz and in the Yucatán peninsula farther to the east. There, in the region that archaeologists call **Mesoamerica,** one of the first civilizations in the Western Hemisphere began to appear.

Early Civilizations in Central America

The first signs of civilization in Mesoamerica appeared in the first millennium B.C.E., with the emergence of what is called Olmec culture in the hot and swampy lowlands along the coast of the Gulf of Mexico south of Veracruz (see Map 6.1). Olmec civilization was characterized by intensive agriculture along the muddy riverbanks in the area and by the carving of stone ornaments, tools, and monuments at sites such as San Lorenzo and La Venta. The site at La Venta includes a ceremonial precinct with a 30-foot-high earthen pyramid, the largest of its date in all Mesoamerica. The Olmec peoples organized a widespread trading network, carried on religious rituals, and devised an as yet undeciphered system of hieroglyphs that is similar in some respects to later Mayan writing (see "Mayan Hieroglyphs and Calendars" later in this chapter) and may be the ancestor of the first true writing systems in the Western Hemisphere.

Olmec society apparently consisted of several classes, including a class of skilled artisans who produced a series of massive stone heads, some of which are more than 10 feet high. The Olmec peoples supported themselves primarily by cultivating crops, such as corn and beans, but also engaged in fishing and hunting.

Eventually, Olmec civilization began to decline and apparently collapsed around the fourth century B.C.E.

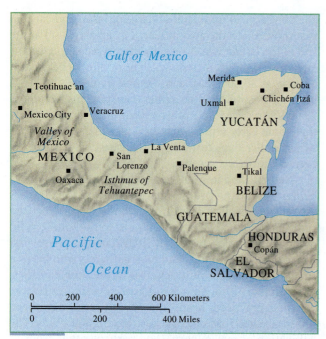

MAP 6.1 The Heartland of Mesoamerica. Mesoamerica was home to some of the first civilizations in the Western Hemisphere. This map shows the major urban settlements in the region. ❓ What areas were most associated with Olmec, Mayan, and Aztec culture?

During its heyday, however, it extended from Mexico City to El Salvador and perhaps to the shores of the Pacific Ocean.

Teotihuacán: America's First Metropolis

The first major metropolis in Mesoamerica was the city of Teotihuacán, capital of an early kingdom about 30 miles northeast of Mexico City that arose around the third century B.C.E. and flourished for nearly a millennium until it collapsed under mysterious circumstances about 800 C.E. Along the main thoroughfare were temples and palaces, all dominated by the massive Pyramid of the Sun (see the comparative illustration "The Pyramid" on p. 127), under which archaeologists have discovered the remains of sacrificial victims, probably put to death during the dedication of the structure. In the vicinity are the remains of a large market where goods from distant regions as well as agricultural produce grown by farmers in the vicinity were exchanged. The products traded included cacao, rubber, feathers, and various types of vegetables and meat. Pulque, a liquor extracted from the agave plant, was used in religious ceremonies. An obsidian mine nearby may explain the location of the city; obsidian is a volcanic glass that was prized in Mesoamerica for use in tools, mirrors, and the blades of sacrificial knives.

Most of the city consisted of one-story stucco apartment compounds; some were as large as 35,000 square feet,

sufficient to house more than a hundred people. Each apartment was divided into several rooms, and the compounds were covered by flat roofs made of wooden beams, poles, and stucco. The compounds were separated by wide streets laid out on a rectangular grid and were entered through narrow alleys.

Living in the fertile Valley of Mexico, an upland plateau surrounded by magnificent snowcapped mountains, the inhabitants of Teotihuacán probably obtained the bulk of their wealth from agriculture. At that time, the valley floor was filled with swampy lakes containing the water runoff from the surrounding mountains. The combination of fertile soil and adequate water combined to make the valley one of the richest farming areas in Mesoamerica.

Sometime during the eighth century C.E., for unknown reasons, the wealth and power of the city began to decline. The next two centuries were a time of troubles throughout the region as principalities fought over limited farmland. The problem was later compounded when peoples from surrounding areas, attracted by the rich farmlands, migrated into the Valley of Mexico and began to compete for territory with small city-states already established there. As the local population expanded, farmers began to engage in more intensive agriculture. They drained the lakes to build *chinampas,* swampy islands crisscrossed by canals that provided water for their crops and easy transportation to local markets for their excess produce.

The Maya

Far to the east of the Valley of Mexico, in the Yucatán peninsula another major civilization had taken form. This was the civilization of the Maya, which was older and just as sophisticated as the society at Teotihuacán.

Origins Like the Aztecs and the inhabitants of Teotihuacán, the Maya trace their origins to the parent Olmec civilization in the lowlands along the Gulf of Mexico. It is not known when human beings first inhabited the Yucatán peninsula, but peoples contemporaneous with the Olmecs were already cultivating such crops as corn, yams, and manioc in the area during the first millennium B.C.E. As the population increased, an early civilization began to emerge along the Pacific coast directly to the south of the peninsula and in the highlands of modern Guatemala. Contacts were already established with the Olmecs to the west.

Since the area was a source for cacao trees and obsidian, the inhabitants soon developed relations with other early civilizations in the region. Cacao trees were the source of chocolate, which was used as a beverage by the upper classes, while cocoa beans, the fruit of the cacao tree, were used as currency in markets throughout the region.

As the population in the area increased, the inhabitants began to migrate into the central Yucatán peninsula

COMPARATIVE ILLUSTRATION

The Pyramid. The monumental structure known as the pyramid was characteristic of two very different civilizations in antiquity. On the left are the three pyramids at Giza, across the Nile River from Cairo. At the rear is the Great Pyramid of Khufu, constructed around 2540 B.C.E. Centuries later, pyramids were also erected by the Maya, Aztecs, and Toltecs in Central America. Shown below is the Pyramid of the Sun at Teotihuacán, erected around 400 C.E. and certainly one of the most impressive pyramids in the Americas. It rises in four tiers to a height of over 200 feet.

Mayan Temple at Tikal. This eighth-century temple, peering over the treetops of a jungle at Tikal, represents the zenith of the engineering and artistry of the Mayan peoples. Erected to house the body of a ruler, such pyramidal tombs contained elaborate works of jade jewelry, polychrome ceramics, and intricate bone carvings depicting the ruler's life and various deities. This temple dominates a great plaza that is surrounded by a royal palace and various religious structures.

The Arranged Marriage. The Maya recorded religious rites, as well as scenes of daily life, on polychrome clay vessels. Used in ritual ceremonies dedicated to the gods, these vessels contained a foamy chocolate beverage called *kakaw,* from which we derive the word *cacao,* the tree that produces the cocoa beans from which chocolate is made. The glyphs accompanying the scenes normally refer to the cacao as well as the vessel's patron, most often the local lord. Here we see three men presenting an offering for an arranged marriage with a lord's daughter, who is shown kneeling behind her father. Mayan rulers often married their daughters to men of lower rank in order to elevate the latter's status and thereby guarantee their allegiance.

to the north. The overcrowding forced farmers in the lowland areas to shift from slash-and-burn cultivation to swamp agriculture of the type practiced in the lake region of the Valley of Mexico. By the middle of the first millennium C.E., the entire area was honeycombed with a patchwork of small city-states competing for land and resources. The most important city-states were probably Tikal and Copán, but it is doubtful that any one was sufficiently powerful to dominate the area. The largest urban centers such as Tikal may have had 100,000 inhabitants at their height.

Political Structures The power of the rulers of the city-states was impressive. One of the monarchs at Copán—known to scholars as "18 Rabbit" from the hieroglyphs composing his name—ordered the construction of a grand palace requiring more than 30,000 person-days of labor. Around the ruler was a class of aristocrats whose wealth was probably based on the ownership of land farmed by their poorer relatives. Eventually, many of the aristocrats became priests or scribes at the royal court or adopted honored professions as sculptors or painters. As the society's wealth

grew, so did the role of artisans and traders, who began to form a small middle class.

The majority of the population on the peninsula, however (estimated at roughly three million at the height of Mayan power), were farmers. They lived on their *chinampa* plots or on terraced hills in the highlands. Houses were built of adobe and thatch and probably resembled the houses of the majority of the population in the area today. There was a fairly clear-cut division of labor along gender lines. The men were responsible for fighting and hunting, the women for homemaking and the preparation of cornmeal, the staple food of much of the population.

Some noblewomen seem to have played important roles in both political and religious life. In the seventh century C.E., for example, Pacal became king of Palenque, one of the most powerful of the Mayan city-states, through the royal line of his mother and grandmother, thereby breaking the patrilineal descent twice. His mother ruled Palenque for three years and was the power behind the throne for her son's first twenty-five years of rule. Pacal legitimized his kingship by transforming his mother into a divine representation of the "first mother" goddess.

THE CREATION OF THE WORLD: A MAYAN VIEW

RELIGION & PHILOSOPHY

Popul Vuh, a sacred work of the ancient Maya, is an account of Mayan history and religious beliefs. No written version in the original Mayan script is extant, but shortly after the Spanish conquest, it was written down in Quiche (the spoken language of the Maya), using the Latin script, apparently from memory. This version was later translated into Spanish. The following excerpt from the opening lines of Popul Vuh recounts the Mayan myth of the creation.

What similarities and differences do you see between this account of the beginning of the world and those of other ancient civilizations?

Popul Vuh: The Sacred Book of the Maya

This is the account of how all was in suspense, all calm, in silence; all motionless, still, and the expanse of the sky was empty.

This is the first account, the first narrative. There was neither man, nor animal, birds, fishes, crabs, trees, stones, caves, ravines, grasses, nor forests; there was only the sky.

The surface of the earth had not appeared. There was only the calm sea and the great expanse of the sky.

There was nothing brought together, nothing which could make a noise, nor anything which might move, or tremble, or could make noise in the sky.

There was nothing standing; only the calm water, the placid sea, alone and tranquil. Nothing existed.

There was only immobility and silence in the darkness, in the night. Only the Creator, the Maker, Tepeu, Gucumatz, the Forefathers, were in the water surrounded with light. They were hidden under green and blue feathers, and were therefore called Gucumatz. By nature they were great sages and great thinkers. In this manner the sky existed and also the Heart of Heaven, which is the name of God and thus He is called.

Then came the word. Tepeu and Gucumatz came together in the darkness, in the night, and Tepeu and Gucumatz talked together. They talked then, discussing and deliberating; they agreed, they united their words and their thoughts.

Then while they meditated, it became clear to them that when dawn would break, man must appear. Then they planned the creation, and the growth of the trees and the thickets and the birth of life and the creation of man. Thus it was arranged in the darkness and in the night by the Heart of Heaven who is called Huracan.

The first is called Caculha Huracan. The second is Chipi-Caculha. The third is Raxa-Caculha. And these three are the Heart of Heaven.

So it was that they made perfect the work, when they did it after thinking and meditating upon it.

CENGAGENOW To read more of Popul Vuh, enter the *CengageNOW* documents area using the access card that is available for *The Essential World History*.

Mayan Religion Mayan religion was polytheistic. Although the names were different, Mayan gods shared many of the characteristics of deities of nearby cultures. The supreme god was named Itzamna (Lizard House). Deities were ranked in order of importance and had human characteristics, as in ancient Greece and India. Some, like the jaguar god of night, were evil rather than good. Some scholars believe that many of the nature deities may have been viewed as manifestations of one supreme godhead (see the box above). As at Teotihuacán, human sacrifice (normally by decapitation) was practiced to propitiate the heavenly forces. Scholars once believed that the Maya were a peaceful people who rarely engaged in violence. Now, however, it is thought that rivalry among Mayan city-states was endemic and often involved bloody clashes. Scenes from paintings and rock carvings depict a society preoccupied with war and the seizure of captives for sacrifice.

Physically, the Mayan cities were built around a ceremonial core dominated by a central pyramid surmounted by a shrine to the gods. Nearby were other temples, palaces, and a sacred ball court. Like many of their modern counterparts, Mayan cities suffered from urban sprawl, with separate suburbs for the poor and the middle class.

The ball court was a rectangular space surrounded by vertical walls with metal rings through which the contestants attempted to drive a hard rubber ball. Although the rules of the game are only imperfectly understood, it apparently had religious significance, and the vanquished players were sacrificed in ceremonies held after the close of the game. Most of the players were men, although there may have been some women's teams. Similar courts have been found at sites throughout Central and South America, with the earliest, located near Veracruz, dating back to around 1500 B.C.E.

Mayan Hieroglyphs and Calendars In some ways, Mayan culture was more advanced than the later Aztec civilization in the Valley of Mexico. The Mayan writing system, which originated in the mid-first millennium C.E., was much more sophisticated than the relatively primitive system used by the Aztecs. Unfortunately, when the Spanish conquered the remains of Mayan civilization, they made no attempt to decipher the language with the assistance of natives familiar with the script. The Spanish bishop

A Ball Court. Throughout Mesoamerica, a dangerous game was played on ball courts such as this one. A large ball of solid rubber was propelled from the hip at such tremendous speed that players had to wear extensive padding. More than an athletic contest, the game had religious significance. The court is thought to have represented the cosmos and the ball the sun, and the losers were sacrificed to the gods in postgame ceremonies. The game is still played today in parts of Mexico.

Diego de Landa, otherwise an astute and sympathetic observer of Mayan culture, remarked, "We found a large number of books in these characters and, as they contained nothing in which there were not to be seen superstition and lies of the devil, we burned them all, which they regretted to an amazing degree, and which caused them much affliction."[1]

The Mayan hieroglyphs remained undeciphered until scholars discovered that many passages contained symbols that recorded dates in the Mayan calendar. This calendar, which measures time back to a particular date in August 3114 B.C.E., required a sophisticated understanding of astronomical events and mathematics to compile. Starting with these known symbols as a foundation, modern scholars have gradually deciphered the script. Like the scripts of the Sumerians and ancient Egyptians, the Mayan hieroglyphs were both ideographic and phonetic and were becoming more phonetic as time passed.

One of the most important repositories of Mayan hieroglyphs is at Palenque, an archaeological site deep in the jungles in the neck of the Mexican peninsula, considerably to the west of the Yucatán. In a chamber located under the Temple of Inscriptions, archaeologists discovered a royal tomb and a massive limestone slab covered with hieroglyphs. By deciphering the message on the slab, archaeologists for the first time identified a historical figure in Mayan history. He was the ruler named Pacal, known from his glyph as "The Shield"; Pacal ordered the construction of the Temple of Inscriptions in the mid-seventh century, and it was his body that was buried in the tomb at the foot of the staircase leading down into the crypt.

As befits their intense interest in the passage of time, the Maya also had a sophisticated knowledge of astronomy and kept voluminous records of the movements of the heavenly bodies. There were practical reasons for their concern. The arrival of the planet Venus in the evening sky, for example, was a traditional time to prepare for war. The Maya also devised the so-called Long Count, a system of calculating time based on the lunar calendar that calls for the end of the current cycle of 5,200 years in the year 2012 (according to the Western solar-based Gregorian calendar).

The Mystery of Mayan Decline   Sometime in the eighth or ninth century, the classical Mayan civilization in the central Yucatán peninsula began to decline. At Copán, for example, it ended abruptly in 822 C.E., when work on various stone sculptures ordered by the ruler suddenly ceased. The end of Palenque, a rival state to the west, soon followed. What caused the decline? Recent evidence supports the theory that overcultivation of the land due to a growing population gradually reduced crop yields. Another theory is that a long drought, which lasted for almost two centuries in the ninth and tenth centuries C.E., may have played a major role. We do know that the period was characterized by an increase in internecine war among the states and the rise of powerful nobles.

Whatever the case, cities like Tikal and Palenque were abandoned to the jungles, though newer urban centers in the northern part of the peninsula, like Uxmal and Chichén Itzá, survived and continued to prosper. According to local history, this latter area was taken over by peoples known as the Toltecs, led by a man known as Kukulcan ("feathered serpent"), who migrated to the peninsula from Tula in central Mexico sometime in the tenth century. Some scholars believe this flight was associated with the legend of the departure of Quetzalcoatl, the feathered serpent who promised that he would someday return to reclaim his homeland.

The Toltecs apparently controlled the upper peninsula from their capital at Chichén Itzá for several centuries, but this area was less fertile and more susceptible to drought than the regions of earlier Mayan settlement, and eventually the Toltecs also declined. When the Spaniards arrived, the area was divided into a number of small principalities, and the cities such as Uxmal and Chichén Itzá, had been abandoned.

The Aztecs

Among the groups moving into the Valley of Mexico after the fall of Teotihuacán were the Mexica (pronounced "Maysheeka"). No one knows their origins, although folk legend held that their original homeland was an island in a lake called Aztlán. From that legendary homeland comes the name *Aztec*, by which they are known to the modern world. Sometime during the early twelfth century, the Aztecs left their original habitat and, carrying an image of their patron deity, Huitzilopochtli, began a lengthy migration that climaxed with their arrival in the Valley of Mexico sometime late in the century.

Less sophisticated than many of their neighbors, the Aztecs were at first forced to seek alliances with stronger city-states. They were excellent warriors, however, and (like Sparta in ancient Greece and the state of Qin in Zhou dynasty China) had become the leading city-state in the lake region by the early fifteenth century. Establishing their capital at Tenochtitlán, on an island in the middle of Lake Texcoco, they set out to bring the entire region under their domination (see Map 6.2).

For the remainder of the fifteenth century, the Aztecs consolidated their control over much of what is modern Mexico, from the Atlantic to the Pacific Ocean and as far south as the Guatemalan border. The new kingdom was not a centralized state but a collection of semiautonomous territories. To provide a unifying focus for the kingdom, the Aztecs promoted their patron god, Huitzilopochtli, as the guiding deity of the entire population, which now numbered several million.

Politics Like all great empires in ancient times, the Aztec state was authoritarian. Power was vested in the monarch, whose authority had both a divine and a secular character. The Aztec ruler claimed descent from the gods and served as an intermediary between the material and the metaphysical worlds. Unlike many of his counterparts in other ancient civilizations, however, the monarch did not obtain his position by a rigid law of succession. On the death of the ruler, his successor was selected from within the royal family by a small group of senior officials, who were also members of the family and were therefore

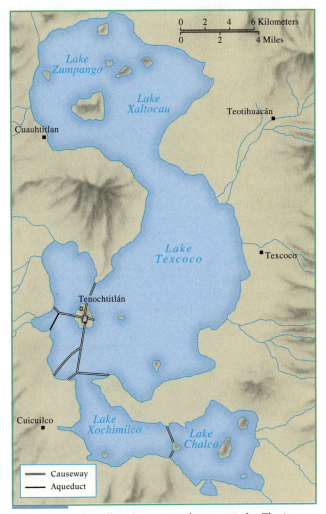

MAP 6.2 **The Valley of Mexico Under Aztec Rule.** The Aztecs were one of the most advanced peoples in pre-Columbian Central America. The capital at Tenochtitlán was located at the site of modern-day Mexico City. Of the five lakes shown here, only Lake Texcoco remains today. ❓ What was the significance of Tenochtitlán's location?

eligible for the position. Once placed on the throne, the Aztec ruler was advised by a small council of lords, headed by a prime minister who served as the chief executive of the government, and a bureaucracy. Beyond the capital, the power of the central government was limited. Rulers of territories subject to the Aztecs were allowed considerable autonomy in return for paying tribute, in the form of goods or captives, to the central government. The most important government officials in the provinces were the tax collectors, who collected the tribute. They used the threat of military action against those who failed to carry out their tribute obligations and therefore, understandably, were not popular with the taxpayers. According to Bernal Díaz, a Spaniard who accompanied Hernán Cortés on his expedition to Tenochtitlán in 1519:

All these towns complained about Montezuma [Moctezuma, the Aztec ruler at the time of the Cortés expedition] and his tax collectors, speaking in private so that the Mexican ambassadors should not hear them, however. They said these officials robbed them of all they possessed, and that if their wives and daughters were pretty they would violate them in front of their fathers and husbands and carry them away. They also said that the Mexicans [that is, the representatives from the capital] made the men work like slaves, compelling them to carry pine trunks and stone and firewood and maize overland and in canoes, and to perform other tasks, such as planting maize fields, and that they took away the people's lands as well for the service of their idols.[2]

Social Structures Positions in the government bureaucracy were the exclusive privilege of the hereditary nobility, all of whom traced their lineage to the founding family of the Aztec clan. Male children in noble families were sent to temple schools, where they were exposed to a harsh regimen of manual labor, military training, and memorization of information about Aztec society and religion. On reaching adulthood, they would select a career in the military service, the government bureaucracy, or the priesthood.

The remainder of the population consisted of commoners, indentured workers, and slaves. Most indentured workers were landless laborers who contracted to work on the nobles' estates, while slaves served in the households of the wealthy. Slavery was not an inherited status, and the children of slaves were considered free citizens.

The vast majority of the population were commoners. All commoners were members of large kinship groups called **calpullis.** Each *calpulli,* often consisting of as many as a thousand members, was headed by an elected chief, who ran its day-to-day affairs and served as an intermediary with the central government. Each *calpulli* was responsible for providing taxes (usually in the form of goods) and conscript labor to the state.

Each *calpulli* maintained its own temples and schools and administered the land held by the community. Farmland within the *calpulli* was held in common and could not be sold, although it could be inherited within the family. In the cities, each *calpulli* occupied a separate neighborhood, where its members often performed a particular function, such as metalworking, stonecutting, weaving, carpentry, or commerce. Apparently, a large proportion of the population engaged in some form of trade, at least in the densely populated Valley of Mexico, where an estimated half of the people lived in an urban environment. Many farmers brought their goods to the markets via the canals and sold them directly to retailers (see the box on p. 133).

Gender roles within the family were rigidly stratified. Male children were trained for war and were expected to serve in the army on reaching adulthood. Women were expected to work in the home, weave textiles, and raise children, although like their brothers they were permitted to enter the priesthood (see the box on p. 134). As in most traditional societies, chastity and obedience were desirable female characteristics. Although women in Aztec society enjoyed more legal rights than women in some traditional Old World civilizations, they were still not equal to men. Women were permitted to own and inherit property and to enter into contracts. Marriage was usually monogamous, although noble families sometimes practiced **polygyny** (the state or practice of having more than one wife at a time). As in most societies at the time, parents usually selected their child's spouse, often for purposes of political or social advancement.

Classes in Aztec society were rigidly stratified. Commoners were not permitted to enter the nobility, although some occasionally rose to senior positions in the army or the priesthood as the result of exemplary service. As in medieval Europe, such occupations often provided a route of upward mobility for ambitious commoners. A woman of noble standing would sometimes marry a commoner because the children of such a union would inherit her higher status, and she could expect to be treated better by her husband's family, who would be proud of the marriage relationship.

Land of the Feathered Serpent: Aztec Religion and Culture

The Aztecs, like their contemporaries throughout Mesoamerica, lived in an environment populated by a multitude of gods. Scholars have identified more than a hundred deities in the Aztec pantheon; some of them were nature spirits, like the rain god, Tlaloc, and some

MARKETS AND MERCHANDISE IN AZTEC MEXICO

INTERACTION & EXCHANGE

One of our most valuable descriptions of Aztec civilization is *The Conquest of New Spain*, written by Bernal Díaz, a Spaniard who accompanied Hernán Cortés on his expedition to Mexico in 1519. In the following passage, Díaz describes the great market at Tenochtitlán.

Which of the items offered for sale in this account might you expect to be available in a market in Asia, Africa, or Europe? What types of goods mentioned here appear to be unique to the Americas?

Bernal Díaz, *The Conquest of New Spain*

Let us begin with the dealers in gold, silver, and precious stones, feathers, cloaks, and embroidered goods, and male and female slaves who are also sold there. They bring as many slaves to be sold in that market as the Portuguese bring Negroes from Guinea. Some are brought there attached to long poles by means of collars round their necks to prevent them from escaping, but others are left loose. Next there were those who sold coarser cloth, and cotton goods and fabrics made of twisted thread, and there were chocolate merchants with their chocolate. In this way you could see every kind of merchandise to be found anywhere in New Spain, laid out in the same way as goods are laid out in my own district of Medina del Campo, a center for fairs, where each line of stalls has its own particular sort. So it was in this great market. There were those who sold sisal cloth and ropes and the sandals they wear on their feet, which are made from the same plant. All these were kept in one part of the market, in the place assigned to them, and in another part were skins of tigers and lions, otters, jackals, and deer, badgers, mountain cats, and other wild animals, some tanned and some untanned, and other classes of merchandise.

There were sellers of kidney beans and sage and other vegetables and herbs in another place, and in yet another they were selling fowls, and birds with great dewlaps, also rabbits, hares, deer, young ducks, little dogs, and other such creatures. Then there were the fruiterers; and the women who sold cooked food, flour and honey cake, and tripe, had their part of the market. Then came pottery of all kinds, from big water jars to little jugs, displayed in its own place, also honey, honey paste, and other sweets like nougat. Elsewhere they sold timber too, boards, cradles, beams, blocks, and benches, all in a quarter of their own.

Then there were the sellers of pitch pine for torches, and other things of that kind, and I must also mention, with all apologies, that they sold many canoe loads of human excrement, which they kept in the creeks near the market. This was for the manufacture of salt and the curing of skins, which they say cannot be done without it. I know that many gentlemen will laugh at this, but I assure them it is true. I may add that on all the roads they have shelters made of reeds or straw or grass so that they can retire when they wish to do so, and purge their bowels unseen by passersby, and also in order that their excrement shall not be lost.

CENGAGENOW To read a description of Aztec imperial life by Díaz, enter the *CengageNOW* documents area using the access card that is available for *The Essential World History*.

---

were patron deities, like the symbol of the Aztecs themselves, Huitzilopochtli. A supreme deity, called Ometeotl, represented the all-powerful and omnipresent forces of the heavens, but he was rather remote, and other gods, notably the feathered serpent Quetzalcoatl, had a more direct impact on the lives of the people. Representing the forces of creation, virtue, and learning and culture, Quetzalcoatl bears a distinct similarity to Shiva in Hindu belief. According to Aztec tradition, this godlike being had left his homeland in the Valley of Mexico in the tenth century, promising to return in triumph (see "The Mystery of Mayan Decline" earlier in this chapter).

Aztec cosmology was based on a belief in the existence of two worlds, the material and the divine. The earth was the material world and took the form of a flat disk surrounded by water on all sides. The divine world, which consisted of both heaven and hell, was the abode of the gods. Human beings could aspire to a form of heavenly salvation but first had to pass through a transitional stage, somewhat like Christian purgatory, before reaching their final destination, where the soul was finally freed from the body. To prepare for the final day of judgment, as well as to help them engage in proper behavior through life, all citizens underwent religious training at temple schools during adolescence and took part in various rituals throughout their lives. The most devout were encouraged to study for the priesthood. Once accepted, they served at temples ranging from local branches at the *calpulli* level to the highest shrines in the ceremonial precinct at Tenochtitlán. In some respects, however, Aztec society may have been undergoing a process of secularization. By late Aztec times, athletic contests at the ball court had apparently lost some of their religious significance. Gambling was increasingly common, and wagering over the results of the matches was widespread. One province reportedly sent sixteen thousand rubber balls to the capital city of Tenochtitlán as its annual tribute to the royal court.

Aztec religion contained a distinct element of fatalism that was inherent in the creation myth, which described

AZTEC MIDWIFE RITUAL CHANTS

FAMILY & SOCIETY

Most Aztec women were burdened with time-consuming family chores, such as grinding corn into flour for tortillas and carrying heavy containers of water from local springs. Like their brothers, Aztec girls went to school, but rather than training for war, they learned spinning, weaving, and how to carry out family rituals. In the sixteenth century c.e., a Spanish priest, Bernardino de Sahagún, interviewed Aztec informants to compile a substantial account of traditional Aztec society. Here we read his narration of ritual chants used by midwives during childhood. For a boy, the highest honor was to shed blood in battle. For a girl, it was to offer herself to the work of domestic life. If a woman died in childbirth, however, she would be glorified as a "warrior woman." Compare the gender roles presented here with those of other ancient civilizations in preceding chapters.

What does this document suggest as to the proper role to be played by a woman in Aztec society? How did the assigned roles for men and women in Mesoamerica compare with those that we have seen in other societies around the world?

Bernardino de Sahagún, *The Florentine Codex*

My precious son, my youngest one. . . . Heed, hearken: Thy home is not here, for thou art an eagle, thou art an ocelot. . . . Thou art the serpent, the bird of the lord of the near, of the nigh. Here is only the place of thy nest. Thou hast only been hatched here; thou hast only come, arrived. . . . Thou belongest out there. . . . Thou hast been sent into warfare. War is the desert, thy task. Thou shalt give drink, nourishment, food to the sun, the lord of the earth. . . . Perhaps thou wilt receive the gift, perhaps thou wilt merit death by the obsidian knife, the flowered death by the obsidian knife.

My beloved maiden. . . . Thou wilt be in the heart of the home, thou wilt go nowhere, thou wilt nowhere become a wanderer, thou becomest the banked fire, the hearth stones. Here our Lord planteth thee, burieth thee. And thou wilt become fatigued, thou wilt become tired, thou art to provide water, to grind maize, to drudge; thou art to sweat by the ashes, by the hearth.

---

an unceasing struggle between the forces of good and evil throughout the universe. This struggle led to the creation and destruction of four worlds, or suns. The world was now living in the time of the fifth sun. But that world, too, was destined to end with the destruction of this earth and all that is within it:

> Even jade is shattered,
> Even gold is crushed,
> Even quetzal plumes are torn. . . .
> One does not live forever on this earth:
> We endure only for an instant![3]

In an effort to postpone the day of reckoning, the Aztecs practiced human sacrifice. The Aztecs believed that by appeasing the sun god, Huitzilopochtli, with sacrifices, they could delay the final destruction of their world. Victims were prepared for the ceremony through elaborate rituals and then brought to the holy shrine, where their hearts were ripped out of their chests and presented to the gods as a holy offering. It was an honor to be chosen for sacrifice, and captives were often used as sacrificial victims, since they represented valor, the trait the Aztecs prized most.

Like the art of the Olmecs, most Aztec architecture, art, and sculpture had religious significance. At the center of the capital city of Tenochtitlán was the sacred precinct, dominated by the massive pyramid dedicated to Huitzilopochtli and the rain god, Tlaloc. According to Bernal Díaz, at its base the pyramid was equal to the plots of six large European town houses and tapered from there to the top, which was surmounted by a platform

containing shrines to the gods and an altar for performing human sacrifices. The entire pyramid was covered with brightly colored paintings and sculptures.

Although little Aztec painting survives, it was evidently of high quality. Bernal Díaz compared the best work with that of Michelangelo. Artisans worked with stone and with soft metals such as gold and silver, which they cast using the lost-wax technique. They did not have the knowledge for making implements in bronze or iron, however. Stoneworking consisted primarily of representations of the gods and bas-reliefs depicting religious ceremonies. Among the most famous is the massive disk called the Stone of the Sun, carved for use at the central pyramid at Tenochtitlán.

The Aztecs had devised a form of writing based on hieroglyphs that represented an object or a concept. The symbols had no phonetic significance and did not constitute a writing system as such but could give the sense of a message and were probably used by civilian or religious officials as notes or memorandums for their orations. A trained class of scribes carefully painted the notes on paper made from the inner bark of fig trees. Unfortunately, many of these notes were destroyed by the Spaniards as part of their effort to eradicate all aspects of Aztec religion and culture.

The Destruction of Aztec Civilization   For a century, the Aztec kingdom dominated much of central Mexico from the Atlantic to the Pacific coast, and its influence penetrated as far south as present-day Guatemala. Most local officials had accepted the sovereignty of the king in

Tenochtitlán, but in Tlaxcallan to the east, the authorities were restive under Aztec rule.

In 1519, a Spanish expedition under the command of Hernán Cortés landed at Veracruz, on the Gulf of Mexico (see Chapter 14). Marching to Tenochtitlán at the head of a small contingent of troops, Cortés received a friendly welcome from the Aztec monarch Moctezuma Xocoyotzin (often called Montezuma), who initially believed his visitor was a representative of Quetzalcoatl, the godlike "feathered serpent". The king and his subjects were astounded to see men on horseback, for the horse had disappeared from the Americas at least ten thousand years earlier.

The Arrival of Hernán Cortés in Mexico

[Map showing: Cortés's route, Gulf of Mexico, Teotihuacán, Veracruz, Tenochtitlán, YUCATÁN, Pacific Ocean, 500 Kilometers, 300 Miles]

But tensions soon erupted between the Spaniards and the Aztecs, provoked in part by demands by Cortés that the Aztecs denounce their native beliefs and accept Christianity. When the Spanish took Moctezuma hostage and began to destroy Aztec religious shrines, the local population revolted and drove the invaders from the city. Receiving assistance from the state of Tlaxcallan, Cortés managed to fight his way back into the city. Meanwhile the Aztecs were beginning to suffer the first effects of the diseases brought by the Europeans, which would eventually wipe out the majority of the local population. In a battle that to many Aztecs must have seemed to symbolize the dying of the legendary fifth sun, the Aztecs were finally vanquished. Within months, their magnificent city and its temples, believed by the conquerors to be the work of Satan, had been destroyed.

© The Granger Collection, New York

The First Civilizations in South America

South America is a vast continent, characterized by extremes in climate and geography. The north is dominated by the mighty Amazon River, which flows through dense tropical jungles carrying a larger flow of water than any other river system in the world (see Map 6.3). Farther to the south, the jungles are replaced by prairies and steppes stretching westward to the Andes Mountains, which extend the entire length of the continent, from the Isthmus of Panama to the Strait of Magellan. Along the Pacific coast, on the western slopes of the mountains, are some of the driest desert regions in the world.

South America has been inhabited by human beings for more than 12,000 years. Wall paintings discovered at the "cavern of the painted rock" in the Amazon region suggest that Stone Age peoples were living in the area at least 11,000 years ago. Early peoples were hunters, fishers, and food gatherers, but there are indications that irrigated farming was practiced in the northern fringe of the Andes Mountains as early as 2000 B.C.E. Other farming communities of similar age have been discovered in the Amazon River valley and on the western slopes of the Andes, where evidence of terraced agriculture dates back about 4,000 years.

By the sixth millennium B.C.E., complex societies had emerge in the central Andes Mountains, in the region of modern Peru, Bolivia, and Ecuador. Archaeologists have discovered the remains of ceremonial precincts, complete with temples, ancestral tombs, and pyramids, similar to those of Mesoamerica. This early Andes civilization may have originated as early as about 2500 B.C.E. (archaeologists have recently discovered the remains of an ancient city in northwestern Peru, with several examples of public architecture and evidence of irrigated agriculture), but it reached its height during the first millennium B.C.E. with the emergence of the Chavín style, named for a site near the modern city of Chavín de Huantar, in the central mountains of modern Peru. The ceremonial precinct at the Chavín site contained an impressive stone temple complete with interior

The Spaniards Conquer a New World. In attempting to subdue the Aztecs, the conquistadors relied on their superior weaponry. They also counted on the support of other Indian peoples, who were increasingly restive under Moctezuma's domination. Here we see two Spanish warriors and their Amerindian allies brandishing their steel weapons against the stones and arrows of the Aztecs. Having learned the value of mounted warfare during the Crusades (see Chapter 12), the Spaniards went to great lengths to bring horses to the Americas, suspending them in slings on their galleons to prevent injury. It is said that Cortés grieved more for the death of a horse than for the death of one of his warriors.

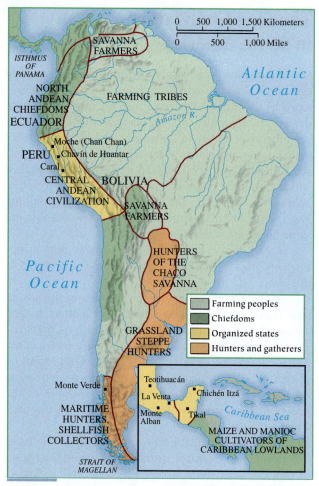

MAP 6.3   Early Peoples and Cultures of Central and South America. This map shows regions of early human settlements in Central and South America. Urban conglomerations appear in Mesoamerica (see inset) and along the western coast of South America. ❓ What do you make of the great distance between organized states in this map?

galleries, a stone-block ceiling, and a system of underground canals that probably channeled water into the temple complex for ritualistic purposes. Evidence of metallurgy, including objects made of copper and gold, has also been found.

Moche

Chavín society had disappeared by 200 B.C.E., but early in the first millennium C.E., another advanced civilization, comprising a total area of over 2,500 square miles, appeared in northern Peru, in the valley of the Moche River, which flows from the foothills of the Andes into the Pacific Ocean. The capital city, large enough in territory to contain over ten thousand people, was dominated by two massive adobe pyramids as high as 100 feet. The largest, known as the Pyramid of the Moon, covered a total of 15 acres and was adorned with painted murals depicting battles, ritual sacrifices, and various local deities.

Artifacts found at Moche, especially the metalwork and stone and ceramic figures, exhibit a high quality of artisanship. They were imitated at river valley sites throughout the surrounding area, which suggests that the authority of the Moche rulers may have extended as far as 400 miles along the coast. The artifacts also indicate that the people at Moche, like those in Central America, were preoccupied with warfare. The Moche were also fascinated by the heavens, and much of their art consisted of celestial symbols and astronomical constellations.

Environmental Problems   The Moche River valley is extremely arid, receiving less than an inch of rain annually. The peoples in the area compensated by building a sophisticated irrigation system to carry water from the river to the parched fields. At its zenith, Moche culture was spectacular. By the eighth century C.E., however, the civilization was in a state of collapse, the irrigation canals had been abandoned, and the remaining population had left the area or suffered from severe malnutrition.

What had happened to bring Moche culture to this untimely end? Archaeologists speculate that environmental changes, perhaps brought on by changes in the water temperature known as **El Niño,** led to periods of drought and then to major floods in the coastal regions and the silting up of the irrigated fields (see the comparative essay "History and the Environment" on p. 137).

Three hundred years later, a new power, the kingdom of Chimor, with its capital at Chan Chan, at the mouth of the Moche River, emerged in the area. Built almost entirely of adobe, Chan Chan housed an estimated thirty thousand residents in an area of over 12 square miles that included a number of palace compounds surrounded by walls nearly 30 feet high. Like the Moche before them, the people of Chimor relied on irrigation to funnel the water from the river into their fields. An elaborate system of canals brought the water through hundreds of miles of hilly terrain to the fields near the coast. Nevertheless, by the fifteenth century, Chimor, too, had disappeared, a victim of floods and a series of earthquakes that destroyed the intricate irrigation system that had been the basis of its survival.

These early civilizations in the Andes were by no means isolated from other societies in the region. As early as 2000 B.C.E., local peoples had been venturing into the Pacific Ocean on wind-powered rafts constructed of balsa wood. By the late first millennium C.E., seafarers from the coast of Ecuador had established a vast trading network that extended southward to central Peru and as far north as western Mexico, over 2,000 miles away. Items transported included jewelry, beads, and metal goods.

The Inka

The Chimor kingdom was eventually succeeded in the late fifteenth century by an invading force from the mountains far to the south. In the late fourteenth century, the Inka were only a small community in the area of Cuzco,

COMPARATIVE ESSAY

HISTORY AND THE ENVIRONMENT

EARTH & ENVIRONMENT

In *The Decline and Fall of the Roman Empire,* published in 1788, the British historian Edward Gibbon raised a question that has fascinated historians ever since: What brought about the collapse of that once-powerful civilization that dominated the Mediterranean region for over five centuries? Traditional explanations have centered on political or cultural factors, such as imperial overreach, moral decay, military weakness, or the impact of invasions. Recently, however, some historians have suggested that environmental factors, such as poisoning due to the use of lead water pipes and cups, the spread of malaria, or a lengthy drought in wheat-growing regions in North Africa, may have been at least contributory causes.

The current interest in the impact of the environment on the Roman Empire reflects a growing awareness among historians that environmental conditions may have been a key factor in the fate of several of the great societies in the ancient world. Climatic changes or natural disasters almost certainly led to the decline and collapse of civilization in the Indus River valley. In the Americas, massive flooding brought about by the El Niño effect (environmental conditions triggered by changes in water temperature in the Pacific Ocean) appears to be one possible cause for the collapse of the Moche civilization in what today is Peru, while drought

and overcultivation of the land are often cited as reasons for the decline of the Maya in Mesoamerica.

Climatic changes continued to affect the fate of nations and peoples after the end of the classical era. Drought conditions and overuse of the land may have led to the gradual decline of Mesopotamia as a focal point of advanced civilization in the Middle East, while soil erosion and colder conditions doomed an early attempt by the Vikings to establish a foothold in Greenland and North America. Sometimes the problems were self-inflicted, as on Easter Island, a remote outpost in the Pacific Ocean, where Polynesian settlers migrating from the west about 900 C.E. so denuded the landscape that by the fifteenth century, what had been a reasonably stable and peaceful society had descended into civil war and cannibalism.

Climatic changes, of course, have not always been detrimental to the health and prosperity of human beings. A warming trend that took place at the end of the last ice age eventually made much of the world more habitable for farming peoples about 10,000 years ago. The effects of El Niño may be beneficial to people living in some areas and disastrous for others. But human misuse of land and water resources is always dangerous to settled societies, especially those living in fragile environments.

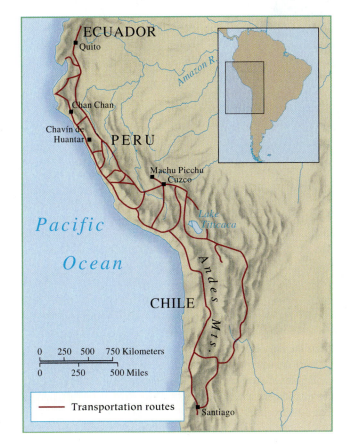

MAP 6.4 **The Inkan Empire About 1500 C.E.** The Inka were the last civilization to flourish in South America prior to the arrival of the Spanish. The impressive system of roads constructed to facilitate communication shows the extent of Inka control throughout the Andes Mountains. ❓ What made the extent of the Inkan Empire such a remarkable achievement?

a city located at an altitude of 10,000 feet in the mountains of southern Peru. In the 1440s, however, under the leadership of their powerful ruler Pachakuti (sometimes called Pachacutec, or "he who transforms the world"), the Inkan peoples launched a campaign of conquest that eventually brought the entire region under their authority. Under Pachakuti and his immediate successors, Topa Inka and Huayna Inka (the word *Inka* means "ruler"), the boundaries of the kingdom were extended as far as Ecuador, central Chile, and the edge of the Amazon basin.

The Four Quarters: Inkan Politics and Society Pachakuti created a highly centralized state (see Map 6.4). With a stunning concern for mathematical precision, he divided his empire, called Tahuantinsuyu, or "the world of the four quarters," into provinces and districts. Each province contained about ten thousand residents (at least in theory) and was ruled by a governor related to the royal family. Excess inhabitants were transferred to other locations. The capital of Cuzco was divided into four quarters, or residential areas, and the social status and economic functions of the residents of each quarter were rigidly defined.

The state was built on forced labor. Often entire communities of workers were moved from one part of the country to another to open virgin lands or engage in massive construction projects. Under Pachakuti, the capital of Cuzco was transformed from a city of mud and thatch into an imposing metropolis of stone. The walls, built of close-fitting stones without the use of mortar, were a wonder to early European visitors. The most impressive structure in the city was a temple dedicated to the sun. According to a Spanish observer, "All four walls of the temple were covered from top to bottom with plates and slabs of gold."[4] Equally impressive are the ruins of the abandoned city of Machu Picchu, built on a lofty hilltop far above the Urubamba River.

Another major construction project was a system of 24,800 miles of highways and roads that extended from the border of modern Colombia to a point south of modern Santiago, Chile. Two major roadways extended in a north-south direction, one through the Andes Mountains and the other along the coast, with connecting routes between them. Rest houses and storage depots were placed along the roads. Suspension bridges made of braided fiber and fastened to stone abutments on opposite banks were built over ravines and waterways. Use of the highways was restricted to official and military purposes. Trained runners carried messages rapidly from one way station to another, enabling information to travel up to 140 miles in a single day.

In rural areas, the population lived mainly by farming. In the mountains, the most common form was terraced agriculture, watered by irrigation systems that carried precise amounts of water into the fields, which were planted with maize, potatoes, and other crops. The plots were tilled by collective labor regulated by the state. Like other aspects of Inkan society, marriage was strictly regulated, and men and women were required to select a marriage partner from within the immediate tribal group. For women, there was one escape from a life of domestic servitude. Fortunate maidens were selected to serve as "chosen virgins" in temples throughout the country (see the box on p. 139). Noblewomen were eligible to compete for service in the Temple of the Sun at Cuzco,

Machu Picchu.   Situated in the Andes in modern Peru, Machu Picchu reflects the glory of Inkan civilization. To farm such rugged terrain, the Inka constructed terraces and stone aqueducts. To span vast ravines, they built suspension bridges made of braided fiber and fastened them to stone abutments on the opposite banks. The most revered of the many temples and stone altars at Machu Picchu was the thronelike "hitching post of the sun," so called because of its close proximity to the sun god.

VIRGINS WITH RED CHEEKS

FAMILY & SOCIETY

A letter from a Peruvian chief to King Philip III of Spain written four hundred years ago gives us a firsthand account of the nature of traditional Inkan society. The purpose of author Huaman Poma was both to justify the history and culture of the Inkan peoples and to record their sufferings under Spanish domination. In his letter, Poma describes Inkan daily life from birth to death in minute detail. He explains the different tasks assigned to men and women, beginning with their early education. Whereas boys were taught to watch the flocks and trap animals, girls were taught to dye, spin and weave cloth, and perform other domestic chores. Most interesting, perhaps, was the emphasis that the Inka placed on virginity, as described in the document presented here. The Inkan tradition of temple virgins is reminiscent of similar practices in ancient Rome, where young girls from noble families were chosen as priestesses to tend the sacred fire in the Temple of Vesta for thirty years. If one lost her virginity, she was condemned to be buried alive in an underground chamber.

In this passage, one of the chief duties of a woman in Inkan society was to spin and weave. In what other traditional societies was textile making a woman's work? Why do you think this was the case?

Huaman Poma, *Letter to a King*

During the time of the Incas certain women, who were called *accla* or "the chosen," were destined for lifelong virginity. Mostly they were confined in houses and they belonged to one of two main categories, namely sacred virgins and common virgins.

The so-called "virgins with red cheeks" entered upon their duties at the age of twenty and were dedicated to the service of the Sun, the Moon, and the Day-Star. In their whole life they were never allowed to speak to a man.

The virgins of the Inca's own shrine of Huanacauri were known for their beauty as well as their chastity. The other principal shrines had similar girls in attendance. At the less important shrines there were the older virgins who occupied themselves with spinning and weaving the silk-like clothes worn by their idols. There was a still lower class of virgins, over forty years of age and no longer very beautiful, who performed unimportant religious duties and worked in the fields or as ordinary seamstresses.

Daughters of noble families who had grown into old maids were adept at making girdles, headbands, string bags, and similar articles in the intervals of their pious observances.

Girls who had musical talent were selected to sing or play the flute and drum at Court, weddings and other ceremonies, and all the innumerable festivals of the Inca year.

There was yet another class of *accla* or "chosen," only some of whom kept their virginity and others not. These were the Inca's beautiful attendants and concubines, who were drawn from noble families and lived in his palaces. They made clothing for him out of material finer than taffeta or silk. They also prepared a maize spirit of extraordinary richness, which was matured for an entire month, and they cooked delicious dishes for the Inca. They also lay with him, but never with any other man.

CENGAGENOW To read more about Inkan society, enter the *CengageNOW* documents area using the access card that is available for *The Essential World History*.

---

while commoners might hope to serve in temples in the provincial capitals. Punishment for breaking the vow of chastity was harsh, and few evidently took the risk.

Inkan Culture Like many other civilizations in pre-Columbian Latin America, the Inkan state was built on war. Soldiers for the 200,000-man Inkan army, the largest and best armed in the region, were raised by universal male conscription. Military units were moved rapidly along the highway system and were housed in the rest houses located along the roadside. Since the Inka had no wheeled vehicles, supplies were carried on the backs of llamas. Once an area was placed under Inka authority, the local inhabitants were instructed in the Quechua language, which became the lingua franca of the state, and were introduced to the state religion. The Inka had no writing system but kept records using a system of knotted strings called **quipu.**

As in the case of the Aztecs and the Maya, the lack of a fully developed writing system did not prevent the Inka from realizing a high level of cultural achievement. Most

of what survives was recorded by the Spanish and consists of entertainment for the elites. The Inka had a highly developed tradition of court theater, including both tragic and comic works. There was also some poetry, composed in blank verse and often accompanied by music played on reed instruments.

The Conquest of the Inka The Inkan Empire was still in existence when the first Spanish expeditions arrived in the central Andes. The leader of the Spanish invaders, Francisco Pizarro, was accompanied by only a few hundred companions, but like Cortés, he possessed steel weapons, gunpowder, and horses, none of which were familiar to his hosts. In the meantime, internal factionalism, combined with the onset of contagious diseases spread unknowingly by the Europeans, had weakened the ruling elite, and the empire fell rapidly to the Spanish forces in 1532. The last Inka ruler was tried by the Spaniards and executed. Pre-Columbian South America's greatest age was over.

Stateless Societies in the Americas

Beyond Central America and the high ridges of the Andes Mountains, on the Great Plains of North America, along the Amazon River in South America, and on the islands of the Caribbean Sea, other communities of Amerindians were also beginning to master the art of agriculture and to build organized societies.

Although human beings had occupied much of the continent of North America during the early phase of human settlement, the switch to farming as a means of survival did not occur until the third millennium B.C.E. at the earliest, and not until much later in most areas of the continent. Until that time, most Amerindian communities lived by hunting, fishing, or foraging.

The Eastern Woodlands

It was probably during the third millennium B.C.E. that peoples in the Eastern Woodlands (the land in eastern North America from the Great Lakes to the Gulf of Mexico) began to cultivate indigenous plants for food in a systematic way. As wild game and food became scarce, some communities began to place more emphasis on cultivating crops. This shift first occurred in the Mississippi River valley from Ohio, Indiana, and Illinois down to the Gulf of Mexico (see Map 6.5). Among the most commonly cultivated crops were maize, squash, beans, and various grasses.

As the population in the area increased, people began to congregate in villages, and sedentary communities began to develop in the alluvial lowlands, where the soil could be cultivated for many years at a time because of the nutrients deposited by the river water. Village councils were established to adjudicate disputes, and in a few cases, several villages banded together under the authority of a local chieftain. Urban centers began to appear, some of them inhabited by ten thousand people or more. At the same time, regional trade increased. The people of the Hopewell culture in Ohio ranged from the shores of Lake Superior to the Appalachian Mountains and the Gulf of Mexico in search of metals, shells, obsidian, and manufactured items to support their economic needs and religious beliefs.

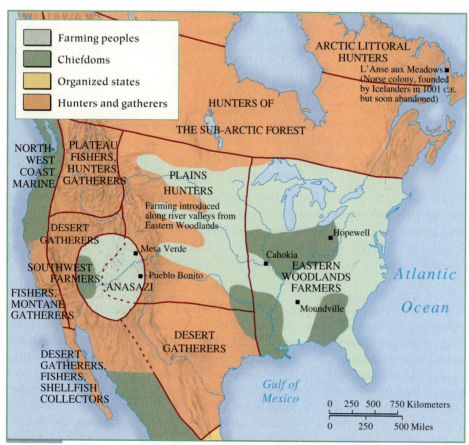

MAP 6.5 **Early Peoples and Cultures of North America.** This map shows regions of human settlement in pre-Columbian North America, including the short-lived Viking colony in Newfoundland. ? Where are the major urban centers located?

Cahokia

At the site of Cahokia, near the modern city of East Saint Louis, Illinois, archaeologists found a burial mound more than 98 feet high with a base larger than that of the Great Pyramid in Egypt. A hundred smaller mounds were also found in the vicinity. The town itself, which covered almost 300 acres and was surrounded by a wooden stockade, was apparently the administrative capital of much of the surrounding territory until its decline in the thirteenth century C.E. With a population of over twenty thousand, it was reportedly the largest city in North America until Philadelphia surpassed that number in the early nineteenth century. Cahokia carried on extensive trade with other communities throughout the region, and there are some signs of regular contacts with the civilizations in Mesoamerica, such as the presence of ball courts in the Central American style. But wars were not uncommon, leading the Iroquois, who inhabited much of the modern states of Pennsylvania and New York as well as parts of southern Canada, to create a tribal alliance called the League of Iroquois.

The "Ancient Ones": The Anasazi

West of the Mississippi River basin, most Amerindian peoples lived by hunting or food gathering. During the first millennium C.E., knowledge of agriculture gradually spread up the rivers to the Great Plains, and farming was practiced as far west as southwestern Colorado, where the Anasazi peoples (Navajo for "alien ancient ones") established an extensive agricultural community in an area extending from northern New Mexico and Arizona to southwestern Colorado and parts of southern Utah. Although they apparently never discovered the wheel or used beasts of burden, the Anasazi created a system of roads that facilitated an extensive exchange of technology, products, and ideas throughout the region. By the ninth century, they had mastered the art of irrigation, which allowed them to expand their productive efforts to squash and beans, and had established an important urban center at Chaco Canyon, in southern New Mexico, where they built a walled city with dozens of three-story communal houses, called *pueblos,* with timbered roofs. Community religious functions were carried out in two large circular chambers called *kivas.* Clothing was made from hides or cotton cloth. At its height, Pueblo Bonito contained several hundred compounds housing several thousand residents. In the mid-twelfth century, the Anasazi moved northward to Mesa Verde in southwestern Colorado. At first, they settled on top of the mesa, but eventually they retreated to the cliff face of the surrounding canyons.

Sometime during the late thirteenth century, however, Mesa Verde was also abandoned, and the inhabitants migrated southward. Their descendants, the Zuni

Courtesy of William J. Duiker

Cliff Palace at Mesa Verde. Mesa Verde is one of the best-developed sites of the Anasazi peoples in southwestern North America. At one time they were farmers who tilled the soil atop the mesas, but eventually they were forced to build their settlements in more protected locations. At Cliff Palace, shown here, adobe houses were hidden on the perpendicular face of the mesa. Access was achieved only by a perilous descent via indented finger-and-toeholds on the rock face.

and the Hopi, now occupy pueblos in central Arizona and New Mexico. For years, archaeologists surmised that a severe drought was the cause of the migration, but in recent years, new evidence has raised doubts that decreasing rainfall, by itself, was a sufficient explanation. An increase in internecine warfare, perhaps brought about by climatic changes, may also have played a role in the decision to relocate. Some archaeologists point to evidence that cannibalism was practiced at Pueblo Bonito and suggest that migrants from the south may have arrived in the area, provoking bitter rivalries within Anasazi society. In any event, with increasing aridity and the importation of the horse by the Spanish in the sixteenth century, hunting revived, and mounted nomads like the Apache and the Navajo came to dominate much of the Southwest.

South America: The Arawak

East of the Andes Mountains in South America, other Amerindian societies were beginning to make the transition to agriculture. Perhaps the most prominent were the Arawak, a people living along the Orinoco River in modern Venezuela. Having begun to cultivate manioc (a tuber used today in the manufacture of tapioca) along the banks of the river, they gradually migrated down to the coast and then proceeded to move eastward along the northern coast of the continent. Some occupied the islands of the Caribbean Sea. In their new island habitat, they lived by a mixture of fishing, hunting, and cultivating maize, beans, manioc, and squash, as well as other crops such as peanuts, peppers, and pineapples. As the population increased, a pattern of political organization above the village level appeared, along with recognizable social classes headed by a chieftain whose authority included control over the economy. The Arawak practiced human sacrifice, and some urban centers contained ball courts, suggesting the possibility of contacts with Mesoamerica.

In most such societies, where clear-cut class stratifications had not as yet taken place, men and women were considered of equal status. Men were responsible for hunting, warfare, and dealing with outsiders, while women were accountable for the crops, the distribution of food, maintaining the household, and bearing and raising the children. Their roles were complementary and were often viewed as a divine division of labor. In such cases, women in the stateless societies of North America held positions of greater respect than their counterparts in the river valley civilizations of the Old World.

CONCLUSION

𝒯HE FIRST HUMAN BEINGS did not arrive in the Americas until quite late in the prehistorical period. For the next several millennia, their descendants were forced to respond to the challenges of the environment in total isolation from other parts of the world. Nevertheless, around 5000 B.C.E., farming settlements began to appear in river valleys and upland areas in both Central and South America. Not long afterward—as measured in historical time—organized communities located along the coast of the Gulf of Mexico and the western slopes of the central Andes Mountains embarked on the long march toward civilization. On the same path were the emerging societies of North America, which were beginning to expand their commercial and cultural links with civilizations farther to the south and had already laid the foundations for future urbanization. Although the total number of people living in the Americas is a matter of debate, some scholars estimate a figure between ten and twenty million.

What is perhaps most striking about the developments in the Western Hemisphere is how closely they paralleled those of other civilizations. Irrigated agriculture, long-distance trade, urbanization, and the development of a writing system were all hallmarks of the emergence of advanced societies of the classical type. One need only point to the awed comments of early Spanish visitors, who said that the cities of the Aztecs were the equal of Seville and the other great metropolitan centers of Spain.

In some respects, the societies that emerged in the Americas were not as advanced in technological terms as their counterparts elsewhere. They were not familiar with the process of smelting iron, for example, and they had not yet invented wheeled vehicles. Their writing systems, by comparison with those in the Old World, were still in their infancy. Several possible reasons have been advanced to explain this technological gap. Certainly, geographic isolation—not only from people of other continents but also, in some cases, from each other—deprived them of the benefits of the diffusion of ideas that had assisted other societies in learning from their neighbors. In some ways, too, they were not as blessed by nature. As the sociologist Jared Diamond has pointed out, the Americas did not possess many indigenous varieties of edible grasses that could encourage hunter-gatherers to take up farming. Nor were there abundant large mammals that could easily be domesticated for food and transport. It was not until the arrival of the Europeans that such familiar attributes of civilization became widely available for human use in the Americas.[5]

At one time, scholars speculated that the societies of the Americas were largely peaceful and devoid of the widespread violence that plagued civilizations elsewhere. Recent evidence, however, suggests that the Amerindian peoples were every bit as addicted to warfare as those of the ancient empires of the Old World. Nevertheless, military prowess was of little help when the peoples of the Americas encountered the first visitors from overseas. The Europeans' advanced military technology and their mastery of horseback riding gave them a major advantage over the local population. Yet it should be noted that in the Americas as elsewhere, many of the first civilizations appear to have been brought to an end as much by environmental changes and disease as by war. In the next chapter, we shall return to the Old World, where new civilizations were in the process of replacing the ancient empires.

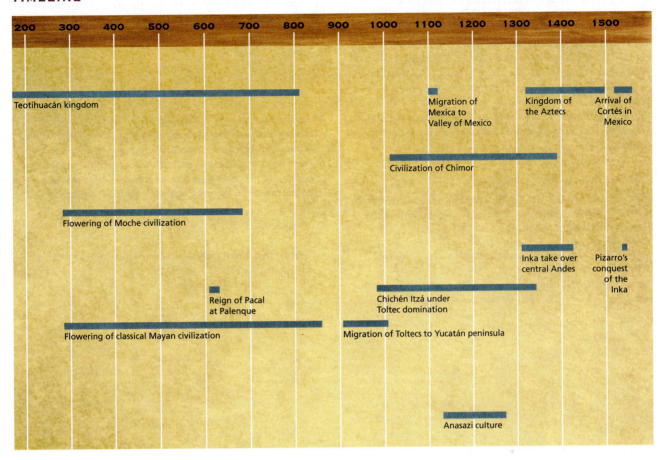

	200	300	400	500	600	700	800	900	1000	1100	1200	1300	1400	1500

Teotihuacán kingdom

Migration of Mexica to Valley of Mexico

Kingdom of the Aztecs

Arrival of Cortés in Mexico

Civilization of Chimor

Flowering of Moche civilization

Inka take over central Andes

Pizarro's conquest of the Inka

Reign of Pacal at Palenque

Chichén Itzá under Toltec domination

Flowering of classical Mayan civilization

Migration of Toltecs to Yucatán peninsula

Anasazi culture

CHAPTER NOTES

1. Quoted in S. Morley and G. W. Brainerd, *The Ancient Maya* (Stanford, Calif., 1983), p. 513.
2. B. Díaz, *The Conquest of New Spain* (Harmondsworth, England, 1975), p. 210.
3. Quoted in M. D. Coe, D. Snow, and E. P. Benson, *Atlas of Ancient America* (New York, 1988), p. 149.
4. G. de la Vega (El Inca), *Royal Commentaries of the Incas and General History of Peru*, pt. 1, trans. H. V. Livermore (Austin, Tex., 1966), p. 180.
5. J. Diamond, *Guns, Germs, and Steel: The Fates of Human Societies* (New York 1997), pp. 187–188.

SUGGESTED READING

For a profusely illustrated and informative overview of the early civilizations of the Americas, see **M. D. Coe, D. Snow,** and **E. P. Benson,** *Atlas of Ancient America* (New York, 1988). The first arrival of human beings in the Americas is discussed in **B. Fagan,** *The Great Journey: The Peopling of Ancient America* (London, 1987).

On Mayan civilization, see **D. Webster,** *The Fall of the Ancient Maya: Solving the Mystery of the Maya Collapse* (London, 2002). See also **M. D. Coe,** *The Maya* (London, 1993), and **J. Sabloff,** *The New Archeology and the Ancient Maya* (New York, 1990).

For an overview of Aztec civilization in Mexico, see **B. Fagan,** *The Aztecs* (New York, 1984). **S. D. Gillespie,** *The Aztec Kings: The Construction of Rulership in Mexican History* (Tucson, Ariz., 1989), is an imaginative effort to uncover the symbolic meaning in Aztec traditions. For a provocative study of religious traditions in a comparative context, see **B. Fagan,** *From Black Land to Fifth Sun* (Reading, Mass., 1998). On the Olmecs and the Zapotecs, see **E. P. Benson,** *The Olmec and Their Neighbors* (Washington, D.C., 1981); **M. D. Coe** and **R. A. Diehl,** *In the Land of the Olmec* (Austin, Tex., 1980); and **R. E. Blanton,** *Monte Alban: Settlement Patterns at the Ancient Zapotec Capital* (New York, 1978).

Much of our information about the lives of the peoples of ancient Central America comes from Spanish writers who visited or lived in the area during the sixteenth and seventeenth centuries. For the original Spanish conquest of Mexico, see **H. Cortés,** *Letters from Mexico* (New Haven, Conn., 1986), and **B. Díaz,** *The Conquest of New Spain* (Harmondsworth, England, 1975).

A worthy account of developments in South America is **G. Bawden,** *The Moche* (Oxford, 1996). On the Inka and their predecessors, see **R. W. Keatinge,** ed., *Peruvian Prehistory: An Overview of Pre-Inca and Inca Society* (Cambridge, 1988). The arrival of the Spanish is chronicled in **C. Howard,** *Pizarro and the Conquest of Peru* (New York, 1967).

On the art and culture of the ancient Americas, see **M. E. Miller,** *Maya Art and Architecture* (London, 1999); **E. Pasztory,** *Pre-Columbian Art* (Cambridge, 1998); and **M. Léon-Portilla** and

E. Shorris, *In the Language of Kings* (New York, 2001). Writing systems are discussed in **M. Coe, *Breaking the Maya Code*** (New York, 1992), and **G. Upton, *Signs of the Inka Quipu*** (Austin, Tex., 2003).

On social issues, see **L. Schele** and **D. Freidel, *A Forest of Kings: The Untold Story of the Ancient Maya*** (New York, 1990); **R. van Zantwijk, *The Aztec Arrangement: The Social History of Pre-Spanish Mexico*** (Norman, Okla., 1985); and **N. Shoemaker, *Negotiators of Change: Historical Perspectives on Native American Women*** (New York, 1995).

For a treatment of the role of the environment, see **B. Fagan, *Floods, Famine, and Emperors: El Niño and the Fate of Civilizations*** (New York, 1999).

InfoTrac College Edition

Visit this chapter's InfoTrac College Edition/Research activities at the *Essential World History* Companion Website for activities related to the ancient Americas.

CENGAGENOW for Duiker and Spielvogel's *The Essential World History, Third Edition*

Enter *CengageNOW* using the access card that is available with this text. *CengageNOW* will assist you in understanding the content in this chapter with lesson plans generated for your needs, as well as provide you with a connection to the *Wadsworth World History Resource Center* (see description below for details).

WORLD HISTORY
RESOURCE CENTER

Enter the Resource Center using either your *CengageNOW* access card or your standalone access card for the *Wadsworth History Resource Center*. Organized by topic, this website includes quizzes; images; over 350 primary source documents; interactive simulations, maps, and timelines; movie explorations; and a wealth of other resources. You can read the following document, and many more, at http://worldrc.wadsworth.com/

Popul Vuh

Visit the *Essential World History* Companion Website for chapter quizzes and more.
academic.cengage.com/history/duiker

FERMENT IN THE MIDDLE EAST: THE RISE OF ISLAM AND ITS IMPACT IN THE REGION

CHAPTER OUTLINE AND FOCUS QUESTIONS

The Rise of Islam

- What were the main tenets of Islam, and how does the religion compare with Judaism and Christianity?

The Arab Empire and Its Successors

- Why did the Arabs undergo such a rapid expansion in the seventh and eighth centuries, and why were they so successful in creating an empire?

Islamic Civilization

- What were the main features of Islamic society and culture during its era of early growth?

Islam and Byzantium

- What were the relations between the Arab states and the Byzantine Empire? Were they marked more by hostility or by cooperation?

CRITICAL THINKING

- What was the overall impact of the rise of Islam on societies and cultures in the Middle East? Compare it with the impact of Christianity in Europe.

Muhammad rises to Heaven

© British Library, London, UK/The Bridgeman Art Library

IN THE YEAR 570, in the Arabian city of Mecca, there was born a child named Muhammad whose life changed the course of world history. The son of a merchant, Muhammad grew to maturity in a time of transition. Old empires that had once ruled the entire Middle East were only a distant memory. The region was now divided into many separate states, and the people adhered to many different faiths.

According to tradition, the young Muhammad became deeply concerned at the corrupt and decadent society of his day and took to wandering in the hills outside the city to meditate on the conditions of his time. On one of these occasions, he experienced visions that he was convinced had been inspired by Allah. Muslims believe that this message had been conveyed to him by the angel Gabriel, who commanded Muhammad to preach the revelations that he would be given. Eventually, they would be transcribed into the holy book of Islam—the Qur'an—and provide inspiration to millions of people throughout the world.

Within a few decades of Muhammad's death, the Middle East was united once again. The initial triumph may have been primarily political and military, based on the transformative power of a dynamic new religion that inspired thousands of devotees to extend their faith to neighboring regions.

Islamic beliefs and culture exerted a powerful influence in all areas occupied by Arab armies. Initially, Arab beliefs and customs, as reflected through the prism of Muhammad's teachings, transformed the societies and cultures of the peoples living in the new empire. But eventually, the distinctive political and cultural forces that had long characterized the region began to reassert themselves. Factional struggles led to the decline and then the destruction of the empire.

Still, the Arab conquest left a powerful legacy that survived the decline of Arab political power. The ideological and emotional appeal of Islam remained strong throughout the Middle East and eventually extended into areas not occupied by Arab armies, such as the Indian subcontinent, Southeast Asia, and sub-Saharan Africa. ◆

The Rise of Islam

The Arabs were a Semitic-speaking people of southwestern Asia with a long history. They were mentioned in Greek sources of the fifth century B.C.E. and even earlier in the Old Testament. The Greek historian Herodotus had applied the name *Arab* to the entire peninsula, calling it Arabia. In 106 B.C.E., the Romans extended their authority to the Arabian peninsula, transforming it into a province of their growing empire.

During Roman times, the region was inhabited primarily by the **Bedouin** Arabs, nomadic peoples who came originally from the northern part of the peninsula. Bedouin society was organized on a tribal basis. The ruling member of the tribe was called the *sheikh* and was selected from one of the leading families by a council of elders called the *majlis.* The *sheikh* ruled the tribe with the consent of the council. Each tribe was autonomous but felt a general sense of allegiance to the larger unity of all the clans in the region. In early times, the Bedouins had supported themselves primarily by sheepherding or by raiding passing caravans, but after the domestication of the camel during the second millennium B.C.E., the Bedouins began to participate in the caravan trade themselves and became major carriers of goods between the Persian Gulf and the Mediterranean Sea.

The Arabs of pre-Islamic times were polytheistic, with a supreme god known as Allah presiding over a community of spirits. It was a communal faith, involving all members of the tribe, and had no priesthood. Spirits were believed to inhabit natural objects, such as trees, rivers, and mountains, while the supreme deity was symbolized by a sacred stone. Each tribe possessed its own stone, but by the time of Muhammad, a massive black meteorite, housed in a central shrine called the Ka'aba in the commercial city of Mecca, had to come to possess especially sacred qualities.

The Role of Muhammad

Into this world came Muhammad (also known as Mohammed), a man whose spiritual visions unified the Arab world (see Map 7.1) with a speed no one would have suspected possible. Born in Mecca to a merchant family and orphaned at the age of six, Muhammad (570–632) grew up to become a caravan manager and eventually married a rich widow, Khadija, who was also his employer. For several years, he lived in Mecca as a merchant but, according to tradition, was apparently troubled by the growing gap between the Bedouin values of honesty and generosity (he himself was a member of the local Hashemite clan of the Quraishi tribe) and the acquisitive behavior of the affluent commercial elites in the city. Deeply concerned, he began to visit the nearby hills to meditate in isolation. It was there that he encountered the angel Gabriel who commanded him to preach the revelations that he would be given.

It is said that Muhammad was acquainted with Jewish and Christian beliefs and came to believe that while Allah had already revealed himself in part through Moses and Jesus—and thus through the Hebraic and Christian traditions—the final revelations were now being given to him. Out of his revelations, which were eventually dictated to scribes, came the Qur'an ("recitation," also spelled Koran), the holy scriptures of Islam (*Islam* means "submission," implying submission to the will of Allah). The Qur'an contained the guidelines by which followers of Allah, known as Muslims (practitioners of Islam), were to live. Like the Christians and the Jews, Muslims (also known as Moslems) were a "people of the Book," believers in a faith based on scripture.

Muslims believe that after returning home, Muhammad set out to comply with Gabriel's command by preaching to the residents of Mecca about his revelations. At first, many were convinced that he was a madman or a charlatan. Others were undoubtedly concerned that his vigorous attacks on traditional beliefs and the corrupt society around him could severely shake the social and political order. After three years of proselytizing, he had only thirty followers.

Discouraged, perhaps, by the systematic persecution of his followers, which was allegedly undertaken with a brutality reminiscent of the cruelties suffered by early Christians, as well as the failure of the Meccans to accept his message, in 622 Muhammad and some of his closest supporters (mostly from his own Hashemite clan) left the city and retreated north to the rival city of Yathrib, later renamed Medina, or "city of the Prophet." That flight, known in history as the **Hegira** (*Hijrah*), marks the first date on the official calendar of Islam. At Medina, Muhammad failed in his original purpose—to convert the Jewish community in Medina to his beliefs. But he was successful in winning support from many residents of the city as well as from Bedouins in the surrounding countryside. From this mixture, he formed the first Muslim community (the **umma**). Returning to his birthplace at the head of a considerable military force, Muhammad conquered Mecca and converted the townspeople to the new faith. In 630, he made a

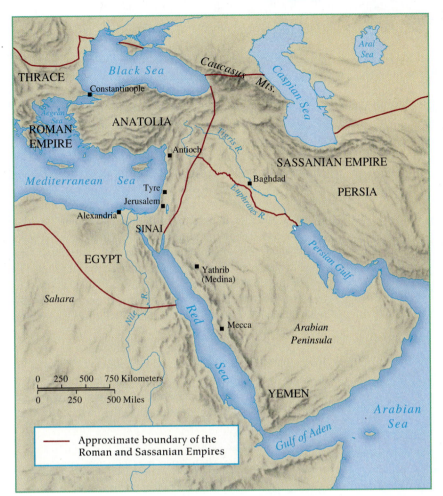

MAP 7.1 The Middle East in the Time of **Muhammad.** When Islam began to spread throughout the Middle East in the early seventh century, the dominant states in the region were the Roman Empire in the eastern Mediterranean and the Sassanian Empire in Persia. **?** How were the territorial boundaries shown here affected by the rise of Muhammad and the new religion of Islam?

symbolic visit to the Ka'aba, where he declared it a sacred shrine of Islam and ordered the destruction of the idols of the traditional faith. Two years later, Muhammad died, just as Islam was beginning to spread throughout the peninsula.

The Teachings of Muhammad

Like Christianity and Judaism, Islam is monotheistic. Allah is the all-powerful being who created the universe and everything in it. Islam is also concerned with salvation and offers the hope of an afterlife. Those who hope to achieve it must subject themselves to the will of Allah. Unlike Christianity, Islam makes no claim to the divinity of its founder. Muhammad, like Abraham, Moses, and other figures of the Old Testament, was a prophet, but he was also a man like other men. Because, according to the Qur'an, earlier prophets had corrupted his revelations, Allah sent his complete revelation through Muhammad.

The Ka'aba in Mecca. The Ka'aba, the shrine containing a black meteorite in the Arabian city of Mecca, is the most sacred site of the Islamic faith. Wherever Muslims pray, they are instructed to face Mecca; each thus becomes a spoke of the Ka'aba, the holy center of the wheel of Islam. If they are able to do so, all Muslims are encouraged to visit the Ka'aba at least once in their lifetime. Called the *hajj*, this pilgrimage to Mecca represents the ultimate in spiritual fulfillment.

THE QUR'AN: THE PILGRIMAGE

RELIGION & PHILOSOPHY

The Qur'an is the sacred book of the Muslims, comparable to the Bible in Christianity. This selection from Sura 22, titled "Pilgrimage," discusses the importance of making a pilgrimage to Mecca, one of the Five Pillars of Islam. The pilgrim's final destination was the Ka'aba at Mecca, containing the Black Stone.

What is the key purpose of undertaking a pilgrimage to Mecca? What is the historical importance of the sacred stone?

Qur'an, Sura 22: "Pilgrimage"

Exhort all men to make the pilgrimage. They will come to you on foot and on the backs of swift camels from every distant quarter; they will come to avail themselves of many a benefit, and to pronounce on the appointed days the name of God over the cattle which He has given them for food. Eat of their flesh, and feed the poor and the unfortunate.

Then let the pilgrims tidy themselves, make their vows, and circle the Ancient House. Such is God's commandment. He that reveres the sacred rites of God shall fare better in the sight of his Lord.

The flesh of cattle is lawful for you, except for that which has been specified before. Guard yourselves against the filth of idols; and avoid the utterance of falsehoods.

Dedicate yourselves to God, and serve none besides Him. The man who serves other deities besides God is like him who falls from heaven and is snatched by the birds or carried away by the wind to some far-off region. Even such is he.

He that reveres the offerings made to God shows the piety of his heart. Your cattle are useful to you in many ways until the time of their slaughter. Then they are offered for sacrifice at the Ancient House.

For every community We have ordained a ritual, that they may pronounce the name of God over the cattle which He has given them for food. Your God is one God; to Him surrender yourselves. Give good news to the humble, whose hearts are filled with awe at the mention of God; who endure adversity with fortitude, attend to their prayers, and give in alms from what We gave them.

We have made the camels a part of God's rites. They are of much use to you. Pronounce over them the name of God as you draw them up in line and slaughter them; and when they have fallen to the ground eat of their flesh and feed the uncomplaining beggar and the demanding suppliant. Thus have We subjected them to your service, so that you may give thanks.

Their flesh and blood does not reach God; it is your piety that reaches Him. Thus has He subjected them to your service, so that you may give glory to God for guiding you.

Give good news to the righteous. God will ward off evil from true believers. God does not love the treacherous and the thankless.

CENGAGENOW To read a full version of the Qur'an, enter the *CengageNOW* documents area using the access card that is available for *The Essential World History*.

At the heart of Islam is the Qur'an, with its basic message that there is no God but Allah and Muhammad is his Prophet. Consisting of 114 *suras* (chapters) drawn together by a committee established after Muhammad's death, the Qur'an is not only the sacred book of Islam but also an ethical guidebook and a code of law and political theory combined.

As it evolved, Islam developed a number of fundamental tenets. At its heart lies the need to obey the will of Allah. This meant following a basic ethical code that consisted of what are popularly termed the **Five Pillars of Islam:** belief in Allah and Muhammad as his Prophet; standard prayer five times a day and public prayer on Friday at midday to worship Allah; observation of the holy month of **Ramadan,** including fasting from dawn to sunset; making a pilgrimage, if possible, to Mecca at least once in one's lifetime (see the box above); and giving alms (*zakat*) to the poor and unfortunate. The faithful who observed the law were guaranteed a place in an eternal paradise (a vision of a luxurious and cool garden shared by some versions of Eastern Christianity) with the sensu-

ous delights so obviously lacking in the midst of the Arabian desert.

Islam was not just a set of religious beliefs but a way of life as well. After the death of Muhammad, Muslim scholars, known as the **ulama,** drew up a law code, called the **Shari'a,** to provide believers with a set of prescriptions to regulate their daily lives. Much of the *Shari'a* was drawn from existing legal regulations or from the **Hadith,** a collection of the sayings of the Prophet that was used to supplement the revelations contained in the holy scriptures.

Believers were subject to strict behavioral requirements. In addition to the Five Pillars, Muslims were forbidden to gamble, to eat pork, to drink alcoholic beverages, and to engage in dishonest behavior. Sexual mores were also strict. Contacts between unmarried men and women were discouraged, and ideally marriages were to be arranged by the parents. In accordance with Bedouin custom, polygyny was permitted, but Muhammad attempted to limit the practice by restricting males to four wives.

The Arab Empire and Its Successors

The death of Muhammad presented his followers with a dilemma. Although Muhammad had not claimed divine qualities, Muslims saw no separation between political and religious authority. Submission to the will of Allah meant submission to his Prophet Muhammad. According to the Qur'an, "Whoso obeyeth the messenger obeyeth Allah."[1] Muhammad's charismatic authority and political skills had been at the heart of his success. But Muslims have never agreed as to whether he named a successor, and although he had several daughters, he left no sons. In the male-oriented society of his day, who would lead the community of the faithful?

Shortly after Muhammad's death, a number of his closest followers selected Abu Bakr, a wealthy merchant from Medina who was Muhammad's father-in-law and one of his first supporters, as **caliph** (*khalifa*, literally "successor"). The caliph was the temporal leader of the Islamic community and was also considered, in general terms, to be a religious leader, or **imam**. Under Abu Bakr's prudent leadership, the movement succeeded in suppressing factional tendencies among some of the Bedouin tribes in the peninsula and began to direct its attention to wider fields. Muhammad had used the Arabic tribal custom of the *razzia* or raid in the struggle against his enemies. Now his successors turned to the same custom to expand the authority of the movement. The Qur'an called this activity "striving in the way of the Lord," or *jihad.* Although sometimes translated as "holy war," the term is ambiguous and has been subject to varying interpretations.

Creation of an Empire

Once the Arabs had become unified under Muhammad's successor, they began directing outward against neighboring peoples the energy they had formerly directed against each other. The Byzantine and Sassanian Empires were the first to feel the strength of the newly united Arabs, now aroused to a peak of zeal by their common faith. At the Yarmuk River near Damascus, in 636, the Muslims defeated the Byzantine army. Four years later, they took possession of the Byzantine province of Syria. To the east, the Arabs defeated a Persian force in 637 and then went on to conquer the entire empire of the Sassanids by 650. In the meantime, Egypt and other areas of North Africa were also brought under Arab authority (see Chapter 8).

What accounts for this rapid expansion of the Arabs after the rise of Islam in the early seventh century? Historians have proposed various explanations, ranging from a prolonged drought on the Arabian peninsula to the desire of Islam's leaders to channel the energies of their new converts. Another hypothesis is that the expansion was deliberately planned by the ruling elites in Mecca to extend their trade routes and bring surplus-producing regions under their control. Whatever the case, Islam's

© British Library, London, UK/The Bridgeman Art Library

Ascension of the Prophet Muhammad. Shown here is an illustration of Muhammad's ascension to Heaven, as described in the Qur'an. Muhammad is veiled, in accordance with the accepted practice of not showing his facial features. Riding a celestial creature with the face of a woman, he arrives in Jerusalem to join Abraham, Jesus, and other prophets in prayer at the site of the Temple of Solomon. From there he ascends to Heaven to meet Allah, thus making the Dome of the Rock one of the sacred sites of the Muslim religion. Then Muhammad returned to Mecca, where he died in the year 632.

To what degree the traditional account of the exposition and inner meaning of the Qur'an can stand up to historical analysis is a matter of debate. The circumstances surrounding the life of Muhammad and his role in founding the religion of Islam, given the lack of verifiable evidence, remain highly speculative, and many Muslims are undoubtedly concerned that the consequences of rigorous examination might undercut key tenets of the Muslim faith. One of the problems connected with such an effort is that the earliest known versions of the Qur'an available today do not contain the diacritical marks that modern Arabic uses to clarify meaning, thus leaving much of the sacred text ambiguous and open to varying interpretations.

ability to unify the Bedouin peoples certainly played a role. Although the Arab triumph was made substantially easier by the ongoing conflict between the Byzantine and Persian Empires, which had weakened both powers, the strength of the Bedouin armies should not be overlooked. Led by a series of brilliant generals, the Arabs put together a large, highly motivated army, whose valor was enhanced by the belief that Muslim warriors who died in battle were guaranteed a place in paradise.

Once the armies had prevailed, Arab administration of the conquered areas was generally tolerant. Sometimes, due to a shortage of trained Arab administrators, government was left to local officials. Conversion to Islam was generally voluntary in accordance with the maxim in the Qur'an that "there shall be no compulsion in religion."[2] Those who chose not to convert were required only to submit to Muslim rule and pay a head tax in return for exemption from military service, which was required of all Muslim males. Under such conditions, the local populations often welcomed Arab rule as preferable to Byzantine rule or that of the Sassanid dynasty in Persia. Furthermore, the simple and direct character of the new religion, as well as its egalitarian qualities (all people were viewed as equal in the eyes of Allah), were undoubtedly attractive to peoples throughout the region.

The Rise of the Umayyads

The main challenge to the growing empire came from within. Some of Muhammad's followers had not agreed with the selection of Abu Bakr as the first caliph and promoted the candidacy of Ali, Muhammad's cousin and son-in-law, as an alternative. Ali's claim was ignored by other leaders, however, and after Abu Bakr's death, the office was passed to Umar, another of Muhammad's followers. In 656, Umar's successor, Uthman, was assassinated, and Ali was finally selected for the position. But according to tradition, Ali's rivals were convinced that he had been implicated in the death of his predecessor, and a factional struggle broke out within the Muslim leadership. In 661, Ali himself was assassinated, and Mu'awiya, the governor of Syria and one of Ali's chief rivals, replaced him in office. Mu'awiya thereupon made the caliphate hereditary in his own family, called the Umayyads, who were a branch of the Quraishi clan. The new caliphate, with its capital at Damascus, remained in power for nearly a century.

The factional struggle within Islam did not bring an end to Arab expansion. At the beginning of the eighth century, new attacks were launched at both the western and the eastern ends of the Mediterranean world (see Map 7.2). Arab armies advanced across North Africa and conquered

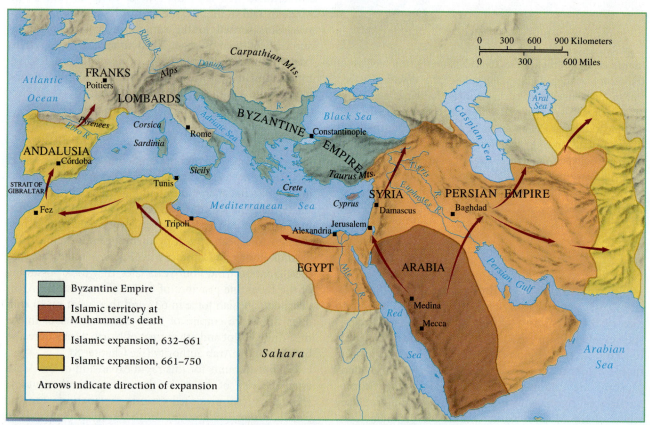

MAP 7.2 **The Expansion of Islam.** This map shows the expansion of the Islamic faith from its origins in the Arabian peninsula. Muhammad's followers carried the religion as far west as Spain and southern France and eastward to India and Southeast Asia. **?** In which of these areas is the Muslim faith still the dominant religion? 🌐 **View an animated version of this map or related maps at** http://worldrc.wadsworth.com/

the Berbers, a primarily pastoral people living along the Mediterranean coast and in the mountains in the interior. Then, around 710, Arab forces, supplemented by Berber allies under their commander, Tariq, crossed the Strait of Gibraltar and occupied southern Spain. The Visigothic kingdom, already weakened by internecine warfare, quickly collapsed, and by 725, most of the Iberian peninsula had become a Muslim state with its center in Andalusia. Seven years later, an Arab force, making a foray into southern France, was defeated by the army of Charles Martel near Poitiers. Some historians think that internal exhaustion would have forced the invaders to retreat even without their defeat at the hands of the Franks. In any event, the Battle of Poitiers would be the high-water mark of Arab expansion in Europe.

In the meantime, in 717, another Muslim force had launched an attack on Constantinople with the hope of destroying the Byzantine Empire. But the Byzantines' use of Greek fire, a petroleum-based compound containing quicklime and sulfur, destroyed the Muslim fleet, thus saving the empire and indirectly Christian Europe, since the fall of Constantinople would have opened the door to an Arab invasion of eastern Europe. The Byzantine Empire and Islam now established an uneasy frontier in southern Asia Minor.

Succession Problems

Arab power also extended to the east, consolidating Islamic rule in Mesopotamia and Persia and northward into Central Asia. But factional disputes continued to plague the empire. Many Muslims of non-Arab extraction resented the favoritism shown by local administrators to Arabs. In some cases, resentment led to revolt, as in Iraq, where Ali's second son, Hussein, disputed the legitimacy of the Umayyads and incited his supporters—to be known in the future as **Shi'ites** (from the Arabic phrase *shi'at Ali*, "partisans of Ali")—to rise up against Umayyad rule in 680. Hussein's forces were defeated, but a schism between Shi'ite and **Sunni** (usually translated as "orthodox") Muslims had been created that continues to this day.

Umayyad rule, always (in historian Arthur Gold-schmidt's words) "more political than pious," created resentment, not only in Mesopotamia, but also in North Africa, where Berber resistance continued, especially in the mountainous areas south of the coastal plains. According to critics, the Umayyads may have contributed to their own demise by their decadent behavior. One caliph allegedly swam in a pool of wine and then imbibed enough of the contents to lower the level significantly. Finally, in 750, a revolt led by Abu al-Abbas, a descendant of Muhammad's uncle, led to the overthrow of the Umayyads and the establishment of the Abbasid dynasty (750–1258) in what is now Iraq.

The Abbasids

The Abbasid caliphs brought political, economic, and cultural change to the world of Islam. While seeking to implant their own version of religious orthodoxy, they tried to break down the distinctions between Arab and non-Arab Muslims. All Muslims were now allowed to hold both civil and military offices. This change helped open Islamic culture to the influences of the occupied civilizations. Many Arabs now began to intermarry with the peoples they had conquered. In many parts of the Islamic world, notably North Africa and the eastern Mediterranean, most Muslim converts began to consider themselves Arabs. In 762, the Abbasids built a new capital city at Baghdad, on the Tigris River far to the east of the Umayyad capital at Damascus. The new capital was strategically positioned to take advantage of river traffic to the Persian Gulf and also lay astride the caravan route from the Mediterranean to Central Asia. The move eastward allowed Persian influence to come to the fore, encouraging a new cultural orientation. Under the Abbasids, judges, merchants, and government officials, rather than warriors, were viewed as the ideal citizens.

Abbasid Rule   The new Abbasid caliphate experienced a period of splendid rule well into the ninth century. Best known of the caliphs of the time was Harun al-Rashid (786–809), or Harun "the Upright," whose reign is often described as the golden age of the Abbasid caliphate. His son al-Ma'mun (813–833) was a patron of learning who founded an astronomical observatory and established a foundation for undertaking translations of classical Greek works. This was also a period of growing economic prosperity. The Arabs had conquered many of the richest provinces of the Roman Empire and now controlled the routes to the east (see Map 7.3). Baghdad became the center of an enormous commercial market that extended into Europe, Central Asia, and Africa, greatly adding to the wealth of the Islamic world and promoting an exchange of culture, ideas, and technology from one end of the known world to the other. Paper was introduced from China and eventually passed on to North Africa and Europe. Crops from India and Southeast Asia such as rice, sugar, sorghum, and cotton moved toward the west, while glass, wine, and indigo dye were introduced into China.

Under the Abbasids, the caliphs became more regal. More kings than spiritual leaders, described by such august phrases as the "caliph of God," they ruled by autocratic means, hardly distinguishable from the kings and emperors in neighboring civilizations. A thirteenth-century Chinese author, who compiled a world geography based on accounts by Chinese travelers, left the following description of one of the later caliphs:

> The king wears a turban of silk brocade and foreign cotton stuff [buckram]. On each new moon and full moon he puts on an eight-sided flat-topped headdress of pure gold, set with the most precious jewels in the world. His robe is of silk brocade and is bound around him with a jade girdle. On his feet he wears golden shoes.... The king's throne is set with pearls and precious stones, and the steps of the throne are covered with pure gold.[3]

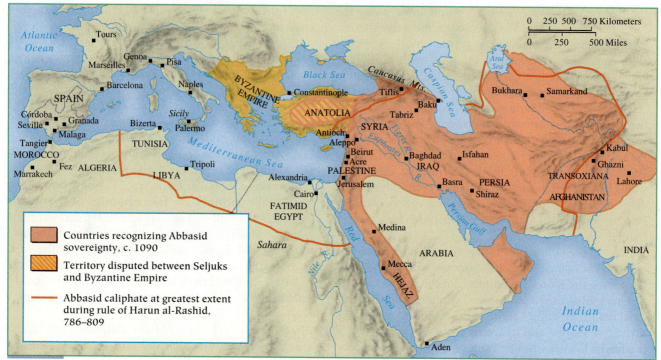

MAP 7.3 **The Abbasid Caliphate at the Height of Its Power.** The Abbasids arose in the eighth century as the defenders of the Muslim faith and established their capital at Baghdad. With its prowess as a trading state, the caliphate was the most powerful and extensive state in the region for several centuries. **?** What were the major urban centers under the influence of Islam, as shown on this map?

View an animated version of this map or related maps at http://worldrc.wadsworth.com/

As the caliph took on more of the trappings of a hereditary autocrat, the bureaucracy assisting him in administering the expanding empire grew more complex as well. The caliph was advised by a council (called a **diwan**) headed by a prime minister, known as a **vizier** (*wazir*). The caliph did not attend meetings of the *diwan* in the normal manner but sat behind a screen and then communicated his divine will to the *vizier*. Some historians have ascribed the change in the caliphate to Persian influence, which permeated the empire after the capital was moved to Baghdad. Persian influence was indeed strong (the mother of the caliph al-Ma'mun, for example, was a Persian), but more likely, the increase in pomp and circumstance was a natural consequence of the growing power and prosperity of the empire.

Instability and Division Nevertheless, an element of instability lurked beneath the surface. The lack of spiritual authority may have weakened the caliphate in competition with its potential rivals, and disputes over succession were common. At Harun's death, the rivalry between his two sons, Amin and al-Ma'mun, led to civil war and the destruction of Baghdad. As described by the tenth-century Muslim historian al-Mas'udi, "Mansions were destroyed, most remarkable monuments obliterated; prices soared. . . . Brother turned his sword against brother, son against father, as some fought for Amin, others for Ma'mun. Houses and palaces fueled the flames; property was put to the sack."[4]

Wealth contributed to financial corruption. By awarding important positions to court favorites, the Abbasid caliphs began to undermine the foundations of their own power and eventually became mere figureheads. Under Harun al-Rashid, members of his Hashemite clan received large pensions from the state treasury, and his wife, Zubaida, reportedly spent huge sums shopping while on a pilgrimage to Mecca. One powerful family, the Barmakids, amassed vast wealth and power until Harun al-Rashid eliminated the entire clan in a fit of jealousy.

The life of luxury enjoyed by the caliph and other political and economic elites in Baghdad seemingly undermined the stern fiber of Arab society as well as the strict moral code of Islam. Strictures against sexual promiscuity were widely ignored, and caliphs were rumored to maintain thousands of concubines in their harems. Divorce was common, homosexuality was widely practiced, and alcohol was consumed in public despite Islamic law's prohibition against imbibing spirits.

The process of disintegration was accelerated by changes that were taking place within the armed forces and the bureaucracy of the empire. Given the shortage of qualified Arabs for key positions in the army and the administration, the caliphate began to recruit officials from among the non-Arab peoples in the empire, such as Persians and Turks from Central Asia. These people gradually became a dominant force in the army and administration.

Provincial rulers also began to break away from central control and establish their own independent dynasties. Already in the eighth century, a separate caliphate had been established in Spain when Abd al-Rahman of the Umayyad dynasty had fled there. In 756, he seized control of southern Spain and then expanded his power into the center of the peninsula. He took the title of **emir,** or commander, and set up the emirate of al-Andalus (the Arabic name for Spain) with its center at Córdoba. The rulers of al-Andalus developed a unique society in which all religions were tolerated. The court also supported writers and artists, creating a brilliant and flourishing culture.

The fragmentation of the Islamic empire accelerated in the tenth century. Morocco became independent, and in 973, a new Shi'ite dynasty under the Fatimids was established in Egypt with its capital at Cairo. With increasing disarray in the empire, the Islamic world was held together only by the common commitment to the Qur'an and the use of the Arabic language as the prevailing means of communication.

The Seljuk Turks

In the eleventh century, the Abbasid caliphate faced yet another serious threat in the form of the Seljuk Turks. The Seljuk Turks were a nomadic people from Central Asia who had converted to Islam and flourished as military mercenaries for the Abbasid caliphate, where they were known for their ability as mounted archers. Moving gradually into Iran and Armenia as the Abbasids weakened, the Seljuk Turks grew in number until by the eleventh century, they were able to occupy the eastern provinces of the Abbasid empire. In 1055, a Turkish leader captured Baghdad and assumed command of the empire with the title of **sultan** ("holder of power"). While the Abbasid caliph remained the chief representative of Sunni religious authority, the real military and political power of the state was in the hands of the Seljuk Turks. The latter did not establish their headquarters in Baghdad, which now entered a period of decline.

By the last quarter of the eleventh century, the Seljuks were exerting military pressure on Egypt and the Byzantine Empire. In 1071, when the Byzantines foolishly challenged the Turks, their army was routed at Manzikert, near Lake Van in eastern Turkey, and the victors took over most of the Anatolian peninsula (see Map 7.4). In dire straits, the Byzantine Empire turned to the west for help, setting in motion the papal pleas that led to the **Crusades** (see the next section).

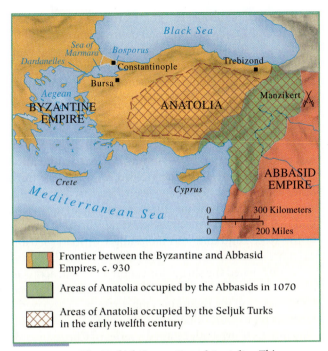

MAP 7.4 **The Turkish Occupation of Anatolia.** This map shows the expansion of Turkic-speaking peoples into the Anatolian peninsula in the eleventh and twelfth centuries. The Ottoman Turks established their capital at Bursa in 1335 and eventually at Constantinople in 1453. ❓ What was the major obstacle to Ottoman expansion into Europe at the time?

In Europe, and undoubtedly within the Muslim world itself, the arrival of the Turks was regarded as a disaster. The Turks were viewed as barbarians who destroyed civilizations and oppressed populations. In fact, in many respects, Turkish rule in the Middle East was probably beneficial. Converted to Islam, the Turkish rulers temporarily brought an end to the fraternal squabbles between Sunni and Shi'ite Muslims while supporting the Sunnites. They put their energies into revitalizing Islamic law and institutions and provided much-needed political stability to the empire, which helped restore its former prosperity. Under Seljuk rule, Muslims began to organize themselves into autonomous brotherhoods, whose relatively tolerant practices characterized Islamic religious attitudes until the end of the nineteenth century, when increased competition with Europe led to confrontation with the West.

Seljuk political domination over the old Abbasid Empire, however, provoked resentment on the part of many Persian Shi'ites, who viewed the Turks as usurping foreigners who had betrayed the true faith of Islam. Among the regime's most feared enemies was Hasan al-Sabahh, a Cairo-trained Persian who formed a rebel group, popularly known as "assassins" (guardians), who for several decades terrorized government officials and other leading political and religious figures from their base in the mountains south of the Caspian Sea. Like their modern-day equivalents, the terrorist organization known as al-Qaeda, Sabahh's followers were highly motivated and were adept in infiltrating the enemy's camp in order to carry out their clandestine activities. The organization was finally eliminated by the invading Mongols in the thirteenth century.

The Crusades

Just before the end of the eleventh century, the Byzantine emperor Alexius I desperately called for assistance from other Christian states in Europe to protect his empire against the invading Seljuk Turks. As part of his appeal, he said that the Muslims were desecrating Christian shrines in the Holy Land and also molesting Christian pilgrims en route to the shrines. In actuality, the Muslims had never threatened the shrines or cut off Christian access to them. But tension between Christendom and Islam was on the rise, and the Byzantine emperor's appeal received a ready response in Europe. Beginning in 1096 and continuing into the thirteenth century, a series of Christian raids on Islamic territories known as the Crusades brought the Holy Land and adjacent areas on the Mediterranean coast from Antioch to the Sinai peninsula under Christian rule (see Chapter 12).

At first, Muslim rulers in the area were taken aback by the invading crusaders, whose armored cavalry presented a new challenge to local warriors, and their response was ineffectual. The Seljuk Turks by that time were preoccupied with events taking place farther to the east and took no action themselves. But in 1169, Sunni Muslims under the leadership of Saladin (Salah al-Din), vizier to the last Fatimid caliph, brought an end to the Fatimid dynasty. Proclaiming himself sultan, Saladin succeeded in establishing his control over both Egypt and Syria, thereby confronting the Christian states in the area with united Muslim power on two fronts. In 1187, Saladin's army invaded the kingdom of Jerusalem and destroyed the Christian forces concentrated there. Further operations reduced Christian occupation in the area to a handful of fortresses along the northern coast. Unlike the Christians, however, Saladin did not permit a massacre of the civilian population and even tolerated the continuation of Christian religious services in conquered territories. For a time, Christian occupation forces even carried on a lively trade relationship with Muslim communities in the region.

The Christians returned for another try a few years after the fall of Jerusalem, but the campaign succeeded only in securing some of the coastal cities. Although the Christians would retain a toehold on the coast for much of the thirteenth century (Acre, their last stronghold, fell to the Muslims in 1291), they were no longer a significant force in Middle Eastern affairs. In retrospect, the Crusades had only minimal importance in the history of the Middle East, although they may have served to unite the forces of Islam against the foreign invaders, thus creating a residue of distrust toward Christians that continues to resonate through the Islamic world today (see the box on p. 155). Far more important in their impact were the Mongols,

© Michael Nicholson/CORBIS

© W. Meier/zefa/CORBIS

COMPARATIVE ILLUSTRATION

SCIENCE & TECHNOLOGY

The Medieval Castle. Beginning in the eighth century, Muslim rulers began to erect fortified stone castles in the desert. So impressed were the crusaders by the innovative defensive features they saw that they began to incorporate similar ideas into their own European castles, which had previously been made of wood. In twelfth-century Syria, the crusaders constructed the imposing citadel known as the Krak des Chevaliers (Castle of the Knights) on the foundation of a Muslim fort (right photo). This new model of a massive fortress of solid masonry spread to western Europe, as is evident in the castle shown in the photo on the left, built in the late thirteenth century in Wales.

THE CRUSADES IN MUSLIM EYES

INTERACTION & EXCHANGE

Usamah, an early-twelfth-century Muslim warrior and gentleman, had close associations with the crusaders. When he was ninety years old, he wrote his memoirs, including many entertaining observations on the crusaders, or "Franks" as he called them. Here Usamah is astounded at the Franks' rudeness to Muslims and at their assumption of cultural superiority.

Why does the author believe it would be a misfortune for his son to visit "the lands of the Franks"? How might his Frankish friend respond?

Usamah, *Book of Reflections*

1. Everyone who is a fresh emigrant from the Frankish lands is ruder in character than those who have become acclimatized and have held long association with the Moslems. Here is an illustration of their rude character.

Whenever I visited Jerusalem I always entered the Aqsa Mosque, beside which stood a small mosque which the Franks had converted into a church. When I used to enter the Aqsa Mosque, which was occupied by the Templars [an order of crusading knights], who were my friends, the Templars would evacuate the little adjoining mosque so that I might pray in it. One day I entered this mosque, repeated the first formula, "Allah is great," and stood up in the act of praying, upon which one of the Franks rushed on me, got hold of me, and turned my face eastward, saying, "This is the way thou shouldst pray!" A group of Templars hastened to him, seized him, and repelled him from me. I resumed my prayer. The same man, while the others were otherwise busy, rushed once more on me and turned my face eastward,

saying, "This is the way thou shouldst pray!" The Templars again came in to him and expelled him. They apologized to me, saying, "This is a stranger who has only recently arrived from the land of the Franks, and he has never before seen anyone praying except eastward." Thereupon I said to myself, "I have had enough prayer." So I went out, and have ever been surprised at the conduct of this devil of a man, at the change in the color of his face, his trembling, and his sentiment at the sight of one praying toward the qiblah.

2. In the army of King Fulk, son of Fulk, was a Frankish reverend knight who had just arrived from their land in order to make the holy pilgrimage and then return home. He was of my intimate fellowship and kept such constant company with me that he began to call me "my brother." Between us were mutual bonds of amity and friendship. When he resolved to return by sea to his homeland, he said to me:

"My brother, I am leaving for my country and I want thee to send with me thy son (my son, who was then fourteen years old, was at that time in my company) to our country, where he can see the knights and learn wisdom and chivalry. When he returns, he will be like a wise man."

Thus there fell upon my ears words which would never come out of the head of a sensible man; for even if my son were to be taken captive, his captivity could not bring him a worse misfortune than carrying him into the lands of the Franks.

CENGAGENOW To read more firsthand accounts of the Crusades, including a story of another rude Frank, enter the *CengageNOW* documents area using the access card that is available for *The Essential World History.*

---

a pastoral people who swept out of the Gobi Desert in the early thirteenth century to seize control over much of the known world (see Chapter 10). Beginning with the advances of Genghis Khan in northern China, Mongol armies later spread across Central Asia, and in 1258, under the leadership of Hulegu, brother of the more famous Khubilai Khan, they seized Persia and Mesopotamia, bringing an end to the caliphate at Baghdad.

The Mongols

Unlike the Seljuk Turks, the Mongols were not Muslims, and they found it difficult to adapt to the settled conditions that they found in the major cities in the Middle East. Their treatment of the local population in conquered territories was brutal (according to one historian, after conquering a city, they wiped out not only entire families but also their household pets) and destructive to the economy. Cities were razed to the ground, and dams and other irrigation works were destroyed,

reducing prosperous agricultural societies to the point of mass starvation. The Mongols advanced as far as the Red Sea, but their attempt to seize Egypt failed, in part because of the effective resistance posed by the Mamluks (a Turkish military class originally composed of slaves; sometimes written as Mamelukes), who had recently overthrown the administration set up by Saladin and seized power for themselves.

Eventually, the Mongol rulers in the Middle East began to take on the coloration of the peoples that they had conquered. Mongol elites converted to Islam, Persian influence became predominant at court, and the cities began to be rebuilt. By the fourteenth century, the Mongol empire began to split into separate kingdoms and then to disintegrate. In the meantime, however, the old Islamic empire originally established by the Arabs in the seventh and eighth centuries had come to an end. The new center of Islamic civilization was in Cairo, now about to promote a renaissance in Muslim culture under the sponsorship of the Mamluks.

To the north, another new force began to appear on the horizon with the rise of the Ottoman Turks on the Anatolian peninsula. In 1453, Sultan Mehmet II seized Constantinople and brought an end to the Byzantine Empire. Then the Ottomans began to turn their attention to the rest of the Middle East (see Chapter 15).

Islamic Civilization

To be a Muslim is not simply to worship Allah but also to live according to his law as revealed in the Qur'an, which is viewed as fundamental and immutable doctrine, not to be revised by human beings.

As Allah has decreed, so must humans behave. Therefore, Islamic doctrine must be consulted to determine questions of politics, economic behavior, civil and criminal law, and social ethics. In Islamic society, there is no demarcation between church and state, between the sacred and the secular.

The Wealth of Araby: Trade and Cities in the Middle East

As we have noted, this era was probably, overall, one of the most prosperous periods in the history of the Middle East. Trade flourished, not only in the Islamic world but also with China (now in a period of efflorescence during the era of the Tang and the Song dynasties—see Chapter 10), with the Byzantine Empire, and with the trading societies in Southeast Asia (see Chapter 9). Trade goods were carried both by ship and by the "fleets of the desert," the camel caravans that traversed the arid land from Morocco in the far west to the countries beyond the Caspian Sea. From West Africa came gold and slaves; from China, silk and porcelain; from East Africa, gold, ivory, and rhinoceros horn; and from the lands of South Asia, sandalwood, cotton, wheat, sugar, and spices. Within the empire, Egypt contributed grain; Iraq, linens, dates, and precious stones; Spain, leather goods, olives, and wine; and western India, various textile goods. The exchange of goods was facilitated by the development of banking and the use of currency and letters of credit (see the comparative essay "Trade and Civilization" on p. 157).

Under these conditions, urban areas flourished. While the Abbasids were in power, Baghdad was probably the greatest city in the empire, but after the rise of the Fatimids in Egypt, the focus of trade shifted to Cairo, described by the traveler Leo Africanus as "one of the greatest and most famous cities in all the whole world, filled with stately and admirable palaces and colleges, and most sumptuous temples."[5] Other great commercial cities included Basra at the head of the Persian Gulf, Aden at the southern tip of the Arabian peninsula, Damascus in modern Syria, and Marrakech in Morocco. In the cities, the inhabitants were generally segregated by religion, with Muslims, Jews, and Christians living in separate neighborhoods. But all were equally subject to the most common threats to urban life—fire, flood, and disease.

CHRONOLOGY	Islam: The First Millennium
Life of Muhammad	570–632
Flight to Medina	622
Conquest of Mecca	630
Fall of Cairo	640
Defeat of Persians	650
Election of Ali to caliphate	656
Muslim entry into Spain	c. 710
Abbasid caliphate	750–1258
Construction of city of Baghdad	762
Reign of Harun al-Rashid	786–809
Founding of Fatimid dynasty in Egypt	973
Capture of Baghdad by Seljuk Turks	1055
Seizure of Anatolia by Seljuk Turks	1071
First Crusade	1096
Saladin destroys Fatimid kingdom	1169
Fourth Crusade	1204
Mongols seize Baghdad	1258
Ottoman Turks capture Constantinople	1453

The most impressive urban buildings were usually the palace for the caliph or the local governor and the great mosque. Houses were often constructed of stone or brick around a timber frame. The larger houses were often built around an interior courtyard, where the residents could retreat from the dust, noise, and heat of the city streets. Sometimes domestic animals such as goats or sheep would be stabled there. The houses of the wealthy were often multistoried, with balconies and windows covered with latticework to provide privacy for those inside. The poor in both urban and rural areas lived in simpler houses composed of clay or unfired bricks. The Bedouins lived in tents that could be dismantled and moved according to their needs.

Eating habits varied in accordance with economic standing and religious preference. Muslims did not eat pork, but those who could afford it often served other meats such as mutton, lamb, poultry, or fish. Fruit, spices, and various sweets were delicacies. The poor were generally forced to survive on boiled millet or peas with an occasional lump of meat or fat. Bread—white or whole meal—could be found on tables throughout the region except in the deserts, where boiled grain was the staple food.

Islamic Society

In some ways, Arab society was probably one of the most egalitarian of its time. Both the principles of Islam, which held that all were equal in the eyes of Allah, and the importance of trade to the prosperity of the state probably contributed to this egalitarianism. Although there was

TRADE AND CIVILIZATION

INTERACTION & EXCHANGE

In 2002, archaeologists unearthed the site of an ancient Egyptian port city on the shores of the Red Sea. Established sometime during the first millennium B.C.E., the city of Berenike linked the Nile River valley with ports as far away as the island of Java in Southeast Asia. The discovery of Berenike is only the latest piece of evidence confirming the importance of interregional trade in the ancient world. The exchange of goods between far-flung societies became a powerful engine driving the rise of advanced civilizations throughout the ancient world. Raw materials such as copper, tin, and obsidian; items of daily necessity like salt, fish, and other foodstuffs; and luxury goods like gold, silk, and precious stones passed from one end of the Eurasian supercontinent to the other, across the desert from the Mediterranean Sea to sub-Saharan Africa, and throughout much of the Americas. Less well known but also important was the maritime trade that stretched from the Mediterranean across the Indian Ocean to port cities on the distant coasts of Southeast and East Asia.

During the first millennium C.E., the level of interdependence among human societies intensified as three major trade routes—across the Indian Ocean, along the Silk Road, and by caravan across the Sahara—created the framework of a single trade system. The new global network was not only commercial but informational as well, transmitting technology and ideas, such as the emerging religions of Buddhism, Christianity, and Islam, to new destinations.

There was a close relationship between missionary activities and trade. Buddhist merchants first brought the teachings of Siddhartha Gautama to China, and Muslim traders carried Muhammad's words to Southeast Asia and sub-Saharan Africa. Indian traders carried Hindu beliefs and political institutions to Southeast Asia.

What caused the rapid expansion of trade during this period? One key factor was the introduction of technology to facilitate transportation. The development of the compass, improved techniques in mapmaking and shipbuilding, and greater knowledge of wind patterns all contributed to the expansion of maritime trade. Caravan trade, once carried by wheeled chariots or on the backs of oxen, now used the camel as the preferred beast of burden through the deserts of Africa, Central Asia, and the Middle East.

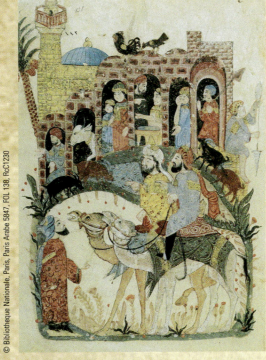

© Bibliotheque Nationale, Paris. Paris Arabe 5847, FOL 138, RcC1230

Another reason for the expansion of commerce during this period was the appearance of several multinational empires that created zones of stability and affluence in key areas of the Eurasian landmass. Most important were the emergence of the Abbasid Empire in the Middle East and the rise of prosperity in China during the Tang and Song dynasties (see Chapter 10). The Mongol invasions in the thirteenth century temporarily disrupted the process but then created a new era of stability that fostered long-distance trade throughout the world.

Arab Merchants in a Caravan. By land or by sea, Arab trade routes extended over half the globe. The world of Islam and the camel, both portrayed in this thirteenth-century miniature, were essential components of Muslim commercial ventures.

a fairly well defined upper class, consisting of the ruling families, senior officials, tribal elites, and the wealthiest merchants, there was no hereditary nobility as in many contemporary societies, and the merchants enjoyed a degree of respect that they did not receive in Europe, China, or India.

Though the Arab Empire was more urbanized than most other societies at the time, the bulk of the population continued to live in the countryside and supported itself by farming or herding animals. During the early stages, most of the farmland was owned by independent peasants, but later some concentration of land in the hands of wealthy owners began to take place. In river valleys like the Tigris and Euphrates and the Nile, the majority of the farmers probably continued to be independent peasants.

"DRAW THEIR VEILS OVER THEIR BOSOMS"

FAMILY & SOCIETY

Prior to the Islamic era, many upper-class women greeted men on the street, entertained their husbands' friends at home, went on pilgrimages to Mecca, and even accompanied their husbands to battle. Such women were neither veiled nor secluded. Muhammad, however, specified that his own wives, who (according to the Qur'an) were "not like any other women," should be modestly attired and should be addressed by men from behind a curtain. Over the centuries, Muslim theologians, fearful that female sexuality could threaten the established order, interpreted Muhammad's "modest attire" and his reference to curtains to mean segregated seclusion and body concealment for all Muslim women. In fact, one strict scholar in fourteenth-century Cairo went so far as to prescribe that ideally a woman should be allowed to leave her home only three times in her life: when entering her husband's home after marriage, after the death of parents, and after her own death.

In traditional Islamic societies, veiling and seclusion were more prevalent among urban women than among their rural counterparts. The latter, who worked in the fields and rarely saw people outside their extended family, were less restricted. In this excerpt from the Qur'an, women are instructed to "guard their modesty" and "draw veils over their bosoms." Nowhere in the Qur'an, however, does it stipulate that women should be sequestered or covered from head to toe.

How does the role of women in Islam compare with what we have seen in other traditional societies, such as India, China, and the Americas?

Qur'an, Sura 24: "The Light"

And say to the believing women
That they should lower
Their gaze and guard
Their modesty: that they
Should not display their
Beauty and ornaments except
What [must ordinarily] appear
Thereof: that they should
Draw their veils over
Their bosoms and not display
Their beauty except
To their husbands, their fathers,
Their husbands' fathers, their sons,
Their husbands' sons,
Their brothers or their brothers' sons,
Or their sisters' sons,
Or their women, or the slaves
Whom their right hands
Possess, or male servants
Free of physical needs,
Or small children who
Have no sense of the shame
Of sex; and that they
Should not strike their feet
In order to draw attention
To their hidden ornaments.

CENGAGE**NOW** To read the Qur'an in its entirety, enter the *CengageNOW* documents area using the access card that is available for *The Essential World History.*

Not all benefited from the high degree of social mobility in the Islamic world, however. Slavery was widespread. Since a Muslim could not be enslaved, the supply came from sub-Saharan Africa or from non-Islamic populations elsewhere in Asia. Most slaves were employed in the army (which was sometimes a road to power, as in the case of the Mamluks) or as domestic servants, who were sometimes permitted to purchase their freedom. The slaves who worked the large estates experienced the worst living conditions and rose in revolt on several occasions.

The Islamic principle of human equality also fell short, as in most other societies of its day, in the treatment of women. Although the Qur'an instructed men to treat women with respect, and women did have the right to own and inherit property, in general the male was dominant in Muslim society. Polygyny was permitted, and the right of divorce was in practice restricted to the husband, although some schools of legal thought permitted women to stipulate that their husband could have only one wife or to seek a separation in certain specific circumstances. Adultery and homosexuality were stringently forbidden (although such prohibitions were frequently ignored in practice), and Islamic custom required that women be cloistered in their homes (thus the tradition of the harem) and prohibited from social contacts with males outside their own family. The custom of requiring women to cover virtually all parts of their body when appearing in public was common in urban areas and continues to be practiced in many Islamic societies today. It should be noted, however, that these customs owed more to traditional Arab practice than to Qur'anic law (see the box above).

The Culture of Islam

The Arabs were truly heirs to many elements of the remaining Greco-Roman culture of the Roman Empire, and they assimilated Byzantine and Persian culture just as readily. In the eighth and ninth centuries, numerous Greek, Syrian, and Persian scientific and philosophical

Preserving the Wisdom of the Greeks. After the fall of the Roman Empire, the philosophical works of ancient Greece were virtually forgotten in Europe or were banned as heretical by the Byzantine Empire. It was thanks to Muslim scholars, who located copies at the magnificent library in Alexandria, Egypt, that many classical Greek writings survived. Here young Muslim scholars are being trained in the Greek language so that they can translate classical Greek writings into Arabic. Later the texts were translated back into Western languages and served as the catalyst for an intellectual revival in medieval and renaissance Europe.

works were translated into Arabic and eventually found their way to Europe. As the chief language in the southern Mediterranean and the Middle East, Arabic became an international language. Later, Persian and Turkish also came to be important in administration and culture.

The spread of Islam led to the emergence of a new culture throughout the Arab Empire. This was true in all fields of endeavor, from literature to art and architecture. But pre-Islamic traditions were not extinguished and frequently combined with Muslim motifs, resulting in creative works of great imagination and originality.

Philosophy and Science During the centuries following the rise of the Arab Empire, it was the Islamic world that was most responsible for preserving and spreading the scientific and philosophical achievements of ancient civilizations. At a time when ancient Greek philosophy was largely unknown in Europe, key works by Aristotle, Plato, and other Greek philosophers were translated into Arabic and stored in a "house of wisdom" in Baghdad, where they were read and studied by Muslim scholars. Through the writings of the Spanish Muslim philosopher Ibn Rushd (known in the West as Averroës), many of these works eventually became known in Europe and influenced Christian thought. Texts on mathematics and linguistics were brought from India. The process was undoubtedly stimulated by the introduction of paper manufacturing from China in the eighth century. By the end of the century, the first paper factories had been established in Baghdad, and booksellers and libraries soon followed. The first paper mill in Europe appeared in the Pyrenees region of Spain in the twelfth century.

Although Islamic scholars are justly praised for preserving much of classical knowledge for the West, they also made considerable advances of their own. Nowhere is this more evident than in mathematics and the natural sciences.

Islamic scholars adopted and passed on the numerical system of India, including the use of the zero, and a ninth-century Persian mathematician founded the mathematical discipline of algebra (*al-jābr*). In astronomy, Muslims set up an observatory at Baghdad to study the position of the stars. They were aware that the earth was round and in the ninth century produced a world map based on the tradition of the Greco-Roman astronomer Ptolemy.

Muslim scholars also made many new discoveries in optics and chemistry and, with the assistance of texts on anatomy by the ancient Greek physician Galen (c.180–200 C.E.), developed medicine as a distinctive field of scientific inquiry. Especially well known was Ibn Sina (980–1037). Known as Avicenna in the West, he compiled a medical encyclopedia that, among other things, emphasized the contagious nature of certain diseases and showed how they could be spread by contaminated water supplies. After its translation into Latin, Avicenna's work became a basic medical textbook for medieval European university students.

Islamic Literature Islam brought major changes to the literature of the Middle East. Muslims regarded the Qur'an as their greatest literary work, but pre-Islamic traditions continued to influence writers throughout the region.

The tradition of Arabic poetry was well established by the time of Muhammad. It extolled Bedouin tribal life, courage in battle, hunting, sports, and respect for the animals of the desert, especially the camel. Because the Arabic language did not possess a written script until the fourth century C.E., poetry was originally passed on by memory. Later, in the eighth and ninth centuries, it was compiled in anthologies.

Pre-Muslim Persia also boasted a long literary tradition, most of it oral and written down in later centuries in the Arabic alphabet. The Persian poetic tradition remained strong under Islam. Rabe'a of Qozdar, Persia's first known woman poet, lived in the second half of the tenth century. Describing the suffering love brings, she wrote: "Beset with impatience I did not know / That the more one seeks to pull away, the tighter becomes the rope."[6]

In the West, the most famous works of Middle Eastern literature are undoubtedly the *Rubaiyat* of Omar Khayyam and *Tales from 1001 Nights* (also called *The Arabian Nights*). Paradoxically, these two works are not as popular with Middle Eastern readers. Both, in fact, were freely translated into Western languages for nineteenth-century European readers, who developed a taste for stories set in exotic foreign places.

Unfortunately, very little is known of the life or the poetry of the twelfth-century poet Omar Khayyam. Skeptical, reserved, and slightly contemptuous of his peers, he combined poetry with scientific works on mathematics and astronomy and a revision of the calendar that was more accurate than the Gregorian version devised in Europe hundreds of years later. Omar Khayyam did not write down his poems but composed them orally over wine with friends at a neighborhood tavern. They were recorded later by friends or scribes. Many poems attributed to him were actually written long after his death. Among them is the well-known couplet translated into English in the nineteenth century: "Here with a loaf of bread beneath the bough, / A flask of wine, a book of verse, and thou."

Omar Khayyam's poetry is simple and down to earth. Key themes are the impermanence of life, the impossibility of knowing God, and disbelief in an afterlife. Ironically, recent translations of his work appeal to modern attitudes of skepticism and minimalist simplicity that may make him even more popular in the West:

> *In youth I studied for a little while;*
> *Later I boasted of my mastery.*
> *Yet this was all the lesson that I learned:*
> *We come from dust, and with the wind are gone.*
>
> *Of all the travelers on this endless road*
> *No one returns to tell us where it leads,*
> *There's little in this world but greed and need;*
> *Leave nothing here, for you will not return. . . .*
>
> *Since no one can be certain of tomorrow,*
> *It's better not to fill the heart with care.*
> *Drink wine by moonlight, darling, for the moon*
> *Will shine long after this, and find us not.*[7]

Like Omar Khayyam's verse, *The Arabian Nights* was loosely translated into European languages and adapted to Western tastes. A composite of folktales, fables, and romances of Indian and indigenous origin, the stories interweave the natural with the supernatural. The earliest stories were told orally and were later transcribed, with many later additions, in Arabic and Persian versions. The famous story of Aladdin and the Magic Lamp, for example, was an eighteenth-century addition. Nevertheless, *The Arabian Nights* has entertained readers for centuries,

allowing them to enter a land of wish fulfillment through extraordinary plots, sensuality, comic and tragic situations, and a cast of unforgettable characters.

Sadi (1210–1292), considered the Persian Shakespeare, remains to this day the favorite author in Iran. His *Rose Garden* is a collection of entertaining stories written in prose sprinkled with verse. He is also renowned for his sonnetlike love poems, which set a model for generations to come. Sadi was a master of the pithy maxim:

> *A cat is a lion in catching mice*
> *But a mouse in combat with a tiger.*
>
> *He has found eternal happiness who lived a good life,*
> *Because, after his end, good repute will keep his name*
>   *alive.*
>
> *When thou fightest with anyone, consider*
> *Whether thou wilt have to flee from him or he from thee.*[8]

Some Arabic and Persian literature reflected the deep spiritual and ethical concerns of the Qur'an. Many writers, however, carried Islamic thought in novel directions. The thirteenth-century poet Rumi, for example, embraced **Sufism,** a form of religious belief that called for a mystical relationship between Allah and human beings (the term *Sufism* stems from the Arabic word for "wool," referring to the rough wool garments that its adherents wore). Converted to Sufism by a wandering dervish (dervishes, from the word for "poor" in Persian, sought to achieve a mystical union with Allah through dancing and chanting in an ecstatic trance), Rumi abandoned orthodox Islam to embrace God directly through ecstatic love. Realizing that love transcends intellect, he sought to reach God through a trance attained by the whirling dance of the dervish, set to mesmerizing music. As he twirled, the poet extemporized some of the most passionate lyrical verse ever conceived. His faith and art remain an important force in Islamic society today (see the box on p. 161).

The Islamic world also made a major contribution to historical writing, another discipline that was stimulated by the introduction of paper manufacturing. The first great Islamic historian was al-Mas'udi. Born in Baghdad in 896, he wrote about both the Muslim and the non-Muslim world, traveling widely in the process. His *Meadows of Gold* is the source of much of our knowledge about the golden age of the Abbasid caliphate. Translations of his work reveal a wide-ranging mind and a keen intellect, combined with a human touch that practitioners of the art in our century might find reason to emulate. Equaling al-Mas'udi in talent and reputation was the fourteenth-century historian Ibn Khaldun. Combining scholarship with government service, Ibn Khaldun was one of the first historians to attempt a philosophy of history.

Islamic Art and Architecture   The art of Islam is a blend of Arab, Turkish, and Persian traditions. Although local influences can be discerned in Egypt, Anatolia, Spain, and other areas and the Mongols introduced an East Asian

THE PASSIONS OF A SUFI MYSTIC

RELIGION & PHILOSOPHY

Sufism was an unorthodox form of Islam that flourished in many parts of the Muslim world. It preached the importance of a highly personal relationship between Allah and the individual believer. Sufi orders began to assume considerable influence by the thirteenth century, perhaps because of the disintegration of the Abbasid Empire and the heightened instability throughout the Islamic world. Sufi missionaries played a major role in efforts to spread Islam to India and Central Asia. In this poem, the thirteenth-century Persian poet Rumi describes the mystical relationship achieved by means of passionate music and dance.

How does this poem celebrate the spiritual side of life? Why might such writings be attacked as contrary to Islamic doctrine?

Rumi, *Call to the Dance*

Come!
But don't join us without music.
We have a celebration here.
Rise and beat the drums.

We are Mansur who said "I am God!"

We are in ecstasy—
Drunk, but not from wine made of grapes.

Whatever your thoughts are about us,
We are far, far from them.

This is the night of the same
When we whirl to ecstasy.

There is light now,
There is light, there is light.

This is true love,
Which means farewell to the mind.
There is farewell today, farewell.

Tonight each flaming heart is a friend of music.
Longing for your lips,
My heart pours out of my mouth.

Hush!
You are made of feeling and thought and passion;
The rest is nothing but flesh and bone.
We are the soul of the world,
Not heavy or sagging like the body.
We are the spirit's treasure,
Not bound to this earth, to time or space.

How can they talk to us of prayer rugs and piety?
We are the hunter and the hunted,
Autumn and spring,
Night and day,
Visible and hidden.
Love is our mother.
We were born of Love.

CENGAGENOW To read more of Rumi's poetry, enter the *CengageNOW* documents area using the access card that is available for *The Essential World History*.

---

accent in the thirteenth century, for a long time Islamic art remained remarkably coherent over a wide area. First and foremost, the Arabs, with their new religion and their writing system, served as a unifying force. Fascinated by the mathematics and astronomy they inherited from the Romans or the Babylonians, they developed a sense of rhythm and abstraction that found expression in their use of repetitive geometric ornamentation. The Turks brought abstraction in figurative and nonfigurative designs, and the Persians added their lyrical poetical mysticism. Much Islamic painting, for example, consists of illustrations of Persian texts.

The ultimate expression of Islamic art is to be found in magnificent architectural monuments beginning in the late seventh century. The first great example is the Dome of the Rock, which was built in 691 to proclaim the spiritual and political legitimacy of the new religion to the ancient world. Set in the sacred heart of Jerusalem on Muhammad's holy rock and touching both the Western Wall of the Jews and the oldest Christian church, the

Dome of the Rock remains one of the most revered Islamic monuments. Constructed on Byzantine lines with an octagonal shape and marble columns and ornamentation, the interior reflects Persian motifs with mosaics of precious stones. Although rebuilt several times and incorporating influences from both East and West, this first monument to Islam represents the birth of a new art.

At first, desert Arabs, whether nomads or conquering armies, prayed in an open court, shaded along the *qibla* (the wall facing the holy city of Mecca) by a thatched roof supported by rows of palm trunks. There was also a ditch where the faithful could wash off the dust of the desert prior to prayer. As Islam became better established, enormous mosques were constructed, but they were still modeled on the open court, which would be surrounded on all four sides with pillars supporting a wooden roof over the prayer area facing the *qibla* wall. The largest mosque ever built, the Great Mosque of Samarra (848–852), covered 10 acres and contained 464 pillars in aisles surrounding the court. Set in the *qibla* wall was a niche, or **mihrab,** containing a decorated panel pointing to Mecca and representing Allah. Remains of the massive 30-foot-high outer wall still stand, but the most famous section of the Samarra mosque was its 90-foot-tall minaret, the tower accompanying a mosque from which the **muezzin** (crier) calls the faithful to prayer five times a day.

No discussion of mosques would be complete without mentioning the famous ninth-century mosque at Córdoba in southern Spain, which is still in remarkable condition. Its 514 columns supporting double horseshoe arches transform this architectural wonder into a unique forest of trees pointing upward, contributing to a light and airy effect. The unparalleled sumptuousness and elegance make the Córdoba mosque one of the wonders of world art, let alone Islamic art.

Since the Muslim religion combines spiritual and political power in one, palaces also reflected the glory of Islam. Beginning in the eighth century with the spectacular castles of Syria, the rulers constructed large brick domiciles reminiscent of Roman design, with protective walls, gates, and baths. With a central courtyard surrounded by two-story arcades and massive gate-towers, they resembled fortresses as much as palaces. Characteristic of such "desert palaces" was the gallery over the entrance gate, with holes through which boiling oil could be poured down on the heads of attacking forces. Unfortunately, none of these structures has survived.

The ultimate remaining Islamic palace is the fourteenth-century Alhambra in Spain. The extensive succession of courtyards, rooms, gardens, and fountains created a fairy-tale castle perched high above the city of Granada. Every inch of surface is decorated in intricate floral and semiabstract patterns; much of the decoration is done in carved plasterwork so fine that it resembles lace. The Lion Court in the center of the harem is world renowned for its lion fountain and surrounding arcade with elegant columns and carvings.

Since antiquity, one of the primary occupations of women has been the spinning and weaving of cloth to make clothing and other useful items for their families. In the Middle East, this skill reached an apogee in the art of the knotted woolen rug. Originating in the pre-Muslim era, rugs were initially used to insulate stone palaces against the cold as well as to warm shepherds' tents. Eventually, they were applied to religious purposes, since every practicing Muslim is required to pray five times a day on clean ground. Small rugs served as prayer mats for individual use, while larger and more elaborate ones were given by rulers as rewards for political favors. Bedouins in the Arabian desert covered their sandy floors with rugs to create a cozy environment in their tents.

In villages throughout the Middle East, the art of rug weaving has been passed down from mother to daughter over the centuries. Small girls as young as four years old took part in the process by helping to spin and prepare the wool shorn from the family sheep. By the age of six, girls would begin their first rug, and before adolescence, their slender fingers would be producing fine carpets.

Skilled artisanship represented an extra enticement to prospective bridegrooms, and rugs often became an important part of a woman's dowry to her future husband. After the wedding, the wife would continue to make rugs for home use, as well as for sale to augment the family income. Eventually, rugs began to be manufactured in workshops by professional artisans, who reproduced the designs from detailed painted diagrams.

Most decorations on the rugs, as well as on all forms of Islamic art, consisted of Arabic script and natural plant and figurative motifs. Repeated continuously in naturalistic or semiabstract geometrical patterns called arabesques, these decorations completely covered the surface and left no area undecorated. This dense decor was also evident in brick, mosaic, and stucco ornamentation and culminated in the magnificent tile work of later centuries.

No representation of the Prophet Muhammad ever adorned a mosque, in painting or in any other art form. Although no passage of the Qur'an forbids representational painting, the *Hadith* warned against any attempt to imitate God through artistic creation or idolatry. From the time of the Dome of the Rock, no figurative representations appear in Islamic religious art.

Human beings and animals could still be represented in secular art, but relatively little survives from the early centuries aside from a very few wall paintings from the royal palaces. Although the Persians used calligraphy and art to decorate their books, the Arabs had no pictorial tradition of their own and only began to develop the art of book illustration in the late twelfth century to illustrate translations of Greek scientific works.

In the thirteenth century, a Mongol dynasty established at Tabriz, west of the Caspian Sea, offered the Middle East its first direct contact with the art of East Asia. Mongol painting, done in the Chinese manner with a full brush and expressing animated movement and intensity (see Chapter 10), freed Islamic painters from traditional confines and enabled them to experiment with new techniques.

Islam and Byzantium

The collapse of Roman power in the Mediterranean led to the emergence of three new civilizations. In the west, Roman elements combined with German influences and Christianity to form a new Christian European civilization (see Chapter 12). Then, beginning in the seventh century, the rise of an Islamic empire resulted in the loss of the southern and eastern Mediterranean lands of the old Roman Empire to a religious power that was neither Roman nor Christian. While new civilizations were forming in the western European and Islamic worlds, the eastern part of the old Roman Empire, increasingly Greek in culture, continued to flourish as the Christian Byzantine Empire. Although the European civilization of the west and the Byzantine civilization of the east came to share a common bond in Christianity, it proved incapable of

Courtesy of William J. Duiker

The Alhambra in Granada. Islamic civilization reached its zenith with the fourteenth-century fairy-tale castle of Alhambra in southern Spain (below). Like the Hindus in India, the Muslims of the Middle East and Spain lived in a hot, dry climate, making water a highly prized commodity both literally and psychologically. The quiet, refreshing coolness of water became a vital component of Muslim architecture, displayed in gardens with fountains and reflecting pools such as this one at the Alhambra. Like the Hindus, Muslims wash prior to religious devotion and can be seen here performing ablutions in the courtyard of a sixteenth-century mosque in Istanbul (left).

Courtesy of William J. Duiker

The Qur'an as Sculptured Design. Muslim sculptors and artists, reflecting the official view that any visual representation of the Prophet Muhammad was blasphemous, turned to geometric patterns, as well as to flowers and animals, as a means of fulfilling their creative urge. The predominant motif, however, was the reproduction of Qur'anic verses in the Arabic script. Calligraphy, which was almost as important in the Middle East as it was in traditional China, used the Arabic script to decorate all of the Islamic arts, from painting to pottery, tile and ironwork, and wall decorations such as this carved plaster panel in a courtyard of the Alhambra palace in Spain. Since a recitation from the Qur'an was an important component of the daily devotional activities for all practicing Muslims, elaborate scriptural panels such as this one perfectly blended the spiritual and the artistic realms.

Courtesy of William J. Duiker

keeping them in harmony politically as the two civilizations continued to move apart. For the Byzantine Empire, the Islamic world also posed a formidable challenge that led to a conflict that lasted for centuries.

The Byzantine Empire

In the fourth century, a noticeable separation between the western and eastern parts of the Roman Empire began to develop. In the course of the fifth century, while the Germans moved into the western part of the empire and established various kingdoms, the Roman Empire in the east, centered on Constantinople, continued to exist and even prosper.

The Reign of Justinian (527–565)

At first, the Byzantine Empire appeared fully capable of maintaining the territories it had inherited from Rome against all rivals. Under the powerful emperor Justinian (r. 527–565), Byzantine armies sailed to North Africa and quickly destroyed the Vandals in two major battles. From North Africa, Byzantine forces invaded the Italian peninsula and briefly appeared to have realized Justinian's dream of restoring the imperial Mediterranean world. His empire included Italy, part of Spain, North Africa, Asia Minor, Palestine, and Syria. To commemorate his victories, Justinian launched a massive project to expand and beautify his capital city of Constantinople.

The Byzantine Empire in the Time of Justinian

Much of Constantinople's appearance for almost the next thousand years was due to Justinian's building projects in the sixth century. The city was dominated by an immense palace complex, a huge arena known as the Hippodrome, and hundreds of churches. Justinian added many new buildings. His public works projects included roads, bridges, walls, public baths, law courts, and colossal underground reservoirs to hold the city's water supply. Churches were his special passion, and in Constantinople alone he built or rebuilt thirty-four of them. His greatest achievement was the famous Hagia Sophia, the Church of the Holy Wisdom.

© Scala/Art Resource, NY

The Emperor Justinian and His Court. As the seat of Byzantine power in Italy, the town of Ravenna became adorned with examples of Byzantine art. The church of San Vitale at Ravenna contains some of the finest examples of sixth-century Byzantine mosaics, in which small pieces of colored glass were attached to the wall to form these figures and their surroundings. The emperor is depicted as both head of state (he wears a jeweled crown and a purple robe) and head of the church (he carries a gold bowl symbolizing the body of Jesus).

Completed in 537, Hagia Sophia was designed by a Greek architect who did not use the simple, flat-roofed basilica of Western architecture. The center of Hagia Sophia consisted of four huge piers crowned by an enormous dome, which seemed to be floating in space. This effect was emphasized by Procopius, the court historian, who, at Justinian's request, wrote a treatise on the emperor's building projects: "From the lightness of the building, it does not appear to rest upon a solid foundation, but to cover the place beneath as though it were suspended from heaven by the fabled golden chain."[9] In part, this impression was created by putting forty-two windows around the base of the dome, which allowed an incredible play of light within the cathedral. Light served to remind the worshipers of God. As darkness is illumined by invisible light, so too it was believed the world is illumined by invisible spirit.

From Eastern Roman to Byzantine Empire Justinian's successes, however, were destined to be short-lived. Shortly after his death, the empire faced threats from the Persians to the east and from Slavic peoples moving into the Balkan peninsula along the northern frontier. But the most serious challenge to the eastern empire was presented by the rise of Islam, which, as noted earlier in the chapter, created a powerful new force that swept through the Middle East. The defeat of the eastern Roman army at the Yarmuk River in 636 resulted in the loss of the provinces of Syria and Palestine. The Arabs also occupied Byzantine territories along the coast of North Africa, including the Nile River valley. The failed Arab attempt to besiege Constantinople—now protected by huge walls—in 717 left Arab and Byzantine forces facing each other along a frontier in southern Asia Minor.

By the middle of the eighth century, the eastern Roman Empire was greatly diminished in size, consisting only of the eastern Balkans, Asia Minor, and the southern coast of Italy. It was now an eastern Mediterranean state. These external challenges had important internal repercussions as well. By the eighth century, the eastern Roman Empire had been transformed into what historians call the Byzantine Empire (sometimes referred to as Byzantium), a civilization with its own unique character that would last until 1453. (Constantinople was built on the site of an older city named Byzantium—hence the term *Byzantine*.)

The Byzantine Empire was a Greek state. Latin fell into disuse as Greek became not only the common language of the Byzantine Empire but its official language as well.

The Byzantine Empire was also a Christian state, built on a faith in Jesus that was shared in a profound way by almost all its citizens. An enormous amount of artistic talent was poured into church construction, church ceremonies, and church decoration. Spiritual principles deeply permeated Byzantine art.

The emperor occupied a crucial position in the Byzantine state. Portrayed as chosen by God, the Byzantine emperor was crowned in sacred ceremonies, and his subjects were expected to prostrate themselves in his presence. His power was considered absolute and was limited in practice only by deposition or assassination. Because the emperor appointed the **patriarch** of Constantinople, the highest Christian church official in the east and second in dignity only to the bishop of Rome (the pope), the emperor also exercised control over both church and state. The Byzantines believed that God had commanded their state to preserve the true faith—Orthodox Christianity or Greek (or Eastern) Orthodoxy (as the Christian religion in the Byzantine Empire was called). Emperor, clergy, and civic officials were all bound together in service to this ideal. It can be said that spiritual values truly held the Byzantine state together.

The Zenith of Byzantine Civilization Despite the problems of the seventh and eighth centuries and new invasions in the ninth century, the Byzantine Empire not only endured but even expanded, reaching its high point in the tenth century. Most important to this renewal was a new dynasty of Byzantine emperors known as the Macedonians (867–1056).

The Macedonian emperors could boast of a remarkable number of achievements in the late ninth and tenth centuries. They fostered a burst of economic prosperity by expanding trade relations with western Europe, especially by selling silks and metalwork. Thanks to this prosperity, the city of Constantinople flourished.

Until the twelfth century, Constantinople was Europe's greatest commercial center. The city was the chief entrepôt for the exchange of products between West and East. Highly desired in Europe were the products of the East: silk from China, spices from Southeast Asia and India, jewelry and ivory from India (the latter used by artisans for church items), wheat and furs from southern Russia, and flax and honey from the Balkans. Many of these eastern goods were then shipped to the Mediterranean area and northern Europe. With a population estimated in the hundreds of thousands, Constantinople was the largest city in Europe during the Middle Ages. It viewed itself as the center of an empire and a special Christian city.

The Byzantine Empire, c. 750

The Byzantine Empire, 1025

Under the Macedonians, Byzantine cultural influence expanded due to the active missionary efforts of Byzantine Christians. Eastern Orthodox Christianity was spread to eastern European peoples, such as the Bulgars and Serbs. Perhaps the greatest missionary success occurred when the prince of Kiev in Russia converted to Christianity in 987.

Under the Macedonian rulers, Byzantium enjoyed a strong civil service, talented emperors, and military advances. In the tenth century, competent emperors combined with a number of talented generals to mobilize the empire's military resources and take the offensive. The Bulgars were defeated, and both the eastern and western parts of Bulgaria were annexed to the empire. The Byzantines went on to add the islands of Crete and Cyprus to the empire and defeat the Muslim forces in Syria, expanding the empire to the upper Euphrates. By 1025, the Byzantine Empire was the largest it had been since the beginning of the seventh century.

New Challenges to the Byzantine Empire The Macedonian dynasty of the tenth and eleventh centuries had restored much of the power of the Byzantine Empire; its incompetent successors, however, reversed most of the gains. After the Macedonian dynasty was extinguished in 1056, the empire was beset by internal struggles for power between ambitious military leaders and aristocratic families.

The growing division between the Catholic church of the West and the Eastern Orthodox church of the Byzantine Empire also weakened the Byzantine state. The Eastern Orthodox church was unwilling to accept the pope's claim that he was the sole head of the church. This dispute reached a climax in 1054 when Pope Leo IX and Patriarch Michael Cerularius, head of the Byzantine church, formally excommunicated each other, initiating a schism between the two great branches of Christianity that has not been completely healed to this day.

The Byzantine Empire faced external threats to its security as well with the rise of the Seljuk Turks. After Byzantine forces were disastrously defeated at Manzikert by a Turkish army in 1071, the Turks advanced into Anatolia, thus reducing the Byzantine Empire to a fraction of its former territories in Asia. To recoup these losses, Emperor Alexius I Comnenus (1081–1118) turned to the West for military assistance. When the emperor's request led to an agreement to launch the Crusades, the threat from Islam appeared to have eased the old rivalries between East and West (see Chapter 12) and reunited Christendom in a common struggle against unbelievers. But the Byzantine Empire would live to regret its request.

Impact of the Crusades

Ultimately, the Crusades had an enormous impact on the Byzantine Empire. In the First Crusade, the mostly French bands of crusading knights ignored their oath of allegiance and promises to Emperor Alexius and organized their own crusader states in Palestine. Then, in 1204, the Fourth Crusade resulted in disaster, as crusading soldiers en route to the Middle East sacked the capital city and briefly set up a Latin Empire of Constantinople. The city was recaptured by Byzantine forces fifty years later, but the empire had been irreparably weakened. Drastically reduced in size to the city proper and the immediately surrounding territories, Constantinople finally succumbed to an attack by the Ottoman Turks in 1453 (see Chapter 15).

CONCLUSION

AFTER THE COLLAPSE of Roman power in the west, the eastern Roman Empire, centered on Constantinople, continued in the eastern Mediterranean and eventually emerged as the unique Christian civilization known as the Byzantine Empire, which flourished for hundreds of years. One of the greatest challenges to the Byzantine Empire, however, came from a new force—Islam—that blossomed in the Arabian peninsula and spread rapidly throughout the Middle East. In the eyes of some Europeans during the Middle Ages, the Arab Empire was a malevolent force that posed a serious threat to the security of Christianity. Their fears were not entirely misplaced, for within half a century after the death of Islam's founder, Muhammad, Arab armies overran Christian states in North Africa and the Iberian peninsula, and Turkish Muslims moved eastward onto the fringes of the Indian subcontinent.

TIMELINE

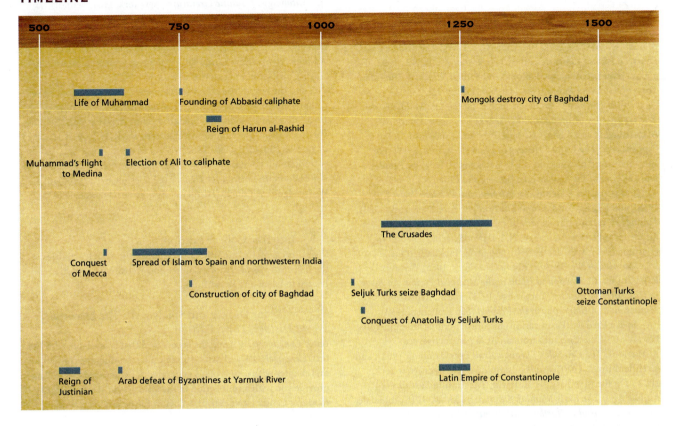

500	750	1000	1250	1500

Life of Muhammad

Founding of Abbasid caliphate

Mongols destroy city of Baghdad

Reign of Harun al-Rashid

Muhammad's flight to Medina

Election of Ali to caliphate

The Crusades

Conquest of Mecca

Spread of Islam to Spain and northwestern India

Construction of city of Baghdad

Seljuk Turks seize Baghdad

Ottoman Turks seize Constantinople

Conquest of Anatolia by Seljuk Turks

Reign of Justinian

Arab defeat of Byzantines at Yarmuk River

Latin Empire of Constantinople

But although the teachings of Muhammad brought war and conquest to much of the known world, they also brought hope and a sense of political and economic stability to peoples throughout the region. Thus, for many people in the medieval Mediterranean world, the arrival of Islam was a welcome event. Islam brought a code of law and a written language to societies that had previously not possessed them. Finally, by creating a revitalized trade network stretching from West Africa to East Asia, it established a vehicle for the exchange of technology and ideas that brought untold wealth to thousands and a better life to millions.

Like other empires in the region, the Arab Empire did not last. It fell victim to a combination of internal and external pressures, and by the end of the thirteenth century, it was no more than a memory. But it left a powerful legacy in Islam, which remains one of the great religions of the world. In succeeding centuries, Islam began to penetrate into new areas beyond the edge of the Sahara and across the Indian Ocean into the islands of the Indonesian archipelago.

CHAPTER NOTES

1. M. M. Pickthall, trans., *The Meaning of the Glorious Koran* (New York, 1953), p. 89.
2. Quoted in T. W. Lippman, *Understanding Islam: An Introduction to the Moslem World* (New York, 1982), p. 118.
3. F. Hirth and W. W. Rockhill, trans., *Chau Ju-kua: His Work on the Chinese and Arab Trade in the Twelfth and Thirteenth Centuries, Entitled Chu-fan-chi* (New York, 1966), p. 115.
4. al-Mas'udi, *The Meadows of Gold: The Abbasids,* ed. P. Lunde and C. Stone (London, 1989), p. 151.
5. L. Africanus, *The History and Description of Africa and of the Notable Things Therein Contained* (New York, n.d.), pp. 820–821.
6. E. Yarshater, ed., *Persian Literature* (Albany, N.Y., 1988), pp. 125–126.
7. Ibid., pp. 154–159.
8. E. Rehatsek, trans., *The Gulistan or Rose Garden of Sa'di* (New York, 1964), pp. 65, 67, 71.
9. Procopius, *Buildings of Justinian* (London, 1897), p. 9.

SUGGESTED READING

Standard works on the Arab Empire and the rise of Islam include **T. W. Lippman,** *Understanding Islam: An Introduction to the Moslem World* (New York, 1982), and **G. E. Perry,** *The Middle East: Fourteen Islamic Centuries,* 2d ed. (Englewood Cliffs, N.J., 1992). For a more recent account, see **J. Bloom** and **S. Blair,** *Islam: A Thousand Years of Faith and Power* (New Haven, Conn., 2002).

Other worthwhile studies include **B. Lewis,** *The Middle East: A Brief History of the Last 2,000 Years* (New York, 1986); **K. Armstrong,** *Islam: A Short History* (New York, 2000); and **J. L. Esposito,** ed., *The Oxford History of Islam* (New York, 1999). For anthropological background, see **D. Bates** and **A. Rassam,** *Peoples and Cultures of the Middle East* (Englewood Cliffs, N.J., 1983).

On Islam, see **F. Denny,** *An Introduction to Islam* (New York, 1985), and **J. L. Esposito,** *Islam: The Straight Path* (New York, 1988). Among the various translations of the Qur'an, two of the best for the introductory student are **N. J. Dawood,** trans., *The Koran* (Harmondsworth, England, 1990), and **M. M. Pickthall,** trans., *The Meaning of the Glorious Koran* (New York, 1953). See also **R. W. Bulliet,** *Conversion to Islam in the Medieval Period: An Essay in Quantitative History* (Cambridge, 1979), and **K. Armstrong,** *Muhammad: A Biography of the Prophet* (San Francisco, 1993).

Specialized works on various historical periods are numerous. For a view of the Crusades from an Arab perspective, see **A. Maalouf,** *The Crusades Through Arab Eyes* (London, 1984), and **C. Hillenbrand,** *The Crusades: Islamic Perspectives* (New York, 2001). On the Mamluks, see **R. Irwin,** *The Middle East in the Middle Ages: The Early Mamluk Sultanate, 1250–1382* (Carbondale, Ill., 1986). In *God of Battles: Christianity and Islam* (Princeton, N.J., 1998), **P. Partner** compares the expansionist tendencies of the two great religions. Also see **R. Fletcher,** *The Cross and the Crescent: Christianity and Islam from Muhammad to the Reform* (New York, 2005).

On the economy, see **E. Ashtor,** *A Social and Economic History of the Near East in the Middle Ages* (Berkeley, Calif., 1976); **K. N. Chaudhuri,** *Asia Before Europe: Economy and Civilization of the Indian Ocean from the Rise of Islam to 1750* (Cambridge, 1990); **C. Issawi,** *The Middle East Economy: Decline and Recovery* (Princeton, N.J., 1995); and **P. Crone,** *Meccan Trade and the Rise of Islam* (Princeton, N.J., 1987).

On women, see **F. Hussain,** ed., *Muslim Women* (New York, 1984); **G. Nashat** and **J. E. Tucker,** *Women in the Middle East and North Africa* (Bloomington, Ind., 1998); **S. S. Hughes** and **B. Hughes,** *Women in World History,* vol. 1 (London, 1995); and **L. Ahmed,** *Women and Gender in Islam* (New Haven, Conn., 1992).

For the best introduction to Islamic literature, consult **J. Kritzeck,** ed., *Anthology of Islamic Literature* (New York, 1964), with its concise commentaries and introduction. An excellent introduction to Persian literature can be found in **E. Yarshater,** *Persian Literature* (Albany, N.Y., 1988). For the student, **H. Haddawy,** trans., *The Arabian Nights* (New York, 1990), is the best version. It presents 271 "nights" in a clear and colorful style.

For the best introduction to Islamic art, consult the concise yet comprehensive work by **D. T. Rice,** *Islamic Art,* rev. ed. (London, 1975). Also see **J. Bloom** and **S. Blair,** *Islamic Arts* (London, 1997). For an excellent overview of world textiles, see **K. Wilson,** *A History of Textiles* (Boulder, Colo., 1982).

Brief but good introductions to Byzantine history can be found in **J. Haldon,** *Byzantium: A History* (Charleston, S.C., 2000) and **W. Treadgold,** *A Concise History of Byzantium* (London, 2001).

InfoTrac College Edition
Visit this chapter's InfoTrac College Edition/Research activities at the *Essential World History* Companion Website for activities related to Islam and Byzantium.

CENGAGENOW **for Duiker and Spielvogel's** *The Essential World History, Third Edition*
Enter *CengageNOW* using the access card that is available with this text. *CengageNOW* will assist you in understanding the content in this chapter with lesson plans generated for your needs, as well as provide you with a connection to the *Wadsworth World History Resource Center* (see description below for details).

WORLD HISTORY RESOURCE CENTER

Enter the Resource Center using either your *CengageNOW* access card or your standalone access card for the *Wadsworth World History Resource Center.* Organized by topic, this website includes quizzes; images; over 350 primary source documents; interactive simulations, maps, and timelines; movie explorations; and a wealth of other resources. You can read the following documents, and many more, at http://worldrc.wadsworth.com/

Muhammad's Last Sermon

Visit the *Essential World History* Companion Website for chapter quizzes and more.
academic.cengage.com/history/duiker

EARLY CIVILIZATIONS IN AFRICA

CHAPTER OUTLINE AND FOCUS QUESTIONS

The Emergence of Civilization

◻ How did the advent of farming and pastoralism affect the various peoples of Africa? How did the consequences of the agricultural revolution in Africa differ from those in other societies in Eurasia and America?

The Coming of Islam

◻ What effects did the coming of Islam have on African religion, society, political structures, trade, and culture?

States and Stateless Societies in Central and Southern Africa

◻ What types of states and societies emerged in central and southern Africa, and what role did migrations play in the evolution of African societies in this area?

African Society

◻ What role did lineage groups, women, and slavery play in African societies? Were there clear and distinct differences between African societies in various parts of the continent? If so, why?

African Culture

◻ What are some of the chief characteristics of African sculpture and carvings, music, and architecture, and what purpose did these forms of creative expression serve in African society?

CRITICAL THINKING

◻ With the exception of the Nile River valley, organized states did not emerge in the continent of Africa until much later than was the case in many regions of the Eurasian supercontinent. Why do you think this was the case?

*I*N 1871, THE GERMAN EXPLORER Karl Mauch began to search southern Africa's central plateau for the colossal stone ruins of a legendary lost civilization. In late August, he found what he had been looking for. According to his diary: "Presently I stood before it and beheld a wall of a height of about 20 feet of granite bricks. Very close by there was a place where a kind of footpath led over rubble into the interior. Following this path I stumbled over masses of rubble and parts of walls and dense thickets. I stopped in front of a towerlike structure. Altogether it rose to a height of about 30 feet." Mauch was convinced that "a civilized nation must once have lived here." Like many other nineteenth-century Europeans, however, Mauch was equally convinced that the Africans who had lived there could never have built such splendid structures as the ones he had found at Great Zimbabwe. To Mauch and other archaeologists, Great Zimbabwe must have been the work of "a northern race closely akin to the Phoenician and Egyptian." It was not until the twentieth century that Europeans could overcome their prejudices and finally admit that Africans south of Egypt had also developed advanced civilizations with spectacular achievements.

169

The continent of Africa has played a central role in the long evolution of humankind. It was in Africa that the first hominids appeared more than three million years ago. It was probably in Africa that the immediate ancestors of modern human beings—*Homo sapiens*—emerged for the first time. The domestication of animals may have occurred first in Africa. Certainly, one of the first states appeared in Africa, in the Nile valley in the northeastern corner of the continent, in the form of the kingdom of the pharaohs. Recent evidence suggests that Egyptian civilization was significantly influenced by cultural developments taking place to the south, in Nubia, in modern Sudan.

After the decline of the Egyptian empire during the first millennium B.C.E., the focus of social change began to shift from the lower Nile valley to other areas of the continent: to West Africa, where a series of major trading states began to take part in the caravan trade with the Mediterranean through the vast wastes of the Sahara; to the region of the upper Nile River, where the states of Kush and Axum dominated trade for several centuries; and to the eastern coast from the Horn of Africa to the straits between the continent and the island of Madagascar, where African peoples began to play an active role in the commercial traffic of the Indian Ocean. In the meantime, a gradual movement of agricultural peoples brought Iron Age farming to the central portion of the continent, leading eventually to the creation of several states in the Congo River basin and the plateau region south of the Zambezi River.

The peoples of Africa, then, have played a significant role in the changing human experience since ancient times. Yet, in many respects, that role was a distinctive one, a fact that continues to affect the fate of the continent in our own day. The landmass of Africa is so vast, and its topography is so diverse, that communications within the continent, and between Africans and peoples living elsewhere in the world, have often been more difficult than in many neighboring regions. As a consequence, African societies are so diverse that generalizations about the nature of the peoples living on the continent are difficult to sustain. ◇

The Emergence of Civilization

After Asia, Africa is the largest of the continents (see Map 8.1). It stretches nearly 5,000 miles from the Cape of Good Hope in the south to the Mediterranean in the north and extends a similar distance from Cape Verde on the west coast to the Horn of Africa on the Indian Ocean.

The Land

Africa is as diverse as it is vast. The northern coast, washed by the Mediterranean Sea, is mountainous for much of its length. South of the mountains lies the greatest desert on earth, the Sahara, which stretches from the Atlantic to the Indian Ocean. To the east is the Nile River,

heart of the ancient Egyptian civilization. Beyond that lies the Red Sea, separating Africa from Asia.

The Sahara acts as a great divide separating the northern coast from the rest of the continent. Africa south of the Sahara is divided into a number of major regions. In the west is the so-called hump of Africa, which juts like a massive shoulder into the Atlantic Ocean. Here the Sahara gradually gives way to grasslands in the interior and then to tropical rain forests along the coast. This region, dominated by the Niger River, is rich in natural resources and was the home of many ancient civilizations.

Far to the east, bordering the Indian Ocean, is a very different terrain of snowcapped mountains, upland plateaus, and lakes. Much of this region is grassland populated by wild beasts, which have given it the modern designation of Safari Country. Here, in the East African Rift valley in the lake district of modern Kenya, early hominids began their long trek toward civilization several million years ago.

Farther to the south lies the Congo basin, with its rain forests watered by the mighty Congo River. The rain forests of equatorial Africa then fade gradually into the hills, plateaus, and deserts of the south. This rich land contains some of the most valuable mineral resources known today.

It is not certain when and where agriculture was first practiced on the continent of Africa. Until recently, historians assumed that crops were first cultivated in the lower Nile valley (the northern part near the Mediterranean) about seven or eight thousand years ago, when wheat and barley were introduced, possibly from the Middle East. Eventually, as explained in Chapter 1, this area gave rise to the civilization of ancient Egypt.

Kush

Recent evidence suggests that this hypothesis may need some revision. South of Egypt, near the junction of the White and the Blue Nile, is the area known historically as Nubia (see Chapter 1). Some archaeologists suggest that agriculture may have appeared first in Nubia rather than in the lower Nile valley. Stone Age farmers from Nubia may have begun to cultivate local crops such as sorghum and millet along the banks of the upper Nile (the southern part near the river's source) as early as the eleventh millennium B.C.E.

Some scholars suggest that the Nubian concept of kingship may have spread to the north, past the cataracts along the Nile, where it eventually gave birth to the better-known civilization of Egypt. Whatever the truth of such conjectures, contacts between the upper and lower Nile clearly had been established by the third millennium B.C.E., when Egyptian merchants traveled to Nubia, which ultimately became an Egyptian tributary. With the disintegration of the Egyptian New Kingdom, Nubia became the independent state of Kush, which developed into a major trading state with its capital at Meroë (see the box on p. 172). Little is known about Kushite society, but it seems

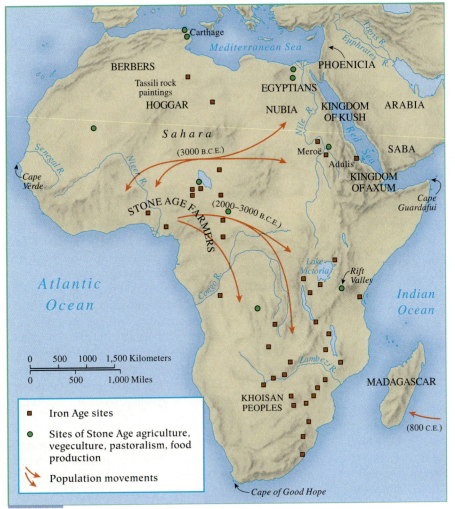

MAP 8.1 Ancient Africa. Modern human beings, known as *Homo sapiens*, first evolved on the continent of Africa. Some key sites of early human settlement are shown on this map. ❓ What factors might have caused the migrations of peoples that are shown on this map? 🌐 **View an animated version of this map or related maps at** http://worldrc.wadsworth.com/

likely that it was predominantly urban. Initially, foreign trade was probably a monopoly of the state, but the extensive luxury goods in the numerous private tombs in the vicinity indicate that at one time, material prosperity was relatively widespread. This suggests that commercial activities were being conducted by a substantial merchant class.

Axum, Son of Saba

In the first millennium C.E., Kush declined and was eventually conquered by Axum, a new power located in the highlands of modern Ethiopia (see Map 8.2). Axum had been founded during the first millennium B.C.E., possibly by migrants from the kingdom of Saba (popularly known as Sheba) across the Red Sea on the southern tip of the Arabian peninsula. During antiquity, Saba was a major trading state, serving as a transit point for goods carried from South Asia into the lands surrounding the Mediterranean. Biblical sources credited the "queen of Sheba" with vast wealth and resources. In fact, much of that

wealth had originated much farther to the east and passed through Saba en route to the countries adjacent to the Mediterranean.

When Saba declined, perhaps because of the desiccation of the Arabian Desert, Axum broke away and survived for centuries as an independent state. Like Saba, Axum owed much of its prosperity to its location on the commercial trade route between India and the Mediterranean, and Greek ships from the Ptolemaic kingdom in Egypt stopped regularly at the port of Adulis on the Red Sea. Axum exported ivory, frankincense, myrrh, and slaves, while its primary imports were textiles, metal goods, wine, and olive oil. For a time, Axum competed for control of the ivory trade with the neighboring state of Kush, and hunters from Axum armed with imported iron weapons scoured the entire region for elephants. Probably as a result of this competition, in the fourth century C.E., the Axumite ruler, claiming he had been provoked, launched an invasion of Kush and conquered it.

Perhaps the most distinctive feature of Axumite civilization was its religion. Originally, the rulers of Axum (who claimed descent from King Solomon through the visit of the queen of Sheba to Israel in biblical times) followed the religion of their predecessors in Saba. But in the fourth century C.E., Axumite rulers adopted Christianity, possibly from Egypt. This commitment to the Egyptian form of Christianity (often called **Coptic,** from the local language of the day) was retained even after the collapse of Axum and the expansion of Islam through the area in later centuries. Later, Axum (now renamed Ethiopia) would be identified by some Europeans as the "hermit kingdom" and the home of Prester John, a legendary Christian king of East Africa (see Chapter 13).

The Sahara and Its Environs

Kush and Axum were part of the ancient trading network that extended from the Mediterranean into the Indian Ocean and were affected in various ways by the cross-cultural contacts that took place throughout that region. Elsewhere in Africa, somewhat different patterns prevailed; they varied from area to area depending on the geography and climate.

THE SLAVE TRADE IN ANCIENT AFRICA

FAMILY & SOCIETY

The practice of slavery was commonplace throughout the African continent from ancient times, but information on the nature of the slave trade is difficult to find. The document below consists of a contract for the purchase of a Nubian slave girl in sixth-century C.E. Egypt. Behind the legal terminology contained in the contract, probably a consequence of the adoption of Roman law in pre-Muslim Egypt, lies the poignant reality of a young Nubian girl, and perhaps her own future children as well, sold into a lifetime of slavery. Tragically, the traffic in slaves continues in the region today as Muslim traders launch periodic raids on Christian villages in the southern Sudan.

Based on what you have learned in this and previous chapters, to what sorts of duties would a young slave like Isidora be assigned? Did she have the option at some future date to obtain her freedom?

Sale of a Nubian Slave Girl

Greeting. We acknowledge that we the aforementioned Pathermuthis and Anatolios, through this our written contract of sale, of our own free will and with voluntary intent and irrevocable and sincere resolution, with steadfast conscience, with correct intention, without any fraud or intimidation or violence or deceit or constraint or any bad faith or deception, that we have sold to you, the aforementioned most well-born Isidora, . . . the girl who belongs to us and who has come to us . . . from the other slave-traders of the Aithiopians, the black slave, Atalous by name, now renamed by you Eutukhia, about twelve years old more or less, an Aloan by race, which afore-mentioned black slave not being previously mortgaged for any principal sum whatsoever or for any business or agreement or afflicted by any old injury or leprosy or beating or concealed ailment, . . . for the mutually agreed, approved, resolved between us, full and just price [of] . . . four gold solidi, of full weight, on the Alexandrian standard, which afore-mentioned price at once we, the vendors, Pathermuthis and Anatolios, have been paid by you . . . for you to possess and to control and to own with every right of ownership, to acquire, to possess, to use her and, with God willing, her children, to manage and to administer concerning her, to sell, to put up as security, to give away, to exchange as dowry and to give . . . and to give to your children and descendants, to leave behind and to transmit to your testamentary heirs, successors, and legal heirs, and in general to do and perform with her all such acts as the laws enjoin upon absolute owners to do with their own property, unhindered and unimpeded, from now for ever, this perpetual warranty and clearance of title and defense of the present sale in regard to every warranty falling on us, the vendors.

CENGAGENOW To read more about the role of women in ancient Nubia, enter the *CengageNOW* documents area using the access card that is available for *The Essential World History*.

At one time, when the world's climate was much colder than it is today, Central Africa may have been one of the few areas that was habitable for the first hominids. Later, from 8000 to 4000 B.C.E., a warm, humid climate prevailed in the Sahara, creating lakes and ponds, as well as vast grasslands (known as savannas) replete with game. Rock paintings found in what are today some of the most uninhabitable parts of the region are a clear indication that the environment was much different several thousand years ago.

By 7000 B.C.E., the peoples of the Sahara were herding animals—first sheep and goats and later cattle. During the sixth and fifth millennia B.C.E., the climate became more arid, however, and the desertification of the Sahara began. From the rock paintings, which for the most part date from the fourth and third millennia B.C.E., we know that by that time, the herds were being supplemented by fishing and limited cultivation of crops such as millet, sorghum, and a drought-resistant form of dry rice. After 3000 B.C.E., as the desiccation of the Sahara proceeded and the lakes dried up, the local inhabitants began to migrate eastward toward the Nile River and southward into the grasslands. As a result, farming began to spread into the savannas on the southern fringes of the desert and eventually into the tropical forest areas to the south, where crops were no longer limited to drought-resistant cereals but could include tropical fruits and tubers.

Historians do not know when goods first began to be exchanged across the Sahara in a north-south direction, but during the first millennium B.C.E., the commercial center of Carthage on the Mediterranean had become a focal point of the trans-Saharan trade. The **Berbers,** a pastoral people of North Africa, served as intermediaries, carrying food products and manufactured goods from Carthage across the desert and exchanging them for salt, gold and copper, skins, various agricultural products, and perhaps slaves (see the box on p. 174).

This trade initiated a process of cultural exchange that would exert a significant impact on the peoples of tropical Africa. Among other things, it may have spread the knowledge of ironworking south of the desert. Although historians once believed that ironworking knowledge reached sub-Saharan Africa from Meroë in the upper Nile valley in the first centuries C.E., recent finds suggest that the peoples along the Niger River were smelting iron five or six hundred years earlier. Some scholars believe that the technique developed independently there, but others believe that it was introduced by the Berbers, who had learned it from the Carthaginians.

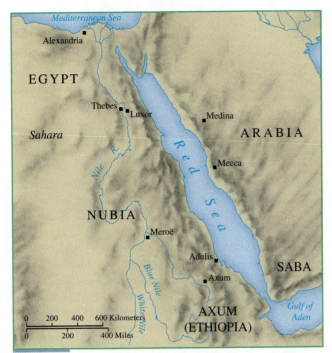

MAP 8.2 **Ancient Ethiopia and Nubia.** The first civilizations to appear on the African continent emerged in the Nile River valley. Early in the first century C.E., the state of Axum emerged in what is modern-day Ethiopia. ❓ Where are the major urban settlements in the region, as shown on this map? Why were they located where they were?

Whatever the case, the **Nok culture** in northern Nigeria eventually became one of the most active iron-working societies in Africa. Excavations have unearthed numerous terra-cotta and metal figures, as well as stone and iron farm implements, dating back as far as 500 B.C.E. The remains of smelting furnaces confirm that the iron was produced locally.

Early in the first millennium C.E., the introduction of the camel provided a major stimulus to the trans-Saharan trade. With its ability to store considerable amounts of food and water, the camel was far better equipped to handle the arduous conditions of the desert than the ox, which had been used previously. The camel caravans of the Berbers became known as the "fleets of the desert."

The Garamantes Recent exploratory work in the Libyan Desert has revealed the existence of an ancient kingdom that for over a thousand years transported goods between societies along the Mediterranean Sea and sub-Saharan Africa. The Garamantes, as they were known to the Romans, carried salt, glass, metal, olive oil, and wine to Central Africa in return for gold, slaves, and various tropical products. To provide food for their communities in the heart of the desert, they constructed a complex irrigation system consisting of several thousand miles of underground channels. The technique is reminiscent of similar systems in Persia and Central Asia (see Chapter 9).

Scholars believe that the kingdom declined as a result of the fall of the Roman Empire and the drying up of the desert.

East Africa

South of Axum, along the shores of the Indian Ocean and in the inland plateau that stretches from the mountains of Ethiopia through the lake district of Central Africa, lived a mixture of peoples, some living by hunting and food gathering and others following pastoral pursuits.

Beginning in the second millennium B.C.E., new peoples began to migrate into East Africa from the west. Farming peoples speaking dialects of the Bantu family of languages began to move from the region of the Niger River into East Africa and the Congo River basin (see the comparative essay "The Migration of Peoples" on p. 175). They were probably responsible for introducing the widespread cultivation of crops and knowledge of ironworking to much of East Africa, although there are signs of some limited iron smelting in the area before their arrival.

The Bantu settled in rural communities based on subsistence farming. The primary crops were millet and sorghum, along with yams, melons, and beans. The land was often tilled with both iron and stone tools, and the former were usually manufactured in a local smelter. Some people kept domestic animals such as cattle, sheep, goats, or chickens or supplemented their diets by hunting and food gathering. Because the population was minimal and an ample supply of cultivable land was available, most settlements were relatively small; each village formed a self-sufficient political and economic entity.

As early as the era of the New Kingdom in the second millennium B.C.E., Egyptian ships had plied the waters off the East African coast in search of gold, ivory, palm oil, and perhaps slaves. By the first century C.E., the region was an established part of a trading network that included the Mediterranean and the Red Sea. In that century, a Greek seafarer from Alexandria wrote an account of his travels down the coast from Cape Guardafui at the tip of the Horn of Africa to the Strait of Madagascar thousands of miles to the south. Called the *Periplus,* this work provides generally accurate descriptions of the peoples and settlements along the African coast and the trade goods they supplied.

According to the *Periplus,* the port of Rhapta (possibly modern Dar es Salaam) was a commercial metropolis, exporting ivory, rhinoceros horn, and tortoiseshell and importing glass, wine, grain, and metal goods such as weapons and tools. The identity of the peoples taking part in this trade is not clear, but it seems likely that the area was already inhabited by a mixture of local peoples and immigrants from the Arabian peninsula. Out of this mixture would eventually emerge an African-Arabian **Swahili** culture (see "East Africa: The Land of Zanj" later in this chapter) that continues to exist in coastal areas today. Beyond Rhapta was "unexplored ocean." Some

FAULT LINE IN THE DESERT

INTERACTION & EXCHANGE

Little is known regarding Antonius Malfante, the Italian adventurer who in 1447 wrote this letter relating his travels along the trade route used by the Hausa city-states of northern Nigeria. In this passage, he astutely described the various peoples who inhabited the Sahara: Arabs, Jews, Tuaregs, and African blacks, who lived in uneasy proximity to one another as they struggled to coexist in the stark conditions of the desert. The mutual hostility between settled and pastoral peoples in the area continues today.

What occupations does Malfante mention? To what degree do they refer to specific peoples living in the area?

Antonius Malfante, Letter to Genoa

Though I am a Christian, no one ever addressed an insulting word to me. They said they had never seen a Christian before. It is true that on my first arrival they were scornful of me, because they all wished to see me, saying with wonder "This Christian has a countenance like ours"—for they believed that Christians had disguised faces. Their curosity was soon satisfied, and now I can go alone anywhere, with no one to say an evil word to me.

There are many Jews, who lead a good life here, for they are under the protection of the several rulers, each of whom defends his own clients. Thus they enjoy very secure social standing. Trade is in their hands, and many of them are to be trusted with the greatest confidence.

This locality is a mart of the country of the Moors [Berbers] to which merchants come to sell their goods: gold is carried hither, and bought by those who come up from the coast. . . .

It never rains here: if it did, the houses, being built of salt in the place of reeds, would be destroyed. It is scarcely ever cold here: in summer the heat is extreme, wherefore they are almost all blacks. The children of both sexes go naked up to the age of fifteen. These people observe the religion and law of Muhammad.

In the lands of the blacks, as well as here, dwell the Philistines [the Tuareg], who live, like the Arabs, in tents. They are without number, and hold sway over the land of Gazola from the borders of Egypt to the shores of the Ocean, as far as Massa and Safi, and over all the neighboring towns of the blacks. They are fair, strong in body and very handsome in appearance. They ride without stirrups, with simple spurs. They are governed by kings, whose heirs are the sons of their sisters—for such is their law. They keep their mouths and noses covered. I have seen many of them here, and have asked them through an interpreter why they cover their mouths and noses thus. They replied: "We have inherited this custom from our ancestors." They are sworn enemies of the Jews, who do not dare to pass hither. Their faith is that of the Blacks. Their sustenance is milk and flesh, no corn or barley, but much rice. Their sheep, cattle, and camels are without number. One breed of camel, white as snow, can cover in one day a distance which would take a horseman four days to travel. Great warriors, these people are continually at war amongst themselves.

The states which are under their rule border upon the land of the blacks . . . which have inhabitants of the faith of Muhammad. In all, the great majority are blacks, but there are a small number of whites [i.e., tawny Moors]. . . .

To the south of these are innumerable great cities and territories, the inhabitants of which are all blacks and idolators, continually at war with each other in defense of their law and faith of their idols. Some worship the sun, others the moon, the seven planets, fire, or water; others a mirror which reflects their faces, which they take to be the images of gods; others groves of trees, the seats of a spirit to whom they make sacrifice; others again, statues of wood and stone, with which, they say, they commune by incantations.

---

contemporary observers believed that the Indian and Atlantic oceans were connected. Others were convinced that the Indian Ocean was an enclosed sea and that the continent of Africa could not be circumnavigated.

Trade across the Indian Ocean and down the coast of East Africa, facilitated by the monsoon winds, would gradually become one of the most lucrative sources of commercial profit in the ancient and medieval worlds. Although the origins of the trade remain shrouded in mystery, traders eventually came by sea from as far away as the mainland of Southeast Asia. Early in the first millennium C.E., Malay peoples bringing cinnamon to the Middle East began to cross the Indian Ocean directly and landed on the southeastern coast of Africa. Eventually, a Malay settlement was established on the island of Madagascar, where the population is still of mixed Malay-African origin. Historians suspect that Malay immigrants were responsible for introducing such Southeast Asian foods as the banana and the yam to Africa. With its high yield and ability to grow in uncultivated rain forest, the banana often became the preferred crop of the Bantu peoples.

The Coming of Islam

As we saw in Chapter 7, the rise of Islam during the first half of the seventh century C.E. had ramifications far beyond the Arabian peninsula. Arab armies swept across North Africa, incorporating it into the Arab Empire and isolating the Christian state of Axum to the south. Although East Africa and West Africa south of the Sahara

COMPARATIVE ESSAY

THE MIGRATION OF PEOPLES

INTERACTION & EXCHANGE

About 50,000 years ago, a small band of *Homo sapiens sapiens* crossed the Sinai peninsula from Africa and began to spread out across the Eurasian supercontinent. Thus began a migration of peoples that continued with accelerating speed throughout the ancient era and beyond. By 40,000 B.C.E., their descendants had spread across Eurasia as far as China and eastern Siberia and had even settled the distant continent of Australia.

Who were these peoples, and what provoked their decision to change their habitat? Undoubtedly, the first migrants were foragers or hunters in search of wild game, but with the advent of agriculture and the domestication of animals about 12,000 years ago, other peoples began to migrate vast distances in search of fertile farming and pasturelands.

The ever-changing climate was undoubtedly a major factor driving the process. In the fourth millennium B.C.E., the drying up of rich pasturelands in the Sahara forced the local inhabitants to migrate eastward toward the Nile River valley and the grasslands of East Africa. At about the same time, Indo-European-speaking farming peoples left the region of the Black Sea and moved gradually into central Europe in search of new farmlands. They were eventually followed by nomadic groups from Central Asia who began to occupy lands along the frontiers of the Roman Empire, while other bands of nomads threatened the plains of northern China from the Gobi Desert. In the meantime, Bantu-speaking farmers migrated from the Niger River southward into the rain forests of Central Africa and beyond. Similar movements took place in Southeast Asia and the Americas.

This steady flow of migrating peoples often had a destabilizing effect on sedentary societies in their path. Nomadic incursions represented a constant menace to the security of China, Egypt, and the Roman Empire and ultimately brought them to an end. But this vast movement of peoples often had beneficial effects as well, spreading new technologies and means of livelihood. Although some migrants, like the Huns, came for plunder and left havoc in their wake, other groups, like the Celtic peoples and the Bantus, prospered in their new environment.

The most famous of all nomadic invasions represents a case in point. In the thirteenth century C.E., the Mongols left their homeland in the Gobi Desert, advancing westward into the Russian steppes and southward in China and Central Asia and leaving death and devastation in their wake. At the height of their empire, the Mongols controlled virtually all of Eurasia except its western and southern fringes, thus creating a zone of stability in which a global trade and informational network could thrive that stretched from China to the shores of the Mediterranean.

© Erich Lessing/Art Resource, NY

Rock Paintings of the Sahara. Even before the Egyptians built their pyramids at Giza, other peoples far to the west in the vast wastes of the Sahara were creating their own art forms. These rock paintings, some of which date back to the fourth millennium B.C.E. and are reminiscent of similar examples from Europe, Asia, and Australia, provide a valuable record of a society that supported itself by a combination of farming, hunting, and herding animals. After the introduction of the horse around 1200 B.C.E., subsequent rock paintings depicted chariots and horseback riding. Eventually, camels began to appear in the paintings, a consequence of the increasing desiccation of the Sahara.

were not conquered by the Arab forces, Islam eventually penetrated these areas as well.

African Religious Beliefs Before Islam

When Islam arrived, most African societies already had well-developed systems of religious beliefs. Like other aspects of African life, early African religious beliefs varied from place to place, but certain characteristics appear to have been shared by most African societies. One of these common features was **pantheism,** belief in a single creator god from whom all things came. Sometimes the creator god was accompanied by a whole pantheon of lesser deities. The Ashanti people of Ghana in West Africa believed in a supreme being called Nyame, whose sons were lesser gods. Each son served a different purpose: one was the rainmaker, another the compassionate, and a third was responsible for the sunshine. This heavenly hierarchy paralleled earthly arrangements: worship of Nyame was the exclusive preserve of the king through his priests; lesser officials and the common people worshiped Nyame's sons, who might intercede with their father on behalf of ordinary Africans.

Many African religions also shared a belief in a form of afterlife during which the soul floated in the atmosphere through eternity. Belief in an afterlife was closely connected to the importance of ancestors and the **lineage group,** or clan, in African society. Each lineage group could trace itself back to a founding ancestor or group of ancestors. These ancestral souls would not be extinguished as long as the lineage group continued to perform rituals in their name. The rituals could also benefit the lineage group on earth, for the ancestral souls, being closer to the gods, had the power to influence, for good or evil, the lives of their descendants.

Such beliefs were challenged but not always replaced by the arrival of Islam. In some ways, the tenets of Islam were in conflict with traditional African beliefs and customs. Although the concept of a single transcendent deity presented no problems in many African societies, Islam's rejection of spirit worship and a priestly class ran counter to the beliefs of many Africans and was often ignored in practice. Similarly, as various Muslim travelers observed, Islam's insistence on the separation of the genders contrasted with the relatively informal relationships that prevailed in many African societies and was probably slow to take root. In the long run, imported ideas were synthesized with native beliefs to create a unique brand of Africanized Islam.

The Arabs in North Africa

In 641, Arab forces advanced into Egypt, seized the delta of the Nile River, and brought two centuries of Byzantine rule to an end. To guard against attacks from the Byzantine fleet, they eventually built a new capital at Cairo, inland from the previous Byzantine capital of Alexandria, and began to consolidate their control over the entire region.

The Arab conquerors were probably welcomed by many, if not the majority, of the local inhabitants. Although Egypt had been a thriving commercial center under the Byzantines, the average Egyptian had not shared in this prosperity. Tax rates were

The Spread of Islam in Africa

generally high, and Christians were subjected to periodic persecution by the Byzantines, who viewed the local Coptic faith and other sects in the area as heresies. Although the new rulers continued to obtain much of their revenue from taxing the local farming population, tax rates were generally lower than they had been under the corrupt Byzantine government, and conversion to Islam brought exemption from taxation. During the next generations, many Egyptians converted to the Muslim faith, but Islam did not move into the upper Nile valley until several hundred years later. As Islam spread southward, it was adopted by many lowland peoples, but it had less success in the mountains of Ethiopia, where Coptic Christianity continued to win adherents (see the next section).

In the meantime, Arab rule was gradually being extended westward along the Mediterranean coast. When the Romans conquered Carthage in 146 B.C.E., they had called their new province Africa, thus introducing a name that would eventually be applied to the entire continent. After the fall of the Roman Empire, much of the area had reverted to the control of local Berber chieftains, but the Byzantines captured Carthage in the mid-sixth century C.E. In 690, the city was seized by the Arabs, who then began to extend their control over the entire area, which they called Al Maghrib ("the west").

At first, the local Berber peoples resisted their new conquerors. The Berbers were tough fighters, and for several generations, Arab rule was limited to the towns and lowland coastal areas. But Arab persistence eventually paid off, and by the early eighth century, the entire North African coast as far west as the Strait of Gibraltar was under Arab rule. The Arabs were now poised to cross the strait and expand into southern Europe and to push south beyond the fringes of the Sahara.

The Kingdom of Ethiopia: A Christian Island in a Muslim Sea

By the end of the sixth century C.E., the kingdom of Axum, long a dominant force in the trade network through the Red Sea, was in a state of decline. Both overexploitation of farmland and a shift in trade routes away from the Red Sea to the Arabian peninsula and Persian Gulf contributed to this decline. By the beginning of the ninth century, the capital had been moved farther into the mountainous interior, and Axum was gradually transformed from a maritime power into an isolated agricultural society.

The rise of Islam on the Arabian peninsula hastened this process, as the Arab world increasingly began to serve as the focus of the regional trade passing through the area. By the eighth century, a number of Muslim trading states had been established on the African coast of the Red Sea, a development that contributed to the transformation of Axum into a landlocked society with primarily agricultural interests. At first, relations between Christian Axum and its Muslim neighbors were relatively peaceful, as the larger and more powerful Axumite kingdom attempted with some success to compel the coastal Islamic states to accept a tributary relationship. Axum's role in the local commercial network temporarily revived, and the area became a prime source for ivory, resins like frankincense and myrrh, and slaves. Slaves came primarily from the south, where Axum had been attempting to subjugate restive tribal peoples living in the Amharic plateau beyond its southern border.

Beginning in the twelfth century, however, relations between Axum and its neighbors deteriorated as the Muslim states along the coast began to move inland to gain control over the growing trade in slaves and ivory. Axum responded with force and at first had some success in reasserting its hegemony over the area. But in the early fourteenth century, the Muslim state of Adal, located at the juncture of the Indian Ocean and the Red Sea, launched a new attack on the Christian kingdom.

Axum also underwent significant internal change during this period. The Zagwe dynasty, which seized control of the country in the mid-twelfth century, centralized the government and extended the Christian faith throughout the kingdom, now known as Ethiopia. Military commanders or civilian officials who had personal or kinship ties with the royal court established vast landed estates to maintain security and facilitate the collection of taxes from the local population. In the meantime, Christian missionaries established monasteries and churches to propagate the faith in outlying areas. Close relations were reestablished with leaders of the Coptic church in Egypt and with Christian officials in the Holy Land. This process was continued by the Solomonids, who succeeded the Zagwe dynasty in 1270. But by the early fifteenth century, the state had become more deeply involved in an expanding conflict with Muslim Adal to the east, a conflict that lasted for over a century and gradually took on the characteristics of a holy war.

East Africa: The Land of Zanj

The rise of Islam also had a lasting impact on the coast of East Africa, which the Greeks had called Azania and the Arabs called Zanj. During the seventh and eighth centuries, peoples from the Arabian peninsula and the Persian Gulf began to settle at ports along the coast and on the small islands offshore. Then, according to legend, in the middle of the tenth century, a Persian from Shiraz, a city in southern Iran, sailed to the area with his six sons. As his small fleet stopped along the coast, each son disembarked on one of the coastal islands and founded a small community; these settlements eventually grew into important commercial centers such as Mombasa, Pemba, Zanzibar (literally, "the coast of Zanj"), and Kilwa.

Although the legend underestimates the degree to which the area had already become a major participant in local commerce as well as the role of the local inhabitants in the process, it does reflect the importance of Arab and Persian immigrants in the formation of a string of trading

CHRONOLOGY Early Africa	
Origins of agriculture in Africa	c. 7000 B.C.E.
Desiccation of the Sahara	Begins c. 5000 B.C.E.
Kingship appears in the Nile valley	c. 3100 B.C.E.
Kingdom of Kush in Nubia	c. 500 B.C.E.
Iron Age begins	c. sixth century B.C.E.
Beginnings of trans-Saharan trade	c. first millennium B.C.E.
Rise of Axum	First century C.E.
Conquest of Kush by Axum	Fourth century C.E.
Bantus spread throughout East Africa	Early centuries C.E.
Arrival of Malays on Madagascar	Second century C.E.
Origins of Ghana	Fifth century C.E.
Arab takeover of lower Nile valley	641 C.E.
Development of Swahili culture	c. first millennium C.E.
Spread of Islam across North Africa	Seventh century C.E.
Spread of Islam in Horn of Africa	Ninth century C.E.
Decline of Ghana	Twelfth century C.E.
Establishment of Zagwe dynasty in Ethiopia	c. 1150
Rise of Mali	c. 1250
Kingdom of Zimbabwe	c. 1300–c. 1450
Portuguese ships explore West African coast	Mid-fifteenth century

ports stretching from Mogadishu (today the capital of Somalia) in the north to Kilwa (south of present-day Dar es Salaam) in the south. Kilwa became especially important as it was near the southern limit for a ship hoping to complete the round-trip journey in a single season. Goods such as ivory, gold, and rhinoceros horn were exported across the Indian Ocean to countries as far away as China, while imports included iron goods, glassware, Indian textiles, and Chinese porcelain. Merchants in these cities often amassed considerable profit, as evidenced by their lavish

The Coast of Zanj

THE COAST OF ZANJ

INTERACTION & EXCHANGE

From early times, the people living on the coast of East Africa took an active part in trade along the coast and across the Indian Ocean. The process began with the arrival of Arab traders early in the first millennium C.E. According to local legends, Arab merchants often married the daughters of the local chieftains and then received title to coastal territories as part of their wife's dowry. This description of the area was written by the Arab traveler al-Mas'udi, who visited the "land of Zanj" in 916.

Why did Arab traders begin to settle along the coast of East Africa? What impact did the Arab presence have on the lives of the local population?

Al-Mas'udi in East Africa

The land of Zanj produces wild leopard skins. The people wear them as clothes, or export them to Muslim countries. They are the largest leopard skins and the most beautiful for making saddles. . . . They also export tortoiseshell for making combs, for which ivory is likewise used. . . . The Zanj are settled in that area, which stretches as far as Sofala, which is the furthest limit of the land and the end of the voyages made from Oman and Siraf on the sea of Zanj. . . . The Zanj use the ox as a beast of burden, for they have no horses, mules or camels in their land. . . . There are many wild elephants in this land but no tame ones. The Zanj do not use them for war or anything else, but only hunt and kill them for their ivory. It is from this country that come tusks weighing fifty pounds and more. They usually go to Oman, and from there are sent to China and India. This is the chief trade route. . . .

The Zanj have an elegant language and men who preach in it. One of their holy men will often gather a crowd and exhort his hearers to please God in their lives and to be obedient to him. He explains the punishments that follow upon disobedience, and reminds them of their ancestors and kings of old. These people have no religious law: their kings rule by custom and by political expediency.

The Zanj eat bananas, which are as common among them as they are in India; but their staple food is millet and a plant called kalari which is pulled out of the earth like truffles. They also eat honey and meat. They have many islands where the coconut grows: its nuts are used as fruit by all the Zanj peoples. One of these islands, which is one or two days' sail from the coast, has a Muslim population and a royal family. This is the island of Kanbulu [thought to be modern Pemba].

CENGAGENOW To read another Arab writer's account of Zanj, enter the *CengageNOW* documents area using the access card that is available for *The Essential World History*.

---

stone palaces, some of which still stand in the modern cities of Mombasa and Zanzibar. Though now in ruins, Kilwa was one of the most magnificent cities of its day. The fourteenth-century Arab traveler Ibn Battuta described it as "amongst the most beautiful of cities and most elegantly built. All of it is of wood, and the ceilings of its houses are of *al-dis* [reeds]."[1] One particularly impressive structure was the Husuni Kubwa, a massive palace with vaulted roofs capped with domes and elaborate stone carvings, surrounding an inner courtyard. Ordinary townspeople and the residents of smaller towns did not live in such luxurious conditions, of course, but even there, affluent urban residents lived in spacious stone buildings, with indoor plumbing and consumer goods imported from as far away as China and southern Europe.

Most of the coastal states were self-governing, although sometimes several towns were grouped together under a single dominant authority. Government revenue came primarily from taxes imposed on commerce. Some trade went on between these coastal city-states and the peoples of the interior, who provided gold and iron, ivory, and various agricultural goods and animal products in return for textiles, manufactured articles, and weapons (see the box above). Relations apparently varied, and the coastal merchants sometimes resorted to force to obtain goods from the inland peoples. A Portuguese visitor recounted that "the men [of Mombasa] are oft-times at war and but seldom at peace with those of the mainland, and they carry on trade with them, bringing thence great store of honey, wax, and ivory."[2]

By the twelfth and thirteenth centuries, a mixed African-Arabian culture, eventually known as Swahili (from the Arabic *sahel* meaning "coast"; thus, "peoples of the coast"), began to emerge throughout the coastal area. Intermarriage between the immigrants and the local population was common, although a distinct Arab community, made up primarily of merchants, persisted in many areas. The members of the ruling class were often of mixed heritage but usually traced their genealogy to Arab or Persian ancestors. By this time, too, many members of the ruling class had converted to Islam. Middle Eastern urban architectural styles and other aspects of Arab culture were implanted within a society still predominantly African. Arabic words and phrases were combined with Bantu grammatical structures to form a mixed language, also known as Swahili; it is the national language of Kenya and Tanzania today.

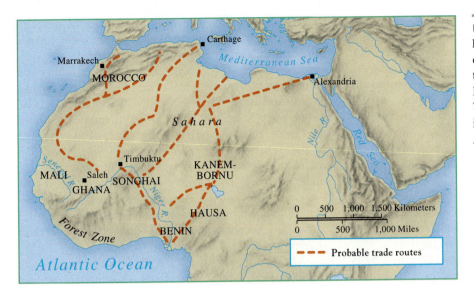

MAP 8.3 **Trans-Saharan Trade Routes.** Trade across the Sahara began during the first millennium B.C.E. With the arrival of the camel from the Middle East, trade expanded dramatically. ❓ Why did similar trade routes not extend into the Congo basin and southern Africa?

The States of West Africa

During the eighth century, merchants from the Maghrib began to carry Muslim beliefs to the savanna areas south of the Sahara. At first, conversion took place on an individual basis rather than through official encouragement. The first rulers to convert to Islam were the royal family of Gao at the end of the tenth century. Five hundred years later, most of the population in the grasslands south of the Sahara had accepted Islam.

The expansion of Islam into West Africa had a major impact on the political system. By introducing Arabic as the first written language in the region and Muslim law codes and administrative practices from the Middle East, Islam provided local rulers with the tools to increase their authority and the efficiency of their governments. Moreover, as Islam gradually spread throughout the region, a common religion united previously diverse peoples into a more coherent community.

When Islam arrived in the grasslands south of the Sahara, the region was beginning to undergo significant political and social change. A number of major trading states were in the making, and they eventually transformed the Sahara into one of the leading avenues of world trade, crisscrossed by caravan routes leading to destinations as far away as the Atlantic Ocean, the Mediterranean, and the Red Sea (see Map 8.3).

Ghana   The first of these great commercial states was Ghana, which emerged in the fifth century C.E. in the upper Niger valley, a grassland region between the Sahara and the tropical forests along the West African coast (the modern state of Ghana, which takes its name from the trading society under discussion here, is located in the forest region to the south). The majority of the people in the area were Iron Age farmers living in villages under the authority of a local chieftain. Gradually, these local communities were united to form the kingdom of Ghana.

Although the people of the region had traditionally lived from agriculture, a primary reason for Ghana's growing importance was gold. The heartland of the state was located near one of the richest gold-producing areas in all of Africa. Ghanaian merchants transported the gold to Morocco, whence it was distributed throughout the known world. This trade began in ancient times, as the Greek historian Herodotus relates:

> The Carthaginians also tell us that they trade with a race of men who live in a part of Libya beyond the Pillars of Heracles [the Strait of Gibraltar]. On reaching this country, they unload their goods, arrange them tidily along the beach, and then, returning to their boats, raise a smoke. Seeing the smoke, the natives come down to the beach, place on the ground a certain quantity of gold in exchange for the goods, and go off again to a distance. The Carthaginians then come ashore and take a look at the gold; and if they think it represents a fair price for their wares, they collect it and go away; if, on the other hand, it seems too little, they go back aboard and wait, and the natives come and add to the gold until they are satisfied. There is perfect honesty on both sides; the Carthaginians never touch the gold until it equals in value what they have offered for sale, and the natives never touch the goods until the gold has been taken away.[3]

Later, Ghana became known to Arab-speaking peoples in North Africa as "the land of gold." Actually, the name was misleading, for the gold did not come from Ghana, but from a neighboring people, who sold it to merchants from Ghana.

Eventually, other exports from Ghana found their way to the bazaars of the Mediterranean coast and beyond—ivory, ostrich feathers, hides, leather goods, and ultimately slaves. The origins of the slave trade in the area probably go back to the first millennium B.C.E., when Berber tribesmen seized African villagers in the regions south of the Sahara and sold them for profit to buyers in Europe and the Middle East. In return, Ghana imported metal goods (especially weapons), textiles, horses, and salt.

Much of the trade across the desert was still conducted by the nomadic Berbers, but Ghanaian merchants played an active role as intermediaries, trading tropical products such as bananas, kola nuts, and palm oil from the forest states of Guinea along the Atlantic coast to the south. By the eighth and ninth centuries, much of this trade was conducted by Muslim merchants, who purchased the goods from local traders (using iron and copper cash or cowrie shells from Southeast Asia as the primary means of exchange) and then sold them to Berbers, who carried them across the desert. The merchants who carried on this trade often became quite wealthy and lived in splendor in cities like Saleh, the capital of Ghana. So did the king, of course, who taxed the merchants as well as the farmers and the producers.

Like other West African kings, the king of Ghana ruled by divine right and was assisted by a hereditary aristocracy composed of the leading members of the prominent clans, who also served as district chiefs responsible for maintaining law and order and collecting taxes. The king was responsible for maintaining the security of his kingdom, serving as an intermediary with local deities, and functioning as the chief law officer to adjudicate disputes. The kings of Ghana did not convert to Islam themselves, although they welcomed Muslim merchants and apparently did not discourage their subjects from adopting the new faith (see the box on p. 181).

Mali   The state of Ghana flourished for several hundred years, but by the twelfth century, weakened by ruinous wars with Berber tribesmen, it had begun to decline; it collapsed at the end of the century. In its place rose a number of new trading societies, including large territorial states like Mali in the west, Songhai and Kanem-Bornu toward the east, and small commercial city-states like the Hausa states, located in what is today northern Nigeria (see Map 8.4).

The greatest of the states that emerged after the destruction of Ghana was Mali. Extending from the Atlantic coast inland as far as the trading cities of Timbuktu and Gao on the Niger River, Mali built its wealth and power on the gold trade. But the heartland of Mali was situated south of the Sahara in the savanna region, where sufficient moisture enabled farmers to grow such crops as sorghum, millet, and rice. The farmers lived in villages ruled by a local chieftain (called a *mansa*), who served as both religious and administrative leader and was responsible for forwarding tax revenues from the village to higher levels of government.

The primary wealth of the country was accumulated in the cities. Here lived the merchants, who were primarily of local origin, although many were now practicing Muslims. Commercial activities were taxed but were apparently so lucrative that both the merchants and the kings prospered. One of the most powerful kings of Mali was Mansa Musa (1312–1337), whose primary contribution to his people was probably not economic prosperity but the Muslim faith. Mansa Musa strongly encouraged the building of mosques and the study of the Qur'an in his kingdom and imported scholars and books to introduce his subjects to the message of Allah. One visitor from Europe, writing in the late fifteenth century, reported that in Timbuktu "are a great store of doctors, judges, priests, and other learned men, that are bountifully maintained at the king's cost and charges. And hither are brought divers manuscripts of written books out of Barbary [North Africa] which are sold for more money than any other merchandise."[4]

Courtesy of William J. Duiker

The Great Gate at Marrakech. The Moroccan city of Marrakech, founded in the ninth century C.E., was a major northern terminus of the trans-Saharan trade and one of the chief commercial centers in premodern Africa. Widely praised by such famous travelers as Ibn Battuta, the city was an architectural marvel in that all its major public buildings were constructed in red sandstone. Shown here is the Great Gate to the city, through which camel caravans passed en route to and from the vast desert. In the Berber language, Marrakech means "pass without making a noise," a reference to the need for caravan traders to be aware of the danger of thieves in the vicinity.

DESCRIPTION OF A GHANAIAN CAPITAL

INTERACTION & EXCHANGE

After its first appearance in West Africa in the decades following the death of Muhammad, Islam competed with native African religions for followers. Eventually, several local rulers converted to the Muslim faith. This passage by the Arab geographer al-Bakri shows how both religions flourished side by side in the state of Ghana during the eleventh century.

Why might an African ruler find it advantageous to adopt the Muslim faith? What kinds of changes would the adoption of Islam entail for the peoples living in West Africa?

Al-Bakri's Description of Ghana

The king's residence comprises a palace and conical huts, the whole surrounded by a fence like a wall. Around the royal town are huts and groves of thorn trees where live the magicians who control their religious rites. These groves, where they keep their idols and bury their kings, are protected by guards who permit no one to enter or find out what goes on in them.

None of those who belong to the imperial religion may wear tailored garments except the king himself and the heir-presumptive, his sister's son. The rest of the people wear wrappers of cotton, silk or brocade according to their means. Most of the men shave their beards and the women their heads. The king adorns himself with female ornaments around the neck and arms. On his head he wears gold-embroidered caps covered with turbans of finest cotton. He gives audience to the people for the redressing of grievances in a hut around which are placed 10 horses covered in golden cloth. Behind him stand 10 slaves carrying shields and swords mounted with gold. On his right are the sons of vassal kings, their heads plaited with gold and wearing costly garments. On the ground around him are seated his ministers, whilst the governor of the city sits before him. On guard at the door are dogs of fine pedigree, wearing collars adorned with gold and silver. The royal audience is announced by the beating of a drum, called daba, made out of a long piece of hollowed-out wood. When the people have gathered, his coreligionists draw near upon their knees sprinkling dust upon their heads as a sign of respect, whilst the Muslims clap hands as their form of greeting.

CENGAGENOW To read more of al-Bakri's account and listen to audio, enter the *CengageNOW* documents area using the access card that is available for *The Essential World History*.

States and Stateless Societies in Central and Southern Africa

In the southern half of the African continent, from the great basin of the Congo River to the Cape of Good Hope, states formed somewhat more slowly than in the north.

Until the eleventh century C.E., most of the peoples in this region lived in what are sometimes called **stateless societies,** characterized by autonomous villages organized by clans and ruled by a local chieftain or clan head. Beginning in the eleventh century, in some parts of southern Africa, these independent villages gradually began to consolidate. Out of these groupings came the first states.

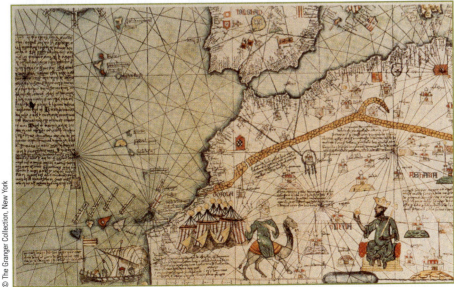

© The Granger Collection, New York

Mansa Musa. Mansa Musa, king of the West African state of Mali, was one of the richest and most powerful rulers of his day. During a famous pilgrimage to Mecca, he arrived in Cairo with a hundred camels laden with gold and gave away so much gold that its value depreciated there for several years. To promote the Islamic faith in his country, he bought homes in Cairo and Mecca to house pilgrims en route to the holy shrine, and he brought back to Mali a renowned Arab architect to build mosques in the trading centers of Gao and Timbuktu. His fame spread to Europe as well, evidenced by this Spanish map of 1375, which depicts Mansa Musa seated on his throne in Mali, holding an impressive gold nugget.

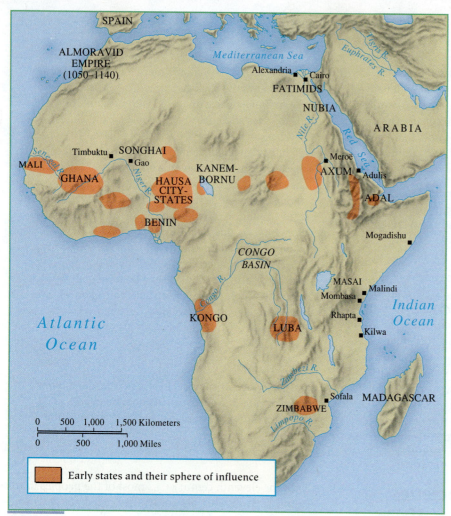

MAP 8.4 **The Emergence of States in Africa.** By the end of the first millennium C.E., organized states had begun to appear in various parts of Africa. ❓ Why did organized states appear at these particular spots and not in other areas of Africa?

expand southward to absorb the mixed farming and pastoral peoples in the area of modern Angola. In the drier grassland area to the south, other small communities continued to support themselves by herding, hunting, or food gathering. We know little about these peoples, however, since they possessed no writing system and had few visitors. A Portuguese sailor who encountered them in the late sixteenth century reported, "These people are herdsmen and cultivators. . . . Their main crop is millet, which they grind between two stones or in wooden mortars to make flour. . . . Their wealth consists mainly in their huge number of dehorned cows. . . . They live together in small villages, in houses made of reed mats, which do not keep out the rain."[5]

Zimbabwe

Farther to the east, the situation was somewhat different. In the grassland regions immediately to the south of the Zambezi River, a mixed economy involving farming, cattle herding, and commercial pursuits had begun to develop during the early centuries of the first millennium C.E. Characteristically, villages in this area were constructed inside walled enclosures to protect the animals at night. The most famous of these communities was Zimbabwe, located on the plateau of the same name between the Zambezi and Limpopo rivers. From the twelfth century to the middle of the fifteenth, Zimbabwe was the most powerful and most prosperous state in the region and played a major role in the gold trade with the Swahili trading communities on the eastern coast.

The ruins of Zimbabwe's capital, known as Great Zimbabwe (the term *Zimbabwe* means "sacred house" in the Bantu language), provide a vivid illustration of the kingdom's power and influence. Strategically situated between substantial gold reserves to the west and a small river leading to the coast, Great Zimbabwe was well placed to benefit from the expansion of trade between the coast and the interior. The town sits on a hill overlooking the river and is surrounded by stone walls, which enclosed an area large enough to hold over ten thousand residents. The houses of the wealthy were built of cement on stone foundations, while those of the common people were of dried mud with thatched roofs.

The Congo River Valley

One area where this process occurred was the Congo River valley, where the combination of fertile land and nearby deposits of copper and iron enabled the inhabitants to enjoy an agricultural surplus and engage in regional commerce. Two new states in particular underwent this transition. Sometime during the fourteenth century, the kingdom of Luba was founded in the center of the continent, in a rich agricultural and fishing area near the shores of Lake Kisale. Luba had a relatively centralized government, in which the king appointed provincial governors, who were responsible for collecting tribute from the village chiefs. At about the same time, the kingdom of Kongo was formed just south of the mouth of the Congo River on the Atlantic coast.

These new states were primarily agricultural, although both had a thriving manufacturing sector and took an active part in the growing exchange of goods throughout the region. As time passed, both began to

Great Zimbabwe. Situated on an important trade route and a center for cattle and agriculture, Great Zimbabwe was originally settled by pastoral peoples during the first millennium B.C.E. Later it became the capital of a prosperous state. Its 30-foot walls were the first in Africa to be constructed without the use of mortar. The walled palace shown here indicates why Great Zimbabwe is generally regarded as the most impressive archaeological site in southern Africa.

In the valley below is the royal palace, surrounded by a stone wall 30 feet high. Artifacts found at the site include household implements and ornaments made of gold and copper, as well as jewelry and even porcelain imported from China.

Most of the royal wealth probably came from two sources: the ownership of cattle and the king's ability to levy heavy taxes on the gold that passed through the kingdom en route to the coast. By the middle of the fifteenth century, however, the city was apparently abandoned, possibly because of environmental damage caused by overgrazing. With the decline of Zimbabwe, the focus of economic power began to shift northward to the valley of the Zambezi River.

Southern Africa

South of the East African plateau and the Congo basin is a vast land of hills, grasslands, and arid desert stretching almost to the Cape of Good Hope at the tip of the continent. As Bantu-speaking farmers spread southward during the final centuries of the first millennium B.C.E., they began to encounter Stone Age peoples in the area who still lived primarily by hunting and foraging.

Available evidence suggests that early relations between these two peoples were relatively harmonious. Intermarriage between members of the two groups was apparently not unusual, and many of the indigenous peoples were gradually absorbed into what became a dominantly Bantu-speaking pastoral and agricultural society that spread throughout much of southern Africa during the first millennium C.E.

The Khoi and the San   Two such peoples were the Khoi and the San, whose language, known as Khoisan, is distinguished by the use of "clicking" sounds. The Khoi were herders, whereas the San were hunter-gatherers who lived in small family communities of twenty to twenty-five members throughout southern Africa from Namibia in the west to the Drakensberg Mountains near the southeastern coast. Scholars have learned about the early life of the San by interviewing their modern descendants and by studying rock paintings found in caves throughout the area. These multicolored paintings, which predate the coming of the Europeans, were drawn with a brush made of small feathers fastened to a reed. They depict various aspects of the San's lifestyle, including their hunting techniques and religious rituals.

African Society

Drawing generalizations about social organization, cultural development, and daily life in traditional Africa is difficult because of the extreme diversity of the continent and its inhabitants. One-quarter of all the languages in the world are spoken in Africa, and five of the major language families are found there. Ethnic divisions are equally pronounced. Because many of these languages did not have a system of writing until fairly recently, historians must rely on accounts of the occasional visitor, such as al-Mas'udi and the famous fourteenth-century chronicler Ibn Battuta. Such travelers, however, tended to come into contact mostly with the wealthy and the powerful, leaving us to speculate about what life was like for ordinary Africans during this early period.

Urban Life

African towns often began as fortified walled villages and gradually evolved into larger communities serving several purposes. Here, of course, were the center of government and the teeming markets filled with goods from distant regions. Here also were artisans skilled in metal- or woodworking, pottery making, and other crafts. Unlike the rural areas, where a village was usually composed of a single lineage group or clan, the towns drew their residents from several clans, although individual clans usually lived in their own compounds and were governed by their own clan heads.

In the states of West Africa, the focal point of the major towns was the royal precinct. The relationship between the ruler and the merchant class differed from the situation in most Asian societies, where the royal family and the aristocracy were largely isolated from the remainder of the population. In Africa, the chasm between the king and the common people was not so great. Often the ruler would hold an audience to allow people to voice their complaints or to welcome visitors from foreign countries. In the city-states of the East African coast as well, the ruler was frequently forced to share political power with a class of wealthy merchants and often, as in the town of Kilwa, "did not possess more country than the city itself."[6]

This is not to say that the king was not elevated above all others in status. In wealthier states, the walls of the audience chamber would be covered with sheets of beaten silver and gold, and the king would be surrounded by hundreds of armed soldiers and some of his trusted advisers. Nevertheless, the symbiotic relationship between the ruler and merchant class served to reduce the gap between the king and his subjects. The relationship was mutually beneficial, since the merchants received honors and favors from the palace while the king's coffers were filled with taxes paid by the merchants. Certainly, it was to the benefit of the king to maintain law and order in his domain so that the merchants could ply their trade. As Ibn Battuta observed, among the good qualities of the peoples of West Africa was the prevalence of peace in the region. "The traveler is not afraid in it," he remarked, "nor is he who lives there in fear of the thief or of the robber by violence."[7]

Village Life

The vast majority of Africans lived in small rural villages. Their identities were established by their membership in a nuclear family and a lineage group. At the basic level was the nuclear family composed of parents and preadult children; sometimes it included an elderly grandparent and other family dependents as well. They lived in small round huts constructed of packed mud and topped with a conical thatch roof. In most African societies, these nuclear family units would in turn be combined into larger kinship communities known as households or lineage groups.

The lineage group was similar in many respects to the clan in China or the class system in India in that it was normally based on kinship ties, although sometimes outsiders such as friends or other dependents may have been admitted to membership. Throughout the precolonial era, lineages served, in the words of one historian, as the "basic building blocks" of African society. The authority of the leading members of the lineage group was substantial. As in China, the elders had considerable power over the economic functions of the other people in the group, which provided mutual support for all members.

A village would usually be composed of a single lineage group, although some communities may have consisted of several unrelated families. At the head of the village was the familiar "big man," who was often assisted by a council of representatives of the various households in the community. Often the "big man" was believed to possess supernatural powers, and as the village grew in size and power, he might eventually be transformed into a local chieftain or monarch.

The Role of Women

Although generalizations are risky, we can say that women were usually subordinate to men in Africa, as in most early societies. In some cases, they were valued for the work they could do or for their role in increasing the size of the lineage group. Polygyny was not uncommon, particularly in Muslim societies. Women often worked in the fields while the men of the village tended the cattle or went on hunting expeditions. In some communities, the women specialized in commercial activities. In one area in southern Africa, young girls were sent into the mines to extract gold because of their smaller physiques.

But there were some key differences between the role of women in Africa and elsewhere. In many African societies, lineage was **matrilinear** rather than **patrilinear.** As Ibn Battuta observed during his travels in West Africa, "A man does not pass on inheritance except to the sons of his sister to the exclusion of his own sons."[8] He said he had never encountered this custom before except among the unbelievers of the Malabar coast in India. Women were often permitted to inherit property, and the husband was often expected to move into his wife's house.

Relations between the genders were also sometimes more relaxed than in China or India, with none of the taboos characteristic of those societies. Again, in the words of Ibn Battuta, himself a Muslim:

> With regard to their women, they are not modest in the presence of men, they do not veil themselves in spite of their perseverance in the prayers. . . . The women there have friends and companions amongst men outside the prohibited degrees of marriage [i.e., other than brothers, fathers, etc.]. Likewise for the men, there are companions from amongst women outside the prohibited degrees. One of them would enter his house to find his wife with her companion and would not disapprove of that conduct.

When Ibn Battuta asked an African acquaintance about these customs, the latter responded: "Women's companionship with men in our country is honorable and takes place in a good way: there is no suspicion about it. They are not like the women in your country." Ibn Battuta noted his astonishment at such a "thoughtless" answer and did not accept further invitations to visit his friend's house.[9]

Such informal attitudes toward the relationship between the genders were not found everywhere in Africa and were probably curtailed as many Africans converted to Islam. But it is a testimony to the tenacity of traditional customs that the relatively puritanical views about the role of women in society brought by Muslims from the Middle East made little impression even among Muslim families in West Africa.

Slavery

African slavery is often associated with the period after 1500. Indeed, the slave trade did reach enormous proportions in the seventeenth and eighteenth centuries, when

European slave ships transported millions of unfortunate victims abroad to Europe or the Americas (see Chapter 14).

Slavery did not originate with the coming of the Europeans, however. It had been practiced in Africa since ancient times and probably originated with prisoners of war who were forced into perpetual servitude. Slavery was common in ancient Egypt and became especially prevalent during the New Kingdom, when slaving expeditions brought back thousands of captives from the upper Nile to be used in labor gangs, for tribute, and even as human sacrifices.

Slavery persisted during the early period of state building, in the first and early second millennia C.E. Berber tribes may have regularly raided agricultural communities south of the Sahara for captives who were transported northward and eventually sold throughout the Mediterranean. Some were enrolled as soldiers, while others, often women, were used as domestic servants in the homes of the well-to-do. The use of captives for forced labor or for sale was apparently also common in African societies farther to the south and along the eastern coast.

Life was difficult for the average slave. The least fortunate were probably those who worked on plantations owned by the royal family or other wealthy landowners. Those pressed into service as soldiers were sometimes more fortunate, since in Muslim societies in the Middle East, they might at some point win their freedom. Many slaves were employed in the royal household or as domestic servants in private homes. In general, these slaves probably had the most tolerable existence. Although they ordinarily were not permitted to purchase their freedom, their living conditions were often decent and sometimes practically indistinguishable from those of the free individuals in the household. In some societies in North Africa, slaves reportedly made up as much as 75 percent of the entire population. Elsewhere the percentage was much lower, in some cases less than 10 percent.

African Culture

In early Africa, as in much of the rest of the world at the time, creative expression, whether in the form of painting, literature, or music, was above all a means of serving religion. Though to the uninitiated a wooden mask or the bronze and iron statuary of southern Nigeria is simply a work of art, to the artist it was often a means of expressing religious convictions. Some African historians reject the use of the term *art* to describe such artifacts because they were produced for religious rather than aesthetic purposes.

Painting and Sculpture

The earliest extant art forms in Africa are rock paintings. The most famous examples are in the Tassili Mountains in the central Sahara, where the earliest paintings may date back as far as 5000 B.C.E., though the majority are a millennium or so younger. Some of the later paintings depict the two-horse chariots used to transport goods prior to the introduction of the camel. Rock paintings are also found elsewhere in the continent, including the Nile valley and in eastern and southern Africa. Those of the San peoples of southern Africa are especially interesting for their illustrations of ritual ceremonies in which village shamans induce rain, propitiate the spirits, or cure illnesses.

More familiar, perhaps, are African wood carvings and sculpture. The remarkable statues, masks, and headdresses were carved from living trees, to the spirit of which the artists had made a sacrifice. Costumed singers and dancers wore these masks and headdresses in performances in honor of the various spirits, revealing the identification and intimate connection of the African with the natural world. In Mali, for example, the 3-foot-tall Ci Wara headdresses, one female, the other male, found meaning in performances that celebrated the mythical hero who had introduced agriculture. Terra-cotta and metal figurines served a similar purpose.

In the thirteenth and fourteenth centuries C.E., metalworkers at Ife in what is now southern Nigeria produced handsome bronze and iron statues using the lost-wax method, in which melted wax is replaced in a mold by molten metal. The Ife sculptures may in turn have influenced artists in Benin, in West Africa, who produced equally impressive works in bronze during the same period. The Benin sculptures include bronze heads, relief plaques depicting life at court, ornaments, and figures of various animals.

Westerners once regarded African wood carvings and metal sculpture as a form of "primitive art," but the label is not appropriate. The metal sculpture of Benin, for example, is highly sophisticated, and some of the best works are considered masterpieces. Such artistic works were often created by artisans in the employ of the royal court.

Music

Like sculpture and wood carving, African music and dance often served a religious function. With their characteristic heavy rhythmic beat, dances were a means of communicating with the spirits, and the frenzied movements that are often identified with African dance were intended to represent the spirits acting through humans.

African music during the traditional period varied to some degree from one society to another. A wide variety of instruments were used, including drums and other percussion instruments, xylophones, bells, horns and flutes, and stringed instruments like the fiddle, harp, and zither. Still, the music throughout the continent had sufficient common characteristics to justify a few generalizations. In the first place, a strong rhythmic pattern was an important feature of most African music, although the desired effect was achieved through a wide variety of means, including gourds, pots, bells, sticks beaten together, and hand clapping as well as drums.

Another important feature of African music was the integration of voice and instrument into a total musical experience. Musical instruments and the human voice were often woven together to tell a story, and instruments, such as the famous "talking drum," were often used to represent the voice. Choral music and individual voices were frequently used in a pattern of repetition and variation, sometimes known as "call and response." Through this technique, the audience participated in the music by uttering a single phrase over and over as a choral response to the changing call sung by the soloist. Sometimes instrumental music achieved a similar result.

Much music was produced in the context of social rituals, such as weddings and funerals, religious ceremonies, and official inaugurations. It could also serve an educational purpose by passing on to the young people information about the history and social traditions of the community. In the absence of written languages in sub-Saharan Africa (except for the Arabic script, used in Muslim societies in East and West Africa), music served as the primary means of transmitting folk legends and religious traditions from generation to generation. Storytelling, which was usually undertaken by a priestly class or a specialized class of storytellers, served a similar function.

Architecture

No aspect of African artistic creativity is more varied than architecture. From the pyramids along the Nile to the ruins of Great Zimbabwe south of the Zambezi River, from the Moorish palaces at Zanzibar to the turreted mud mosques of West Africa, African architecture shows a striking diversity of approach and technique that is unmatched in other areas of creative endeavor.

The earliest surviving architectural form found in Africa is the pyramid. The Kushite kingdom at Meroë apparently adopted the pyramidal form from Egypt during the last centuries of the first millennium B.C.E. Although used for the same purpose as their earlier counterparts at Giza, the pyramids at Meroë were distinctive in style; they were much smaller and were topped with a flat platform rather than rising to a point. Remains of temples with massive carved pillars at Meroë also reflect Egyptian influence.

Farther to the south, the kingdom of Axum was developing its own architectural traditions. Most distinctive were the carved stone pillars, known as stelae, that were used to mark the tombs of dead kings. Some stood as high as 100 feet. The advent of Christianity eventually had an impact on Axumite architecture. During the Zagwe dynasty in the twelfth and thirteenth centuries C.E., churches carved out of solid rock were constructed throughout the country (see the comparative illustration on p. 193 in Chapter 9). Stylistically, they combined indigenous techniques inherited from the pre-Christian

© Angela Fisher/Robert Estall Photographs

The Mosque at Jenne, Mali. With the opening of the gold fields south of Mali, in present-day Ghana, Jenne became an important trading center for gold. Shown here is its distinctive fourteenth-century mosque made of unbaked clay without reinforcements. The projecting timbers offer easy access for repairing the mud exterior, as was regularly required.

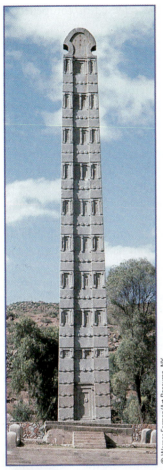

© Werner Forman/Art Resource, NY

© Réunion des Musées Nationaux/Art Resource, NY

© Borromeo/Art Resource

ARTS & IDEAS

COMPARATIVE ILLUSTRATION

The Stele. A stele is a stone slab or pillar, usually decorated or inscribed, and placed upright. Stelae were often used to commemorate the accomplishments of a ruler or significant figure. Shown at the left is the tallest of the Axum stelae still standing, in present-day Ethiopia. The stone stelae in Axum in the fourth century B.C.E. marked the location of royal tombs with inscriptions commemorating the glories of the kings. An earlier famous stele, seen in the center, is that of Hammurabi (who ruled from 1792 to 1750 B.C.E.; see Chapter 1), which depicts Hammurabi standing in front of a seated god. Below the scene is an inscription of the Code of Hammurabi. A similar kind of stone pillar, shown at the right, was erected in India during the reign of Asoka in the third century B.C.E. (see Chapter 2) to commemorate events in the life of the Buddha. Archaeologists have also found stelae in ancient China, Greece, and Mexico.

period with elements borrowed from Christian churches in the Holy Land.

In West Africa, buildings constructed in stone were apparently a rarity until the emergence of states during the first millennium C.E. At that time, the royal palace, as well as other buildings of civic importance, was often built of stone or cement, while the houses of the majority of the population continued to be constructed of dried mud. On his visit to the state of Guinea on the West African coast, the sixteenth-century traveler Leo Africanus noted that the houses of the ruler and other elites were built of chalk with roofs of straw. Even then, however, well into the state-building period, mosques were often built of mud.

Along the east coast, the architecture of the elite tended to reflect Middle Eastern styles. In the coastal towns and islands from Mogadishu to Kilwa, the houses of the wealthy were built of stone and reflected Moorish influence. As elsewhere, the common people lived in huts of mud, thatch, or palm leaves. Mosques were built of stone.

The most famous stone buildings in sub-Saharan Africa are those at Great Zimbabwe. Constructed of carefully cut stones that were set in place without mortar, the great wall and the public buildings at Great Zimbabwe are an impressive monument to the architectural creativity of the peoples of the region.

Literature

Literature in the sense of written works did not exist in sub-Saharan Africa during the early traditional period, except in regions where Islam had brought the Arabic script from the Middle East. But African societies compensated for the absence of a written language with a rich tradition of oral lore. The bard, or professional storyteller, was an ancient African institution by which history was transmitted orally from generation to generation. In many West African societies, bards were highly esteemed and served as counselors to kings as well as protectors of local tradition. Bards were revered for their oratory and singing skills, phenomenal memory, and astute interpretation of history. As one African scholar wrote, the death of a bard was equivalent to the burning of a library.

Bards served several necessary functions in society. They were chroniclers of history, preservers of social customs and proper conduct, and entertainers who possessed a monopoly over the playing of several musical instruments, which accompanied their narratives. Because of their unique position above normal society, bards often played the role of mediator between hostile families or clans in a community. They were also credited with possessing occult powers and could read divinations and give blessings and curses. Traditionally, bards also served as advisers to the king, sometimes inciting him to action (such as going to battle) through the passion of their poetry. When captured by the enemy, bards were often treated with respect and released or compelled to serve the victor with their art.

One of the most famous West African epics is *The Epic of Son-Jara* (also known as *Sunjata* or *Sundiata*). Passed down orally by bards for more than seven hundred years, it relates the heroic exploits of Son-Jara, the founder and ruler (1230–1255) of Mali's empire. Although Mansa Musa is famous throughout the world because of his flamboyant pilgrimage to Mecca in the fourteenth century, Son-Jara is more celebrated in West Africa because of the dynamic and unbroken oral traditions of the West African peoples.

In addition to the bards, women too were appreciated for their storytelling talents, as well as for their role as purveyors of the moral values and religious beliefs of African societies. In societies that lacked a written tradition, women represented the glue that held the community together. Through the recitation of fables, proverbs, poems, and songs, mothers conditioned the communal bonding and moral fiber of succeeding generations in a way that was rarely encountered in the patriarchal societies of Europe, eastern and southern Asia, and the Middle East. Such activities were not only vital aspects of education in traditional Africa, but they also offered a welcome respite from the drudgery of everyday life and a spark to develop the imagination and artistic awareness of the young. Renowned for its many proverbs, Africa also offers the following: "A good story is like a garden carried in the pocket."

CONCLUSION

*T*HANKS TO THE DEDICATED WORK of a generation of archaeologists, anthropologists, and historians, we now have a much better understanding of the evolution of human societies in Africa than we did a few decades ago. Intensive efforts by archaeologists have demonstrated beyond reasonable doubt that the first hominids lived there. Recent evidence suggests that farming may have been practiced in Africa more than twelve thousand years ago, and the concept of kingship may have originated not in Sumer or in Egypt but in the upper Nile valley as long ago as the fourth millennium B.C.E.

Less is known about more recent African history, partly because of the paucity of written records. Still, historians have established that the first civilizations had begun to take shape in sub-Saharan Africa by the first millennium C.E., while the continent as a whole was an active participant in emerging regional and global trade with the Mediterranean world and across the Indian Ocean.

Thus, the peoples of Africa were not as isolated from the main currents of human history as was once assumed. Although the state-building process in sub-Saharan Africa was still in its early stages compared with the ancient civilizations of India, China, and Mesopotamia, in many respects these new states were as impressive and sophisticated as their counterparts elsewhere in the world.

In the fifteenth century, a new factor was added to the equation. Urged on by the tireless efforts of Prince Henry the Navigator, Portuguese fleets began to probe southward along the coast of West Africa. At first, their sponsors were in search of gold and slaves, but at the end of the century, Vasco da Gama's voyage around the Cape of Good Hope signaled Portugal's determination to dominate the commerce of the Indian Ocean in the future. The new situation posed a challenge to the peoples of Africa, whose nascent states and technology would be severely tested by the rapacious demands of the Europeans.

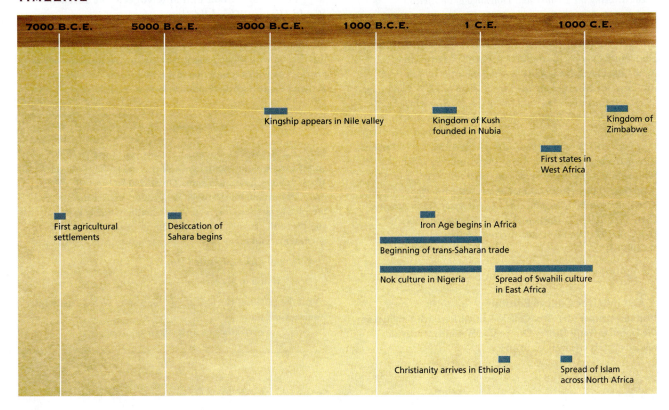

| 7000 B.C.E. | 5000 B.C.E. | 3000 B.C.E. | 1000 B.C.E. | 1 C.E. | 1000 C.E. |

Kingship appears in Nile valley

Kingdom of Kush founded in Nubia

Kingdom of Zimbabwe

First states in West Africa

First agricultural settlements

Desiccation of Sahara begins

Iron Age begins in Africa

Beginning of trans-Saharan trade

Nok culture in Nigeria

Spread of Swahili culture in East Africa

Christianity arrives in Ethiopia

Spread of Islam across North Africa

CHAPTER NOTES

1. S. Hamdun and N. King, eds., *Ibn Battuta in Africa* (London, 1975), p. 19.
2. *The Book of Duarte Barbosa* (Nedeln, Liechtenstein, 1967), p. 28.
3. Herodotus, *The Histories,* trans. A. de Sélincourt (Baltimore, 1964), p. 307.
4. Quoted in M. Shinnie, *Ancient African Kingdoms* (London, 1965), p. 60.
5. C. R. Boxer, ed., *The Tragic History of the Sea, 1589–1622* (Cambridge, 1959), pp. 121–122.
6. Quoted in D. Nurse and T. Spear, *The Swahili: Reconstructing the History and Language of an African Society 800–1500* (Philadelphia, 1985), p. 84.
7. Hamdun and King, *Ibn Battuta in Africa,* p. 47.
8. Ibid., p. 28.
9. Ibid., pp. 28–30.

SUGGESTED READING

In few areas of world history is scholarship advancing as rapidly as in African history. New information is constantly forcing archaeologists and historians to revise their assumptions about the early history of the continent. Standard texts therefore quickly become out-of-date as their conclusions are supplanted by new evidence.

Still, there are several worthwhile general surveys that provide a useful overview of the early period of African history. The dean of African historians, and certainly one of the most readable, is **B. Davidson.** For a sympathetic portrayal of the African people, see his *African History* (New York, 1968) and *Lost Cities in Africa,* rev. ed. (Boston, 1970). Other respected accounts are **R. Oliver** and

J. D. Fage, *A Short History of Africa* (Middlesex, England, 1986), and **V. B. Khapoya,** *The African Experience: An Introduction* (Englewood Cliffs, N.J., 1994). For a readable treatment incorporating fairly recent evidence, see **K. Shillington,** *History of Africa* (New York, 1989). **R. O. Collins,** ed., *Problems in African History: The Precolonial Centuries* (New York, 1993), provides a useful collection of scholarly articles on key issues in precolonial Africa.

Specialized studies are beginning to appear with frequency on many areas of the continent. For a popular account of archaeological finds, see **B. Fagan,** *New Treasures of the Past: Fresh Finds That Deepen Our Understanding of the Archaeology of Man* (Leicester, England, 1987). For a more detailed treatment of the early period, see the multi-volume *General History of Africa,* sponsored by UNESCO (Berkeley, Calif., 1998). **R. O. Collins** has provided a useful service with his *African History in Documents* (Princeton, N.J., 1990). **C. Ehret,** *An African Classical Age: Eastern and Southern Africa in World History, 1000 B.C. to 400 A.D.* (Charlottesville, Va., 1998), applies historical linguistics to make up for the lack of documentary evidence in the precolonial era. **J. D. Clarke** and **S. A. Brandt,** eds., *From Hunters to Farmers* (Berkeley, Calif., 1984), takes an economic approach. Also see **D. A. Welsby,** *The Kingdom of Kush: The Napataean Meroitic Empire* (London, 1996), and **J. Middleton,** *Swahili: An African Mercantile Civilization* (New Haven, Conn., 1992). For a fascinating account of trans-Saharan trade, see **E. W. Bovill,** *The Golden Trade of the Moors: West African Kingdoms in the Fourteenth Century,* 2d ed. (Princeton, N.J., 1995). On the cultural background, see **R. Olaniyan,** ed., *African History and Culture* (Lagos, Nigeria, 1982), and **J. Vansina,** *Paths in the Rainforest: Toward a History of Political Tradition in Equatorial Africa* (Madison, Wis., 1990). Although there exist many editions of *The Epic of Son-Jara,* based on recitations of different bards, the most conclusive edition is by **F. D. Sisòkò,** translated and annotated by **J. W. Johnson** (Bloomington, Ind., 1992).

On East Africa, see **D. Nurse** and **T. Spear**, *The Swahili: Reconstituting the History and Language of an African Society, 800–1500* (Philadelphia, 1985). The maritime story is recounted with documents in **G. S. P. Freeman-Grenville**, *The East African Coast: Select Documents from the First to the Earlier Nineteenth Century* (Oxford, 1962). For the larger picture, see **K. N. Chaudhuri**, *Trade and Civilization in the Indian Ocean: An Economic History from the Rise of Islam to 1750* (Cambridge, 1985). On the early history of Ethiopia, see **S. Burstein**, ed., *Ancient African Civilizations: Kush and Axum* (Princeton, N.J., 1998).

For useful general surveys of southern Africa, see **N. Parsons**, *A New History of Southern Africa* (New York, 1983), and **K. Shillington**, *A History of Southern Africa* (Essex, England, 1987), a profusely illustrated account. For an excellent introduction to African art, see **M. B. Visond** et al., *A History of Art in Africa* (New York, 2001); **R. Hackett**, *Art and Religion in Africa* (London, 1996); and **F. Willet**, *African Art,* rev. ed. (New York, 1993).

InfoTrac College Edition

Visit this chapter's InfoTrac College Edition/Research activities at the *Essential World History* Companion Website for activities related to early civilizations in Africa.

CENGAGENOW **for Duiker and Spielvogel's** *The Essential World History, Third Edition*

Enter *CengageNOW* using the access card that is available with this text. *CengageNOW* will assist you in understanding the content in this chapter with lesson plans generated for your needs, as well as provide you with a connection to the *Wadsworth World History Resource Center* (see description below for details).

WORLD HISTORY RESOURCE CENTER

Enter the Resource Center using either your *CengageNOW* access card or your standalone access card for the *Wadsworth World History Resource Center*. Organized by topic, this website includes quizzes; images; over 350 primary source documents; interactive simulations, maps, and timelines; movie explorations; and a wealth of other resources. You can read the following documents, and many more, at http://worldrc.wadsworth.com/

    An African Creation Story

    Hymn to Mawari

Visit the *Essential World History* Companion Website for chapter quizzes and more.

    academic.cengage.com/history/duiker

THE EXPANSION OF CIVILIZATION IN SOUTHERN ASIA

One of the two massive carved statues of the Buddha formerly at Bamiyan

CHAPTER OUTLINE AND FOCUS QUESTIONS

The Silk Road

▢ What were some of the chief destinations along the Silk Road, and what kinds of products and ideas traveled along the route?

India After the Mauryas

▢ How did Buddhism change in the centuries after Siddhartha Gautama's death, and why did the religion ultimately decline in popularity in India?

The Arrival of Islam

▢ How did Islam arrive in the Indian subcontinent, and why were Muslim peoples able to establish states here?

Society and Culture

▢ What impact did Muslim rule have on Indian society? To what degree did the indigenous population convert to the new religion, and why?

▢ What are some of the most important cultural achievements of Indian civilization in the era between the Mauryas and Mughals?

The Golden Region: Early Southeast Asia

▢ What were the main characteristics of Southeast Asian social and economic life, culture, and religion before 1500 C.E.?

CRITICAL THINKING

▢ New religions had a significant impact on the social and cultural life of peoples living in southern Asia during the period covered in this chapter. What factors caused the spread of these religions in the first place? What changes occurred as a result of the introduction of these new faiths? Were the religions themselves affected by their spread into new regions of Asia?

WHILE TRAVELING from his native China to India along the Silk Road in the early fifth century C.E., the Buddhist monk Fa Xian stopped en route at a town called Bamiyan, a rest stop located deep in the mountains of what is today known as Afghanistan. At that time, Bamiyan was a major center of Buddhist studies, with dozens of temples and monasteries filled with students, all overlooked by two giant standing statues of the Buddha hewn directly out of the side of a massive cliff. Fa Xian was thrilled at the sight. "The law of Buddha," he remarked with satisfaction in his account of the experience, "is progressing and flourishing." He then continued southward to India, where he spent several years visiting Buddhists throughout the country. Because little of the literature from that period survives, Fa Xian's observations are a valuable resource for our knowledge of the daily lives of the Indian people.

The India that Fa Xian visited was no longer the unified land it had been under the Mauryan dynasty. The overthrow of the Mauryas in the early second century B.C.E. had been followed by several hundred years of disunity, when the subcontinent was divided into a number of separate kingdoms and principalities. The dominant force in the north

191

was the Kushan state, established by Indo-European-speaking peoples who had been driven out of what is now China's Xinjiang province by the Xiongnu (see Chapter 3). The Kushans penetrated into the mountains north of the Indus River, where they eventually formed a kingdom with its capital at Bactria, not far from modern Kabul. Over the next two centuries, the Kushans expanded their supremacy along the Indus River and into the central Ganges valley.

Meanwhile, to the south, a number of kingdoms arose among the Dravidian-speaking peoples of the Deccan Plateau, which had been only partly under Mauryan rule. The most famous of these kingdoms was Chola (sometimes spelled Cola) on the southeastern coast. Chola developed into a major trading power and sent merchant fleets eastward across the Bay of Bengal, where they introduced Indian culture as well as Indian goods to the peoples of Southeast Asia. In the fourth century C.E., Chola was overthrown by the Pallavas, who ruled from their capital at Kanchipuram (known today as Kanchi), just southwest of modern Chennai (Madras), for the next four hundred years. ◆

The Silk Road

The Kushan kingdom, with its power base beyond the Khyber Pass in modern Afghanistan, became the dominant political force in northern India in the centuries immediately after the fall of the Mauryas. Sitting astride the main trade routes across the northern half of the subcontinent, the Kushans thrived on the commerce that passed through the area (see Map 9.1). The bulk of that trade was between the Roman Empire and China and was transported along the route known as the Silk Road, one segment of which passed through the mountains northwest of India (see Chapter 10). From there, goods were shipped to Rome through the Persian Gulf or the Red Sea.

Trade between India and Europe had begun even before the rise of the Roman Empire, but it expanded rapidly in the first century C.E., when sailors mastered the pattern of the monsoon winds in the Indian Ocean (from the southwest in the summer and the northeast in the winter). Commerce between the Mediterranean and the Indian Ocean, as described in the *Periplus*, a first-century C.E. account by a Greek participant, was extensive and often profitable, and it resulted in the establishment of several small trading settlements along the Indian coast. Rome imported ivory, indigo, textiles, precious stones, and pepper from India and silk from China. The Romans sometimes paid cash for these goods but also exported silver, wine, perfume, slaves, and glass and cloth from Egypt. Overall, Rome appears to have imported much more than it sold to the Far East, leading Emperor Tiberius to grumble that "the ladies and their baubles are transferring our money to foreigners."

The Silk Road was a conduit not only of material goods but also of technology and of ideas. The first Indian monks

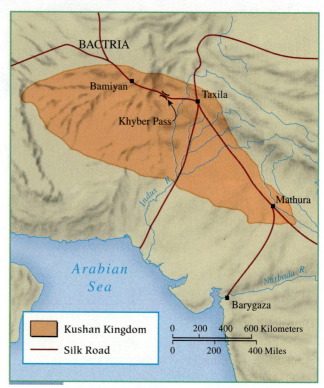

MAP 9.1 The Kushan Kingdom and the Silk Road. After the collapse of the Mauryan Empire, a new state formed by recent migrants from the north arose north of the Indus River valley. For the next four centuries, the Kushan kingdom played a major role in regional trade via the Silk Road until it declined in the third century C.E. ❓ What were the major products shipped along the Silk Road? Which countries beyond the borders of this map took an active part in trade along the Silk Road?

to visit China may have traveled over the road during the second century C.E. By the time of Fa Xian, Buddhist monks from China were beginning to arrive in increasing numbers to visit holy sites in India. The exchange of visits not only enriched the study of Buddhism in the two countries but also led to a fruitful exchange of ideas and technological advances in the realms of astronomy, mathematics, and linguistics. According to one scholar, the importation of Buddhist writings from India encouraged the development of printing in China, while the Chinese obtained lessons in health care from monks returned from the Asian subcontinent.

Indeed, the emergence of the Kushan kingdom as a major commercial power was due not only to its role as an intermediary in the Rome-China trade but also to the rising popularity of Buddhism. During the second century C.E., Kanishka, the greatest of the Kushan monarchs, began to patronize Buddhism. Under Kanishka and his successors, an intimate and mutually beneficial relationship was established between Buddhist monasteries and the local merchant community in thriving urban centers like Taxila and Varanasi. Merchants were eager to build stupas and donate money to monasteries in return for social prestige

COMPARATIVE ILLUSTRATION

Portrayals of the Buddha. By their sheer size, the two towering Buddhas cut out of a mountain cliff in Afghanistan expressed the builder's perception of the Buddha as encompassing the entire universe. Their purpose was to attract monks and merchants along the Silk Road and to spread the wisdom and compassion of the Buddha. For over a millennium, the extensive cave complex, which contained over a thousand frescoes and statues of various sizes, was a major religious center in Central Asia. The statues were painted and gilded, as in ancient Greece. The drapery on the 175-foot statue on the left reflects the fusion of cultural influences from several regions along the Silk Road, combining Chinese, Indian, Persian, and Greco-Roman styles. The influence of the Bamiyan style soon spread eastward, as is shown by the sixth-century statue of a standing Buddha, from a site in eastern China, on the right. Tragically, in 2001, Muslim extremists destroyed the two large Buddhist statues at Bamiyan, along with all other shrines in the vicinity, decrying them as "idols of the gods of the infidels."

and the implied promise of a better life in this world or the hereafter.

For their part, the wealthy monasteries ceased to be simple communities where monks could find a refuge from the material cares of the world; instead they became major consumers of luxury goods provided by their affluent patrons. Monasteries and their inhabitants became increasingly involved in the economic life of society, and Buddhist architecture began to be richly decorated with precious stones and glass purchased from local merchants

or imported from abroad. The process was very similar to the changes that would occur in the Christian church in medieval Europe.

It was from the Kushan kingdom that Buddhism began its long journey across the wastes of Central Asia to China and other societies in eastern Asia. As trade between the two regions increased, merchants and missionaries flowed from Bactria over the trade routes snaking through the mountains toward the northeast. At various stopping points on the trail, pilgrims erected statues and

THE GOOD LIFE IN MEDIEVAL INDIA

INTERACTION & EXCHANGE

Much of what we know about life in medieval India comes from the accounts of Chinese missionaries who visited the subcontinent in search of documents recording the teachings of the Buddha. Here the Buddhist monk Fa Xian, who spent several years there in the fifth century c.e., reports on conditions in the kingdom of Mathura (Mo-tu-lo), a vassal state in western India that was part of the Gupta Empire. Although he could not have been pleased that the Gupta monarchs in India had adopted the Hindu faith, he found that the people were contented and prosperous except for the untouchables, whom he called Chandalas.

To what degree do the practices described here appear to conform to the principles established by Siddhartha Gautama in his own teachings? Would political advisers such as Kautilya and the Chinese philosopher Mencius have approved of governmental policies?

Fa Xian, *The Travels of Fa Xian*

Going southeast from this somewhat less than 80 *joyanas,* we passed very many temples one after another, with some myriad of priests in them. Having passed these places, we arrived at a certain country. This country is called Mo-tu-lo. Once more we followed the Pu-na river. On the sides of the river, both right and left, are twenty *sangharamas,* with perhaps 3,000 priests. The law of Buddha is progressing and flourishing. Beyond the deserts are the countries of western India. The kings of these countries are all firm believers in the law of Buddha. They remove their caps of state when they make offerings to the priests. The members of the royal household and the chief ministers personally direct the food giving; when the distribution of food is over, they spread a carpet on the ground opposite the chief seat (the president's seat) and sit down before it. They dare not sit on couches in the presence of the priests. The rules relating to the almsgiving of kings have been handed down from the time of Buddha till now. Southward from this is the so-called middle country (Madhyadesa). The climate of this country is warm and equable, without frost or snow. The people are very well off, without poll tax or official restrictions. Only those who till the royal lands return a portion of profit of the land. If they desire to go, they go; if they like to stop, they stop. The kings govern without corporal punishment; criminals are fined, according to circumstances, lightly or heavily. Even in cases of repeated rebellion they only cut off the right hand. The king's personal attendants, who guard him on the right and left, have fixed salaries. Throughout the country the people kill no living thing nor drink wine, nor do they eat garlic or onions, with the exception of Chandalas only. The Chandalas are named "evil men" and dwell apart from others; if they enter a town or market, they sound a piece of wood in order to separate themselves; then men, knowing who they are, avoid coming in contact with them. In this country they do not keep swine nor fowls, and do not deal in cattle; they have no shambles [slaughterhouses] or wine shops in their marketplaces. In selling they use cowrie shells. The Chandalas only hunt and sell flesh.

CENGAGENOW To read more about Fa Xian's travels, enter the *CengageNOW* documents area using the access card that is available for *The Essential World History.*

---

decorated mountain caves with magnificent frescoes depicting the life of the Buddha and his message to his followers. One of the most prominent of these centers was at Bamiyan, not far from modern-day Kabul, where believers carved two mammoth statues of the Buddha out of a sheer sandstone cliff. According to the Chinese pilgrim Fa Xian (see the box above), when he visited the area in 400 C.E., over a thousand monks were attending a religious ceremony at the site.

India After the Mauryas

The Kushan kingdom came to an end under uncertain conditions sometime in the third century C.E. In 320, a new state was established in the central Ganges valley by a local raja named Chandragupta (no relation to Chandragupta Maurya, the founder of the Mauryan dynasty). Chandragupta located his capital at Pataliputra, the site of the now decaying palace of the Mauryas. Under his successor Samudragupta, the territory under Gupta rule was extended into surrounding areas, and eventually the new kingdom became the dominant political force throughout northern India. It also established a loose suzerainty over the state of Pallava to the south, thus becoming the greatest state in the subcontinent since the decline of the Mauryan Empire. Under a succession of powerful, efficient, and highly cultured monarchs, notably Samudragupta and Chandragupta II, India enjoyed a new "classical age" of civilization (see Map 9.2).

The Gupta Dynasty: A New Golden Age?

Historians of India have traditionally viewed the Gupta era as a time of prosperity and thriving commerce with China, Southeast Asia, and the Mediterranean. Great cities, notable for their temples and Buddhist monasteries as well as for their economic prosperity, rose along the main trade routes throughout the subcontinent. The religious trade also prospered, as pilgrims from across

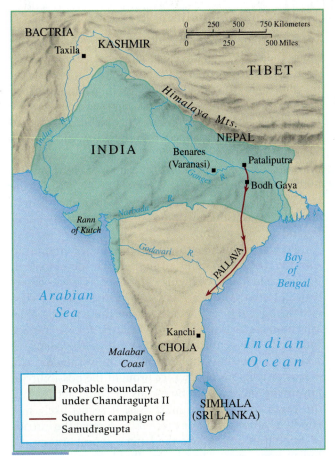

MAP 9.2 **The Gupta Empire.** This map shows the extent of the Gupta Empire, the only major state to arise in the Indian subcontinent during the first millennium C.E. The arrow indicates the military campaign into southern India led by King Samudragupta. **?** How did the Gupta Empire differ in territorial extent from its great predecessor, the Mauryan Empire? **🌐** **View an animated version of this map or related maps at** http://worldrc.wadsworth.com/

India and as far away as China came to visit the major religious centers.

As in the Mauryan Empire, much of the trade in the Gupta Empire was managed or regulated by the government. The Guptas owned mines and vast crown lands and earned massive profits from their commercial dealings. But there was also a large private sector, dominated by great *jati* (caste) guilds that monopolized key sectors of the economy. A money economy had probably been in operation since the second century B.C.E., when copper and gold coins had been introduced from the Middle East. This in turn led to the development of banking. Nevertheless, there are indications that the circulation of coins was limited. The Chinese missionary Xuan Zang, who visited India early in the seventh century, remarked that most commercial transactions were conducted by barter.[1]

But the good fortunes of the Guptas proved to be relatively short-lived. Beginning in the late fifth century

C.E., incursions by nomadic warriors from the northwest gradually reduced the power of the empire. Soon northern India was once more divided into myriad small kingdoms engaged in seemingly constant conflict.

The Transformation of Buddhism

The Chinese pilgrims who traveled to India during the Gupta era found a Buddhism that had changed in a number of ways in the centuries since the time of Siddhartha Gautama. They also found a doctrine that was beginning to decline in popularity in the face of the rise of Hinduism.

The transformation in Buddhism had come about in part because the earliest written sources were transcribed two centuries after Siddhartha's death and in part because his message was reinterpreted as it became part of the everyday life of the people. Abstract concepts of a Nirvana that cannot be described began to be replaced, at least in the popular mind, with more concrete visions of heavenly salvation, and Siddhartha was increasingly regarded as a divinity rather than as a sage. The Buddha's teachings that all four classes were equal gave way to the familiar Brahmanic conviction that some people, by reason of previous reincarnations, were closer to Nirvana than others.

Theravada These developments led to a split in the movement. Purists emphasized what they insisted were the original teachings of the Buddha (describing themselves as the school of **Theravada,** or "the teachings of the elders"). Followers of Theravada considered Buddhism a way of life, not a salvationist creed. Theravada stressed the importance of strict adherence to personal behavior and the quest for understanding as a means of release from the wheel of life.

Mahayana In the meantime, another interpretation of Buddhist doctrine was emerging in the northwest. Here Buddhist believers, perhaps hoping to compete with other salvationist faiths circulating in the region, began to promote the view that Nirvana could be achieved through devotion and not just through painstaking attention to one's behavior. According to advocates of this school, eventually to be known as **Mahayana** ("greater vehicle"), Theravada teachings were too demanding or too strict for ordinary people to follow and therefore favored the wealthy, who were more apt to have the time and resources to spend weeks or months away from their everyday occupations. Mahayana Buddhists referred to their rivals as **Hinayana,** or "lesser vehicle," because in Theravada fewer would reach enlightenment. Mahayana thus attempted to provide hope for the masses in their efforts to reach Nirvana, but to the followers of Theravada, it did so at the expense of an insistence on proper behavior.

To advocates of the Mahayana school, salvation could also come from the intercession of a **bodhisattva** ("he who possesses the essence of Buddhahood"). According to Mahayana beliefs, some individuals who had achieved bodhi and were thus eligible to enter the state of Nirvana after death chose instead, because of their great compassion, to remain on earth in spirit form to help all human beings achieve release from the life cycle. Followers of Theravada, who believed the concept of bodhisattva applied only to Siddhartha Gautama himself, denounced such ideas as "the teaching of demons." But to their proponents, such ideas extended the hope of salvation to the masses. Mahayana Buddhists revered the saintly individuals who, according to tradition, had become bodhisattvas at death and erected temples in their honor where the local population could pray and render offerings.

A final distinguishing characteristic of Mahayana Buddhism was its reinterpretation of Buddhism as a religion rather than as a philosophy. Although Mahayana had philosophical aspects, its adherents increasingly regarded the Buddha as a divine figure, and an elaborate Buddhist cosmology developed. Nirvana was not a form of extinction but a true heaven.

Under Kushan rule, Mahayana achieved considerable popularity in northern India and for a while even made inroads in such Theravada strongholds as the island of Sri Lanka. But in the end, neither Mahayana nor Theravada was able to retain its popularity in Indian society. By the seventh century C.E., Theravada had declined rapidly on the subcontinent, although it retained its foothold in Sri Lanka and across the Bay of Bengal in Southeast Asia, where it remained an influential force to modern times. Mahayana prospered in the northwest for centuries, but eventually it was supplanted by a revived Hinduism and later by a new arrival, Islam. But Mahayana too would find better fortunes abroad, as it was carried over the Silk Road or by sea to China and then to Korea and Japan (see Chapters 10 and 11). In all three countries, Buddhism has coexisted with Confucian doctrine and indigenous beliefs to the present.

The Decline of Buddhism in India

Why was Buddhism unable to retain its popularity in its native India, although it became a major force elsewhere in Asia? Some have speculated that in denying the existence of the soul, Buddhism ran counter to traditional Indian belief. Perhaps, too, one of Buddhism's strengths was also a weakness. In rejecting the class divisions that defined the Indian way of life, Buddhism appealed to those very groups who lacked an accepted place in Indian society, such as the untouchables. But at the same time, it represented a threat to those with a higher status. Moreover, by emphasizing the responsibility of each person to seek an individual path to Nirvana, Buddhism undermined the strong social bonds of the Indian class system.

Perhaps a final factor in the decline of Buddhism was the rise of Hinduism. In its early development, Brahminism had been highly elitist. Not only was observance of court ritual a monopoly of the *brahmin* class (see the box on p. 197), but the major route to individual salvation, asceticism, was hardly realistic for the average Indian. In the centuries after the fall of the Mauryas, however, a growing emphasis on devotion (**bhakti**) as a means of religious observance brought the possibility of improving one's *karma* by means of ritual acts within the reach of Indians of all classes. It seems likely that Hindu devotionalism rose precisely to combat the inroads of Buddhism and reduce the latter's appeal among the Indian population. The Chinese Buddhist missionary Fa Xian, who visited India in the mid-Gupta era, reported that mutual hostility between the Buddhists and the *brahmins* was quite strong:

> Leaving the southern gate of the capital city, on the east side of the road is a place where Buddha once dwelt. Whilst here he bit [a piece from] the willow stick and fixed it in the earth; immediately it grew up seven feet high, neither more nor less. The unbelievers and Brahmans, filled with jealousy, cut it down and scattered the leaves far and wide, but yet it always sprang up again in the same place as before.[2]

For a while, Buddhism was probably able to stave off the Hindu challenge by its own salvationist creed of Mahayana, which also emphasized the role of devotion, but the days of Buddhism as a dominant faith in the subcontinent were numbered.

The Arrival of Islam

While India was still undergoing a transition after the collapse of the Gupta Empire, a new and dynamic force in the form of Islam was arising in the Arabian peninsula to the west. As we have seen, during the seventh and eighth centuries, Arab armies carried the new faith westward to the Iberian peninsula and eastward across the arid wastelands of Persia and into the rugged mountains of the Hindu Kush. Islam first reached India through the Arabs in the eighth century, but a second onslaught in the tenth

THE EDUCATION OF A *BRAHMIN*

RELIGION & PHILOSOPHY

Although the seventh-century Chinese traveler Xuan Zang was a Buddhist, he faithfully recorded his impressions of the Hindu religion in his memoirs. Here he describes the education of a brahmin, the highest class in Indian society.

How would you compare the educational practices described here with the training provided to young men in other traditional societies in Europe, Asia, and the Americas? What is distinctive, if anything, about the educational system in India?

Xuan Zang, *Records of Western Countries*

The Brahmans study the four *Veda Sastras*. The first is called *Shau* [longevity]; it relates to the preservation of life and the regulation of the natural condition. The second is called *Sse* [sacrifice]; it relates to the [rules of] sacrifice and prayer. The third is called *Ping* [peace or regulation]; it relates to decorum, casting of lots, military affairs, and army regulations. The fourth is called *Shue* [secret mysteries]; it relates to various branches of science, incantations, medicine.

The teachers [of these works] must themselves have closely studied the deep and secret principles they contain, and penetrated to their remotest meaning. They then explain their general sense, and guide their pupils in understanding the words that are difficult. They urge them on and skillfully conduct them. They add luster to their poor knowledge, and stimulate the desponding. If they find that their pupils are satisfied with their acquirements, and so wish to escape to attend to their worldly duties, then they use means to keep them in their power. When they have finished their education, and have attained thirty years of age, then their character is formed and their knowledge ripe. When they have secured an occupation they first of all thank their master for his attention. There are some, deeply versed in antiquity, who devote themselves to elegant studies, and live apart from the world, and retain the simplicity of their character. These rise above mundane presents, and are as insensible to renown as to the contempt of the world. Their name having spread afar, the rulers appreciate them highly, but are unable to draw them to the court. The chief of the country honors them on account of their [mental] gifts, and the people exalt their fame and render them universal homage. . . . They search for wisdom, relying on their own resources. Although they are possessed of large wealth, yet they will wander here and there to seek their subsistence. There are others who, whilst attaching value to letters, will yet without shame consume their fortunes in wandering about for pleasure, neglecting their duties. They squander their substance in costly food and clothing. Having no virtuous principle, and no desire to study, they are brought to disgrace, and their infamy is widely circulated.

CENGAGENOW To read more about the travels of Xuan Zang, enter the *CengageNOW* documents area using the access card that is available for *The Essential World History*.

---

and eleventh centuries by Turkic-speaking converts had a more lasting effect (see Map 9.3).

Although Arab merchants had been active along the Indian coasts for centuries, Arab armies did not reach India until the early eighth century. When Indian pirates attacked Arab shipping near the delta of the Indus River, the Muslim ruler in Iraq demanded an apology from the ruler of Sind, a Hindu state in the Indus valley. When the latter refused, Muslim forces conquered lower Sind in 711 and then moved northward into the Punjab, bringing Arab rule into the frontier regions of the subcontinent for the first time.

The Empire of Mahmud of Ghazni

For the next three centuries, Islam made no further advances into India. But a second phase began at the end of the tenth century with the rise of the state of Ghazni, located in the area of the old Kushan kingdom in present-day Afghanistan. The new kingdom was founded in 962 when Turkic-speaking slaves seized power from the Samanids, a Persian dynasty. When the founder of the new state died in 997, his son, Mahmud of Ghazni (997–1030), succeeded him. Brilliant and ambitious, Mahmud used his patrimony as a base of operations for sporadic forays against neighboring Hindu kingdoms to the southeast. Before his death in 1030, he was able to extend his rule throughout the upper Indus valley and as far south as the Indian Ocean (see Map 9.4). In wealth and cultural brilliance, his court at Ghazni rivaled that of the Abbasid dynasty in neighboring Baghdad. But his achievements had a dark side. Describing Mahmud's conquests in northwestern India, the contemporary historian al-Biruni wrote:

> Mahmud utterly ruined the prosperity of the country, and performed wonderful exploits by which the Hindus became like atoms scattered in all directions, and like a tale of old in the mouth of the people. Their scattered remains cherish, of course, the most inveterate aversion towards all Muslims. This is the reason, too, why Hindu sciences have retired far away from those parts of the country conquered by us, and have fled to places which our hand cannot yet reach, to Kashmir, Benares, and other places.[3]

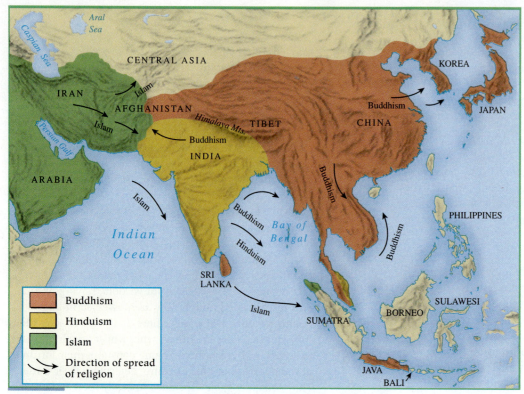

MAP 9.3 **The Spread of Religions in Southern and Eastern Asia, 600–1900 C.E.**
Between 600 and 1900 C.E., three of the world's great religions—Buddhism,
Hinduism, and Islam—continued to spread from their original sources to different
parts of Southern and Eastern Asia. **?** Which religion had the greatest impact?
How might the existence of major trade routes help explain the spread of
these religions?

Resistance against the advances of Mahmud and his successors into northern India was led by the Rajputs, aristocratic Hindu clans who were probably descended from tribal groups that had penetrated into northwestern India from Central Asia in earlier centuries. The Rajputs possessed a strong military tradition and fought bravely, but their military tactics, based on infantry supported by elephants, were no match for the fearsome cavalry of the invaders, whose ability to strike with lightning speed contrasted sharply with the slow-footed forces of their adversaries. Although the power of Ghazni declined after Mahmud's death, a successor state in the area resumed the advance in the late twelfth century, and by 1200, Muslim power, in the form of a new Delhi sultanate, had been extended over the entire plain of northern India.

The Delhi Sultanate

South of the Ganges River valley, Muslim influence spread more slowly and in fact had little immediate impact. Muslim armies launched occasional forays into the Deccan Plateau, but at first, they had little success, even though the area was divided among a number of

warring kingdoms, including the Cholas along the eastern coast and the Pandyas far to the south.

One reason the Delhi sultanate failed to take advantage of the disarray of its rivals was the threat posed by the Mongols on the northwestern frontier (see Chapter 10). Mongol armies unleashed by the great tribal warrior Genghis Khan occupied Baghdad and destroyed the Abbasid caliphate in the 1250s, while other forces occupied the Punjab around Lahore, from which they threatened Delhi on several occasions. For the next half-century, the attention of the sultanate was focused on the Mongols. That threat finally declined in the early fourteenth century with the gradual breakup of the Mongol Empire, and a new Islamic state emerged in the form of a new Tughluq dynasty (1320–1413), which extended its power into the Deccan Plateau. In praise of his sovereign, the Tughluq monarch Ala-ud-din, the poet Amir Khusrau exclaimed:

Happy be Hindustan, with its splendor of religion,
Where Islamic law enjoys perfect honor and dignity;
In learning Delhi now rivals Bukhara;
Islam has been made manifest by the rulers.
From Ghazni to the very shore of the ocean
You see Islam in its glory.[4]

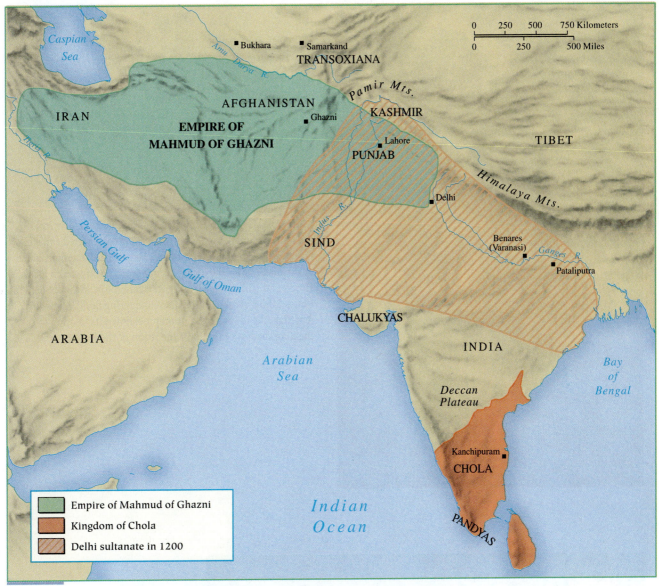

MAP 9.4 **India, 1000–1200.** Beginning in the tenth century, Turkic-speaking peoples invaded northwestern India and introduced Islam to the peoples in the area. Most famous was the empire of Mahmud of Ghazni. ❓ Locate the major trade routes passing through the area. What geographic features explain the location of those routes?

Such happiness was not destined to endure, however. During the latter half of the fourteenth century, the Tughluq dynasty gradually fell into decline. In 1398, a new military force crossed the Indus River from the northwest, raided the capital of Delhi, and then withdrew. According to some contemporary historians, as many as 100,000 Hindu prisoners were massacred before the gates of the city. Such was India's first encounter with Tamerlane.

Tamerlane

Tamerlane (b. 1330s), also known as Timur-i-lang (Timur the Lame), was the ruler of a Mongol khanate based in Samarkand to the north of the Pamir Mountains. His kingdom had been founded on the ruins of the Mongol Empire, which had begun to disintegrate as a result of succession struggles in the thirteenth century. Tamerlane, the son of a local aristocrat, seized power in Samarkand in 1369 and immediately launched a program of conquest. During the 1380s, he brought the entire region east of the Caspian Sea under his authority and then conquered Baghdad and occupied Mesopotamia (see Map 9.5). After his brief foray into northern India, he turned to the west and raided the Anatolian peninsula. Defeating the army of the Ottoman Turks, he advanced almost as far as the Bosporus before withdrawing. "The last of the great nomadic conquerors," as one recent historian described him, died in 1405 in the midst of a final military campaign.

Kutub Minar. To commemorate their religious victory in 1192, the Muslim conquerors of northern India constructed a magnificent mosque on the site of Delhi's largest Hindu temple. Much of the material for the mosque came from twenty-seven local Hindu and Jain shrines (right). Adjacent to the mosque soars the Kutub Minar, symbol of the new conquering faith. Originally 238 feet high, the tower's inscription proclaimed its mission to cast the long shadow of God over the realm of the Hindus.

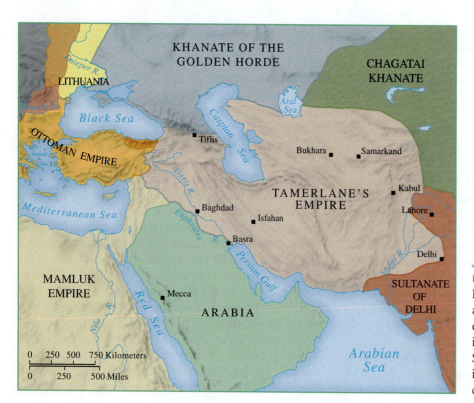

MAP 9.5 **The Empire of Tamerlane.** In the fourteenth century, Tamerlane, a feared conqueror of Mongolian extraction, established a brief empire in Central Asia with his capital at Samarkand. **?** Which of the states in this map were part of Muslim civilization?

Samarkand, Gem of an Empire. The city of Samarkand has a long history. Originating during the first millennium B.C.E. as a caravan stop on the Silk Road, it was later occupied by Alexander the Great, the Abbasids, and the Mongols before becoming the capital of Tamerlane's expanding empire. Tamerlane expended great sums in creating a city worthy of his own imperial ambitions. Shown here is the great square, known as the Registan. Site of a mosque, a library, and a Muslim university, all built in the exuberant Persian style, Samarkand was the jumping-off point for trade with China far to the east.

The passing of Tamerlane removed a major menace from the diverse states of the Indian subcontinent. But the respite from external challenge was not a long one. By the end of the fifteenth century, two new challenges had appeared from beyond the horizon: the Mughals, a newly emerging nomadic power beyond the Khyber Pass in the north, and the Portuguese traders, who arrived by sea from the eastern coast of Africa in search of gold and spices. Both, in different ways, would exert a major impact on the later course of Indian civilization.

Society and Culture

The establishment of Muslim rule over the northern parts of the subcontinent had a significant impact on the society and culture of the Indian people.

Religion

Like their counterparts in other areas that came under Islamic rule, many Muslim rulers in India were relatively tolerant of other faiths and used peaceful means, if any, to encourage nonbelievers to convert to Islam. Even the more enlightened, however, could be fierce when their religious zeal was aroused. One ruler, on being informed that a Hindu fair had been held near Delhi, ordered the promoters of the event put to death. Hindu temples were razed, and mosques were erected in their place. Eventually, however, most Muslim rulers realized that not all Hindus could be converted and recognized the necessity of accepting what to them was an alien and repugnant

religion. While Hindu religious practices were generally tolerated, non-Muslims were compelled to pay a tax to the state. Some Hindus likely converted to Islam to avoid paying the tax, but they were then expected to make the traditional charitable contribution required of Muslims in all Islamic societies.

Over time, millions of Hindus did turn to the Muslim faith. Some were individuals or groups in the employ of the Muslim ruling class, such as government officials, artisans, or merchants catering to the needs of the court. But many others were probably peasants from the *sudra* class or even untouchables who found in the egalitarian message of Islam a way of removing the stigma of low-class status in the Hindu social hierarchy.

Seldom have two major religions been so strikingly different. Whereas Hinduism tolerated a belief in the existence of several deities (although admittedly they were all considered by some to be manifestations of one supreme god), Islam was uncompromisingly monotheistic. Whereas Hinduism was hierarchical, Islam was egalitarian. Whereas Hinduism featured a priestly class to serve as an intermediary with the ultimate force of the universe, Islam permitted no one to come between believers and their god. Such differences contributed to the mutual hostility that developed between the adherents of the two faiths in the Indian subcontinent, but more mundane issues, such as the Muslim habit of eating beef and the idolatry and sexual frankness in Hindu art, were probably a greater source of antagonism at the popular level (see the box on p. 202).

In other cases, the two peoples borrowed from each other. Some Muslim rulers found the Indian idea of

THE ISLAMIC CONQUEST OF INDIA

INTERACTION & EXCHANGE

One consequence of the Muslim conquest of northern India was the imposition of many Islamic customs on Hindu society. In this excerpt, the fourteenth-century Muslim historian Zia-ud-din Barani describes the attempt of one Muslim ruler, Ala-ud-din, to prevent the use of alcohol and gambling, two practices expressly forbidden in Muslim society. Ala-ud-din had seized power in Delhi from a rival in 1294.

The ruler described here is a Muslim, establishing regulations for moral behavior in a predominantly Hindu society. Based on information available to you in Chapter 8, was a similar approach often adopted by Muslim rulers in African societies?

A Muslim Ruler Suppresses Hindu Practices

He forbade wine, beer, and intoxicating drugs to be used or sold; dicing, too, was prohibited. Vintners and beer sellers were turned out of the city, and the heavy taxes which had been levied from them were abolished. All the china and glass vessels of the Sultan's banqueting room were broken and thrown outside the gate of Badaun, where they formed a mound. Jars and casks of wine were emptied out there till they made mire as if it were the season of the rains. The Sultan himself entirely gave up wine parties. Self-respecting people at once followed his example; but the ne'er-do-wells went on making wine and spirits and hid the leather bottles in loads of hay or firewood and by various such tricks smuggled it into the city. Inspectors and gatekeepers and spies diligently sought to seize the contraband and the smugglers; and when seized the wine was given to the elephants, and the importers and sellers and drinkers [were] flogged and given short terms of imprisonment. So many were they, however, that holes had to be dug for their incarceration outside the great thoroughfare of the Badaun gate, and many of the wine bibbers died from the rigor of their confinement and others were taken out half-dead and were long in recovering their health. The terror of these holes deterred many from drinking. Those who could not give it up had to journey ten or twelve leagues to get a drink, for at half that distance, four or five leagues from Delhi, wine could not be publicly sold or drunk. The prevention of drinking proving very difficult, the Sultan enacted that people might distill and drink privately in their own homes, if drinking parties were not held and the liquor not sold. After the prohibition of drinking, conspiracies diminished.

divine kingship appealing. In their turn, Hindu rajas learned by bitter experience the superiority of cavalry mounted on horses instead of elephants, the primary assault weapon in early India. Some upper-class Hindu males were attracted to the Muslim tradition of **purdah** and began to keep their women in seclusion (termed locally "behind the curtain") from everyday society. Hindu sources claimed that one reason for adopting the custom was to protect Hindu women from the roving eyes of foreigners. But it is likely that many Indian families adopted the practice for reasons of prestige or because they were convinced that *purdah* was a practical means of protecting female virtue.

All in all, Muslim rule probably did not have a significant impact on the lives of most Indian women (see the comparative essay "Caste, Class, and Family" on p. 203). *Purdah* was more commonly practiced among the higher classes than among the lower classes. Though it was probably of little consolation, sexual relations in poor and low-class families were relatively egalitarian, as men and women worked together on press gangs or in the fields. Muslim customs apparently had little effect on the Hindu tradition of *sati*. In fact, in many respects, Muslim women had more rights than their Hindu counterparts. They had more property rights than Hindu women and were legally permitted to divorce under certain conditions and to remarry after the death of their husband. The primary role for Indian women in general, however, was to produce children. Sons were preferred over daughters, not only because they alone could conduct ancestral rites but also because a daughter was a financial liability. A father had to provide a costly dowry for a daughter when she married, yet after the wedding, she would transfer her labor assets to her husband's family. Still, women shared with men a position in the Indian religious pantheon. The Hindu female deity, known as Devi, was celebrated by both men and women as the source of cosmic power, bestower of wishes, and symbol of fertility.

Overall the Muslims continued to view themselves as foreign conquerors and generally maintained a strict separation between the Muslim ruling class and the mass of the Hindu population. Although a few Hindus rose to important positions in the local bureaucracy, most high posts in the central government and the provinces were reserved for Muslims. Only with the founding of the Mughal dynasty was a serious effort undertaken to reconcile the differences.

One result of this effort was the religion of the Sikhs ("disciples"). Founded by the guru Nanak in the early sixteenth century in the Punjab, **Sikhism** attempted to integrate the best of the two faiths in a single religion. Sikhism originated in the devotionalist movement in Hinduism, which taught that God was the single true reality. All else is illusion. But Nanak rejected the Hindu

CASTE, CLASS, AND FAMILY

FAMILY & SOCIETY

Why have men and women played such different roles throughout human history? Why have some societies historically adopted the nuclear family, while others preferred the joint family or the clan? Such questions are controversial and often subject to vigorous debate, yet they are crucial to our understanding of the human experience.

As we know, the first human beings practiced hunting and foraging, living in small bands composed of one or more lineage groups and moving from place to place in search of sustenance. Individual members of the community were assigned different economic and social roles—usually with men as the hunters and women as the food gatherers—but such roles were not rigidly defined. The concept of private property did not exist, and all members shared the goods possessed by the community according to need.

The agricultural revolution brought about dramatic changes in human social organizations. Although women, as food gatherers, may have been the first farmers, men—now increasingly deprived of their traditional role as hunters—began to replace them in the fields. As communities gradually adopted a sedentary lifestyle, women were increasingly assigned to domestic tasks in the home while raising the children. As farming communities grew in size and prosperity, vocational specialization and the concept of private property appeared, leading to the family as a legal entity and the emergence of a class system composed of elites, commoners, and slaves. Women were deemed inferior to men and placed in a subordinate status.

This trend toward job specialization and a rigid class system was less developed in pastoral societies, some of which still practiced a nomadic style of life and shared communal goods on a roughly equal basis within the community. Even within sedentary societies, there was considerable variety in the nature of social organizations. In some areas, the nuclear family consisted of parents and their dependent children. Other societies, however, adopted (either in theory or in practice) the idea of the joint family (ideally consisting of three generations of a family living under one roof) and sometimes even going a step further, linking several families under the larger grouping of the caste or the clan. Prominent examples of the latter tendency include India and China, although the degree to which such concepts conformed to reality is a matter of debate.

Such large social organizations, where they occurred, often established a rigid hierarchy of status within the community, including the subordination of women. On the other hand, they sometimes played a useful role in society, providing a safety net or a ladder of upward mobility for disadvantaged members of the group, as well as a form of stability in societies where legitimate and effective authority at the central level was lacking.

---

tradition of asceticism and mortification of the flesh and, like Muhammad, taught his disciples to participate in the world. Sikhism achieved considerable popularity in northwestern India, where Islam and Hinduism confronted each other directly, and eventually evolved into a militant faith that fiercely protected its adherents against its two larger rivals. In the end, Sikhism did not reconcile Hinduism and Islam but provided an alternative to them.

One complication for both Muslims and Hindus as they tried to come to terms with the existence of a mixed society was the problem of class and caste. Could non-Hindus form castes, and if so, how were they related to the Hindu castes? Where did the Turkic-speaking elites who made up the ruling class in many of the Islamic states fit into the equation?

The problem was resolved in a pragmatic manner that probably followed an earlier tradition of assimilating non-Hindu tribal groups into the system. Members of the Turkic ruling groups formed social groups that were roughly equivalent to the Hindu *brahmin* or *kshatriya* class. Ordinary Indians who converted to Islam also formed Muslim castes, although at a lower level on the social scale. Many who did so were probably artisans who converted en masse to obtain the privileges that conversion could bring.

In most of India, then, Muslim rule did not substantially disrupt the class and caste systems. One perceptive European visitor in the early sixteenth century reported that in Malabar, along the southwestern coast, there were separate castes for fishing, pottery making, weaving, carpentry and metalworking, salt mining, sorcery, and labor on the plantations. There were separate castes for doing the laundry, one for the elite and the other for the common people.

Economy and Daily Life

India's landed and commercial elites lived in the cities, often in conditions of considerable opulence. The rulers, of course, possessed the most wealth. One maharaja of a relatively small state in southern India, for example, had over 100,000 soldiers in his pay along with nine hundred elephants and twenty thousand horses. Another maintained a thousand high-class women to serve as sweepers of his palace. Each carried a broom and a brass basin containing a mixture of cow dung and water and followed him from one house to another, plastering the path where he was to tread. Most urban dwellers, of course, did not live in such style. Xuan Zang, the Chinese Buddhist missionary, left us a description of ordinary homes in a seventh-century urban area:

> Their houses are surrounded by low walls, and form the suburbs. The earth being soft and muddy, the walls of the towns are mostly built of brick or tiles. The towers on the walls are constructed of wood or bamboo; the houses have balconies and belvederes, which are made of wood, with a coating of lime or mortar, and covered with tiles. The different buildings have the same form as those in China; rushes, or dry branches, or tiles, or boards are used for covering them. The walls are covered with lime and mud, mixed with cow's dung for purity. At different seasons they scatter flowers about. Such are some of their different customs.[5]

Agriculture   The majority of India's population (estimated at slightly more than 100 million in the first millennium C.E.), however, lived on the land. Most were peasants who tilled small plots with a wooden plow pulled by oxen and paid a percentage of the harvest to their landlord. The landlord in turn forwarded part of the payment to the local ruler. In effect, the landlord functioned as a tax collector for the king, who retained ultimate ownership of all farmland in his domain. At best, most peasants lived at the subsistence level. At worst, they were forced into debt and fell victim to moneylenders who charged exorbitant rates of interest.

In the north and in the upland regions of the Deccan Plateau, the primary grain crops were wheat and barley. In the Ganges valley and the southern coastal plains, the main crop was rice. Vegetables were grown everywhere, and southern India produced many spices, fruits, sugarcane, and cotton. The cotton plant apparently originated in the Indus River valley and spread from there. Although some cotton was cultivated in Spain and North Africa by the eighth and ninth centuries, India remained the primary producer of cotton goods. Spices such as cinnamon, pepper, ginger, sandalwood, cardamom, and cumin were also major export products.

Foreign Trade   Agriculture, of course, was not the only source of wealth in India. Since ancient times, the subcontinent had served as a major entrepôt for trade between the Middle East and the Pacific basin, as well as the source of other goods shipped throughout the known world. Although civil strife and piracy, heavy taxation of the business community by local rulers to finance their fratricidal wars, and increased customs duties between principalities may have contributed to a decline in internal trade, the level of foreign trade remained high, particularly in the kingdoms in the south and along the northwestern coast, which were located along the traditional trade routes to the Middle East and the Mediterranean Sea. Much of this foreign trade was carried on by wealthy Hindu castes with close ties to the royal courts. But there were other participants as well, including such non-Hindu minorities as the Muslims, the Parsis, and the Jain community. The Parsis, expatriates from Persia who practiced the Zoroastrian religion, dominated banking and the textile industry in the cities bordering the Rann of Kutch. Later they would become a dominant economic force in the modern city of Mumbai (Bombay). The Jains became prominent in trade and manufacturing even though their faith emphasized simplicity and the rejection of materialism.

According to early European travelers, merchants often lived quite well. One Portuguese observer described the "Moorish" population in Bengal as follows:

> They have girdles of cloth, and over them silk scarves; they carry in their girdles daggers garnished with silver and gold, according to the rank of the person who carries them; on their fingers many rings set with rich jewels, and cotton turbans on their heads. They are luxurious, eat well and spend freely, and have many other extravagances as well. They bathe often in great tanks which they have in their houses. Everyone has three or four wives or as many as he can maintain. They keep them carefully shut up, and treat them very well, giving them great store of gold, silver and apparel of fine silk.[6]

Outside these relatively small, specialized trading communities, most manufacturing and commerce were in the hands of petty traders and artisans, who were generally limited to local markets. This failure to build on the promise of antiquity has led some historians to ask why India failed to produce an expansion of commerce and growth of cities similar to the developments that began in Europe during the High Middle Ages or even in China during the Song dynasty (see Chapter 10). Some have pointed to the traditionally low status of artisans and merchants in Indian society, symbolized by the comment in the *Arthasastra* that merchants were "thieves that are not called by the name of thief."[7] Yet commercial activities were frowned on in many areas in Europe throughout the Middle Ages, a fact that did not prevent the emergence of capitalist societies in much of the West.

Another factor may have been the monopoly on foreign trade held by the government in many areas of India. More important, perhaps, was the impact of the class and caste system, which reduced the ability of entrepreneurs to expand their activities and have dealings with other members of the commercial and manufacturing community. Successful artisans, for example, normally could not set up as merchants to market their products, nor could merchants compete for buyers outside their normal area of operations. The complex interlocking relationships among the various classes in a given region were a powerful factor inhibiting the development of a thriving commercial sector in medieval India.

The Wonder of Indian Culture

The era between the Mauryas and the Mughals in India was a period of cultural evolution as Indian writers and artists built on the literary and artistic achievements of their predecessors. This is not to say, however, that Indian

Courtesy of William J. Duiker

© Werner Forman/Art Resource, NY

ARTS & IDEAS

COMPARATIVE ILLUSTRATION

Rock Architecture. Along with the caves at Ajanta, one of the greatest examples of Indian rock architecture remains the eighth-century temple at Ellora, in central India, shown on the left. Named after Shiva's holy mountain in the Himalayas, the temple is approximately the size of the Parthenon in Athens but was literally carved out of a hillside. The builders dug nearly 100 feet straight down into the top of the mountain to isolate a single block of rock, removing over 3 million cubic feet of stone in the process. Unlike earlier rock-cut shrines, which had been constructed in the form of caves, the Ellora temple is open to the sky and filled with some of India's finest sculpture. The overall impression is one of massive grandeur.

This form of architecture also found expression in parts of Africa. In 1200 C.E., Christian monks in Ethiopia began to construct a remarkable series of eleven churches carved out of solid volcanic rock (right). After a 40-foot trench was formed by removing the bedrock, the central block of stone was hewed into the shape of a Greek cross; then it was hollowed out and decorated. These churches, which are still in use today, testify to the fervor of Ethiopian Christianity, which plays a major role in preserving the country's cultural and national identity.

culture rested on its ancient laurels. To the contrary, it was an era of tremendous innovation in all fields of creative endeavor.

Art and Architecture At the end of antiquity, the primary forms of religious architecture were the Buddhist cave temples and monasteries. The next millennium witnessed the evolution of religious architecture from underground cavity to monumental structure.

The twenty-eight caves of Ajanta in the Deccan Plateau are one of India's greatest artistic achievements. They are as impressive for their sculpture and painting as for their architecture. Except for a few examples from the second century B.C.E., most of the caves were carved out of solid rock over an incredibly short period of eighteen years, from 460 to 478 C.E. (see the comparative illustration above). In contrast to the early unadorned temple halls, these temples were exuberantly decorated with ornate pillars, friezes, beamed ceilings, and statues of the Buddha and bodhisattvas. Several caves served as monasteries, which by then had been transformed from simple

holes in the wall to large complexes with living apartments, halls, and shrines to the Buddha.

All of the inner surfaces of the caves, including the ceilings, sculptures, walls, door frames, and pillars, were painted in vivid colors. Perhaps best known are the wall paintings, which illustrate the various lives and incarnations of the Buddha. Similar rock paintings focusing on secular subjects can be found at Sigiriya, a fifth-century royal palace on the island of Sri Lanka.

Among the most impressive rock carvings in southern India are the cave temples at Mamallapuram (also known as Mahabalipuram), south of the modern city of Madras. The sculpture, called *Descent of the Ganges River*, depicts the role played by Shiva in intercepting the heavenly waters of the Ganges and allowing them to fall gently on the earth. Mamallapuram also boasts an eighth-century shore temple, which is one of the earliest surviving freestanding structures in the subcontinent.

From the eighth century until the time of the Mughals, Indian architects built a multitude of magnificent Hindu temples, now constructed exclusively above ground. Each temple consisted of a central shrine surmounted by a sizable tower, a hall for worshipers, a vestibule, and a porch, all set in a rectangular courtyard that might also contain other minor shrines. Temples became progressively more ornate until the eleventh century, when the sculpture began to dominate the structure itself. The towers became higher and the temple complexes more intricate, some becoming virtual walled compounds set one within the other and resembling a town in themselves.

The greatest example of medieval Hindu temple art is probably Khajuraho. Of the original eighty-five temples, dating from the tenth century, twenty-five remain standing today. All of the towers are buttressed at various levels on the sides, giving the whole a sense of unity and creating a vertical movement similar to Mount Kailasa in the Himalayas, sacred to Hindus. Everywhere the viewer is entertained by voluptuous temple dancers bringing life to the massive structures. One is removing a thorn from her foot, another is applying eye makeup, and yet another is wringing out her hair.

Literature   During this period, Indian authors produced a prodigious number of written works, both religious and secular. Indian religious poetry was written in Sanskrit and also in the languages of southern India. As Hinduism was transformed from a contemplative to a more devotional religion, its poetry became more ardent and erotic and prompted a sense of divine ecstasy. Much of the religious verse extolled the lives and heroic acts of Shiva, Vishnu, Rama, and Krishna by repeating the same themes over and over, which is also a characteristic of Indian art. In the eighth century, a tradition of poet-saints inspired by intense mystical devotion to a deity emerged in southern India. Many were women who sought to escape the drudgery of domestic toil through an imagined sexual union with the god-lover. Such was the case for the twelfth-century mystic whose poem here expresses her sensuous joy in the physical-mystical union with her god:

> It was like a stream
> running into the dry bed
> of a lake,
> like rain pouring on plants
> parched to sticks.
> It was like this world's pleasure
> and the way to the other,
> both walking towards me.
> Seeing the feet of the master,
> O lord white as jasmine
> I was made worthwhile.[8]

The great secular literature of traditional India was also written in Sanskrit in the form of poetry, drama, and prose. Some of the best medieval Indian poetry is found in single-stanza poems, which create an entire emotional scene in just four lines. Witness this poem by the poet Amaru:

> We'll see what comes of it, I thought,
>   and I hardened my heart against her.

> What, won't the villain speak to me? she
>   thought, flying into a rage.
> And there we stood, sedulously refusing to look one
>   another in the face,
> Until at last I managed an unconvincing laugh,
>   and her tears robbed me of my resolution.[9]

One of India's most famous authors was Kalidasa, who lived during the Gupta dynasty. Although little is known of him, including his dates, he probably wrote for the court of Chandragupta II (375–415 C.E.). Even today, Kalidasa's hundred-verse poem, *The Cloud Messenger*, remains one of the most popular Sanskrit poems.

In addition to being a poet, Kalidasa was also a great dramatist. He wrote three plays, all dramatic romances that blend the erotic with the heroic and the comic. *Shakuntala*, perhaps the best-known play in all Indian literature, tells the story of a king who, while out hunting, falls in love with the maiden Shakuntala. He asks her to marry him and offers her a ring of betrothal but is suddenly recalled to his kingdom on urgent business. Shakuntala, who is pregnant, goes to him, but the king has been cursed by a hermit and no longer recognizes her. With the help of the gods, the king eventually does recall their love and is reunited with Shakuntala and their son.

Like poetry, prose developed in India from the Vedic period. The use of prose was well established by the sixth and seventh centuries C.E. This is truly astonishing considering that the novel did not appear until the tenth century in Japan and until the seventeenth century in Europe.

One of the greatest masters of Sanskrit prose was Dandin, who lived during the seventh century. In *The Ten Princes*, he created a fantastic and exciting world that fuses history and fiction. His keen powers of observation, details of low life, and humor give his writing considerable vitality.

Music   Another area of Indian creativity that developed during this era was music. Ancient Indian music had come from the chanting of the Vedic hymns and thus inevitably had a strong metaphysical and spiritual flavor. The actual physical vibrations of music (*nada*) were considered to be related to the spiritual world. An off-key or sloppy rendition of a sacred text could upset the harmony and balance of the entire universe.

In form, Indian classical music is based on a scale, called a **raga**. There are dozens, if not hundreds, of separate scales, which are grouped into separate categories depending on the time of day during which they are to be performed. The performers use a stringed instrument called a *sitar* and various types of wind instruments and drums. The performers select a basic *raga* and then are free to improvise the melodic structure and rhythm. A good performer never performs a particular *raga* the same way twice. As with jazz music in the West, the audience is concerned not so much with faithful reproduction as with the performer's creativity.

The Golden Region: Early Southeast Asia

Between China and India lies the region that today is called Southeast Asia. It has two major components: a mainland region extending southward from the Chinese border down to the tip of the Malayan peninsula and an extensive archipelago, most of which is part of present-day Indonesia and the Philippines. Travel between the islands and regions to the west, north, and east was not difficult, so Southeast Asia has historically served as a vast land bridge for the movement of peoples between China, the Indian subcontinent, and the more than 25,000 islands of the South Pacific.

Mainland Southeast Asia consists of several north-south mountain ranges, separated by river valleys that run in a southerly or southeasterly direction. Between the sixth and the thirteenth centuries C.E., two groups of migrants—the Thai from southwestern China and the Burmese from the Tibetan highlands—came down these valleys in search of new homelands, as earlier peoples had done before them. Once in Southeast Asia, most of these migrants settled in the fertile deltas of the rivers—the Irrawaddy and the Salween in Burma, the Chao Phraya in Thailand, and the Red River and the Mekong in Vietnam—or in lowland areas in the islands to the south.

Although the river valleys facilitated north-south travel on the Southeast Asian mainland, movement between east and west was relatively difficult. The mountains are densely forested and often infested with malaria-carrying mosquitoes. Consequently, the lowland peoples in the river valleys were often isolated from each other and had only limited contacts with the upland peoples in the mountains. These geographic barriers may help explain why Southeast Asia is one of the few regions in Asia that was never unified under a single government.

Given Southeast Asia's location between China and India, it is not surprising that both civilizations influenced developments in the region. In 111 B.C.E., Vietnam was conquered by the Han dynasty and remained under Chinese control for more than a millennium (see Chapter 11). The Indian states never exerted much political control over Southeast Asia, but their influence was pervasive nevertheless. By the first centuries C.E., Indian merchants were sailing to Southeast Asia; they were soon followed by Buddhist and Hindu missionaries. Indian influence can be seen in many aspects of Southeast Asian culture, from political institutions to religion, architecture, language, and literature.

Paddy Fields and Spices: The States of Southeast Asia

The traditional states of Southeast Asia can generally be divided between agricultural societies and trading societies. The distinction between farming and trade

MAP 9.6 **Southeast Asia in the Thirteenth Century.** This map indicates the major states that arose in Southeast Asia in the early second millennium C.E. Some, like Angkor and Dai Viet, were predominantly agricultural. Others, like Srivijaya and Champa, were commercial. [?] Which of these empires were soon to disappear? Why?

was a product of the environment. The agricultural societies—notably, Vietnam, Angkor in what is now Cambodia, and the Burmese state of Pagan—were situated in rich river deltas that were conducive to the development of a wet rice economy (see Map 9.6). Although all produced some goods for regional markets, none was tempted to turn to commerce as the prime source of national income. In fact, none was situated astride the main trade routes that crisscrossed the region.

The Mainland States The kingdom of Angkor, which took shape in the ninth century, was the most powerful state to emerge in mainland Southeast Asia before the sixteenth century. The remains of its capital city, Angkor Thom, give a sense of the magnificence of Angkor civilization. The city formed a square 2 miles on each side. Its massive stone walls were several feet thick

THE KINGDOM OF ANGKOR

INTERACTION & EXCHANGE

Angkor (known to the Chinese as Chen-la) was the greatest kingdom of its time in Southeast Asia. This passage was probably written in the thirteenth century by Chau Ju-kua, an inspector of foreign trade in the city of Quanzhou (sometimes called Zayton) on the southern coast of China. His account, compiled from reports of seafarers, includes a brief description of the capital city, Angkor Thom, which is still one of the great archaeological sites of the region. Angkor was already in decline when Chau Ju-kua described the kingdom, and the capital was abandoned soon afterward, in 1432.

Because of the paucity of written records about Angkor society, documents such as this one by a Chinese source are important in providing knowledge about local conditions. What does this excerpt tell us about the political system, religious belief, and land use in thirteenth-century Angkor?

Chau Ju-kua, *Records of Foreign Nations*

The officials and the common people dwell in houses with sides of bamboo matting and thatched with reeds. Only the king resides in a palace of hewn stone. It has a granite lotus pond of extraordinary beauty with golden bridges, some three hundred odd feet long. The palace buildings are solidly built and richly ornamented. The throne on which the king sits is made of gharu wood and the seven precious substances; the dais is jewelled, with supports of veined wood [ebony?]; the screen [behind the throne] is of ivory.

When all the ministers of state have audience, they first make three full prostrations at the foot of the throne; they then kneel and remain thus, with hands crossed on their breasts, in a circle round the king, and discuss the affairs of state. When they have finished, they make another prostration and retire. . . .

[The people] are devout Buddhists. There are serving [in the temples] some three hundred foreign women; they dance and offer food to the Buddha. They are called *a-nan* or slave dancing girls.

As to their customs, lewdness is not considered criminal; theft is punished by cutting off a hand and a foot and by branding on the chest.

The incantations of the Buddhist and Taoist priests [of this country] have magical powers. Among the former those who wear yellow robes may marry, while those who dress in red lead ascetic lives in temples. The Taoists clothe themselves with leaves; they have a deity called P'o-to-li which they worship with great devotion.

[The people of this country] hold the right hand to be clean, the left unclean, so when they wish to mix their rice with any kind of meat broth, they use the right hand to do so and also to eat with.

The soil is rich and loamy; the fields have no bounds. Each one takes as much as he can cultivate. Rice and cereals are cheap; for every tael of lead one can buy two bushels of rice.

The native products comprise elephants' tusks, the *chan* and *su* [varieties of gharu wood], good yellow wax, kingfisher's feathers, . . . resin, foreign oils, ginger peel, gold-colored incense, . . . raw silk and cotton fabrics.

The foreign traders offer in exchange for these gold, silver, porcelainware, sugar, preserves, and vinegar.

Angkor

and were surrounded by a moat. Four main gates led into the city, which at its height had a substantial population (see the box above). By the fourteenth century, however, Angkor had begun to decline, and in 1432, Angkor Thom was destroyed by the Thai, who had migrated into the region from southwestern China in the thirteenth century and established their capital at Ayuthaya, in lower Thailand, in 1351.

The Malay World   In the Malayan peninsula and the Indonesian archipelago, a different pattern emerged. For centuries, this area had been linked to regional trade networks, and much of its wealth had come from the export of tropical products to China, India, and the Middle East. The vast majority of the inhabitants of the region were of Malay ethnic stock, a people who spread from their original homeland in southeastern China into island Southeast Asia and even to more distant locations in the South Pacific, such as Tahiti, Hawaii, and Easter Island.

Eventually, the islands of the Indonesian archipelago gave rise to two of the region's most notable trading societies—Srivijaya and Majapahit. Both were based in large part on spices. As the wealth of the Arab Empire in the Middle East and then of western Europe increased, so did the demand for the products of East Asia. Merchant fleets from India and the Arabian peninsula sailed to the Indonesian islands to buy cloves, pepper, nutmeg, cinnamon, precious woods, and other exotic products coveted by the wealthy. In the eighth century, Srivijaya, located along the eastern coast of Sumatra, became a powerful commercial state that dominated the trade route passing through the Strait of Malacca, at that time the most convenient route from East Asia into the Indian Ocean. The rulers of Srivijaya had helped bring

Chinese conquest of Vietnam	111 B.C.E.
Arrival of Burmese peoples	c. seventh century
Formation of Srivijaya	c. 670
Construction of Borobudur	c. eighth century
Creation of Angkor kingdom	c. ninth century
Thai migrations into Southeast Asia	c. thirteenth century
Rise of Majapahit empire	1292
Fall of Angkor kingdom	1432

the route to prominence by controlling the pirates who had previously plagued shipping in the strait. Another inducement was Srivijaya's capital at Palembang, a deep-water port where sailors could wait out the change in the monsoon season before making their return voyage. In 1025, however, Chola, one of the kingdoms of southern India and a commercial rival of Srivijaya, inflicted a devastating defeat on the island kingdom. Although Srivijaya survived, it was unable to regain its former dominance, in part because the main trade route had shifted to the east, through the Strait of Sunda and directly out into the Indian Ocean. In the late thirteenth century, this shift in trade patterns led to the founding of a new kingdom of Majapahit on the island of Java. In the mid-fourteenth century, Majapahit succeeded in uniting most of the archipelago and perhaps even part of the Southeast Asian mainland under its rule.

The Role of India

Indian influence was evident in all of these societies to various degrees. Based on models from the kingdoms of southern India, Southeast Asian kings were believed to possess special godlike qualities that set them apart from ordinary people. In some societies such as Angkor, the most prominent royal advisers constituted a *brahmin* class on the Indian model. In Pagan and Angkor, some division of the population into separate classes based on occupation and ethnic background seems to have occurred, although these divisions do not seem to have developed the rigidity of the Indian class system.

India also supplied Southeast Asians with a writing system. The societies of the region had no written scripts for their spoken languages before the arrival of the Indian merchants and missionaries. Indian phonetic symbols were borrowed and used to record the spoken language. Initially, Southeast Asian literature was written in the Indian Sanskrit but eventually came to be written in the local languages. Southeast Asian authors borrowed popular Indian themes, such as stories from the Buddhist scriptures and tales from the Ramayana.

A popular form of entertainment among the common people, the **wayang kulit,** or shadow play, may have come originally from India or possibly China, but it became a distinctive art form in Java and other islands of the Indonesian archipelago. In a shadow play, flat leather puppets were manipulated behind an illuminated screen while the narrator recited tales from the Indian classics. The plays were often accompanied by gamelan, a type of music performed by an orchestra composed primarily of percussion instruments such as gongs and drums that apparently originated in Java.

Daily Life

Because of the diversity of ethnic backgrounds, religions, and cultures, making generalizations about daily life in Southeast Asia during the early historical period is difficult. Nevertheless, it appears that Southeast Asian societies did not always apply the social distinctions that were sometimes imported from India.

Social Structures

Still, traditional societies in Southeast Asia had some clearly hierarchical characteristics. At the top of the social ladder were the hereditary aristocrats, who monopolized both political power and economic wealth and enjoyed a borrowed aura of charisma by virtue of their proximity to the ruler. Most aristocrats lived in the major cities, which were the main source of power, wealth, and foreign influence. Beyond the major cities lived the mass of the population, composed of farmers, fishers, artisans, and merchants. In most Southeast Asian societies, the vast majority were probably rice farmers, living at a bare level of subsistence and paying heavy rents or taxes to a landlord or a local ruler.

The average Southeast Asian peasant was not actively engaged in commerce except as a consumer of various necessities. But accounts by foreign visitors indicate that in the Malay world, some were involved in growing or mining products for export, such as tropical food products, precious woods, tin, and precious gems. Most of the regional trade was carried on by local merchants, who purchased products from local growers and then transported them to the major port cities. During the early state-building era, roads were few and relatively primitive, so most of the trade was transported by small boats down rivers to the major ports along the coast. There the goods were loaded onto larger ships for delivery outside the region. Growers of export goods in areas near the coast were thus indirectly involved in the regional trade network but received few economic benefits from the relationship.

As we might expect from an area of such ethnic and cultural diversity, social structures differed significantly from country to country. In the Indianized states on the mainland, the tradition of a hereditary tribal aristocracy was probably accentuated by the Hindu practice of dividing the population into separate classes, called *varna* in imitation of the Indian model. In Angkor and Pagan, for example, the divisions were based on occupation or ethnic background. Some people were considered free subjects of the king, although there may have been legal restrictions against changing occupations. Others, however, may have been indentured to an employer. Each community was under a chieftain, who in turn was subordinated to a higher official responsible for passing on the tax revenues of each group to the central government.

In the kingdoms in the Malayan peninsula and the Indonesian archipelago, social relations were generally less formal. Most of the people in the region, whether farmers, fishers, or artisans, lived in small *kampongs* (Malay for "villages") in wooden houses built on stilts to avoid flooding during the monsoon season. Some of the farmers were probably sharecroppers who paid a part of their harvest to a landlord, who was often a member of the aristocracy. But in other areas, the tradition of free farming was strong.

Women and the Family   The women of Southeast Asia during this era have been described as the most fortunate in the world. Although most women worked side by side with men in the fields, as in Africa they often played an active role in trading activities. Not only did this lead to a higher literacy rate among women than among their male counterparts, but it also allowed them more financial independence than their counterparts in China and India, a fact that was noticed by the Chinese traveler Zhou Daguan at the end of the thirteenth century: "In Cambodia it is the women who take charge of trade. For this reason a Chinese arriving in the country loses no time in getting himself a mate, for he will find her commercial instincts a great asset."[10]

Although, as elsewhere, warfare was normally part of the male domain, women sometimes played a role as bodyguards as well. According to Zhou Daguan, women were used to protect the royal family in Angkor, as well as in kingdoms located on the islands of Java and Sumatra. Though there is no evidence that such female units ever engaged in battle, they did give rise to wondrous tales of amazon warriors in the writings of foreign travelers such as the fourteenth-century Muslim adventurer Ibn Battuta.

One reason for the enhanced status of women in traditional Southeast Asia is that the nuclear family was more common than the joint family system prevalent in China and the Indian subcontinent. Throughout the region, wealth in marriage was passed from the male to the female, in contrast to the dowry system applied in China and India. In most societies, virginity was usually not a valued commodity in brokering a marriage, and divorce proceedings could be initiated by either party. Still, most marriages were monogamous, and marital fidelity was taken seriously.

The relative availability of cultivable land in the region may help explain the absence of joint families. Joint families under patriarchal leadership tend to be found in areas where land is scarce and individual families must work together to conserve resources and maximize income. With the exception of a few crowded river valleys, few areas in Southeast Asia had a high population density per acre of cultivable land. Throughout most of the area, water was plentiful, and the land was relatively fertile. In parts of Indonesia, it was possible to survive by living off the produce of wild fruit trees—bananas, coconuts, mangoes, and a variety of other tropical fruits.

World of the Spirits: Religious Belief

Indian religions also had a profound effect on Southeast Asia. Traditional religious beliefs in the region took the familiar form of spirit worship and animism that we have seen in other cultures. Southeast Asians believed that spirits dwelled in the mountains, rivers, streams, and other sacred places in their environment. Mountains were probably particularly sacred, since they were considered to be the abode of ancestral spirits, the place to which the souls of all the departed would retire after death.

When Hindu and Buddhist ideas began to penetrate the area early in the first millennium C.E., they exerted a strong appeal among local elites. Not only did the new doctrines offer a more convincing explanation of the nature of the cosmos, but they also provided local rulers with a means of enhancing their prestige and power and conferred an aura of legitimacy on their relations with their subjects. In Angkor, the king's duties included performing sacred rituals on the mountain in the capital city; in time, the ritual became a state cult uniting Hindu gods with local nature deities and ancestral spirits in a complex pantheon.

This state cult, financed by the royal court, eventually led to the construction of temples throughout the country. Many of these temples housed thousands of priests and retainers and amassed great wealth, including vast estates farmed by local peasants. It has been estimated that there were as many as 300,000 priests in Angkor at the height of its power. This vast wealth, which was often exempt from taxes, may be one explanation for the gradual decline of Angkor in the thirteenth and fourteenth centuries.

Initially, the spread of Hindu and Buddhist doctrines took place mostly among the elite. Although the common people participated in the state cult and helped construct the temples, they did not give up their traditional beliefs in local deities and ancestral spirits. A major transformation began in the eleventh century, however, when Theravada Buddhism began to penetrate the kingdom of Pagan in mainland Southeast Asia from the island of Sri Lanka. From Pagan, it spread rapidly to other areas in Southeast Asia and eventually became the religion of the masses throughout the mainland west of the Annamite Mountains.

Theravada's appeal to the peoples of Southeast Asia is reminiscent of the original attraction of Buddhist thought centuries earlier on the Indian subcontinent. By teaching that individuals could seek Nirvana through their own actions rather than through the intercession of the ruler or a priest, Theravada was more accessible to the masses than the state cults promoted by the rulers. During the

Angkor Wat. The Khmer rulers of Angkor constructed a number of remarkable temples and palaces. Devised as either Hindu or Buddhist shrines, the temples also reflected the power and sanctity of the king. This twelfth-century temple known as Angkor Wat is renowned both for its spectacular architecture and for the thousands of fine bas-reliefs relating Hindu legends and Khmer history. Most memorable are the heavenly dancing maidens and the royal processions with elephants and soldiers.

next centuries, Theravada gradually undermined the influence of state-supported religions and became the dominant faith in several mainland societies, including Burma, Thailand, Laos, and Cambodia.

Theravada did not penetrate far into the Malayan peninsula or the Indonesian island chain, perhaps because it entered Southeast Asia through Burma farther to the north. But the Malay world found its own popular alternative to state religions when Islam began to enter the area in the thirteenth and fourteenth centuries. Because Islam's expansion into Southeast Asia took place for the most part after 1500, its emergence as a major force in the region will be discussed in a later chapter.

Not surprisingly, Indian influence extended to the Buddhist and Hindu temples of Southeast Asia. Temple architecture reflecting Gupta or southern Indian styles began to appear in Southeast Asia during the first centuries C.E. Most famous is the Buddhist temple at Borobudur, in central Java. Begun in the late eighth cen-

tury at the behest of a king of Sailendra (an agricultural kingdom based in eastern Java), Borobudur is a massive stupa with nine terraces. Sculpted on the sides of each terrace are bas-reliefs depicting the nine stages in the life of Siddhartha Gautama, from childhood to his final release from the chain of human existence. Surmounted by hollow bell-like towers containing representations of the Buddha and capped by a single stupa, the structure dominates the landscape for miles around.

Second only to Borobudur in technical excellence and even more massive in size are the ruins of the old capital city of Angkor Thom. The temple of Angkor Wat is the most famous and arguably the most beautiful of all the existing structures at Angkor Thom. Built on the model of the legendary Mount Meru (the home of the gods in Hindu tradition), it combines Indian architectural techniques with native inspiration in a structure of impressive delicacy and grace. In existence for more than six hundred years, Angkor Wat serves as a bridge between the Hindu and Buddhist architectural styles.

The Temple of Borobudur.   The colossal pyramid temple at Borobudur, on the island of Java, is one of the greatest Buddhist monuments. Constructed in the eighth century, it depicts the path to spiritual enlightenment in stone. Sculptures and relief portrayals of the life of the Buddha at the lower level depict the world of desire. At higher elevations, they give way to empty bell towers (see inset) and culminate at the summit with an empty and closed stupa, signifying the state of Nirvana. Shortly after it was built, Borobudur was abandoned as a new ruler switched his allegiance to Hinduism and ordered the erection of the Hindu temple of Prambanan nearby. Buried for a thousand years under volcanic ash and jungle, Borobudur was rediscovered in the nineteenth century and has recently been restored to its former splendor.

CONCLUSION

DURING THE MORE THAN fifteen hundred years from the fall of the Mauryas to the rise of the Mughals, Indian civilization faced a number of severe challenges. One challenge was primarily external and took the form of a continuous threat from beyond the mountains in the northwest. A second was generated by internal causes and stemmed from the tradition of factionalism and internal rivalry that had marked relations within the aristocracy since the Aryan invasion in the second millennium B.C.E. (see Chapter 2). Despite the abortive efforts of the Guptas, that tradition continued almost without interruption down to the founding of the Mughal Empire in the sixteenth century.

The third challenge was primarily cultural and appeared in the religious divisions between Hindus and Buddhists, and later between Hindus and Muslims, that took place throughout much of this period. It is a measure of the strength and resilience of

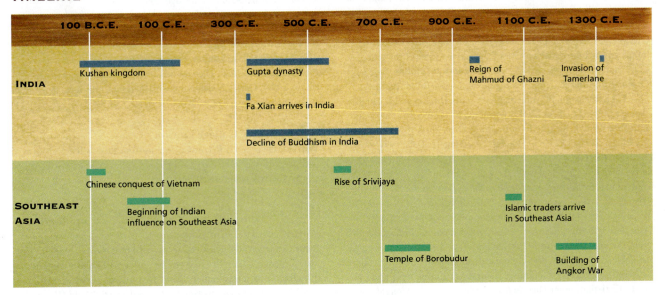

Hindu tradition that it was able to surmount the challenge of Buddhism and by the late first millennium C.E. reassert its dominant position in Indian society. But that triumph was short-lived. Like so many other areas in the region of southern Asia, by 1000 C.E., it was beset by a new challenge presented by nomadic forces from Central Asia. One result of the foreign conquest of northern India was the introduction of Islam into the region.

During the same period that Indian civilization faced these challenges at home, it was having a profound impact on the emerging states of Southeast Asia. Situated at the crossroads between two oceans and two great civilizations, Southeast Asia has long served as a bridge linking peoples and cultures, and it is not surprising that as complex societies began to develop in the area, they were strongly influenced by the older civilizations of neighboring China and India. At the same time, the Southeast Asian peoples put their own unique stamp on the ideas that they adopted and eventually rejected those that were inappropriate to local conditions.

The result was a region characterized by an almost unparalleled cultural richness and diversity, reflecting influences from as far away as the Middle East, yet preserving indigenous elements that were deeply rooted in the local culture. Unfortunately, that very diversity posed potential problems for the peoples of Southeast Asia as they faced a new challenge from beyond the horizon. We shall deal with that challenge when we return to the region in a later chapter. In the meantime, we must turn our attention to the other major civilization that spread its shadow over the societies of southern Asia—China.

CHAPTER NOTES

1. Hiuen Tsiang, *Si-Yu-Ki: Buddhist Records of the Western World*, trans. S. Beal (London, 1982), pp. 89–90.
2. "Fo-Kwo-Ki" (Travels of Fa Xian), ch. 20, p. 43, in ibid.
3. E. C. Sachau, *Alberoni's India* (London, 1914), vol. 1, p. 22.
4. Quoted in S. M. Ikram, *Muslim Civilization in India* (New York, 1964), p. 68.
5. Hiuen Tsiang, *Si-Yu-Ki*, pp. 73–74.
6. D. Barbosa, *The Book of Duarte Barbosa* (Nedeln, Liechtenstein, 1967), pp. 147–148.
7. Quoted in R. Lannoy, *The Speaking Tree: A Study of Indian Culture and Society* (London, 1971), p. 232.
8. Quoted in S. Tharu and K. Lalita, *Women Writing in India*, vol. 1 (New York, 1991), p. 77.
9. Quoted in A. L. Basham, *The Wonder That Was India* (London, 1954), p. 426.
10. Quoted in S. Hughes and B. Hughes, *Women in World History*, vol. 1 (Armonk, N.Y., 1995), p. 217.

SUGGESTED READING

The period from the decline of the Mauryas to the rise of the Mughals in India is not especially rich in terms of materials in English. Still, a number of the standard texts on Indian history contain useful sections on the period. Particularly good are **A. L. Basham, *The Wonder That Was India*** (London, 1954), and **S. Wolpert, *New History of India*** (New York, 1989).

A number of studies of Indian society and culture deal with this period. See, for example, **R. Lannoy, *The Speaking Tree*** (Oxford,

1971), for a sophisticated interpretation of Indian culture during the medieval period. On Buddhism, see **H. Nakamura,** *Indian Buddhism: A Survey with Bibliographical Notes* (Delhi, 1987), and **H. Akira,** *A History of Indian Buddhism from Sakyamuni to Early Mahayana* (Honolulu, 1990). For an interesting treatment of the Buddhist influence on commercial activities that is reminiscent of the role of Christianity in Europe, see **L. Xinru,** *Ancient India and Ancient China: Trade and Religious Changes, A.D. 1–600* (Delhi, 1988).

For a discussion of women's issues, see **S. Hughes** and **B. Hughes,** *Women in World History,* vol. 1 (Armonk, N.Y., 1995); **S. Tharu** and **K. Lalita,** *Women Writing in India,* vol. 1 (New York, 1991); and **V. Dehejia,** *Devi: The Great Goddess* (Washington, D.C., 1999).

The most comprehensive treatment of the Indian economy and, in particular, the regional trade throughout the Indian Ocean is **K. N. Chaudhuri,** *Trade and Civilization in the Indian Ocean: An Economic History from the Rise of Islam to 1750* (Cambridge, 1985), a ground-breaking comparative study. See also his more recent and massive *Asia Before Europe: Economy and Civilization of the Indian Ocean from the Rise of Islam to 1750* (Cambridge, 1990), which owes a considerable debt to F. Braudel's classic work on the Mediterranean region.

For an overview of events in Central Asia during this period, see **D. Christian,** *Inner Eurasia from Prehistory to the Mongol Empire* (Oxford, 1998), and **C. E. Bosworth,** *The Later Ghaznavids: Splendor and Decay* (New York, 1977). On the career of Tamerlane, see **B. F. Manz,** *The Rise and Rule of Tamerlane* (Cambridge, 1989).

For Indian art during the medieval period, see **S. Huntington,** *The Art of Ancient India: Buddhist, Hindu, and Jain* (New York, 1985), and **V. Dehejia,** *Indian Art* (London, 1997).

The early history of Southeast Asia is not as well documented as that of China or India. Except for Vietnam, where histories written in Chinese appeared shortly after the Chinese conquest, written materials on societies in the region are relatively sparse. Historians were therefore compelled to rely on stone inscriptions and the accounts of travelers and historians from other countries. As a result, the history of precolonial Southeast Asia was presented, as it were, from the outside looking in. For an overview of modern scholarship on the region, see **N. Tarling,** ed., *The Cambridge History of Southeast Asia,* vol. 1 (Cambridge, 1999).

Impressive advances are now being made in the field of prehistory. See **P. Bellwood,** *Prehistory of the Indo-Malaysian Archipelago* (Honolulu, 1997), and **C. Higham,** *The Archaeology of Mainland Southeast Asia* (Cambridge, 1989). Also see **C. Higham,** *The Bronze Age of Southeast Asia* (Cambridge, 1996).

The role of commerce has recently been highlighted as a key aspect in the development of the region. For two fascinating accounts, see **K. R. Hall,** *Maritime Trade and State Development in Early Southeast Asia* (Honolulu, 1985), and **A. Reid,** *Southeast Asia in the Era of Commerce, 1450–1680: The Lands Below the Winds* (New Haven, Conn., 1989). The latter is also quite useful on the role of women.

InfoTrac College Edition

Visit this chapter's InfoTrac College Edition/Research activities at the *Essential World History* Companion Website for activities related to early southern Asia.

CENGAGENOW **for Duiker and Spielvogel's *The Essential World History,* Third Edition**

Enter *CengageNOW* using the access card that is available with this text. *CengageNOW* will assist you in understanding the content in this chapter with lesson plans generated for your needs, as well as provide you with a connection to the *Wadsworth World History Resource Center* (see description below for details).

WORLD HISTORY RESOURCE CENTER

Enter the Resource Center using either your *CengageNOW* access card or your standalone access card for the *Wadsworth World History Resource Center.* Organized by topic, this website includes quizzes; images; over 350 primary source documents; interactive simulations, maps, and timelines; movie explorations; and a wealth of other resources. You can read the following documents, and many more, at http://worldrc.wadsworth.com/

Acts and Rewards of Devotion to the Buddha

The Buddhist Conception of the Intermediate State

Visit the *Essential World History* Companion Website for chapter quizzes and more.

academic.cengage.com/history/duiker

10

THE FLOWERING OF TRADITIONAL CHINA

Detail of a Chinese scroll, Spring Festival on the River

The Metropolitan Museum of Art, From the Collection of A. W. Bahr, Purchase, Fletcher Fund, 1947, The A. W. Bahr Collection, (47.18.1) Photograph ©1978 The Metropolitan Museum of Art

CHAPTER OUTLINE AND FOCUS QUESTIONS

China After the Han

▢ After the decline of the Han dynasty, China went through several centuries of internal division. Why do you think this occurred, and what impact did it have on Chinese society?

China Reunified: The Sui, the Tang, and the Song

▢ What major changes in political structures and social and economic life occurred during the Sui, Tang, and Song dynasties?

Explosion in Central Asia: The Mongol Empire

▢ Why were the Mongols able to amass an empire, and what were the main characteristics of their rule in China?

The Ming Dynasty

▢ What were the chief initiatives taken by the early rulers of the Ming dynasty to enhance the role of China in the world? Why did the imperial court order the famous voyages of Zhenghe, and then why were they discontinued?

In Search of the Way

▢ What roles did Buddhism, Daoism, and Neo-Confucianism play in Chinese intellectual life in the period between the Sui dynasty and the Ming?

The Apogee of Chinese Culture

▢ What were the main achievements in Chinese literature and art in the period between the Tang dynasty and the Ming, and what technological innovations and intellectual developments contributed to these achievements?

CRITICAL THINKING

▢ The civilization of ancient China fell under the onslaught of nomadic invasions, as had some of its counterparts elsewhere in the world. But China, unlike other classical empires, was later able to reconstitute itself on the same political and cultural foundations. How do you account for the difference?

*O*N HIS FIRST VISIT to the city, the traveler was mightily impressed. Its streets were so straight and wide that he could see through the city from one end to the other. Along the wide boulevards were beautiful palaces and inns in great profusion. The city was laid out in squares like a chessboard, and within each square were spacious courts and gardens. Truly, said the visitor, this must be one of the largest and wealthiest cities on earth–a city "planned out to a degree of precision and beauty impossible to describe."

The visitor was Marco Polo, and the city was Khanbaliq (later known as Beijing), capital of the Yuan dynasty (1279–1368) and one of the great urban centers of the Chinese Empire. Marco Polo was an Italian merchant who had traveled to China in the late thirteenth century and then served as an official at the court of Khubilai Khan. In later travels in China, Polo visited a number of other great cities, including the commercial hub of Kaifeng (ken-Zan-fu) on the Yellow River. It is a city, he remarked,

of great commerce, and eminent for its manufactures. Raw silk is produced in large quantities, and tissues of gold and every other kind of silk are woven there. At this place likewise they prepare every article necessary for the equipment of an army. All species of provisions are in abundance, and to be procured at a moderate price."[1]

Polo's diary, published after his return to Italy almost twenty years later, astonished readers with tales of this magnificent but unknown civilization far to the east.

When Marco Polo arrived, China was ruled by the Mongols, a nomadic people from Central Asia who had recently assumed control of the Chinese Empire. The Yuan dynasty, as the Mongol rulers were called, was only one of a succession of dynasties to rule China after the collapse of the Han in the third century C.E. The end of the Han had led to a period of internal division that lasted nearly four hundred years and was aggravated by the threat posed by nomadic peoples from the north. This time of troubles ended in the early seventh century, when a dynamic new dynasty, the Tang, came to power.

To this point, Chinese history appeared to be following a pattern similar to that of India, where the passing of the Mauryan dynasty in the second century B.C.E. unleashed a period of internal division that, except for the interval of the Guptas, lasted for several hundred years. But China did not recapitulate the Indian experience. The Tang dynasty led China to some of its finest achievements and was succeeded by the Song, who ruled most of China for nearly three hundred years. The Song were in turn overthrown by the Mongols in the late thirteenth century, who then gave way to a powerful new native dynasty, the Ming, in 1368. Dynasty followed dynasty, with periods of extraordinary cultural achievement alternating with periods of internal disorder, but in general, Chinese society continued to build on the political and cultural foundations of the Zhou and the Han.

Chinese historians, viewing this vast process as it evolved over time, began to hypothesize that Chinese history was cyclical, driven by the dynamic interplay of the forces of good and evil, *yang* and *yin,* growth and decay. Beyond the forces of conflict and change lay the essential continuity of Chinese history, based on the timeless principles established by Confucius and other thinkers during the Zhou dynasty in antiquity. If India often appeared to be a politically and culturally diverse entity, only sporadically knit together by ambitious rulers, China, in the eyes of its historians, was a coherent civilization struggling to relive the glories of its ancient golden age while contending against the divisive forces operating throughout the cosmos. ◇

China After the Han

After the collapse of the Han dynasty at the beginning of the third century C.E., China fell into an extended period of division and civil war. Taking advantage of the absence of organized government in China, nomadic forces from the Gobi Desert penetrated south of the Great Wall and established their own rule over northern China. In the Yangtze valley and farther to the south, native Chinese rule was maintained, but constant civil war and instability led later historians to refer to the period as the "era of the six dynasties."

The collapse of the Han Empire had a marked effect on the Chinese psyche. The Confucian principles that emphasized hard work, the subordination of the individual to community interests, and belief in the essentially rational order of the universe came under severe challenge, and many Chinese intellectuals began to reject the stuffy moralism and complacency of State Confucianism and sought emotional satisfaction in hedonistic pursuits or philosophical Daoism.

Eccentric behavior and a preference for philosophical Daoism became a common response to a corrupt age. A group of writers known as the "seven sages of the bamboo

The Big Goose Pagoda.   When the Buddhist pilgrim Xuan Zang returned to China from India in the mid-seventh century C.E., he settled in the capital of Chang'an, where, under orders from the Tang emperor, he began to translate Buddhist texts in his possession from Sanskrit into Chinese. The Big Goose Pagoda, shown here, was erected shortly afterward to house them. Originally known as the Pagoda of the Classics, the structure consists of seven stories and is over 240 feet tall.

forest" exemplified the period. Among the best known was the poet Liu Ling, whose odd behavior is described in this oft-quoted passage:

> Liu Ling was an inveterate drinker and indulged himself to the full. Sometimes he stripped off his clothes and sat in his room stark naked. Some men saw him and rebuked him. Liu Ling said, "Heaven and earth are my dwelling, and my house is my trousers. Why are you all coming into my trousers?"[2]

But neither popular beliefs in the supernatural nor philosophical Daoism could satisfy deeper emotional needs or provide solace in time of sorrow or the hope of a better life in the hereafter. Instead Buddhism filled that gap.

Buddhism was brought to China in the first or second century C.E., probably by missionaries and merchants traveling over the Silk Road. The concept of rebirth was probably unfamiliar to most Chinese, and the intellectual hairsplitting that often accompanied discussion of Buddha's message in India was somewhat too esoteric for Chinese tastes. Still, in the difficult years surrounding the decline of the Han dynasty, Buddhist ideas, especially those of the Mahayana school, began to find adherents among intellectuals and ordinary people alike. As Buddhism increased in popularity, it was frequently attacked by supporters of Confucianism and Daoism for its foreign origins. But such sniping did not halt the progress of Buddhism, and eventually the new faith was assimilated into Chinese culture, assisted by the efforts of such tireless advocates as the missionaries Fa Xian and Xuan Zang and the support of ruling elites in both northern and southern China (see "The Rise and Decline of Buddhism and Daoism" later in this chapter).

China Reunified: The Sui, the Tang, and the Song

After nearly four centuries of internal division, China was unified once again in 581 when Yang Jian (Yang Chien), a member of a respected aristocratic family in northern China, founded a new dynasty, known as the Sui (581–618 C.E.). Yang Jian (who is also known by his reign title of Sui Wendi, or Sui Wen Ti) established his capital at the historic metropolis of Chang'an and began to extend his authority throughout the heartland of China.

The Sui Dynasty

Like his predecessors, the new emperor sought to create a unifying ideology for the state to enhance its efficiency. But whereas Liu Bang, the founder of the Han dynasty, had adopted Confucianism as the official doctrine to hold the empire together, Yang Jian turned to Daoism and Buddhism. He founded monasteries for both doctrines in the capital and appointed Buddhist monks to key positions as political advisers.

Yang Jian was a builder as well as a conqueror, ordering the construction of a new canal from the capital to the confluence of the Wei and Yellow rivers nearly 100 miles to the east. His son, Emperor Sui Yangdi (Sui Yang Ti), continued the process, and the 1,400-mile-long Grand Canal, linking the two great rivers of China, the Yellow and the Yangtze, was completed during his reign. The new canal facilitated the shipment of grain and other commodities from the rice-rich southern provinces to the densely populated north. Sui Yangdi also used the canal as an imperial highway for inspecting his empire and dispatching troops to troubled provinces.

Despite such efforts to project the majesty of the imperial personage, the Sui dynasty came to an end immediately after Sui Yangdi's death. The Sui emperor was a tyrannical ruler, and his expensive military campaigns aroused widespread unrest. After his return from a failed campaign against Korea in 618, the emperor was murdered in his palace. One of his generals, Li Yuan, took advantage of the instability that ensued and declared the foundation of a new dynasty, known as the Tang (T'ang). Building on the successes of its predecessor, the Tang lasted for three hundred years, until 907.

The Tang Dynasty

Li Yuan ruled for a brief period and then was elbowed aside by his son, Li Shimin (Li Shih-min), who assumed the reign title Tang Taizong (T'ang T'ai-tsung). Under his vigorous leadership, the Tang launched a program of internal renewal and external expansion that would make it one of the greatest dynasties in the long history of China (see Map 10.1). Under the Tang, the northwest was pacified and given the name of Xinjiang, or "new region." A long conflict with Tibet led for the first time to the extension of Chinese control over the vast and desolate plateau north of the Himalaya Mountains. The southern provinces below the Yangtze were fully assimilated into the Chinese Empire, and the imperial court established commercial and diplomatic relations with the states of Southeast Asia. With reason, China now claimed to be the foremost power in East Asia, and the emperor demanded fealty and tribute from all his fellow rulers beyond the frontier. Korea accepted tribute status and attempted to adopt the Chinese model, and the Japanese dispatched official missions to China to learn more about its customs and institutions (see Chapter 11).

Finally, the Tang dynasty witnessed a flowering of Chinese culture. Many modern observers feel that the era represents the apogee of Chinese creativity in poetry and sculpture. One reason for

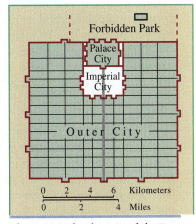

Chang'an Under the Sui and the Tang

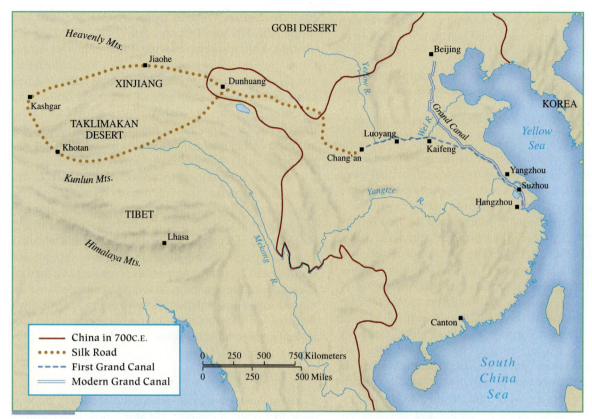

MAP 10.1 **China Under the Tang.** The era of the Tang dynasty was one of the greatest periods in the long history of China. Tang influence spread from heartland China into neighboring regions, including Central and Southeast Asia. ❓ What was the main function of the Grand Canal during this period, and why was it built? 🌐 **View an animated version of this map or related maps at** http://worldrc.wadsworth.com/

this explosion of culture was the influence of Buddhism, which affected art, literature, and philosophy, as well as religion and politics. Monasteries sprang up throughout China, and (as under the Sui) Buddhist monks served as advisers at the Tang imperial court. The city of Chang'an, now restored to the glory it had known as the capital of the Han dynasty, once again became the seat of the empire. It was possibly the greatest city in the world of its time, with an estimated population of nearly two million. The city was filled with temples and palaces, and its markets teemed with goods from all over the known world (see the box on p. 219).

But the Tang, like the Han, sowed the seeds of their own destruction. Tang rulers could not prevent the rise of internal forces that would ultimately weaken the dynasty and bring it to an end. Two ubiquitous problems were court intrigues and official corruption. In 755, rebellious forces briefly seized control of the capital of Chang'an. Although the revolt was eventually suppressed, the Tang never fully recovered from the catastrophe. The loss of power by the central government led to increased influence by great landed families inside China and chronic instability along the northern and western frontiers, where local military commanders ruled virtually without central government

interference. It was an eerie repetition of the final decades of the Han.

The end finally came in the early tenth century, when border troubles with northern nomadic peoples called the Khitan increased, leading to the final collapse of the dynasty in 907. The Tang had followed the classic strategy of "using a barbarian to oppose a barbarian" by allying with a trading people called the Uighurs (a Turkic-speaking people who had taken over many of the caravan routes along the Silk Road) against their old rivals. But yet another nomadic people called the Kirghiz defeated the Uighurs and then turned on the Tang government in its moment of weakness and overthrew it.

The Song Dynasty

China slipped once again into chaos. This time, the period of foreign invasion and division was much shorter. In 960, a new dynasty, known as the Song (960–1279), rose to power. From the start, however, the Song (Sung) rulers encountered more problems than their predecessors. Although the founding emperor, Song Taizu (Sung T'ai-tsu), was able to co-opt many of the powerful military commanders whose rivalry had brought the Tang

THE GOOD LIFE IN THE HIGH TANG

ARTS & IDEAS

At the height of the Tang dynasty, China was at the apex of its power and magnificence. Here the Tang poet Du Fu (Tu Fu) describes a gala festival in the capital of Chang'an (Ch'ang-an) attended by the favored elite. The author's distaste for the spectacle of arrogance and waste is expressed in muted sarcasm.

Why does the author of this poem appear to be so angry at the site of the festival he described here?

Du Fu, "A Poem"

Third day of the third month
The very air seems new
In Ch'ang-an along the water
Many beautiful girls . . .
Firm, plump contours,
Flesh and bone proportioned.
Dresses of gauze brocade
Mirror the end of spring
Peacocks crimped in thread of gold
Unicorns in silver. . . .
Some are kin to the imperial favorite
Among them the Lady of Kuo and the
    Lady of Ch'in [Qin].
Camel-humps of purple meat

Brought in shining pans
The white meat of raw fish
Served on crystal platters
Don't tempt the sated palate.
All that is cut with fancy and
Prepared with care—left untouched.
Eunuchs, reins a-flying
Disturb no dust
Bring the "eight chef d'oeuvres"
From the palace kitchens.
Music of strings and pipes . . .
Accompanying the feasting
Moving the many guests
All of rank and importance.
Last comes a horseman
See him haughtily
Dismount near the screen
And step on the flowery carpet. . . .
The chancellor is so powerful
His mere touch will scorch
Watch you don't come near
Lest you displease him.

CENGAGE**NOW** To read more Tang poetry, enter the *CengageNOW* documents area using the access card that is available for *The Essential World History.*

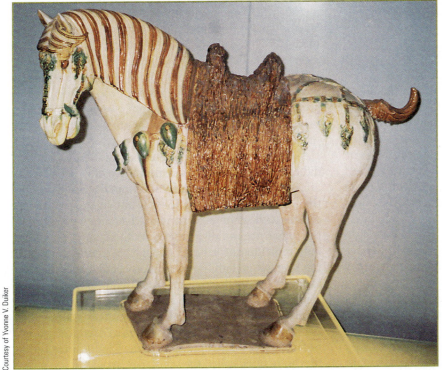

Courtesy of Yvonne V. Duiker

A Tang Horse. During the Tang dynasty, trade between China, India, and the Middle East along the famous Silk Road increased rapidly and introduced new Central Asian motifs to Chinese culture. Ceramic representations of the sturdy Central Asian horse and the two-humped Bactrian camel were often produced as decorative objects in the homes of the wealthy or as tomb figures. Preserved for us today, these ceramic studies of horses and camels, as well as of officials, court ladies, and servants, painted in brilliant gold, green, and blue lead glazes, are impressive examples of Tang cultural achievement.

dynasty to an end, he was unable to reconquer the north-western part of the country from the nomadic Khitan peoples. The emperor therefore established his capital farther to the east, at Kaifeng, where the Grand Canal intersected the Yellow River. Later, when pressures from the nomads in the north increased, the court was forced to move the capital even farther south, to Hangzhou (Hangchow), on the coast just south of the Yangtze River delta; the emperors who ruled from Hangzhou are known as the southern Song. The Song also lost control over Tibet. Despite its political and military weaknesses, the dynasty nevertheless ruled during a period of economic expansion, prosperity, and cultural achievement and is therefore considered among the more successful Chinese dynasties. The population of the empire had risen to an estimated forty million people, slightly more than that of the continent of Europe.

Yet the Song dynasty was never able to surmount the external challenge from the north, and that failure eventually brought about the end of the dynasty. During its final decades, the Song rulers were forced to pay tribute to the Jurchen peoples from Manchuria. In the early thirteenth century, the Song, ignoring precedent and the fate of the Tang, formed an alliance with the Mongols, a new and obscure nomadic people from the Gobi Desert. As under the Tang, the decision proved to be a disaster. Within a few years, the Mongols had become a much more serious threat to China than the Jurchen. After defeating the Jurchen, the Mongols turned their attention to the Song, advancing on Song territory from both the north and the west. By this time, the Song Empire had been weakened by internal factionalism and a loss of tax revenues. After a series of river battles and sieges marked by the use of catapults and gunpowder, the Song were defeated, and the conquerors announced the creation of a new Yuan (Mongol) dynasty. Ironically, the Mongols had first learned about gunpowder from the Chinese.

Political Structures: The Triumph of Confucianism

During the nearly seven hundred years from the Sui to the end of the Song, a mature political system based on principles originally established during the Qin and Han dynasties gradually emerged in China. After the Tang dynasty's brief flirtation with Buddhism, State Confucianism became the ideological cement that held the system together. The development of this system took several centuries, and it did not reach its height until the period of the Song dynasty.

Equal Opportunity in China: The Civil Service Examination   At the apex of the government hierarchy was the **Grand Council,** assisted by a secretariat and a chancellery; it included representatives from all three authorities—civil, military, and censorate. Under the Grand Council was the Department of State Affairs, composed of ministries responsible for justice, military affairs, personnel, public works, revenue, and rites (ritual).

This department was in effect the equivalent of a modern cabinet.

The Tang dynasty adopted the practice of selecting bureaucrats through civil service examinations. One way of strengthening the power of the central administration was to make the civil service examination system the primary route to an official career. To reduce the power of the noble families, relatives of individuals serving in the imperial court, as well as eunuchs, were prohibited from taking the examinations. But if the Song rulers' objective was to make the bureaucracy more subservient to the court, they may have been disappointed. The rising professionalism of the bureaucracy, which numbered about ten thousand in the imperial capital, with an equal number at the local level, provided it with an esprit de corps and an influence that sometimes enabled it to resist the whims of individual emperors.

Under the Song, the examination system attained the form that it would retain in later centuries. In general, three levels of examinations were administered. The first was a qualifying examination given annually at the provincial capital. Candidates who succeeded in this first stage were considered qualified but normally were not given positions in the bureaucracy except at the local level. Many stopped at this level and accepted positions as village teachers to train other candidates. Candidates who wished to go on could take a second examination given at the capital every three years. Successful candidates could apply for an official position. Some went on to take the final examination, which was given in the imperial palace once every three years. Those who passed were eligible for high positions in the central bureaucracy or for appointments as district magistrates.

By Song times, examinations were based entirely on the Confucian classics. Candidates were expected to memorize passages and to be able to define the moral lessons they contained. The system guaranteed that successful candidates—and therefore officials—would have received a full dose of Confucian political and social ethics. Many students complained about the rigors of memorization and the irrelevance of the process. Others brought crib notes into the examination hall (one enterprising candidate concealed an entire Confucian text in the lining of his cloak).

The Song authorities ignored such criticisms, but they did open the system to more people by allowing all males except criminals or members of certain restricted occupations to take the examinations. To provide potential candidates with schooling, training academies were set up at the provincial and district level. Without such academies, only individuals fortunate enough to receive training in the classics in family-run schools would have had the expertise to pass the examinations. In time, the majority of candidates came from the landed gentry, nonaristocratic landowners who controlled much of the wealth in the countryside. Because the gentry prized education and became the primary upholders of the Confucian tradition, they were often called the **scholar-gentry.**

But certain aspects of the system still prevented it from truly providing equal opportunity to all. In the first place, only males were eligible. Then again, the Song did not attempt to establish a system of universal elementary education. In practice, only those who had been given a basic education in the classics at home were able to enter the state-run academies and compete for a position in the bureaucracy. The poor had little chance.

Nor could the system guarantee an honest, efficient bureaucracy. Official arrogance, bureaucratic infighting, corruption, and legalistic interpretations of government regulations were as prevalent in medieval China as in bureaucracies the world over. Nepotism was a particular problem, since many Chinese, following Confucius, held that filial duty transcended loyalty to the community.

Despite such weaknesses, the civil service examination system was an impressive achievement for its day and probably provided a more efficient government and more opportunity for upward mobility than were found in any other civilization of its time. Most Western governments, for example, only began to recruit officials on the basis of merit in the nineteenth century. Furthermore, by regulating the content of the examinations, the system helped provide China with a cultural uniformity lacking in empires elsewhere in Asia.

Local Government   The Song dynasty maintained the local government institutions that it had inherited from its predecessors. At the base of the government pyramid was the district (or county), governed by a magistrate. The magistrate, assisted by his staff of three or four officials and several other menial employees, was responsible for maintaining law and order and collecting taxes within his jurisdiction. A district could exceed 100,000 people. Below the district was the basic unit of Chinese government, the village. Because villages were so numerous in China, the central government did not appoint an official at that level and allowed the villages to administer themselves. Village government was normally in the hands of a council of elders, usually assisted by a chief. The council, usually made up of the heads of influential families in the village, maintained the local irrigation and transportation network, adjudicated local disputes, organized and maintained a militia, and assisted in collecting taxes (usually paid in grain) and delivering them to the district magistrate.

The Economy

During the long period between the Sui and the Song, the Chinese economy, like the government, grew considerably in size and complexity. China was still an agricultural society, but major changes were taking place within the economy and the social structure. The urban sector of the economy was becoming increasingly important, new social classes were beginning to appear, and the economic focus of the empire was beginning to shift from the Yellow River valley in the north to the Yangtze River valley in the

center—a process that was encouraged both by the expansion of cultivation in the Yangtze delta and by the control exerted over the north by nomadic peoples during the Song.

Land Reform   The economic revival began shortly after the rise of the Tang. During the long period of internal division, land had become concentrated in the hands of aristocratic families, with most peasants reduced to serfdom or slavery. The early Tang tried to reduce the power of the landed nobility and maximize tax revenues by adopting the ancient "equal field" system, in which land was allocated to farmers for life in return for an annual tax payment and three weeks of conscript labor.

At first, the new system was vigorously enforced and led to increased rural prosperity and government revenue. But eventually, the rich and the politically influential learned to manipulate the system for their own benefit and accumulated huge tracts of land. The growing population, caused by a rise in food production and the extended period of social stability, also put steady pressure on the system. Finally, the government abandoned the effort to equalize landholdings and returned the land to private hands while attempting to prevent inequalities through the tax system. The failure to resolve the land problem contributed to the fall of the Tang dynasty in the early tenth century.

The Song tried to resolve the land problem by returning to the successful programs of the early Tang and reducing the power of the wealthy landed aristocrats. During the late eleventh century, the reformist official Wang Anshi (Wang An-shih) attempted to limit the size of landholdings through progressive land taxes and provided cheap credit to poor farmers to help them avoid bankruptcy. His reforms met with some success, but other developments probably contributed more to the general agricultural prosperity under the Song. These included the opening of new lands in the Yangtze River valley, improvements in irrigation techniques such as the chain pump (a circular chain of square pallets on a treadmill that enabled farmers to lift considerable amounts of water or mud to a higher level), and the introduction of a new strain of quick-growing rice from Southeast Asia, which permitted farmers in warmer regions to plant and harvest two crops each year.

The Urban Economy   Major changes also took place in the Chinese urban economy, which witnessed a significant increase in trade and manufacturing. Despite the restrictive policies of the state, the urban sector grew steadily larger and more complex, helped by several new technological developments (see the comparative essay "The Spread of Technology" on p. 222). During the Tang, the Chinese mastered the art of manufacturing steel by mixing cast iron and wrought iron. The blast furnace was heated to a high temperature by burning coal, which had been used as a fuel in China from about the fourth century C.E. The resulting product was used in the manufacture of swords, sickles,

The Spread of Technology

SCIENCE & TECHNOLOGY

From the invention of stone tools and the discovery of fire to the introduction of agriculture and the writing system, mastery of technology has been a driving force in the history of human evolution. But why do some human societies appear to be much more advanced in their use of technology than others? People living on the island of New Guinea, for example, began cultivating local crops like taro and the banana as early as ten thousand years ago but never took the next steps toward creating a complex society until the arrival of Europeans many millennia later. Advanced societies had begun to emerge in the Western Hemisphere during the classical era, but none had discovered the use of the wheel or the smelting of metals for toolmaking. Writing was in its infancy there.

Technological advances appear to take place for two reasons: need and opportunity. Farming peoples throughout the world needed to control the flow of water, so in areas where water was scarce or unevenly distributed, they learned how to practice irrigation to make resources available throughout the region. Sometimes, however, opportunity strikes by accident (as in the legendary story of the Chinese princess who dropped a silkworm cocoon in her cup of hot tea) or when new technology is introduced from a neighboring region (as when the discovery of tin in Anatolia launched the Bronze Age throughout the Middle East).

The most important factor enabling societies to keep abreast of the latest advances in technology, it would appear, is participation in the global trade and communications network. In this respect, the relative ease of communications between the Mediterranean Sea and the Indus River valley represented a major advantage for the Abbasid Empire, enabling the peoples living there to have rapid access to all the resources and technological advances in that part of the world. China was more isolated from such developments because of distance and the obstacle represented by the Himalaya Mountains. But because of its size and high level of cultural achievement, China was almost a continent in itself and was soon communicating with countries to the west via the Silk Road.

Societies that were not linked to this vast network were at an enormous disadvantage in keeping up with new developments in the field of technology. The peoples of New Guinea, at the far end of the Indonesian archipelago, had little or no contact with the outside world. In the Western Hemisphere, a trade network did begin to take shape between societies in the Andes and their counterparts in Mesoamerica. But because of difficulties in communication (see Chapter 6), contacts were more intermittent. As a result, technological developments taking place in distant Eurasia did not reach the Americas until the arrival of the conquistadors.

and even suits of armor. By the eleventh century, more than 35,000 tons of steel were being produced annually. The introduction of cotton offered new opportunities in textile manufacturing. Gunpowder was invented by the Chinese during the Tang dynasty and used primarily for explosives and a primitive form of flamethrower; it reached the West via the Arabs in the twelfth century.

The Silk Road The nature of trade was also changing. In the past, most long-distance trade had been undertaken by state monopoly. By the time of the Song, private commerce was being actively encouraged, and many merchants engaged in shipping as well as in wholesale and retail trade. Guilds began to appear, along with a new money economy. Paper currency began to be used in the eighth and ninth centuries. Credit (at first called "flying money") also made its first appearance during the Tang. With the increased circulation of paper money, banking began to develop as merchants found that strings of copper coins were too cumbersome for their increasingly complex operations. Equally useful, if more prosaic, was the invention of the abacus, an early form of calculator that simplified the calculations needed for commercial transactions.

Long-distance trade, both overland and by sea, expanded under the Tang and the Song. Trade with countries and peoples to the west had been carried on for centuries (see Chapter 5), but it had declined dramatically between the fourth and sixth centuries C.E. as a result of the collapse of the Han and Roman Empires. It began to revive with the rise of the Tang and the simultaneous unification of much of the Middle East under the Arabs. During the Tang era, the Silk Road revived and then reached its zenith. Much of the trade was carried by the Turkic-speaking Uighurs. During the Tang, Uighur caravans of two-humped Bactrian camels (a hardy variety native to Iran and regions to the northeast) carried goods back and forth between China and the countries of South Asia and the Middle East.

In actuality, the Silk Road was composed of a number of separate routes. The first to be used, probably because of the jade found in the mountains south of Khotan, ran along the southern rim of the Taklimakan Desert via Kashgar and thence through the Pamir Mountains into Bactria. Eventually, however, this area began to dry up, and traders were forced to seek other routes. From a climatic standpoint, the best route for the Silk Road was to the north of the Tian Shan (Heavenly Mountains), where

Arrival of Buddhism in China	c. first century C.E.
Fall of the Han dynasty	220 C.E.
Sui dynasty	581–618
Tang dynasty	618–907
Li Bo (Li Po) and Du Fu (Tu Fu)	700s
Song dynasty	960–1279
Wang Anshi	1021–1086
Southern Song dynasty	1127–1279
Mongol conquest of China	1279
Reign of Khubilai Khan	1260–1294
Fall of the Yuan dynasty	1368
Ming dynasty	1369–1644

created by the water runoff from winter snows in the mountains, which then dried up in the searing heat of the desert.

The Maritime Route The Silk Road was so hazardous that shipping goods by sea became increasingly popular. China had long been engaged in sea trade with other countries in the region, but most of the commerce was originally in the hands of Korean, Japanese, or Southeast Asian merchants. Chinese maritime trade, however, was stimulated by the invention of the compass and technical improvements in shipbuilding such as the sternpost rudder and the lug sail (which enabled ships to sail close to the wind). If Marco Polo's observations can be believed, by the thirteenth century, Chinese junks (a type of seagoing ship popular in Asian waters that employed square sails and a flat bottom) had multiple sails and weighed up to 2,000 tons, much more than contemporary ships in the West. The Chinese governor of Canton in the early twelfth century remarked:

> According to the government regulations concerning seagoing ships, the larger ones can carry several hundred men, and the smaller ones may have more than a hundred men on board. . . . The ship's pilots are acquainted with the configuration of the coasts; at night they steer by the stars, and in the daytime by the Sun. In dark weather they look at the south-pointing needle. They also use a line a hundred feet long with a hook at the end, which they let down to take samples of mud from the seabottom; by its appearance and smell they can determine their whereabouts.[3]

moisture-laden northwesterly winds created pastures where animals could graze. But the area was frequently infested by bandits who preyed on unwary travelers. Most caravans therefore followed the southern route, which passed along the northern fringes of the Taklimakan Desert to Kashgar and down into northwestern India. Travelers avoided the direct route through the desert (in the Uighur language, the name means "go in and you won't come out") and trudged from oasis to oasis along the southern slopes of the Tian Shan. The oases were

Ladies Preparing Silk. Although the Tang dynasty was a very prolific period in the development of Chinese painting, very few examples survive to the present day. Fortunately, copying the works of previous masters was a common tradition in China. Here we see a twelfth-century copy of a Tang painting showing ladies preparing newly woven silk. Two women are stretching a bolt of silk while a third irons the cloth with a pan containing burning coals. Silk was a highly prized luxury item in elite circles throughout the imperial period in China.

A wide variety of goods passed through Chinese ports. The Chinese exported tea, silk, and porcelain to the countries beyond the South China Sea, receiving exotic woods, precious stones, and various tropical goods in exchange. Seaports on the southern China coast exported sweet oranges, lemons, and peaches in return for grapes, walnuts, and pomegranates. Along the Silk Road to China came raw hides, furs, and horses. Chinese aristocrats, their appetite for material consumption stimulated by the affluence of Chinese society during much of the Tang and Song periods, were fascinated by the exotic goods and the flora and fauna of the desert and the tropical lands of the South Seas. The city of Chang'an became the eastern terminus of the Silk Road and perhaps the wealthiest city in the world during the Tang era. The major port of exit in southern China was Canton, where an estimated 100,000 merchants lived.

Some of this trade was a product of the tribute system, which the Chinese rulers used as an element of their foreign policy. The Chinese viewed the outside world as they viewed their own society—in a hierarchical manner. Rulers of smaller countries along the periphery were viewed as "younger brothers" of the Chinese emperor and owed fealty to him. Foreign rulers who accepted the relationship were required to pay tribute and to promise not to harbor enemies of the Chinese Empire. In return, they obtained legitimacy and access to the vast Chinese market.

Society in Traditional China

These political and economic changes affected Chinese society during the Tang and Song eras. For one thing, it became much more complex. Whereas previously China had been almost exclusively rural, with a small urban class of merchants, artisans, and workers almost entirely dependent on the state, the cities had now grown into an important, if statistically still insignificant, part of the population. Urban life, too, had changed. Cities were no longer primarily administrative centers dominated by officials and their families but now included a much broader mix of officials, merchants, artisans, touts, and entertainers. Unlike the situation in Europe, however, Chinese cities did not possess special privileges that protected their residents from the rapacity of the central government.

In the countryside, equally significant changes were taking place, as the relatively rigid demarcation between the landed aristocracy and the mass of the rural population gave way to a more complex mixture of landed gentry, free farmers, sharecroppers, and landless laborers. There was also a class of "base people," consisting of actors, butchers, and prostitutes, who possessed only limited legal rights and were not permitted to take the civil service examination.

The Rise of the Gentry Perhaps the most significant development was the rise of the landed gentry as the most

influential force in Chinese society. The gentry class controlled much of the wealth in the rural areas and produced the majority of the candidates for the bureaucracy. By virtue of their possession of land and specialized knowledge of the Confucian classics, the gentry had replaced the aristocracy as the political and economic elite of Chinese society. Unlike the aristocracy, however, the gentry did not form an exclusive class separated by the accident of birth from the remainder of the population. Upward and downward mobility between the scholar-gentry class and the remainder of the population was not uncommon and may have been a key factor in the stability and longevity of the system. A position in the bureaucracy opened the doors to wealth and prestige for the individual and his family but was no guarantee of success, and the fortunes of individual families might experience a rapid rise and fall. The soaring ambitions and arrogance of China's landed gentry are vividly described in the following wish list set in poetry by a young bridegroom of the Tang dynasty:

> Chinese slaves to take charge of treasury and barn,
> Foreign slaves to take care of my cattle and sheep.
> Strong-legged slaves to run by saddle and stirrup
>   when I ride,
> Powerful slaves to till the fields with might and main,
> Handsome slaves to play the harp and hand the wine;
> Slim-waisted slaves to sing me songs, and dance;
> Dwarfs to hold the candle by my dining-couch.[4]

For affluent Chinese in this era, life offered many more pleasures than had been available to their ancestors. There were new forms of entertainment, such as playing cards and chess (brought from India, although an early form had been invented in China during the Zhou dynasty); new forms of transportation, such as the paddle-wheel boat and horseback riding (made possible by the introduction of the stirrup); better means of communication (block printing was first invented in the eighth century C.E.); and new tastes for the palate introduced from lands beyond the frontier (see the comparative illustration on p. 225). Tea had been introduced from the Burmese frontier by monks as early as the Han dynasty, and brandy and other concentrated spirits produced by the distillation of alcohol made their appearance in the seventh century.

Village China The vast majority of the Chinese people still lived off the land in villages ranging in size from a few dozen residents to several thousand. The life of the farmers was bounded by their village. Although many communities were connected to the outside world by roads or rivers, the average Chinese rarely left the confines of their native village except for an occasional visit to a nearby market town.

An even more basic unit than the village in the lives of most Chinese, of course, was the family. The ideal was the joint family with at least three generations under one roof. Because of the heavy labor requirements of rice farming,

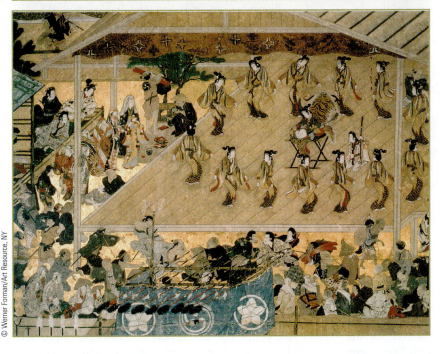

 COMPARATIVE ILLUSTRATION

FAMILY & SOCIETY

Public Entertainment in China and Japan. Besides being an artistic masterpiece, the Chinese scroll shown at the top, known as *Spring Festival on the River,* is one of the most remarkable social documents of early twelfth-century China. Nearly 33 feet long, it records with encyclopedic detail various aspects of Chinese society, from the imperial court down to the lowliest peasants, as they prepare for the spring festival. The screen painting on the bottom, probably from the fifteenth century, depicts a form of Japanese public entertainment (see Chapter 11). On the left, the well-behaved upper-class spectators observe the graceful dancers on stage in a dignified manner, while the ordinary people down at the front are depicted as a rowdy crowd.

of the house. He had traditional legal rights over his wife, and if she did not provide him with a male heir, he was permitted to take a second wife. She, however, had no recourse to divorce. As the old saying went, "Marry a chicken, follow the chicken; marry a dog, follow the dog." Wealthy Chinese might keep concubines, who lived in a separate room in the house and sometimes competed with the legal wife for precedence.

In accordance with Confucian tradition, children were expected, above all, to obey their parents, who not only determined their children's careers but also selected their marriage partners. Filial piety was viewed as an absolute moral good, above virtually all other moral obligations.

The Role of Women The tradition of male superiority continued from ancient times into the medieval era, especially under the southern Song when it was reinforced by Neo-Confucianism (see the box on p. 226). Female children were considered less desirable than males because they could not undertake heavy work in the fields or carry on the family traditions. Poor families often sold their daughters to wealthy villagers to serve as concubines, and in times of famine, female infanticide was not uncommon to ensure there would be food for the remainder of the family. Concubines had few legal rights; female domestic servants, even fewer.

the tradition of the joint family was especially prevalent in the south. When a son married, he was expected to bring his new wife back to live in his parents' home.

Chinese village architecture reflected these traditions. Most family dwellings were simple, consisting of one or at most two rooms. They were usually constructed of dried mud, stone, or brick, depending on available materials and the prosperity of the family. Roofs were of thatch or tile, and the floors were usually of packed dirt. Large houses were often built in a square around an inner courtyard, thus guaranteeing privacy from the outside world.

Within the family unit, the eldest male theoretically ruled as an autocrat. He was responsible for presiding over ancestral rites at an altar, usually in the main room

THE SAINTLY MISS WU

FAMILY & SOCIETY

The idea that a wife should sacrifice her wants to the needs of her husband and family was deeply embedded in traditional Chinese society. Widows in particular had few rights, and their remarriage was strongly condemned. In this account from a story by Hung Mai, a twelfth-century writer, the widowed Miss Wu wins the respect of the entire community by faithfully serving her mother-in-law.

What is the moral of this story? How do the supernatural elements in the account strengthen the lesson intended by the author?

Hung Mai, *A Song Family Saga*

Miss Wu served her mother-in-law very filially. Her mother-in-law had an eye ailment and felt sorry for her daughter-in-law's solitary and poverty-stricken situation, so suggested that they call in a son-in-law for her and thereby get an adoptive heir. Miss Wu announced in tears, "A woman does not serve two husbands. I will support you. Don't talk this way." Her mother-in-law, seeing that she was determined, did not press her. Miss Wu did spinning, washing, sewing, cooking, and cleaning for her neighbors, earning perhaps a hundred cash a day, all of which she gave to her mother-in-law to cover the cost of firewood and food. If she was given any meat, she would wrap it up to take home. . . .

Once when her mother-in-law was cooking rice, a neighbor called to her, and to avoid overcooking the rice she dumped it into a pan. Owing to her bad eyes, however, she mistakenly put it in the dirty chamber pot. When Miss Wu returned and saw it, she did not say a

word. She went to a neighbor to borrow some cooked rice for her mother-in-law and took the dirty rice and washed it to eat herself.

One day in the daytime neighbors saw [Miss Wu] ascending into the sky amid colored clouds. Startled, they told her mother-in-law, who said, "Don't be foolish. She just came back from pounding rice for someone, and is lying down on the bed. Go and look." They went to the room and peeked in and saw her sound asleep. Amazed, they left.

When Miss Wu woke up, her mother-in-law told her what happened, and she said, "I just dreamed of two young boys in blue clothes holding documents and riding on the clouds. They grabbed my clothes and said the Emperor of Heaven had summoned me. They took me to the gate of heaven and I was brought in to see the emperor, who was seated beside a balustrade. He said 'Although you are just a lowly ignorant village woman, you are able to serve your old mother-in-law sincerely and work hard. You really deserve respect.' He gave me a cup of aromatic wine and a string of cash, saying, 'I will supply you. From now on you will not need to work for others.' I bowed to thank him and came back, accompanied by the two boys. Then I woke up."

There was in fact a thousand cash on the bed, and the room was filled with a fragrance. They then realized that the neighbors' vision had been a spirit journey. From this point on even more people asked her to work for them, and she never refused. But the money that had been given to her she kept for her mother-in-law's use. Whatever they used promptly reappeared, so the thousand cash was never exhausted. The mother-in-law also regained her sight in both eyes.

During the Song era, two new practices emerged that changed the equation for women seeking to obtain a successful marriage contract. First, a new form of dowry appeared. Whereas previously the prospective husband offered the bride's family a bride price, now the reverse became the norm, with the bride's parents paying the groom's family a dowry. With the prosperity that characterized Chinese society during much of the Song era, affluent parents sought to buy a satisfactory husband for their daughter, preferably one with a higher social standing and good prospects for an official career.

A second source of marital bait during the Song period was the promise of a bride with tiny bound feet. The process of **foot binding,** carried out on girls aged five to thirteen, was excruciatingly painful, since it bent and compressed the foot to half its normal size by imprisoning it in restrictive bandages. But the procedure was often performed by ambitious mothers intent on assuring their daughters of the best possible prospects for marriage. Bound feet represented submissiveness and self-discipline, two required attributes for the ideal Confucian wife.

Throughout northern China, foot binding became a common practice for women of all social classes. It was less common in southern China, where the cultivation of wet rice could not be carried out with bandaged feet; there it tended to be limited to the scholar-gentry class. Still, most Chinese women with bound feet contributed to the labor force to supplement the family income. Although foot binding was eventually prohibited, the practice lasted into the twentieth century, particularly in rural villages.

As in most traditional societies, there were exceptions to the low status of women in Chinese society. Women had substantial property rights and retained control over their dowries even after divorce or the death of the husband. Wives were frequently an influential force within the home, often handling the accounts and taking primary responsibility for raising the children. Some were active in politics. The outstanding example was Wu Zhao (c. 625–c. 706), popularly known as Empress Wu. Selected by Emperor Tang Taizong as a concubine, after his death she rose to a position of supreme power at court. At first, she was content to rule through her sons, but in 690, she declared herself empress of China. For her presumption, she has been vilified by later Chinese historians, but she was actually a quite capable ruler. She was responsible for giving meaning to the civil service examination system and was the first to select graduates of the examinations for the highest positions in government. During her last years, she reportedly fell under the influence of courtiers and was deposed in 705, when she was probably around eighty.

Explosion in Central Asia: The Mongol Empire

The Mongols, who succeeded the Song as the rulers of China in 1279, rose to power in Asia with stunning rapidity. When Genghis Khan (also known as Chinggis Khan), the founder of Mongol greatness, was born, the Mongols were a relatively obscure pastoral people in the region of modern Outer Mongolia. Like most of the nomadic peoples in the region, they were organized loosely into clans and tribes and even lacked a common name for themselves. Rivalry among the various tribes over pasture, livestock, and booty was intense and increased at the end of the twelfth century as a result of a growing population and the consequent overgrazing of pastures.

The Creation of the Mongol Empire

Born in 1162, Genghis Khan (his original name was Temuchin, or Temujin) was the son of one of the more impoverished nobles of his tribe. While he was still a child, his father was murdered by a rival, and the youngster was temporarily forced to seek refuge in the wilderness. Nevertheless, through his prowess and the power of his personality, he gradually unified the Mongol tribes. In 1206, he was elected Genghis Khan ("universal ruler") at a massive tribal meeting. From that time on, he devoted himself to military pursuits. Mongol nomads were now forced to pay taxes and were subject to military conscription. "Man's highest joy," Genghis Khan reportedly remarked, "is in victory: to conquer one's enemies, to pursue them, to deprive them of their possessions, to make their beloved weep, to ride on their horses, and to embrace their wives and daughters."[5]

The army that Genghis Khan unleashed on the world was not

The Mongol Conquest of China

exceptionally large—less than 130,000 men in 1227, at a time when the total Mongol population numbered between one and two million. But their mastery of military tactics set the Mongols apart from their rivals. Their tireless flying columns of mounted warriors surrounded their enemies and harassed them like cattle, luring them into pursuit, then ambushing them with flank attacks. John Plano Carpini, a contemporary Franciscan friar, described their tactics:

> As soon as they discover the enemy they charge and each one unleashes three or four arrows. If they see that they can't break him, they retreat in order to entice the enemy to pursue, thus luring him into an ambush prepared in advance. . . . Their military stratagems are numerous. At the moment of an enemy cavalry attack, they place prisoners and foreign auxiliaries in the forefront of their own position, while positioning the bulk of their own troops on the right and left wings to envelop the adversary, thus giving the enemy the impression that they are more numerous than in reality. If the adversary defends himself well, they open their ranks to let him pass through in flight, after which they launch in pursuit and kill as many as possible.[6]

In the years after the election of Temuchin as universal ruler, the Mongols, now in possession of a new type of compound bow, which added both power and distance, defeated tribal groups to their west and then turned their attention to the seminomadic non-Chinese kingdoms in northern China. There they discovered that their adversaries were armed with a weapon called a fire-lance, an early form of flamethrower. Gunpowder had been invented in China during the late Tang period, and by the early thirteenth century, a type of fire-lance had been developed that could spew out a combination of flame and projectiles that could travel 30 or 40 yards and inflict considerable damage on the enemy. By the end of the thirteenth century, the fire-lance had evolved into the much more effective handgun and cannon. These inventions came too late to save China from the Mongols, however, and were transmitted to Europe by the early fourteenth century by foreigners employed by the Mongol rulers of China.

While some Mongol armies were engaged in the conquest of northern China, others traveled farther afield and advanced as far as central Europe (see the box on p. 228). Only the death of the Great Khan may have prevented an all-out Mongol attack on western Europe. In 1231, the Mongols attacked Persia and then defeated the Abbasids at Baghdad in 1258 (see Chapter 7). Mongol forces attacked the Song from the west in the 1260s and finally defeated the remnants of the Song navy in 1279.

By then, the Mongol Empire was quite different from what it had been under its founder. Prior to the conquests of Genghis Khan, the Mongols had been purely nomadic. They lived in round tents covered with felt (called yurts) that were easily transported. For food, the Mongols depended on milk and meat from their herds and game from hunting.

A LETTER TO THE POPE

In 1243, Pope Innocent IV dispatched the Franciscan friar John Plano Carpini to the Mongol headquarters at Karakorum to appeal to the great khan Kuyuk to cease his attacks on Christians. After a considerable wait, Carpini was given the following reply, which could not have pleased the pope. The letter was discovered recently in the Vatican archives.

Based on the account shown here, what message was the pope seeking to convey to the great khan in Karakorum? What is the nature of the latter's reply?

A Letter from Kuyuk Khan to Pope Innocent IV

By the power of the Eternal Heaven, We are the all-embracing Khan of all the Great Nations. It is our command:

This is a decree, sent to the great Pope that he may know and pay heed.

After holding counsel with the monarchs under your suzerainty, you have sent us an offer of subordination, which we have accepted from the hands of your envoy.

If you should act up to your word, then you, the great Pope, should come in person with the monarchs to pay us homage and we should thereupon instruct you concerning the commands of the Yasak.

Furthermore, you have said it would be well for us to become Christians. You write to me in person about this matter, and have addressed to me a request. This, your request, we cannot understand.

Furthermore, you have written me these words: "You have attacked all the territories of the Magyars and other Christians, at which I am astonished. Tell me, what was their crime?" These, your words, we likewise cannot understand. Jenghiz Khan and Ogatai Khakan revealed the commands of Heaven. But those whom you name would not believe the commands of Heaven. Those of whom you speak showed themselves highly presumptuous and slew our envoys. Therefore, in accordance with the commands of the Eternal Heaven the inhabitants of the aforesaid countries have been slain and annihilated. If not by the command of Heaven, how can anyone slay or conquer out of his own strength?

And when you say: "I am a Christian. I pray to God. I arraign and despise others," how do you know who is pleasing to God and to whom He allots His grace? How can you know it, that you speak such words?

Thanks to the power of the Eternal Heaven, all lands have been given to us from sunrise to sunset. How could anyone act other than in accordance with the commands of Heaven? Now your own upright heart must tell you: "We will become subject to you, and will place our powers at your disposal." You in person, at the head of the monarchs, all of you, without exception, must come to tender us service and pay us homage, then only will we recognize your submission. But if you do not obey the commands of Heaven, and run counter to our orders, we shall know that you are our foe.

That is what we have to tell you. If you fail to act in accordance therewith, how can we foresee what will happen to you? Heaven alone knows.

CENGAGENOW To read an account of Carpini's journey, enter the *CengageNOW* documents area using the access card that is available for *The Essential World History*.

To administer the new empire, Genghis Khan set up a capital city at Karakorum, in present-day Outer Mongolia, but prohibited his fellow Mongols from practicing sedentary occupations or living in cities. But under his successors, Mongol aristocrats began to enter administrative positions, and commoners took up sedentary occupations as farmers or merchants. As one khan remarked, quoting his Chinese adviser, "Although you inherited the Chinese Empire on horseback, you cannot rule it from that position."[7]

The territorial nature of the empire also changed. Following tribal custom, at the death of the ruling khan, the territory was distributed among his heirs. Genghis Khan's empire was thus divided into several separate **khanates,** each under the autonomous rule of one of his sons by his principal wife (see Map 10.2). One of his sons was awarded the khanate of Chaghadai in Central Asia with its capital at Samarkand; another ruled Persia from the conquered city of Baghdad; a third took charge of the khanate of Kipchak (commonly known as the Golden Horde). But it was one of his grandsons, named Khubilai Khan (who ruled from 1260 to 1294), who completed the conquest of the Song and established a new Chinese dynasty, called the Yuan. Khubilai moved the capital of China northward to Khanbaliq ("city of the khan"), which was located on a major trunk route from the Great Wall to the plains of northern China. Later the city would be known by the Chinese name Beijing, or Peking ("northern capital").

Mongol Rule in China

At first, China's new rulers exhibited impressive vitality. Mongol rulers adapted to the Chinese political system and made use of local talents in the bureaucracy, although the highest positions were usually reserved for Mongols. The tripartite division of the administration into civilian, military, and censorate was retained, as were the six ministries. Eventually, even the civil service system was revived, as was the state cult of Confucius, although Khubilai Khan himself was a Buddhist. Some leading Mongols followed their ruler in converting to Buddhism,

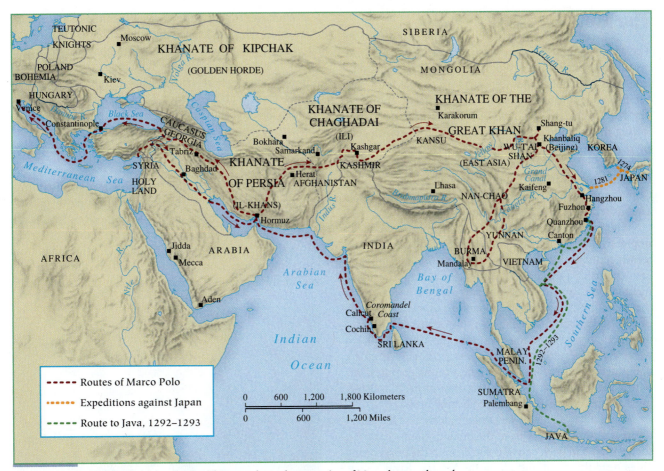

MAP 10.2 **Asia Under the Mongols.** This map shows the expansion of Mongol power throughout Eurasia in the thirteenth century. After the death of Genghis Khan, the empire was divided into four separate khanates. ❓ Why was the Mongol Empire divided into four separate khanates?

🌐 View an animated version of this map or related maps at http://worldrc.wadsworth.com/

but most commoners retained their traditional religion. In general, the Mongols remained apart as a separate class with their own laws.

The Mongols' greatest achievement may have been the prosperity they fostered. They continued the relatively tolerant economic policies of the southern Song, and by bringing the entire Eurasian landmass under a single rule, they encouraged long-distance trade, particularly along the Silk Road, now dominated by Muslim merchants from Central Asia. To promote trade, the Grand Canal was extended from the Yellow River to the capital. Adjacent to the canal, a paved highway was constructed that extended all the way from the Song capital of Hangzhou to its Mongol counterpart at Khanbaliq. According to the Italian merchant Marco Polo, who resided there during the reign of Khubilai Khan, the new capital was a magnificent city 24 miles in diameter where "so many pleasures may be found that one fancies himself to be in Paradise." The urban area was surrounded by thick walls of earth penetrated by twelve massive gates.

From the Yuan to the Ming

But the Yuan eventually fell victim to the same fate that had afflicted other powerful dynasties in China. Excessive spending on foreign campaigns, inadequate tax revenues, factionalism and corruption at court and in the bureaucracy, and growing internal instability all contributed to the dynasty's demise. Khubilai Khan's successors lacked his administrative genius, and by the middle of the fourteenth century, the Yuan dynasty in China, like the Mongol khanates elsewhere in Central Asia, had fallen into a rapid decline.

The immediate instrument of Mongol defeat was Zhu Yuanzhang (Chu Yuan-chang), the son of a poor peasant in the lower Yangtze valley. After losing most of his family in the famine of the 1340s, Zhu became an itinerant monk and then the leader of a band of bandits. In the 1360s, unrest spread throughout the country, and after defeating a number of rivals, Zhu Yuanzhang put an end to the disintegrating Yuan regime and declared the foundation of a new Ming ("bright") dynasty (which lasted from 1369 to 1644).

The Ming Dynasty

The Ming inaugurated a new era of greatness in Chinese history. Under a series of strong rulers, China extended its rule into Mongolia and Central Asia. The Ming even briefly reconquered Vietnam, which, after a thousand years of Chinese rule, had reclaimed its independence following the collapse of the Tang dynasty in the tenth century. Along the northern frontier, the emperor Yongle (Yung Lo, 1402–1424) strengthened the Great Wall and pacified the nomadic tribespeople who had troubled China in previous centuries. A tributary relationship was established with the Yi dynasty in Korea.

The internal achievements of the Ming were equally impressive. When they replaced the Mongols in the fourteenth century, the Ming turned to traditional Confucian institutions as a means of ruling their vast empire. These included the six ministries at the apex of the bureaucracy, the use of the civil service examinations to select members of the bureaucracy, and the division of the empire into provinces, districts, and counties. As before, Chinese villages were relatively autonomous, and local councils of elders continued to be responsible for adjudicating disputes, initiating local construction and irrigation projects, mustering a militia, and assessing and collecting taxes.

The society that was governed by this vast hierarchy of officials was a far cry from the predominantly agrarian society that had been ruled by the Han. In the burgeoning cities near the coast and along the Yangtze River valley, factories and workshops were vastly increasing the variety and output of their manufactured goods. The population had doubled, and new crops had been introduced, greatly expanding the food output of the empire.

The Voyages of Zhenghe

In 1405, in a splendid display of Chinese maritime might, Yongle sent a fleet of Chinese trading ships under the eunuch admiral Zhenghe (Cheng Ho) through the Strait of Malacca and out into the Indian Ocean; there they traveled as far west as the east coast of Africa, stopping on the way at ports in South Asia. The size of the fleet was impressive: it included nearly 28,000 sailors on sixty-two ships, some of them junks larger by far than any other oceangoing vessels the world had yet seen. China seemed about to become a direct participant in the vast trade network that extended as far west as the Atlantic Ocean, thus culminating the process of opening China to the wider world that had begun with the Tang dynasty.

Why the expeditions were undertaken has been a mater of some debate. Some historians assume that economic profit was the main reason. Others point to Yongle's native curiosity and note that the voyage—and the six others that followed it—returned not only with goods but also with a plethora of information about the outside world as well as with some items unknown in China (the emperor was especially intrigued by the giraffes and placed them in the imperial zoo).

Whatever the case, the voyages resulted in a dramatic increase in Chinese knowledge about the world and the nature of ocean travel. They also brought massive profits for their sponsors, including individuals connected with Admiral Zhenghe at court. This aroused resentment among conservatives within the bureaucracy, some of whom viewed commercial activities with a characteristic measure of Confucian disdain.

The Ming Turn Inward

Shortly after Yongle's death, the voyages were discontinued, never to be revived. The decision had long-term consequences and in the eyes of many modern historians marks a turning inward of the Chinese state, away from commerce and toward a more traditional emphasis on agriculture, away from the exotic lands to the south and toward the heartland of the country in the Yellow River

The Great Wall of China. Although the Great Wall is popularly believed to be over two thousand years old, the part of the wall that is most frequently visited by tourists was a reconstruction undertaken during the early Ming dynasty as a means of protection against invasion from the north. Part of that wall, which was built to protect the imperial capital of Beijing, is shown here.

valley. The imperial capital was moved from Nanjing, in central China, back to Beijing.

Why the Ming government discontinued Zhenghe's voyages and turned its attention back to domestic concerns has long been a matter of scholarly debate. Was it simply a consequence of court intrigues or the replacement of one emperor by another, or were deeper issues involved? A recent theory that has gained wide attention even speculated that the Chinese fleets did not limit their explorations to the Indian Ocean but actually circled the earth and discovered the existence of the Western Hemisphere. The voyages, and their abrupt discontinuance, remain one of the most fascinating enigmas in the history of China.

In Search of the Way

By the time of the Sui dynasty, Buddhism and Daoism had emerged as major rivals of Confucianism as the ruling ideology of the state. But during the last half of the Tang dynasty, Confucianism revived and once again became dominant at court, a position it would retain to the end of the dynastic period in the early twentieth century. Buddhist and Daoist beliefs, however, remained popular at the local level.

The Rise and Decline of Buddhism and Daoism

As noted earlier, Buddhism arrived in China with merchants from India and found its first adherents among the merchant community and intellectuals intrigued by the new ideas. During the chaotic centuries following the collapse of the Han dynasty, Buddhism and Daoism appealed to those who were searching for more emotional and spiritual satisfaction than Confucianism could provide. Both faiths reached beyond the common people and found support among the ruling classes as well.

The Sinification of Buddhism As Buddhism attracted more followers, it began to take on Chinese characteristics and divided into a number of separate sects. Some, like the **Chan** (**Zen** in Japanese) sect, called for mind training and a strict regimen as a means of seeking enlightenment (see the box on p. 232). Others, like the **Pure Land** sect, stressed the role of devotion, an approach that was more appealing to ordinary Chinese, who lacked the time and inclination for strict monastic discipline. Still others were mystical sects, like **Tantrism,** which emphasized the importance of magical symbols and ritual in seeking a preferred way to enlightenment. Some Buddhist groups, like their Daoist counterparts, had political objectives. The **White**

The Spread of Buddhism in Asia

Lotus sect, founded in 1133, often adopted the form of a rebel movement, seeking political reform or the overthrow of a dynasty and forecasting a new era when a "savior Buddha" would come to earth to herald the advent of a new age. Most believers, however, assimilated Buddhism into their daily lives, where it joined Confucian ideology and spirit worship as an element in the highly eclectic and tolerant Chinese worldview.

The burgeoning popularity of Buddhism continued into the early years of the Tang dynasty. Early Tang rulers lent their support to the Buddhist monasteries that had been established throughout the country. But ultimately, Buddhism and Daoism lost favor at court and were increasingly subjected to official persecution. Envious Daoists and Confucianists made a point of criticizing the foreign origins of Buddhist doctrines, which one prominent Confucian scholar characterized as nothing but "silly relics." But another reason for this change of heart may have been financial. The great Buddhist monasteries had accumulated thousands of acres of land and serfs that were exempt from paying taxes to the state. Such wealth contributed to the corruption of the monks and other Buddhist officials and in turn aroused popular resentment and official disapproval. As the state attempted to eliminate the great landholdings of the aristocracy, the large monasteries also attracted its attention. During the later Tang, countless temples and monasteries were destroyed, and over 100,000 monks were compelled to leave the monasteries and return to secular life.

Yet there were probably deeper political and ideological reasons for the growing antagonism between Buddhism and the state. By preaching the illusory nature of the material world, Buddhism was denying the very essence of Confucian teachings—the necessity for filial piety and hard work. By encouraging young Chinese to abandon their rice fields and seek refuge and wisdom in the monasteries, Buddhism was undermining the foundation stones of Chinese society—the family unit and the work ethic. In the last analysis, Buddhism was incompatible with the activist element in Chinese society, an orientation that was most effectively expressed by State Confucianism. In the competition with Confucianism for support by the state, Buddhism, like Daoism, was almost certain to lose.

Neo-Confucianism: The Investigation of Things

Into the vacuum left by the decline of Buddhism and Daoism stepped a revived Confucianism. Challenged by Buddhist and Daoist ideas about the nature of the universe, Confucian thinkers began to flesh out the spare metaphysical structure of classical Confucian doctrine with a set of sophisticated theories about the nature of the cosmos and humans' place in it.

The fundamental purpose of **neo-Confucianism,** as the new doctrine was called, was to unite the metaphysical speculations of Buddhism and Daoism with the pragmatic Confucian approach to society. In response to Buddhism and Daoism, neo-Confucianism maintained that the world

THE WAY OF THE GREAT BUDDHA

According to Buddhists, it is impossible to describe the state of Nirvana, which is sometimes depicted as an extinction of self. Yet Buddhist scholars found it difficult to avoid trying to interpret the term for their followers. The following passage by the Chinese monk Shen-Hui, one of the leading exponents of Chan Buddhism, dates from the eighth century and attempts to describe the means by which an individual may hope to seek enlightenment. There are clear similarities with philosophical Daoism.

What are the similarities with philosophical Daoism expressed in this passage? Compare and contrast the views expressed here with the Neo-Confucian worldview.

Shen-Hui, *Elucidating the Doctrine*

"Absence of thought" is the doctrine.
"Absence of action" is the foundation.
True Emptiness is the substance.
And all wonderful things and beings are the function.
True Thusness is without thought; it cannot be known through conception and thought.
The True State is noncreated—can it be seen in matter and mind?
There is no thought except that of True Thusness.
There is no creation except that of the True State.
Abiding without abiding, forever abiding in Nirvana.
Acting without acting, immediately crossing to the Other Shore.
Thusness does not move, but its motion and functions are inexhaustible.
In every instant of thought, there is no seeking; the seeking itself is no thought.
Perfect wisdom is not achieved, and yet the Five Eyes all become pure and the Three Bodies are understood.
Great Enlightenment has no knowledge, and yet the Six Supernatural Powers of the Buddha are utilized and the Four Wisdoms of the Buddha are made great.
Thus we know that calmness is at the same time no calmness, wisdom at the same time no wisdom, and action at the same time no action.
The nature is equivalent to the void and the substance is identical with the Realm of Law.
In this way, the Six Perfections are completed.
None of the ways to arrive at Nirvana is wanting.
Thus we know that the ego and the dharmas are empty in reality and being and nonbeing are both obliterated.
The mind is originally without activity; the Way is always without thought.
No thought, no reflection, no seeking, no attainment;
No this, no that, no coming, no going.
With such reality one understands the True Insight [into previous and future mortal conditions and present mortal suffering].
With such a mind one penetrates the Eight Emancipations [through the eight stages of mental concentration].
By merits one accomplishes the Ten Powers of the Buddha.

CENGAGENOW To read "Buddha Enters Nirvana," enter the *CengageNOW* documents area using the access card that is available for *The Essential World History.*

---

is real, not illusory, and that fulfillment comes from participation, not withdrawal.

The primary contributor to this intellectual effort was the philosopher Zhu Xi (Chu Hsi). Raised during the southern Song era, Zhu Xi accepted the division of the world into a material world and a transcendent world (called by neo-Confucianists the **Supreme Ultimate,** or *Tai Ji*). The latter was roughly equivalent to the *Dao*, or Way, in classical Confucian philosophy. To Zhu Xi, this Supreme Ultimate was a set of abstract principles governed by the law of *yin* and *yang* and the five elements.

Human beings served as a link between the two halves of this bifurcated universe. Although human beings live in the material world, each individual has an identity that is linked with the Supreme Ultimate, and the goal of individual action is to transcend the material world in a Buddhist sense to achieve an essential identity with the Supreme Ultimate. According to Zhu Xi and his followers, the means of transcending the material world is self-cultivation, which is achieved by the "investigation of things." During the remainder of the Song dynasty and into the early years of the Ming, Zhu Xi's ideas became the central core of Confucian ideology and a favorite source of questions for the civil service examinations.

Neo-Confucianism remained the state doctrine until the end of the dynastic system in the twentieth century. Some historians have asked whether the doctrine can help to explain why China failed to experience scientific and industrial revolutions of the sort that occurred in the West. In particular, it has been suggested that neo-Confucianism tended to encourage an emphasis on the elucidation of moral principles rather than the expansion of scientific knowledge. Though the Chinese excelled in practical technology, inventing gunpowder, the compass (first used by seafarers during the Song dynasty), printing and paper, and cast iron, among other things, they had less interest in scientific theory. Their relative backwardness in mathematics is a good example. Chinese scholars had no knowledge of the principles of geometry and

Longmen Caves Buddhist Sculpture. The Silk Road, which stretched through Central Asia from the Middle East to China, was an avenue for ideas as well as trade. Over the centuries, Christian, Buddhist, and Muslim teachings came to China across the sandy wastes of the Taklimakan Basin. In the seventh century, the Tang emperor Gaozong commissioned this massive temple carving as part of the large complex of cave art devoted to Buddha at Longmen in central China. Bold and grandiose in their construction, these statues reflect the glory that was the Tang dynasty.

emerged as the highest form of Chinese ceramics, and sculpture flourished under the influence of styles imported from India and Central Asia.

Literature

The development of Chinese literature was stimulated by two technological innovations: the invention of paper during the Han dynasty and the invention of woodblock printing during the Tang. At first, paper was used for clothing, wrapping material, toilet tissue, and even armor, but by the first century B.C.E., it was being used for writing as well.

In the seventh century C.E., the Chinese developed the technique of carving an entire page of text into a wooden block, inking it, and then pressing it onto a sheet of paper. Ordinarily, a text was printed on a long sheet of paper like a scroll. Then the paper was folded and stitched together to form a book. The earliest printed book known today is a Buddhist text published in 868 C.E.; it is more than 16 feet long. Although the Chinese eventually developed movable type as well, block printing continued to be used until relatively modern times because of the large number of Chinese characters needed to produce a lengthy text. Even with printing, books remained too expensive for most Chinese, but they did help popularize all forms of literary writing among the educated elite.

During the post-Han era, historical writing and essays continued to be favorite forms of literary activity. Each dynasty produced an official dynastic history of its predecessor to elucidate sober maxims about the qualities of good and evil in human nature, and local gazetteers added to the general knowledge about the various regions.

Poetry But it was in poetry, above all, that Chinese of the Tang to the Ming dynasties most effectively expressed their literary talents. Chinese poems celebrated the beauty of nature, the changes of the seasons, the joys of friendship and drink, and sadness at the brevity of life, old age, and parting. Love poems existed but were neither as intense as Western verse nor as sensual as Indian poetry.

The nature of the Chinese language imposed certain characteristics on Chinese poetry, the first being compactness. The most popular forms were four-line and eight-line poems, with five or seven words in each line. Because Chinese grammar does not rely on case or gender and makes no distinction between verb tenses,

lagged behind other advanced civilizations in astronomy, physics, and optics. Until the Mongol era, they had no knowledge of Arabic numerals and lacked the concept of zero. Even after that time, they continued to use a cumbersome numbering system based on Chinese characters.

Furthermore, intellectual affairs in China continued to be dominated by the scholar-gentry, the chief upholders of neo-Confucianism, who not only had little interest in the natural sciences or economic change but also viewed them as a threat to their own dominant status in Chinese society. The commercial middle class, who lacked social status and an independent position in society, had little say in intellectual matters. In contrast, in the West, an urban middle class emerged that was a source not only of wealth but also of social prestige, political power, and intellectual ideas. The impetus for the intellectual revolution in the West came from the members of the commercial bourgeoisie, who were interested in the conquest of nature and the development of technology. In China, however, the scholar-gentry continued to focus on the sources of human behavior and a correct understanding of the relationship between humankind and the universe. The result was an intellectual environment that valued continuity over change and tradition over innovation.

The Apogee of Chinese Culture

The period between the Tang and the Ming dynasties was in many ways the great age of achievement in Chinese literature and art. Enriched by Buddhist and Daoist images and themes, Chinese poetry and painting reached the pinnacle of their creativity. Porcelain

five-character Chinese poems were not only brief but often cryptic and ambiguous.

Two Tang poets, Li Bo (Li Po, sometimes known as Li Bai or Li Taibo) and Du Fu (Tu Fu), symbolized the genius of the era as well as the two most popular styles. Li Bo was a free spirit. His writing often centered on nature and shifted easily between moods of revelry and melancholy. One of his best-known poems is entitled "Quiet Night Thoughts":

> Beside my bed the bright moonbeams bound
> Almost as if there were frost on the ground.
> Raising up, I gaze at the Mountain moon;
> Lying back, I think of my old hometown.

Whereas Li Bo was a carefree Daoist, Du Fu was a sober Confucian. His poems often dealt with historical issues or ethical themes, befitting a scholar-official living during the chaotic times of the late Tang era. Many of his works reflect a concern with social injustice and the plight of the unfortunate rarely to be found in the writings of his contemporaries (see the box on p. 219). Neither the poetry nor the prose of the great writers of the Tang and Song dynasties was written for or ever reached the majority of the Chinese population.

Popular Culture   By the Song dynasty, China had sixty million people, one million in Hangzhou alone. With the growth of cities came an increased demand for popular entertainment. Although the Tang dynasty had imposed a curfew on urban residents, the Song did not. The city gates and bridges were closed at dark, but food stalls and entertainment continued through the night. At fairgrounds throughout the year, one could find comedians, musicians, boxers, fencers, wrestlers, acrobats, puppets and marionettes, shadow plays, and especially storytellers.

The Chinese Novel   During the Yuan dynasty, new forms of literary creativity, including popular theater and the novel, began to appear. One of the most famous novels was *Tale of the Marshes,* an often violent tale of bandit heroes who at the end of the northern Song banded together to oppose government taxes and official oppression. They rob from those in power to share with the poor. *Tale of the Marshes* is the first prose fiction that describes the daily ordeal of ordinary Chinese people in their own language. Unlike the picaresque novel in the West, *Tale of the Marshes* does not limit itself to the exploits of one hero, offering instead 108 different story lines. This multitude of plots is a natural outgrowth of the tradition of the professional storyteller, who attempts to keep the audience's attention by recounting as many adventures as the market will bear.

Art

Although painting flourished in China under the Han and reached a level of artistic excellence under the Tang, little remains from those periods. The painting of the Song and the Yuan, however, is considered the apogee of painting in traditional China.

Like literature, Chinese painting found part of its inspiration in Buddhist and Daoist sources. Some of the best surviving examples of the Tang period are the Buddhist wall paintings in the caves at Dunhuang, in Central Asia. Like the few surviving Tang scroll paintings, these wall paintings display a love of color and refinement that are reminiscent of styles in India and Iran.

Daoism ultimately had a greater influence than Buddhism on Chinese painting. From early times, Chinese artists removed themselves to the mountains to write and paint and find the *Dao,* or Way, in nature. In the fifth century, one Chinese painter, who was too old to travel, began to paint mountain scenes from memory and announced that depicting nature could function as a substitute for contemplating nature itself. Painting, he said, could be the means of realizing the *Dao.* This explains in part the emphasis on nature in traditional Chinese painting. The word *landscape* in Chinese means "mountain-water," and the Daoist search for balance between earth and water, hard and soft, *yang* and *yin,* is at play in the tradition of Chinese painting.

To represent the totality of nature, Chinese artists attempted to reveal the quintessential forms of the landscape. Rather than depicting the actual realistic shape of a specific mountain, they tried to portray the idea of "mountain." Empty spaces were left in the paintings because in the Daoist vision, one cannot know the whole truth. Daoist influence was also evident in the tendency to portray human beings as insignificant in the midst of nature. In contrast to the focus on the human body and personality in Western art, Chinese art presented people as tiny figures fishing in a small boat, meditating on a cliff, or wandering up a hillside trail, coexisting with but not dominating nature.

The Chinese displayed their paintings on long scrolls of silk or paper that were attached to a wooden cylindrical bar at the bottom. Varying in length from 3 to 20 feet, the paintings were unfolded slowly so that the eye could enjoy each segment, one after the other, beginning at the bottom with water or a village and moving upward into the hills to the mountain peaks and the sky.

By the tenth century, Chinese painters began to eliminate color from their paintings, preferring the challenge of capturing the distilled essence of the landscape in washes of black ink on white silk. Borrowing from calligraphy, now a sophisticated and revered art, they emphasized the brush stroke and created black-and-white landscapes characterized by a gravity of mood and dominated by overpowering mountains.

Second only to painting in creativity was the field of ceramics, notably, the manufacture of porcelain. Made of fine clay baked at unusually high temperatures in a kiln, porcelain was first produced during the period after the fall of the Han and became popular during the Tang era. During the Song, porcelain came into its own. The translucent character of Chinese porcelain represented the final product of a technique that did not reach Europe until the eighteenth century.

Emperor Ming-huang Traveling to Shu. Although the Tang dynasty was a prolific period in the development of Chinese painting, few examples have survived. Fortunately, the practice of copying the works of previous masters was a common tradition in China. Here we see an eleventh-century copy of an eighth-century painting depicting the precipitous journey of Emperor Ming-huang as he was driven by a revolt from the capital into the mountains of southwest China. Rather than portraying the bitterness of the emperor's precarious escape, however, the artist reflected the confidence and brilliance of the Tang dynasty through cheerful color and an idyllic landscape.

CONCLUSION

TRADITIONALLY CHINESE HISTORIANS believed that Chinese history tended to be cyclical. The pattern of history was marked by the rise and fall of great dynasties, interspersed with periods of internal division and foreign invasion. Underlying the waxing and waning of dynasties was the essential continuity of Chinese civilization.

This view of the dynamic forces of Chinese history was long accepted as valid by historians in China and in the West and led many to assert that Chinese history was unique and could not be placed in a European or universal framework. Whereas Western history was linear, leading steadily away from the past, China's always returned to its moorings and was rooted in the values and institutions of antiquity.

In recent years, however, this traditional view of a changeless China has come under increasing challenge from historians who see patterns of change that made the China of the late fifteenth century a very different place from the country that had existed at the rise of the Tang dynasty in 600. To these scholars, China had passed through its own version of the "middle ages" and was on the verge of beginning a linear evolution into a posttraditional society.

As we have seen, China at the beginning of the Ming had advanced in many ways since the end of the great Han dynasty over a thousand years earlier. The industrial and commercial sector had grown considerably in size, complexity, and technological capacity,

TIMELINE

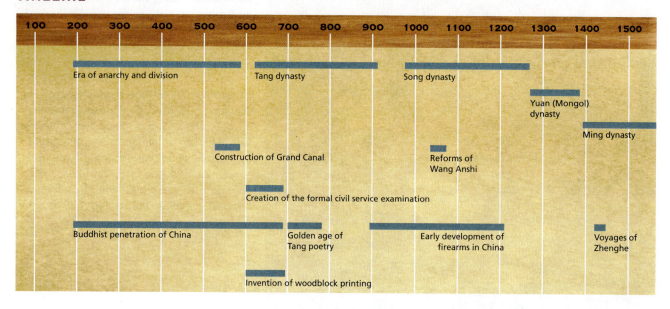

while in the countryside, the concentration of political and economic power in the hands of the aristocracy had been replaced by a more stable and equitable mixture of landed gentry, freehold farmers, and sharecroppers. In addition, Chinese society had achieved a level of stability and social tranquillity that was the envy of observers from other lands near and far. The civil service provided an avenue of upward mobility that was unavailable elsewhere in the world, and the state tolerated a diversity of beliefs that responded to the emotional needs and preferences of the Chinese people. In many respects, China's achievements were unsurpassed throughout the world and marked a major advance beyond the world of antiquity.

Yet there were also some key similarities between the China of the Ming and the China of late antiquity. Ming China was still a predominantly agrarian society,

with wealth based primarily on the ownership of land. Commercial activities flourished but remained under a high level of government regulation and by no means represented a major proportion of the national income. China also remained a relatively centralized empire based on an official ideology that stressed the virtue of hard work, social conformity, and hierarchy.

Thus, the significant change that China experienced during its medieval era can probably be best described as change within continuity, an evolutionary working out of trends that had first become visible during the Han dynasty or even earlier. The result was a civilization that was the envy of its neighbors and of the world. It also influenced other states in the region, including Japan, Korea, and Vietnam. It is to these societies along the Chinese rimlands that we now turn.

CHAPTER NOTES

1. *The Travels of Marco Polo* (New York, n.d.), pp. 128, 179.
2. Quoted in A. F. Wright, *Buddhism in Chinese History* (Stanford, Calif., 1959), p. 30.
3. Chu-yu, *P'ing-chow Table Talks,* quoted in R. Temple, *The Genius of China: 3,000 Years of Science, Discovery, and Invention* (New York, 1986), p. 150.
4. Quoted in E. H. Schafer, *The Golden Peaches of Samarkand: A Study of T'ang Exotics* (Berkeley, Calif., 1963), p. 43.
5. Quoted in J. K. Fairbank, E. O. Reischauer, and A. M. Craig, *East Asia: Tradition and Transformation* (Boston, 1973), p. 164.
6. Quoted in R. Grousset, *L'Empire des Steppes* (Paris, 1939), p. 285.
7. A. M. Khazanov, *Nomads and the Outside World* (Cambridge, 1983), p. 241.

SUGGESTED READING

For an authoritative overview of the early imperial era in China, see **M. Elvin, *The Pattern of the Chinese Past*** (Stanford, Calif., 1973). A global perspective is presented in **S. A. M. Adshead, *China in World History*** (New York, 1988).

A vast body of material is available on almost all periods of early Chinese history. For the post-Han period, see **A. E. Dien,** ed., ***State and Society in Early Medieval China*** (Stanford, Calif., 1990); **F. Mote, *Imperial China*** (Cambridge, 1999); and **D. Twitchett** and **M. Loewe, *Cambridge History of China,*** vol. 3, ***Medieval China*** (Cambridge, 1986).

For a readable treatment of the brief but tempestuous Sui dynasty, see **A. F. Wright, *The Sui Dynasty*** (New York, 1978). The Song dynasty has been studied in considerable detail by historians. For an excellent interpretation, see **J. T. C. Liu, *China Turning***

Inward: Intellectual Changes in the Early Twelfth Century
(Cambridge, Mass., 1988). Song problems with the northern frontier are chronicled in **Tao Jing-shen**, *Two Sons of Heaven: Studies
in Sung-Liao Relations* (Tucson, Ariz., 1988).

There are a number of good studies on the Mongol period
in Chinese history. See, for example, **W. A. Langlois**, *China Under
Mongol Rule* (Princeton, N.J., 1981). **M. Rossabi**, *Khubilai Khan:
His Life and Times* (Berkeley, Calif., 1988), is a good biography of
the dynasty's greatest emperor, while **M. Rossabi**, ed., *China
Among Equals: The Middle Kingdom and Its Neighbors*
(Berkeley, Calif., 1983), deals with foreign affairs. For a provocative
interpretation of Chinese relations with nomadic peoples, see
T. J. Barfield, *The Perilous Frontier: Nomadic Empires and
China* (Cambridge, 1989). An analytic account of the dynamics
of nomadic society is **A. M. Khazanov**, *Nomads and the Outside
World* (Cambridge, 1983).

The emergence of urban culture during this era is analyzed in
C. K. Heng, *Cities of Aristocrats and Bureaucrats: The Development of Medieval Chinese Cityscapes* (Honolulu, 1999). For
perspectives on China as viewed from the outside, see **J. Spence**,
The Chan's Great Continent: China in a Western Mirror (New York,
1998). China's contacts with foreign cultures are discussed in
J. Waley-Cohen, *The Sextants of Beijing* (New York, 1999). On
the controversial belief that Chinese fleets circled the globe in the
fifteenth century, see **G. Menzies**, *1421: The Year China Discovered
America* (New York, 2002).

For an introduction to women's issues during this period, con-
sult **P. B. Ebrey**, *The Inner Quarters: Marriage and the Lives of
Chinese Women in the Sung Period* (Berkeley Calif., 1993); *Chu Hsi's
Family Rituals* (Princeton, N.J., 1991); and *"Women, Marriage, and
the Family in Chinese History,"* in **P. S. Ropp**, *Heritage of China:
Contemporary Perspectives on Chinese Civilization* (Berkeley, Calif.,
1990). For an overview of Chinese foot binding, see **C. F. Blake**,
*"Foot-Binding in Neo-Confucian China and the Appropriation of
Female Labor," Signs* **19** (Spring 1994).

On Central Asia, two popular accounts are **J. Myrdal**, *The Silk
Road* (New York, 1979), and **N. Marty**, *The Silk Road* (Methuen,
Mass., 1987). A more interpretive approach is found in **S. A. M.
Adshead**, *Central Asia in World History* (New York, 1993). See also
E. T. Grotenhuis, ed., *Along the Silk Road* (Washington, D.C., 2002).
Xuan Zang's journey to India is re-created in **R. Bernstein**, *Ultimate
Journey: Retracing the Path of an Ancient Buddhist Monk Who
Crossed Asia in Search of Enlightenment* (New York, 2000).

The classic work on Chinese literature is **Liu Wu-Chi**, *An
Introduction to Chinese Literature* (Bloomington, Ind., 1966). Also
consult the more recent and scholarly **S. Owen**, *An Anthology of
Chinese Literature: Beginnings to 1911* (New York, 1996), and

V. Mair, *The Columbia Anthology of Traditional Chinese
Literature* (New York, 1994). For poetry, see **Liu Wu-Chi** and **I.
Yucheng Lo**, *Sunflower Splendor: Three Thousand Years of
Chinese Poetry* (Bloomington, Ind., 1975), and **S. Owen**, *The Great
Age of Chinese Poetry: The High T'ang* (New Haven, Conn., 1981),
the latter presenting poems in both Chinese and English.

For a comprehensive introduction to Chinese art, see the classic
M. Sullivan, *The Arts of China,* 4th ed. (Berkeley, Calif., 1999);
M. Tregear, *Chinese Art,* rev. ed. (London, 1997); and **C. Clunas**, *Art
in China* (Oxford, 1997). The standard introduction to Chinese
painting can be found in **J. Cahill**, *Chinese Painting* (New York,
1985), and **Yang Xin** et al., *Three Thousand Years of Chinese
Painting* (New Haven, Conn., 1997).

InfoTrac College Edition

Visit this chapter's InfoTrac College Edition/Research activities at
the *Essential World History* Companion Website for activities
related to traditional China.

CENGAGENOW for Duiker and Spielvogel's *The Essential
World History, Third Edition*

Enter *CengageNOW* using the access card that is available with
this text. *CengageNOW* will assist you in understanding the
content in this chapter with lesson plans generated for your
needs, as well as provide you with a connection to the *Wadsworth
World History Resource Center* (see description below for details).

WORLD HISTORY
RESOURCE CENTER

Enter the Resource Center using either your *CengageNOW* access
card or your standalone access card for the *Wadsworth World
History Resource Center*. Organized by topic, this website includes
quizzes; images; over 350 primary source documents; interactive
simulations, maps, and timelines; movie explorations; and a wealth
of other resources. You can read the following documents, and
many more, at http://worldrc.wadsworth.com/

Dao De Jing, *Daoism*

Confucius, *The Doctrine of the Mean*

Visit the *Essential World History* Companion Website for chapter
quizzes and more.

academic.cengage.com/history/duiker

11

THE EAST ASIAN RIMLANDS: EARLY JAPAN, KOREA, AND VIETNAM

CHAPTER OUTLINE AND FOCUS QUESTIONS

Japan: Land of the Rising Sun

☐ How did Japan's geographic location affect the course of its early history, and how did it influence the political structures and social institutions that arose there?

Korea: Bridge to the East

☐ What were the main characteristics of economic and social life in early Korea?

Vietnam: The Smaller Dragon

☐ What were the main developments in Vietnamese history before 1500? Why were the Vietnamese able to restore their national independence after a millennium of Chinese rule?

CRITICAL THINKING

☐ How did Chinese civilization influence the societies that arose in Japan, Korea, and Vietnam during their early history?

Vietnamese troops defending their homeland against Chinese invaders

Maurice Durand Collection, Yale University Library

WHEN THE FIRST EMPEROR OF QIN laid his eyes on the rhinoceros horn, the elephant tusks, and the kingfisher plumes that had been brought to him from the land of Yueh, he knew that he must have more of them, so he ordered Commissioner T'u Sui to lead a vast army to extend his imperial authority over the small land to the south of his empire. The battle raged for three years, but the Yueh were not so easy to conquer. According to a Chinese account of the event, "The Yueh people entered the wilderness and lived there with the animals; none consented to be a slave of [Qin]. . . . [They] attacked by night, inflicting on them a great defeat and killing Commissioner T'u Sui."[1]

The event described here occurred sometime in the late third century B.C.E., and the land of Yueh is today known as Vietnam. Although the Qin were eventually able to subdue the rebellion, another revolt erupted in 39 C.E. when Trung Trac and Trung Nhi, the widows of local lords, organized an uprising against Chinese occupation forces. This attempt failed as well, but future dynasties continued to have difficulties in controlling the region, and in the tenth century C.E., the people of Yueh rose up once more and restored their independence. To this day, the relationship between China and Vietnam is an uneasy one, marked by alternating periods of cooperation and conflict.

The Qin emperor's disdainful attitude toward his small neighbor should not surprise us. During ancient times, China was the most technologically advanced society in East Asia. To the north and west were pastoral peoples whose military exploits were often impressive but whose political and cultural attainments were still limited, at least by comparison with the great river valley civilizations of the day. In inland areas south of the Yangtze River were scattered clumps of rice farmers and hill peoples, most of whom had not yet entered the era of state building and had little knowledge of the niceties of Confucian ethics. Along the fringes of Chinese civilization were a number of other agricultural societies that were beginning to follow a pattern of development similar to that of China, although somewhat later in time. One of these was the land of Yueh, where a relatively advanced agricultural civilization had been in existence for several hundred years before the area was finally conquered by the Han dynasty in the second century C.E. Another was in the islands of Japan, where an organized society was beginning to take shape just as Chinese administrators were attempting to consolidate imperial rule over the Vietnamese people. On the Korean peninsula, an advanced Neolithic society had already begun to develop a few centuries earlier.

All of these early agricultural societies were eventually influenced to some degree by their great neighbor, China. Vietnam remained under Chinese rule for a thousand years. Korea retained its separate existence but was long a tributary state of China and in many ways followed the cultural example of its larger patron. Only Japan retained both its political independence and its cultural uniqueness. Yet even the Japanese were strongly influenced by the glittering culture of their powerful neighbor, and today many Japanese institutions and customs still bear the imprint of several centuries of borrowing from China. In this chapter, we will take a closer look at these emerging societies along the Chinese rimlands and consider how their cultural achievements reflected or contrasted with those of the Chinese Empire. ◆

Japan: Land of the Rising Sun

The geographic environment helps explain some of the historical differences between Chinese and Japanese society. Whereas China is a continental civilization, Japan is an island country. It consists of four main islands (see Map 11.1): Hokkaido in the north, the main island of Honshu in the center, and the two smaller islands of Kyushu and Shikoku in the southwest. Its total

MAP 11.1 **Early Japan.** This map shows key cities in Japan during the early development of the Japanese state. ❓ Why were the original Japanese capitals in early Japan located where they were? 🖱 View an animated version of this map or related maps at http://worldrc.wadsworth.com/

land area is about 146,000 square miles, about the size of the state of Montana. Japan's main islands are at approximately the same latitude as the eastern seaboard of the United States.

Like the eastern United States, Japan is blessed with a temperate climate. It is slightly warmer on the east coast, which is washed by the Pacific current that sweeps up from the south, and has a number of natural harbors that provide protection from the winds and high waves of the Pacific Ocean. As a consequence, in recent times, the majority of the Japanese people have tended to live along the east coast, especially in the flat plains surrounding the cities of Tokyo, Osaka, and Kyoto. In these favorable environmental conditions, Japanese farmers have been able to harvest two crops of rice annually since early times.

By no means, however, is Japan an agricultural paradise. Like China, much of the country is mountainous, with only about 20 percent of the total land area suitable for cultivation. These mountains are of volcanic origin, since the Japanese islands are located at the juncture of the Asian and Pacific tectonic plates. This location is both an advantage and a disadvantage. Volcanic soils are extremely fertile, which helps explain the exceptionally high productivity of Japanese farmers. At the same time, the area is prone to earthquakes, such as the famous earthquake of 1923, which destroyed almost the entire city of Tokyo.

The fact that Japan is an island country has had a significant impact on Japanese history. As we have seen, the continental character of Chinese civilization, with its constant threat of invasion from the north, had a number of consequences for Chinese history. One effect was to make the Chinese more sensitive to the preservation of their culture from destruction at the hands of non-Chinese invaders. Proud of their own considerable cultural achievements and their dominant position throughout the region, the Chinese have traditionally been reluctant to dilute the purity of their culture with foreign innovations. Culture more than race is a determinant of the Chinese sense of identity.

By contrast, the island character of Japan probably had the effect of strengthening the Japanese sense of ethnic and cultural distinctiveness. Although the Japanese view of themselves as the most ethnically homogeneous people in East Asia may not be entirely accurate (the modern Japanese probably represent a mix of peoples, much like their neighbors on the continent), their sense of racial and cultural homogeneity has enabled them to import ideas from abroad without worrying that the borrowings will destroy the uniqueness of their own culture.

A Gift from the Gods: Prehistoric Japan

According to an ancient legend recorded in historical chronicles written in the eighth century C.E., the islands of Japan were formed as a result of the marriage of the god Izanagi and the goddess Izanami. After giving birth to Japan, Izanami gave birth to a sun goddess whose name was Amaterasu. A descendant of Amaterasu later descended to earth and became the founder of the Japanese nation. This Japanese creation myth is reminiscent of similar beliefs in other ancient societies, which often saw themselves as the product of a union of deities. What is interesting about the Japanese version is that it has survived into modern times as an explanation for the uniqueness of the Japanese people and the divinity of the Japanese emperor, who is still believed by some Japanese to be a direct descendant of the sun goddess Amaterasu (see the box on p. 242).

Modern scholars have a more prosaic explanation for the origins of Japanese civilization. According to archaeological evidence, the Japanese islands have been occupied by human beings for at least 100,000 years. The earliest known Neolithic inhabitants, known as the Jomon people from the cord pattern of their pottery, lived in the islands as much as 10,000 years ago. They lived by hunting, fishing, and food gathering and probably had not mastered the techniques of agriculture.

Agriculture probably first appeared in Japan sometime during the first millennium B.C.E., although some archaeologists believe that the Jomon people had already learned how to cultivate some food crops considerably earlier than that. About 400 B.C.E., rice cultivation was introduced, probably by immigrants from the mainland by way of the Korean peninsula. Until recently, historians believed that these immigrants drove out the existing inhabitants of the area and gave rise to the emerging Yayoi culture (named for the site near Tokyo where pottery from the period was found).

It is now thought, however, that Yayoi culture was a product of a mixture between the Jomon people and the new arrivals, enriched by imports such as wet-rice agriculture, which had been brought by the immigrants from the mainland. In any event, it seems clear that the Yayoi peoples were the ancestors of the vast majority of present-day Japanese.

At first, the Yayoi lived primarily on the southern island of Kyushu, but eventually they moved northward onto the main island of Honshu, conquering, assimilating, or driving out the previous inhabitants of the area, some of whose descendants, known as the Ainu, still live in the northern islands. Finally, in the first centuries C.E., the Yayoi settled in the Yamato plain in the vicinity of the modern cities of Osaka and Kyoto. Japanese legend recounts the story of a "divine warrior" (in Japanese, *Jimmu*) who led his people eastward from the island of Kyushu to establish a kingdom in the Yamato plain.

The Yamato Plain

In central Honshu, the Yayoi set up a tribal society based on a number of clans, called **uji.** Each **uji** was ruled by a hereditary chieftain, who provided protection to the local population in return for a proportion of the annual harvest. The population itself was divided between a small aristocratic class and the majority of the population, composed of rice farmers, artisans, and other household servants of the aristocrats. Yayoi society was highly decentralized, although eventually the chieftain of the dominant clan in the Yamato region, who claimed to be descended from the sun goddess Amaterasu, achieved a kind of titular primacy. There is no evidence, however, of a central ruler equivalent in power to the Chinese rulers of the Shang and the Zhou eras.

The Rise of the Japanese State

Although the Japanese had been aware of China for centuries, they paid relatively little attention to their more advanced neighbor until the early seventh century, when the rise of the centralized and expansionistic Tang dynasty presented a challenge. The Tang began to meddle in the affairs of the Korean peninsula, conquering the southwestern coast and arousing anxiety in Japan. Yamato rulers attempted to deal with the potential threat posed by the Chinese in two ways. First, they sought alliances with the remaining Korean states. Second, they attempted to centralize their authority so that they could mount a more effective resistance in the event of a Chinese invasion. The key figure in this effort was Shotoku Taishi (572–622), a leading aristocrat in one of the dominant clans in the Yamato region. Prince Shotoku sent missions

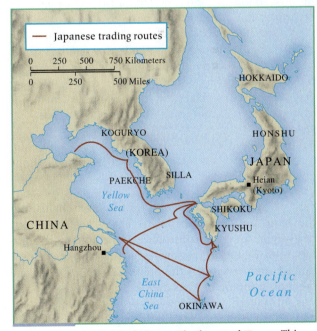

COMPARATIVE ILLUSTRATION

The Longhouse. Many early peoples built longhouses of wood and thatch to store their goods and carry on community activities. Many such structures were erected on heavy pilings to protect the interior from flooding, from insects, or from wild animals. On the left is a model of a sixth century C.E. warehouse in Osaka, Japan. The original was apparently used by local residents to store grain and other foodstuffs. In the center is the reconstruction of a similar structure built originally by Vikings in Denmark. The longhouses on the right are still occupied by families living on Nias, a small island off the coast of Sumatra. The outer walls were built to resemble the hulls of Dutch galleons that plied the seas near Nias during the seventeenth and eighteenth centuries.

to the Tang capital, Chang'an, to learn about the political institutions already in use in the relatively centralized Tang kingdom (see Map 11.2).

Emulating the Chinese Model Shotoku Taishi then launched a series of reforms to create a new system based roughly on the Chinese model. In the so-called seventeen-article constitution, he called for the creation of a centralized government under a supreme ruler and a merit system for selecting and ranking public officials (see the box on p. 243). His objective was to limit the powers of the hereditary nobility and enhance the prestige and authority of the Yamato ruler, who claimed divine status and was now emerging as the symbol of the unique character of the Japanese nation. In reality, there is evidence that places the origins of the Yamato clan on the Korean peninsula.

After Shotoku Taishi's death in 622, his successors continued to introduce reforms based on the Chinese model to make the government more efficient. In a series of so-called Taika ("great change") reforms that began in the mid-seventh century, the Grand Council of State was established, presiding over a cabinet of eight ministries. To the traditional six ministries of Tang China were added ministers representing the central secretariat and the imperial household. The territory of Japan was divided into administrative districts on the Chinese pattern. The

MAP 11.2 **Japan's Relations with China and Korea.** This map shows the Japanese islands at the time of the Yamato state. Maritime routes taken by Japanese traders and missionaries to China are indicated. ❓ Where did Japanese traders travel after reaching the mainland? 🪶 **View an animated version of this map or related maps at** http://worldrc.wadsworth.com/

THE EASTERN EXPEDITION OF EMPEROR JIMMU

POLITICS & GOVERNMENT

Japanese myths maintained that the Japanese nation could be traced to the sun goddess Amaterasu, who was the ancestor of the founder of the Japanese imperial family, Emperor Jimmu. This passage from the *Nihon Shoki (The Chronicles of Japan)* describes the campaign in which the "divine warrior" Jimmu occupied the central plains of Japan, symbolizing the founding of the Japanese nation. Legend dates this migration to about 660 B.C.E., but modern historians believe that it took place much later (perhaps as late as the fourth century C.E.) and that the account of the "divine warrior" may represent an effort by Japanese chroniclers to find a local equivalent to the Sage Kings of prehistoric China.

How does the author of this document justify the actions taken by Emperor Jimmu to defeat his enemies? What evidence does he present to demonstrate that Jimmu has the support of divine forces?

The Chronicles of Japan

Emperor Jimmu was forty-five years of age when he addressed the assemblage of his brothers and children: "Long ago, this central land of the Reed Plains was bequeathed to our imperial ancestors by the heavenly deities, Takamimusubi-no-Kami and Amaterasu Omikami. . . . However, the remote regions still do not enjoy the benefit of our imperial rule, with each town having its own master and each village its own chief. Each of them sets up his own boundaries and contends for supremacy against other masters and chiefs."

"I have heard from an old deity knowledgeable in the affairs of the land and sea that in the east there is a beautiful land encircled by blue mountains. This must be the land from which our great task of spreading our benevolent rule can begin, for it is indeed the center of the universe. . . . Let us go there, and make it our capital. . . .'"

In the winter of that year . . . the Emperor personally led imperial princes and a naval force to embark on his eastern expedition. . . .

When Nagasunehiko heard of the expedition, he said: "The children of the heavenly deities are coming to rob me of my country." He immediately mobilized his troops and intercepted Jimmu's troops at the hill of Kusaka and engaged in a battle. . . . The imperial forces were unable to advance. Concerned with the reversal, the Emperor formulated a new divine plan and said to himself: "I am the descendant of the Sun Goddess, and it is against the way of heaven to face the sun in attacking my enemy. Therefore our forces must retreat to make a show of weakness. After making sacrifice to the deities of heaven and earth, we shall march with the sun on our backs. We shall trample down our enemies with the might of the sun. In this way, without staining our swords with blood, our enemies can be conquered." . . . So, he ordered the troops to retreat to the port of Kusaka and regroup there. . . .

[After withdrawing to Kusaka, the imperial forces sailed southward, landed at a port in the present-day Kita peninsula, and again advanced north toward Yamato.]

The precipitous mountains provided such effective barriers that the imperial forces were not able to advance into the interior, and there was no path they could tread. Then one night Amaterasu Omikami appeared to the Emperor in a dream: "I will send you the Yatagarasu, let it guide you through the land." The following day, indeed, the Yatagarasu appeared flying down from the great expanse of the sky. The Emperor said: "The coming of this bird signifies the fulfillment of my auspicious dream. How wonderful it is! Our imperial ancestor, Amaterasu Omikami, desires to help us in the founding of our empire."

CENGAGE*NOW* To read more about Emperor Jimmu, enter the *CengageNOW* documents area using the access card that is available for *The Essential World History*.

---

rural village, composed ideally of fifty households, was the basic unit of government. The village chief was responsible for "the maintenance of the household registers, the assigning of the sowing of crops and the cultivation of mulberry trees, the prevention of offenses, and the requisitioning of taxes and forced labor." A law code was introduced, and a new tax system was established; now all farmland technically belonged to the state, so taxes were paid directly to the central government rather than through the local nobility, as had previously been the case.

As a result of their new acquaintance with China, the Japanese also developed a strong interest in Buddhism.

Some of the first Japanese to travel to China during this period were Buddhist pilgrims hoping to learn more about the exciting new doctrine and bring back scriptures. Buddhism became quite popular among the aristocrats, who endowed wealthy monasteries that became active in Japanese politics. At first, the new faith did not penetrate to the masses, but eventually, popular sects such as the Pure Land sect, an import from China, won many adherents among the common people.

The Nara Period Initial efforts to build a new state modeled roughly after the Tang state were successful. After Shotoku Taishi's death in 622, political influence fell into

THE SEVENTEEN-ARTICLE CONSTITUTION

POLITICS & GOVERNMENT

The following excerpt from the *Nihon Shoki (The Chronicles of Japan)* is a passage from the seventeen-article constitution promulgated in 604 C.E. Although the opening section reflects Chinese influence in its emphasis on social harmony, there is also a strong focus on obedience and hierarchy. The constitution was put into practice during the reign of the famous Prince Shotoku.

What are the key components in this first constitution in the history of Japan? To what degree do its provisions conform to Confucian principles in China?

The Chronicles of Japan

Summer, 4th month, 3rd day [12th year of Empress Suiko, 604 C.E.]. The Crown Prince personally drafted and promulgated a constitution consisting of seventeen articles, which are as follows:

I. Harmony is to be cherished, and opposition for opposition's sake must be avoided as a matter of principle. Men are often influenced by partisan feelings, except a few sagacious ones. Hence there are some who disobey their lords and fathers, or who dispute with their neighboring villages. If those above are harmonious and those below are cordial, their discussion will be guided by a spirit of conciliation, and reason shall naturally prevail. There will be nothing that cannot be accomplished.

II. With all our heart, revere the three treasures. The three treasures, consisting of Buddha, the Doctrine, and the Monastic Order, are the final refuge of the four generated beings, and are the supreme objects of worship in all countries. Can any man in any age ever fail to respect these teachings? Few men are utterly devoid of goodness, and men can be taught to follow the teachings. Unless they take refuge in the three treasures, there is no way of rectifying their misdeeds.

III. When an imperial command is given, obey it with reverence. The sovereign is likened to heaven, and his subjects are likened to earth. With heaven providing the cover and earth supporting it, the four seasons proceed in orderly fashion, giving sustenance to all that which is in nature. If earth attempts to overtake the functions of heaven, it destroys everything. . . . If there is no reverence shown to the imperial command, ruin will automatically result. . . .

VII. Every man must be given his clearly delineated responsibility. If a wise man is entrusted with office, the sound of praise arises. If a wicked man holds office, disturbances become frequent. . . . In all things, great or small, find the right man, and the country will be well governed. . . . In this manner, the state will be lasting and its sacerdotal functions will be free from danger.

CENGAGENOW To read the entire constitution, enter the *CengageNOW* documents area using the access card that is available for *The Essential World History.*

---

the hands of the powerful Fujiwara clan, which managed to marry into the ruling family and continue the reforms Shotoku had begun. In 710, a new capital, laid out on a grid similar to the great Tang city of Chang'an, was established at Nara, on the eastern edge of the Yamato plain. The Yamato ruler began to use the title "son of Heaven" in the Chinese fashion. In deference to the allegedly divine character of the ruling family, the mandate remained in perpetuity in the imperial house rather than being bestowed on an individual who was selected by Heaven because of his talent and virtue, as was the case in China.

Had these reforms succeeded, Japan might have followed the Chinese pattern and developed a centralized bureaucratic government. But as time passed, the central government proved unable to curb the power of the aristocracy. Unlike in Tang China, the civil service examinations in Japan were not open to all but were restricted to individuals of noble birth. Leading officials were awarded large tracts of land, and they and other powerful families were able to keep the taxes from the lands for themselves. Increasingly starved for revenue, the central government steadily lost power and influence.

The Heian Period   In 794, the emperor moved the capital to his family's original power base at nearby Heian, on the site of present-day Kyoto. The new capital was laid out in the now familiar Chang'an checkerboard pattern, but on a larger scale than at Nara. Now increasingly self-confident, the rulers ceased to emulate the Tang and sent no more missions to Chang'an. At Heian, the emperor—as the head of the royal line descended from the sun goddess was now officially styled—continued to rule in name, but actual power was in the hands of the Fujiwara clan, which had managed through intermarriage to link its fortunes closely with the imperial family. A senior member of the clan began to serve as regent (in practice, the chief executive of the government) for the emperor (see the comparative essay "Feudal Orders Around the World" on p. 244).

FEUDAL ORDERS AROUND THE WORLD

POLITICS & GOVERNMENT

When we use the word *feudalism,* we usually think of European knights on horseback clad in iron coats and armed with sword and lance. However, between 800 and 1500, a form of social organization that modern historians called feudalism developed in different parts of the world. By the term *feudalism,* these historians meant a decentralized political order in which local lords owed loyalty and provided military service to a king or more powerful lord. In Europe, a feudal order based on lords and vassals arose between 800 and 900 and flourished for the next four hundred years.

In Japan, a feudal order much like that found in Europe developed between 800 and 1500. By the end of the ninth century, powerful nobles in the countryside, while owing a loose loyalty to the Japanese emperor, began to exercise political and legal power in their own extensive lands. To protect their property and security, these nobles retained samurai, warriors who owed loyalty to the nobles and provided military service for them. Like knights in Europe, the samurai followed a warrior code and fought on horseback, clad in iron. They carried a sword and bow and arrow, however, rather than a sword and lance.

In some respects, the political relationships among the Indian states beginning in the fifth century took on the character of the feudal system that emerged in Europe in the Middle Ages. Like medieval European lords, local Indian rajas were technically vassals of the king, but unlike in European feudalism, the relationship was not a contractual one. Still, the Indian model became highly complex, with "inner" and "outer" vassals, depending on their physical or political proximity to the king, and "greater" or "lesser" vassals, depending on their power and influence. As in Europe, the vassals themselves often had vassals.

In the Valley of Mexico, between 1300 and 1500 the Aztecs developed a political system that bore some similarities to the Japanese, Indian, and European feudal orders. Although the Aztec king was a powerful, authoritarian ruler, the local rulers of lands outside the capital city were allowed considerable freedom. Nevertheless, they paid tribute to the king and also provided him with military forces. Unlike the knights and samurai of Europe and Japan, however, Aztec warriors were armed with sharp knives made of stone and spears of wood fitted with razor-sharp blades cut from stone.

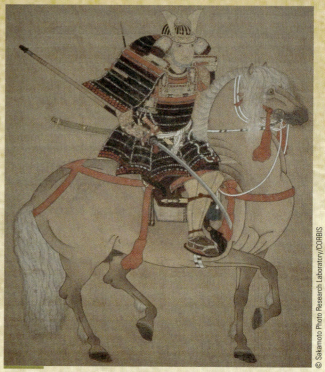

© Sakamoto Photo Research Laboratory/CORBIS

Samurai. During the Kamakura period, painters began to depict the adventures of the new warrior class. Here is an imposing mounted samurai warrior, the Japanese equivalent of the medieval knight in fief-holding Europe. Like his European counterpart, the samurai was supposed to live by a strict moral code and was expected to maintain an unquestioning loyalty to his liege lord. Above all, a samurai's life was one of simplicity and self-sacrifice.

What was occurring was a return to the decentralization that had existed prior to Shotoku Taishi. The central government's attempts to impose taxes directly on the rice lands failed, and rural areas came under the control of powerful families whose wealth was based on the ownership of tax-exempt farmland (called **shoen**). To avoid paying taxes, peasants would often surrender their lands to a local aristocrat, who would then allow the peasants to cultivate the lands in return for the payment of rent. To obtain protection from government officials, these local aristocrats might in turn grant title of their lands to a more powerful aristocrat with influence at court. In return, these individuals would receive inheritable rights to a portion of the income from the estate.

With the decline of central power at Heian, local aristocrats tended to take justice into their own hands and increasingly used military force to protect their interests. A new class of military retainers called the **samurai** emerged whose purpose was to protect the security and property of their patron. They frequently drew their leaders from disappointed aristocratic office seekers, who thus began to occupy a prestigious position in local society, where they often served an administrative as well as a military function. The samurai lived a life of simplicity and self-sacrifice

JAPAN'S WARRIOR CLASS

POLITICS & GOVERNMENT

The samurai was the Japanese equivalent of the medieval European knight. Like the knight, he was expected to adhere to a strict moral code. Although this passage comes from a document dating only to the seventeenth century, it shows the importance of hierarchy and duty in a society influenced by the doctrine of Confucius. Note the similarity with Krishna's discourse on the duties of an Indian warrior in Chapter 2.

How would you compare the duties of the samurai with those of a knight in medieval Europe? Are his responsibilities closer to those of a Confucian "gentleman" in China?

The Way of the Samurai

The master once said: . . . Generation after generation men have taken their livelihood from tilling the soil, or devised and manufactured tools, or produced profit from mutual trade, so that peoples' needs were satisfied. Thus the occupations of farmer, artisan, and merchant necessarily grew up as complementary to one another. However, the samurai eats food without growing it, uses utensils without manufacturing them, and profits without buying or selling. . . . The samurai is one who does not cultivate, does not manufacture, and does not engage in trade, but it cannot be that he has no function at all as a samurai. . . .

If one deeply fixes his attention on what I have said and examines closely one's own function, it will become clear what the business of the samurai is. The business of the samurai consists in reflecting on his own station in life, in discharging loyal service to his master if he has one, in

deepening his fidelity in associations with friends, and, with due consideration of his own position, in devoting himself to duty above all. . . . The samurai dispenses with the business of the farmer, artisan, and merchant and confines himself to practicing this Way; should there be someone in the three classes of the common people who transgresses against these moral principles, the samurai summarily punishes him and thus upholds proper moral principles in the land. . . . Outwardly he stands in physical readiness for any call to service, and inwardly he strives to fulfill the Way of the lord and subject, friend and friend, father and son, older and younger brother, and husband and wife. Within his heart he keeps to the ways of peace, but without he keeps his weapons ready for use. The three classes of the common people make him their teacher and respect him. By following his teachings, they are enabled to understand what is fundamental and what is secondary.

Herein lies the Way of the samurai, the means by which he earns his clothing, food, and shelter; and by which his heart is put at ease, and he is enabled to pay back at length his obligation to his lord and the kindness of his parents. Were there no such duty, it would be as though one were to steal the kindness of one's parents, greedily devour the income of one's master, and make one's whole life a career of robbery and brigandage. This would be very grievous.

CENGAGENOW To read the samurai creed, enter the *CengageNOW* documents area using the access card that is available for *The Essential World History*.

---

and were expected to maintain an intense and unquestioning loyalty to their lord. Bonds of loyalty were also quite strong among members of the samurai class, and homosexuality was common. Like the knights of medieval Europe, the samurai fought on horseback (although a samurai carried a sword and a bow and arrows rather than lance and shield) and were supposed to live by a strict warrior code, known in Japan as *Bushido*, or "way of the warrior" (see the box above). As time went on, they became a major force and almost a surrogate government in much of the Japanese countryside.

The Kamakura Shogunate and After   By the end of the twelfth century, as rivalries among noble families led to almost constant civil war, once again centralizing forces asserted themselves. This time the instrument was a powerful noble from a warrior clan named Minamoto Yoritomo (1142–1199), who defeated several rivals and set up his power base on the Kamakura peninsula, south of the modern city of Tokyo. To strengthen the state, he created a more centralized government (the *bakufu*, or "tent government")

under a powerful military leader, known as the **shogun** (general). The shogun attempted to increase the powers of the central government while reducing rival aristocratic clans to vassal status. This **shogunate system,** in which the emperor was the titular authority while the shogun exercised actual power, served as the political system in Japan until the second half of the nineteenth century.

The system worked effectively, and it was fortunate that it did, because during the next century, Japan faced the most serious challenge it had yet confronted. The Mongols, who had destroyed the Song dynasty in China, were now attempting to assert their hegemony throughout all of Asia (see Chapter 10). In 1266, Emperor Khubilai Khan demanded tribute from Japan. When the Japanese refused, he invaded with an army of over 30,000 troops. Bad weather and difficult conditions forced a retreat, but the Mongols tried again in 1281. An army nearly 150,000 strong landed on the northern coast of Kyushu. The Japanese were able to contain them for two months until virtually the entire Mongol fleet was destroyed by a massive typhoon—a "divine wind" (*kamikaze*). Japan would not face a foreign invader again until American forces landed on the Japanese islands in the summer of 1945.

The resistance to the Mongols had put a heavy strain on the system, however, and in 1333, the Kamakura shogunate was overthrown by a coalition of powerful clans. A new shogun, supplied by the Ashikaga family, arose in Kyoto and attempted to continue the shogunate system. But the Ashikaga were unable to restore the centralized power of their predecessors. With the central government reduced to a shell, the power of the local landed aristocracy increased to an unprecedented degree. Heads of great noble families, now called **daimyo** ("great names"), controlled vast landed estates that owed no taxes to the government or to the court in Kyoto. As clan rivalries continued, the daimyo relied increasingly on the samurai for protection, and political power came into the hands of a loose coalition of noble families.

By the end of the fifteenth century, Japan was again close to anarchy. A disastrous civil conflict known as the Onin War (1467–1477) led to the virtual destruction of the capital city of Kyoto and the disintegration of the shogunate. With the disappearance of any central authority, powerful aristocrats in rural areas now seized total control over large territories and ruled as independent great lords. Territorial rivalries and claims of precedence led to almost constant warfare in this period of "warring states," as it is called (in obvious parallel with a similar era during the Zhou dynasty in China). The trend back toward central authority did not begin until the last quarter of the sixteenth century.

CHRONOLOGY Formation of the Japanese State

Shotoku Taishi	572–622
Era of Taika reforms	Mid-seventh century
Nara period	710–784
Heian (Kyoto) period	794–1185
Murasaki Shikibu	978–c. 1016
Minamoto Yoritomo	1142–1199
Kamakura shogunate	1185–1333
Mongol invasions	Late thirteenth century
Ashikaga period	1333–1600
Onin War	1462–1477

Economic and Social Structures

From the time the Yayoi culture was first established on the Japanese islands, Japan was a predominantly agrarian society. Although Japan lacked the spacious valleys and deltas of the river valley societies, its inhabitants were able to take advantage of their limited amount of tillable land and plentiful rainfall to create a society based on the cultivation of wet rice.

Trade and Manufacturing   As in China, commerce was slow to develop in Japan. During ancient times, each *uji* had a local artisan class, composed of weavers, carpenters, and ironworkers, but trade was essentially local and was

The Burning of the Palace.   The Kamakura era is represented in this action-packed thirteenth-century scene from the *Scroll of the Heiji Period,* which depicts the burning of a retired emperor's palace in the middle of the night. Servants and ladies of the court flee in vain from the massive flames. Confusion and violence reign. The determined faces of the samurai warriors only add to the ferocity of the attack.

COMPARATIVE ILLUSTRATION

Urban Life in Medieval Japan and Europe. Like Europe in the Middle Ages, medieval Japan was largely an agricultural society, but during their medieval periods, both began to develop trade and manufacturing in growing urban areas. Intraregional trade was transported by horse-drawn carts or by boats on rivers or along the coast. Portrayed at the top is a detail from a thirteenth-century scroll depicting the bustle and general confusion of the city of Edo (now Tokyo). On the bottom is a similar scene from a fourteenth-century painting by Ambrogio Lorenzetti. He portrays a street scene in Siena, Italy. In the street are donkeys loaded with goods, a goatherd driving his flock through the town, and two women from the country bringing their goods into the town. In the background, a shoemaker is at work in his shop, a teacher is instructing his students, a man is selling spices, and a tailor is cutting a piece of cloth.

FAMILY & SOCIETY

regulated by the local clan leaders. With the rise of the Yamato state, a money economy gradually began to develop, although most trade was still conducted through barter until the twelfth century, when metal coins introduced from China became more popular.

Trade and manufacturing began to develop more rapidly during the Kamakura period, with the appearance of trimonthly markets in the larger towns and the emergence of such industries as paper, iron casting, and porcelain. Foreign trade, mainly with Korea and China, began during the eleventh century. Japan exported raw materials, paintings, swords, and other manufactured items in return for silk, porcelain, books, and copper cash. Some Japanese traders were so aggressive in pressing their interests that authorities in China and Korea attempted to limit the number of Japanese commercial missions that could visit each year. Such restrictions were often ignored, however, and encouraged some Japanese traders to turn to piracy.

Significantly, manufacturing and commerce developed rapidly during the more decentralized period of the Ashikaga shogunate and the era of the warring states, perhaps because of the rapid growth in the wealth and

autonomy of local daimyo families. Market towns, now operating on a full money economy, began to appear, and local manufacturers formed guilds to protect their mutual interests. Sometimes local peasants would sell products made in their homes, such as clothing made of silk or hemp, household items, or food products, at the markets. In general, however, trade and manufacturing remained under the control of the local daimyo, who would often provide tax breaks to local guilds in return for other benefits. Although Japan remained a primarily agricultural society, it was on the verge of a major advance in manufacturing.

Daily Life One of the first descriptions of the life of the Japanese people comes from a Chinese dynastic history from the third century C.E. It describes lords and peasants living in an agricultural society that was based on the cultivation of wet rice. Laws had been enacted to punish offenders, local trade was conducted in markets, and government granaries stored the grain that was paid as taxes.

Life for the common people probably changed very little over the next several hundred years. Most were peasants who worked on land owned by their lord or, in some cases, by the state or by Buddhist monasteries. By no means, however, were all peasants equal either economically or socially. Although in ancient times, all land was owned by the state and peasants working the land were taxed at an equal rate depending on the nature of the crop, after the Yamato era variations began to develop. At the top were local officials who were often well-to-do peasants. They were responsible for organizing collective labor services and collecting tax grain from the peasants and in turn were exempt from such obligations themselves.

The mass of the peasants were under the authority of these local officials. In theory, peasants were free to dispose of their harvest as they saw fit after paying their tax quota, but in practical terms, their freedom was limited. Those who were unable to pay the tax sank to the level of **genin,** or landless laborers, who could be bought and sold by their proprietors like slaves along with the land on which they worked. Some fled to escape such a fate and attempted to survive by clearing plots of land in the mountains or by becoming bandits.

In addition to the *genin*, the bottom of the social scale was occupied by the **eta,** a class of hereditary slaves who were responsible for what were considered degrading occupations, such as curing leather and burying the dead. The origins of the *eta* are not entirely clear, but they probably were descendants of prisoners of war, criminals, or mountain dwellers who were not related to the dominant Yamato peoples. As we shall see, the *eta* are still a distinctive part of Japanese society, and although their full legal rights are guaranteed under the current constitution, discrimination against them is not uncommon.

Daily life for ordinary people in early Japan resembled that of their counterparts throughout much of Asia. The vast majority lived in small villages, several of which normally made up a single *shoen*. Housing was simple. Most lived in small two-room houses of timber, mud, or thatch, with dirt floors covered by straw or woven mats (the origin, perhaps, of the well-known *tatami*, or woven-mat floor, of more modern times). Their diet consisted of rice (if some was left after the payment of the grain tax), wild grasses, millet, roots, and some fish and birds. Life must have been difficult at best; as one eighth-century poet lamented:

> Here I lie on straw
> Spread on bare earth,
> With my parents at my pillow,
> My wife and children at my feet,
> All huddled in grief and tears.
> No fire sends up smoke
> At the cooking place,
> And in the cauldron
> A spider spins its web.[2]

The Role of Women Evidence about the relations between men and women in early Japan presents a mixed picture. The Chinese dynastic history reports that "in their meetings and daily living, there is no distinction between . . . men and women." It notes that a woman "adept in the ways of shamanism" had briefly ruled Japan

in the third century C.E. But it also remarks that polygyny was common, with nobles normally having four or five wives and commoners two or three.[3] An eighth-century law code guaranteed the inheritance rights of women, and wives abandoned by their husbands were permitted to obtain a divorce and remarry. A husband could divorce his wife if she did not produce a male child, committed adultery, disobeyed her parents-in-law, talked too much, engaged in theft, was jealous, or had a serious illness.[4]

When Buddhism was introduced, women were initially relegated to a subordinate position in the new faith. Although they were permitted to take up monastic life—many widows entered a monastery at the death of their husbands—they were not permitted to visit Buddhist holy places, nor were they even (in the accepted wisdom) equal with men in the afterlife. One Buddhist commentary from the late thirteenth century said that a woman could not attain enlightenment because "her sin is grievous, and so she is not allowed to enter the lofty palace of the great Brahma, nor to look upon the clouds which hover over his ministers and people."[5] Other Buddhist scholars were more egalitarian: "Learning the Law of Buddha and achieving release from illusion have nothing to do with whether one happens to be a man or a woman."[6] Such views ultimately prevailed, and women were eventually allowed to participate fully in Buddhist activities in medieval Japan.

Although women did not possess the full legal and social rights of their male counterparts, they played an active role at various levels of Japanese society. Aristocratic women were prominent at court, and some, such as the author Murasaki Shikibu, known as Lady Murasaki (978–c. 1016), became renowned for their artistic or literary talents. Though few commoners could aspire to such prominence, women often appear in the scroll paintings of the period along with men, doing the spring planting, threshing and hulling the rice, and acting as carriers, peddlers, salespersons, and entertainers.

In Search of the Pure Land: Religion in Early Japan

In Japan, as elsewhere, religious belief began with the worship of nature spirits. Early Japanese worshiped spirits, called **kami,** who resided in trees, rivers and streams, and mountains. They also believed in ancestral spirits present in the atmosphere. In Japan, these beliefs eventually evolved into a kind of state religion called **Shinto** (the "Sacred Way" or the "Way of the Gods"), which is still practiced today. Shinto still serves as an ideological and emotional force that knits the Japanese into a single people and nation.

Shinto does not have a complex metaphysical superstructure or an elaborate moral code. It does require certain ritual acts, usually undertaken at a shrine, and a process of purification, which may have originated in primitive concerns about death, childbirth, illness, and menstruation. This traditional concern about physical purity may help explain the strong Japanese concern for personal cleanliness and the practice of denying women entrance to the holy places.

Another feature of Shinto is its stress on the beauty of nature and the importance of nature itself in Japanese life. Shinto shrines are usually located in places of exceptional beauty and are often dedicated to a nearby physical feature. As time passed, such primitive beliefs contributed to the characteristic Japanese love of nature. In this sense, early Shinto beliefs have been incorporated into the lives of all Japanese.

In time, Shinto evolved into a state doctrine that was linked with belief in the divinity of the emperor and the sacredness of the Japanese nation. A national shrine was established at Ise, north of the early capital of Nara, where the emperor annually paid tribute to the sun goddess. But although Shinto had evolved well beyond its primitive origins, like its counterparts elsewhere it could not satisfy all the religious and emotional needs of the Japanese people. For those needs, the Japanese turned to Buddhism.

Buddhism   As we have seen, Buddhism was introduced into Japan from China during the sixth century C.E. and had begun to spread beyond the court to the general population by the eighth century. As in China, most Japanese saw no contradiction between worshiping both the Buddha and their local nature gods, many of whom were considered to be later manifestations of the Buddha. Most of the Buddhist sects that had achieved popularity in China were established in Japan, and many of them attracted powerful patrons at court. Great monasteries were established that competed in wealth and influence with the noble families that had traditionally ruled the country.

Perhaps the two most influential Buddhist sects were the Pure Land (Jodo) sect and **Zen** (in Chinese, Chan or Ch'an). The Pure Land sect, which taught that devotion alone could lead to enlightenment and release, was very popular among the common people, for whom monastic life was one of the few routes to upward mobility. Among the aristocracy, the most influential school was Zen, which exerted a significant impact on Japanese life and culture during the era of the warring states. In its emphasis on austerity, self-discipline, and communion with nature, Zen complemented many traditional beliefs in Japanese society and became an important component of the samurai warrior's code.

In Zen teachings, there were various ways to achieve enlightenment (**satori** in Japanese). Some stressed that it could be achieved suddenly. One monk, for example, reportedly achieved satori by listening to the sound of a bamboo striking against roof tiles; another, by carefully watching the opening of peach blossoms in the spring. But other practitioners, sometimes called adepts, said that enlightenment could come only through studying the scriptures and arduous self-discipline (known as zazen, or "seated Zen"). Seated Zen involved a lengthy process of meditation that cleansed the mind of all thoughts so that it could concentrate on the essential.

In the Garden.   In traditional China and Japan, gardens were meant to free the observer's mind from mundane concerns, offering spiritual refreshment in the quiet of nature. Chinese gardens were designed to reconstruct an orderly microcosm of nature, where the harassed Confucian official could find spiritual renewal. Wandering within a constantly changing perspective consisting of ponds, trees, rocks, and pavilions, he could imagine himself immersed in a monumental landscape. In this garden in Suzhou on the left, the rocks represent towering mountains to suggest the Daoist sense of withdrawal and eternity, reducing the viewer to a tiny speck in the grand flow of life.

In Japan, the traditional garden reflected the Zen Buddhist philosophy of simplicity, restraint, allusion, and tranquillity. In this garden at the Ryoanji temple in Kyoto, the rocks are meant to suggest mountains rising from a sea of pebbles. Such gardens served as an aid to meditation, inspiring the viewer to join with comrades in composing "linked verse."

Sources of Traditional Japanese Culture

Nowhere is the Japanese genius for blending indigenous and imported elements into an effective whole better demonstrated than in culture. In such widely diverse fields as art, architecture, sculpture, and literature, the Japanese from early times showed an impressive capacity to borrow selectively from abroad without destroying essential native elements.

Growing contact with China during the period of the rise of the Yamato state stimulated Japanese artists. Missions sent to China and Korea during the seventh and eighth centuries returned with examples of Tang literature, sculpture, and painting, all of which influenced the Japanese.

Literature Borrowing from Chinese models was somewhat complicated, however, since the early Japanese had no writing system for recording their own spoken language and initially adopted the Chinese written language for writing. But resourceful Japanese soon began to adapt the Chinese written characters so that they could be used for recording the Japanese language. In some cases, Chinese characters were given Japanese pronunciations. But Chinese characters ordinarily could not be used to record Japanese words, which normally contain more than one syllable. Sometimes the Japanese simply used Chinese characters as phonetic symbols that were combined to form Japanese words. Later they simplified the characters into phonetic symbols that were used alongside Chinese characters. This hybrid system continues to be used today.

At first, most educated Japanese preferred to write in Chinese, and a court literature—consisting of essays, poetry, and official histories—appeared in the classical Chinese language. But spoken Japanese never totally disappeared among the educated classes and eventually became the instrument of a unique literature. With the lessening of Chinese cultural influence in the tenth century, Japanese verse resurfaced. Between the tenth and fifteenth centuries, twenty imperial anthologies of poetry were compiled. Initially, they were written primarily by courtiers, but with the fall of the Heian court and the rise of the warrior and merchant classes, all literate segments of society began to produce poetry.

Japanese poetry is unique. It expresses its themes in a simple form, a characteristic stemming from traditional Japanese aesthetics, Zen religion, and the language itself. The aim of the Japanese poet was to create a mood, perhaps the melancholic effect of gently falling cherry blossoms or leaves. With a few specific references, the poet suggested a whole world, just as Zen Buddhism sought enlightenment from a sudden perception. Poets often alluded to earlier poems by repeating their images with small changes, a technique that was viewed not as plagiarism but as an elaboration on the meaning of the earlier poem.

By the fourteenth century, the technique of the "linked verse" had become the most popular form of Japanese poetry. Known as **haiku,** it is composed of seventeen syllables divided into lines of five, seven, and five syllables. The poems usually focused on images from nature and called attention to the mutability of life. Often the poetry was written by several individuals alternately composing verses and linking them together into long sequences of hundreds and even thousands of lines.

Poetry served a unique function at the Heian court, where it was the initial means of communication between lovers. By custom, aristocratic women were isolated from all contact with men outside their immediate family and spent their days hidden behind screens. Some amused themselves by writing poetry. When courtship began, poetic exchanges were the only means a woman had to attract her prospective lover, who would be enticed solely by her poetic art.

During the Heian period, male courtiers wrote in Chinese, believing that Chinese civilization was superior and worthy of emulation. Like the Chinese, they viewed prose fiction as "vulgar gossip." Nevertheless, from the ninth century to the twelfth, Japanese women were prolific writers of prose fiction in Japanese. Excluded from school, they learned to read and write at home and wrote diaries and stories to pass the time. Some of the most talented women were invited to court as authors in residence.

In the increasingly pessimistic world of the warring states of the Kamakura period (1185–1333), Japanese novels typically focused on a solitary figure who is aloof from the refinements of the court and faces battle and possibly death. Another genre, that of the heroic war tale, came out of the new warrior class. These works described the military exploits of warriors, coupled with an overwhelming sense of sadness and loneliness.

The famous classical Japanese drama known as *No* also originated during this period. *No* developed out of a variety of entertainment forms, such as dancing and juggling, that were part of the native tradition or had been imported from China and other regions of Asia. The plots were normally based on stories from Japanese history or legend. Eventually, *No* evolved into a highly stylized drama in which the performers wore masks and danced to the accompaniment of instrumental music. Like much of Japanese culture, *No* was restrained, graceful, and refined.

Art and Architecture In art and architecture, as in literature, the Japanese pursued their interest in beauty, simplicity, and nature. To some degree, Japanese artists and architects were influenced by Chinese forms. As they became familiar with Chinese architecture, Japanese rulers and aristocrats tried to emulate the splendor of Tang civilization and began constructing their palaces and temples in Chinese style.

During the Heian period (794–1185), the search for beauty was reflected in various art forms, such as narrative hand scrolls, screens, sliding door panels, fans, and lacquer decoration. As in the case of literature, nature themes dominated, such as seashore scenes, a spring rain, moon and mist, or flowering wisteria and cherry blossoms. All were intended to evoke an emotional response on the part of the viewer. Japanese painting suggested the frail beauty of nature by presenting it on a smaller scale. The majestic mountain in a Chinese painting became a more intimate Japanese landscape with rolling hills and a rice field. Faces were rarely shown, and human drama was indicated by a woman lying prostrate or hiding her face in her sleeve. Tension was shown by two people talking at a great distance or with their backs to one another.

During the Kamakura period (1185–1333), the hand scroll with its physical realism and action-packed paintings of the new warrior class achieved great popularity. Reflecting these chaotic times, the art of portraiture flourished, and a scroll would include a full gallery of warriors and holy men in starkly realistic detail, including such unflattering features as stubble, worry lines on a forehead, and crooked teeth. Japanese sculptors also produced naturalistic wooden statues of generals, nobles, and saints. By far the most distinctive, however, were the fierce heavenly "guardian kings," who still intimidate the viewer today.

Zen Buddhism, an import from China in the thirteenth century, also influenced Japanese aesthetics. With its emphasis on immediate enlightenment without recourse to intellectual analysis and elaborate ritual, Zen reinforced the Japanese predilection for simplicity and self-discipline. During this era, Zen philosophy found expression in the Japanese garden, the tea ceremony, the art of flower arranging, pottery and ceramics, and miniature plant display (the famous **bonsai,** literally "pot scenery").

Landscapes served as an important means of expression in both Japanese art and architecture. Japanese gardens were initially modeled on Chinese examples. Early court texts during the Heian period emphasized the importance of including a stream or pond when creating a garden. The landscape surrounding the fourteenth-century Golden Pavilion in Kyoto displays a harmony of garden, water, and architecture that makes it one of the treasures of the world. Because of the shortage of water in the city, later gardens concentrated on rock composition, using white pebbles to represent water.

Like the Japanese garden, the tea ceremony represents the fusion of Zen and aesthetics. Developed in the fifteenth century, it was practiced in a simple room devoid of external ornament except for a **tatami** floor, sliding doors, and an alcove with a writing desk and asymmetrical shelves. The participants could therefore focus completely on the activity of pouring and drinking tea. "Tea and Zen have the same flavor," goes the Japanese saying. Considered the ultimate symbol of spiritual deliverance, the tea ceremony had great aesthetic value and moral significance in traditional times just as it does today.

Japan and the Chinese Model

Few societies in Asia have historically been as isolated as Japan. Cut off from the mainland by 120 miles of frequently turbulent ocean, the Japanese had only minimal contact with the outside world during most of their early development.

Whether this isolation was ultimately beneficial to Japanese society cannot be determined. On the one hand, the lack of knowledge of developments taking place elsewhere probably delayed the process of change in Japan. On the other hand, the Japanese were spared the destructive invasions that afflicted other ancient civilizations. Certainly, once the Japanese became acquainted with Chinese culture at the height of the Tang era, they were quick to take advantage of the opportunity. In the space of a few decades, the young state adopted many aspects of Chinese society and culture and thereby introduced major changes into Japanese life.

Courtesy of William J. Duiker

The Golden Pavilion in Kyoto. The landscape surrounding the Golden Pavilion displays a harmony of garden, water, and architecture that makes it one of the treasures of the world. Constructed in the fourteenth century as a retreat where the shoguns could withdraw from their administrative chores, the pavilion is named for the gold foil that covered its exterior. Completely destroyed by an arsonist in 1950 as a protest against the commercialism of modern Buddhism, it was rebuilt and reopened in 1987. The use of water as a backdrop is especially noteworthy in Chinese and Japanese landscapes, as well as in the Middle East.

Nevertheless, Japanese political institutions failed to follow all aspects of the Chinese pattern. Despite Prince Shotoku's effort to make effective use of the imperial traditions of Tang China, the decentralizing forces inside Japanese society remained dominant throughout the period under discussion in this chapter. Adoption of the Confucian civil service examination did not lead to a breakdown of Japanese social divisions; instead the examination was administered in a manner that preserved and strengthened them. Although Buddhist and Daoist doctrines made a significant contribution to Japanese religious practices, Shinto beliefs continued to play a major role in shaping the Japanese worldview.

Why Japan did not follow the Chinese road to centralized authority has been the subject of some debate among historians. Some argue that the answer lies in differing cultural traditions, while others suggest that Chinese institutions and values were introduced too rapidly to be assimilated effectively by Japanese society. One factor may have been the absence of a foreign threat (except for the Mongols) in Japan. A recent view holds that diseases (such as smallpox and measles) imported inadvertently from China led to a marked decline in the population of the islands, reducing the food output and preventing the population from coalescing in more compact urban centers.

In any event, Japan was not the only society in Asia to assimilate ideas from abroad while at the same time preserving customs and institutions inherited from the past. Across the Sea of Japan to the west and several thousand miles to the south, other Asian peoples were embarked on a similar journey. We now turn to their experience.

Korea: Bridge to the East

No society in East Asia was more strongly influenced by the Chinese model than Korea. Slightly larger than the state of Minnesota, the Korean peninsula was probably first settled by Altaic-speaking fishing and hunting peoples from neighboring Manchuria during the Neolithic Age. Because the area is relatively mountainous (only about one-fifth of the peninsula is adaptable to cultivation), farming was apparently not practiced until about 2000 B.C.E. The other aspect of Korea's geography that has profoundly affected its history is its proximity to both China and Japan.

In 109 B.C.E., the northern part of the peninsula came under direct Chinese rule. During the next several generations, the area was ruled by the Han dynasty, which divided the territory into provinces and introduced Chinese institutions. With the decline of the Han in the third century C.E., power gradually shifted to local tribal leaders, who drove out the Chinese administrators but continued to absorb Chinese cultural influence. Eventually, three separate kingdoms emerged on the peninsula: Koguryo in the north,

Paekche in the southwest, and Silla in the southeast. The Japanese, who had recently established their own state on the Yamato plain, maintained a small colony on the southern coast.

Korea's Three Kingdoms

The Three Kingdoms

From the fourth to the seventh centuries, the three kingdoms were bitter rivals for influence and territory on the peninsula. At the same time, all began to absorb Chinese political and cultural institutions. Chinese influence was most notable in Koguryo, where Buddhism was introduced in the late fourth century C.E. and the first Confucian academy on the peninsula was established in the capital at Pyongyang. All three kingdoms also appear to have accepted a tributary relationship with one or another of the squabbling states that emerged in China after the fall of the Han. The kingdom of Silla, less exposed than its two rivals to Chinese influence, was at first the weakest of the three, but eventually its greater internal cohesion—perhaps a consequence of the tenacity of its tribal traditions—enabled it to become the dominant power on the peninsula. Then the rulers of Silla forced the Chinese to withdraw from all but the area adjacent to the Yalu River. To pacify the haughty Chinese, Silla accepted tributary status under the Tang dynasty. The remaining Japanese colonies in the south were eliminated.

With the country unified for the first time, the rulers of Silla attempted to use Chinese political institutions and ideology to forge a centralized state. Buddhism, now rising in popularity, became the state religion, and Korean monks followed the paths of their Japanese counterparts on journeys to the Middle Kingdom. Chinese architecture and art became dominant in the capital at Kyongju and other urban centers, and the written Chinese language became the official means of communication at court. But powerful aristocratic families, long dominant in the southeastern part of the peninsula, were still influential at court. They were able to prevent the adoption of the Tang civil service examination system and resisted the distribution of manorial lands to the poor. The failure to adopt the Chinese model was fatal. Squabbling among noble families steadily increased, and after the assassination of the king of Silla in 780, the country sank into civil war.

The Rise of the Koryo Dynasty

In the early tenth century, a new dynasty called Koryo (the root of the modern word for Korea) arose in the north. The new kingdom adopted Chinese political institutions in an effort to strengthen its power and unify its

The Sokkuram Buddha. As Buddhism spread from India to other parts of Asia, so did the representation of the Buddha in human form. From the first century C.E., statues of the Buddha began to absorb various cultural influences. Some early sculptures, marked by flowing draperies, reflected the Greco-Roman culture introduced to India during the era of Alexander the Great. Others were reminiscent of traditional male earth spirits, with broad shoulders and staring eyes. Under the Guptas, artists emphasized the Indian ideal of spiritual and bodily perfection.

As the faith spread along the Silk Road, representations of the Buddha began to reflect cultural influence from Persia and China, and eventually from Korea and Japan. Shown here is the eighth-century Sokkuram Buddha, created in the kingdom of Silla. Unable to construct a structure similar to the cave temples in China and India because of the hardness of the rock in the nearby hills, Korean builders erected a small domed cave out of granite blocks and a wooden veranda (see inset). Today, pilgrims still climb the steep hill to pay homage to this powerful and serene Buddha, one of the finest in Asia.

territory. The civil service examination system was introduced in 958, but as in Japan, the bureaucracy continued to be dominated by influential aristocratic families.

The Koryo dynasty remained in power for four hundred years, protected from invasion by the absence of a strong dynasty in neighboring China. Under the Koryo, industry and commerce slowly began to develop, but as in China, agriculture was the prime source of wealth. In theory, all land was the property of the king, but in actuality, noble families controlled their holdings. The lands were worked by peasants who were subject to burdens similar to those of European serfs. At the bottom of society was a class of "base people" (*chonmin*), composed of slaves, artisans, and other specialized workers.

From a cultural point of view, the Koryo era was one of high achievement. Buddhist monasteries, run by sects introduced from China, including Pure Land and Zen (Chan), controlled vast territories, while their monks served as royal advisers at court. At first, Buddhist themes dominated in Korean art and sculpture, and the entire Tripitaka (the "three baskets" of the Buddhist canon) was printed using wooden blocks. Eventually, however, with the appearance of landscape painting and porcelain, Confucian themes began to predominate.

Under the Mongols

Like its predecessor in Silla, the kingdom of Koryo was unable to overcome the power of the nobility and the absence of a reliable tax base. In the thirteenth century, the Mongols seized the northern part of the country and assimilated it into the Yuan Empire. The weakened kingdom of Koryo became a tributary of the Great Khan in Khanbaliq (see Chapter 10).

The era of Mongol rule was one of profound suffering for the Korean people, especially the thousands of peasants and artisans who were compelled to perform forced labor to help build the ships in preparation for Khubilai Khan's invasion of Japan. On the positive side, the Mongols introduced many new ideas and technology from China and farther afield. The Koryo dynasty had managed to survive, but only by accepting Mongol authority, and when the power of the Mongols declined, the kingdom declined with it. With the rise to power of the Ming in China, Koryo collapsed, and power was seized by the military commander Yi Song-gye, who declared the founding of the new Yi dynasty in 1392. Once again, the Korean people were in charge of their own destiny.

Vietnam: The Smaller Dragon

While the Korean people were attempting to establish their own identity in the shadow of the powerful Chinese Empire, the peoples of Vietnam, on China's southern frontier, were trying to do the same. The Vietnamese, then known as the Viet, or Yueh in Chinese, began to practice irrigated agriculture in the flooded regions of the Red River delta at an early date and entered the Bronze Age sometime during the second millennium B.C.E. By about 200 B.C.E., a young state had begun to form in the area but immediately encountered the expanding power of the Qin Empire (see Chapter 3). The Vietnamese were not easy to subdue, however, and the collapse of the Qin dynasty temporarily enabled them to preserve their independence. Nevertheless, a century later, they were absorbed into the Han Empire.

At first, the Han were satisfied to rule the delta as an autonomous region under the administration of the local landed aristocracy. But Chinese taxes were oppressive, and in 39 C.E., a revolt led by the Trung Sisters (widows of local nobles who had been executed by the Chinese) briefly brought Han rule to an end. The Chinese soon suppressed the rebellion, however, and began to rule the area directly through officials dispatched from China. In time, however, these foreign officials began to intermarry with the local nobility and form a Sino-Vietnamese ruling class who, though trained in Chinese culture, began to identify with the cause of Vietnamese autonomy.

For nearly a thousand years, the Vietnamese were exposed to the art, architecture, literature, philosophy, and written language of China as the Chinese attempted to integrate the area culturally as well as politically and administratively into their empire. To all intents and purposes, the Red River delta, then known to the Chinese as the "pacified South" (Annam), became a part of China.

The Rise of Great Viet

Despite the Chinese efforts to assimilate Vietnam, the Vietnamese sense of ethnic and cultural identity proved inextinguishable, and in the tenth century, the Vietnamese took advantage of the collapse of the Tang dynasty in China to overthrow Chinese rule.

The new Vietnamese state, which called itself Dai Viet (Great Viet), became a dynamic new force on the Southeast Asian mainland. As the population of the Red River delta expanded, Dai Viet soon came into conflict with Champa, its neighbor to the south. Located along the central coast of modern Vietnam, Champa was a trading society based on Indian cultural traditions. Over the next several centuries, the two states fought on numerous occasions. By the end of the fifteenth century, Dai Viet had conquered Champa. The Vietnamese then resumed their march southward, establishing agricultural settlements in the newly conquered territory. By the seventeenth century, the Vietnamese had reached the Gulf of Siam.

The Vietnamese faced an even more serious challenge from the north. The Song dynasty in China, beset with its own problems on the northern frontier, eventually accepted the Dai Viet ruler's offer of tribute status (see the box on p. 255), but later dynasties attempted to reintegrate the Red River delta into the Chinese Empire. The first effort was made in the late thirteenth century by the Mongols, who attempted on two occasions to conquer the Vietnamese. After a series of bloody battles, during which the Vietnamese displayed an impressive capacity for guerrilla warfare, the invaders were driven out. A little over a century later, the Ming dynasty tried again, and for twenty years Vietnam was once more under Chinese rule. In 1428, the Vietnamese evicted the Chinese again, but the experience had contributed to the strong sense of Vietnamese identity.

The Kingdom of Dai Viet, 1100

The Chinese Legacy Despite their stubborn resistance to Chinese rule, after the restoration of independence in the tenth century, Vietnamese rulers quickly discovered the convenience of the Confucian model in administering a river valley society and therefore attempted to follow Chinese practice in forming their own state. The ruler styled himself an emperor like his counterpart to the north (although he prudently termed himself a king in his direct dealings with the Chinese court), adopted Chinese court rituals, claimed the Mandate of Heaven, and arrogated to himself the same authority and privileges in his dealings with his subjects. But unlike a Chinese emperor, who had no particular symbolic role as defender of the Chinese people or Chinese culture, a Vietnamese monarch was viewed, above all, as the symbol and defender of Vietnamese independence.

Like their Chinese counterparts, Vietnamese rulers fought to preserve their authority from the challenges of powerful aristocratic families and turned to the Chinese bureaucratic model, including civil service examinations, as a means of doing so. Under the pressure of strong monarchs, the concept of merit eventually took hold, and the power of the landed aristocracy was weakened if not entirely broken. The Vietnamese adopted much of the Chinese administrative structure, including the six ministries, the censorate, and the various levels of provincial and local administration.

A Plea to the Emperor

POLITICS & GOVERNMENT

Like many other societies in premodern East and Southeast Asia, the kingdom of Vietnam regularly paid tribute to the imperial court in China. The arrangement was often beneficial to both sides, as the tributary states received a form of international recognition from the relationship, as well as trade privileges in the massive Chinese market. China, for its part, assured itself that neighboring areas would not harbor dissident elements hostile to its own security.

In this document, contained in a historical chronicle written by Le Tac in the fourteenth century, a claimant to the Vietnamese throne seeks recognition from the Song emperor while offering tribute to the Son of Heaven in China. Note the way in which the claimant, Le Hoan, founder of the early Le dynasty (980–1009), demeans the character of the Vietnamese people in comparison with the sophisticated ways of imperial China.

What is the tribute system as described in this document? Does it provide benefits to both parties in the arrangement, and if so, how and why?

Le Tac, *Essay on Annam*

My ancestors have received favors from the Imperial Court. Living in a faraway country at a corner of the sea [Annam], they have been granted the seals of investiture for that barbarian area and have always paid to the Imperial ministers the tribute and respect they owed. But recently our House has been little favored by Heaven; however, the death of our ancestors has not prevented us from promptly delivering the tribute. . . .

But now the leadership of the country is in dispute and investiture has not yet been conferred by China. My father, Pou-ling, and my eldest brother, Lienn, formerly enjoyed the favors of the [Chinese] Empire, which endowed them with the titles and functions of office. They zealously and humbly protected their country, neither daring to appear lazy or negligent. . . . [But then] the good fortune of our House began to crumble. The mandarins [officials], the army, the people, the court elders, and members of my family, all . . . entreated me to lead the army. . . . My people, who are wild mountain-dwellers, have unpleasant and violent customs; they are a people who live in caves and have disorderly and impetuous habits. I feared that trouble would arise if I did not yield to their wishes. From prudence I therefore assumed power temporarily. . . . I hope that His Majesty will place my country among His other tributary states by granting me the investiture. He will instill peace in the heart of His little servant by allowing me to govern the patrimony my parents left me. Then shall I administer my barbarian and remote people. . . . I shall send tributes of precious stones and ivory, and before the Golden Gate I shall express my loyalty.

Courtesy of William J. Duiker

The Temple of Literature, Hanoi
When the Vietnamese regained their independence from China in the tenth century C.E., they retained Chinese institutions that they deemed beneficial. A prime example was the establishment of the Temple of Literature, Vietnam's first university, in 1076. Here the sons of mandarins (officials) were educated in the Confucian classics in preparation for an official career. Beginning in the fifteenth century, those receiving doctorates had stelae erected to identify their achievements. Shown here is the central hall of the temple, where advanced students took the metropolitan examinations for the doctorate.

Another aspect of the Chinese legacy was the spread of Buddhist, Daoist, and Confucian ideas, which supplemented the Viets' traditional belief in nature spirits. Buddhist precepts became popular among the local population, who integrated the new faith into their existing belief system by founding Buddhist temples dedicated to the local village deity in the hope of guaranteeing an abundant harvest. Upper-class Vietnamese educated in the Confucian classics tended to follow the more agnostic Confucian doctrine, but some joined Buddhist monasteries. Daoism also flourished at all levels of society and, as in China, provided a structure for animistic beliefs and practices that still predominated at the village level.

During the early period of independence, Vietnamese culture also borrowed liberally from its larger neighbor. Educated Vietnamese tried their hand at Chinese poetry, wrote dynastic histories in the Chinese style, and followed Chinese models in sculpture, architecture, and porcelain. Many of the notable buildings of the medieval period, such as the Temple of Literature and the famous One-Pillar Pagoda in Hanoi, are classic examples of Chinese architecture.

But there were signs that Vietnamese creativity would eventually transcend the bounds of Chinese cultural norms. Although most classical writing was undertaken in literary Chinese, the only form of literary expression deemed suitable by Confucian conservatives, an adaptation of Chinese written characters, called *chu nom* ("southern characters"), was devised to provide a written system for spoken Vietnamese. In use by the early ninth century, it eventually began to be used for the composition of essays and poetry in the Vietnamese language. Such pioneering efforts would lead in later centuries to the emergence of a vigorous national literature totally independent of Chinese forms.

Society and Family Life

Vietnamese social institutions and customs were also strongly influenced by those of China. As in China, the introduction of a Confucian system and the adoption of civil service examinations undermined the role of the old landed aristocrats and led eventually to their replacement by the scholar-gentry class. Also as in China, the examinations were open to most males, regardless of family background, which opened the door to a degree of social mobility unknown in most of the states elsewhere in the region. Candidates for the bureaucracy read many of the same Confucian classics and absorbed the same ethical principles as their counterparts in China. At the same time, they were also exposed to the classic works of Vietnamese history, which strengthened their sense that Vietnam was a distinct culture similar to, but separate from, that of China.

The vast majority of the Vietnamese people, however, were peasants. Most were small landholders or

CHRONOLOGY	Early Korea and Vietnam
Chinese conquest of Korea and Vietnam	First century B.C.E
Trung Sisters' Revolt	39 C.E.
Foundation of Champa	192
Era of Three Kingdoms in Korea	Fourth–seventh centuries
Restoration of Vietnamese independence	939
Mongol invasion of Korea and Vietnam	1257–1285
Foundation of Yi dynasty in Korea	1392
Vietnamese conquest of Champa	1471

sharecroppers who rented their plots from wealthier farmers, but large estates were rare due to the systematic efforts of the central government to prevent the rise of a powerful local landed elite.

Family life in Vietnam was similar in many respects to that in China. The Confucian concept of family took hold during the period of Chinese rule, along with the related concepts of filial piety and gender inequality. Perhaps the most striking difference between family traditions in China and Vietnam was that Vietnamese women possessed more rights both in practice and by law. Since ancient times, wives had been permitted to own property and initiate divorce proceedings. One consequence of Chinese rule was a growing emphasis on male dominance, but the tradition of women's rights was never totally extinguished and was legally recognized in a law code promulgated in 1460.

Moreover, Vietnam had a strong historical tradition associating heroic women with the defense of the homeland. The Trung Sisters were the first but by no means the only example. In the following passage, a Vietnamese historian of the eighteenth century recounts their story:

The imperial court was far away; local officials were greedy and oppressive. At that time the country of one hundred sons was the country of the women of Lord To. The ladies [the Trung Sisters] used the female arts against their irreconcilable foe; skirts and hairpins sang of patriotic righteousness, uttered a solemn oath at the inner door of the ladies' quarters, expelled the governor, and seized the capital. . . . Were they not grand heroines? . . . Our two ladies brought forward an army of all the people, and, establishing a royal court that settled affairs in the territories of the sixty-five strongholds, shook their skirts over the Hundred Yueh [the Vietnamese people].[7]

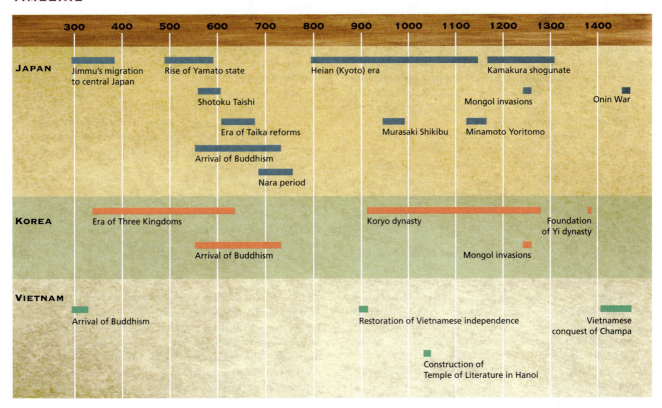

CONCLUSION

THERE ARE SOME TANTALIZING similarities among the three countries we have examined in this chapter. All borrowed liberally from the Chinese model. At the same time, all adapted Chinese institutions and values to the conditions prevailing in their own societies. Though all expressed admiration and respect for China's achievement, all sought to keep Chinese power at a distance.

As an island nation, Japan was the most successful of the three in protecting its political sovereignty and its cultural identity. Both Korea and Vietnam were compelled on various occasions to defend their independence by force of arms. That experience may have shaped their strong sense of national distinctiveness, which we shall discuss further in a later chapter.

The appeal of Chinese institutions can undoubtedly be explained by the fact that Japan, Korea, and Vietnam were all agrarian societies, much like their larger neighbor. But it is also significant that the aspect of Chinese political culture that was least amenable to adoption abroad was the civil service examination system. The Confucian concept of meritocracy ran directly counter to the strong aristocratic tradition that flourished in all three societies during their early stage of development. Even when the system was adopted, it was put to quite different uses. Only in Vietnam did the concept of merit eventually triumph over that of birth, as strong rulers of Dai Viet attempted to initiate the Chinese model as a means of creating a centralized system of government.

CHAPTER NOTES

1. Keith W. Taylor, *The Birth of Vietnam* (Berkeley, Calif., 1983), p. 18.
2. Quoted in David John Lu, *Sources of Japanese History,* vol. 1 (New York, 1974), p. 7.
3. From "The History of Wei," quoted in ibid., p. 10.
4. From "The Law of Households," quoted in ibid., p. 32.
5. From "On the Salvation of Women," quoted in ibid., p. 127.
6. Quoted in Barbara Ruch, "The Other Side of Culture in Medieval Japan," in Kozo Yamamura, ed., *The Cambridge History of Japan,* vol. 3, *Medieval Japan* (Cambridge, 1990), p. 506.
7. Quoted in Taylor, *The Birth of Vietnam,* pp. 336–337.

SUGGESTED READING

Some of the standard treatments of the rise of Japanese civilization appear in textbooks dealing with the early history of East Asia. Two of the best are **J. K. Fairbank, E. O. Reischauer,** and **A. M. Craig,** *East Asia: Tradition and Transformation* (Boston, 1973), and **C. Schirokauer,** *A Brief History of Chinese and Japanese Civilizations* (San Diego, Calif., 1989). For more recent scholarship on the early period, see the first three volumes of **The Cambridge History of Japan,** ed. **J. W. Hall** et al. (Cambridge, 1988).

The best available collections of documents on the early history of Japan are **D. J. Lu,** ed., *Sources of Japanese History,* vol. 1 (New York, 1974), and **Theodore de Bary** et al., eds., *Sources of Japanese Tradition,* vol. 1 (New York, 2002).

For specialized books on the early historical period, see **R. J. Pearson,** ed., *Windows on the Japanese Past: Studies in Archaeology and Prehistory* (Ann Arbor, Mich., 1986). **J. W. Hall,** *Government and Local Power in Japan, 500–1700* (Princeton, N.J., 1966), provides a detailed analysis of the development of Japanese political institutions. The relationship between disease and state building is analyzed in **W. W. Farris,** *Population, Disease, and Land in Early Japan, 645–900* (Cambridge, 1985). The Kamakura period is covered in **J. P. Mass,** ed., *Court and Bakufu in Japan: Essays in Kamakura History* (New Haven, Conn., 1982). See also **H. P. Varley,** *The Onin War* (New York, 1977). For Japanese Buddhism, see **W. T. de Bary,** ed., *The Buddhist Tradition in India, China, and Japan* (New York, 1972).

A concise and provocative introduction to women's issues during this period in Japan, as well as in other parts of the world, can be found in **S. S. Hughes** and **B. Hughes,** *Women in World History* (Armonk, N.Y., 1995). For a tenth-century account of daily life for women at the Japanese court, see **I. Morris,** trans. and ed., *The Pillow Book of Sei Shonagon* (New York, 1991). For the changes that took place from matrilocal and matrilineal marriages to a patriarchal society, consult **H. Tonomura,** "*Black Hair and Red Trousers: Gendering the Flesh in Medieval Japan,*" in **American Historical Review** 99 (1994).

The best introduction to Japanese literature for college students is still the concise and insightful **D. Keene,** *Japanese Literature: An Introduction for Western Readers* (London, 1953). The most comprehensive anthology is **D. Keene,** *Anthology of Japanese Literature* (New York, 1955), while the best history of Japanese literature, also by **D. Keene,** is *Seeds in the Heart: Japanese Literature from Earlier Times to the Late Sixteenth Century* (New York, 1993).

For the most comprehensive introduction to Japanese art, consult **P. Mason,** *History of Japanese Art* (New York, 1993). Also see the concise **J. Stanley-Baker,** *Japanese Art* (London, 1984). For a stimulating text with magnificent illustrations, see **D. Elisseeff** and **V. Elisseeff,** *Art of Japan* (New York, 1985). See also **J. E. Kidder Jr.,** *The Art of Japan* (London, 1985), for an insightful text accompanied by beautiful photographs.

For an informative and readable history of Korea, see **Lee Ki-baik,** *A New History of Korea* (Cambridge, 1984). **P. H. Lee,** ed., *Sourcebook of Korean Civilization,* vol. 1 (New York, 1993), is a rich collection of documents dating from the period prior to the sixteenth century.

Vietnam often receives little attention in general studies of Southeast Asia because it was part of the Chinese Empire for much of the traditional period. For a detailed investigation of the origins of Vietnamese civilization, see **K. W. Taylor,** *The Birth of Vietnam* (Berkeley, Calif., 1983). **T. Hodgkin,** *Vietnam: The Revolutionary Path* (New York, 1981), provides an overall survey of Vietnamese history to modern times.

InfoTrac College Edition

Visit this chapter's InfoTrac College Edition/Research activities at the *Essential World History* Companion Website for activities related to early East Asia.

CENGAGENOW™ for Duiker and Spielvogel's *The Essential World History, Third Edition*

Enter *CengageNOW* using the access card that is available with this text. *CengageNOW* will assist you in understanding the content in this chapter with lesson plans generated for your needs, as well as provide you with a connection to the *Wadsworth World History Resource Center* (see description below for details).

WORLD HISTORY
RESOURCE CENTER

Enter the Resource Center using either your *CengageNOW* accesss card or your standalone access card for the *Wadsworth World History Resource Center.* Organized by topic, this website includes quizzes; images; over 350 primary source documents; interactive simulations, maps, and timelines; movie explorations; and a wealth of other resources. You can read the following documents, and many more, at http://worldrc.wadsworth.com/

    Japanese Creation Myth

    The Legend of King Onjo of Paekche

    Story of the Trung Sisters

Visit the *Essential World History* Companion Website for chapter quizzes and more.

    academic.cengage.com/history/duiker

12

THE MAKING OF EUROPE

A medieval French manuscript illustration of the coronation of Charlemagne by Pope Leo III

© Scala/Art Resource, NY

IN 800, CHARLEMAGNE, the king of the Franks, journeyed to Rome to help Pope Leo III, head of the Catholic church, who was barely clinging to power in the face of rebellious Romans. On Christmas Day, Charlemagne and his family, attended by Romans and Franks, crowded into Saint Peter's Basilica to hear Mass. Quite unexpectedly, according to a Frankish writer, "as the king rose from praying before the tomb of the blessed apostle Peter, Pope Leo placed a golden crown on his head." The people in the church shouted, "Long life and victory to Charles Augustus, crowned by God the great and peace-loving Emperor of the Romans." Seemingly, the Roman Empire in the west had been reborn, and Charles had become the first Roman emperor since 476. But this "Roman emperor" was actually a German king, and he had been crowned by the head of the western Christian church. In truth, the coronation of Charlemagne was a sign not of the rebirth of the Roman Empire but of the emergence of a new European civilization that came into being in western Europe after the collapse of the western Roman Empire.

This new civilization—European civilization—was formed by the coming together of three major elements:

the legacy of the Romans, the Christian church, and the Germanic peoples who moved in and settled the western empire. European civilization developed during a period that historians call the Middle Ages, or the medieval period, which lasted from about 500 to about 1500. To the historians who first used the name, the Middle Ages was a middle period between the ancient world and the modern world. During the Early Middle Ages, from about 500 to 1000 C.E., the Roman world of the western empire was slowly transformed into a new Christian European society. ◇

The Emergence of Europe in the Early Middle Ages

As we saw in Chapter 10, China descended into political chaos and civil wars after the end of the Han Empire, and it was almost four hundred years before a new imperial dynasty established political order. After the collapse of the western Roman Empire in the fifth century, it would also take hundreds of years to establish the foundations for a new society.

The New Germanic Kingdoms

Already in the third century C.E., Germanic peoples had begun to move into the lands of the Roman Empire, and by 500, the western Roman Empire had been replaced politically by a series of successor states ruled by German kings. The fusion of Romans and Germans took different forms in the various Germanic kingdoms. Both the kingdom of the Ostrogoths in Italy and the kingdom of the Visigoths in Spain (see Map 12.1) maintained the Roman structure for the larger native populations, while a Germanic warrior caste came to dominate. Over a period of time, Germans and natives began to fuse. In Britain, however, after the Roman armies withdrew at the beginning of the fifth century, the Angles and Saxons, Germanic tribes from Denmark and northern Germany, moved in and settled there.

Only one of the German states on the European continent proved long-lasting—the kingdom of the Franks. The establishment of a Frankish kingdom was the work of Clovis (c. 482–511), who became a Catholic Christian around 500. By 510, Clovis had established a powerful new Frankish kingdom stretching from the Pyrenees in the west to German lands in the east (modern France and western Germany). After Clovis's death, however, as was the Frankish custom, his sons divided his newly created kingdom, and during the sixth and seventh centuries, the once-united Frankish kingdom came to be divided into three major areas: Neustria, Austrasia, and Burgundy.

The Role of the Christian Church

By the end of the fourth century, Christianity had become the predominant religion of the Roman Empire. As the official Roman state disintegrated, the Christian church played an increasingly important role in the growth of the new European civilization.

The Organization of the Church   By the fourth century, the Christian church had developed a system of government. The Christian community in each city was headed by a bishop, whose area of jurisdiction was known as a bishopric, or **diocese;** the bishoprics of each Roman province were joined together under the direction of an archbishop. The bishops of four great cities—Rome, Jerusalem, Alexandria, and Antioch—held positions of special power in church affairs. Soon, however, one of them—the bishop of Rome—claimed that he was the sole leader of the western Christian church, which came to be known as the Roman Catholic church. According to church tradition, Jesus had given the keys to the kingdom of heaven to Peter, who was considered the chief apostle and the first bishop of Rome. Subsequent bishops of Rome were considered Peter's successors and came to be known as popes (from the Latin word *papa*, meaning "father"). By the sixth century, popes had been successful in extending papal authority over the Christian church in the west and converting the pagan peoples of Germanic Europe. Their primary instrument of conversion was the monastic movement.

The Monks and Their Missions   A **monk** (in Latin, *monachus,* meaning "someone who lives alone") was a man who sought to live a life divorced from the world, cut off from ordinary human society, in order to pursue an ideal of total dedication to God. As the monastic ideal spread, a new form of **monasticism** based on living together in a community soon became the dominant form. Saint Benedict (c. 480–c. 543), who founded a monastic house for which he wrote a set of rules, established the basic form of monastic life in the western Christian church.

Benedict's rule divided each day into a series of activities. All monks were required to do physical work of some kind for several hours a day because idleness was "the enemy of the soul." At the very heart of community practice was prayer, the proper "work of God." Although this included private meditation and reading, all of the monks gathered together seven times during the day for common prayer and chanting of psalms. The Benedictine life was a communal one. Monks ate, worked, slept, and worshiped together.

Each Benedictine monastery was strictly ruled by an **abbot,** or "father" of the monastery, who had complete authority over his fellow monks. Unquestioning obedience to the will of the abbot was expected of every monk. Each Benedictine monastery held lands that enabled it to be a self-sustaining community, isolated from and independent of the world surrounding it. Within the monastery, however, monks were to fulfill their vow of poverty: "Let all things be common to all, as it is written, lest anyone should say that anything is his own."[1] Only

Women played an important role in the monastic missionary movement and the conversion of the Germanic kingdoms. Some served as **abbesses** (an abbess was the head of a monastery or a convent for nuns); many abbesses came from aristocratic families, especially in Anglo-Saxon England. In the kingdom of Northumbria, for example, Saint Hilda founded the monastery of Whitby in 657. As abbess, she was responsible for making learning an important part of the life of the monastery.

Charlemagne and the Carolingians

During the seventh and eighth centuries, as the kings of the Frankish kingdom gradually lost their power, the mayors of the palace—the chief officers of the king's household—assumed more control of the kingdom. One of these mayors, Pepin, finally took the logical step of assuming the kingship of the Frankish state for himself and his family. Upon his death in 768, his son came to the throne of the Frankish kingdom.

This new king was the dynamic and powerful ruler known to history as Charles the Great (768–814), or Charlemagne (from the Latin *Carolus Magnus*). He was determined and decisive, intelligent and inquisitive, a strong statesman, and a pious Christian. Though he himself was unable to read or write, he was a wise patron of learning. In a series of military campaigns, he greatly expanded the territory he had inherited and created what came to be known as the Carolingian Empire. At its height, Charlemagne's empire covered much of western and central Europe.

As Charlemagne's power grew, so did his prestige as the most powerful Christian ruler; one monk even wrote that he ruled the "kingdom of Europe." In 800, Charlemagne acquired a new title: emperor of the Romans. Charlemagne's coronation as Roman emperor demonstrated the strength, even after three hundred years, of the concept of an enduring Roman Empire. More important, it symbolized the fusion of the

MAP 12.1 **The Germanic Kingdoms of the Old Western Empire.** The Germanic tribes filled the power vacuum caused by the demise of the Roman Empire, building states that blended elements of Germanic customs and laws with those of Roman culture, including large-scale conversions to Christianity. The Franks established the most durable of these Germanic states. **?** Which Germanic tribes settled in the present-day countries of Europe?

View an animated version of this map or related maps at http://worldrc.wadsworth.com/

men could be monks, but women, called **nuns,** also began to withdraw from the world to dedicate themselves to God.

Monasticism played an indispensable role in early medieval civilization. Monks became the new heroes of Christian civilization, and their dedication to God became the highest ideal of Christian life. They were the social workers of their communities: monks provided schools for the young, hospitality for travelers, and hospitals for the sick. Monks also copied Latin works and passed on the legacy of the ancient world to the new European civilization. Monasteries became centers of learning wherever they were located, and monks worked to spread Christianity to all of Europe.

Charlemagne's Empire

The Coronation of Charlemagne. After a rebellion in 799 forced Pope Leo III to seek refuge at Charlemagne's court, Charlemagne went to Rome to settle the affair. There, on Christmas Day 800, he was crowned emperor of the Romans by the pope. This manuscript illustration shows Leo III placing a crown on Charlemagne's head.

Roman, Christian, and Germanic elements that formed the base of European civilization. A Germanic king had been crowned emperor of the Romans by the spiritual leader of western Christendom. A new civilization had emerged.

The World of Lords and Vassals

The Carolingian Empire began to disintegrate soon after Charlemagne's death in 814, and less than thirty years later, in 843, it was divided among his grandsons into three major sections. Invasions in different parts of the old Carolingian world added to the process of disintegration.

Invasions of the Ninth and Tenth Centuries In the ninth and tenth centuries, western Europe was beset by a wave of invasions. Muslims attacked the southern coasts of Europe and sent raiding parties into southern France. The Magyars, a people from western Asia, moved into central Europe at the end of the ninth century and settled on the plains of Hungary, from where they made forays into western Europe. Finally crushed at the Battle of Lechfeld in Germany in 955, the Magyars converted to Christianity and settled down to create the kingdom of Hungary.

The most far-reaching attacks of the time came from the Northmen or Norsemen of Scandinavia, also known to us as the Vikings. The Vikings were warriors whose love of adventure and search for booty and new avenues of trade may have led them to invade other areas of Europe. Viking ships were the best of the period. Their shallow draft enabled them to sail up European rivers and attack places at some distance inland. In the ninth century, Vikings sacked villages and towns, destroyed churches, and easily defeated small local armies.

By the mid-ninth century, the Northmen had begun to build winter settlements in different areas of Europe. By 850, groups of Norsemen from Norway had settled in Ireland, and Danes occupied northeastern England by 878. Beginning in 911, the ruler of the western Frankish lands gave one band of Vikings land at the mouth of the Seine River, forming a section of France that came to be known as Normandy. This policy of settling the Vikings and converting them to Christianity was a deliberate one; by their conversion to Christianity, the Vikings were soon made a part of European civilization.

The Development of Fief-Holding The disintegration of central authority in the Carolingian world and the invasions by Muslims, Magyars, and Vikings led to the emergence of a new type of relationship between free individuals. When governments ceased to be able to defend their subjects, it became important to find some powerful lord who could offer protection in return for service. The contract sworn between a lord and his subordinate (known as a **vassal**) is the basis of a form of social organization that later generations of historians viewed as an organized system of government, which they called *feudalism*. But feudalism was never a system, and many historians today prefer to avoid using the term (see the comparative essay "Feudal Orders Around the World" on p. 244).

With the breakdown of royal governments, powerful nobles took control of large areas of land. They needed men to fight for them, so the practice arose of giving grants of land to vassals who in return would fight for their lord. The Frankish army had originally consisted of foot soldiers, dressed in coats of mail and armed with swords. But in the eighth century, a military change began to occur when larger horses and the stirrup were introduced. Earlier, horsemen had been throwers of spears. Now they came to be armored in coats of mail (the larger horse could carry the weight) and wielded long lances that enabled them to act as battering rams (the stirrup kept them on their horses). For almost five hundred years, warfare in Europe would be dominated by these mounted warriors, or *knights,* as they were called.

Of course, a horse, armor, and weapons were expensive, and it took time and much practice to learn to wield these instruments skillfully from horseback. Consequently, lords who wanted men to fight for them had to grant each vassal a piece of land that provided for the support of the vassal and his family. In return for the land, the vassal provided his lord with his fighting skills. Each needed the other. In the Early Middle Ages, when there was little trade and wealth was based primarily on land, land became the most important gift a lord could give to a vassal in return for his military service.

By the ninth century, the grant of land made to a vassal had become known as a **fief.** A fief was a piece of land held from the lord by a vassal in return for military service, but vassals who held such grants of land also came to exercise rights of jurisdiction or political and legal authority within these fiefs. As the Carolingian world disintegrated politically under the impact of internal dissension and invasions, an increasing number of powerful lords arose who were now responsible for keeping order.

Fief-holding came to be characterized by a set of practices that determined the relationship between a lord and his vassal. The major obligation of a vassal to his lord was to perform military service, usually about forty days a year. A vassal was also required to appear at his lord's court when summoned to give advice to the lord. He might also be asked to sit in judgment in a legal case, since the important vassals of a lord were peers and only they could judge each other. Finally, vassals were also responsible for aids, or financial payments to the lord, on a number of occasions. In turn, a lord also had responsibilities toward his vassals. His major obligation was to protect his vassal, either by defending him militarily or by taking his side in a court of law. The lord was also responsible for the maintenance of the vassal, usually by granting him a fief.

The Manorial System   The landholding class of nobles and knights contained a military elite whose ability to function as warriors depended on having the leisure time to pursue the arts of war. Landed estates, located on the fiefs given to a vassal by his lord and worked by a dependent peasant class, provided the economic sustenance that made this way of life possible. A **manor** was simply an agricultural estate operated by a lord and worked by peasants. Although a large class of free peasants continued to exist, increasing numbers of free peasants became **serfs**—persons bound to the land and required to provide labor services, pay rents, and be subject to the lord's jurisdiction. By the ninth century, probably 60 percent of the population of western Europe had become serfs.

Labor services consisted of working the lord's **demesne,** the land retained by the lord, which might consist of one-third to one-half of the cultivated lands scattered throughout the manor. The rest would be used by the peasants for themselves. Building barns and digging ditches were also part of the labor services. Serfs usually worked about three days a week for their lord and paid rents by giving the lord a share of every product they raised.

Serfs were legally bound to the lord's lands and could not leave without his permission. Although free to marry, serfs could not marry anyone outside their manor without the lord's approval. Moreover, lords sometimes exercised public rights or political authority on their lands, which gave them the right to try peasants in their own courts.

Europe in the High Middle Ages

The new European civilization that had emerged in the Early Middle Ages began to flourish in the High Middle Ages (1000–1300). New agricultural practices that increased the food supply helped give rise to commercial and urban expansion. Both lords and vassals recovered from the invasions and internal dissension of the Early Middle Ages, while medieval kings began to exert a centralizing authority. The recovery of the Catholic church made it a forceful presence in every area of life. The High Middle Ages also gave birth to a cultural revival.

Land and People

In the Early Middle Ages, Europe had a relatively small population, but in the High Middle Ages, the number of people nearly doubled, from 38 to 74 million. What accounted for this dramatic increase? For one thing, conditions in Europe were more settled and more peaceful after the invasions of the Early Middle Ages had ended. For another, agricultural production surged after 1000.

The New Agriculture   During the High Middle Ages, Europeans began to farm in new ways. An improvement in climate resulted in better growing conditions, but an important factor in increasing food production was the expansion of cultivated or arable land, accomplished by clearing forested areas. Peasants of the eleventh and twelfth centuries cut down trees and drained swamps.

Technological changes also furthered the development of farming. The Middle Ages saw an explosion of labor-saving devices, many of which were made from iron, which was mined in different areas of Europe. Iron was used to make scythes, axes, and hoes for use on farms as well as saws, hammers, and nails for building purposes. Iron was crucial in making the *carruca,* a heavy, wheeled plow with an iron plowshare pulled by teams of horses, which could turn over the heavy clay soil north of the Alps.

Besides using horsepower, the High Middle Ages harnessed the power of water and wind to do jobs formerly done by humans or animals. Located along streams, mills powered by water were used to grind grains and produce flour. Where rivers were lacking or not easily dammed, Europeans developed windmills to harness the power of the wind.

COMPARATIVE ILLUSTRATION

The New Agriculture in the Medieval World. New agricultural methods and techniques in the Middle Ages enabled peasants in both Europe and China to increase food production. This general improvement in diet was a factor in supporting noticeably larger populations in both areas. At the bottom, a thirteenth-century illustration shows a group of English peasants harvesting grain. Overseeing their work is a bailiff, or manager. At the right, a twelfth-century painting shows Chinese peasants transplanting month-old seedlings from the nursery bed to their permanent field. Rice became the staple food in China. What is the significance of the bailiff's presence in the English image?

Freer Gallery of Art, Smithsonian Institution, Washington, D.C.: Purchase F1954.21

The Art Archive/British Library/British Library

The shift from a two-field to a three-field system also contributed to the increase in food production (see the comparative illustration above). In the Early Middle Ages, peasants planted one field while another of equal size was allowed to lie fallow to regain its fertility. Now estates were divided into three parts. One field was planted in the fall with winter grains, such as rye and wheat, and spring grains, such as oats or barley, and vegetables, such as peas or beans, were planted in the second field. The third was allowed to lie fallow. By rotating their use, only one-third rather than one-half of the land lay fallow at any time. The rotation of crops also kept the soil from being exhausted so quickly, and more crops could now be grown.

Daily Life of the Peasantry The lifestyle of the peasants was quite simple. Their cottages consisted of wood frames surrounded by sticks with the space between them filled with rubble and then plastered over with clay. Roofs were simply thatched. The houses of poorer peasants consisted of a single room, but others had at least two rooms—a main room for cooking, eating, and other activities and another room for sleeping.

Peasant women occupied both an important and a difficult position in manorial society. They were expected to carry and bear their children and at the same time fulfill their obligation to labor in the fields. Their ability to manage the household might determine whether a peasant family would starve or survive in difficult times.

Though simple, a peasant's daily diet was adequate when food was available. The staple of the peasant diet, and the medieval diet in general, was bread. Women made the dough for the bread at home, then brought their loaves to be baked in community ovens, which were owned by the lord of the manor. Peasant bread was highly nutritious, containing not only wheat and rye but also barley, millet, and oats, giving it a dark appearance and a very heavy, hard texture. Bread was supplemented by numerous vegetables from the household gardens, cheese from cow's or goat's milk, nuts and berries from woodlands, and fruits, such as apples, pears, and cherries. Chickens provided eggs and sometimes meat.

The Nobility of the Middle Ages

In the High Middle Ages, European society, like that of Japan during the same period, was dominated by men whose chief concern was warfare. Like the Japanese samurai, many nobles loved war. As one nobleman wrote:

> And well I like to hear the call of "Help" and see the
>   wounded fall,
> Loudly for mercy praying,
> And see the dead, both great and small,
> Pierced by sharp spearheads one and all.[2]

The men of war were the lords and vassals of medieval society.

The lords were the kings, dukes, counts, barons, and viscounts (and even bishops and archbishops) who had extensive landholdings and wielded considerable political influence. They formed an **aristocracy** or nobility of people who held real political, economic, and social power. Both the great lords and ordinary knights were warriors, and the institution of knighthood united them. But there were also social divisions among them based on extremes of wealth and landholdings.

Although aristocratic women could legally hold property, most women remained under the control of men—their fathers until they married and their husbands after that. Nevertheless, these women had many opportunities for playing important roles. Because the lord was often away at war or at court, the lady of the castle had to manage the estate. Households could include large numbers of officials and servants, so this was no small responsibility.

Although women were expected to be subservient to their husbands, there were many strong women who advised and sometimes even dominated their husbands. Perhaps most famous was Eleanor of Aquitaine (c. 1122–1204). Married to King Louis VII of France, Eleanor accompanied her husband on a Crusade, but her alleged affair with her uncle during the Crusade led Louis to have their marriage annulled. Eleanor then married Henry, duke of Normandy, who became King Henry II of England (1154–1189). She took an active role in politics, even assisting her sons in rebelling against Henry in 1173 and 1174.

The New World of Trade and Cities

Medieval Europe was overwhelmingly an agrarian society, with most people living in small villages. In the eleventh and twelfth centuries, however, new elements were introduced that began to transform the economic foundation of European civilization: a revival of trade, the emergence of specialized craftspeople and artisans, and the growth and development of towns.

The Revival of Trade

The revival of trade was a gradual process. During the chaotic conditions of the Early Middle Ages, large-scale trade had declined in western Europe except for Byzantine contacts with Italy and the Jewish traders who moved back and forth between the Muslim and Christian worlds. By the end of the tenth century, however, people were emerging in Europe with both the skills and the products for commercial activity. Cities in northern Italy took the lead in this revival of trade.

While the northern Italian cities were busy trading in the Mediterranean, the towns of Flanders were doing likewise in northern Europe. Flanders, the area along the coast of present-day Belgium and northern France, was known for its high-quality woolen cloth. The location of Flanders made it an ideal center for the traders of northern Europe. Merchants from England, Scandinavia, France, and Germany converged there to trade their goods for woolen cloth. Flanders prospered in the eleventh and twelfth centuries. By the twelfth century, a regular exchange of goods had developed between Flanders and Italy, the two major centers of northern and southern European trade.

As trade increased, both gold and silver came to be in demand at fairs and trading markets of all kinds. Slowly a money economy began to emerge. New trading companies and banking firms were set up to manage the exchange and sale of goods. All of these new practices were part of the rise of **commercial capitalism,** an economic system in which people invested in trade and goods in order to make profits.

Trade Outside Europe

In the High Middle Ages, Italian merchants became even more daring in conducting trade. They established trading posts in Cairo, Damascus, and a number of Black Sea ports, where they acquired spices, silks, jewelry, dyestuffs, and other goods brought by Muslim merchants from India, China, and Southeast Asia.

The rise of the Mongol Empire in the thirteenth century (see Chapter 10) also opened the door to Italian merchants in the markets of Central Asia, India, and China (see the box on p. 266). As nomads who relied on trade with settled communities, the Mongols maintained safe trade routes for merchants moving through their lands. Two Venetian merchants, Niccolò and Maffeo Polo, began to travel in the Mongol Empire around 1260.

The creation of the crusader states in Syria and Palestine in the twelfth and thirteenth centuries (see "the First Crusades" later in this chapter) was especially favorable for Italian merchants. In return for taking the crusaders to the east, Italian merchant fleets received trading concessions in Syria and Palestine. Venice, for example, which profited the most from this trade, was given a quarter in Tyre on the coast of what is now Lebanon. Soon this quarter, known as "a little Venice in the east," and similar quarters in other cities became bases for carrying on lucrative trade.

An Italian Banker Discusses Trading Between Europe and China

INTERACTION & EXCHANGE

Working on behalf of a banking guild in Florence, Francesco Balducci Pegolotti journeyed to England and Cyprus. As a result of his contacts with many Italian merchants, he acquired considerable information about long-distance trade between Europe and China. In this account, written in 1340, he provides advice for Italian merchants.

What were Francesco Pegolotti's impressions of China? Were they positive or negative? Explain your answer.

Francesco Balducci Pegolotti, *An Account of Traders Between Europe and China*

In the first place, you must let your beard grow long and not shave. And at Tana [modern Rostov] you should furnish yourself with a guide. And you must not try to save money in the matter of guides by taking a bad one instead of a good one. For the additional wages of the good one will not cost you so much as you will save by having him. And besides the guide it will be well to take at least two good menservants who are acquainted with the Turkish tongue. . . .

The road you travel from Tana to China is perfectly safe, whether by day or night, according to what the merchants say who have used it. Only if the merchant, in going or coming, should die upon the road, everything belonging to him will become the possession of the lord in the country in which he dies. . . . And in like manner if he dies in China. . . .

China is a province which contains a multitude of cities and towns. Among others there is one in particular, that is to say the capital city, to which many merchants are attracted, and in which there is a vast amount of trade; and this city is called Khanbaliq [modern Beijing]. And the said city has a circuit of one hundred miles, and is all full of people and houses and of dwellers in the said city. . . .

Whatever silver the merchants may carry with them as far as China, the emperor of China will take from them and put into his treasury. And to merchants who thus bring silver they give that paper money of theirs in exchange . . . and with this money you can readily buy silk and all other merchandise that you have a desire to buy. And all the people of the country are bound to receive it. And yet you shall not pay a higher price for your goods because your money is of paper.

The Growth of Cities   The revival of trade led to a revival of cities. Towns had greatly declined in the Early Middle Ages, especially in Europe north of the Alps. Old Roman cities continued to exist but had dwindled in size and population. With the revival of trade, merchants began to settle in these old cities, followed by craftspeople or artisans, people who on manors or elsewhere had developed skills and now saw an opportunity to ply their trade and make goods that could be sold by the merchants. In the course of the eleventh and twelfth centuries, the old Roman cities came alive with new populations and growth.

Beginning in the late tenth century, many new cities or towns were also founded, particularly in northern Europe. Usually, a group of merchants established a settlement near some fortified stronghold, such as a castle or monastery. (This explains why so many place names in Europe end in *borough, burgh, burg,* or *bourg,* which means "fortress" or "walled enclosure.") Castles were particularly favored because they were generally located along trade routes; the lords of the castle also offered protection. If the settlement prospered and expanded, new walls were built to protect it.

Although lords wanted to treat towns and townspeople as they would their vassals and serfs, cities had totally different needs and a different perspective. Townspeople needed mobility to trade. Consequently, these merchants and artisans (who came to be called *burghers* or *bourgeois,* from the same root as *borough* and *burg*) needed their own unique laws to meet their requirements and were willing to pay for them. In many instances, lords and

kings saw that they could also make money and were willing to sell to the townspeople the liberties they were beginning to demand, including the right to bequeath goods and sell property, freedom from any military obligation to the lord, and written urban laws that guaranteed their freedom. Some towns also obtained the right to govern themselves by choosing their own officials and administering their own courts of law.

As time went on, medieval cities developed their own governments for running the affairs of the community. Only males who were born in the city or had lived there for a particular length of time could be citizens. In many cities, these citizens elected members of a city council who served as judges and city officials and passed laws.

Medieval cities remained relatively small in comparison to either ancient or modern cities. A large trading city would number about 5,000 inhabitants. By 1200, London was the largest city in England with 30,000 people. Otherwise, north of the Alps, only a few great urban centers of commerce, such as Bruges and Ghent, had a population close to 40,000. Italian cities tended to be larger, with Venice, Florence, Genoa, Milan, and Naples numbering almost 100,000. Even the largest European city, however, seemed small alongside the Byzantine capital of Constantinople or the Arab cities of Damascus, Baghdad, and Cairo.

Daily Life in the Medieval City   Medieval towns were surrounded by stone walls that were expensive to build, so the space within was precious. Consequently, most medieval cities featured narrow, winding streets with houses crowded against each other and second and third stories extending out over the streets. Because dwellings were built mostly of wood before the fourteenth century and candles and wood fires were used for light and heat, fire was a constant threat. Medieval cities burned rapidly once a fire started.

Most of the people who lived in cities were merchants involved in trade and artisans engaged in manufacturing a wide range of goods, such as cloth, metalwork, shoes, and leather goods. Generally, merchants and artisans had their own sections within a city. The merchant area included warehouses, inns, and taverns. Artisan sections were usually divided along craft lines. From the twelfth century on, craftspeople began to organize themselves into **guilds,** and by the thirteenth century, there were individual guilds for virtually every craft. Each craft had its own street where its activity was pursued.

The physical environment of medieval cities was not pleasant. They were often dirty and rife with smells from animal and human waste deposited in backyard privies or on the streets. Cities were unable to stop water pollution, especially from the tanning and animal-slaughtering industries, which dumped their waste products into the river.

In medieval cities, women, in addition to supervising the household, purchasing food, preparing meals, raising the children, and managing the family finances, were also often expected to help their husbands in their trades. Some women also developed their own trades to earn extra money. When some master craftsmen died, their widows even carried on their trades. Some women in medieval towns were thus able to lead lives of considerable independence.

Evolution of the European Kingdoms

The recovery and growth of European civilization in the High Middle Ages also affected the state. Although lords and vassals seemed forever mired in endless petty conflicts, some medieval kings inaugurated the process of developing new kinds of monarchical states that were based on the centralization of power rather than the decentralized political order that was characteristic of fief-holding. By the thirteenth century, European monarchs were solidifying their governmental institutions in pursuit of greater power.

England in the High Middle Ages   On October 14, 1066, an army of heavily armed knights under William of Normandy landed on the coast of England and soundly defeated King Harold and his Anglo-Saxon foot soldiers. William was crowned king of England at Christmastime in London and then began the process of combining Anglo-Saxon and Norman institutions to create a new England. Many of the Norman knights were given parcels of land that they held as fiefs from the new English king. William made all nobles swear an oath of loyalty to him as sole ruler of England and insisted that all people owed loyalty to the king. All in all, William of Normandy established a strong, centralized monarchy.

In the twelfth century, the power of the English monarchy was greatly enlarged during the reign of Henry II (1154–1189). Henry was particularly successful in strengthening the royal courts. By increasing the number of criminal cases to be tried in the king's courts and taking other steps to expand the power of the royal courts, he expanded the power of the king. Moreover, since the royal courts were now found throughout England, a body of **common law** (law that was common to the whole kingdom) began to replace the different law codes that often varied from place to place.

Many English nobles came to resent the ongoing growth of the king's power, however, and rose in rebellion during the reign of King John (1199–1216). At Runnymeade in 1215, John was forced to seal the Magna Carta (the Great Charter) guaranteeing feudal liberties. Feudal custom had always recognized that the relationship between king and vassals was based on mutual rights and obligations. The Magna Carta gave written recognition to that fact and was used in later years to support the idea that a monarch's power was limited.

During the reign of Edward I (1272–1307), the English Parliament emerged. Originally, the word *parliament* was applied to meetings of the king's Great Council, in which the greater barons and chief prelates of the church met with the king's judges and principal advisers to deal with judicial affairs. But in 1295, needing money, Edward I invited two knights from every county and two residents from each town to meet with the Great Council to consent to new taxes. This was the first Parliament.

The English Parliament, then, came to be composed of two knights from every county and two burgesses from every borough as well as the barons and ecclesiastical lords. Eventually, barons and church lords formed the House of Lords; knights and burgesses, the House of Commons. The Parliaments of Edward I approved taxes, discussed politics, passed laws, and handled judicial business. The law of the realm was beginning to be determined not by the king alone but by the king in consultation with representatives of various groups that constituted the community.

Growth of the French Kingdom   In 843, the Carolingian Empire had been divided into three major sections. The western Frankish lands formed the core of the eventual kingdom of France. In 987, after the death of the last Carolingian king, the western Frankish nobles chose Hugh Capet as the new king, thus establishing the Capetian dynasty of French kings. Although they carried the title of kings, the Capetians had little real power. They controlled as the royal domain only the lands around Paris known as the Île-de-France. As kings of France, the Capetians were formally the overlords of the great lords of France, such as the dukes of Normandy, Brittany, Burgundy, and Aquitaine.

In reality, however, many of the dukes were considerably more powerful than the Capetian kings.

The reign of King Philip II Augustus (1180–1223) was an important turning point in the growth of the French monarchy. Philip II waged war against the Plantagenet rulers of England, who also ruled the French territories of Normandy, Maine, Anjou, and Aquitaine, and was successful in gaining control of most of these territories, thus enlarging the power of the French monarchy (see Map 12.2). To administer justice and collect royal revenues in his new territories, Philip appointed new royal officials, thus inaugurating a French royal bureaucracy in the thirteenth century.

Capetian rulers after Philip II continued to add lands to the royal domain. Philip IV the Fair (1285–1314) was especially effective in strengthening the French monarchy. He reinforced the royal bureaucracy and also brought a French parliament into being by asking representatives of the three estates, or classes—the clergy (first estate), the nobles (second estate), and the townspeople

(third estate)—to meet with him. They did so in 1302, inaugurating the Estates-General, the first French parliament, although it had little real power. By the end of the thirteenth century, France was the largest, wealthiest, and best-governed monarchical state in Europe.

The Lands of the Holy Roman Empire   In the tenth century, the powerful dukes of the Saxons became kings of the eastern Frankish kingdom (or Germany, as it came to be called). The best known of the Saxon kings of Germany was Otto I (936–973), who intervened in Italian politics and for his efforts was crowned by the pope in 962 as emperor of the Romans, reviving a title that had seldom been used since the time of Charlemagne.

As leaders of a new Roman Empire, the German kings attempted to rule both German and Italian lands. Frederick I Barbarossa (1152–1190) and Frederick II (1212–1250) tried to create a new kind of empire. Previous German kings had focused on building a strong German kingdom, to which Italy might be added as an

MAP 12.2   Europe in the High Middle Ages. Although the nobility dominated much of European society in the High Middle Ages, kings began the process of extending their power in more effective ways, creating the monarchies that would form the European states. **❓** Which were the strongest monarchical states by 1300? Why? What about Germany and Italy? 🖐 View an animated version of this map or related maps at http://worldrc.wadsworth.com/

appendage. Emperor Frederick I, however, planned to get his chief revenues from Italy as the center of a "holy empire," as he called it (hence the name Holy Roman Empire). But his attempt to conquer northern Italy ran into severe opposition from the pope and the cities of northern Italy. An alliance of these cities and the pope defeated Frederick's forces in 1176.

The main goal of Frederick II was the establishment of a strong centralized state in Italy, but he too became involved in a deadly conflict with the popes and the north Italian cities. Frederick waged a bitter struggle in northern Italy, winning many battles but ultimately losing the war.

The struggle between popes and emperors had dire consequences for the Holy Roman Empire. By spending their time fighting in Italy, the German emperors left Germany in the hands of powerful German lords who ignored the emperor and created their own independent kingdoms. This ensured that the German monarchy would remain weak and incapable of building a centralized monarchical state; thus, the German Holy Roman Emperor had no real power over either Germany or Italy. Unlike France and England, neither Germany nor Italy created a centralized national monarchy in the Middle Ages. Both Germany and Italy consisted of many small, independent states, a situation that changed little until the nineteenth century.

The Slavic Peoples of Central and Eastern Europe

The Slavic peoples were originally a single people in central Europe, but they gradually divided into three major groups: the western, southern, and eastern Slavs (see Map 12.3). The western Slavs eventually formed the Polish and Bohemian kingdoms. German Christian missionaries converted both the Czechs in Bohemia and the Slavs in Poland by the tenth century. The non-Slavic kingdom of Hungary, which emerged after the Magyars settled down after their defeat in 955, was also converted to Christianity by German missionaries. The Poles, Czechs, and Hungarians all accepted Catholic or western Christianity and became closely tied to the Roman Catholic church and its Latin culture.

The southern and eastern Slavic populations took a different path: the Slavic peoples of Moravia were converted to the Orthodox Christianity of the Byzantine Empire by two Byzantine missionary brothers, Cyril and Methodius,

who began their activities in 863. The southern Slavic peoples included the Croats, Serbs, and Bulgarians. For the most part, they too embraced Eastern Orthodoxy, although the Croats came to accept the Roman Catholic church. The acceptance of Eastern Orthodoxy by the Serbs and Bulgarians tied their cultural life to the Byzantine state.

The eastern Slavic peoples, from whom the modern Russians, Byelorussians, and Ukrainians are descended, had settled in the territory of present-day Ukraine and European Russia. There, beginning in the late eighth century, they began to encounter Swedish Vikings who moved down the extensive network of rivers into the lands of the eastern Slavs in search of booty and new trade routes (see the box on p. 270). These Vikings built trading settlements and eventually came to dominate the native peoples, who called them "the Rus," from which the name *Russia* is derived.

The Development of Russia   A Viking leader named Oleg (c. 873–913) settled in Kiev at the beginning of the tenth century and created the Rus state known as the principality of Kiev. His successors extended their control over the eastern Slavs and expanded the territory of Kiev until it included the territory between the Baltic and

MAP 12.3   **The Migrations of the Slavs.** Originally from east-central Europe, the Slavic people broke into three groups. The western Slavs converted to Catholic Christianity, while most of the eastern Slavs and southern Slavs, under the influence of the Byzantine Empire, embraced the Eastern Orthodox faith. ❓ What connections do these Slavic migrations have with what we today characterize as eastern Europe? 🌐 View an animated version of this map or related maps at http://worldrc.wadsworth.com/

A Muslim's Description of the Rus

Despite the difficulties that travel presented, early medieval civilization did witness some contact among the various cultures. This might occur through trade, diplomacy, or the conquest and migration of peoples. This document is a description of the Swedish Rus, who eventually merged with the native Slavic peoples to form the principality of Kiev, commonly regarded as the first Russian state. It was written by Ibn Fadlan, a Muslim diplomat sent from Baghdad in 921 to a settlement on the Volga River. His comments on the filthiness of the Rus reflect the Muslim preoccupation with cleanliness.

What was Ibn Fadlan's impression of the Rus? Why do you think he was so critical of their behavior?

Ibn Fadlan, Description of the Rus

I saw the Rus folk when they arrived on their trading mission and settled at the river Atul (Volga). Never had I seen people of more perfect physique. They are tall as date palms, and reddish in color. They wear neither coat nor kaftan, but each man carried a cape which covers one half of his body, leaving one hand free. No one is ever parted from his axe, sword, and knife. Their swords are Frankish in design, broad, flat, and fluted. Each man has a number of trees, figures, and the like from the fingernails to the neck. Each woman carried on her bosom a container made of iron, silver, copper, or gold—its size and substance depending on her man's wealth.

They [the Rus] are the filthiest of God's creatures. They do not wash after discharging their natural functions, neither do they wash their hands after meals. They are as lousy as donkeys. They arrive from their distant lands and lay their ships alongside the banks of the Atul, which is a great river, and there they build big houses on its shores. Ten or twenty of them may live together in one house, and each of them has a couch of his own where he sits and diverts himself with the pretty slave girls whom he had brought along for sale. He will make love with one of them while a comrade looks on; sometimes they indulge in a communal orgy, and, if a customer should turn up to buy a girl, the Rus man will not let her go till he has finished with her.

They wash their hands and faces every day in incredibly filthy water. Every morning the girl brings her master a large bowl of water in which he washes his hands and face and hair, then blows his nose into it and spits into it. When he has finished the girl takes the bowl to his neighbor—who repeats the performance. Thus the bowl goes the rounds of the entire household. . . .

If one of the Rus folk falls sick they put him in a tent by himself and leave bread and water for him. They do not visit him, however, or speak to him, especially if he is a serf. Should he recover he rejoins the others; if he dies they burn him. But if he happens to be a serf they leave him for the dogs and vultures to devour. If they catch a robber they hang him to a tree until he is torn to shreds by wind and weather.

Black seas and the Danube and Volga rivers. By marrying Slavic wives, the Viking ruling class was gradually assimilated into the Slavic population.

The growth of the principality of Kiev attracted religious missionaries, especially from the Byzantine Empire. One Rus ruler, Vladimir (c. 980–1015), married the Byzantine emperor's sister and officially accepted Christianity for himself and his people in 987. From the end of the tenth century, Byzantine Christianity became the model for Russian religious life.

The Kievan Rus state prospered and reached its high point in the first half of the eleventh century. But civil wars and new invasions by Asiatic nomads caused the principality of Kiev to collapse, and the sack of Kiev by north Russian princes in 1169 brought an end to the first Russian state. That first Russian state had remained closely tied to the Byzantine Empire, not to the new Europe.

Impact of the Mongols   In the thirteenth century, the Mongols conquered Russia and cut it off even more from Europe, but they were not numerous enough to settle the vast Russian lands. They occupied only part of Russia and required the Russian princes to pay tribute to them. One Russian prince soon emerged as more powerful than the others. Alexander Nevsky, prince of Novgorod, defeated a German invading army in northwestern Russia in 1242. His cooperation with the Mongols won him their favor. The khan, leader of the western part of the Mongol Empire, rewarded Alexander Nevsky with the title of grand-prince, enabling his descendants to become the princes of Moscow and eventually leaders of all Russia.

Christianity and Medieval Civilization

Christianity was an integral part of the fabric of European society and the consciousness of Europe. Papal directives affected the actions of kings and princes alike, and Christian teachings and practices touched the lives of all Europeans.

The Papal Monarchy   Since the fifth century, the popes of the Catholic church had reigned supreme over the affairs of the church. They had also come to exercise control over the territories in central Italy that came to be known as the Papal States, which kept the popes involved

England	
Norman conquest	1066
William the Conqueror	1066–1087
Henry II	1154–1189
John	1199–1216
Magna Carta	1215
Edward I	1272–1307
First Parliament	1295
France	
Philip II Augustus	1180–1223
Philip IV	1285–1314
First Estates-General	1302
Germany and the Empire	
Otto I	936–973
Frederick I Barbarossa	1152–1190
Frederick II	1212–1250
The Eastern World	
Mongol conquest of Russia	1230s
Alexander Nevsky, prince of Novgorod	c. 1220–1263

in political matters, often at the expense of their spiritual obligations. At the same time, the church became increasingly entangled in the evolving feudal relationships. High officials of the church, such as bishops and abbots, came to hold their offices as fiefs from nobles. As vassals, they were obliged to carry out the usual duties, including military service. Of course, lords assumed the right to choose their vassals and thus came to appoint bishops and abbots.

By the eleventh century, church leaders realized the need to free the church from the interference of lords in the appointment of church officials. **Lay investiture** was the practice by which secular rulers both chose nominees to church offices and invested them with the symbols of their office. Pope Gregory VII (1073–1085) decided to fight this practice. Gregory claimed that he—the pope—was God's "vicar on earth" and that the pope's authority extended over all of Christendom, including its rulers. In 1075, he issued a decree forbidding high-ranking clerics from receiving their investiture from lay leaders.

Gregory VII soon found himself in conflict with the king of Germany over his actions. King Henry IV (1056–1106) of Germany was also a determined man who had appointed high-ranking clerics, especially bishops, as his vassals in order to use them as administrators. Henry had no intention of obeying a decree that challenged the very heart of his administration.

The struggle between Henry IV and Gregory VII, which is known as the Investiture Controversy, was one of the great conflicts between church and state in the High Middle Ages. It dragged on until a new German king and a new pope reached a compromise in 1122 called the Concordat of Worms. Under this agreement, a bishop in Germany was first elected by church officials. After election, the nominee paid homage to the king as his lord, who then invested him with the symbols of temporal office. A representative of the pope, however, then invested the new bishop with the symbols of his spiritual office.

The Church Supreme   The popes of the twelfth century did not abandon the reform ideals of Pope Gregory VII, but they were more inclined to consolidate their power and build a strong administrative system. During the papacy of Pope Innocent III (1198–1216), the Catholic church reached the height of its power. At the beginning of his pontificate, in a letter to a priest, the pope made a clear statement of his views on papal supremacy:

> As God, the creator of the universe, set two great lights in the firmament of heaven, the greater light to rule the day, and the lesser light to rule the night, so He set two great dignities in the firmament of the universal church, . . . the greater to rule the day, that is, souls, and the lesser to rule the night, that is, bodies. These dignities are the papal authority and the royal power. And just as the moon gets her light from the sun, and is inferior to the sun . . . so the royal power gets the splendor of its dignity from the papal authority.[3]

Innocent III's actions were those of a man who believed that he, the pope, was the supreme judge of European affairs. To achieve his political ends, he did not hesitate to use the spiritual weapons at his command, especially the **interdict**, which forbade priests to dispense the **sacraments** of the church in the hope that the people, deprived of the comforts of religion, would exert pressure against their ruler.

New Religious Orders and New Spiritual Ideals   Between 1050 and 1150, a wave of religious enthusiasm seized Europe, leading to a spectacular growth in the number of monasteries and the emergence of new monastic orders. Most important was the Cistercian order, founded in 1098 by a group of monks dissatisfied with the moral degeneration and lack of strict discipline at their own Benedictine monastery. The Cistercians were strict. They ate a simple diet and possessed only a single robe apiece. More time for prayer and manual labor was provided by shortening the number of hours spent at religious services. The Cistercians played a major role in developing a new, activist spiritual model for twelfth-century Europe. A Benedictine monk often spent hours in prayer to honor God. The Cistercian ideal had a different emphasis: "Arise, soldier of Christ, arise! Get up off the ground and return to the battle from which you have fled! Fight more boldly after your flight, and triumph in glory!"[4]

A Group of Nuns.   Although still viewed by the medieval church as inferior to men, women were as susceptible to the spiritual fervor of the twelfth century as men, and female monasticism grew accordingly. This miniature shows a group of Flemish nuns listening to the preaching of an abbot, Gilles li Muisis. The nun wearing a white robe at the far left is a novice.

Women were also actively involved in the spiritual movements of the age. The number of women joining religious houses grew dramatically in the High Middle Ages. Most nuns were from the ranks of the landed aristocracy. Convents were convenient for families unable or unwilling to find husbands for their daughters and for aristocratic women who did not wish to marry. Female intellectuals found them a haven for their activities. Most of the learned women of the Middle Ages were nuns.

In the thirteenth century, two new religious orders emerged that had a profound impact on the lives of ordinary people. Like their founder, Saint Francis of Assisi (1182–1226), the Franciscans lived among the people, preaching repentance and aiding the poor. Their calls for a return to the simplicity and poverty of the early church, reinforced by their own example, were especially effective and made them very popular.

Dominicans arose out of the desire of a Spanish priest, Dominic de Guzmán (1170–1221), to defend church teachings from **heresy**—beliefs contrary to official church doctrine. Dominic was an intellectual who came to believe that a new religious order of men who lived lives of poverty but were learned and capable of preaching effectively would best be able to attack heresy. The Dominicans became especially well known for their roles as the inquisitors of the papal Inquisition.

The Holy Office, as the papal Inquisition was formally called, was a court that had been established by the church to find and try heretics. Anyone accused of heresy who refused to confess was still considered guilty and was turned over to the state for execution. To the Christians of the thirteenth century, who believed that there was only one path to salvation, heresy was a crime against God and against humanity. In their minds, force should be used to save souls from damnation.

The Culture of the High Middle Ages

The High Middle Ages was a time of extraordinary intellectual and artistic vitality. It witnessed the birth of universities and a building spree that left Europe bedecked with churches and cathedrals.

The Rise of Universities   The university as we know it—with faculty, students, and degrees—is a product of the High Middle Ages. The word *university* is derived from the Latin word *universitas,* meaning a corporation or guild, and referred to either a corporation of teachers or a corporation of students. Medieval universities were educational guilds or corporations that produced educated and trained individuals.

The first European university appeared in Bologna, Italy, where a great teacher named Irnerius (1088–1125), who taught Roman law, attracted students from all over Europe. To protect themselves, students at Bologna formed a guild or *universitas,* which was recognized by Emperor Frederick Barbarossa and given a charter in 1158. Kings, popes, and princes soon competed to found new universities, and by the end of the Middle Ages, there were eighty universities in Europe, most of them in England, France, Italy, and Germany.

University students (all men—women did not attend universities in the Middle Ages) began their studies with the traditional **liberal arts** curriculum, which consisted of grammar, rhetoric, logic, arithmetic, geometry, music, and astronomy. Teaching was done by the lecture method. The word *lecture* is derived from the Latin verb for "read." Before the development of the printing press in the fifteenth century, books were expensive and few students could afford them, so teachers read from a basic text (such as a collection of laws if the subject was law) and then added their explanations. No exams were given after a series of lectures, but when a student applied for a degree, he was given a comprehensive oral examination by a committee of teachers. The exam was taken after a four- or six-year period of study. The first degree a student could earn was a bachelor of arts; later he might receive a master of arts.

After completing the liberal arts curriculum, a student could go on to study law, medicine, or theology. A student who passed his final oral examinations was granted a doctor's degree, which officially enabled him to teach his subject. Students who received degrees from medieval universities could pursue other careers besides teaching that proved to be much more lucrative. A law degree was necessary for those who wished to serve as advisers to kings and princes.

The Development of Scholasticism

The importance of Christianity in medieval society ensured that theology would play a central role in the European intellectual world. Theology, the formal study of religion, was "queen of the sciences" in the new universities.

Beginning in the eleventh century, the effort to apply reason or logical analysis to the church's basic theological doctrines had a significant impact on the study of theology. The word *scholasticism* is used to refer to the philosophical and theological system of the medieval schools. **Scholasticism** tried to reconcile faith and reason, to demonstrate that what was accepted on faith was in harmony with what could be learned by reason.

The overriding task of scholasticism was to harmonize Christian teachings with the work of the Greek philosopher Aristotle. In the twelfth century, due largely to the work of Muslim and Jewish scholars in Spain, western Europe was introduced to a large number of Greek scientific and philosophical works, including the works of Aristotle. However, Aristotle's works threw many theologians into consternation. Aristotle had arrived at his conclusions by rational thought, not by faith, and some of his doctrines contradicted the teachings of the church. The most famous attempt to reconcile Aristotle and the doctrines of Christianity was that of Saint Thomas Aquinas (1225–1274).

Aquinas's reputation derives from his masterful attempt to reconcile faith and reason. He took it for granted that there were truths derived by reason and truths derived by faith. He was certain, however, that the two truths could not be in conflict. The natural mind, unaided by faith, could arrive at truths concerning the physical universe. Without the help of God's grace, however, reason alone could not grasp spiritual truths, such as the Trinity (the manifestation of God in three separate yet identical

persons—Father, Son, and Holy Spirit) or the Incarnation (Jesus' simultaneous identity as God and human).

The Gothic Cathedral

Begun in the twelfth century and brought to perfection in the thirteenth, the Gothic cathedral remains one of the greatest artistic triumphs of the High Middle Ages. Soaring skyward, as if to reach heaven, it was a fitting symbol for medieval people's preoccupation with God.

Two fundamental innovations of the twelfth century made Gothic cathedrals possible. The combination of ribbed vaults and pointed arches replaced the barrel vault of earlier churches and enabled builders to make Gothic churches higher. The use of pointed arches and ribbed vaults created an impression of upward movement. Another technical innovation, the flying buttress, basically a heavy arched pier of stone built onto the outside of the walls, made it possible to distribute the weight of the church's vaulted ceilings outward and down and thus

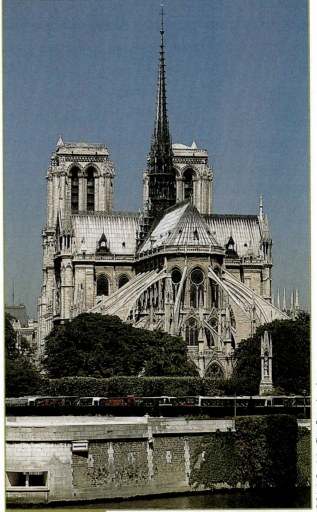

The Gothic Cathedral. The Gothic cathedral was one of the great artistic triumphs of the High Middle Ages. Seen here is the cathedral of Notre-Dame in Paris. Begun in 1163, it was not completed until the beginning of the fourteenth century.

© Sylvain Grandadam/Photo Researchers, Inc.

eliminate the heavy walls used in earlier churches to hold the weight of the massive barrel vaults. Thus, Gothic cathedrals could be built with thin walls containing magnificent stained-glass windows, which created a play of light inside that varied with the sun at different times of the day. The use of light reflected the belief that natural light was a symbol of the divine light of God.

The first fully Gothic church was the abbey of Saint-Denis near Paris, inspired by its famous Abbot Suger (1122–1151) and built between 1140 and 1150. Although the Gothic style was a product of northern France, by the mid-thirteenth century, French Gothic architecture had spread to virtually all of Europe. French Gothic architecture was seen most brilliantly in cathedrals in Paris (Notre-Dame), Reims, Amiens, and Chartres.

A Gothic cathedral was the work of the entire community. All classes contributed to its construction. Master masons, who were both architects and engineers, designed them, and stonemasons and other craftspeople were paid a daily wage and provided the skilled labor to build them. A Gothic cathedral symbolized the chief preoccupation of a medieval Christian community, its dedication to a spiritual ideal. The largest buildings of an era reflect the values of its society. The Gothic cathedral, with its towers soaring toward heaven, gave witness to an age when a spiritual impulse underlay most aspects of life.

Medieval Europe and the World

As it developed, European civilization remained largely confined to one geographic area. Although some Europeans, especially merchants, had contacts with parts of Asia and Africa, and Viking explorers even reached the eastern fringes of North America in the tenth and eleventh centuries, such efforts to reach beyond Europe were limited. But at the end of the eleventh century, Europeans began their first concerted attempt to expand beyond the frontiers of Europe by conquering the land of Palestine.

The First Crusades

The Crusades were based on the idea of a holy war against the infidels or unbelievers. The wrath of Christians was directed against the Muslims, and at the end of the eleventh century, Christian Europe found itself with a glorious opportunity to attack them. The immediate impetus for the Crusades came when the Byzantine emperor, Alexius I, asked Pope Urban II for help against the Seljuk Turks, who were Muslims. The pope saw a golden opportunity to provide papal leadership for a great cause: to rally the warriors of Europe for the liberation of Jerusalem and the Holy Land (Palestine) from the infidel. At the Council of Clermont in southern France near the end of 1095, Urban II challenged Christians to take up their weapons and join in a holy war to recover the Holy Land.

Three organized crusading bands of noble warriors, most of them French, made their way eastward. After the capture of Antioch in 1098, much of the crusading host proceeded down the Palestinian coast, evading the well-defended coastal cities, and reached Jerusalem in June 1099. After a five-week siege, the Holy City was taken amid a horrible massacre of the inhabitants—men, women, and children (see the box on p. 275).

After further conquest of Palestinian lands, the crusaders ignored the wishes of the Byzantine emperor and organized four Latin crusader states. Because the crusader kingdoms were surrounded by Muslims hostile to them, they grew increasingly dependent on the Italian commercial cities for supplies from Europe. Some Italian cities, such as Genoa, Pisa, and, above all, Venice, grew rich and powerful in the process.

But it was not easy for the crusader kingdoms to maintain themselves. Already by the 1120s, the Muslims had begun to strike back. The fall of one of the Latin kingdoms in 1144 led to renewed calls for another Crusade, especially from the monastic firebrand Saint Bernard of Clairvaux. He exclaimed: "Now, on account of our sins, the enemies of the cross have begun to show their faces. . . . What are you doing, you servants of the cross? Will you throw to the dogs that which is most holy? Will you cast pearls before swine?"[5] Bernard even managed to enlist two powerful rulers, but their Second Crusade proved to be a total failure.

The Third Crusade was a reaction to the fall of the Holy City of Jerusalem in 1187 to the Muslim forces under Saladin. Now all of Christendom was ablaze with calls for a new Crusade. Three major monarchs agreed to lead their forces in person: Emperor Frederick Barbarossa of Germany, Richard I the Lionhearted of England (1189–1199), and Philip II Augustus, king of France. Some of the crusaders finally arrived in the East by 1189 only to encounter problems. Frederick Barbarossa drowned while swimming in a local river, and his army quickly disintegrated. The English and French arrived by sea and met with success against the coastal cities, where they had the support of their fleets, but when they moved inland, they failed miserably. Eventually, after Philip went home, Richard the Lionhearted negotiated a settlement whereby Saladin agreed to allow Christian pilgrims free access to Jerusalem.

The Later Crusades

After the death of Saladin in 1193, Pope Innocent III initiated the Fourth Crusade. On its way to the East, the crusading army became involved in a dispute over the succession to the Byzantine throne. The Venetian leaders of the Fourth Crusade saw an opportunity to neutralize their greatest commercial competitor, the Byzantine Empire. Diverted to Constantinople, the crusaders sacked the great capital city of Byzantium in 1204 and set up the new Latin Empire of Constantinople. Not until 1261 did a Byzantine army recapture Constantinople.

The Siege of Jerusalem: Christian and Muslim Perspectives

INTERACTION & EXCHANGE

During the First Crusade, Christian knights laid siege to Jerusalem in June 1099. The first excerpt is taken from an account by Fulcher of Chartres, who accompanied the crusaders to the Holy Land. The second selection is by a Muslim writer, Ibn al-Athir, whose account of the First Crusade can be found in his history of the Muslim world.

How do these two accounts differ? What was the fate of the Muslims in Jerusalem?

Fulcher of Chartres, *Chronicle of the First Crusade*

Then the Franks entered the city magnificently at the noonday hour on Friday, the day of the week when Christ redeemed the whole world on the cross. With trumpets sounding and with everything in an uproar, exclaiming: "Help, God!" they vigorously pushed into the city, and straightaway raised the banner on the top of the wall. All the heathen, completely terrified, changed their boldness to swift flight through the narrow streets of the quarters. The more quickly they fled, the more quickly they were put to flight.

Count Raymond and his men, who were bravely assailing the city in another section, did not perceive this until they saw the Saracens [Muslims] jumping from the top of the wall. Seeing this, they joyfully ran to the city as quickly as they could, and helped the others pursue and kill the wicked enemy.

Then some, both Arabs and Ethiopians, fled into the Tower of David; others shut themselves in the Temple of the Lord and of Solomon, where in the halls a very great attack was made on them. Nowhere was there a place where the Saracens could escape swordsmen.

On the top of Solomon's Temple, to which they had climbed in fleeing, many were shot to death with arrows and cast down headlong from the roof. Within this Temple, about ten thousand were beheaded. If you had been there, your feet would have been stained up to the ankles with the blood of the slain. What more shall I tell? Not one of them was allowed to live. They did not spare the women and children.

Account of Ibn al-Athir

In fact Jerusalem was taken from the north on the morning of Friday 22 Sha'ban 492/15 July 1099. The population was put to the sword by the Franks, who pillaged the area for a week. A band of Muslims barricaded themselves into the Oratory of David and fought on for several days. They were granted their lives in return for surrendering. The Franks honored their word, and the group left by night for Ascalon. In the Masjid al-Aqsa the Franks slaughtered more than 70,000 people, among them a large number of Imams and Muslim scholars, devout and ascetic men who had left their homelands to live lives of pious seclusion in the Holy Place. The Franks stripped the Dome of the Rock of more than forty silver candelabra, each of them weighing 3,600 drams, and a great silver lamp weighing forty-four Syrian pounds, as well as a hundred and fifty smaller candelabra and more than twenty gold ones, and a great deal more booty. Refugees from Syria reached Baghdad in Ramadan, among them the qadi Abu sa'd al-Harawi. They told the Caliph's ministers a story that wrung their hearts and brought tears to their eyes. On Friday they went to the Cathedral Mosque and begged for help, weeping so that their hearers wept with them as they described the sufferings of the Muslims in the Holy City: the men killed, the women and children taken prisoner, the homes pillaged. Because of the terrible hardships they had suffered, they were allowed to break the fast.

CENGAGENOW To read a number of accounts of the siege, enter the *CengageNOW* documents area using the access card that is available for *The Essential World History*.

In the meantime, additional Crusades were undertaken to reconquer the Holy Land. All of them were largely disasters, and by the end of the thirteenth century, the European military effort to capture Palestine was recognized as a complete failure.

The Crises of the Late Middle Ages

At the beginning of the fourteenth century, changes in weather patterns in Europe ushered in what has been called a "little ice age." Shortened growing seasons and disastrous weather conditions, including heavy storms and constant rain, led to widespread famine and hunger. Soon an even greater catastrophe struck.

The Black Death

The **Black Death** of the mid-fourteenth century was the most devastating natural disaster in European history, ravaging Europe's population and causing economic, social, political, and cultural upheaval. People were horrified by an evil force they could not understand and by the subsequent breakdown of all normal human relations.

Bubonic plague was the most common and most important form of plague in the diffusion of the Black Death and was spread by black rats infested with fleas who were host to the deadly bacterium *Yersinia pestis*. This great plague originated in Asia. After disappearing from Europe and the Middle East in the Early Middle Ages, bubonic plague had continued to haunt areas of

THE ROLE OF DISEASE

INTERACTION & EXCHANGE

When Hernán Cortés and his fellow conquistadors arrived in Mesoamerica in 1519, the local inhabitants were frightened of the horses and the firearms that accompanied the Spaniards. What they did not know was that the most dangerous enemies brought by these strange new arrivals were invisible—the disease-bearing microbes that would soon kill them by the millions.

Diseases have been the scourge of animal species since the dawn of prehistory, making the lives of human beings, in the words of the English philosopher Thomas Hobbes, "nasty, brutish, and short." With the increasing sophistication of forensic evidence, archaeologists today are able to determine from recently discovered human remains that our immediate ancestors were plagued by such familiar ailments as anemia, arthritis, tuberculosis, and malaria.

With the explosive growth of the human population brought about by the agricultural revolution, the problems posed by the presence of disease intensified. As people began to congregate in villages and cities, bacteria settled in their piles of refuse and were carried by lice in their clothing. The domestication of animals made humans more vulnerable to diseases carried by their livestock. As population density increased, the danger of widespread epidemics increased with it.

As time went on, succeeding generations gradually developed a partial or complete immunity to many of these diseases, which became chronic rather than fatal to their victims, as occurred with malaria in parts of Africa, for example, and chicken pox in the Americas. But when a disease was introduced to a particular society that had not previously been exposed to it, the consequences were often fatal. The most dramatic example was the famous Black Death, the plague that ravaged Europe and China during the fourteenth century, killing up to one-half of the inhabitants in the affected regions. Smallpox had the same impact in the Americas after the arrival of Christopher Columbus, and malaria was fatal to many Europeans on their arrival in West Africa.

How were these diseases transmitted? In most instances, they followed the trade routes. Such was the case with the Black Death, which was initially carried by fleas living in the saddlebags of Mongol warriors as they advanced toward Europe in the thirteenth and fourteenth centuries and thereafter by rats in the holds of cargo ships. Smallpox and other diseases were brought to the Americas by the conquistadors. Epidemics, then, are a price that humans pay for having developed the network of rapid communications that has accompanied the evolution of human society.

---

southwestern China. Rats accompanying Mongol troops spread the plague into central and northwestern China and into Central Asia in the mid-thirteenth century. From there, trading caravans brought the plague to Caffa, on the Black Sea, in 1346 (see the comparative essay "The Role of Disease" above).

The plague reached Europe in October 1347 when Genoese merchants brought it from Caffa to the island of Sicily off the coast of Italy. It quickly spread to southern Italy and southern France by the end of 1347. Diffusion of the Black Death followed commercial trade routes. In 1348, it spread through Spain, France, and the Low Countries and into Germany. By the end of that year, it had moved to England, ravaging it in 1349. By the end of 1349, the plague had reached northern Europe and Scandinavia. Eastern Europe and Russia were affected by 1351.

Mortality figures for the Black Death were incredibly high. Especially hard hit were Italy's crowded cities, where 50 to 60 percent of the people died. One citizen of Florence wrote, "A great many breathed their last in the public streets, day and night; a large number perished in their homes, and it was only by the stench of their decaying bodies that they proclaimed their deaths to their neighbors. Everywhere the city was teeming with corpses."[6] In England and Germany, entire villages simply disappeared.

It has been estimated that out of a total European population of 75 million, as many as 38 million people may have died of the plague between 1347 and 1351.

The attempt of contemporaries to explain the Black Death and mitigate its harshness led to extreme sorts of behavior. To many, either the plague had been sent by God as a punishment for humans' sins, or it had been caused by the devil. Some, known as the flagellants, resorted to extreme measures to gain God's forgiveness. Groups of flagellants, both men and women, wandered from town to town, flogging each other with whips to beg the forgiveness of a God who, they felt, had sent the plague to punish humans for their sinful ways. One contemporary chronicler described their activies:

The penitents went about, coming first out of Germany. They were men who did public penance and scourged themselves with whips of hard knotted leather with little iron spikes. Some made themselves bleed very badly between the shoulder blades and some foolish women had cloths ready to catch the blood and smear it on their eyes, saying it was miraculous blood. While they were doing penance, they sang very mournful songs about the nativity and the passion of Our Lord. The object of this penance was to put a stop to the mortality, for in that time . . . at least a third of all the people in the world died.[7]

A Medieval Holocaust: The Cremation of the Strasbourg Jews

RELIGION & PHILOSOPHY

In their attempt to explain the widespread horrors of the Black Death, medieval Christian communities looked for scapegoats. As at the time of the Crusades, the Jews were accused of poisoning wells and hence spreading the plague. This selection by a contemporary chronicler, written in 1349, gives an account of how Christians in the town of Strasbourg in the Holy Roman Empire dealt with their Jewish community. It is apparent that financial gain was also an important factor in killing the Jews.

What charges were made against the Jews in regard to the Black Death? Can it be said that these charges were economically motivated? Why or why not? Why did the anti-Semitism of towns such as Strasbourg lead to the establishment of large Jewish populations in eastern Europe?

Jacob von Königshofen, "The Cremation of the Strasbourg Jews"

In the year 1349 there occurred the greatest epidemic that ever happened. Death went from one end of the earth to the other. . . . And from what this epidemic came, all wise teachers and physicians could only say that it was God's will. . . . This epidemic also came to Strasbourg in the summer of the above-mentioned year, and it is estimated that about sixteen thousand people died.

In the matter of this plague the Jews throughout the world were reviled and accused in all lands of having caused it through the poison which they are said to have put into the water and the wells—that is what they were accused of—and for this reason the Jews were burnt all the way from the Mediterranean into Germany. . . .

[The account then goes on to discuss the situation of the Jews in the city of Strasbourg.]

On Saturday . . . they burnt the Jews on a wooden platform in their cemetery. There were about two thousand people of them. Those who wanted to baptize themselves were spared. [Some say that about a thousand accepted baptism.] Many small children were taken out of the fire and baptized against the will of their fathers and mothers. And everything that was owed to the Jews was canceled, and the Jews had to surrender all pledges and notes that they had taken for debts. The council, however, took the cash that the Jews possessed and divided it among the workingmen proportionately. The money was indeed the thing that killed the Jews. If they had been poor and if the feudal lords had not been in debt to them, they would not have been burnt. . . .

Thus were the Jews burnt at Strasbourg, and in the same year in all the cities of the Rhine, whether Free Cities or Imperial Cities or cities belonging to the lords. In some towns they burnt the Jews after a trial; in others, without a trial. In some cities the Jews themselves set fire to their houses and cremated themselves.

It was decided in Strasbourg that no Jew should enter the city for a hundred years, but before twenty years had passed, the council and magistrates agreed that they ought to admit the Jews again into the city for twenty years. And so the Jews came back again to Strasbourg in the year 1368 after the birth of our Lord.

The flagellants created mass hysteria wherever they went, and authorities worked overtime to crush the movement.

An outbreak of virulent anti-Semitism also accompanied the Black Death. Jews were accused of causing the plague by poisoning town wells. The worst **pogroms** against this minority were carried out in Germany, where more than sixty major Jewish communities had been exterminated by 1351 (see the box above). Many Jews fled eastward to Russia and especially to Poland, where the king offered them protection. Eastern Europe became home to large Jewish communities.

Economic Dislocation and Social Upheaval

The death of so many people in the fourteenth century also had severe economic consequences. Trade declined, and some industries suffered greatly. A shortage of workers caused a dramatic rise in the price of labor, while the decline in the number of people lowered the demand for food, resulting in falling prices. Landlords were now paying more for labor at the same time that their rental income was declining. Concurrently, the decline in the number of peasants after the Black Death made it easier for some to convert their labor services to rent, thus freeing them from serfdom. But there were limits to how much the peasants could advance. They faced the same economic hurdles as the lords, who also attempted to impose wage restrictions and reinstate old forms of labor service. Peasant complaints became widespread and soon gave rise to rural revolts.

Although the peasant revolts sometimes resulted in short-term gains for the participants, the uprisings were easily crushed and their gains quickly lost. Accustomed to ruling, the established classes easily combined and stifled dissent.

Political Instability

Famine, plague, economic turmoil, and social upheaval were not the only problems of the fourteenth century. War and political instability must also be added to the list. Of all the struggles that ensued in the fourteenth century, the Hundred Years' War was the most violent.

The Hundred Years' War In the thirteenth century, England still held one small possession in France known as the duchy of Gascony. As duke of Gascony, the English king pledged loyalty as a vassal to the French king, but when King Philip VI of France (1328–1350) seized Gascony in 1337, the duke of Gascony—King Edward III of England (1327–1377)—declared war on Philip.

The Hundred Years' War began in a burst of knightly enthusiasm. The French army of 1337 still relied largely on heavily armed noble cavalrymen, who looked with contempt on foot soldiers and crossbowmen, whom they regarded as social inferiors. The English, too, used heavily armed cavalry, but they relied even more on large numbers of paid foot soldiers. Armed with pikes, many of these soldiers had also adopted the longbow, invented by the Welsh. The longbow had greater striking power, longer range, and more rapid speed of fire than the crossbow.

The first major battle of the Hundred Years' War occurred in 1346 at Crécy, just south of Flanders. The larger French army followed no battle plan but simply attacked the English lines in a disorderly fashion. The arrows of the English archers decimated the French cavalry. As the chronicler Froissart described it, "[With their longbows] the English continued to shoot into the thickest part of the crowd, wasting none of their arrows. They impaled or wounded horses and riders, who fell to the ground in great distress, unable to get up again without the help of several men."[8] It was a stunning victory for the English and the foot soldier.

The Battle of Crécy was not decisive, however. The English simply did not possess the resources to subjugate all of France, but they continued to try. The English king, Henry V (1413–1422), was especially eager to achieve victory. At the Battle of Agincourt in 1415, the heavy, armor-plated French knights attempted to attack across a field turned to mud by heavy rain; the result was a disastrous French defeat and the death of fifteen hundred French nobles. The English were masters of northern France.

The seemingly hopeless French cause fell into the hands of the dauphin Charles, the heir to the throne, who governed the southern two-thirds of French lands. Charles's cause seemed doomed until a French peasant woman quite unexpectedly saved the timid monarch. Born in 1412, the daughter of well-to-do peasants, Joan of Arc was a deeply religious person who came to believe that her favorite saints had commanded her to free France. In February 1429, Joan made her way to the dauphin's court and persuaded Charles to allow her to accompany a French army to Orléans. Apparently inspired by the faith of the peasant girl called "the Maid of Orléans," the French armies found new confidence in themselves and liberated Orléans and the entire Loire valley.

But Joan did not live to see the war concluded. Captured in 1430, she was turned over to the Inquisition on charges of witchcraft. In the fifteenth century, spiritual visions were thought to be inspired by either God or the devil. Joan was condemned to death as a heretic and burned at the stake in 1431. Twenty-five years later, a new

ecclesiastical court exonerated her of these charges, and five centuries later, in 1920, she was made a saint of the Roman Catholic church.

Joan of Arc's accomplishments proved decisive. Although the war dragged on for another two decades, defeats of English armies in Normandy and Aquitaine led to French victory by 1453. Important to the French success was the use of the cannon, a new weapon made possible by the invention of gunpowder. The Chinese had invented gunpower in the eleventh century and devised a simple cannon by the thirteenth century. The Mongols greatly improved this technology, developing more accurate cannons and cannonballs; both spread to the Middle East in the thirteenth century and to Europe by the fourteenth. The use of gunpowder eventually brought drastic changes to European warfare by making castles, city walls, and armored knights obsolete.

Political Disintegration By the fourteenth century, the feudal order had begun to break down. With money from taxes, kings could now hire professional soldiers, who tended to be more reliable than feudal knights anyway. Fourteenth-century kings had their own problems, however. Many dynasties in Europe failed to produce male heirs, and the founders of new dynasties had to fight for their positions as groups of nobles, trying to gain advantages for themselves, supported opposing candidates. Rulers encountered financial problems too. Hiring professional soldiers left them always short of cash, adding yet another element of uncertainty and confusion to fourteenth-century politics.

The Decline of the Church

The papacy of the Roman Catholic church reached the height of its power in the thirteenth century. But problems in the fourteenth century led to a serious decline for the church. By that time, the monarchies of Europe were no longer willing to accept papal claims of temporal supremacy, as is evident in the struggle between Pope Boniface VIII (1294–1303) and King Philip IV of France. In need of new revenues, Philip claimed the right to tax the clergy of France, but Boniface VIII insisted that the clergy of any state could not pay taxes to their secular ruler without the consent of the pope, who, he argued, was supreme over both the church and the state.

Philip IV refused to accept the pope's position and sent French forces to capture Boniface and bring him back to France for trial. The pope escaped but soon died from the shock of his experience. To ensure his position, Philip IV engineered the election of a Frenchman, Clement V (1305–1314), as pope. The new pope took up residence in Avignon on the east bank of the Rhone River.

From 1305 to 1377, the popes resided in Avignon, leading to an increase in antipapal sentiment. The pope was the bishop of Rome, and it was unseemly that the head of the Catholic church should reside in Avignon instead of Rome. Moreover, the splendor in which the pope and cardinals were living in Avignon led to a highly vocal criticism of the papacy. At last, Pope Gregory XI (1370–1378), perceiving the disastrous decline in papal prestige, returned to Rome in 1377, but died there the spring after his return.

When the college of cardinals met to elect a new pope, the citizens of Rome threatened that the cardinals would not leave Rome alive unless they elected an Italian as pope. Wisely, the terrified cardinals duly elected the Italian archbishop of Bari as Pope Urban VI (1378–1389). Five months later, however, a group of French cardinals declared Urban's election invalid and chose a Frenchman as pope, who promptly returned to Avignon. Because Urban remained in Rome, there were now two popes, beginning what has been called the Great Schism of the church.

The Great Schism divided Europe. France and its allies supported the pope in Avignon, whereas France's enemy England and its allies supported the pope in Rome. The Great Schism was also damaging to the faith of Christian believers. The pope was widely believed to be the true leader of Christendom; when both lines of popes denounced the other as the Antichrist, people's faith in the papacy and the church were undermined. Finally, a church council met at Constance, Switzerland, in 1417. After the competing popes resigned or were deposed, a new pope was elected who was acceptable to all parties.

By the mid-fifteenth century, as a result of these crises, the church had lost much of its temporal power. Even worse, the papacy and the church had also lost much of their moral prestige.

Recovery: The Renaissance

People who lived in Italy between 1350 and 1550 or so believed that they were witnessing a rebirth of classical antiquity—the world of the Greeks and Romans. To them, this marked a new age, which historians later called the **Renaissance** (French for "rebirth") and viewed as a distinct period of European history, which began in Italy and then spread to the rest of Europe.

Renaissance Italy was largely an urban society. The city-states became the centers of Italian political, economic, and social life. Within this new urban society, a secular spirit emerged as increasing wealth created new possibilities for the enjoyment of worldly things.

The Renaissance was also an age of recovery from the disasters of the fourteenth century, including the Black Death, political disorder, and economic recession. In pursuing that recovery, Italian intellectuals became intensely interested in the glories of their own past, the Greco-Roman culture of antiquity.

A new view of human beings emerged as people in the Italian Renaissance began to emphasize individual ability. The fifteenth-century Florentine architect Leon Battista Alberti expressed the new philosophy succinctly:

"Men can do all things if they will."[9] This high regard for human worth and for individual potentiality gave rise to a new social ideal of the well-rounded personality or "universal person" (*l'uomo universale*) who was capable of achievements in many areas of life.

The Intellectual Renaissance

The emergence and growth of individualism and secularism as characteristics of the Italian Renaissance are most noticeable in the intellectual and artistic realms. The most important literary movement associated with the Renaissance is humanism.

Renaissance humanism was an intellectual movement based on the study of the classics, the literary works of Greece and Rome. Humanists studied the liberal arts—grammar, rhetoric, poetry, moral philosophy or ethics, and history—all based on the writings of ancient Greek and Roman authors. We call these subjects the humanities.

Petrarch (1304–1374), who has often been called the father of Italian Renaissance humanism, did more than any other individual in the fourteenth century to foster its development. Petrarch sought to find forgotten Latin manuscripts and also began the humanist emphasis on the use of pure classical Latin. Humanists used the works of Cicero as a model for prose and those of Virgil for poetry. As Petrarch said, "Christ is my God; Cicero is the prince of the language."

In Florence, the humanist movement took a new direction at the beginning of the fifteenth century. The humanists who worked as secretaries for the city council of Florence took a new interest in civic life. They came to believe that intellectuals had a duty to live an active life for their state and that their study of the humanities should be put to the service of the state.

Also evident in the humanism of the first half of the fifteenth century was a growing interest in classical Greek civilization. One of the first Italian humanists to gain a thorough knowledge of Greek was Leonardo Bruni, who became an enthusiastic pupil of the Byzantine scholar Manuel Chrysoloras, who taught in Florence from 1396 to 1400.

The Artistic Renaissance

Renaissance artists sought to imitate nature in their works of art. Their search for naturalism became an end in itself: to persuade onlookers of the reality of the object or event they were portraying. At the same time, the new artistic standards reflected the new attitude of mind in which human beings became the focus of attention, the "center and measure of all things," as one artist proclaimed.

This new Renaissance style was developed by Florentine painters in the fifteenth century. Especially important were two major developments. One emphasized the technical side of painting—understanding the

Leonardo da Vinci, *The Last Supper*.   Leonardo da Vinci was the impetus behind the High Renaissance concern for the idealization of nature, moving from a realistic portrayal of the human figure to an idealized form. Evident in Leonardo's *Last Supper* is his effort to depict a person's character and inner nature by the use of gesture and movement. Unfortunately, Leonardo used an experimental technique in this fresco, which soon led to its physical deterioration.

laws of perspective and the geometrical organization of outdoor space and light. The second development was the investigation of movement and anatomical structure. The realistic portrayal of the human nude became one of the foremost preoccupations of Italian Renaissance art.

By the end of the fifteenth century, Italian artists had mastered the new techniques for scientific observation of the world around them and were ready to move into new forms of creative expression. This marked the shift to the High Renaissance, which was dominated by the work of three artistic giants, Leonardo da Vinci (1452–1519), Raphael (1483–1520), and Michelangelo (1475–1564). Leonardo carried on the fifteenth-century experimental tradition by studying everything and even dissecting human bodies in order to see how nature worked. But Leonardo stressed the need to advance beyond such realism and initiated the High Renaissance's preoccupation with the idealization of nature, an attempt to generalize from realistic portrayal to an ideal form.

At twenty-five, Raphael was already regarded as one of Italy's best painters. He was acclaimed for his numerous madonnas, in which he attempted to achieve an ideal of beauty far surpassing human standards. He is well known for his frescoes in the Vatican Palace, which reveal a world of balance, harmony, and order—the underlying principles of the art of the classical world of Greece and Rome.

Michelangelo, an accomplished painter, sculptor, and architect, was fiercely driven by a desire to create, and he worked with great passion and energy on a remarkable number of projects. Michelangelo was influenced by Neoplatonism, which viewed the ideal beauty of the human form as a reflection of divine beauty; the more beautiful the body, the more God-like the figure. Another manifestation of Michelangelo's search for ideal beauty was his *David*, a colossal marble statue commissioned by the government of Florence in 1501 and completed in 1504.

The State in the Renaissance

In the second half of the fifteenth century, attempts were made to reestablish the centralized power of monarchical governments after the political disasters of the fourteenth century. Some historians called these states the "new monarchies," especially those of France, England, and Spain.

The Italian States   The Italian states provided the earliest examples of state building in the fifteenth century. During the Middle Ages, Italy had failed to develop a centralized territorial state, and by the fifteenth century, five major powers dominated the Italian peninsula: the duchy of Milan, the republics of Florence and Venice, the Papal States, and the kingdom of Naples.

Milan, Florence, and Venice proved especially adept at building strong, centralized states. Under a series of dukes, Milan became a highly centralized territorial state in which the rulers devised systems of taxation that generated enormous revenues for the government. The

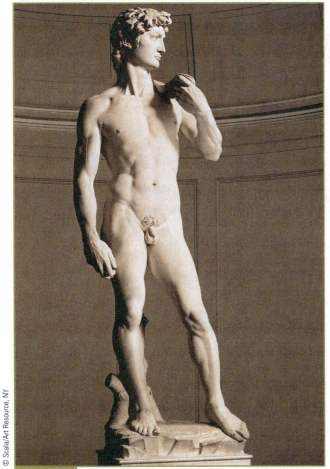

Michelangelo, *David*. This statue of David, cut from an 18-foot-high block of marble, exalts the beauty of the human body and is a fitting symbol of the Italian Renaissance's affirmation of human power. Completed in 1504, *David* was moved by Florentine authorities to a special location in front of the Palazzo Vecchio, the seat of the Florentine government.

maritime republic of Venice remained an extremely stable political entity governed by a small oligarchy of merchant-aristocrats. Its commercial empire brought in vast revenues and gave it the status of an international power. In Florence, Cosimo de' Medici took control of the merchant oligarchy in 1434. Through lavish patronage and careful courting of political allies, he and his family dominated the city at a time when Florence was the center of the cultural Renaissance.

As strong as these Italian states became, they still could not compete with the powerful monarchical states to the north and west. Beginning in 1494, Italy became a battlefield for the great power struggle between the French and Spanish monarchies, a conflict that led to Spanish domination of Italy in the sixteenth century.

Western Europe The Hundred Years' War left France prostrate. But it had also engendered a certain degree of French national feeling toward a common enemy that the kings could use to reestablish monarchical power. The development of a French territorial state was greatly advanced by King Louis XI (1461–1483), who strengthened the use of the *taille*—an annual direct tax usually on land or property—as a permanent tax imposed by royal authority, giving him a sound, regular source of income and creating the foundations of a strong French monarchy.

As the first Tudor king, Henry VII (1485–1509) worked to establish a strong monarchical government in England. Henry ended the petty wars of the nobility by abolishing their private armies. He was also very thrifty. By not overburdening the nobility and the middle class with taxes, Henry won their favor, and they provided him much support.

Spain, too, experienced the growth of a strong national monarchy by the end of the fifteenth century. During the Middle Ages, several independent Christian kingdoms had emerged in the course of the long reconquest of the Iberian peninsula from the Muslims. Two of the strongest were Aragon and Castile. When Isabella of Castile (1474–1504) married Ferdinand of Aragon (1479–1516) in 1469, it was a major step toward unifying Spain. The two rulers worked to strengthen royal control of government. They filled the royal council with middle-class lawyers who operated on the belief that the monarchy embodied the power of the state. Ferdinand and Isabella also reorganized the military forces of Spain, making the new Spanish army the best in Europe by the sixteenth century.

Central and Eastern Europe Unlike France, England, and Spain, the Holy Roman Empire failed to develop a strong monarchical authority. The failure of the German emperors in the thirteenth century ended any chance of centralized monarchical authority, and Germany became a land of hundreds of virtually independent states. After 1438, the position of Holy Roman emperor was held by members of the Habsburg dynasty. Having gradually acquired a number of possessions along the Danube, known collectively as Austria, the house of Habsburg had become one of the wealthiest landholders in the empire.

In eastern Europe, rulers struggled to achieve the centralization of the territorial states. Religious differences troubled the area, as Roman Catholics, Eastern Orthodox Christians, and other groups, including the Mongols, confronted each other. In Poland, the nobles gained the upper hand and established the right to elect their kings, a policy that drastically weakened royal authority.

Since the thirteenth century, Russia had been under the domination of the Mongols. Gradually, the princes of Moscow rose to prominence by using their close relationship to the Mongol khans to increase their wealth and expand their possessions. During the reign of the great Prince Ivan III (1462–1505), a new Russian state was born. Ivan annexed other Russian principalities and took advantage of dissension among the Mongols to throw off their yoke by 1480.

TIMELINE

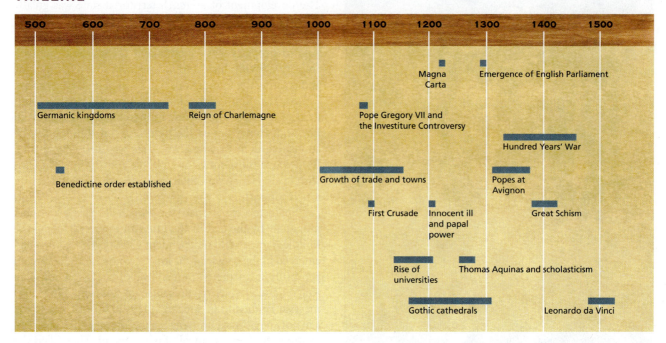

| 500 | 600 | 700 | 800 | 900 | 1000 | 1100 | 1200 | 1300 | 1400 | 1500 |

Germanic kingdoms

Reign of Charlemagne

Magna Carta

Emergence of English Parliament

Pope Gregory VII and the Investiture Controversy

Hundred Years' War

Benedictine order established

Growth of trade and towns

Popes at Avignon

First Crusade

Innocent III and papal power

Great Schism

Rise of universities

Thomas Aquinas and scholasticism

Gothic cathedrals

Leonardo da Vinci

CONCLUSION

*T*HE COLLAPSE OF THE HAN dynasty in China in the third century C.E. led to nearly four centuries of internal chaos. The fall of the Roman Empire in the fifth century brought a quite different result as three new civilizations emerged out of the collapse of Roman power in the Mediterranean. Islam emerged in the Middle East. The eastern part of the old Roman Empire, increasingly Greek in culture, continued to survive as the Christian Byzantine Empire. And a new Christian European civilization was establishing its roots in the west.

The coronation of Charlemagne, the descendant of a Germanic tribe converted to Christianity, as Roman emperor in 800 symbolized the fusion of the three chief components of the new European civilization: the German tribes, the Roman legacy, and the Christian church. Charlemagne's Carolingian Empire fostered the idea of a distinct European identity, which has led one recent historian to call him a "father of Europe."[10] With the disintegration of that empire, power fell into the hands of many different lords, who came to constitute a powerful group of nobles that dominated the political, economic, and social life of Europe. But quietly and surely, within this world of castles and private power, kings gradually began to extend their public power and laid the foundations for the European kingdoms that in one form or another have dominated European politics ever since.

European civilization began to flourish in the High Middle Ages. The revival of trade, the expansion of towns and cities, and the development of a money economy did not mean the end of a predominantly rural European society, but they did open the door to new ways to make a living and new opportunities for people to expand and enrich their lives. At the same time, the High Middle Ages also gave birth to an intellectual and spiritual revival that transformed European society.

Fourteenth-century Europe was challenged by an overwhelming number of disintegrative forces, but European society proved remarkably resilient. Elements of recovery in the age of the Renaissance made the fifteenth century a period of significant artistic, intellectual, and political change in Europe. By the second half of the fifteenth century, the growth of strong, centralized monarchical states made possible the dramatic expansion of Europe into other parts of the world.

CHAPTER NOTES

1. Norman F. Cantor, ed., *The Medieval World, 300–1300* (New York, 1963), p. 104.
2. Quoted in Marvin Perry, Joseph Peden, and Theodore Von Laue, *Sources of the Western Tradition*, vol. 1 (Boston, 1987), p. 218.
3. Oliver J. Thatcher and Edgar H. McNeal, eds., *A Source Book for Medieval History* (New York, 1905), p. 208.
4. Quoted in R. H. C. Davis, *A History of Medieval Europe from Constantine to Saint Louis,* 2d ed. (New York, 1988), p. 252.
5. Quoted in Hans E. Mayer, *The Crusades,* trans. John Gillingham (New York, 1972), pp. 99–100.

6. Giovanni Boccaccio, *The Decameron,* trans. Frances Winwar (New York, 1955), p. xiii.

7. Jean Froissart, *Chronicles,* ed. and trans. Geoffrey Brereton (Harmondsworth, England, 1968), p. 111.

8. Ibid., p. 89.

9. Quoted in J. Burckhardt, *The Civilization of the Renaissance in Italy,* trans. S. G. C. Middlemore (London, 1960), p. 81.

10. A. Barbero, *Charlemagne: Father of a Continent,* trans. A. Cameron (Berkeley, Calif., 2004), p. 4.

SUGGESTED READING

For general histories of the Middle Ages, see **D. Nicholas,** *The Evolution of the Medieval World: Society, Government, and Thought in Europe, 312–1500* (London, 1993), and **B. Rosenwein,** *A Short History of the Middle Ages* (Orchard Park, N.Y., 2002). A brief history of the Early Middle Ages can be found in **R. Collins,** *Early Medieval Europe, 300–1000* (New York, 1991).

Carolingian Europe is examined in **P. Riche,** *The Carolingians: A Family Who Forged Europe* (Philadelphia, 1993). On Charlemagne, see **A. Barbero,** *Charlemagne: Father of a Continent,* trans. **A. Cameron** (Berkeley, Calif., 2004).

Two introductory works on fief-holding are **J. R. Strayer,** *Feudalism* (Princeton, N.J., 1985), and the classic work by **M. Bloch,** *Feudal Society* (London, 1961). For an important revisionist view, see **S. Reynolds,** *Fiefs and Vassals* (Oxford, 1994).

For a good introduction to the High Middle Ages, see **W. C. Jordan,** *Europe in the High Middle Ages* (New York, 2003); **J. H. Mundy,** *Europe in the High Middle Ages, 1150–1309,* 3d ed. (New York, 1999); and **M. Barber,** *The Two Cities: Medieval Europe, 1050–1320* (London, 1992). Urban history is covered in **D. Nicholas,** *The Growth of the Medieval City: From Late Antiquity to the Early Fourteenth Century* (New York, 1997). On women in general, see **D. J. Herlihy,** *Opera Muliebria: Women and Work in Medieval Europe* (New York, 1990).

There are numerous works on the various medieval states. On England, see **R. Frame,** *The Political Development of the British Isles, 1100–1400* (Oxford, 1990). On Germany, see **H. Fuhrmann,** *Germany in the High Middle Ages, c. 1050–1250* (Cambridge, 1986), an excellent account. On France, see **J. Dunbabib,** *France in the Making, 843–1180* (Oxford, 1985). On Italy, see **D. J. Herlihy,** *Cities and Society in Medieval Italy* (London, 1980).

For a general survey of Christianity in the Middle Ages, see **J. H. Lynch,** *The Medieval Church: A Brief History* (London, 1992). For a superb introduction to early Christianity, see **P. Brown,** *The Rise of Western Christendom: Triumph and Adversity, A.D. 200–1000,* 2d ed. (Oxford, 2002). On the papacy in the High Middle Ages, see **I. S. Robinson,** *The Papacy* (Cambridge, 1990).

On medieval intellectual life, see **M. L. Colish,** *Medieval Foundations of the Western Intellectual Tradition, 400–1400* (New Haven, Conn., 1997). On the Gothic movement, see **M. Camille,** *Gothic Art: Glorious Visions* (New York, 1996).

Two general surveys on the Crusades are **H. E. Mayer,** *The Crusades,* 2d ed. (New York, 1988), and **J. Riley-Smith,** *The Crusades: A Short History* (New Haven, Conn., 1987). On the First Crusade, see **T. Asbridge,** *The First Crusade: A New History* (Oxford, 2004).

On the Black Death, see **J. Kelly,** *The Great Mortality* (New York, 2005); and **D. J. Herlihy,** *The Black Death and the Transformation of the West,* ed. S. K. Cohn Jr. (Cambridge, Mass., 1997).

General works on the Renaissance in Europe include **P. Burke,** *The European Renaissance: Centres and Peripheries* (Oxford, 1998), and **J. R. Hale,** *The Civilization of Europe in the Renaissance* (New York, 1994). For a beautifully illustrated introduction to the Renaissance, see **G. Holmes,** *Renaissance* (New York, 1996).

A brief introduction to Renaissance humanism can be found in **C. G. Nauert Jr.,** *Humanism and the Culture of Renaissance Europe* (Cambridge, 1995). Good surveys of Renaissance art include **R. Turner,** *Renaissance Florence: The Invention of a New Art* (New York, 1997), and **F. Hartt,** *History of Italian Renaissance Art,* 4th ed. (Englewood Cliffs, N.J., 1994).

For a general work on the political development of Europe in the Renaissance, see **J. H. Shennan,** *The Origins of the Modern European State, 1450–1725* (London, 1974). The best overall study of the Italian states is **L. Martines,** *Power and Imagination: City-States in Renaissance Italy* (New York, 1979).

InfoTrac College Edition

Visit this chapter's InfoTrac College Edition/Research activities at the *Essential World History* Companion Website for activities related to medieval Europe.

CENGAGENOW **for Duiker and Spielvogel's** *The Essential World History, Third Edition*

Enter *CengageNOW* using the access card that is available with this text. *CengageNOW* will assist you in understanding the content in this chapter with lesson plans generated for your needs, as well as provide you with a connection to the *Wadsworth World History Resource Center* (see description below for details).

WORLD HISTORY
RESOURCE CENTER

Enter the Resource Center using either your *CengageNOW* access card or your standalone access card for the *Wadsworth World History Resource Center.* Organized by topic, this website includes quizzes; images; over 350 primary source documents; interactive simulations, maps, and timelines; movie explorations; and a wealth of other resources. You can read the following documents, and many more, at http://worldrc.wadsworth.com/

Grant of an Estate to the Monks of Saint-Denis

Thomas Aquinas, *Summa Theologica*

Visit the *Essential World History* Companion Website for chapter quizzes and more.

academic.cengage.com/history/duiker

LOOKING BACK, LOOKING AHEAD

THE MILLENNIUM FOLLOWING the destruction of the ancient empires brought about enormous changes in human society. During the era of Mongol expansion, there was widespread death and suffering throughout the known world. At the same time, the world had witnessed a significant expansion in the technological and material capacity of human societies and in the depth of contact among them. The era of widespread peace

TIMELINE

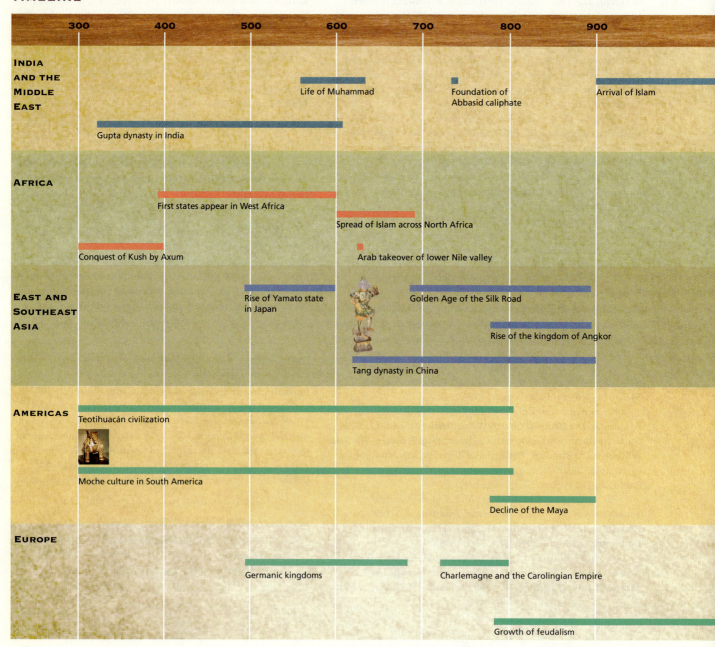

	300	400	500	600	700	800	900

INDIA AND THE MIDDLE EAST
- Life of Muhammad
- Foundation of Abbasid caliphate
- Arrival of Islam
- Gupta dynasty in India

AFRICA
- First states appear in West Africa
- Spread of Islam across North Africa
- Conquest of Kush by Axum
- Arab takeover of lower Nile valley

EAST AND SOUTHEAST ASIA
- Rise of Yamato state in Japan
- Golden Age of the Silk Road
- Rise of the kingdom of Angkor
- Tang dynasty in China

AMERICAS
- Teotihuacán civilization
- Moche culture in South America
- Decline of the Maya

EUROPE
- Germanic kingdoms
- Charlemagne and the Carolingian Empire
- Growth of feudalism

brought about as the result of the Mongol conquests also inaugurated what one scholar has described as the "idea of the unified conceptualization of the globe," creating a "basic information circuit" that spread commodities, ideas, and inventions from one end of the Eurasian supercontinent to the other. The way was prepared for a new stage of world history.

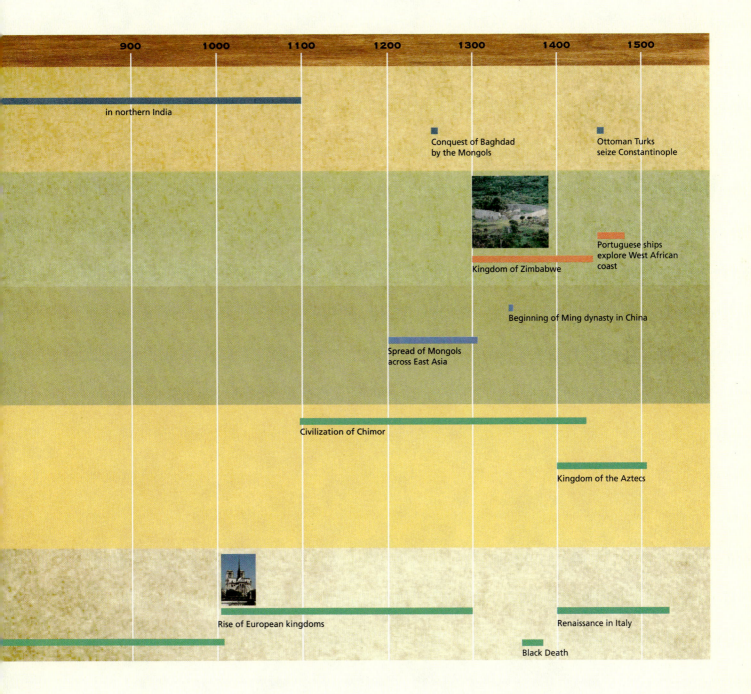

900 | 1000 | 1100 | 1200 | 1300 | 1400 | 1500

in northern India

Conquest of Baghdad by the Mongols

Ottoman Turks seize Constantinople

Kingdom of Zimbabwe

Portuguese ships explore West African coast

Beginning of Ming dynasty in China

Spread of Mongols across East Asia

Civilization of Chimor

Kingdom of the Aztecs

Rise of European kingdoms

Renaissance in Italy

Black Death

GLOSSARY

absolutism a form of government where the sovereign power or ultimate authority rested in the hands of a monarch who claimed to rule by divine right and was therefore responsible only to God.

Abstract Expressionism a post–World War II artistic movement that broke with all conventions of form and structure in favor of total abstraction.

Agricultural (Neolithic) Revolution the shift from hunting animals and gathering plants for sustenance to producing food by systematic agriculture that occurred gradually between 10,000 and 4000 B.C.E. (the Neolithic or "New Stone" Age).

agricultural revolution the application of new agricultural techniques that allowed for a large increase in productivity in the eighteenth century.

Amerindian earliest inhabitants of North and South America. Original theories suggested migration from Siberia across the Bering Land Bridge; more recent evidence suggests migration also occurred by sea from regions of the South Pacific to South America.

anarchism a political theory that holds that all governments and existing social institutions are unnecessary and advocates a society based on voluntary cooperation.

ANC the African National Congress. Founded in 1912, it was the beginning of political activity by South African blacks. Banned by politically dominant European whites in 1960, it was not officially "unbanned" until 1990. It is now the official majority party of the South African government.

Analects the body of writing containing conversations between Confucius and his disciples that preserves his worldly wisdom and pragmatic philosophies.

anti-Semitism hostility toward or discrimination against Jews.

apartheid the system of racial segregation practiced in the Republic of South Africa until the 1990s, which involved political, legal, and economic discrimination against nonwhites.

appeasement the policy, followed by the European nations in the 1930s, of accepting Hitler's annexation of Austria and Czechoslovakia in the belief that meeting his demands would assure peace and stability.

Aramaic A Semitic language dominant in the Middle East in the first century B.C.E.; still in use in small regions of the Middle East and southern Asia.

Arianism a Christian heresy that taught that Jesus was inferior to God. Though condemned by the Council of Nicaea in 325, Arianism was adopted by many of the Germanic peoples who entered the Roman Empire over the next centuries.

aristocracy a class of hereditary nobility in medieval Europe; a warrior class who shared a distinctive lifestyle based on the institution of knighthood, although there were social divisions within the group based on extremes of wealth.

Arthasastra an early Indian political treatise that sets forth many fundamental aspects of the relationship of rulers and their subjects. It has been compared to Machiavelli's well-known book, *The Prince,* and has provided principles upon which many aspects of social organization have developed in the region.

Aryans Indo–European-speaking nomads who entered India from the Central Asian steppes between 1500 and 1000 B.C.E. and greatly affected Indian society, notably by establishing the caste system. The term was later adopted by German Nazis to describe their racial ideal.

asceticism a lifestyle involving the denial of worldly pleasures. Predominantly associated with Hindu, Buddhist, or Christian religions, adherents perceive their practices as a path to greater spitiuality.

ASEAN the Association for the Southeast Asian Nations formed in 1967 to promote the prosperity and political stability of its member nations. Currently Brunei, Indonesia, Laos, Malaysia, Myanmar, the Philippines, Singapore, Thailand, and Vietnam are members. Other countries in the region participate as "observer" members.

Ausgleich the "Compromise" of 1867 that created the dual monarchy of Austria-Hungary. Austria and Hungary each had its own capital, constitution, and legislative assembly, but were united under one monarch.

authoritarian state a state that has a dictatorial government and some other trappings of a totalitarian state, but does not demand that the masses be actively involved in the regime's goals as totalitarian states do.

auxiliaries troops enlisted from the subject peoples of the Roman Empire to supplement the regular legions composed of Roman citizens.

bakufu the centralized government set up in Japan in the twelfth century. See shogunate system.

balance of power a distribution of power among several states such that no single nation can dominate or interfere with the interests of another.

Banners Originally established in 1639 by the Qing empire, the Eight Banners were administrative divisions into which all Manchu families were placed. Banners quickly evolved into the basis of Manchu military organization with each required to raise and support a prescribed number of troops.

Bao-jia system the Chinese practice, reportedly originated by the Qin dynasty in the third century B.C.E., of organizing families into groups of five or ten to exercise mutual control and surveillance and reduce loyalty to the family.

Baroque a style that dominated Western painting, sculpture, architecture and music from about 1580 to 1730, generally characterized by elaborate ornamentation and dramatic effects. Important practitioners included Bernini, Rubens, Handel, and Bach.

Bedouins nomadic tribes originally from northern Arabia, who became important traders after the domestication of the camel during the first millennium B.C.E. Early converts to Islam, their values and practices deeply affected Muhammad.

benefice in the Christian church, a position, such as a bishopric, that consisted of both a sacred office and the right of the holder to the annual revenues from the position.

Berbers an ethnic group indigenous to western North Africa.

bey a provincial governor in the Ottoman Empire.

bhakti in Hinduism, devotion as a means of religious observance open to all persons regardless of class.

bodhi Wisdom. Sometimes described as complete awareness of the true nature of the universe.

bicameral legislature a legislature with two houses.

Black Death the outbreak of plague (mostly bubonic) in the mid-fourteenth century that killed from 25 to 50 percent of Europe's population.

Blitzkrieg "lightning war." A war conducted with great speed and force, as in Germany's advance at the beginning of World War II.

bodhisattvas in some schools of Buddhism, individuals who have achieved enlightenment but, because of their great compassion, have chosen to renounce Nirvana and to remain on earth in spirit form to help all human beings achieve release from reincarnation.

Bolsheviks a small faction of the Russian Social Democratic Party who were led by Lenin and dedicated to violent revolution; seized power in Russia in 1917 and were subsequently renamed the Communists.

bonsai Originating in China in the first millenium B.C.E. and known there as *penzai*, it was imported to Japan between 700–900 C.E. Bonsai combines patience and artistry in the cultivation of stunted trees and shrubs to create exquisite nature scenes in miniature.

boyars the Russian nobility.

Brahman The Hindu word roughly equivalent to God; the Divine basis of all being; regarded as the source and sum of the cosmos.

brahmin A member of the Hindu priestly caste or class; literally "one who has realized or attempts to realize Brahman." Traditionally, duties of a brahmin include studying Hindu religious scriptures and transmitting them to others orally. The priests of Hindu temples are brahmin.

Brezhnev Doctrine the doctrine, enunciated by Leonid Brezhnev, that the Soviet Union had a right to intervene if socialism was threatened in another socialist state; used to justify the use of Soviet troops in Czechoslovakia in 1968.

Buddhism A religion and philosophy based on the teachings of Siddhartha Gautama in about 500 B.C.E. Principally practiced in China, India, and other parts of Asia, Buddhism has 360 million followers and is considered a major world releigion.

Burakumin A Japanese minority similar to dalits (or untouchables) in Indian culture. Past and current discrimination has resulted in lower educational attainment and socioeconomic status for members of this group. Movements with objectives ranging from "liberation" to integration have tried over the years to change this situation.

Bushido The code of conduct observed by samurai warriors; comparable to the European concept of chilvalry.

caliph the secular leader of the Islamic community.

calpulli In Aztec society, a kinship group, often of a thousand or more, which served as an intermediary with the central government, providing taxes and conscript labor to the state.

capital material wealth used or available for use in the production of more wealth.

caste system a system of rigid social hierarchcy in which all members of that society are assigned by birth to specific "ranks," and inherit specific roles and privileges.

cartel a combination of independent commercial enterprises that work together to control prices and limit competition.

Cartesian dualism Descartes's principle of the separation of mind and matter (and mind and body) that enabled scientists to view matter as something separate from themselves that could be investigated by reason.

caudillos strong leaders in nineteenth-century Latin America, who were usually supported by the landed elites and ruled chiefly by military force, though some were popular; they included both modernizers and destructive dictators.

censorate one of the three primary Chinese ministries, originally established in the Qin dynasty, whose inspectors surveyed the efficiency of officials throughout the system.

chaebol a South Korean business structure similar to the Japanese keiretsu.

Chan Buddhism a Chinese sect (Zen in Japanese) influenced by Daoist ideas, which called for mind training and a strict regimen as a means of seeking enlightenment.

chansons de geste a form of vernacular literature in the High Middle Ages that consisted of heroic epics focusing on the deeds of warriors.

chinampas in Mesoamerica, artifical islands crisscrossed by canals that provided water for crops and easy transportation to local markets.

chivalry the ideal of civilized behavior that emerged among the nobility in the eleventh and twelfth centuries under the influence of the church; a code of ethics knights were expected to uphold.

Christian (northern) humanism an intellectual movement in northern Europe in the late fifteenth and early sixteenth centuries that combined the interest in the classics of the Italian Renaissance with an interest in the sources of early Christianity, including the New Testament and the writings of the church fathers.

civic humanism an intellectual movement of the Italian Renaissance that saw Cicero, who was both an intellectual and a statesman, as the ideal and held that humanists should be involved in government and use their rhetorical training in the service of the state.

civil rights the basic rights of citizens including equality before the law, freedom of speech and press, and freedom from arbitrary arrest.

civil service examination an elaborate Chinese system of selecting bureaucrats on merit, first introduced in 165 C.E., developed by the Tang dynasty in the seventh century C.E. and refined under the Song dynasty; later adopted in Vietnam and with less success in Japan and Korea. It contributed to efficient government, upward mobility, and cultural uniformity.

class struggle the basis of the Marxist analysis of history, which says that the owners of the means of production have always oppressed the workers and predicts an inevitable revolution. See Marxism.

Cold War the ideological conflict between the Soviet Union and the United States after World War II.

collective farms large farms created in the Soviet Union by Stalin by combining many small holdings into one large farm worked by the peasants under government supervision.

collective security the use of an international army raised by an association of nations to deter aggression and keep the peace.

coloni free tenant farmers who worked as sharecroppers on the large estates of the Roman Empire (singular: *colonus*).

Comintern a worldwide organization of Communist parties, founded by Lenin in 1919, dedicated to the advancement of world revolution; also known as the Third International.

common law law common to the entire kingdom of England; imposed by the king's courts beginning in the twelfth century to replace the customary law used in county and feudal courts that varied from place to place.

commune in medieval Europe, an association of townspeople bound together by a sworn oath for the purpose of obtaining basic liberties from the lord of the territory in which the town was located; also, the self-governing town after receiving its liberties.

communalism in South Asia, the tendency of people to band together in mutually antagonistic social sub-groups; elsewhere used to describe unifying trends in the larger community.

conciliarism a movement in fourteenth- and fifteenth-century Europe that held that final authority in spiritual matters resided with a general church council, not the pope; emerged in response to the Avignon papacy and the Great Schism and used to justify the summoning of the Council of Constance (1414–1418).

condottieri leaders of bands of mercenary soldiers in Renaissance Italy who sold their services to the highest bidder.

Confucianism a system of thought based on the teachings of Confucius (551–479 B.C.E.) that developed into the ruling ideology of the Chinese state. See Neo-Confucianism.

conquistadors "conquerors." Leaders in the Spanish conquests in the Americas, especially Mexico and Peru, in the sixteenth century.

conscription a military draft.

conservatism an ideology based on tradition and social stability that favored the maintenance of established institutions, organized religion, and obedience to authority and resisted change, especially abrupt change.

consuls the chief executive officers of the Roman Republic. Two were chosen annually to administer the government and lead the army in battle.

consumer society a term applied to Western society after World War II as the working classes adopted the consumption patterns of the middle class and installment plans, credit cards, and easy credit made consumer goods such as appliances and automobiles widely available.

containment   a policy adopted by the United States in the Cold War. Its goal was to use whatever means, short of all-out war, to limit Soviet expansion.

Continental System   Napoleon's effort to bar British goods from the Continent in the hope of weakening Britain's economy and destroying its capacity to wage war.

Contras   in Nicaragua in the 1980s, an anti-Sandinista guerrilla movement supported by the U.S. Reagan administration.

Coptic   a form of Christianity, originally Egyptian, that has thrived in Ethiopia since the fourth century C.E.

cosmopolitanism   the quality of being sophisticated and having wide international experience.

cottage industry   a system of textile manufacturing in which spinners and weavers worked at home in their cottages using raw materials supplied to them by capitalist entrepreneurs.

Crusade   in the Middle Ages, a military campaign in defense of Christendom.

cultural relativism   the belief that no culture is superior to another because culture is a matter of custom, not reason, and derives its meaning from the group holding it.

cuneiform   "wedge-shaped." A system of writing developed by the Sumerians that consisted of wedge-shaped impressions made by a reed stylus on clay tablets.

daimyo   prominent Japanese families who provided allegiance to the local shogun in exchange for protection; similar to vassals in Europe.

dalits   commonly referred to as untouchables; the lowest level of Indian society, technically outside the caste system and considered less than human; renamed harijans ("children of God") by Gandhi, they remain the object of discrimination despite affirmative action programs.

Dao   a Chinese philosophical concept, literally "The Way," central to both Confucianism and Daoism, that describes the behavior proper to each member of society; somewhat similar to the Indian concept of dharma.

Daoism   a Chinese philosophy traditionally ascribed to the perhaps legendary Lao Tzu, which holds that acceptance and spontaneity are the keys to harmonious interaction with the universal order; an alternative to Confucianism.

decolonization   the process of becoming free of colonial status and achieving statehood; occurred in most of the world's colonies between 1947 and 1962.

deism   belief in God as the creator of the universe who, after setting it in motion, ceased to have any direct involvement in it and allowed it to run according to its own natural laws.

deficit spending   the concept, developed by John Maynard Keynes in the 1930s, that in times of economic depression governments should stimulate demand by hiring people to do public works, such as building highways, even if this increased public debt.

demesne   the part of a manor retained under the direct control of the lord and worked by the serfs as part of their labor services.

denazification   after World War II, the Allied policy of rooting out any traces of Nazism in German society by bringing prominent Nazis to trial for war crimes and purging any known Nazis from political office.

depression   a very severe, protracted economic downturn with high levels of unemployment.

destalinization   the policy of denouncing and undoing the most repressive aspects of Stalin's regime; begun by Nikita Khrushchev in 1956.

détente   the relaxation of tension between the Soviet Union and the United States that occurred in the 1970s.

devshirme   in the Ottoman Empire, a system (literally, "collection") of training talented children to be administrators or members of the sultan's harem; originally meritocratic, by the seventeenth century, it degenerated into a hereditary caste.

dharma   in Hinduism and Buddhism, the law that governs the universe, and specifically human behavior.

dialectic   logic, one of the seven liberal arts that made up the medieval curriculum. In Marxist thought, the process by which all change occurs through the clash of antagonistic elements.

Diaspora   the scattering of Jews throughout the ancient world after the Babylonian captivity in the sixth century B.C.E.

dictator   in the Roman Republic, an official granted unlimited power to run the state for a short period of time, usually six months, during an emergency.

diocese   the area under the jurisdiction of a Christian bishop; based originally on Roman administrative districts.

direct representation   a system of choosing delegates to a representative assembly in which citizens vote directly for the delegates who will represent them.

divination   the practice of seeking to foretell future events by interpreting divine signs, which could appear in various forms, such as in entrails of animals, in patterns in smoke, or in dreams.

divine-right monarchy   a monarchy based on the belief that monarchs receive their power directly from God and are responsible to no one except God.

domino theory   the belief that if the Communists succeeded in Vietnam, other countries in Southeast and East Asia would also fall (like dominoes) to communism; a justification for the U.S. intervention in Vietnam.

dualism   the belief that the universe is dominated by two opposing forces, one good and the other evil.

dyarchy   during the Qing dynasty in China, a system in which all important national and provincial admininstrative positions were shared equally by Chinese and Manchus, which helped to consolidate both Manchu rule and their assimilation.

dynastic state   a state where the maintenance and expansion of the interests of the ruling family is the primary consideration.

economic imperialism   the process in which banks and corporations from developed nations invest in underdeveloped regions and establish a major presence there in the hope of making high profits; not necessarily the same as colonial expansion in that businesses invest where they can make a profit, which may not be in their own nation's colonies.

El Niño   periodic changes in water temperature at the surface of the Pacific Ocean, which can lead to major environmental changes and may have led to the collapse of the Moche civilization in what is now Peru.

emir   "commander" (Arabic), used by Muslim rulers in southern Spain and elsewhere.

empiricism   the practice of relying on observation and experiment.

enclosure movement   in the eighteenth century, the fencing in of the old open fields, combining many small holdings into larger units that could be farmed more efficiently.

encomienda   a grant from the Spanish monarch to colonial conquistadors; see *encomienda system.*

encomienda system   the system by which Spain first governed its American colonies. Holders of an encomienda were supposed to protect the Indians as well as using them as laborers and collecting tribute but in practice exploited them.

encyclical   a letter from the pope to all the bishops of the Roman Catholic church.

enlightened absolutism   an absolute monarchy where the ruler follows the principles of the Enlightenment by introducing reforms for the improvement of society, allowing freedom of speech and the press, permitting religious toleration, expanding education, and ruling in accordance with the laws.

Enlightenment   an eighteenth-century intellectual movement, led by the philosophes, that stressed the application of reason and the scientific method to all aspects of life.

entrepreneur   one who organizes, operates, and assumes the risk in a business venture in the expectation of making a profit.

Epicureanism a philosophy founded by Epicurus in the fourth century C.E. that taught that happiness (freedom from emotional turmoil) could be achieved through the pursuit of pleasure (intellectual rather than sensual pleasure).

equestrians a group of extremely wealthy men in the late Roman Republic who were effectively barred from high office, but sought political power commensurate with their wealth; called equestrians because many had gotten their start as cavalry officers (*equites*).

eta in feudal Japan, a class of hereditary slaves who were responsible for what were considered degrading occupations, such as curing leather and burying the dead.

ethnic cleansing the policy of killing or forcibly removing people of another ethnic group; used by the Serbs against Bosnian Muslims in the 1990s.

eucharist a Christian sacrament in which consecrated bread and wine are consumed in celebration of Jesus' Last Supper; also called the Lord's Supper or communion.

eunuch a man whose testicles have been removed; a standard feature of the Chinese imperial system, the Ottoman Empire, and the Mughal Dynasty, among others.

evolutionary socialism a socialist doctrine espoused by Eduard Bernstein who argued that socialists should stress cooperation and evolution to attain power by democratic means rather than by conflict and revolution.

fascism an ideology or movement that exalts the nation above the individual and calls for a centralized government with a dictatorial leader, economic and social regimentation, and forcible suppression of opposition; in particular, the ideology of Mussolini's Fascist regime in Italy.

feminism the belief in the social, political, and economic equality of the sexes; also, organized activity to advance women's rights.

fief a landed estate granted to a vassal in exchange for military services.

filial piety in traditional China, in particular, a hierarchical system in which every family member has his or her place, subordinate to a patriarch who has in turn reciprocal responsibilities.

Final Solution the physical extermination of the Jewish people by the Nazis during World War II.

five pillars of Islam the core requirements of the faith, observation of which would lead to paradise: belief in Allah and his Prophet Muhammad; prescribed prayers; observation of Ramadan; pilgrimage to Mecca; and giving alms to the poor.

five relationships in traditional China, the hierarchical interpersonal associations considered crucial to social order, within the family, between friends, and with the king.

folk culture the traditional arts and crafts, literature, music, and other customs of the people; something that people make, as opposed to modern popular culture, which is something people buy.

foot binding an extremely painful process, common in China throughout the second millenium C.E., that compressed girls' feet to half their natural size, representing submissiveness and self-discipline, which were considered necessary attributes for an ideal wife.

four modernizations the slogan for radical reforms of Chinese industry, agriculture, technology, and national defense, instituted by Deng Xiaoping after his accession to power in the late 1970s.

free trade the unrestricted international exchange of goods with low or no tariffs.

fundamentalism a movement that emphasizes rigid adherence to basic religious principles; often used to describe evangelical Christianity, it also characterizes the practices of Islamic conservatives.

general strike a strike by all or most workers in an economy; espoused by Georges Sorel as the heroic action that could be used to inspire the workers to destroy capitalist society.

genin landless laborers in feudal Japan, who were effectively slaves.

gentry well-to-do English landowners below the level of the nobility; played an important role in the English Civil War of the seventeenth century.

geocentric theory the idea that the earth is at the center of the universe and that the sun and other celestial objects revolve around the earth.

glasnost "openness." Mikhail Gorbachev's policy of encouraging Soviet citizens to openly discuss the strengths and weaknesses of the Soviet Union.

Gleichschaltung the coordination of all government institutions under Nazi control in Germany from 1933.

global civilization human society considered as a single world-wide entity, in which local differences are less important than overall similarities.

good emperors the five emperors who ruled from 96 to 180 (Nerva, Trajan, Hadrian, Antoninus Pius, and Marcus Aurelius), a period of peace and prosperity for the Roman Empire.

Grand Council the top of the government hierarchy in the Song dynasty in China.

grand vezir (*also*, vizier) the chief executive in the Ottoman Empire, under the sultan.

Great Leap Forward a short-lived, radical experiment in China, started in 1958, which created vast rural communes and attempted to replace the family as the fundamental social unit.

Great Proletarian Cultural Revolution an attempt to destroy all vestiges of tradition in China, in order to create a totally egalitarian society; launched by Mao Zedong in 1966, it became virtually anarchic and lasted only until Mao's death in 1976.

Great Schism the crisis in the late medieval church when there were first two and then three popes; ended by the Council of Constance (1414–1418).

green revolution the introduction of technological agriculture, especially in India in the 1960s, which increased food production substantially but also exacerbated rural inequality because only the wealthier farmers could afford fertilizer.

guest workers foreign workers working temporarily in European countries.

guided democracy the name given by President Sukarno of Indonesia in the late 1950s to his style of government, which theoretically operated by consensus.

guild an association of people with common interests and concerns, especially people working in the same craft. In medieval Europe, guilds came to control much of the production process and to restrict entry into various trades.

guru teacher, especially in the Hindu, Buddhist and Sikh religious traditions, where it is an important honorific.

gymnasium in classical Greece, a place for athletics; in the Hellenistic Age, a secondary school with a curriculum centered on music, physical exercise, and literature.

Hadith a collection of the sayings of the Prophet Muhammad, used to supplement the revelations contained in the Qur'an.

Hanseatic League a commercial and military alliance of north German coastal towns, increasingly powerful in the fifteenth century C.E.

harem the private domain of a ruler such as the sultan in the Ottoman Empire or the caliph of Baghdad, generally large and mostly inhabited by the extended family.

Hegira the flight of Muhammad from Mecca to Medina in 622, which marks the first date on the official calendar of Islam.

heliocentric theory the idea that the sun (not the earth) is at the center of the universe.

Hellenistic literally, "to imitate the Greeks"; the era after the death of Alexander the Great when Greek culture spread into the Near East and blended with the culture of that region.

helots serfs in ancient Sparta, who were permanently bound to the land that they worked for their Spartan masters.

heresy the holding of religious doctrines different from the official teachings of the church.

Hermeticism an intellectual movement beginning in the fifteenth century that taught that divinity is embodied in all aspects of nature; included works on alchemy and magic as well as theology and philosophy. The tradition continued into the seventeenth century and influenced many of the leading figures of the Scientific Revolution.

hetairai highly sophisticated courtesans in ancient Athens who offered intellectual and musical entertainment as well as sex.

hieroglyphics a highly pictorial system of writing most often associated with ancient Egypt. Also used (with different "pictographs") by other ancient peoples such as the Mayans.

high culture the literary and artistic culture of the educated and wealthy ruling classes.

Hinayana the scornful name for Theravada Buddhism ("lesser vehicle") used by devotees of Mahayana Buddhism.

Hinduism the main religion in India, it emphasizes reincarnation, based on the results of the previous life, and the desirability of escaping this cycle. Its various forms feature both asceticism and the pleasures of ordinary life, and encompass a multitude of gods as different manifestations of one ultimate reality.

Holocaust the mass slaughter of European Jews by the Nazis during World War II.

Hopewell culture a Native American society that flourished from about 200 B.C.E. to 400 C.E., noted for large burial mounds and extensive manufacture. Largely based in Ohio, its traders ranged as far as the Gulf of Mexico.

hoplites heavily armed infantry soldiers used in ancient Greece in a phalanx formation.

Huguenots French Calvinists.

humanism an intellectual movement in Renaissance Italy based upon the study of the Greek and Roman classics.

Hundred Schools (of philosophy) in China around the third century B.C.E., a wide-ranging debate over the nature of human beings, society, and the universe. The Schools included Legalism and Daoism, as well as Confucianism.

hydraulic society a society organized around a large irrigation system.

iconoclasm an eighth-century Byzantine movement against the use of icons (pictures of sacred figures), which was condemned as idolatry.

ideology a political philosophy such as conservatism or liberalism.

imam an Islamic religious leader; some traditions say there is only one per generation, others use the term more broadly.

imperialism the policy of extending one nation's power either by conquest or by establishing direct or indirect economic or cultural authority over another. Generally driven by economic self-interest, it can also be motivated by a sincere (if often misguided) sense of moral obligation.

imperium "the right to command." In the Roman Republic, the chief executive officers (consuls and praetors) possessed the *imperium;* a military commander was an *imperator.* In the Roman Empire, the title *imperator,* or emperor, came to be used for the ruler.

indirect representation a system of choosing delegates to a representative assembly in which citizens do not choose the delegates directly but instead vote for electors who choose the delegates.

indirect rule a colonial policy of foreign rule in cooperation with local political elites; implemented in much of India and Malaya, and parts of Africa, it was not feasible where resistance was greater.

individualism emphasis on and interest in the unique traits of each person.

indulgence the remission of part or all of the temporal punishment in purgatory due to sin; granted for charitable contributions and other good deeds. Indulgences became a regular practice of the Christian church in the High Middle Ages, and their abuse was instrumental in sparking Luther's reform movement in the sixteenth century.

infanticide the practice of killing infants.

inflation a sustained rise in the price level.

intifada the "uprising" of Palestinians living under Israeli control, especially in the 1980s and 1990s.

intendants royal officials in seventeenth-century France who were sent into the provinces to execute the orders of the central government.

intervention, principle of the idea, after the Congress of Vienna, that the great powers of Europe had the right to send armies into countries experiencing revolution to restore legitimate monarchs to their thrones.

Islam the religion derived from the revelations of Muhammad, the Prophet of Allah; literally, "submission" (to the will of Allah); also the culture and civilization based upon the faith.

isolationism a foreign policy in which a nation refrains from making alliances or engaging actively in international affairs.

Jainism an Indian religion, founded in the fifth century B.C.E., which stresses extreme simplicity.

Janissaries an elite core of eight thousand troops personally loyal to the sultan of the Ottoman Empire.

jati a kinship group, the basic social organization of traditional Indian society, to some extent specialized by occupation.

jihad In Islam, "striving in the way of the Lord." The term is ambiguous and has been subject to varying interpretations, from the practice of conducting raids against local neighbors to the conduct of "holy war" against unbelievers.

joint-stock company a company or association that raises capital by selling shares to individuals who receive dividends on their investment while a board of directors runs the company.

joint-stock investment bank a bank created by selling shares of stock to investors. Such banks potentially have access to much more capital than do private banks owned by one or a few individuals.

Jomon the earliest known Neolithic inhabitants of Japan, named for the cord pattern of their pottery.

justification by faith the primary doctrine of the Protestant Reformation; taught that humans are saved not through good works, but by the grace of God, bestowed freely through the sacrifice of Jesus.

Kabuki a form of Japanese theater which developed in the seventeenth century C.E.; originally disreputable, it became a highly stylized art form.

kami spirits who were worshiped in early Japan, and resided in trees, rivers and streams. See Shinto.

karma a fundamental concept in Hindu (and later Buddhist, Jain, and Sikh) philosophy, that rebirth in a future life is determined by actions in this or other lives; the word refers to the entire process, to the individual's actions, and also to the cumulative result of those actions, for instance a store of good or bad karma.

keiretsu a type of powerful industrial or financial conglomerate that emerged in post–World War II Japan following the abolition of zaibatsu.

khanates Mongol kingdoms, in particular the subdivisions of Genghis Khan's empire ruled by his heirs.

kokutai the core ideology of the Japanese state, particularly during the Meiji Restoration, stressing the uniqueness of the Japanese system and the supreme authority of the emperor.

kolkhoz a collective farm in the Soviet Union, in which the great bulk of the land was held and worked communally. Between 1928 and 1934, 250,000 kolkhozes replaced 26 million family farms.

kshatriya originally, the warrior class of Aryan society in India; ranked below (sometimes equal to) brahmins, in modern times often government workers or soldiers.

laissez-faire "to let alone." An economic doctrine that holds that an economy is best served when the government does not interfere but allows the economy to self-regulate according to the forces of supply and demand.

latifundia large landed estates in the Roman Empire (singular: *latifundium*).

lay investiture the practice in which a layperson chose a bishop and invested him with the symbols of both his temporal office and his spiritual office; led to the Investiture Controversy, which was ended by compromise in the Concordat of Worms in 1122.

Lebensraum "living space." The doctrine, adopted by Hitler, that a nation's power depends on the amount of land it occupies; thus, a nation must expand to be strong.

Legalism a Chinese philosophy that argued that human beings were by nature evil and would follow the correct path only if coerced by harsh laws and stiff punishments. Adopted as official ideology by the Qin dynasty, it was later rejected but remained influential.

legitimacy, principle of the idea that after the Napoleonic wars peace could best be reestablished in Europe by restoring legitimate monarchs who would preserve traditional institutions; guided Metternich at the Congress of Vienna.

Leninism Lenin's revision of Marxism that held that Russia need not experience a bourgeois revolution before it could move toward socialism.

liberal arts the seven areas of study that formed the basis of education in medieval and early modern Europe. Following Boethius and other late Roman authors, they consisted of grammar, rhetoric, and dialectic or logic (the *trivium*) and arithmetic, geometry, astronomy, and music (the *quadrivium*).

liberalism an ideology based on the belief that people should be as free from restraint as possible. Economic liberalism is the idea that the government should not interfere in the workings of the economy. Political liberalism is the idea that there should be restraints on the exercise of power so that people can enjoy basic civil rights in a constitutional state with a representative assembly.

limited liability the principle that shareholders in a joint-stock corporation can be held responsible for the corporation's debts only up to the amount they have invested.

limited (constitutional) monarchy a system of government in which the monarch is limited by a representative assembly and by the duty to rule in accordance with the laws of the land.

lineage group the descendants of a common ancestor; relatives, often as opposed to immediate family.

Longshan a Neolithic society from near the Yellow River in China, sometimes identified by its black pottery.

maharaja originally, a king in the Aryan society of early India (a great raja); later used more generally to denote an important ruler.

Mahayana a school of Buddhism that promotes the idea of universal salvation through the intercession of bodhisattvas; predominant in north Asia.

majlis a council of elders among the Bedouins of the Roman era.

mandate of Heaven the justification for the rule of the Zhou dynasty in China; the king was charged to maintain order as a representative of Heaven, which was viewed as an impersonal law of nature.

mandates a system established after World War I whereby a nation officially administered a territory (mandate) on behalf of the League of Nations. Thus, France administered Lebanon and Syria as mandates, and Britain administered Iraq and Palestine.

Manichaeanism an offshoot of the ancient Zoroastrian religion, influenced by Christianity; became popular in central Asia in the eighth century C.E.

manor an agricultural estate operated by a lord and worked by peasants who performed labor services and paid various rents and fees to the lord in exchange for protection and sustenance.

Marshall Plan the European Recovery Program, under which the United States provided financial aid to European countries to help them rebuild after World War II.

Marxism the political, economic, and social theories of Karl Marx, which included the idea that history is the story of class struggle and that ultimately the proletariat will overthrow the bourgeoisie and establish a dictatorship en route to a classless society.

mass education a state-run educational system, usually free and compulsory, that aims to ensure that all children in society have at least a basic education.

mass leisure forms of leisure that appeal to large numbers of people in a society including the working classes; emerged at the end of the nineteenth century to provide workers with amusements after work and on weekends; used during the twentieth century by totalitarian states to control their populations.

mass politics a political order characterized by mass political parties and universal male and (eventually) female suffrage.

mass society a society in which the concerns of the majority—the lower classes—play a prominent role; characterized by extension of voting rights, an improved standard of living for the lower classes, and mass education.

materialism the belief that everything mental, spiritual, or ideal is an outgrowth of physical forces and that truth is found in concrete material existence, not through feeling or intuition.

matrilinear passing through the female line, for example from a father to his sister's son rather than his own, as practiced in some African societies; not necessarily, or even usually, combined with matriarchy, in which women rule.

megaliths large stones, widely used in Europe from around 4000 to 1500 B.C.E. to create monuments, including sophisticated astronomical observatories.

Meiji Restoration the period during the late 19th and early 20th century in which fundamental economic and cultural changes occured in Japan, tranforming it from a feudal and agrarian society to an industrial and technological society.

mercantilism an economic theory that held that a nation's prosperity depended on its supply of gold and silver and that the total volume of trade is unchangeable; therefore, advocated that the government play an active role in the economy by encouraging exports and discouraging imports, especially through the use of tariffs.

Mesoamerica the region stretching roughly from modern central Mexico to Honduras, in which the Olmec, Mayan, Aztec and other civilizations developed.

Mesolithic Age the period from 10,000 to 7000 C.E., characterized by a gradual transition from a food-gathering/hunting economy to a food-producing economy.

mestizos the offspring of intermarriage between Europeans, originally Spaniards, and native American Indians.

metics resident foreigners in ancient Athens; not permitted full rights of citizenship but did receive the protection of the laws.

Middle Passage the journey of slaves from Africa to the Americas as the middle leg of the triangular trade.

Middle Path a central concept of Buddhism, which advocates avoiding extremes of both materialism and asceticism; also known as the Eightfold Way.

mihrab the niche in a mosque's wall that indicates the direction of Mecca, usually containing an ornately decorated panel representing Allah.

militarism a policy of aggressive military preparedness; in particular, the large armies based on mass conscription and complex, inflexible plans for mobilization that most European nations had before World War I.

millet an administrative unit in the Ottoman empire used to organize religious groups.

ministerial responsibility a tenet of nineteenth-century liberalism that held that ministers of the monarch should be responsible to the legislative assembly rather than to the monarch.

Modernism the new artistic and literary styles that emerged in the decades before 1914 as artists rebelled against traditional efforts to portray reality as accurately as possible (leading to Impressionism and Cubism) and writers explored new forms.

monotheistic/monotheism having only one god; the doctrine or belief that there is only one god.

muezzin the man who calls Muslims to prayer at the appointed times; nowadays often a tape-recorded message played over loudspeakers.

mulattoes the offspring of Africans and Europeans, particularly in Latin America.

Munich syndrome a term used to criticize efforts to appease an aggressor, as in the Munich agreement of 1938, on the grounds that they only encourage his appetite for conquest.

mutual deterrence   the belief that nuclear war could best be prevented if both the United States and the Soviet Union had sufficient nuclear weapons so that even if one nation launched a preemptive first strike, the other could respond and devastate the attacker.

mystery religions   religions that involve initiation into secret rites that promise intense emotional involvement with spiritual forces and a greater chance of individual immortality.

nationalism   a sense of national consciousness based on awareness of being part of a community—a "nation"—that has common institutions, traditions, language, and customs and that becomes the focus of the individual's primary political loyalty.

nationalities problem   the dilemma faced by the Austro-Hungarian Empire in trying to unite a wide variety of ethnic groups including, among others, Austrians, Hungarians, Poles, Croats, Czechs, Serbs, Slovaks, and Slovenes in an era when nationalism and calls for self-determination were coming to the fore.

nationalization   the process of converting a business or industry from private ownership to government control and ownership.

nation in arms   the people's army raised by universal mobilization to repel the foreign enemies of the French Revolution.

nation-state   a form of political organization in which a relatively homogeneous people inhabits a sovereign state, as opposed to a state containing people of several nationalities.

NATO   the North Atlantic Treaty Organization; a military alliance formed in 1949 in which the signatories (Belgium, Canada, Denmark, France, Great Britain, Iceland, Italy, Luxembourg, the Netherlands, Norway, Portugal, and the United States) agreed to provide mutual assistance if any one of them was attacked; later expanded to include other nations, including former members of the Warsaw Pact—Poland, the Czech Republic, and Hungary.

natural laws   a body of laws or specific principles held to be derived from nature and binding upon all human society even in the absence of positive laws.

natural rights   certain inalienable rights to which all people are entitled; include the right to life, liberty, and property, freedom of speech and religion, and equality before the law.

natural selection   Darwin's idea that organisms that are most adaptable to their environment survive and pass on the variations that enabled them to survive, while other, less adaptable organisms become extinct; "survival of the fittest."

Nazi New Order   the Nazis' plan for their conquered territories; included the extermination of Jews and others considered inferior, ruthless exploitation of resources, German colonization in the east, and the use of Poles, Russians, and Ukrainians as slave labor.

negritude   a philosophy shared among African blacks that there exists a distinctive "African personality" that owes nothing to Western values and provides a common sense of purpose and destiny for black Africans.

Neo-Confucianism   the dominant ideology of China during the second millennium C.E., it combined the metaphysical speculations of Buddhism and Daoism with the pragmatic Confucian approach to society, maintaining that the world is real, not illusory, and that fulfillment comes from participation, not withdrawal. It encouraged an intellectual environment that valued continuity over change and tradition over innovation.

neocolonialism   the use of economic rather than political or military means to maintain Western domination of developing nations.

Neolithic Revolution   the development of agriculture, including the planting of food crops and the domestication of farm animals, around 10,000 B.C.E.

Neoplatonism   a revival of Platonic philosophy; in the third century C.E., a revival associated with Plotinus; in the Italian Renaissance, a revival associated with Marsilio Ficino who attempted to synthesize Christianity and Platonism.

New Course   a short-lived, liberalizing change in Soviet policy to its Eastern European allies instituted after the death of Stalin in 1953.

New Culture Movement   a protest launched at Peking University after the failure of the 1911 revolution, aimed at abolishing the remnants of the old system and introducing Western values and institutions into China.

New Deal   the reform program implemented by President Franklin Roosevelt in the 1930s, which included large public works projects and the introduction of Social Security.

New Democracy   the initial program of the Chinese Communist government, from 1949 to 1955, focusing on honest government, land reform, social justice, and peace rather than on the utopian goal of a classless society.

New Economic Policy   a modified version of the old capitalist system introduced in the Soviet Union by Lenin in 1921 to revive the economy after the ravages of the civil war and war communism.

new imperialism   the revival of imperialism after 1880 in which European nations established colonies throughout much of Asia and Africa.

new monarchies   the governments of France, England, and Spain at the end of the fifteenth century, where the rulers were successful in reestablishing or extending centralized royal authority, suppressing the nobility, controlling the church, and insisting upon the loyalty of all peoples living in their territories.

Nirvana   in Buddhist thought, enlightenment, the ultimate transcendence from the illusion of the material world; release from the wheel of life.

nobiles   "nobles." The small group of families from both patrician and plebeian origins who produced most of the men who were elected to office in the late Roman Republic.

Nok culture   in northern Nigeria, one of the most active early iron-working societies in Africa, artifacts from which date back as far as 500 B.C.E.

nuclear family   a family group consisting only of father, mother, and children.

nun   female religious monk.

old regime/old order   the political and social system of France in the eighteenth century before the Revolution.

oligarchy   rule by a few.

Open Door notes   a series of letters sent in 1899 by U.S. Secretary of State John Hay to Great Britain, France, Germany, Italy, Japan and Russia, calling for equal economic access to the China market for all states and for the maintenance of the territorial and administrative integrity of the Chinese Empire.

optimates   "best men." Aristocratic leaders in the late Roman Republic who generally came from senatorial families and wished to retain their oligarchical privileges.

opium trade   the sale of the addictive product of the poppy, specifically by British traders to China in the 1830s. Chinese attempts to prevent it led to the Opium War of 1839–1842, which resulted in British access to Chinese ports and has traditionally been considered the beginning of modern Chinese history.

orders/estates   the traditional tripartite division of European society based on heredity and quality rather than wealth or economic standing, first established in the Middle Ages and continuing into the eighteenth century; traditionally consisted of those who pray (the clergy), those who fight (the nobility), and those who work (all the rest).

organic evolution   Darwin's principle that all plants and animals have evolved over a long period of time from earlier and simpler forms of life.

Organization of African Unity   founded in Addis Ababa in 1963, it was intended to represent the interests of all the newly independent countries of Africa and provided a forum for the discussion of common problems until 2001, when it was replaced by the African Union.

Paleolithic Age   the period of human history when humans used simple stone tools (c. 2,500,000–10,000 B.C.E.).

pan-Africanism the concept of African continental unity and solidarity in which the common interests of African countries transcend regional boundaries.

pantheism a doctrine that equates God with the universe and all that is in it.

pariahs members of the lowest level of traditional Indian society, technically outside the class system itself; also known as untouchables.

pasha an administrative official of the Ottoman empire, responsible for collecting taxes and maintaining order in the provinces; later, some became hereditary rulers.

paterfamilias the dominant male in a Roman family whose powers over his wife and children were theoretically unlimited, though they were sometimes circumvented in practice.

patriarchal/patriarchy a society in which the father is supreme in the clan or family; more generally, a society dominated by men.

patriarchal family a family in which the husband/father dominates his wife and children.

patricians great landowners who became the ruling class in the Roman Republic.

patrilinear passing through the male line, from father to son; often combined with patriarchy.

patronage the practice of awarding titles and making appointments to government and other positions to gain political support.

Pax Romana "Roman peace." A term used to refer to the stability and prosperity that Roman rule brought to the Mediterranean world and much of western Europe during the first and second centuries C.E.

peaceful coexistence the policy adopted by the Soviet Union under Khrushchev in 1955, and continued by his successors, that called for economic and ideological rivalry with the West rather than nuclear war.

Pentateuch the first five books of the Hebrew Bible (Genesis, Exodus, Leviticus, Numbers, and Deuteronomy).

peoples' democracies a term invented by the Soviet Union to define a society in the early stage of socialist transition, applied to Eastern European countries in the 1950s.

perestroika "restructuring." A term applied to Mikhail Gorbachev's economic, political, and social reforms in the Soviet Union.

permissive society a term applied to Western society after World War II to reflect the new sexual freedom and the emergence of a drug culture.

Petrine supremacy the doctrine that the bishop of Rome—the pope—as the successor of Saint Peter (traditionally considered the first bishop of Rome) should hold a preeminent position in the church.

phalanx a rectangular formation of tightly massed infantry soldiers.

philosophes intellectuals of the eighteenth-century Enlightenment who believed in applying a spirit of rational criticism to all things, including religion and politics, and who focused on improving and enjoying this world, rather than on the afterlife.

plebeians the class of Roman citizens who included nonpatrician landowners, craftspeople, merchants, and small farmers in the Roman Republic. Their struggle for equal rights with the patricians dominated much of the Republic's history.

pluralism the practice in which one person holds several church offices simultaneously; a problem of the late medieval church.

pogroms organized massacres of Jews.

polis an ancient Greek city-state encompassing both an urban area and its surrounding countryside; a small but autonomous political unit where all major political and social activities were carried out in a central location.

political democracy a form of government characterized by universal suffrage and mass political parties.

politiques a group who emerged during the French Wars of Religion in the sixteenth century; placed politics above religion and believed that no religious truth was worth the ravages of civil war.

polygyny the practice of having more than one wife at a time.

polytheistic/polytheism having many gods; belief in or the worship of more than one god.

popular culture as opposed to high culture, the unofficial, written and unwritten culture of the masses, much of which was passed down orally; centers on public and group activities such as festivals. In the twentieth century, refers to the entertainment, recreation, and pleasures that people purchase as part of mass consumer society.

populares "favoring the people." Aristocratic leaders in the late Roman Republic who tended to use the people's assemblies in an effort to break the stranglehold of the *nobiles* on political offices.

popular sovereignty the doctrine that government is created by and subject to the will of the people, who are the source of all political power.

portolani charts of landmasses and coastlines made by navigators and mathematicians in the thirteenth and fourteenth centuries.

Poststructuralism a theory formulated by Jacques Derrida in the 1960s, holding that there is no fixed, universal truth since culture is created and can therefore be analyzed in various ways.

praetorian guard the military unit that served as the personal bodyguard of the Roman emperors.

praetors the two senior Roman judges, who had executive authority when the consuls were away from the city and could also lead armies.

Prakrit an ancient Indian language, a simplified form of Sanskrit.

predestination the belief, associated with Calvinism, that God, as a consequence of his foreknowledge of all events, has predetermined those who will be saved (the elect) and those who will be damned.

price revolution the dramatic rise in prices (inflation) that occurred throughout Europe in the sixteenth and early seventeenth centuries.

primogeniture an inheritance practice in which the eldest son receives all or the largest share of the parents' estate.

principate the form of government established by Augustus for the Roman Empire; continued the constitutional forms of the Republic and consisted of the *princeps* ("first citizen") and the senate, although the *princeps* was clearly the dominant partner.

proletariat the industrial working class. In Marxism, the class who will ultimately overthrow the bourgeoisie.

Protestant Reformation the western European religious reform movement in the sixteenth century C.E. that divided Christianity into Catholic and Protestant groups.

purdah the Indian term for the practice among Muslims and some Hindus of isolating women and preventing them from associating with men outside the home.

Pure Land a Buddhist sect, originally Chinese but later popular in Japan, which taught that devotion alone could lead to enlightenment and release.

Puritans English Protestants inspired by Calvinist theology who wished to remove all traces of Catholicism from the Church of England.

querelles des femmes "arguments about women." A centuries-old debate about the nature of women that continued during the Scientific Revolution as those who argued for the inferiority of women found additional support in the new anatomy and medicine.

quipu an Inka record-keeping system that used knotted strings rather than writing.

raj common name for the British colonial regime in India.

raja originally, a chieftain in the Aryan society of early India, a representative of the gods; later used more generally to denote a ruler.

Ramadan the holy month of Islam, during which believers fast from dawn to sunset; since the Islamic calendar is lunar, Ramadan migrates through the seasons.

rationalism a system of thought based on the belief that human reason and experience are the chief sources of knowledge.

realism in medieval Europe, the school of thought that, following Plato, held that the individual objects we perceive are not real but merely manifestations of universal ideas existing in the mind of God. In the nineteenth century, a school of painting that emphasized the everyday life of ordinary people, depicted with photographic realism.

Realpolitik "politics of reality." Politics based on practical concerns rather than theory or ethics.

real wages/income/prices wages/income/prices that have been adjusted for inflation.

reason of state   the principle that a nation should act on the basis of its long-term interests and not merely to further the dynastic interests of its ruling family.

reincarnation   the idea that the individual soul is reborn in a different form after death; in Hindu and Buddhist thought, release from this cycle is the objective of all living souls.

relativity theory   Einstein's theory that holds, among other things, that (1) space and time are not absolute but are relative to the observer and interwoven into a four-dimensional space-time continuum and (2) matter is a form of energy ($E = mc^2$).

Renaissance   the "rebirth" of classical culture that occurred in Italy between c. 1350 and c. 1550; also, the earlier revivals of classical culture that occurred under Charlemagne and in the twelfth century.

rentier   a person who lives on income from property and is not personally involved in its operation.

reparations   payments made by a defeated nation after a war to compensate another nation for damage sustained as a result of the war; required from Germany after World War I.

revisionism   a socialist doctrine that rejected Marx's emphasis on class struggle and revolution and argued instead that workers should work through political parties to bring about gradual change.

revolution   a fundamental change in the political and social organization of a state.

revolutionary socialism   the socialist doctrine espoused by Georges Sorel who held that violent action was the only way to achieve the goals of socialism.

rhetoric   the art of persuasive speaking; in the Middle Ages, one of the seven liberal arts.

Rococo   a style, especially of decoration and architecture, that developed from the Baroque and spread throughout Europe by the 1730s. While still elaborate, it emphasized curves, lightness, and charm in the pursuit of pleasure, happiness, and love.

ronin   Japanese warriors made unemployed by developments in the early modern era, since samurai were forbidden by tradition to engage in commerce.

rural responsibility system   post-Maoist land reform in China, under which collectives leased land to peasant families, who could consume or sell their surplus production and keep the profits.

sacraments   rites considered imperative for a Christian's salvation. By the thirteenth century consisted of the eucharist or Lord's Supper, baptism, marriage, penance, extreme unction, holy orders, and confirmation of children; Protestant reformers of the sixteenth century generally recognized only two—baptism and communion (the Lord's Supper).

samurai   literally "retainer"; similar to European knights. Usually in service to a particular shogun, these Japanese warriors lived by a strict code of ethics and duty.

Sanskrit   an early Indo-European language, in which the Vedas were composed, beginning in the second millenium B.C.E. It survived as the language of literature and the bureaucracy for centuries after its decline as a spoken tongue.

sans-culottes   the common people who did not wear the fine clothes of the upper classes (sans-culottes means "without breeches") and played an important role in the radical phase of the French Revolution.

sati   the Hindu ritual requiring a wife to throw herself upon her deceased husband's funeral pyre.

satori   enlightenment, in the Japanese, especially Zen, Buddhist tradition.

satrap/satrapy   a governor with both civil and military duties in the ancient Persian Empire, which was divided into satrapies, or provinces, each administered by a satrap.

satyagraha   the Hindi term for the practice of nonviolent resistance, as advocated by Mohandas Gandhi; literally, "hold fast to the truth".

scholar-gentry   in Song dynasty China, candidates who passed the civil service examinations and whose families were non-aristocratic landowners; eventually, a majority of the bureaucracy.

scholasticism   the philosophical and theological system of the medieval schools, which emphasized rigorous analysis of contradictory authorities; often used to try to reconcile faith and reason.

School of Mind   a philosophy espoused by Wang Yangming during the mid-Ming era of China, which argued that mind and the universe were a single unit and knowledge was therefore obtained through internal self-searching rather than through investigation of the outside world; for a while, a significant but unofficial rival to neo-Confucianism.

scientific method   a method of seeking knowledge through inductive principles; uses experiments and observations to develop generalizations.

Scientific Revolution   the transition from the medieval worldview to a largely secular, rational, and materialistic perspective; began in the seventeenth century and was popularized in the eighteenth.

secularization   the process of becoming more concerned with material, worldly, temporal things and less with spiritual and religious things.

self-determination   the doctrine that the people of a given territory or a particular nationality should have the right to determine their own government and political future.

self-strengthening   a late-nineteenth-century Chinese policy, by which Western technology would be adopted while Confucian principles and institutions were maintained intact.

senate/senators   the leading council of the Roman Republic; composed of about 300 men (senators) who served for life and dominated much of the political life of the Republic.

sepoys   native troops hired by the East India Company to protect British interests in south Asia, who formed the basis of the British Indian Army.

serf   a peasant who is bound to the land and obliged to provide labor services and pay various rents and fees to the lord; considered unfree but not a slave because serfs could not be bought and sold.

Shari'a   a law code, originally drawn up by Muslim scholars shortly after the death of Muhammad, that provides believers with a set of prescriptions to regulate their daily lives.

sheikh   originally, the ruler of a Bedouin tribe; later, also used as a more general honorific.

Shi'ite   the second largest tradition of Islam, which split from the majority Sunni soon after the death of Muhammad, in a disagreement over the succession; especially significant in Iran and Iraq.

Shinto   a kind of state religion in Japan, derived from beliefs in nature spirits and until recently linked with belief in the divinity of the emperor and the sacredness of the Japanese nation.

shogun   a powerful Japanese leader, originally military, who ruled under the titular authority of the emperor.

shogunate system   the system of government in Japan in which the emperor exercised only titular authority while the shogun (regional military dictators) exercised actual political power.

Sikhism   a religion, founded in the early sixteenth century in the Punjab, which began as an attempt to reconcile the Hindu and Muslim traditions and developed into a significant alternative to both.

sipahis   in the Ottoman empire, local cavalry elites, who held fiefdoms and collected taxes.

skepticism   a doubtful or questioning attitude, especially about religion.

Social Darwinism   the application of Darwin's principle of organic evolution to the social order; led to the belief that progress comes from the struggle for survival as the fittest advance and the weak decline.

socialism   an ideology that calls for collective or government ownership of the means of production and the distribution of goods.

social security/social insurance   government programs that provide social welfare measures such as old age pensions and sickness, accident, and disability insurance.

Socratic method   a form of teaching that uses a question-and-answer format to enable students to reach conclusions by using their own reasoning.

Sophists wandering scholars and professional teachers in ancient Greece who stressed the importance of rhetoric and tended toward skepticism and relativism.

soviets councils of workers' and soldiers' deputies formed throughout Russia in 1917; played an important role in the Bolshevik Revolution.

sphere of influence a territory or region over which an outside nation exercises political or economic influence.

Star Wars nickname of the Strategic Defense Initiative, proposed by President Reagan, which was intended to provide a shield that would destroy any incoming missiles; named after a popular science-fiction movie series.

stateless societies the pre-Columbian communities in much of the Americas who developed substantial cultures without formal nation states.

State Confucianism the integration of Confucian doctrine with Legalist practice under the Han dynasty in China, which became the basis of Chinese political thought until the modern era.

Stoicism a philosophy founded by Zeno in the fourth century C.E. that taught that happiness could be obtained by accepting one's lot and living in harmony with the will of God, thereby achieving inner peace.

stupa originally a stone tower holding relics of the Buddha, more generally a place for devotion, often architecturally impressive and surmounted with a spire.

subinfeudation the practice in which a lord's greatest vassals subdivided their fiefs and had vassals of their own, and those vassals, in turn, subdivided their fiefs and so on down to simple knights whose fiefs were too small to subdivide.

Sublime Porte the office of the grand vezir in the Ottoman empire.

sudras the classes that represented the great bulk of the Indian population from ancient time, mostly peasants, artisans or manual laborers; ranked below brahmins, kshatriyas, and vaisyas, but above the pariahs.

suffrage the right to vote.

suffragists those who advocate the extension of the right to vote (suffrage), especially to women.

Sufism a mystical school of Islam, noted for its music, dance, and poetry, which became prominent in about the thirteenth century.

sultan "holder of power," a title commonly used by Muslim rulers in the Ottoman Empire, Egypt, and elsewhere; still in use in parts of Asia, sometimes for regional authorities.

Sunni the largest tradition of Islam, from which the Shi'ites split soon after the death of Muhammad, in a disagreement over the succession.

Supreme Ultimate according to Neo-Confucianists, a transcendent world, distinct from the material world in which humans live, but to which humans may aspire; a set of abstract principles, roughly equivalent to the Dao.

surplus value in Marxism, the difference between a product's real value and the wages of the worker who produced the product.

Swahili a mixed African-Arabian culture that developed by the twelfth century along the east coast of Africa; also, the national language of Kenya and Tanzania.

syncretism the combining of different forms of belief or practice, as, for example, when two gods are regarded as different forms of the same underlying divine force and are fused together.

Taika reforms the seventh-century "great change" reforms that established the centralized Japanese state.

taille a French tax on land or property, developed by King Louis XI in the fifteenth century as the financial basis of the monarchy. It was largely paid by the peasantry; the nobility and the clergy were exempt.

Tantrism a mystical Buddhist sect, which emphasized the importance of magical symbols and ritual in seeking a path to enlightenment.

tariffs duties (taxes) imposed on imported goods; usually imposed both to raise revenue and to discourage imports and protect domestic industries.

tetrarchy rule by four; the system of government established by Diocletian (284–305) in which the Roman Empire was divided into two parts, each ruled by an "Augustus" assisted by a "Caesar."

theocracy a government based on a divine authority.

Theravada a school of Buddhism that stresses personal behavior and the quest for understanding as a means of release from the wheel of life, rather than the intercession of bodhisattvas; predominant in Sri Lanka and Southeast Asia.

three-field system in medieval agriculture, the practice of dividing the arable land into three fields so that one could lie fallow while the others were planted in winter grains and spring crops.

three kingdoms Koguryo, Paekche, and Silla, rivals but all under varying degrees of Chinese influence, which together controlled virtually all of Korea from the fourth to the seventh centuries.

three obediences the traditional duties of Japanese women, in permanent subservience: child to father, wife to husband, and widow to son.

tithe a tenth of one's harvest or income; paid by medieval peasants to the village church.

Tongmenghui the political organization—"Revolutionary Alliance"—formed by Sun Yat-sen in 1905, which united various revolutionary factions and ultimately toppled the Manchu dynasty.

Torah the body of law in Hebrew Scripture, contained in the Pentateuch (the first five books of the Hebrew Bible).

totalitarian state a state characterized by government control over all aspects of economic, social, political, cultural, and intellectual life, the subordination of the individual to the state, and insistence that the masses be actively involved in the regime's goals.

total war warfare in which all of a nation's resources, including civilians at home as well as soldiers in the field, are mobilized for the war effort.

trade union an association of workers in the same trade, formed to help members secure better wages, benefits, and working conditions.

transubstantiation a doctrine of the Roman Catholic church that teaches that during the eucharist the substance of the bread and wine is miraculously transformed into the body and blood of Jesus.

trench warfare warfare in which the opposing forces attack and counterattack from a relatively permanent system of trenches protected by barbed wire; characteristic of World War I.

tribunes of the plebs beginning in 494 B.C.E., Roman officials who were given the power to protect plebeians against arrest by patrician magistrates.

tribute system an important element of Chinese foreign policy, by which neighboring states paid for the privilege of access to Chinese markets, received legitimation and agreed not to harbor enemies of the Chinese Empire.

Truman Doctrine the doctrine, enunciated by Harry Truman in 1947, that the United States would provide economic aid to countries that said they were threatened by Communist expansion.

twice-born the males of the higher castes in traditional Indian society, who underwent an initiation ceremony at puberty.

tyrant/tyranny in an ancient Greek *polis* (or an Italian city-state during the Renaissance), a ruler who came to power in an unconstitutional way and ruled without being subject to the law.

uhuru "freedom" (Swahili), and so a key slogan in the African independence movements, especially in Kenya.

uji a clan in early Japanese tribal society.

ulama a convocation of leading Muslim scholars, the earliest of which shortly after the death of Muhammad drew up a law code, called the Shari'a, based largely on the Koran and the sayings of the Prophet, to provide believers with a set of prescriptions to regulate their daily lives.

umma the Muslim community, as a whole.

uncertainty principle a principle in quantum mechanics, posited by Heisenberg, that holds that one cannot determine the path of an electron because the very act of observing the electron would affect its location.

unconditional surrender complete, unqualified surrender of a nation.

uninterrupted revolution   the goal of the Great Proletarian Cultural Revolution launched by Mao Zedong in 1966.

utopian socialists   intellectuals and theorists in the early nineteenth century who favored equality in social and economic conditions and wished to replace private property and competition with collective ownership and cooperation; deemed impractical and "utopian" by later socialists.

vaisya   the third-ranked class in traditional Indian society, usually merchants.

varna   Indian classes, or castes. See caste system.

vassal   a person granted a fief, or landed estate, in exchange for providing military services to the lord and fulfilling certain other obligations such as appearing at the lord's court when summoned and making a payment on the knighting of the lord's eldest son.

veneration of ancestors   the extension of filial piety to include care for the deceased, for instance by burning replicas of useful objects to accompany them on their journey to the next world.

vernacular   the everyday language of a region, as distinguished from a language used for special purposes. For example, in medieval Paris, French was the vernacular, but Latin was used for academic writing and for classes at the University of Paris.

Vietnam syndrome   the presumption, from the 1970s on, that the U.S. public would object to a protracted military entanglement abroad, such as another Vietnam-type conflict.

vizier   (*also*, vezir) the prime minister in the Abbasid caliphate and elsewhere, a chief executive.

volkish thought   the belief that German culture is superior and that the German people have a universal mission to save Western civilization from inferior races.

war communism   Lenin's policy of nationalizing industrial and other facilities and requisitioning the peasants' produce during the civil war in Russia.

War Guilt Clause   the clause in the Treaty of Versailles that declared that Germany (and Austria) were responsible for starting World War I and ordered Germany to pay reparations for the damage the Allies had suffered as a result of the war.

Warsaw Pact   a military alliance, formed in 1955, in which Albania, Bulgaria, Czechoslovakia, East Germany, Hungary, Poland, Romania, and the Soviet Union agreed to provide mutual assistance. Dissolved in 1991, most former members eventually joined NATO.

welfare state   a social/political system in which the government assumes the primary responsibility for the social welfare of its citizens by providing such things as social security, unemployment benefits, and health care.

well field system   the theoretical pattern of land ownership in early China, named for the appearance of the Chinese character for "well," in which farmland was divided into nine segments and a peasant family would cultivate one for their own use and cooperate with seven others to cultivate the ninth for the landlord.

wergeld   "money for a man." In early Germanic law, a person's value in monetary terms, which was paid by a wrongdoer to the family of the person who had been injured or killed.

White Lotus   a Chinese Buddhist sect, founded in 1133 C.E., that sought political reform; in 1796–1804, a Chinese peasant revolt.

women's liberation movement   the struggle for equal rights for women, which has deep roots in history but achieved new prominence under this name in the 1960s, building on the work of, among others, Simone de Beauvoir and Betty Friedan.

world-machine   Newton's conception of the universe as one huge, regulated, and uniform machine that operated according to natural laws in absolute time, space, and motion.

Yangshao   a Neolithic society from near the Yellow River in China, sometimes identified by its painted pottery.

Young Turks   a successful Turkish reformist group in the late nineteenth and early twentieth centuries.

zaibatsu   powerful business cartels formed in Japan during the Meiji era and outlawed following World War II.

zamindars   Indian tax collectors, who were assigned land, from which they kept part of the revenue; the British revived the system in a misguided attempt to create a landed gentry.

Zen Buddhism   (in Chinese, Chan or Ch'an) a school of Buddhism particularly important in Japan, some of whose adherents stress that enlightenment (satori) can be achieved suddenly, though others emphasize lengthy meditation.

ziggurat   a massive stepped tower upon which a temple dedicated to the chief god or goddess of a Sumerian city was built.

Zionism   an international movement that called for the establishment of a Jewish state or a refuge for Jews in Palestine.

Zoroastrianism   a religion founded by the Persian Zoroaster in the seventh century C.E.; characterized by worship of a supreme god Ahuramazda who represents the good against the evil spirit, identified as Ahriman.

Abbasid   uh-BAH-sid *or* AB-uh-sid
Abd al-Rahman   ub-duh-rahkh-MAHN
Abu al-Abbas   uh-BOOL-uh-BUSS
Abu Bakr   uh-boo-BAHK-ur
Achebe, Chinua   ah-CHAY-bay, CHIN-wah
Achilles   uh-KIL-eez
Adenauer, Konrad   AD-uh-now-ur
aediles   EE-dylz
Aegospotami   ee-guh-SPOT-uh-mee
Aeolians   ee-OH-lee-unz
Aequi   EE-kwy
Aeschylus   ESS-kuh-luss
Aetius   ay-EE-shuss
Afrikaners   ah-fri-KAH-nurz
Agesilaus   uh-jess-uh-LAY-uss
Agincourt   AH-zhen-koor
Aguinaldo, Emilio   ah-gwee-NAHL-doh, ay-MEEL-yoh
Ahlwardt, Hermann   AHL-vart, hayr-MAHN
Ahuramazda   uh-hoor-uh-MAHZ-duh
Aix-la-Chapelle   ex-lah-shah-PELL
Ajanta   uh-JUHN-tuh
Akhenaten   ah-khuh-NAH-tun
Akhetaten   ah-khuh-TAH-tun
Akkadians   uh-KAY-dee-unz
Alaric   AL-uh-rik
Alberti, Leon Battista   al-BAYR-tee, LAY-un buh-TEESS-tuh
Albigensians   al-buh-JEN-see-unz
Albuquerque, Afonso de   AL-buh-kur-kee, ah-FAHN-soh day
Alcibiades   al-suh-BY-uh-deez
Alcuin   AL-kwin
Alemanni   al-uh-MAH-nee
al-Fatah   al-FAH-tuh
al-Hakim   al-hah-KEEM
Alia, Ramiz   AH-lee-uh, rah-MEEZ
al-Khwarizmi   al-KHWAR-iz-mee
Allah   AH-lah
al-Ma'mun   al-muh-MOON
Almeida, Francesco da   ahl-MAY-duh, frahn-CHAYSS-koh
al-Sadat, Anwar   ah-sah-DAHT, ahn-WAHR
Aidoo, Ama Ata   ah-EE-doo, AH-mah AH-tah
Amaterasu   ah-muh-teh-RAH-suh
Amenhotep   ah-mun-HOH-tep
Anasazi   ah-nuh-SAH-zee
Andreotti, Giulio   ahn-dray-AH-tee, JOOL-yoh
Andropov, Yuri   ahn-DRAHP-awf, YOOR-ee
Anjou   AHN-zhoo
Antigonid   an-TIG-uh-nid
Antigonus Gonatus   an-TIG-oh-nuss guh-NAH-tuss
Antiochus   an-TY-uh-kuss
Antonescu, Ion   an-tuh-NESS-koo, YON
Antoninus Pius   an-tuh-NY-nuss PY-uss
Anyang   ahn-YAHNG
apella   uh-PELL-uh
Apollonius   ap-uh-LOH-nee-uss
Aquinas, Thomas   uh-KWY-nuss
Arafat, Yasir   ah-ruh-FAHT, yah-SEER
aratrum   uh-RAH-trum
Arawak   AR-uh-wahk
Archimedes   ahr-kuh-MEE-deez
Argonautica   ahr-guh-NAWT-uh-kuh
Aristarchus   ar-iss-TAR-kus

Aristotle   AR-iss-tot-ul
Arjuna   ahr-JOO-nuh
Arsinoë   ahr-SIN-oh-ee
artium baccalarius   ar-TEE-um bak-uh-LAR-ee-uss
artium magister   ar-TEE-um muh-GISS-ter
Aryan   AR-ee-un
Ashikaga   ah-shee-KAH-guh
Ashkenazic   ash-kuh-NAH-zik
Ashoka   uh-SHOH-kuh
Ashurbanipal   ah-shur-BAH-nuh-pahl
Ashurnasirpal   ah-shur-NAH-zur-pahl
asiento   ah-SYEN-toh
assignat   ah-see-NYAH
Assyrians   uh-SEER-ee-unz
Astell, Mary   AST-ul
Atahualpa   ah-tuh-WAHL-puh
Attalid   AT-uh-lid
audiencias   ow-dee-en-SEE-uss
Auerstadt   OW-urr-shtaht
augur   AW-gurr
Augustine   AW-guh-steen
Aum Shinri Kyo   awm-shin-ree-KYO
Aung San Huu Kyi   AWNG-sawn-soo-chee
Aurelian   aw-REEL-yun
Auschwitz-Birkenau   OW-shvitz-BEER-kuh-now
Ausgleich   OWSS-glykh
auspices   AWSS-puh-sizz
Austerlitz   AWSS-tur-litz
Australopithecines   aw-stray-loh-PITH-uh-synz
Austrasia   awss-TRAY-zhuh
Autun   oh-TUNH
Avalokitesvara   uh-VAH-loh-kee-TESH-vuh-ruh
Avicenna   av-i-SENN-uh
Avignon   ah-veen-YOHNH
Ayacucho   ah-ya-KOO-choh
Ayodhya   ah-YOHD-hyah
Ayuthaya   ah-yoo-TY-yuh
Azerbaijan   az-ur-by-JAN
Ba'ath   BAHTH
Baader-Meinhof   BAH-durr-MYN-huff
Babeuf, Gracchus   bah-BUFF, GRAK-uss
Babur   BAH-burr
Bach, Johann Sebastian   BAKH, yoh-HAHN suh-BASS-chun
Baden-Powell, Robert   BAD-un-POW-ul
Bai Hua   by HWA
bakufu   buh-KOO-foo *or Japanese* bah-KOO-fuh
Bakunin, Michael   buh-KOON-yun
Balboa, Vasco Nuñez de   bal-BOH-uh, BAHS-koh NOON-yez day
Ballin, Albert   BAH-leen
Bandaranaike, Sirimavo   bahn-dur-uh-NY-uh-kuh, see-ree-MAH-voh
Banque de Belgique   BAHNK duh bel-ZHEEK
Ban Zhao   bahn ZHOW
Bao-jia   BOW-jah
Barbarossa   bar-buh-ROH-suh
Baroque   buh-ROHK
Barth, Karl   BAHRT
Basho   BAH-shoh
Bastille   bass-STEEL
Basutoland   buh-SOO-toh-land
Batista, Fulgencio   bah-TEES-tuh, full-JEN-see-oh

Bauhaus   BOW-howss
Bayazid   by-uh-ZEED
Bayle, Pierre   BELL, PYAYR
Beauharnais, Josephine de   boh-ar-NAY, zhoh-seff-FEEN duh
Beauvoir, Simone de   boh-VWAR, see-MUHN duh
Bebel, August   BAY-bul, ow-GOOST
Beccaria, Cesare   buh-KAH-ree-uh, CHAY-zuh-ray
Bechuanaland   bech-WAH-nuh-land
Bede   BEED
Begin, Menachem   BAY-gin, muh-NAH-khum
Beguines   bay-GEENZ
Beiderbecke, Bix   BY-der-bek, BIKS
Beijing   bay-ZHING
Belarus   bell-uh-ROOSS
Belgioioso, Cristina   bell-joh-YOH-soh
Belisarius   bell-uh-SAH-ree-uss
benefice   BEN-uh-fiss
Benin   bay-NEEN
Bergson, Henri   BAYRK-suhn, ahn-REE
Berlioz, Hector   BAYR-lee-ohz, hek-TOR
Berlusconi, Silvio   bayr-loo-SKOH-nee, SEEL-vee-oh
Bernhardi, Friedrich von   bayrn-HAR-dee, FREED-reekh fun
Bernini, Gian Lorenzo   bur-NEE-nee, JAHN loh-RENT-zoh
Bernstein, Eduard   BAYRN-shtyn, AY-doo-art
Bethman-Hollweg, Theobald von   BET-mun-HOHL-vek, TAY-oh-bahlt fun
Bhagavad Gita   bah-guh-vahd-GEE-tuh
Bharata Janata   BAR-ruh-tuh JAH-nuh-tuh
Bhutto, Zulfikar Ali   BOO-toh, ZOOL-fee-kahr ah-LEE
Bismarck, Otto von   BIZ-mark, OH-toh fun
Blanc, Louis   BLAHNH, LWEE
Blitzkrieg   BLITZ-kreeg
Blum, Léon   BLOOM, LAY-ohnh
Boccaccio, Giovanni   boh-KAH-choh, joe-VAH-nee
Bodichon, Barbara   boh-di-SHOHNH
Boer   BOOR *or* BOR
Boethius   boh-EE-thee-uss
Boleyn, Anne   BUH-lin *or* buh-LIN
Bolívar, Simón   boh-LEE-var, see-MOHN
Bologna   boh-LOHN-yuh
Bolsheviks   BOHL-shuh-viks
Bora, Katherina von   BOH-rah, kat-uh-REE-nuh fun
Borobudur   boh-roh-buh-DOOR
Bosnia   BAHZ-nee-uh
Bosporus   BAHSS-pruss
Bossuet, Jacques   baw-SWAY, ZHAHK
Botswana   baht-SWAH-nuh
Botta, Giuseppe   BOH-tah, joo-ZEP-pay
Botticelli, Sandro   bot-i-CHELL-ee, SAHN-droh
Boulanger, Georges   boo-lahnh-ZHAY, ZHORZH
boule   BOOL
Bracciolini, Poggio   braht-choh-LEE-nee, POH-djoh
Brahe, Tycho   BRAH, TY-koh
Brahmo Samaj   BRAH-moh suh-MAHJ
Bramante, Donato   brah-MAHN-tay, doh-NAH-toh
Brandt, Willy   BRAHNT, VIL-ee
Brasidas   BRASS-i-duss
Brest-Litovsk   BREST-li-TUFFSK
Brétigny   bray-tee-NYEE
Brezhnev, Leonid   BREZH-neff, lyee-oh-NYEET
Briand, Aristide   bree-AHNH, ah-ruh-STEED
Broz, Josip   BRAWZ, yaw-SEEP
Brunelleschi, Filippo   BROO-nuh-LESS-kee, fee-LEE-poh
Brüning, Heinrich   BRUR-ning, HYN-rikh
Bückeberg   BURK-uh-bayrk
Bulganin, Nicolai   bool-GAN-yin, nyik-uh-LY
Bund Deutscher Mädel   BOONT DOIT-chur MAY-dul
Bundesrat   BOON-duss-raht
Burckhardt, Jacob   BOORK-hart, YAK-ub
Burschenschaften   BOOR-shun-shahf-tun
Bushido   BOO-shee-doh
Cabral, Pedro   kuh-BRAL, PAY-droh
cahiers de doléances   ka-YAY duh doh-lay-AHNSS

Cai Yuanpei   TSY yoo-wan-PAY
Calais   ka-LAY
Calas, Jean   ka-LAH, ZHAHNH
Caligula   kuh-LIG-yuh-luh
caliph   KAY-liff
caliphate   KAY-luh-fayt
Callicrates   kuh-LIK-ruh-teez
Calonne, Charles de   ka-LUNN, SHAHRL duh
Cambyses   kam-BY-seez
Camus, Albert   ka-MOO, ahl-BAYR
Can Vuong   kahn VWAHNG
Canaanites   KAY-nuh-nytss
Cannae   KAH-nee
Cao Cao   TSOW-tsow
Capet, Hugh   ka-PAY, YOO
Capetian   kuh-PEE-shun
Caracalla   kuh-RAK-uh-luh
Caraffa, Gian Pietro   kuh-RAH-fuh, JAHN PYAY-troh
carbonari   kar-buh-NAH-ree
Cárdenas, Lázaro   KAHR-day-nahss, LAH-zah-roh
Carolingian   kar-uh-LIN-jun
carruca   kuh-ROO-kuh
Carthage   KAHR-thij
Carthaginian   kahr-thuh-JIN-ee-un
Cartier, Jacques   kahr-TYAY, ZHAK
Casa de Contratación   KAH-sah day KOHN-trah-tahk-SYOHN
Cassiodorus   kass-ee-uh-DOR-uss
Castiglione, Baldassare   ka-steel-YOH-nay, bal-duh-SAH-ray
Castro, Fidel   KASS-troh, fee-DELL
Çatal Hüyük   chaht-ul-hoo-YOOK
Catharism   KATH-uh-riz-um
Catullus   kuh-TULL-uss
Cavendish, Margaret   KAV-un-dish
Cavour, Camillo di   kuh-VOOR, kuh-MEEL-oh dee
Ceauşescu, Nicolae   chow-SHES-koo, nee-koh-LY
celibacy   SELL-uh-buh-see
cenobitic   sen-oh-BIT-ik
Cereta, Laura   say-RAY-tuh, LOW-ruh
Cerularius, Michael   sayr-yuh-LAR-ee-uss
Cézanne, Paul   say-ZAHN, POHL
Chacabuco   chahk-ah-BOO-koh
Chaeronea   ker-uh-NEE-uh
Chaldean   kal-DEE-un
Chamorro, Violeta Barrios de   chah-MOH-roh, vee-oh-LET-uh bah-REE-ohss day
Champlain, Samuel de   shonh-PLENH *or* sham-PLAYN, sahm-WEL duh
Chandragupta Maurya   chun-druh-GOOP-tuh MOWR-yuh
Chang'an   CHENG-AHN
chanson de geste   shahn-SONH duh ZHEST
Chao Phraya   chow-PRY-uh
Charlemagne   SHAR-luh-mayn
Chateaubriand, François-René de   shah-TOH-bree-AHNH, frahnh-SWAH-ruh-NAY duh
Châtelet, marquise du   shat-LAY, mahr-KEEZ duh
Chauvet   shoh-VAY
Chavín de Huántar   chah-VEEN day HWAHN-tahr
Chechnya   CHECH-nyuh
Cheka   CHEK-uh
Chennai   CHEN-ny
Chen Shuibian   CHEN-shwee-BYAHN
Chiang Kai-shek   CHANG ky-SHEK
Chichén Itzá   chee-CHEN-eet-SAH
Chimor   chee-MAWR
Chirac, Jacques   shee-RAK, ZHAHK
Chongqing   chung-CHING
Chrétien de Troyes   kray-TYEN duh TRWAH
Chrétien, Jean   kray-TYEN, ZHAHNH
Chrysoloras, Manuel   kriss-uh-LAWR-uss, man-WEL
Cicero   SIS-uh-roh
Cincinnatus   sin-suh-NAT-uss
ciompi   CHAHM-pee
Cistercians   sis-TUR-shunz

Cixi   TSEE-chee
Clairvaux   klayr-VOH
Claudius   KLAW-dee-uss
Cleisthenes   KLYSS-thuh-neez
Clemenceau, Georges   kluh-mahn-SOH, ZHORZH
Clovis   KLOH-viss
Codreanu, Corneliu   kaw-dree-AH-noo, kor-NELL-yoo
Colbert, Jean-Baptiste   kohl-BAYR, ZHAHN-bap-TEEST
Colonia Agrippinensis   kuh-LOH-nee-uh uh-grip-uh-NEN-suss
colonus   kuh-LOH-nuss
Columbanus   kah-lum-BAY-nuss
comitia centuriata   kuh-MISH-ee-uh sen-choo-ree-AH-tuh
Commodus   KAHM-uh-duss
Comnenus   kahm-NEE-nuss
Comte, Auguste   KOHNT, ow-GOOST
concilium plebis   kahn-SILL-ee-um PLEE-biss
Concordat of Worms   kun-KOR-dat uv WURMZ or VORMPS
Condorcet, Marie-Jean de   konh-dor-SAY, muh-REE-ZHAHNH duh
condottieri   kahn-duh-TYAY-ree
Confucius   kun-FYOO-shuss
conquistador   kahn-KEESS-tuh-dor
consul   KAHN-sull
Contarini, Gasparo   kahn-tuh-REE-nee, GAHS-puh-roh
conversos   kohn-VAYR-sohz
Copán   koh-PAHN
Copernicus, Nicolaus   kuh-PURR-nuh-kuss, NEE-koh-lowss
Córdoba   KOR-duh-buh
Corinth   KOR-inth
Corpus Hermeticum   KOR-pus hur-MET-i-koom
Corpus Iuris Civilis   KOR-pus YOOR-iss SIV-i-liss
corregidores   kuhr-reg-uh-DOR-ayss
Cortés, Hernán   kor-TAYSS or kor-TEZ, hayr-NAHN
Corvinus, Matthias   kor-VY-nuss, muh-THY-uss
Courbet, Gustave   koor-BAY, goo-STAHV
Crassus   KRASS-uss
Crécy   kray-SEE
Credit Anstalt   KRAY-deet AHN-shtahlt
Crédit Mobilier   kray-DEE moh-bee-LYAY
Croatia   kroh-AY-shuh
Croesus   KREE-suss
cum manu   koom MAH-noo
Curie, Marie   kyoo-REE
Cypselus   SIP-suh-luss
Cyrenaica   seer-uh-NAY-uh-kuh
Dadaism   DAH-duh-iz-um
Daimler, Gottlieb   DYM-lur, GUHT-leeb
daimyo   DYM-yoh
Dai Viet   dy VYET
d'Albret, Jeanne   dahl-BRAY, ZHAHN
Dalí, Salvador   dah-LEE, sahl-vah-DOR
Dandin   DUN-din
Danton, Georges   dahn-TONH, ZHORZH
Dao de Jing   DOW-deh-JING
Darius   duh-RY-uss
Darmstadt   DARM-shtaht
dauphin   DAW-fin
David, Jacques-Louis   dah-VEED, ZHAHK-LWEE
de Gaulle, Charles   duh GOHL, SHAHRL
De Rerum Novarum   day RAY-rum noh-VAR-um
Debelleyme, Louis-Maurice   duh-buh-LAYM, LWEE-moh-REESS
Debussy, Claude   duh-byoo-SEE, KLOHD
décades   day-KAD
Decameron   dee-KAM-uh-run
decarchies   DEK-ar-keez
decemviri   duh-SEM-vuh-ree
Deffand, marquise du   duh-FAHNH, mar-KEEZ doo
Dei-Anang   DAY-ah-NAHNG
Deir el Bahri   dayr-ahl-BAH-ree
Delacroix, Eugène   duh-lah-KRWAH, oo-ZHEN
Démar, Claire   DAY-mar
Demosthenes   duh-MAHSS-thuh-neez
Deng Xiaoping   DENG-show-PING
Denikin, Anton   dyin-YEE-kin, ahn-TOHN

Desai, Anita   dess-SY
descamisados   dayss-kah-mee-SAH-dohss
Descartes, René   day-KART, ruh-NAY
Dessau   DESS-ow
d'Este, Isabella   DESS-tay, ee-suh-BELL-uh
détente   day-TAHNT
devshirme   dev-SHEER-may
dharma   DAR-muh
d'Holbach, Paul   dohl-BAHK, POHL
dhoti   DOH-tee
Diaghilev, Sergei   DYAHG-yuh-lif, syir-GAY
Dias, Bartholomeu   DEE-ush, bar-toh-loh-MAY-oo
Diaspora   dy-ASS-pur-uh
Diderot, Denis   dee-DROH, duh-NEE
Ding Ling   DING LING
Diocletian   dy-uh-KLEE-shun
Disraeli, Benjamin   diz-RAY-lee
Djibouti   juh-BOO-tee
Djoser   ZHOH-sur
Dollfuss, Engelbert   DAWL-fooss, ENG-ul-bayrt
Domesday Book   DOOMZ-day book
Domitian   doh-MISH-un
Donatello, Donato di   doh-nuh-TELL-oh, doh-NAH-toh dee
Donatist   DOH-nuh-tist
Donatus   duh-NAY-tus
Dopolavoro   duh-puh-LAH-vuh-roh
Dorians   DOR-ee-unz
Doryphoros   doh-RIF-uh-rohss
Dostoevsky, Fyodor   dus-tuh-YEF-skee, FYUD-ur
Douhet, Giulio   doo-AY, JOOL-yoh
Dreyfus, Alfred   DRY-fuss
Du Bois, W. E. B.   doo-BOISS
Dubček, Alexander   DOOB-chek
Dufay, Guillaume   doo-FAY, gee-YOHM
Duma   DOO-muh
Duong Thu Huong   ZHWAHNG too HWAHNG
Dupleix, Joseph-François   doo-PLEKS
Dürer, Albrecht   DOO-rur, AHL-brekht
Dzerzhinksy, Felix   djur-ZHIN-skee
Ebert, Friedrich   AY-bayrt, FREE-drikh
ecclesia   ek-KLEE-zee-uh
Eckhart, Meister   EK-hart, MY-stur
Einsatzgruppen   YN-zahtz-groop-un
Einstein, Albert   YN-styn
Ekaterinburg   i-kat-tuh-RIN-burk
Emecheta, Buchi   ay-muh-CHAY-tuh, BOO-chee
encomienda   en-koh-MYEN-duh
Engels, Friedrich   ENG-ulz, FREE-drikh
Enki   EN-kee
Enlil   EN-lil
Entente Cordiale   ahn-TAHNT kor-DYAHL
entrepôt   ahn-truh-POH
Epaminondas   i-PAM-uh-NAHN-duss
Ephesus   EFF-uh-suss
ephor   EFF-ur
Epicureanism   ep-i-kyoo-REE-uh-ni-zum
Epicurus   ep-i-KYOOR-uss
episcopos   i-PIS-kuh-puss
equestrians   i-KWES-tree-unz
equites   EK-wuh-teez
Erasistratus   er-uh-SIS-truh-tuss
Erasmus, Desiderius   i-RAZZ-mus, dez-i-DEER-ee-uss
Eratosthenes   er-uh-TAHSS-thuh-neez
eremitical   er-uh-MIT-i-kul
Erhard, Ludwig   AYR-hart, LOOD-vik
Estonia   ess-TOH-nee-uh
Etruscans   i-TRUSS-kunz
Euclid   YOO-klid
Euripides   yoo-RIP-uh-deez
exchequer   EKS-chek-ur
Execrabilis   ek-suh-KRAB-uh-liss
Eylau   Y-low
Falange   fuh-LANJ

Fang Lizhu   FAHNG lee-ZHOO
fasces   FASS-eez
Fascio di Combattimento   FASH-ee-oh dee com-bat-ee-MEN-toh
Fatimid   FAT-i-mid
Fedele, Cassandra   FAY-duh-lee
Feltre, Vittorino da   FELL-tray, vee-tor-EE-noh dah
Ficino, Marsilio   fee-CHEE-noh, mar-SIL-yoh
Fischer, Joschka   FISH-ur, YUSH-kah
Flaubert, Gustave   floh-BAYR, goo-STAHV
Fleury, Cardinal   floo-REE
fluyt   FLYT
Foch, Ferdinand   FUSH, fayr-di-NAWNH
Fontainebleau   FAWNH-ten-bloh
Fontenelle, Bernard de   fawnt-NELL, bayr-NAHR duh
Fouquet, Nicolas   foo-KAY, nee-koh-LAH
Fourier, Charles   foo-RYAY, SHAHRL
Francesca, Piero della   frahn-CHESS-kuh, PYAY-roh del-luh
Freud, Sigmund   FROID, SIG-mund *or* ZIG-munt
Friedan, Betty   free-DAN
Friedland   FREET-lahnt
Friedrich, Caspar David   FREED-rikh, kass-PAR dah-VEET
Froissart, Jean   frwah-SAR, ZHAHNH
Fronde   FROHND
Fu Xi   foo SHEE
Fu Xuan   foo SHWAHN
fueros   FWYA-rohss
Führerprinzip   FYOOR-ur-prin-TSEEP
Fujiwara   foo-jee-WAH-rah
gabelle   gah-BELL
Gaiseric   GY-zuh-rik
Galba   GAHL-buh
Galilei, Galileo   GAL-li-lay, gal-li-LAY-oh
Gama, Vasco da   GAHM-uh, VAHSH-koh dah
Gandhi, Mohandas (Mahatma)   GAHN-dee, moh-HAHN-dus (mah-HAHT-muh)
Garibaldi, Giuseppe   gar-uh-BAHL-dee, joo-ZEP-pay
Gasperi, Alcide de   GAHSS-puh-ree, ahl-SEE-day day
Gatti de Gamond, Zoé   gah-TEE duh gah-MOHNH, zoh-AY
Gaugamela   gaw-guh-MEE-luh
Gelasius   juh-LAY-shuss
Genghis Khan   JING-uss *or* GENG-uss KAHN
genin   gay-NIN
Gentileschi, Artemisia   jen-tuh-LESS-kee, ar-tuh-MEE-zhuh
Geoffrin, Marie-Thérèse de   zhoh-FRENH, ma-REE-tay-RAYZ duh
gerousia   juh-ROO-see-uh
Gesamtkunstwerk   guh-ZAHMT-koonst-vayrk
Gierek, Edward   GYER-ek, ED-vahrt
Gilgamesh   GILL-guh-mesh
Giolitti, Giovanni   joh-LEE-tee, joe-VAHN-nee
Giotto   JOH-toh
Girondins   juh-RAHN-dinz
glasnost   GLAHZ-nohst
Gleichschaltung   glykh-SHAHL-toonk
Goebbels, Joseph   GUR-bulz
Goethe, Johann Wolfgang von   GUR-tuh, yoh-HAHN VULF-gahnk fun
Gokhale, Gopal   GOH-ku-lay, goh-PAHL
Gömbös, Julius   GUM-buhsh
Gomulka, Wladyslaw   goh-MOOL-kuh, vlah-DIS-lahf
gonfaloniere   gun-fah-loh-NYAY-ray
Gonzaga, Gian Francesco   gun-DZAH-gah, JAHN frahn-CHES-koh
Gorbachev, Mikhail   GOR-buh-chof, meek-HAYL
Göring, Hermann   GUR-ing, hayr-MAHN
Gottwald, Clement   GAWT-valt, klay-MENT
Gouges, Olympe   GOOZH, oh-LAMP
Gracchus, Tiberius and Gaius   GRAK-us, ty-BEER-ee-uss *and* GY-uss
grandi   GRAHN-dee
Grieg, Edvard   GREEG, ED-vart
Groote, Gerard   GROH-tuh
Gropius, Walter   GROH-pee-uss, VAHL-tuh
Grossdeutsch   GROHS-doich
Groza, Petra   GRO-zhuh, PET-ruh

Guan Yin   gwahn-YIN
Guangdong   gwahng-DUNG
Guangxu   gwahng-SHOO
Guangzhou   gwahng-JOH
Guaraní   gwahr-uh-NEE
Guicciardini, Francesco   gwee-char-DEE-nee, frahn-CHESS-koh
Guindorf, Reine   GWIN-dorf, RY-nuh
Guise   GEEZ
Guizot, François   gee-ZOH, frahnh-SWAH
Gujarat   goo-juh-RAHT
Guomindang   gwoh-min-DAHNG
Gustavus Adolphus   goo-STAY-vus uh-DAHL-fuss
Gutenberg, Johannes   GOO-ten-bayrk, yoh-HAH-nuss
Guzman, Gaspar de   goos-MAHN, gahs-PAR day
Habsburg   HAPS-burg
Hadith   huh-DEETH
Hadrian   HAY-dree-un
Hagia Sophia   HAG-ee-uh soh-FEE-uh
hajj   HAJ
Hammurabi   hahm-uh-RAH-bee
Han Gaozu   HAHN gow-DZOO
Han Wudi   HAHN woo-DEE
Handel, George Friedrich   HAN-dul
Hankou   HAHN-kow
Hannibal   HAN-uh-bul
Hanukkah   HAH-nuh-kuh
Harappa   huh-RAP-uh
Hardenberg, Karl von   HAR-den-bayrk, KARL fun
Harun al-Rashid   huh-ROON ah-rah-SHEED
Hassan ben Sabbah   khah-SAHN ben shah-BAH
Hatshepsut   hat-SHEP-soot
Haushofer, Karl   HOWSS-hoh-fuh
Haussmann, Baron   HOWSS-mun
Havel, Vaclav   HAH-vul, VAHT-slahf
Haydn, Franz Joseph   HY-dun, FRAHNTS YO-zef
Hedayat, Sadeq   hay-DY-yaht, sah-DEK
hegemon   HEJ-uh-mun
Hegira   hee-JY-ruh
Heian   hay-AHN
Heisenberg, Werner   HY-zun-bayrk, VAYR-nur
heliaea   HEE-lee-ee
Hellenistic   hel-uh-NIS-tik
helots   HEL-uts
Heraclius   he-ruh-KLY-uss *or* huh-RAK-lee-uss
Herculaneum   hur-kyuh-LAY-nee-um
Herodotus   huh-ROD-uh-tuss
Herophilus   huh-ROF-uh-luss
Herzegovina   HAYRT-suh-guh-VEE-nuh
Herzen, Alexander   HAYRT-sun
Herzl, Theodor   HAYRT-sul, TAY-oh-dor
Heshen   HEH-shen
Hesiod   HEE-see-ud
Hesse, Hermann   HESS-uh, hayr-MAHN
hetairai   huh-TY-ry
Heydrich, Reinhard   HY-drikh, RYN-hart
Hideyoshi, Toyotomi   hee-day-YOH-shee, toh-yoh-TOH-mee
hieroglyph   HY-uh-roh-glif
Hildegard of Bingen   HIL-duh-gard uv BING-un
Hindenburg, Paul von   HIN-den-boork, POWL fun
Hiroshima   hee-roh-SHEE-muh
Hisauchi, Michio   hee-sah-OO-chee, mee-CHEE-OH
Hitler Jugend   HIT-luh YOO-gunt
Ho Chi Minh   HOH CHEE MIN
Höch, Hannah   HURKH
Hohenstaufen   hoh-en-SHTOW-fen
Hohenzollern   hoh-en-TSULL-urn
Hohenzollern-Sigmaringen   hoh-en-TSULL-urn-zig-mah-RING-un
Hokkaido   hoh-KY-doh
Hokusai   HOH-kuh-sy
Holtzendorf   HOHLT-sen-dorf
Homo sapiens   HOH-moh SAY-pee-unz
Honecker, Erich   HOH-nek-uh, AY-reekh
Hong Xiuquan   HOONG shee-oo-CHWAHN

Honorius   hoh-NOR-ee-uss
hoplites   HAHP-lyts
Horace   HOR-uss
Horthy, Miklós   HOR-tee, MIK-lohsh
Hosokawa, Mirohiro   hoh-soh-KAH-wah, mee-roh-HEE-roh
Höss, Rudolf   HURSS
Hoxha, Enver   HAW-jah, EN-vayr
Huang Di   hwahng-DEE
Huayna Inca   WY-nuh INK-uh
Huê   HWAY
Huguenots   HYOO-guh-nots
Huitzilopochtli   WEET-see-loh-POHCHT-lee
Humayun   hoo-MY-yoon
Husák, Gustav   HOO-sahk, goo-STAHV
Ibn Saud   ib-un-sah-OOD
Ibn Sina   ib-un SEE-nuh
iconoclasm   y-KAHN-uh-claz-um
Ictinus   ik-TY-nuss
Ife   EE-fay
Ignatius of Loyola   ig-NAY-shuss uv loi-OH-luh
Il Duce   eel DOO-chay
Île-de-France   EEL-duh-fronhss
illustrés   ee-loo-STRAY
illustrissimi   ee-loo-STREE-see-mee
imperator   im-puh-RAH-tur
imperium   im-PEER-ee-um
intendant   anh-tahnh-DAHNH *or* in-TEN-dunt
Irigoyen, Hipólito   ee-ree-GOH-yen, ee-POH-lee-toh
Isis   Y-sis
Issus   ISS-uss
Iturbide, Agustín de   ee-tur-BEE-day, ah-goo-STEEN dat
ius civile   YOOSS see-VEE-lay
ius gentium   YOOSS GEN-tee-um
ius naturale   YOOSS nah-too-RAH-lay
Izanagi   ee-zah-NAH-gee
Izanami   ee-zah-NAH-mee
Izvestia   iz-VESS-tee-uh
Jacobin   JAK-uh-bin
Jacquerie   zhak-REE
Jadwiga   yahd-VEE-guh
Jagiello   yahg-YEL-oh
Jahn, Friedrich Ludwig   YAHN, FREED-rikh LOOD-vik
jati   JAH-tee
Jaufré Rudel   zhoh-FRAY roo-DEL
Jaurès, Jean   zhaw-RESS, ZHAHNH
Jena   YAY-nuh
Jiang Qing   jahng-CHING
Jiang Zemin   JAHNG zuh-MIN
Jiangxi   JAHNG-shee
jihad   jee-HAHD
Jinnah, Mohammed Ali   JIN-uh, moh-HAM-ed ah-LEE
Joffre, Joseph   ZHUFF-ruh, zhoh-ZEFF
Journal des Savants   zhoor-NAHL day sah-VAHNH
Juana Inés de la Cruz, Sor   HWAH-nuh ee-NAYSS day lah KROOZ, SAWR
Judaea   joo-DEE-uh
Judas Maccabaeus   JOO-dus mak-uh-BEE-uss
Jung, Carl   YOONG
Junkers   YOONG-kurz
Jupiter Optimus Maximus   JOO-puh-tur AHP-tuh-muss MAK-suh-muss
Jurchen   roor-ZHEN
Justinian   juh-STIN-ee-un
Juvenal   JOO-vuh-nul
Ka'aba   KAH-buh
Kádár, János   KAH-dahr, YAH-nush
Kalidasa   kah-lee-DAH-suh
kamikaze   kah-mi-KAH-zee
Kanagawa   kah-nah-GAH-wah
Kanchipuram   kahn-CHEE-poo-rum
Kandinsky, Wassily   kan-DIN-skee, vus-YEEL-yee
Kang Youwei   KAHNG yow-WAY

Kangxi   GANG-zhee
Kanishka   kuh-NISH-kuh
Kant, Immanuel   KAHNT, i-MAHN-yoo-el
Karisma Kapoor   kuh-RIZ-muh kuh-POOR
Karlowitz   KARL-oh-vits
Karlsbad   KARLSS-baht
Kaunitz, Wenzel von   KOW-nits, VENT-sul fun
Kautilya   kow-TIL-yuh
Kazakhstan   ka-zak-STAN *or* kuh-zahk-STAHN
Kemal Atatürk, Mustafa   kuh-MAHL ah-tah-TIRK, moos-tah-FAH
Kenyatta, Jomo   ken-YAHT-uh, JOH-moh
Kerensky, Alexander   kuh-REN-skee
Keynes, John Maynard   KAYNZ
Khadija   kaha-DEE-jah
Khajuraho   khah-joo-RAH-hoh
Khanbaliq   khahn-bah-LEEK
Khomeini, Ayatollah Ruholla   khoh-MAY-nee, ah-yah-TUL-uh roo-HUL-uh
Khrushchev, Nikita   KHROOSH-chawf, nuh-KEE-tuh
Khubilai Khan   KOO-bluh KAHN
Kikuya   ki-KOO-yuh
Kilwa   KIL-wuh
Kim Dae Jung   kim day JOONG
Kim Il Sung   kim il SOONG
Kirghiz   keer-GEEZ
Kleindeutsch   KLYN-doich
Knesset   kuh-NESS-it
Koguryo   koh-GOOR-yoh
Kohl, Helmut   KOHL, HEL-moot
koiné   koi-NAY
Koizumi, Junichero   koh-ee-ZOO-mee, joo-nee-CHAY-roh
kokutai   koh-kuh-TY
Kolchak, Alexander   kul-CHAHK
Kollantai, Alexandra   kul-lun-TY
Kongxi   koong-SHEE
Königgrätz   kur-nig-GRETS
Kornilov, Lavr   kor-NYEE-luff, LAH-vur
Koryo   KAWR-yoh
Kosciuszko, Thaddeus   kaw-SHOOS-koh, tah-DAY-oosh
Kosovo   KAWSS-suh-voh
Kossuth, Louis   KAWSS-uth *or* KAW-shoot
Kostunica, Vojislav   kuh-STOO-nit-suh, VOH-yee-slav
Kosygin, Alexei   kuh-SEE-gun, uh-LEK-say
kouros   KOO-rohss
Koyaanisqatsi   koh-YAH-niss-kaht-see
Kraft durch Freude   KRAHFT doorkh FROI-duh
Kreditanstalt   kray-deet-AHN-shtalt
Krishna   KRISH-nuh
Kristallnacht   kri-STAHL-nahkht
Krupp, Alfred   KROOP
Kuchuk-Kainarji   koo-CHOOK-ky-NAR-jee
Kukulcan   koo-kul-KAHN
kulaks   KOO-lahks
Kulturkampf   kool-TOOR-kahmpf
Kun, Béla   KOON, BAY-luh
Kundera, Milan   koon-DAYR-uh, MEE-lahn
Kursk   KOORSK
Kushanas   koo-SHAH-nuz
Kwasniewski, Aleksander   kwahsh-NYEF-skee
Kyangyi   kyang-YEE
Kyoto   KYOH-toh
Kyushu   KYOO-shoo
la belle époque   lah BEL ay-PUK
Lafayette, marquis de   lah-fay-ET, mar-KEE duh
laissez-faire   less-ay-FAYR
Lamarck, Jean-Baptiste   lah-MARK, ZHAHNH-bah-TEEST
Lancaster   LAN-kas-tur
Lao Tzu   LOW-dzuh
La Rochefoucauld-Liancourt, duc de   lah-RUSH-foo-koh-lee-ahnh-KOOR, dook duh
Las Navas de Tolosa   lahss nah-vahss day toh-LOH-suh
latifundia   lat-i-FOON-dee-uh
Latium   LAY-shum

Latvia   LAT-vee-uh
Launay, marquis de   loh-NAY, mar-KEE duh
Laurier, Wilfred   LOR-ee-ay
Lavoisier, Antoine   lah-vwah-ZYAY, an-TWAHN
Lazar   lah-ZAR
Le Tellier, François Michel   luh tel-YAY, frahnh-SWAH mee-SHEL
Lebensraum   LAY-benz-rowm
Lee Kuan-yew   LEE-kwahn-YOO
Les Demoiselles d'Avignon   lay dem-wah-ZEL dah-vee-NYOHNH
Lespinasse, Julie de   less-pee-NAHSS, zhoo-LEE duh
Lévesque, René   lay-VEK, ruh-NAY
Leviathan   luh-VY-uh-thun
Leyster, Judith   LESS-tur
Liège   lee-EZH
Li Su   lee SOO
Li Yuan   lee YWAHN
Li Zicheng   lee zee-CHENG
Liaodong   LYOW-doong
Licinius   ly-SIN-ee-uss
Liebenfels, Lanz von   LEE-bun-felss, LAHNTS fun
Liebknecht, Karl   LEEP-knekht
Liebknecht, Wilhelm   LEEP-knekht, VIL-helm
Liliuokalani   LIL-ee-uh-woh-kuh-LAH-nee
Lin Zexu   LIN dzeh-SHOO
Lindisfarne   LIN-dis-farn
Lionne, Hugues de   LYUN, OOG duh
List, Friedrich   LIST, FREED-rikh
Liszt, Franz   LIST, FRAHNTS
Lithuania   lith-WAY-nee-uh
Liu Bang   lyoo BAHNG
Liu Ling   lyoo LING
Liu Shaoqi   lyoo show-CHEE
Livy   LIV-ee
Longshan   loong-SHAHN
L'Ouverture, Toussaint   loo-vayr-TOOR, too-SANH
Louvois   loo-VWAH
Lu Xun   loo SHUN
Lucretius   loo-KREE-shus
Luddites   LUD-yts
Ludendorff, Erich   LOO-dun-dorf
Lueger, Karl   LOO-gur
Luftwaffe   LOOFT-vahf-uh
l'uomo universale   LWOH-moh OO-nee-vayr-SAH-lay
Luoyang   LWOH-yahng
Lützen   LURT-sun
Luxemburg, Rosa   LOOK-sum-boork
Lyons   LYOHNH
Maastricht   MAHSS-trikht
Ma'at   MAH-ut
Macao   muh-KOW
Machiavelli, Niccolò   mahk-ee-uh-VEL-ee, nee-koh-LOH
Maginot Line   MA-zhi-noh lyn
Magna Graecia   MAG-nuh GREE-shuh
Magyars   MAG-yarz
Mahabharata   muh-hahb-huh-RAH-tuh
maharaja   mah-huh-RAH-juh
Mahavira   mah-hah-VEE-ruh
Mahayana   mah-huh-YAH-nuh
Mahfouz, Naguib   mahkh-FOOZ, nah-GEEB
Mahmud of Ghazni   MAHKH-mood uv GAHZ-nee
Maimonides   my-MAH-nuh-deez
Maistre, Joseph de   MESS-truh, zhoh-ZEF duh
maius imperium   MY-yoos im-PEE-ree-um
Malaysia   muh-LAY-zhuh
Malaya   muh-LAY-uh
Malenkov, Georgy   muh-LEN-kuf, gyee-OR-gyee
Mallarmé, Stéphane   mah-lahr-MAY, stay-FAHN
Malleus Maleficarum   mal-EE-uss mal-uh-FIK-uh-rum
Malthus, Thomas   MAWL-thuss
Mamallapuram   muh-MAH-luh-poor-um
Manchukuo   man-CHOO-kwoh
Manetho   MAN-uh-thoh
Mao Dun   mow DOON

Mao Zedong   mow zee-DOONG
Marconi, Guglielmo   mahr-KOH-nee, gool-YEL-moh
Marcus Aurelius   MAR-kuss aw-REE-lee-uss
Marcuse, Herbert   mar-KOO-zuh
Marie Antoinette   muh-REE an-twuh-NET
Marius   MAR-ee-uss
Marquez, Gabriel Garcia   mar-KEZ
Marseilles   mar-SAY
Marsiglio of Padua   mar-SIL-yoh uv PAD-juh-wuh
Masaccio   muh-ZAH-choh
Masaryk, Thomas   MAS-uh-rik
Mästlin, Michael   MEST-lin
Matteotti, Giacomo   mat-tay-AHT-tee, JAHK-uh-moh
Maxentius   mak-SEN-shuss
Maximian   mak-SIM-ee-un
Maya   MY-uh
Mazarin   maz-uh-RANH
Mazzini, Giuseppe   maht-SEE-nee, joo-ZEP-pay
Megasthenes   muh-GAS-thuh-neez
Mehmet   meh-MET
Meiji   MAY-jee
Mein Kampf   myn KAHMPF
Meir, Golda   may-EER
Melanchthon, Philip   muh-LANK-tun
Menander   muh-NAN-dur
Mencius   MEN-shuss
Mendeleyev, Dmitri   men-duh-LAY-ef, di-MEE-tree
Mensheviks   MENS-shuh-viks
Mercator, Gerardus   mur-KAY-tur, juh-RAHR-dus
Merian, Maria Sibylla   MAY-ree-un
Merovingian   meh-ruh-VIN-jee-un
Mesopotamia   mess-uh-puh-TAY-mee-uh
Messiaen, Olivier   meh-SYANH, oh-lee-VYAY
mestizos   mess-TEE-zohz
Metaxas, John   muh-tahk-SAHSS
Metternich, Klemens von   MET-ayr-nikh, KLAY-menss fun
Mexica   meh-SHEE-kuh
Michel, Louise   mee-SHEL
Michelangelo   my-kuh-LAN-juh-loh
Mieszko   MYESH-koh
millet   mi-LET
Millet, Jean-François   mi-YEH, ZHAHNH-frahnh-SWAH
Milošević, Slobodan   mi-LOH-suh-vich, sluh-BOH-dahn
Miltiades   mil-TY-uh-deez
Minamoto Yoritomo   mee-nah-MOH-toh, yoh-ree-TOH-moh
Minseito   MEEN-say-toh
Mirandola, Pico della   mee-RAN-doh-lah, PEE-koh DELL-uh
Mishima, Yukio   mi-SHEE-muh, yoo-KEE-oh
missi dominici   MISS-ee doh-MIN-i-chee
Mitterrand, François   MEE-tayr-rahnh, frahnh-SWAH
Moche   moh-CHAY
Moctezuma   mahk-tuh-ZOO-muh
Mogadishu   moh-guh-DEE-shoo
Mohács   MOH-hach
Mohenjo-Daro   mo-HEN-jo-DAH-roh
Moldavia   mohl-DAY-vee-uh
Moldova   mohl-DOH-vuh
Molière, Jean-Baptiste   mohl-YAYR, ZHAHNH-bah-TEEST
Molotov, Vyacheslav   MAHL-uh-tawf, vyich-chiss-SLAHF
Mombasa   mahm-BAH-suh
Monet, Claude   moh-NEH, KLOHD
Mongkut   MAWNG-koot
Montaigne, Michel de   mahn-TAYN, mee-SHEL duh
Montefeltro, Federigo da   mahn-tuh-FELL-troh,
    fay-day-REE-goh dah
Montesquieu   MOHN-tess-kyoo
Montessori, Maria   mahn-tuh-SOR-ee
Morisot, Berthe   mor-ee-ZOH, BAYRT
Mozambique   moh-zam-BEEK
Mozart, Wolfgang Amadeus   MOH-tsart, VULF-gahng
    ah-muh-DAY-uss
Muawiya   moo-AH-wee-yah
Mudejares   moo-theh-KHAH-rayss

Mughal   MOO-gul
Muhammad   moh-HAM-ud *or* moh-HAHM-ud
Mühlberg   MURL-bayrk
Mukden   MOOK-dun
mulattoes   muh-LAH-tohz
Mumbai   MUM-by
Müntzer, Thomas   MURN-tsur
Murad   moo-RAHD
Musharraf, Pervaiz   moo-SHAHR-uf, pur-VEZ
Muslim   MUZ-lum
Mutsuhito   moo-tsoo-HEE-toh
Myanmar   MYAN-mahr
Mycenaean   my-suh-NEE-un
Nabonidas   nab-uh-NY-duss
Nabopolassar   nab-uh-puh-LASS-ur
Nagasaki   nah-gah-SAH-kee
Nagy, Imry   NAHJ, IM-ray
Nanjing   nan-JING
Nantes   NAHNT
Nara   NAH-rah
Nasrin, Taslima   naz-REEN, tah-SLEE-muh
Nasser, Gamal Abdul   NAH-sur, juh-MAHL ahb-DOOL
Navarre   nuh-VAHR
Nebuchadnezzar   neb-uh-kud-NEZZ-ur
Nehru, Jawaharlal   NAY-roo, juh-WAH-hur-lahl
Nero   NEE-roh
Nerva   NUR-vuh
Netanyahu, Benjamin   net-ahn-YAH-hoo
Neumann, Balthasar   NOI-mahn, BAHL-tuh-zahr
Neumann, Solomon   NOI-mahn
Neustria   NOO-stree-uh
Nevsky, Alexander   NYEF-skee
Newcomen, Thomas   NYOO-kuh-mun *or* nyoo-KUM-mun
Ngo Dinh Diem   GOH din DYEM
Nguyen   NGWEN
Nicias   NISS-ee-uss
Nietzsche, Friedrich   NEE-chuh, FREED-rikh
Nimwegen   NIM-vay-gun
Ninhursaga   nin-HUR-sah-guh
Nkrumah, Kwame   en-KROO-muh, KWAH-may
nobiles   no-BEE-layz
Nobunaga, Oda   noh-buh-NAH-guh, OH-dah
Nogarola, Isotta   noh-guh-ROH-luh, ee-ZAHT-uh
Novalis, Friedrich   noh-VAH-lis, FREED-rikh
Novotny, Antonin   noh-VAHT-nee, AHN-toh-nyeen
novus homo   NOH-vuss HOH-moh
nuoc mam   NWAHK MAHM
Nyame   NYAH-may
Nystadt   NEE-shtaht
Oaxaca   wah-HAH-kuh
Octavian   ahk-TAY-vee-un
Odoacer   oh-doh-AY-sur
Odysseus   oh-DISS-ee-uss
Oe, Kenzaburo   OH-ay, ken-zuh-BOO-roh
Olivares   oh-lee-BAH-rayss
Olmec   AHL-mek *or* OHL-mek
Omar Khayyam   OH-mar ky-YAHM
Ometeotl   oh-met-tee-AH-tul
optimates   ahp-tuh-MAH-tayz
Oresteia   uh-res-TY-uh
Orkhan   or-KHAHN
Osaka   oh-SAH-kuh
Osama bin Laden   oh-SAH-muh bin LAH-dun
Osiris   oh-SY-russ
Ostara   oh-STAH-ruh
Ostpolitik   OHST-poh-lee-teek
ostrakon   AHSS-truh-kahn
Ostrogoths   AHSS-truh-gahthss
Ovid   OH-vid
Oxenstierna, Axel   OOK-sen-shur-nah, AHK-sul
Pacal   pa-KAL
Pachakuti   pah-chah-KOO-tee
Paekche   bayk-JEE

Pagan   puh-GAHN
Paleologus   pay-lee-AWL-uh-guss
Panaetius   puh-NEE-shuss
Pankhurst, Emmeline   PANK-hurst
papal curia   PAY-pul KYOOR-ee-uh
Papen, Franz von   PAH-pun, FRAHNTS fun
Paracelsus   par-uh-SELL-suss
Parlement   par-luh-MAHNH
Parti Québécois   par-TEE kay-bek-KWAH
Pascal, Blaise   pass-KAHL, BLEZ
Pasternak, Boris   PASS-tur-nak, buh-REESS
Pasteur, Louis   pass-TOOR, LWEE
Pataliputra   pah-tah-lee-POO-truh
paterfamilias   pay-tur-fuh-MEEL-yus
Pensées   pahnh-SAY
Pentateuch   PEN-tuh-took
Pepin   PEP-in *or* pay-PANH
perestroika   per-uh-STROI-kuh
Pergamum   PUR-guh-mum
Pericles   PER-i-kleez
perioeci   per-ee-EE-see
Perpetua   pur-PET-choo-uh
Pétain, Henri   pay-TANH, AHN-ree
Petite Roquette   puh-TEET raw-KET
Petrarch   PEE-trark *or* PET-trark
Petronius   pi-TROH-nee-uss
phalansteries   fuh-LAN-stuh-reez
philosophe   fee-loh-ZAWF
Phintys   FIN-tiss
Phoenicians   fuh-NEE-shunz
Photius   FOH-shuss
Picasso, Pablo   pi-KAH-soh
Pietism   PY-uh-tiz-um
Pilsudski, Joseph   peel-SOOT-skee
Piscator, Erwin   PIS-kuh-tor, AYR-vin
Pisistratus   puh-SIS-truh-tuss
Pissarro, Camille   pee-SAH-roh, kah-MEEL
Pizan, Christine de   pee-ZAHN, kris-TEEN duh
Pizarro, Francesco   puh-ZAHR-oh, frahn-CHESS-koh
Planck, Max   PLAHNK
Plantagenet   plan-TAJ-uh-net
Plassey   PLASS-ee
Plato   PLAY-toh
Plautus   PLAW-tuss
plebiscita   pleb-i-SEE-tuh
Poincaré, Raymond   pwanh-kah-RAY, ray-MOHNH
polis   POH-liss
politiques   puh-lee-TEEKS
Pollaiuolo, Antonio   pohl-ly-WOH-loh
Poltava   pul-TAH-vuh
Polybius   puh-LIB-ee-uss
Pombal, marquis de   pum-BAHL, mar-KEE duh
Pompadour, madame de   POM-puh-door, mah-DAHM duh
Pompeii   pahm-PAY
Pompey   PAHM-pee
pontifex maximus   PAHN-ti-feks MAK-si-muss
Popul Vuh   puh-PUL VOO
populares   PAWP-oo-lahr-ayss
populo grasso   PAWP-oo-loh GRAH-soh
Postumus   PAHS-choo-muss
Potosí   poh-toh-SEE
Potsdam   PAHTS-dam
Poussin, Nicholas   poo-SANH, NEE-koh-lah
Praecepter Germaniae   PREE-sep-tur gayr-MAHN-ee-ee
praetor   PREE-tur
Prakrit   PRAH-krit
Pravda   PRAHV-duh
Primo de Rivera   PREE-moh day ri-VAY-ruh
primogeniture   pree-moh-JEN-i-chur
princeps   PRIN-seps
Principia   prin-SIP-ee-uh
Procopius   pruh-KOH-pee-uss
procurator   PROK-yuh-ray-tur

Ptolemaic tahl-uh-MAY-ik
Ptolemy TAHL-uh-mee
Pugachev, Emelyan poo-guh-CHAWF, yim-yil-YAHN
Punic PYOO-nik
Putin, Vladimir POO-tin
Pyongyang pyawng-YANG
Pyrrhic PEER-ik
Pyrrhus PEER-uss
Pythagoras puh-THAG-uh-russ
Qajar kuh-JAHR
Qianlong CHAN-loong
Qin CHIN
Qin Shi Huangdi chin shee hwang-DEE
Qing CHING
Qiu Jin chee-oo-JIN
Qu CHOO
quadrivium kwah-DRIV-ee-um
quaestors KWES-turs
querelle des femmes keh-REL day FAHM
Quesnay, François keh-NAY, frahnn-SWAH
Quetzelcoatl KWET-sul-koh-AHT-ul
Quraishi koo-RY-shee
Qur'an kuh-RAN *or* kuh-RAHN
Rabe'a of Qozdar rah-BAY-uh uv kuz-DAHR
Racine, Jean-Baptiste ra-SEEN, ZHAHNH-buh-TEEST
Rahner, Karl RAH-nur
Rajput RAHJ-poot
Rama RAH-mah
Ramayana rah-mah-YAH-nah
Ramcaritmanas RAM-kah-rit-MAH-nuz
Rameses RAM-uh-seez
Raphael RAFF-ee-ul
Rasputin rass-PYOO-tin
Rathenau, Walter RAH-tuh-now, VAHL-tuh
Realpolitik ray-AHL-poh-lee-teek
Realschule ray-AHL-shoo-luh
Reichsrat RYKHSS-raht
Reichstag RYKHSS-tahk
Rembrandt van Rijn REM-brant vahn RYN
Rémy, Nicholas ray-MEE, nee-koh-LAH
Renan, Ernst re-NAHNH
Rhee, Syngman REE, SING-mun
Ricci, Matteo REE-chee, ma-TAY-oh
Richelieu REESH-uh-lyuh
Ricimer RISS-uh-mur
Rig Veda RIK-vee-duh
Rikstag RIKS-tahk
Rilke, Rainer Maria RILL-kuh, RY-nuh mah-REE-uh
Rimbaud, Arthur ram-BOH, ar-TOOR
risorgimento ree-SOR-jee-men-toh
Riza-i-Abassi ree-ZAH-yah-BAH-see
Robespierre, Maximilien ROHBZ-pyayr, mak-see-meel-YENH
Rococo ruh-KOH-koh
Rocroi roh-KRWAH
Röhm, Ernst RURM
Rommel, Erwin RAHM-ul
Romulus Augustulus RAHM-yuh-luss ow-GOOS-chuh-luss
Rossbach RAWSS-bahkh
Rousseau, Jean-Jacques roo-SOH, ZHAHNH-ZHAHK
Rurik ROO-rik
Ryswick RYZ-wik
Sacrosancta sak-roh-SANK-tuh
Saikaku sy-KAH-koo
Saint-Just sanh-ZHOOST
Saint-Simon, Henri de sanh-see-MOHNH, ahnh-REE duh
Sakharov, Andrei SAH-kuh-rawf, ahn-DRAY
Saladin SAL-uh-din
Salazar, Antonio SAL-uh-zahr
Sallust SAL-ust
Samnite SAM-nyt
Samudragupta suh-mood-ruh-GOOP-tuh
samurai SAM-uh-ry
San Martín, José de san mar-TEEN, hoh-SAY day

Sandinista san-duh-NEES-tuh
sans-culottes sahnh-koo-LUT *or* sanz-koo-LAHTSS
Sarraut, Albert sah-ROH, ahl-BAYR
Sartre, Jean-Paul SAR-truh, ZHAHNH-POHL
Sassanid suh-SAN-id
sati suh-TEE
satrap SAY-trap
satrapy SAY-truh-pee
Satyricon sa-TEER-uh-kahn
Schaumburg-Lippe SHOWM-boorkh-LEE-puh
Schleswig-Holstein SHLESS-vik-HOHL-shtyn
Schlieffen, Alfred von SHLEE-fun, AHL-fret fun
Schliemann, Heinrich SHLEE-mahn, HYN-rikh
Schmidt, Helmut SHMIT, HEL-moot
Schönberg, Arnold SHURN-bayrk, AR-nawlt
Schönborn SHURN-bawn
Schönerer, Georg von SHURN-uh-ruh, GAY-ork fun
Schröder, Gerhard SHRUR-duh, GAYR-hahrt
Schuschnigg, Karl von SHOOSH-nik, KAHRL fun
Schutzmannschaft SHOOTS-mahn-shahft
Scipio Aemilianus SEE-pee-oh ee-mil-YAY-nuss
Scipio Africanus SEE-pee-oh af-ree-KAY-nuss
scriptoria skrip-TOR-ee-uh
Ségur say-GOO-uh
Sejm SAYM
Seleucid suh-LOO-sid
Seleucus suh-LOO-kuss
Seljuk SEL-jook
Seneca SEN-uh-kuh
Sephardic suh-FAHR-dik
Septimius Severus sep-TIM-ee-uss se-VEER-uss
serjents sayr-ZHAHNH
Sforza, Ludovico SFORT-sah, loo-doh-VEE-koh
Shakuntala shah-koon-TAH-lah
Shalmaneser shal-muh-NEE-zur
Shandong SHAHN-doong
Shang SHAHNG
Shari'a shah-REE-uh
Shen Nong shun-NOONG
Shi'ite SHEE-YT
Shidehara shee-de-HAH-rah
Shiga Naoya SHEE-gah NOW-yah
Shikoku shee-KOH-koo
Shimonoseki shee-moh-noh-SEK-ee
Shiva SHIV-uh
Shotoku Taishi shoh-TOH-koo ty-EE-shee
Sichuan SEECH-wahn
Siddhartha Gautama si-DAR-tuh GAW-tuh-muh
Sieveking, Amalie SEE-vuh-king, uh-MAHL-yuh
Sieyès, Abbé syay-YESS, ab-BAY
Sigiriya see-gee-REE-uh
signoria seen-YOR-ee-uh
Silla SIL-uh
Silva, Luis Inácio Lula de LWEES ee-NAH-syoh LOO-luh duh-SEEL-vuh
Sima Qian SEE-mah chee-AHN
sine manu sy-nee-MAY-noo
sipahis suh-PAH-heez
Sita SEE-tuh
Slovenia sloh-VEE-nee-uh
Société Générale soh-see-ay-TAY zhay-nay-RAHL
Socrates SAHK-ruh-teez
Solon SOH-lun
Solzhenitsyn, Alexander sohl-zhuh-NEET-sin
Somme SUM
Song Taizu SOONG ty-DZOO
Soong, Mei-ling SOONG, may-LING
Sophocles SAHF-uh-kleez
Sorel, Georges soh-RELL, ZHORZH
Spartacus SPAR-tuh-kuss
Spartiates spar-tee-AH-teez
Speer, Albert SHPAYR
Speransky, Michael spyuh-RAHN-skee

Spinoza, Benedict de   spi-NOH-zuh
squadristi   skwah-DREES-tee
Srebrenica   sreb-bruh-NEET-suh
stadholder   STAD-hohl-dur
Staël, Germaine de   STAHL, zhayr-MEN duh
Stakhanov, Alexei   stuh-KHAH-nuf, uh-LEK-say
Stasi   SHTAH-see
Stauffenberg, Claus von   SHTOW-fen-berk, KLOWSS fun
Stein, Heinrich von   SHTYN, HYN-rikh fun
Stilicho   STIL-i-koh
Stoicism   STOH-i-siz-um
Stolypin, Peter   stuh-LIP-yin
strategoi   strah-tay-GOH-ee
Stravinsky, Igor   struh-VIN-skee, EE-gor
Stresemann, Gustav   SHTRAY-zuh-mahn, GOOS-tahf
Strozzi, Alessandra   STRAWT-see
Struensee, John Frederick   SHTROO-un-zay
Sturmabteilung   SHTOORM-ap-ty-loonk
Sudetenland   soo-DAY-tun-land
sudra   SOO-druh *or* SHOO-druh
Suger   soo-ZHAYR
Suharto   soo-HAHR-toh
Sui Wendi   SWEE wen-DEE
Sui Yangdi   SWEE yahng-DEE
Sukarno   soo-KAHR-noh
Sukarnoputri, Megawati   soo-kahr-noh-POO-tree, meg-uh-WAH-tee
Suleiman   SOO-lay-mahn
Suleymaniye   soo-lay-MAHN-ee-eh
Sulla   SUL-uh
Sumerians   soo-MER-ee-unz *or* soo-MEER-ee-unz
Summa Theologica   SOO-muh tay-oh-LAH-jee-kuh
Sun Yat-sen   SOON yaht-SEN
Suppululiumas   suh-PIL-oo-LEE-uh-muss
Suttner, Bertha von   ZOOT-nuh, BAYR-tuh fun
Swaziland   SWAH-zee-land
Symphonie Fantastique   SANH-foh-nee fahn-tas-TEEK
Taaffe, Edward von   TAH-fuh, ED-vahrt fun
Taban lo Liyong   tuh-BAN loh-lee-YAWNG
Tacitus   TASS-i-tuss
Tahuantinsuyu   tuh-HWAHN-tin-SOO-yoo
Taika   TY-kuh
taille   TY
Taiping   ty-PING
Talleyrand, Prince   tah-lay-RAHNH
Tanganyika   tang-an-YEE-kuh
Tanizaki, Junichiro   tan-i-ZAH-kee, jun-i-CHEE-roh
Tanzania   tan-zuh-NEE-uh
Temuchin   TEM-yuh-jin
Tenochtitlán   tay-nawch-teet-LAHN
Teotihuacán   tay-noh-tee-hwa-KAHN
Tertullian   tur-TUL-yun
Texcoco   tess-KOH-koh
Thales   THAY-leez
Theocritus   thee-AHK-ruh-tuss
Theodora   thee-uh-DOR-uh
Theodoric   thee-AHD-uh-rik
Theodosius   thee-uh-DOH-shuss
Theognis   thee-AHG-nuss
Theravada   thay-ruh-VAH-duh
Thermopylae   thur-MAHP-uh-lee
Thiers, Adolphe   TYAYR, a-DAWLF
Thucydides   thoo-SID-uh-deez
Thutmosis   thoot-MOH-suss
Tiananmen   TYAHN-ahn-men
Tianjin   TYAHN-jin
Tiberius   ty-BEER-ee-uss
Tiglath-pileser   TIG-lath-py-LEE-zur
Tikal   tee-KAHL
Tirpitz, Admiral von   TEER-pits
Tisza, István   TISS-ah, ISHT-vun
Tito   TEE-toh
Titus   TY-tuss

Tlaloc   tuh-lah-LOHK
Tlaltelolco   tuh-lahl-teh-LOH-koh
Tlaxcala   tuh-lah-SKAH-lah
Toer, Pramoedya   TOOR, pra-MOO-dyah
Tojo, Hideki   TOH-joh, hee-DEK-ee
Tokugawa Ieyasu   toh-koo-GAH-wah ee-yeh-YAH-soo
Tolstoy, Leo   TOHL-stoy
Tongmenghui   toong-meng-HWEE
Topa Inca   TOH-puh INK-uh
Topkapi   tawp-KAH-pee
Torah   TOR-uh
Tordesillas   tor-day-SEE-yass
Touré, Sékou   too-RAY, say-KOO
Trajan   TRAY-jun
Trevithick, Richard   TREV-uh-thik
Tristan, Flora   TRISS-tun
trivium   TRIV-ee-um
Trotsky, Leon   TRAHT-skee
Troyes   TRWAH
Trudeau, Pierre   troo-DOH, PYAYR
Trufaut, François   troo-FOH, frahnh-SWAH
Tsara, Tristan   TSAHR-rah, TRISS-tun
Tübingen   TUR-bing-un
Tughluq   tug-LUK
Tulsidas   tool-see-DAHSS
Tutankhamun   too-tang-KAH-mun
Tyche   TY-kee
Uccello, Paolo   oo-CHEL-oh, POW-loh
uhuru   oo-HOO-roo
uji   OO-jee
Ulbricht, Walter   OOL-brikht, VAHL-tuh
Ulianov, Vladimir   ool-YA-nuf
Umayyads   oo-MY-adz
Unam Sanctam   OO-nahm **SAHNK-tahm**
universitas   yoo-nee-VAYR-see-tahss
Utamaro   OO-tah-mah-roh
Uzbekistan   ooz-BEK-i-stan
vaisya   VISH-yuh
Vajpayee, Atal Behari   VAHJ-py-ee, AH-tahl bi-HAH-ree
Valens   VAY-linz
Valentinian   val-en-TIN-ee-un
Valéry, Paul   vah-lay-REE, POHL
Valois   val-WAH
Van de Velde, Theodore   vahn duh VEL-duh, TAY-oh-dor
van Eyck, Jan   vahn YK *or* van AYK, YAHN
van Gogh, Vincent   van GOH
Vasa, Gustavus   VAH-suh, GUSS-tuh-vuss
Vega, Lope de   VAY-guh, LOH-pay day
Velde, Theodor van de   VEL-duh, tay-oh-DOR vahn duh
Vendée   vahnh-DAY
Venetia   vuh-NEE-shuh
Verdun   vur-DUN
Vergerio, Pietro Paolo   vur-JEER-ee-oh, PYAY-troh POW-loh
Versailles   vayr-SY
Vesalius, Andreas   vuh-SAY-lee-uss, ahn-DRAY-uss
Vespasian   vess-PAY-zhun
Vespucci, Amerigo   vess-POO-chee, ahm-ay-REE-goh
Vesuvius   vuh-SOO-vee-uss
Vichy   VISH-ee
Vierzehnheiligen   feer-tsayn-HY-li-gen
Virchow, Rudolf   FEER-khoh, ROO-dulf
Virgil   VUR-jul
Visconti, Giangaleazzo   vees-KOHN-tee, jahn-gah-lay-AH-tsoh
Vishnu   VISH-noo
Visigoths   VIZ-uh-gathz
Voilquin, Suzanne   vwahl-KANH, soo-ZAHN
Volk   FULK
Volkschulen   FULK-shoo-lun
Voltaire   vohl-TAYR
Wafd   WAHFT
Wagner, Richard   VAG-nur, RIKH-art
Walesa, Lech   vah-WENT-sah, LEK
Wallachia   wah-LAY-kee-uh

Wallenstein, Albrecht von   VAHL-en-shtyn, AWL-brekht
Wang Anshi   WAHNG ahn-SHEE
Wang Shuo   wahng-SHWOH
Wang Tao   wahng-TOW
Wannsee   VAHN-zay
Watteau, Antoine   wah-TOH, AHN-twahn
Weill, Kurt   VYL
Weizsäcker, Richard von   VYTS-zek-ur, RIKH-art
wergeld   WUR-geld
Windischgrätz, Alfred   VIN-dish-grets
Winkelmann, Maria   VINK-ul-mahn
Witte, Sergei   VIT-uh, syir-GYAY
Wittenberg   VIT-ten-bayrk
Wojtyla, Karol   voy-TEE-wah, KAH-rul
Wollstonecraft, Mary   WULL-stun-kraft
Wu Zhao   woo-ZHOW
Würzburg   VURTS-boork
Wyclif, John   WIK-lif
Xavier, Francis   ZAY-vee-ur
Xerxes   ZURK-seez
Xhosa   KHOH-suh
Xia   SHEE-ah
Xian   SHEE-ahn
Xiangyang   SHYAHNG-yahng
Ximenes   khee-MAY-ness
Xinjiang   SHIN-jyahng
Xiongnu   SHYAHNG-noo
Xui Tong   shwee-TOONG
Yahweh   YAH-way
Yan'an   yuh-NAHN
Yang Guifei   yahng gwee-FAY
Yangshao   yahng-SHOW
Yangtze   YANG-tsee

Yayoi   yah-YO-ee
Yeats, William Butler   YAYTS
Yeltsin, Boris   YELT-sun
Yi Jing   yee-JING
Yi Song-gye   YEE song-YEE
yishuv   YISH-uv
Yuan Shikai   yoo-AHN shee-KY
Yudhoyono, Susilo   yood-hoh-YOH-noh, soo-SEE-loh
Yue   yoo-EH
zaibatsu   zy-BAHT-soo *or Japanese* DZY-bahtss
Zanj   ZANJ
Zanzibar   ZAN-zi-bar
Zasulich, Vera   tsah-SOO-likh
Zemsky Sobor   ZEM-skee suh-BOR
zemstvos   ZEMPST-vohz
Zeno   ZEE-noh
Zenobia   zuh-NOH-bee-uh
zeppelin   ZEP-puh-lin
Zeus   ZOOSS
Zhang Zhidong   JANG jee-DOONG
Zhao Ziyang   JOW dzee-YAHNG
Zhenotdel   zhen-ut-DEL
Zhivkov, Todor   ZHIV-kuff, toh-DOR
Zia ul-Haq, Mohammad   ZEE-uh ool-HAHK
ziggurat   ZIG-uh-rat
Zimmermann, Dominikus   TSIM-ur-mahn, doh-MEE-nee-kooss
Zinzendorf, Nikolaus von   TSIN-sin-dorf, NEE-koh-LOWSS fun
Zola, Émile   ZOH-lah, ay-MEEL
zollverein   TSOHL-fuh-ryn
Zoroaster   ZOR-oh-ass-tur
Zuanzong   zwahn-ZOONG
Zuni   ZOO-nee
Zwingli, Ulrich   TSFING-lee, OOL-rikh

MAP CREDITS

The authors wish to acknowledge their use of the following books as reference in preparing the maps listed here:

SPOT MAP, PAGE 31   Geoffrey Barraclough, ed., *Times Atlas of World History*, (Maplewood, N.J.: Hammond Inc., 1978), p. 65.

MAP 3.1   Geoffrey Barraclough, ed., *Times Atlas of World History*, (Maplewood, N.J.: Hammond Inc., 1978), p. 63.

MAP 5.4   Hammond Past Worlds: *The Times Atlas of Archeology*, (Maplewood, N.J.: Hammond Inc. 1988), pp. 190–191.

MAP 5.5   Conrad Schirokauer, *A Brief History of Chinese and Japanese Civilizations*, 2d ed. (San Diego: Harcourt Brace Jovanovich, 1989), p. 52.

MAP 6.2   Michael Coe, Dean Snow and Elizabeth Benson, *Atlas of Ancient America* (New York: Facts on File, 1988), p. 144.

MAP 6.3   Geoffrey Barraclough, ed., *Times Atlas of World History*, (Maplewood, N.J.: Hammond Inc., 1978), p. 47.

MAP 6.4   Phillipa Fernandez-Arnesto, *Atlas of World Exploration*, (New York: Harper Collins, 1991), p. 35.

MAP 6.5   Geoffrey Barraclough, ed., *Times Atlas of World History*, (Maplewood, N.J.: Hammond Inc., 1978), p. 47.

MAP 7.3   Geoffrey Barraclough, ed., *Times Atlas of World History*, (Maplewood, N.J.: Hammond Inc., 1978), pp. 134–135.

MAP 7.4   Geoffrey Barraclough, ed., *Times Atlas of World History*, (Maplewood, N.J.: Hammond Inc., 1978), p. 135.

MAP 8.1   Geoffrey Barraclough, ed., *Times Atlas of World History*, (Maplewood, N.J.: Hammond Inc., 1978), pp. 44–45.

MAP 8.4   Geoffrey Barraclough, ed., *Times Atlas of World History*, (Maplewood, N.J.: Hammond Inc., 1978), pp. 136–137.

MAP 9.2   Michael Edwardes, *A History of India* (London: Thames and Hudson, 1961), p. 79.

MAP 10.1   John K. Fairbank, Edwin O. Reischauer, and Albert M. Craig, *East Asia: Tradition and Transformation* (Boston: Houghton Mifflin, 1973), p. 103.

SPOT MAP, PAGE 273   Albert Hermann, *An Historical Atlas of China* (Chicago: Aidine, 1966), p. 13.

MAP 11.1   John K. Fairbank, Edwin O. Reischauer, and Albert M. Craig, *East Asia: Tradition and Transformation* (Boston: Houghton Mifflin, 1973), p. 363.

DOCUMENTS

This page constitutes an extension of the copyright page. We have made every effort to trace the ownership of all copyrighted material and to secure permission from copyright holders. In the event of any question arising as to the use of any material, we will be pleased to make the necessary corrections in future printings. Thanks are due to the following authors, publishers, and agents for permission to use the material indicated.

CHAPTER 1

THE CODE OF HAMMURABI 12
Pritchard, James B., ed., *Ancient Near Eastern Texts Relating to the Old Testament*, 3rd Edition with Supplement. Copyright © 1950, 1955, 1969, renewed 1978 by Princeton University Press. Reprinted by permission of Princeton University Press.

THE SIGNIFICANCE OF THE NILE RIVER AND THE PHARAOH 15
Pritchard, James B., ed., *Ancient Near Eastern Texts Relating to the Old Testament*, 3rd Edition with Supplement. Copyright © 1950, 1955, 1969, renewed 1978 by Princeton University Press. Reprinted by permission of Princeton University Press. "Hymn to the Pharoah": Reprinted from The Literature Of The Ancient Egyptians, Adolf Ermann. Copyright © 1927 by E. P. Dutton.

THE COVENANT AND THE LAW: THE BOOK OF EXODUS 22
Reprinted from the Holy Bible, New International Version.

THE ASSYRIAN MILITARY MACHINE 24
"King Sennacherib (704–681 B.C.E.) Describes a battle with the Elamites in 691": Reprinted with permission from Pan Macmillan, London, from *The Might That Was Assyria* by H. W. Saggs. Copyright © 1984 by Sidgwick & Jackson Limited. Pritchard, James B., ed., Ancient Near Eastern Texts Relating to the Old Testament, 3rd Edition with Supplement. Copyright © 1950, 1955, 1969, renewed 1978 by Princeton University Press. Reprinted by permission of Princeton University Press.

CHAPTER 2

THE ORIGINS OF KINGSHIP 35
Excerpt from *Sources of Indian Tradition*, by William Theodore de Bary. Copyright © 1988 by Columbia University Press.

THE DUTIES OF A KING 36
Excerpt from *Sources of Indian Tradition*, by William Theodore de Bary. Copyright © 1988 by Columbia University Press. Reprinted with the permission of the publisher.

SOCIAL CLASSES IN ANCIENT INDIA 37
Excerpt from *Sources of Indian Tradition*, by William Theodore de Bary. Copyright © 1988 by Columbia University Press. Reprinted with the permission of the publisher.

HOW TO ACHIEVE ENLIGHTENMENT 44
From *The Teachings of the Compassionate Buddha*, E. A. Burtt, ed. Copyright 1955 by Mentor. Used by permission of the E. A. Burtt Estate.

CHAPTER 3

THE WAY OF THE GREAT LEARNING 60
Excerpt from *Sources of Chinese Tradition*, by William Theodore de Bary. Copyright © 1960 by Columbia University Press. Reprinted with the permission of the publisher.

THE DAOIST ANSWER TO CONFUCIANISM 62
From *The Way of Lao Tzu (Tao-te Ching)*, by Wing-Tsit Chan, trans. Copyright © 1963 by Macmillan College Publishing Company, Inc.

THE ART OF WAR 64
From *Sun Tzu: The Art of War*, Ralph D. Sawyer (Boulder: Westview Press, 1994), pp. 177–179.

MEMORANDUM ON THE BURNING OF BOOKS 65
Excerpt from *Sources of Chinese Tradition*, by William Theodore de Bary. Copyright © 1960 by Columbia University Press. Reprinted with the permission of the publisher.

CHAPTER 4

HOMER'S IDEAL OF EXCELLENCE 78
From *The Iliad* by Homer, translated by E. V. Rieu (Penguin Classics 1950). Copyright © the Estate of R. V. Rieu, 1946. Reproduced by permission of Penguin Books Ltd.

THE LYCURGAN REFORMS 81
From Plutarch, *The Lives of the Noble Grecians and Romans*, translated by John Dryden, and revised by Arthur Hugh Clough. (New York: Modern Library).

HOUSEHOLD MANAGEMENT AND THE ROLE OF THE ATHENIAN WIFE 88
From *Xenophon: Memoribilia and Oeconomicus*, Volume IV, Loeb Classical Library 168, translated by E. C. Marchant, Cambridge, Mass.: Harvard University Press, 1923. The Loeb Classical Library ® is a registered trademark of the President and Fellows of Harvard College.

ALEXANDER MEETS AN INDIAN KING 91
From *The Campaigns of Alexander* by Arrian, translated by Aubrey de Selincourt. Viking Press, 1976.

CHAPTER 5

CINCINNATUS SAVES ROME: A ROMAN MORALITY TALE 98
From *The Early History of Rome* by Livy, translated by Aubrey de Selincourt (Penguin Classics, 1960). Copyright © Aubrey de Selincourt, 1960. Reproduced by permission of Penguin Books Ltd.

in Classical Greece, 88–89
in India, 30–31, 38–40, 203–04
in Latin America, 132, **139b**
in medieval Europe, 264–65
in Roman Empire, 105–07
in Southeast Asia, 209–10
in Sumerian city-states, 10
in Vietnam, 256
Socrates (philosopher), 86
Solomon (Israelite king 970-930 B.C.E.), 21
Solon (Athenian ruler), 81
Somalia, 177–78
Song Taizu (Chinese emperor), 218
Son-Jara (African ruler), 188
Sophocles (Greek author), 85
South America, **136m**
　Arawak civilization, 142
　emergence of civilization in, 9, 135
　Inca Empire of, 136–39
　Moche civilization, 136
　timelines in history, **143b**
Southeast Asia, **198m**
　agriculture c.5000 B. C. E., 6
　area and geography defined, 207
　chronology of, **209t**
　discovery of bronze, 8, **56b**
　Indian influence on, 209
　religion in, 210–12
　society and daily life in, 209–10
　states and societies of, 207–09
　timelines in history, **212b**, **284b**
　trade with Middle East, **157b**
　See also specific country byname
"Southern ape-men" (*australopithecines*), 5
Southwest Asia, **92m**
　Arab civilization of, 146
　colonization by Greece, 91–92
　Indo-European peoples in, 20, 45–46
　Seljuk Turk expansion into, 153–54
　See also specific country byname
Spain, **150m**
　Byzantine Empire in, 164
　expansion of Islam to, **163p**
　Greek colonization in, 79
　Muslim control of, 151, 281
　New World conquests by, 124, 135, 139–40,
　　276b
　Paleolithic Age activities in, 5–6
　Roman conquests in, 100–101
　Visigoth kingdom, 109, 151, 260
Spartacus (Roman gladiator), 107
Sri Lanka (Ceylon), 30, 45–47, 210
Stoicism, 93–94, 106
Stone tools, 5, 7
　See also Tools
Stonehenge (c.2100-1900 B.C.E.), **20p**
Sudan, 18, 170, **172b**
Sufism, 160–**61b**, **161b**
Sui Wendi (Chinese emperor), 217
Sui Yangdi (Chinese emperor), 217
Sumerian civilization, **4p**, 9, **10m**, **11m**
Sun Tzu (military strategist), **64b**
Sunni Muslims, 151–54
Swahili peoples, 173, 178
Syria
　Arab expansion in, 149, 154, 166
　Byzantine Empire in, 164
　conquest by Alexander the Great, 89
　Egyptian armies in, 16–17
　Hellenistic Seleucids kingdom of, 91–**92m**
　importance in Middle East trade, 265
Syriac, Semitic language of, **11t**

Tacitus (Roman historian), **108b**
Tale of the Marshes, 234
Tales from 1001 Nights(Khayyam), 160

Tamerlane (Timur-i-lang, Mongol ruler), 199,
　200m, 201
Tang Taizong (Li Shimin, Chinese emperor),
　217, 226
Tantrism, 231
Tanzania, 178
Taoism. *See* Daoism (Taoism)
Tariq (Berber commander), 151
Tea/tea industry
　Chinese trade in, 223–24
　Japanese tea ceremony, 251
　origins in Burma, 224
Technological development
　bronze and iron casting, 68–69
　in China, 57–58, 113–14, 221–22
　Hellenistic period and, 93
　invention of the wheel, 10
　maps and maritime navigation, **157b**
　role of Silk Road in, 192
　in weapons and warfare, 227
　See also Architecture;Metals, use of
The Ten Princes (Dandin), 206
Tenochtitlán (Aztec city-state), 124, 131–35
Teotihuacán (Valley of Mexico city-state),
　126
Terra cotta army, Qin Empire, 68–69, **70p**
Territorial states, civilization and the concept
　of, 3
Terrorism, **24b**, **153m**
Thailand, 211
Theater. *See* Entertainment;Music and theater
Theodosius the Great (Roman emperor), 112
Thucydides (Greek historian), 84
Thutmosis III (pharaoh c.1480-1450 B.C.E.), 17
Tiberius (Roman emperor), 103, 192
Tibet, 52–53, 217, 220
Tigris and Euphrates River, 4–5, 9–14
Tikal's Temple of the Inscriptions, 13
Timelines in history
　Africa, **189b**
　in the Americas, **143b**
　China, **72b**, **118b**, **120–21b**, **236b**
　Egypt, **120–21b**
　Europe, **282b**, **284b**
　Greece, **95b**
　India, **49b**, **120–21b**, **212b**
　Israel, **27b**
　Japan, **257b**
　Korea, **257b**
　Latin America, **284b**
　Mediterranean region, **120–21b**
　Mesopotamia, **27b**
　Middle East, **120–21b**, **167b**, **284b**
　North Africa, **27b**
　Persian Empire, **27b**
　Rome, **118b**, **120–21b**
　Southeast Asia, **212b**, **284b**
　Vietnam, **257b**
　Western Hemisphere, **143b**
　See also Chronologies
Tools
　African use of iron, 173
　Chinese use of iron, 57–58
　Egyptian use of bronze, 17
　for expanding civilization and trade, **157b**
　labor-saving devices in agriculture, 265
　Neolithic Age and use of metals for, 8
　See also Stone tools
Torture, **24b**, 66
Totalitarianism, in ancient China, **65b**
Trade
　advances of civilization from, 8, **157b**
　Egyptian civilization and, 18
　sea and land routes for, **115m**, **179m**
　spread of civilization by, **157b**
　spread of disease by, **276b**

Trade, overland
　inAfrica, 19, 170–74, 177–78
　Arab influence on, 151, 156
　Central Asia origins of, 3
　from China, 58, 113–14, 222–24
　from Egypt, 16, 18
　between Europe and China, **266b**
　from India, 31, 40
　in medieval India, 204
　Phoenician sea routes and, 20
　of the Roman Empire, 104–05
　Sumerian city-states and, 10
　See also Silk Road
Trade, overseas/maritime, **115m**, **241m**
　Chinese, 223–24
　Indian Ocean, 40
　Roman Empire, 114–15
Trade, regional
　inthe Americas, 140
　Chinese, 123
　in India, 40, 46
　Japanese, **241m**
　Middle East, 3, 176
　Middle East origins of, 3
　Neolithic agriculture and, 7
　Southeast Asia, 192, 208–09
　spread of civilization by, **157b**
Trans-Jordan. *See* Jordan, kingdom of
Transportation systems
　civilization and the role of, 14, **99p**
　creation of trade and markets, **157b**
　technology development in, 224
Tribute system/payments
　inAfrica, 182, 185
　in China, 217, 220, 224
　in Japan, 245, 249
　Korea status with China, 217
　in Russia, 270
　in South America, 131, 133, **244b**
　Vietnam status with China, 254–**55b**
Trojan War, 77–**78b**
Turkestan, Chinese. *See* China,Xinjiang ("New
　Region")
Turkey, **153m**
　emergence of civilization in, 20
　Greek colonization in, 79
　origin of Crusades in, 153
Turkmenistan, 9
Tutankhamen (pharaoh c.1347 B.C.E.), 17, **54p**
Tyranny, 80–82

Ukraine (former Soviet republic), 269
Umar (caliph), 150
Umma (Sumerian city-state), 9
Universities
　creation of medieval, 272–73
　Muslim influence on, 159, **201p**
　women at, 272
　See also Education
Ur(Sumerian city-state), 9
Urban II (Pope), 274
Urbanization, 8, 142
　See also Cities
Uruinimgina, Cone of, 13
Uruk (Sumerian city-state), **4p**, 9
Uthman (caliph), 150
Uzbekistan (former Soviet republic), 9

Valley of Mexico. *See* CentralAmerica; Mexico
Vandals, 109, 164, **261m**
Vietnam, **254m**
　Chinese conquest of, 65, 207, 230, 238–39,
　　254
　Le dynasty (980-1009 C.E.), **255b**
　rise of Dai Viet, 254–55
　timelines in history, **257b**